Shareholders' Rights

Jurisdictional comparisons   **First edition 2011**

General Editors:
Alessandro Varrenti, CBA Studio Legale e Tributario;
Fernando de las Cuevas, Gómez-Acebo & Pombo
Matthew Hurlock, Kirkland & Ellis International LLP

THE
EUROPEAN LAWYER
REFERENCE
THE QUEEN'S AWARDS
FOR ENTERPRISE
INTERNATIONAL TRADE
2006

General Editors
Alessandro Varrenti, CBA Studio Legale e Tributario;
Fernando de las Cuevas, Gómez-Acebo & Pombo
Matthew Hurlock, Kirkland & Ellis International LLP

Publisher
Mark Wyatt

International Director
Michele O'Sullivan

Commercial Manager
Katie Burrington

Publishing Services Director
Ben Martin

Publishing and Production Manager
Emily Kyriacou

Production Editor
Caroline Pearce

Chief Sub Editor
Lisa Naylor

Sub Editors
Lucie Nason & Angie Gibson

Design and Production
Dawn McGovern

Published by
The European Lawyer
Futurelex Limited
23-24 Smithfield Street
London EC1A 9LF
T: +44 (0) 20 7332 2582
F: +44 (0) 20 7332 2599
www.europeanlawyer.co.uk

Printed in the UK by CPI William Clowes Beccles NR34 7TL
ISBN: 978-0-9565440-8-7
© Futurelex Limited 2011

Contents

Foreword

Alessandro Varrenti, CBA Studio Legale e Tributario

At the time when my friends Fernando de las Cuevas, Matthew Hurlock and I undertook the task of coordinating the work of contributors from some of the greatest law firms around the world, we all felt strongly that this book would be of great use to many. For that reason we wanted to ensure it was an indispensable guide which covered as many jurisdictions as possible.

Lots of different thoughts and ideas crossed our minds at the beginning of this project, and doubts too. How should we structure the book? Which method – essay or questionnaire – would be the right way to approach our colleagues, and how many countries, and which ones, should we cover?

Despite the dilemmas we all shared the same belief. The process of globalisation has certainly not come to an end, although it is correct to say that it came to a halt, or at least a pause, in recent years. Yet, the need for interaction between lawyers from different countries is stronger than ever, so also is the need to know, at least in broad terms initially, how other legal systems function in the main jurisdictions where clients intend to operate and the main rights in a given country for corporate businesses planning an investment abroad.

When some of the co-editors first started our legal practice, differences between corporate legal systems in the various European countries were many, substantial, and significant in terms of their relevance; not to mention the differences that existed between legal systems in countries in the western and the eastern world. European directives have certainly helped to shape a somewhat unified (or rather, 'harmonised') system of corporate laws over time, but differences and peculiarities still exist. These can be found at any given instance in national court interpretations and rulings.

The political expansion of the European boundaries in the past 20 years has brought together countries from the old Warsaw Pact and those of the western world, making evident at once the cultural differences between people who thus far had been used to economic, industrial and legal systems that had very little, if anything, in common. One of the consequences of political unification has been the need on the part of companies for comprehension of the very basics of local corporate laws, to determine where they would be best protected by the law, or if and how they should seek legal protection through agreements or other sorts of contractual arrangements.

The unprecedented development of business in Russia, China and India and the fast growth of big companies and even conglomerates in the Middle East and the Gulf area over this same time span has also signalled the need for lawyers to learn more. Had this book been written 20 years ago, it would probably have aroused the curiosity of some of those who were already fortunate to belong to the then much smaller community of international lawyers, and it would possibly have been a sensible tool to use for the few of them that worked on cross-border transactions. Nowadays, we pretentiously feel that this book is indispensable in any law library. The number and size of international transactions has simply become bigger over time, and so has their volume. Readers may not find here every answer to the numerous legal questions that they may have in respect to the corporate rights that can be enjoyed here or there around the world, but each chapter is definitely a terrific starting point for anyone willing to understand shareholder rights elsewhere in the world.

This book does not purport to be exhaustive with regard to the topics that it addresses, but we feel it is a good road map because it contains some very useful indications for those who operate internationally in respect to the main rights for shareholders in various countries, and how they can be enforced. When we started out, one of the recurring issues that surfaced was the need to ensure that we would address questions to our contributors that would be sensible and practical to deal with in each of the jurisdictions involved. And as we went on expanding the number of jurisdictions and reached 29, we realised that the objective to extend our work to as many countries as possible was proportionally inverse with respect to the initial idea to tailor the book as a very technical tool. Making this book a sort of doctoral thesis in some very sophisticated areas of corporate law would doubtless have been a stimulating exercise, but of little use to many readers. Rather, we trust that our deliberate choice to make this a sort of 'first aid' publication will prove correct over time.

We do hope that our publisher will give us the opportunity to update the book as new rules come into force in each of the different jurisdictions. We also hope to extend the list of countries covered in the next edition.

No foreword seems to end without expressing personal thanks to particular people and this will be no exception. We all owe, and I do in particular, heartfelt and special thanks to Michele O'Sullivan at *The European Lawyer* for the idea to put us together in one book, and to Katie Burrington, also at *The European Lawyer*, for pushing us all along to do more and better. We trust that we have done well, as time will hopefully tell.

Also on behalf of my friends Fernando and Matthew, our thanks to all our contributors and their outstanding firms for their efforts and patience.

Milan, December 2010

Argentina

Estudio Beccar Varela Roberto H. Crouzel, Miguel C. Remmer, Constanza P. Connolly, Germán G. Pennimpede & Nicolás C. D'Odorico

BASIC INFORMATION ON THE TYPES OF LIMITED LIABILITY COMPANIES AND ON THE RIGHTS OF SHAREHOLDERS

1. What types of companies enjoy limited liability? If more than one, which ones have shareholders, ie holders of share certificates? Which one is the most common? Which one is mostly used by foreign investors?

The *Sociedad Anónima (SA) and the Sociedad de Responsabilidad Limitada* (SRL) are the most common types of companies that enjoy limited liability, due to their proven efficiency over other types, which have become rare or have been completely forgotten due to lack of use. For this reason, we will only refer to the former. However, please be aware that joint stock companies (*Sociedad en Comandita por Acciones*), in which only the non-managing partner (*socio comanditario*) limits their liability to the capital they subscribe, also exist.

Due to the foregoing, foreign companies doing business in Argentina usually choose between an SA and an SRL. Of the two, SAs are more common, yet SRLs are popular among American investors due to the tax benefits that entail the principle of 'look-through qualification', which allows the consolidation of profits and losses with their respective parent company.

Unless we make an express distinction herein, we are referring to both the SA and the SRL types of company.

Unlike the SA whose capital stock is represented by shares, the capital stock of an SRL is represented by quotas. Only shares may be either represented in physical certificates or kept as book-entry stock. Quotas, on the other hand, are registered with the General Inspection of Corporations (GIC). (Note: we refer to this supervisory authority due to the fact that the great majority of limited liability companies are incorporated in the City of Buenos Aires. Therefore, every time we refer herein to the GIC, we are considering companies registered in the City of Buenos Aires. Other jurisdictions usually follow the criteria of the GIC; however, it is necessary to study the subject on a case-by-case basis.) Both are freely transferable unless the by-laws provide otherwise (provisions that may limit but not prohibit their transfer).

It is true that foreign companies often operate in Argentina through a branch, instead of a subsidiary. The reason for this is that branches are easier to operate (a mere power of attorney would do) and they have fewer bookkeeping requirements than the SA and the SRL. In contrast, Argentine law considers branches to be one and the same entity with their head offices, and as a consequence of this the head office may be held jointly liable with its Argentine branch. Conversely, if an Argentine subsidiary is incorporated, the liability of the head office will generally be limited to the assets contributed to that subsidiary (ie, the subsidiary's equity capital).

2. Are there minimum capital requirements and/or thin capitalisation rules in force?

Yes, for the incorporation of an SA the Argentine Business Association Law 19,550 (as amended, BAL) requires a minimum capital stock of AR$12,000 (AR$ stands for Argentine pesos), which is about US$3,000 at the current exchange rate. Further, companies must have a degree of capital that in the GIC's judgment is sufficient to allow them to attain their corporate purpose. Consequently, the minimum capital requirements will be assessed on a case-by-case basis, depending on the corporate purpose.

Highly-regulated businesses, such as banks and insurance companies, have specific regulations requiring significantly higher minimum capital requirements.

Finally, as a general rule, no limitations apply to the deductibility of interest. However, local entities will apply 'thin capitalisation rules' for the deductibility of interest payments (other than those that are subject to a 35 per cent withholding tax) made by local taxpayers (excluding financial entities) to foreign related parties. In such a case, this interest will be subject to a thin capitalisation rule by which liabilities related to the interest cannot exceed 200 per cent of the net worth at the end of the fiscal year. Interest that is not deductible pursuant to such a rule, must be treated as 'dividend'.

3. Describe the types of shares that can be issued by a company and the different rights that they attribute to their owners, as well as any other financial instruments (bonds or other) and other instruments of a participatory nature in the company's capital that can also be issued by the company.

As far as equity capital is concerned, the SA can issue common shares or preferred shares.

Common shares are voting shares. As a general rule, each common share gives the right to one vote. The by-laws may create classes of shares entitled to up to five votes each. The issuance of multi-voting shares is forbidden once the company has gone public. Likewise, multi-voting quotas are forbidden in SRLs (ie, each quota grants the right to one vote).

Preferred stock usually has a priority right to receive the profits of the company with preference over common stock. Preferred stock may lack voting rights, except for some special matters (eg, in the case of a default in the payment of the dividends, decisions related to the transformation or dissolution of the company, a change of its corporate purpose, etc). Preferred stock cannot be multi-voting stock.

An irrevocable capital contribution is allowed to be recorded in a special account within the net worth of the company during a specific amount of time. After some time, the contribution will have to be either capitalised into shares or repaid, or it will have to be recorded as a liability.

Another common form of debt is the commercial bond, which could be convertible or non-convertible into shares and, if placed through a public offering procedure, may grant certain tax benefits.

Finally, participation bonds (*bonos de participación*) may be issued in exchange for a consideration that is not a contribution of capital. They only give the right to participate in the profits of the fiscal year. The participation bonds may also be given to personnel of the corporation. The profits that correspond to them are computed as expenses. They are non-transferable and are forfeited upon termination of the employment relationship, whatever the cause may be.

4. Can a company have only one shareholder and still enjoy limited liability?

Companies in Argentina must have at least two partners. Should the number of partners be reduced to one (due to buyout, death, or for any other reason), the remaining partner becomes unlimitedly liable, and has three months to find another partner or the company will be forcibly dissolved and liquidated.

5. Are the rights of shareholders the same in any type of company?

Yes, they are the same. However, different classes of shares or quotas may grant different rights within a company.

6. What are the basic rights of any shareholder? Describe briefly the rights of minority shareholders and indicate which thresholds, if any, are required to allow the minority shareholders to exercise any such rights.

The basic rights of any shareholder may be classified as political and economic rights.

Regarding the first class, the main political right is the right to vote in the general meetings of the company. Other political rights are the right to request a shareholders' meeting (see question 11 below), the right to control and review the books and records of the company (a right that is only available in an SA when there are no appointed syndics) and the right to withdraw from the company if certain decisions are enforced (eg, early liquidation of the company, merger, spin-off, etc), among others. Regarding the government, administration and control bodies of the SA, please see question 19 below.

The main economic right is to receive the profits of the company in the same proportion as the contribution made or as provided for in the by-laws. Stipulations by virtue of which one or some of the members receive all the profits or are excluded from them or are exempted from contributing to the losses are void.

Economic as well as political rights may be modified, and the latter may even be suppressed. For instance, preferred stock grants its holder a special economic right, and for these shares the law considers it legitimate to restrain their voting rights.

The BAL has created several mechanisms to protect the right of minority shareholders. Among them there exists a right of first refusal and a right of accrual every time there is a capital increase (both widespread, anti-dilution mechanisms). Also, in the SA, minority shareholders may force the appointment of board members by means of the 'cumulative voting system', which basically works as follows:

- Each shareholder that votes by cumulating their votes shall have a number of votes equal to that which results from multiplying the votes that they normally would possess by the number of directors to be elected. They can distribute or accumulate their votes in a number of candidates not exceeding one-third of the vacancies to be filled.
- The shareholders that vote using the regular or plural system and those that vote by cumulating their votes shall compete in the election of one-third of the vacancies to be filled. The remaining two-thirds shall be filled by the regular or plural method. The shareholders that do not use the cumulative voting system shall vote for all of the vacancies to be filled, giving to each of the candidates all of the votes that correspond to such shareholders in accordance with their shares with voting rights.

Finally, through classes of shares, the by-laws may provide for the appointment, on behalf of the minority, of one or more directors and one or more syndics.

Concerning the existing thresholds required in the SA to allow the minority shareholders to exercise some of their rights, please see answers to questions 11 and 23 below. There are no minimum thresholds required in the SRL.

7. Do all shareholders enjoy the same rights or can some shareholders be attributed specific rights, whether by reason of the particular class of stock owned or other? Are such rights generally provided for at the level of the company's by-laws and/or in shareholders' agreements?

As a general rule, shareholders and quota holders have the same rights within the same class of stock. That is, different classes may provide for different rights, especially as far as economic preference and voting rights are concerned. Shareholders' and quota holders' rights may be provided for either in the by-laws or in a shareholders' agreement. The latter usually provides for those rights and obligations that the partners do not want to disclose to third parties.

8. May the rights of shareholders, generally speaking, be limited, modified, suppressed or waived in any way? If so, how? Are such modifications or limitations provided for in the company's by-laws and/or in shareholders' agreements?

Certain rights may be waived, whereas others may not. As a general rule the

BAL considers that all partners may share profits and liabilities alike, and that is why the right to collect dividends and afford liabilities may not be waived beforehand (but once they are vested).

Voting rights may be waived only for preferred stock, and in general (that is, for all preferred shares of the same class, not for an individual partner). The remaining political and economic rights may also be waived within a certain class of stock. Individual partners may only waive their rights after they are vested, but not beforehand.

Regarding this matter, please also see question 34 below.

GENERAL MEETING OF SHAREHOLDERS (GM) AND VOTING RIGHTS

9. Which decisions are reserved to the competence of the GM?

The BAL covers two classes of GM in the SA: the Ordinary GM (OGM) and the Extraordinary GM (EGM).

Decisions reserved to the competence of the OGM include those on the following matters:

(i) consideration and approval of the general balance sheet, profit and loss statement, distribution of profits, management report, syndic's opinion and all other measures relating to the management of the corporation that it is competent to decide in accordance with the law and the by-laws or that are submitted for its decision by the board, the supervisory council or the syndics;

(ii) appointment and removal of directors, syndics or members of the supervisory council and determination of their remunerations;

(iii) responsibilities of the directors and syndics and members of the supervisory council; and

(iv) increases of capital, in accordance with section 188 (ie, when the increase of the capital stock is up to five times its amount and the by-laws provide that such an increase may be decided by the OGM).

The EGM has authority over all those matters that are not within the authority of the OGM and with respect to the modifications of the by-laws. Therefore, in the system of the BAL, the EGM has a residual competence.

10. How does a shareholder participate in a GM? Are there any limitations to having a minimum number of shares? May a shareholder delegate attendance to another shareholder or to the board? May a shareholder obtain assistance from the courts or any other governmental body to intervene in a GM or to cause one to be held in some particular cases?

To attend a GM, shareholders must notify their attendance in order to be registered in the Ledger of Attendance at Shareholders' Meetings, not less than three working days prior to the date of the meeting. The company will furnish them with appropriate vouchers of receipt which will serve for their admission to the GM.

Shareholders may have themselves represented at a GM. However, directors, syndics, members of the supervisory council, managers and other company employees may not be their representatives. It is sufficient to grant the proxy via a private instrument, with the affixed signature certified judicially, by a notary public or by a bank, save in the event of provisions to the contrary established in the by-laws.

OGM and EGM shall be called by the board of directors or the syndic in those cases established by law or whenever either may deem it necessary or when so required by shareholders representing at least five per cent of the capital stock, provided the by-laws do not fix a lesser percentage. Should the board of directors or syndic fail to do so, the meeting may be called by the corporate supervisory authority or by court order, upon request by a shareholder.

In the case of the SRL, please see question 13 below.

11. May a GM be called and held at the request of any shareholder? Is there a threshold regarding the percentage of the stock interest owned in the company that may entitle a shareholder to such a right?

No, a GM may not be called and held at the request of any shareholder. A GM may only be called by shareholders representing at least five per cent of the capital stock, provided the by-laws do not fix a lesser percentage. In this last case, the motion will list the matters to be dealt with and the GM shall be summoned by the board or, failing that, by the syndic.

12. May a shareholder bring up an issue to be resolved upon and put it to a vote if it is not included on the agenda? May a shareholder require more information from the GM and/or the board concerning the agenda of the GM, to be put in a better position to exercise their vote?

All decisions on matters other than those included on the agenda are null and void, except when the entire capital is present and decisions are adopted unanimously by the shares vested with voting rights.

A shareholder may require further information concerning the agenda of the GM prior to the the latter being held. Likewise, during the GM the shareholder may also require further information and thus, if such a request is accepted by the majority, the meeting may be postponed once but must be reconvened within the following 30 days.

13. May a GM be held by telecommunication means and/or by correspondence (ie by written consent)?

For the SRL, the BAL states that the by-laws shall provide the form of deliberation and adoption of social resolutions. In the absence of rules, those resolutions adopted in response to a simultaneous and authentic consultation, taken through a vote of the partners within 10 days of such consultation and made known to the management through any method that assures its authenticity; or those resolutions resulting from a written statement in which all partners express the sense in which they vote, shall be valid.

The BAL does not foresee these possibilities for the SA. Further, the GIC considers they are forbidden in the case of the SA.

Finally, public companies are allowed to hold a GM by telecommunication means as long as such a possibility is stated in their by-laws.

14. Are voting rights always proportionate to the stock held by each shareholder or can they vary by share class?
Please see the answer to question 7 above.

15. Are there non-voting shares? Is there a maximum percentage of capital represented by non-voting shares?
Regarding the first question, please see the answer to question 3 above.

In addition, please be aware that there is no maximum percentage of capital represented by non-voting shares.

16. Can shareholders group their shares in order to exercise their voting rights (eg by trust, shareholders' agreement or otherwise)?
Yes, shareholders can group their shares in what is called 'voting syndicates' in order to exercise their voting rights. The voting syndicates are usually instrumented in shareholders' agreements which, as it is explained below, are not opposable to the company nor to third parties.

Please also note that the general principle of the BAL regarding a GM is the 'deliberative principle' by means of which shareholders shall deliberate and vote in the GM, no matter if they previously agreed on how to vote on a specific subject.

17. Under what circumstances can a shareholder challenge the resolutions adopted by the GM? Are there thresholds concerning the stock interest owned to be able to bring such a claim?
Every resolution of the GM adopted in violation of the law or the by-laws may be opposed within three months as a nullity by the shareholders who did not cast their votes in favour of the respective decision and by those absent who are able to demonstrate that at the time the decision was taken, they held the requisite qualification to be considered shareholders. Those who voted in favour may also object to the decision if their votes are voidable for defects in their consent.

There are no thresholds concerning the stock interest owned to be able to bring such a claim.

18. What are the terms and procedures to challenge a resolution of the GM?
The action must be brought against the corporation, before the judge of its domicile, within three months of the closing of the meeting. However, certain court decisions have allowed the filing of an action even after three months as long as it is considered a clear violation of the public order.

SHAREHOLDERS' RIGHTS VERSUS DIRECTORS AND DUTIES OF OTHER CORPORATE BODIES IN THE COMPANY

19. What is the procedure for the appointment/replacement/ revocation of directors and of statutory auditors, if any?

Please see the table below with the names of the government, administration and control bodies of the SA following:

Government body	Shareholders' meeting
Administration body	Board of directors
Control body	Control body Syndic/Supervisory committee (composed of syndics)/ Supervisory council (composed of shareholders)

The appointment of directors, syndics and members of the supervisory council shall be carried out by a shareholders' meeting. In some cases, the appointment of directors may be done by the supervisory council.

Their removal is always a faculty of the shareholder's meeting, which may remove directors and syndics even without cause.

Regarding their replacement, the by-laws may direct the election of alternatives to overcome the lack of directors for any reason. This provision is mandatory in the case of corporations that do not have a syndic. In the case of a vacancy, the syndics shall appoint a replacement until the next shareholders' meeting if the by-laws do not establish another method of appointment.

20. May shareholders challenge the resolutions of the board of directors? Is there a minimum percentage of capital required to challenge a board resolution?

Unlike what it does regarding the decisions of the shareholders' meeting, the BAL does not regulate a process for challenging resolutions of the board, which has caused some debate among judges and scholars.

Recent commercial court decisions on the matter and the great majority of authors have considered the possibility of having the shareholders challenge a decision of the board before the court, as can be done with the decisions of a shareholders' meeting. Further, they do not call for a minimum percentage of capital to pursue such a purpose.

21. Are shareholders entitled to bring a legal action against the directors of the company? In which circumstances? Please describe briefly the principles of director's liabilities.

In fact, the action for liability against the directors pertains to the company, after a resolution by a shareholders' meeting. Such a resolution may be adopted even when it is not on the agenda of the meeting, if it is the direct consequence of the resolution of a matter that is included therein. The resolution will produce the removal of the director or directors affected and will make their replacement mandatory. However, the action referred to above may also be filed by the shareholders who have opposed the approval of the directors' performance at the shareholders' meeting and represent at least five per cent of the company's capital stock.

The directors have unlimited, joint and several liability to the corporation, the shareholders and third parties for mismanagement – according to the criteria of loyalty and the performance of a good businessman – as well as for infringement of the law, of the by-laws or of the regulations thereof, and for any other damage produced by fraud, abuse of authority and gross negligence.

Liability shall be imputed considering the individual performance whenever functions had been assigned in accordance with the by-laws, the regulations or a shareholders' meeting resolution.

What is stated in the paragraphs above notwithstanding, a director who participated in the deliberation or resolution or who acknowledged it, is exempt from liability if they put their written protest on the record and gave notice to the syndic before their liability is reported to the board, the syndic, the shareholders' meeting, the competent authority or before judicial action is exercised.

22. What are the rights in connection with transactions where the directors have a conflict of interest situation?
When a director has an interest adverse to that of the corporation, they must inform the board and the syndics and abstain from participating in the deliberation, under the penalty of incurring responsibility for mismanagement (as explained in question 21 above).

A director can only enter into contracts with the corporation that are in the corporation's normal business whenever such agreements are entered into under market conditions. Agreements that do not conform to these requisites may only be entered into after the approval of the board or consent of the syndics if there is no quorum. Likewise, these transactions must be reported to the shareholders' meeting.

If the shareholder's meeting disapproves the agreements already entered into, the directors, or the syndics in their case, shall be joint and severally liable for the damages caused to the company.

Contracts entered into in violation of the rules explained earlier and which are not ratified by the shareholders' meeting are null and void without impairment of the liability stated for the directors or syndics in the paragraph immediately above.

INFORMATION RIGHTS ON THE COMPANY'S BUSINESS
23. What information may be requested by the shareholders from the board concerning the general state of the company's business or any specific transaction? Are information rights different depending on the number of shares owned? Are shareholders entitled to receive written information before, during or after the GM about the meeting agenda and to what extent? Is it possible for a shareholder to obtain a copy of the minutes of the GM?
The shareholders can examine the company's books and records, and obtain

upon request the reports that they think are relevant. They may also obtain, at their cost, a signed copy of the minutes. In the SA and SRL this faculty of individual control by the shareholders is excluded whenever the company has a syndic. Syndics will only investigate the written accusations that are made by shareholders who represent no less than two per cent of the capital stock of the company and provide information if required by shareholders representing such percentage.

Before each GM, the shareholders should be provided with the necessary information in order to be able to vote on the points included in the agenda. In the particular case of a GM where the financial statement is considered, the shareholders shall be provided with the balance sheet and its complementary documentation 15 days prior to the GM. Additionally, a copy of the financial documentation treated by the GM must be kept in the headquarters of the company.

24. Do shareholders have the right/duty to resolve in the GM upon matters which were not on the agenda?
All decisions on matters not included in the agenda of the meeting are invalid, except:
(i)   if all the capital is present and the decision is adopted unanimously by the shareholders with the right to vote;
(ii) the exceptions that are expressly authorised in the BAL; and
(iii) the election of those entrusted with signing the minutes of the meeting.

25. Are shareholders entitled to inspect the corporate books and/or any other corporate or accounting documents? To what extent? Can they do it through external counsel or advisors?
In order to participate and vote in a GM, shareholders have the right to receive the relevant documentation relating to the items on the GM's agenda. In addition, as has been explained above, shareholders are entitled to inspect corporate books and/or any other corporate or accounting documents – except when the company has a syndic. Although the BAL remains silent regarding this point, the extent of such an inspection shall be reasonable and cannot hinder the normal business of the company.

Further, the National Civil and Commercial Procedural Code establishes the possibility that in order to inspect the company's books, evidence of the character of the shareholder must be put before the court.

Shareholders must obtain the authorisation of the board of directors if they want an inspection to be done through external advisors. Several judicial precedents have established that such an authorisation shall not be unreasonably denied.

SHAREHOLDERS' AGREEMENTS
26. Are shareholders' agreements validly enforceable? What are their typical contents and term of duration? Are they enforceable by or against third parties and, if so, to what extent?
Shareholders' agreements are not regulated in the BAL due to the fact that

they are private agreements that fall outside the scope of the BAL. However, the courts and the authors agree on holding these kinds of agreements valid under Argentine law, as long as they do not violate public order regulations.

The content of shareholders' agreements typically relates to subjects such as:

- the government of the company (management policies);
- voting syndicates;
- the resolution of conflicts;
- the appointment of directors, syndics and auditors;
- supermajorities (which may increase but never decrease);
- limitations to the transferability of the shares (right of first refusal, drag- and tag-along rights, etc); and
- options on the capital stock (put and call).

The content of shareholders' agreements vary on a case-by-case basis according to the number of shareholders and percentage of shares they hold.

There seems to be no limitation regarding the term of duration. However, some authors believe that this kind of agreement should be specific in terms of time and content.

Shareholders' agreements are not enforceable against third parties –this includes the company itself, although *bona fide* principles will still apply.

27. Do shareholders' agreements have to be disclosed to the public or registered in any public registry?

There are some public institutions that compel the disclosure of the shareholders' agreements, such as the Argentine Securities and Exchange Commission (*Comisión Nacional de Valores*) for listed companies, but the BAL does not include this obligation for non-listed companies.

ECONOMIC RIGHTS AND RIGHTS OVER THE STOCK

28. Is the stock always freely transferable? Are there any legal limitations? Are there any restrictions on contractual limitations?

The rule fixed by the BAL is that the stock is freely transferable. However, the by-laws may limit the transferability of nominative or book-entry shares, provided the limitation does not mean to prohibit their transference. The limitation, whenever it exists, must be evidenced on the share certificate and in the account registration, its written statements and the status reports.

Apart from a specific limitation that may be stated in the by-laws of the company, a restriction on the transferability of stock may arise from an agreement or from a law. Further, certain specific industries provide for a prior authorisation of the relevant regulatory authority in order to become a shareholder of the regulated company. In addition, section 1277 of the Civil Code requires the spouse's consent in order to transfer recordable assets owned by a married person (eg in order to transfer the stock owned by a married person).

Regarding contractual limitations, the typical clauses foreseen to limit the transferability of the stock are the right of first refusal, the prohibition of the transfer of stock during a certain term, put and call options and tag- and drag-along rights. Please see question 26 above.

29. Are shareholders entitled to pledge their stock?

Yes, shareholders are entitled to pledge their stock.

Section 219 of the BAL states that a pledge – or judicial attachment – of the rights granted to the position of shareholder, shall correspond to the owner of the shares (ie the pledgor). Therefore, there is an obligation on the creditor to facilitate the exercise of the owner's rights by means of depositing the shares or by other proceedings that guarantee their rights. However, the owner shall bear the pertinent expenses.

The above notwithstanding, in our opinion, the political rights corresponding to the position of shareholder may be also assigned to the creditor.

30. Are there financial assistance issues to be considered and other prohibitions to be evaluated in the context of a leveraged buyout transaction?

In the context of a leveraged buyout transaction it is considered against the interest of the company to issue a guarantee or to provide financial assistance for the acquisition of treasury shares. This prohibition arises from judicial precedents and not from the BAL itself.

31. May a company buy back its own stock and, if so, under what circumstances and subject to which limitations?

A corporation may only acquire stock issued by itself under the following conditions:

i)   to cancel them subsequent to an agreement to reduce capital;
ii) in exceptional cases, with realised and liquid profits or free reserves when they are fully paid, in order to prevent serious damage, justifying evidence whereof being submitted to the following shareholders' meeting; and
iii) because they form part of the assets of a concern that is acquired or the equity of a corporation that is absorbed.

The board of directors shall dispose of the treasury shares acquired in cases ii) and iii) of the paragraph above within a one-year term, unless otherwise extended by the shareholders' meeting. The right of first refusal shall apply to these sales. The rights vested in such treasury shares shall be suspended until the shares are disposed of and they will not be counted for either quorum or majority purposes.

Finally, according to Argentine law, companies may not receive their own shares in guarantee.

32. Is there a legal right to withdraw from the company and, if so, under what circumstances? How is the shareholders' stock valuated and paid in such a case?

Yes, there is a legal right to withdraw from the company. In this respect, shareholders who disagree with decisions relating to the transformation of the company's type, the extension of the duration or re-formation of the company, the transfer abroad of the corporate domicile, the fundamental change of the corporate purpose and the total or partial repayment of capital, may withdraw from the corporation with reimbursement of the value of the shares they own. The shareholders of the absorbed corporation in the case of a merger or a division may also withdraw from the company.

They may also withdraw in the case of an increase of capital when the decision corresponds to the extraordinary shareholders' meeting and implies a disbursement by a shareholder, in the case of a voluntary withdrawal from the public offering or from the quotation of the stock on a stock exchange, and in the case of the continuation of the corporation once it has decided the exclusion of the company from public offer or from quotation of its shares on a stock exchange.

The right of withdrawal can only be exercised by those who voted against the resolution, within the fifth day, and by those absent who demonstrate their qualification as shareholders at the time of the shareholders' meeting, within 15 days of the conclusion of the meeting.

The shares shall be reimbursed at their value resulting from the last balance sheet made or that must be made in compliance with statutory or regulatory provisions. However, some judicial precedents have objected to this solution in cases in which the market value of the shares essentially differs from their book value. As a general principle, the appropriate amount must be paid within one year of the closing of the shareholders' meeting that originated the withdrawal or 60 days from the closing of the shareholder's meeting or publication, as the case may be. The amount of the debt shall be adjusted up to the date of payment.

The withdrawal right and the legal action emerging therefrom lapse if the resolution that originated them is revoked by a shareholders' meeting held within 60 days after the expiration of the period of time granted for its exercise to the absentees. In this case the withdrawing shareholders forthwith reacquire the exercise of their rights, and likewise their economic rights shall be backdated to the time when they served notice of their withdrawal.

33. In which circumstances can dividends be distributed among shareholders? Is it possible to exclude or limit the right of certain shareholders to dividends? Does a certain portion of the profits need to be set aside in a reserve fund where it cannot be distributed to the shareholders? Are advances on dividends allowed and, if so, under which circumstances? Can advances on dividends be reclaimed by the company?

The distribution of dividends to shareholders is only lawful if it results from realised and liquidated profits (meaning after the payment of pending losses) corresponding to a balance sheet of the fiscal year that has been regularly drawn up and approved. It is prohibited to distribute interest or dividends in advance or provisional or resulting from special balance sheets except in the case of corporations included in section 299 of the BAL (ie those corporations that are regularly and continuously monitored by the state).

As was explained in question 6 above, it is not possible to exclude certain shareholders from their right to dividends. However, it is possible to limit that right by subordinating it to preferred shares or by stating in the by-laws that, for instance, dividends will not be distributed for a certain term.

Furthermore, the BAL requires limited liability companies and stock companies to create a reserve of not less than five per cent of the liquid and realised profits shown in the profit and loss statement of the fiscal year, until the aggregate reaches 20 per cent of the company's capital. When this reserve is diminished for any reason, profits may not be distributed until it has been refunded.

Apart from the legal reserve, other reserves may be established, provided that they are reasonable and appropriate to prudent management (voluntary reserves). Finally, the by-laws may set forth the constitution of statutory reserves. These reserves – voluntary and statutory – may also limit the right to dividends.

In any event, the amount of dividends to be distributed shall be determined by majority vote at the shareholders' meeting, provided that shareholders shall not continuously and repeatedly vote to refuse to distribute any dividends.

It is prohibited to distribute dividends in advance or provisional or resulting from special balance sheets, except in the case of corporations included in section 299 (ie those that are regularly and continuously monitored by the state). In all these cases the directors, the members of the supervisory council and the syndics shall have unlimited and joint and several liability for such payments and distributions.

The above notwithstanding, dividends received in good faith are not reimbursable by the company.

34. What are the rights of shareholders in the case of an issue of new stock (increase of the company's corporate capital) (pre-emption rights)?

Common shares with either a single or plural vote, grant their holders the right of first refusal to subscribe for new shares of the same class in proportion to those which they possess. They also entitle their holders to the right to increase *pro rata* the shares subscribed for on each occasion (accrual right). Regarding the right of first refusal, the extraordinary shareholders' meeting, with qualified majorities, may resolve in special and exceptional cases, when required by the interests of the corporation, to limit or suspend the preferential right for the subscription of new shares, under the following conditions: (i) that the discussion about this decision be included in the agenda of the meeting; and (ii) that the stock in question is to be paid for by contributions in kind or is given in payment for pre-existing liabilities.

These rights may be extended by the by-laws to preferred stock.

35. May minority shareholders ban or limit the company's capital structure in any manner?

In principle, minority shareholders are not able to ban or limit the company's capital structure in any manner. However, whenever a GM must adopt resolutions that affect the rights of a class of stock (provided that the company's stock is divided into classes), the consent or ratification of that class is required. Such consent will be given in a special shareholders' meeting governed by the rules applicable to the regular shareholders' meeting.

36. Which are the financial assistance prohibitions in force?

Transactions carried on between an Argentine resident and: i) related parties, or ii) foreign parties located in tax haven jurisdictions, are subject to the arm's length principle. Failure to apply the arm's-length principle results in adjustments of profits under one of the following methods: comparable uncontrolled price, resale price, cost plus, profit split and transactional net margin.

Taxpayers subject to compliance with a transfer pricing regime are deemed to provide information regarding transactions with affiliated companies, information concerning the transfer pricing method used and details of activities of the affiliated companies.

37. Apart from publicly-listed companies, in which cases (if any) are shareholders obligated to obtain an authorisation from, or provide information to, a public authority about events that have an impact on their stock interest in the company?

Even though shareholders are not obliged to obtain any authorisation from or provide information to a public authority about events that have an impact on their stock interest in the company, there are some resolutions that oblige either the company or some representatives to do so.

In this respect, General Resolution 1375 (GR 1375) and General Resolution 4120 (GR 4120, as amended) issued by the National Tax Authority establish a registration and information regime applicable to companies and to local representatives of foreign individuals and entities.

Pursuant to the GR 1375, the local tax authorities must be informed of all economic transactions between Argentine residents and representatives of foreign counterparties. GR 1375 also establishes an official registry where all representatives of foreign entities must be registered before the closing of the economic transaction. The filing of the information concerning the transaction, if any, must be done every four months.

In accordance with GR 4120, every 31 December, all the stock companies – such as SAs and SRLs - shall submit to the National Tax Authority certain information about the owners of their capital stock. The information requested will vary on a case-by-case basis, depending on the nature of the owner (for example, if it is an individual or a company, etc).

Finally, when a quota holder transfers their quotas in an SRL, the transfer shall be registered with the GIC.

SHAREHOLDERS' RIGHTS IN THE CASE OF EXTRAORDINARY TRANSACTIONS AND/OR WINDING-UP

38. What rights are available to shareholders in the case of a sale of all or a substantial portion of the company's assets? In the case of a merger or de-merger?

When a company is merged into another, the shareholders of the absorbed company may exercise the withdrawal right, in accordance with the terms and conditions described in question 32 above. The same right is granted to the shareholders of the existing company in the case of a spin-off.

Please note that the decision to sell the assets of the company is generally incumbent on the board of directors, therefore the shareholders do not have specific rights in such cases. However, in the case of the sale of significant assets of the company, it is advisable to have such a decision ratified by a shareholders' meeting.

39. Which rights are available to shareholders in the case of conversion of the company into a European Company (SE) or into another type of company?

In the case of a transformation of the company's type into an SE or into another type of company, shareholders may exercise the withdrawal right, in accordance with the terms and conditions described in question 32 above.

40. Which rights are available to shareholders of a company in liquidation?

There are no restrictions on shareholders' rights in the case of a company in liquidation. Once the company's liabilities have been cancelled, the liquidators – who may be the directors or the persons appointed by the shareholders' meeting for the purpose – will prepare the final balance sheet and the distribution proposal, which shall be approved by the shareholders. Afterwards, the liquidators will refund the capital participation to each shareholder and, except as otherwise is provided for in the company's by-laws, the surplus shall be distributed in proportion to the participation of each member in the profits.

41. Can shareholders cause the liquidation of the company? How?

Yes, shareholders may cause the liquidation of the company by voting for it in the corresponding shareholders' meeting. Section 244 is applicable for such a purpose and, thus, the resolution, in order to be valid, shall be decided by the favourable vote of those holding the majority of shares with the right to vote, without applying plurality of votes.

COMPANY GROUPS

42. Is the concept of 'group' recognised as such under specific legislation? What are the implications?

The BAL does not refer expressly to the concept of 'group'. However, section 33 of the BAL refers to controlled and linked companies. Companies are considered 'controlled' whenever another company, directly or through another company that is in turn controlled: i) possesses a participation, by any title, that grants to it the votes necessary to form the company's will in social meetings or regular assemblies; ii) exercises a dominant influence as a consequence of the possession of shares, quotas or parts of interest, or as a consequence of the special links existing among the companies.

Companies are considered 'linked' when one company holds more than 10 per cent of the capital of the other. When a company holds more than 25 per cent of the capital of the other, it must make it known to the other so that its next regular assembly takes notice of the fact.

Section 62 of the BAL requires controlling companies to file with the supervisory authority – as complementary information – annual consolidated financial statements, prepared pursuant to generally accepted accounting principles and to the regulations of the supervisory authority. There are also technical resolutions issued by the Professional Councils of Economic Sciences, which establish technical requirements on the matter.

Unlike the BAL, the Executive Order 677/01 of the Public Offering Transparency System, refers expressly to the concepts of 'controlling', 'controlling group' or 'control groups' defining them as any individual or legal person that holds, either directly or indirectly, individually or jointly, whichever the case may be, a share in the capital stock or voting rights that, *de jure or de facto*, providing they are stable, grant enough votes to take a corporate decision in shareholders' general meetings or to choose or remove the majority of the directors or syndics. In this sense, one of the implications for a company of being part of the group may be the obligation to inform transactions. For example if any individual or legal person, or all the persons belonging to groups, acting in a coordinated way, purchase or sell shares of stock in a company making a public offering of its negotiable securities for an amount that implies changes in the stakes held by the controlling group or groups and thus affecting the structure, the listed company should inform the Securities and Excange Commission.

43. Does a controlling company have any particular duties *vis-à-vis* its controlled company shareholders?
Apart from what is stated in this chapter, there are no other essential duties of a holding company *vis-à-vis* its controlled company shareholders.

44. What are the rights of company shareholders when the controlling company puts in place actions and/or transactions that can be prejudicial to the shareholders?
Besides the rights concerning: (i) the challenge of shareholders' meeting's decisions and/or board of director's decisions against the law, the by-laws or any other internal rules of the company; (ii) the disapproval of the director's performance, which are treated above; and (iii) the preventive suspension upon the petition of a party of the execution of a measure that could cause damage (injunction), damages caused to the company by fraud or negligence of those who control the company, makes the authors liable to indemnify the company without being able to allege that it has been compensated with

the profits that their actions have provided in other businesses.

The controlling parties that apply the funds or assets of the company to their own use or own business or to that of a third party are obliged to hand the resulting profits to the company, bearing the losses or damages exclusively to their own account.

Finally, when an action by a company covers the prosecution of objectives beyond those of the company, or constitutes a mere device to violate the law, the public order or good faith or to frustrate third-party rights, such an action shall be directly imputed to the members or controlling parties that made it possible; and shall be imposed upon them jointly, several and unlimited liability for the damages caused (disregard theory).

45. What are the limitations, if any, to the possibility of owning reciprocal stock interests in companies?

In accordance with the BAL's regime on the matter, the establishment of companies or the increase of their capital by means of reciprocal participation is void, even if through an intermediary person. The breach of this prohibition will impose upon the founders, managers, directors and syndics jointly, several and unlimited liability. The capital unlawfully subscribed for must be reduced within the term of three months and, if it is not, the company will be dissolved as a matter of law.

Furthermore, a controlled company will neither hold shares in its parent company nor in another subsidiary of its parent company for an amount that exceeds, according to the balance sheet, its reserves excluding the legal reserve.

The shares of interest, quotas or stock that exceed the limits established above must be transferred within six months following the date of approval of the balance sheet from which the infringement results. The non-fulfilment of the transfer of the excess interest causes the loss of voting rights and of the profits that correspond to such excess participation until these provisions are complied with.

Brazil

Pinheiro Neto Advogados
Alexandre Bertoldi, Roberta S. R. Bilotti Demange, Sofia Toledo Piza & Vânia Marques Ribeiro Moyano

BASIC INFORMATION ON THE TYPES OF LIMITED LIABILITY COMPANIES AND ON THE RIGHTS OF SHAREHOLDERS

1. What types of companies enjoy limited liability? If more than one, which ones have shareholders, ie holders of share certificates? Which one is the most common? Which one is mostly used by foreign investors?

Although Brazilian law provides for several forms of business organisations, the only ones that enjoy limited liability are the *sociedades limitadas* (limited companies) governed by Law 10.406/02, as amended, and the *sociedades anônimas* (joint stock companies) governed by Law 6.404/76, as amended (Corporation Law). In both cases, the liability of partners is limited to the amount they contributed to pay up the company's capital; in principle, the partners are not held liable for any amount in excess of such contributions, unless illicit acts are held to occur. However, differently from joint stock companies (in which shareholders are not held liable for any shares subscribed and not paid up by other shareholders), the quota holders of limited companies may be held liable for the subscribed and unpaid corporate capital of the company, including that which was subscribed by other quota holders.

The equity held in joint stock companies is represented by shares and their ownership is evidenced in the share register book. Shares do not need to have a par value and may be represented by certificates. The equity held in limited companies is represented by quotas and its amount and respective par value held by each quota holder is reflected in its articles of association.

Both types are very common and widely adopted in Brazil, by either Brazilian residents or foreign investors. The choice between both types will depend mostly on the level of corporate governance required. Joint stock companies offer the possibility to adopt higher standards of corporate governance, but are also more complex and costly.

2. Are there minimum capital requirements and/or thin capitalisation rules in force?

In principle, there are no minimum capital requirements for the incorporation of companies in Brazil; except when the law specifies a minimum amount due to a specific corporate purpose which shall be performed by the company, for instance, financial institutions which due to the Central Bank rules must be incorporated with a minimum capital.

The Brazilian government enacted Provisional Measure No 472, of 15 December 2009, that was recently converted into Law 12.249/10 to regulate thin capitalisation in Brazil. Pursuant to the current Brazilian legislation, the debt/equity ratios to be used for the purposes of determining the limitations for interest payment deductions under the thin capitalisation rules may vary depending on the place in which the foreign creditor is resident or domiciled, as provided below:

- Related parties not resident in a tax haven jurisdiction: as a general rule, the debt/equity ratio is 2 for 1 for loan transactions entered into between a Brazilian legal entity and a foreign related party not resident in a tax haven jurisdiction or favourable tax regime. This test should be made in two steps: (i) with respect to the specific creditor; and (ii) with respect to all loans with related parties.
- Foreign parties resident in tax haven and favourable tax regime jurisdictions: as a general rule, the debt/equity ratio is 0.3 for 1 for loan transactions entered into between a Brazilian legal entity and a foreign party resident in a tax haven or favourable tax regime jurisdiction (irrespective of not being related to the Brazilian party). In this sense, pursuant to the applicable tax legislation, interest payments made to a foreign party resident in a tax haven or favourable tax regime jurisdiction are not deductible for corporate taxation purposes if the debt raised by the Brazilian entity with the foreign tax haven/favourable tax regime parties happens to exceed 30 per cent of the equity value (net worth) of the Brazilian entity (in this case, only the interest applied over the principal amount of the debt that exceeds the 0.3 for 1 ratio for all the debt borrowed from parties resident in a tax haven or favourable tax regime jurisdiction is not deductible).

3. Describe the types of shares that can be issued by a company and the different rights that they attribute to their owners, as well as any other financial instruments (bonds or other) and other instruments of a participatory nature in the company's capital that can also be issued by the company.

Shares may be common, preferred or fruition, depending on the nature of the rights conferred to shareholders. Common shares entitle each of their holders to one vote in the resolutions of a general meeting (GM). Preferred shares may grant their holders:
(i)   priority in the distribution of fixed or minimum dividends;
(ii) priority in capital repayment, with or without a premium; or
(iii) cumulative advantages dealt with in items (i) and (ii).

Preferred shares will be granted voting rights if the company fails to distribute fixed or minimum dividends for more than three consecutive years.

Common shares in non listed companies may belong to different classes, depending on:
(i)   their non-convertibility into preferred shares;
(ii) the requirement that the shareholder be Brazilian; or

(iii) the right to vote separately for the election of certain officers of the company.

Preferred shares in listed or non listed companies may belong to one or more classes, and carry rights that may include the possibility to elect certain members for the company's administrative bodies, even if such preferred shares are granted with no other voting rights.

Other securities that may be issued by a joint stock company are:

- participation certificates (*partes beneficiárias*): non-par securities issued by non listed companies only that confer on their holders the right to participate in up to 10 per cent of annual profits;
- subscription warrants (*bônus de subscrição*): negotiable securities that can only be issued by a company with authorised capital. These securities entitle their holders to subscribe for shares when the capital is increased, subject to the conditions stated on the corresponding certificates; and
- debentures (*debêntures*): securities that give their holders credit rights against the issuing company. Debentures may be converted into shares, and will be necessarily secured by the issuing company. Unless otherwise permitted by law, the total amount of outstanding debentures cannot exceed the capital of the company.

4.　Can a company have only one shareholder and still enjoy limited liability?

Brazilian law sets forth the exceptional cases in which it is possible to maintain limited liability despite having only one shareholder:

- in limited companies for up to 180 days; and
- in joint stock companies until the annual GM in the year following the company being left with one single shareholder.

If at least two partners are not in place within the terms mentioned above, the company may be subject to dissolution.

The Corporation Law also provided for a specific type of joint stock company that can have only one shareholder: the wholly owned subsidiary (*subsidiária integral*).

5.　Are the rights of shareholders the same in any type of company?

The rights of shareholders vary in accordance with the type of company. In limited companies, for instance, the rights of shareholders are simpler and fewer than in joint stock companies. Even in the same type of company, the rights of a shareholder vary in accordance with the type (common or preferred) and class of shares. However, shares of the same type and class always confer equal rights on their holders.

6.　What are the basic rights of any shareholder? Describe briefly the rights of minority shareholders and indicate which thresholds, if any, are required to allow the minority shareholders to exercise any such rights.

Shareholders' basic rights are:

- to participate in the profits;

- to participate in the assets of the company in the case of its liquidation;
- to monitor the management of the company;
- to exercise the pre-emptive right in the subscription of shares, participation certificates convertible into shares, debentures convertible into shares and/or subscription warrants; and
- to withdraw from the company in the case of certain fundamental changes in the company.

General minority shareholders' rights are:
- to request the judicial liquidation of the company if the officers or the majority of the shareholders fail to provide for liquidation or oppose it in cases in which dissolution of the company is required by law;
- to call a GM if management delays more than 60 days for such a call in cases provided for in the by-laws or by the Corporation Law;
- to file derivative actions against officers for losses caused to the company, provided such an action is not filed by the company within three months of a GM decision; and
- to attend meetings of shareholders and discuss any matter in the agenda.

Rights of shareholders representing 0.5 per cent of the total capital are:
- to request a list of the addresses of the shareholders to which the company sends proxy solicitations for powers of attorney, so as to send them their own proxy request.

Rights of shareholders representing five per cent or more of the total capital include:
- apply for a court order requiring a complete disclosure of corporate books when acts violate the law or the by-laws, or in the event of grounds to suspect that management has committed serious irregularities;
- request the instatement and elect one member of the audit committee;
- request copies of management reports, accounts and financial statements, and opinions of independent auditors, if any;
- file a derivative action against the company's officers to claim losses caused to the company according to a resolution passed at the GM, in the event that the GM decides not to file such an action;
- request that the audit committee furnish information on the matters within its competence;
- request the winding-up of the company by court action, provided the company is not achieving its corporate objectives;
- sue the controlling company to recover damages caused by breach of its controlling shareholder fiduciary duties; and
- call a GM whenever the officers do not, within eight days, comply with their justifiable request that a meeting be called, indicating the matters to be discussed, or whenever the officers do not, within eight days,

comply with the request that a meeting be called in order to appoint an audit committee.

Rights of shareholders representing 10 per cent or more of the voting capital include:

- shareholders with at least 10 per cent of the voting capital may request the adoption of cumulative voting procedures in the election of the members of the board of directors, regardless of whether such a procedure is or is not provided for in the by-laws;
- the holders of at least 15 per cent of the voting capital or 10 per cent of the non-voting shares, excluding the controlling shareholder, have the right to elect one of the board members (if the necessary number of votes is not obtained by 10 per cent of the share capital in preferred shares, or by 15 per cent of the voting capital, these classes may aggregate their share capital to have the right to elect one board member); and
- shareholders representing at least 10 per cent of the voting capital can further elect one member of the audit committee and the respective alternate.

7. Do all shareholders enjoy the same rights or can some shareholders be attributed specific rights, whether by reason of the particular class of stock owned or other? Are such rights generally provided for at the level of the company's by-laws and/or in shareholders' agreements?

As mentioned, the rights of shareholders can vary in accordance with the type (common or preferred) and class of shares. The rights of shareholders are generally provided for at the level of company by-laws, but in some cases can be provided for in the shareholders' agreement as well.

8. May the rights of shareholders, generally speaking, be limited, modified, suppressed or waived in any way? If so, how? Are such modifications or limitations provided for in the company's by-laws and/or in shareholders' agreements?

The rights of shareholders can be modified or suppressed through shareholders' agreements. The by-laws must always respect the minimum standards established in Brazilian law.

GENERAL MEETING OF SHAREHOLDERS (GM) AND VOTING RIGHTS
9. Which decisions are reserved to the competence of the GM?

The GM has exclusive authority to:
- amend the by-laws;
- elect or discharge the company's management and audit committee members at any time;
- receive the annual accounts of the management and resolve on the

financial statements presented by them;
- authorise the issuance of debentures;
- suspend the exercise of rights by a shareholder;
- resolve on the appraisal of assets contributed by any shareholder to the company's capital;
- authorise the issuance of participation certificates;
- resolve on the transformation, merger, consolidation, spin-off, winding-up and liquidation of the company; to elect and dismiss liquidators; and to examine the liquidators' accounts; and
- authorise the managers to admit bankruptcy of the company and to file for debt rehabilitation.

10. How does a shareholder participate in a GM? Are there any limitations to having a minimum number of shares? May a shareholder delegate attendance to another shareholder or to the board? May a shareholder obtain assistance from the courts or any other governmental body to intervene in a GM or to cause one to be held in some particular cases?
The attendees of a GM must bring forth evidence of their shareholder status, and may be represented by proxy. There are no requirements of a minimum number of shares and all common shares are entitled to one vote in the GM.

A shareholder may be represented at a GM by a proxy appointed less than one year before, who shall be a shareholder, a company officer or a lawyer; in a listed company, the proxy may also be a financial institution. A condominium shall be represented by its investment fund officer.

A shareholder may obtain assistance through the courts or the Brazilian Securities Commission (CVM) to intervene in a GM or cause a GM to be held in specific cases.

11. May a GM be called and held at the request of any shareholder? Is there a threshold regarding the percentage of the stock interest owned in the company that may entitle a shareholder to such a right?
A GM must be called by the board of directors (if any) or the executive officers as determined in the company's by-laws. GMs may also be called by:
- the audit committee, in the cases prescribed by law;
- any shareholder, whenever the officers delay the call to resolve on a matter required by law or the by-laws for more than 60 days;
- shareholders representing at least five per cent of the capital, whenever the corporation officers do not, within eight days, comply with their justifiable request that a meeting be called, indicating the matters to be discussed; and
- shareholders representing at least five per cent of the voting capital, or five per cent of non-voting shareholders, whenever the corporation officers do not, within eight days, comply with the request to call a meeting in order to appoint an audit committee.

12. May a shareholder bring up an issue to be resolved upon and put it to a vote if it is not included on the agenda? May a shareholder require more information from the GM and/or the board, concerning the agenda of the GM, to be put in a better position to exercise their vote?
Only if all shareholders are present at the GM is it possible for a shareholder to bring up an issue to be resolved and put it to a vote if it has not been included in the GM agenda. Shareholders may require more information from the GM and from the board of directors to be able to vote.

13. May a GM be held by telecommunication means and/or by correspondence (ie by written consent)?
In accordance with the Corporation Law, shareholders' meetings must be held live, in the company's headquarters, unless prevented by force majeure. In limited liability companies, however, it is possible to have written resolutions of the quota holders instead of quota holders' meetings, if all quota holders decide in writing on a matter that would be the object of a quota holders' meeting.

14. Are voting rights always proportionate to the stock held by each shareholder or can they vary by share class?
Each common share grants its holder one vote in the shareholders' meeting. The only exception is the cumulative voting procedures in the election of the members of the board of directors, more detailed in question 6 above.

15. Are there non-voting shares? Is there a maximum percentage of capital represented by non-voting shares?
Preferred shares can be non-voting. Companies may issue non-voting preferred shares up to 50 per cent of the company's total capital stock. If provided for in the by-laws, non-voting preferred shares of a company established prior to the enactment of Law 10.303/01, which amended the Corporation Law, may represent up to two-thirds of its capital stock.

16. Can shareholders group their shares in order to exercise their voting rights (eg, by trust, shareholders' agreement or otherwise)?
Shareholders may group their shares; usually the shares are grouped to exercise the right to call a shareholders' meeting, receive information or in the context of cumulative voting procedures.

17. Under what circumstances can a shareholder challenge the resolutions adopted by the GM? Are there thresholds concerning the stock interest owned to be able to bring such a claim?
In general terms, any shareholder has three tracks to protect its rights, including against resolutions adopted by the GM that are against the law, the by-laws or the shareholders' agreement:
(i)   within the company, chasing the management bodies, the audit committee or the GM;
(ii) administratively, filing a claim with the CVM (if it is a listed company);

or

(iii) judicially, filing a claim before the courts or the arbitration tribunal, as the case may be.

In addition, under certain specific circumstances, the shareholders have some specific rights that can be viewed as ways of challenging the GM's resolution, such as:

(i)   the withdrawal rights (please refer to question 32 below); and
(ii) the right of shareholders owning 10 per cent or more of the share capital of a listed company to request a new valuation of the company in the context of a mandatory public offer.

18. What are the terms and procedures to challenge a resolution of the GM?

The Corporation Law does not establish any specific mechanism for the shareholders to challenge the resolutions adopted by the GM, but in general, shareholders have 15 to 30 days as from the date of the publication of the resolution to file the appropriate claims.

SHAREHOLDERS' RIGHTS VERSUS DIRECTORS AND DUTIES OF OTHER CORPORATE BODIES IN THE COMPANY

19. What is the procedure for the appointment/replacement/ revocation of directors and of statutory auditors, if any?

The appointment/replacement/revocation of directors and of the audit committee is within the competence of the annual GM, which must take place during the first four months of every year, and is approved by the majority of the shareholders present at the meeting (except for the special rights of preferred and minority shareholders to elect one member each).

Except when otherwise provided in the by-laws, in the event of a vacancy in a position on the board of directors a replacement shall be appointed by the remaining board members and shall serve until the next GM. Should vacancies occur in the majority of positions, a GM shall be called to hold a new election.

20. May shareholders challenge the resolutions of the board of directors? Is there a minimum percentage of capital required to challenge a board resolution?

The Corporation Law does not establish a specific mechanism for shareholders to challenge the resolutions of the board of directors, but as a general rule, a duly called and convened GM is empowered to decide all matters relating to the objects of the company and to adopt such resolutions as it deems necessary for the protection of the company as an ongoing concern.

21. Are shareholders entitled to bring a legal action against the directors of the company? In which circumstances? Please describe briefly the principles of directors' liability.

By a resolution adopted in a GM, the company may bring an action for civil liability against any manager (directors or officers) for the losses caused to the company's property. Any shareholder may bring this suit if proceedings are not instituted within three months from the date of the resolution of the GM. Should the GM decide not to file a liability suit, it may be brought by shareholders representing at least five per cent of the capital stock.

Any damages recovered by a liability suit brought by a shareholder shall accrue to the company, but the company shall reimburse them for all expenses incurred, up to the limit of such damages.

This liability suit does not preclude any action available to any shareholder or third party directly harmed by the acts of the manager.

The general rule concerning directors' liability is that they will not be personally liable for the damages caused by actions undertaken on behalf of the company in the normal course of business, which are performed in the best interests of the company, and pursuant to the provisions of existing laws or the by-laws. The company may nevertheless be liable for damages to third parties which arise as a consequence of these actions. Liability of the company in this case would arise as a consequence of its status as a legal entity and liability could range from contractual (for example, breach of contract) to strict liability (for example, supply of defective products).

The directors will, however, be liable for any loss caused when they act negligently or fraudulently ('subjective liability') in breach of their fiduciary duties or in breach of existing laws or by-laws ('objective liability'). Directors' fiduciary duties may be summarised as follows:
(i)   duty of diligence to fulfil the company's purpose;
(ii) duty of loyalty;
(iii) duty of confidentiality; and
(iv) duty to disclose any personal conflict of interest situation.

It should be noted that a director will also be held personally liable for the acts performed by their fellow directors, if they do not expressly state their disagreement and if they do not ensure that such disagreement is registered in the minutes of the meeting during which the decision was taken, or if they do not communicate to the next management level in writing their dissenting vote or the information with regard to irregularities that are within their knowledge.

22. What are the rights in connection with transactions where the directors have a conflict of interest situation?

A manager (directors or officers) is prohibited by the law to take part in any corporate transaction in which they have an interest that conflicts with an interest of the company, or in the decisions made by the other managers on the matter. They must disclose their disqualification to the other managers and must cause the nature and extent of their interest to be recorded in the minutes of the board of directors or executive office meeting.

Notwithstanding the foregoing, a manager may only contract with the company at arm's length terms. Any business contracted other than in accordance with this rule is voidable, and the manager concerned will be compelled to transfer to the company all benefits which they may have obtained in such business.

INFORMATION RIGHTS ON THE COMPANY'S BUSINESS

23. What information may be requested by the shareholders from the board concerning the general state of the company's business or any specific transaction? Are information rights different depending on the number of shares owned? Are shareholders entitled to receive written information before, during or after the GM about the meeting agenda and to what extent? Is it possible for a shareholder to obtain a copy of the minutes of the GM?

All documents related to the matters subject to the approval of the GM must be available to the shareholders at the company's headquarters at the time that the GM is called.

One month before the date of the annual GM, the managers must make available to the shareholders (including to take copies):

(i)   the management report on the company's affairs and major administrative events of the last financial year;
(ii) copies of the accounts and financial statements;
(iii) the opinion of the independent auditors, if any;
(iv) the audit committee's opinion, including dissenting opinions, if any; and
(v)   other documents relating to matters included in the agenda.

The company managers or at least one of them and the independent auditor, if any, shall be present at the GM to deal with any request by shareholders for clarification, but the managers may not vote as shareholders or as proxies on the documents mentioned above.

Should the GM require further clarification, it may postpone the resolution and order an investigation; subject to a waiver by the shareholders present at the meeting, the resolution may also be deferred if a manager, a member of the statutory audit committee or the independent auditor fails to attend the meeting.

Every shareholder is entitled to obtain a copy of the minutes of the GM.

In addition, any shareholder owning at least 0.5 per cent of the share capital has the right to request the addresses of the shareholders for the purposes of exercising the proxy rights.

24. Do shareholders have the right/duty to resolve in the GM upon matters which were not on the agenda?

No.

25. Are shareholders entitled to inspect the corporate books and/or any other corporate or accounting documents? To what extent? Can they do it through external counsel or advisors?

In addition to the right to inspect the accounting documents as set forth above, at the request of shareholders representing at least five per cent of the capital stock, a full disclosure of the company's books may be ordered by the court whenever acts contrary to law or to the by-laws occur or there is a grounded fear of serious irregularities committed by any of the company's management bodies.

SHAREHOLDERS' AGREEMENTS
26. Are shareholders' agreements validly enforceable? What are their typical contents and term of duration? Are they enforceable by or against third parties and, if so, to what extent?
Shareholders' agreements regulating the purchase and sale of shares, the right of first refusal to acquire shares, the exercise of voting rights or the existing controlling powers shall be observed by the company when filed at its headquarters.

The commitments or burdens resulting from such an agreement may only be enforced against a third party after the agreement has been duly entered in the registration books and on the share certificates, if any.

The chairman of the meeting or of the company's decision-making board shall not compute the vote cast in violation of the shareholders' agreement on file.

The term of duration of the shareholders' agreements may vary a lot, but usually they have long-term duration (10 to 20 years) or they last for as long as the shareholders concerned continue to own a certain percentage of the share ownership.

27. Do shareholders' agreements have to be disclosed to the public or registered in any public registry?
Shareholders' agreements of listed companies are publicly available through the CVM. Shareholders' agreements of privately held companies are filed in the company's headquarters and should be available only to interested parties upon justifiable request.

ECONOMIC RIGHTS AND RIGHTS OVER THE STOCK
28. Is the stock always freely transferable? Are there any legal limitations? Are there any restrictions on contractual limitations?
The by-laws of non listed companies may impose restrictions on the transfer of registered shares, provided that restrictions are defined in detail and do not preclude their negotiability nor subject the shareholder to discretionary decisions of the company's management bodies or majority shareholders. A restriction on the transfer of shares created by an amendment to the by-laws shall only apply to shares whose owners have expressly consented to such a restriction, by requesting its annotation in the registered shares register.

Shares of listed companies may only be traded after 30 per cent of their issue price has been paid. Non-compliance with this provision shall render the act void.

29. Are shareholders entitled to pledge their stock?
The pledge of shares is effected by recording the respective instrument in the registered shares register. A pledge of book-entry shares is effected by the entry of the respective instrument in the books of the financial institution; such an entry shall be annotated on the deposit account statement provided to the shareholder. The company or financial institution is always entitled to request a copy of the pledge instrument for its files.

30. Are there financial assistance issues to be considered and other prohibitions to be evaluated in the context of a leveraged buyout transaction?

A limitation to be considered in the case of financial assistance is related to thin capitalisation rules (please refer to question 2 above).

31. May a company buy back its own stock and, if so, under what circumstances and subject to which limitations?

A company may not trade in its own shares. This prohibition does not apply to:

(i) redemption, repayment or amortisation operations provided for by law;
(ii) shares acquired to be held in the company treasury or cancelled, in an amount up to the outstanding balance of profits or reserves, the statutory reserve excepted, and without entailing a reduction in the corporate capital, or by donation;
(iii) the disposal of shares acquired under item (ii) above, and held in treasury; or
(iv) the purchase of shares when, it being resolved that the capital will be reduced through a cash redemption of part of the share value, their stock exchange price is less than or equal to the amount to be repaid.

Listed companies may purchase shares issued by themselves, for cancellation or holding in treasury for further disposal, if authorised by its by-laws and provided that the total amount of purchased shares does not exceed 10 per cent of each class of outstanding shares (including existing shares held in treasury by controlled and associated companies).

The purchase price of the shares may not exceed the market value. While held in treasury, the shares shall have no rights to dividends or vote.

32. Is there a legal right to withdraw from the company and, if so, under what circumstances? How is the shareholders' stock valued and paid in such a case?

The approval of the following matters gives the dissenting shareholder the right to withdraw from the company against repayment of its shares:

(i) creation of preferred shares or increase in an existing class of preferred shares, without maintaining the existing ratio to the other classes of preferred shares, unless already provided for or authorised by the by-laws;
(ii) change in the priorities, advantages and conditions of redemption or authorisation of one or more classes of preferred shares, or the creation of a more favoured new class;
(iii) reduction of the compulsory dividend;
(iv) consolidation of the company, or its merger into another;
(v) participation in a group of companies;
(vi) change in the objects of the company; or
(vii) spin-off of the company.

The withdrawal rights are subject to the following rules:
• in the events of items (i) and (ii), only the holder of shares of adversely

affected kinds or classes will have the right to withdraw;

- in the cases of items (iv) and (v), the right to withdraw from the company shall not apply to holders of shares of a type or class which has liquidity and dispersion in the market. There will be: (a) liquidity, when the type or class of share is part of a general securities portfolio index eligible for trading on the securities market in Brazil or abroad, as defined by the CVM; and (b) dispersion, when the controlling shareholder, the parent company or other companies under its common control hold less than half of the shares of a certain type or class;
- in the case of item (vii), the right to withdraw shall only apply if the spin-off results in: (a) a change of the corporate objective, unless the spun-off equity is transferred to a company with the same core activity as that of the resulting company; (b) a reduction in the compulsory dividends; or (c) the participation in a group of companies; and
- share redemption shall be demanded from the company within 30 days from the publication of the minutes of the GM.

Shareholders dissenting from a resolution of the GM, including the holders of non-voting preferred shares, may exercise the right to repay those shares of which they were the holders of record on the date of the first publication of the meeting call notice, or on the date of communication of the relevant fact underlying the resolution, whichever is earlier.

Within the 10-day period following expiration of the term dealt with under the last bullet point above, the management bodies may call a GM to affirm or overturn the resolution, should they deem that payment of the redemption price for the shares to the dissenting shareholders that exercised the right to withdraw will threaten the financial stability of the company.

The by-laws may establish rules for determining the repayment amount, which in any event may only be less than the shareholders' equity shown in the latest balance sheet approved by the GM, if based on the company's economic value ascertained by valuation procedures.

If the GM resolution is adopted more than 60 days after the date of the latest approved balance sheet, the dissenting shareholder may demand, together with the repayment claim, that a special balance sheet be prepared as of a date within said 60-day period. In this case, the company shall forthwith pay 80 per cent of the repayment amount calculated according to the latest balance sheet and, after the special balance sheet is ready, the balance shall be paid within 120 days from the GM resolution date.

If the by-laws stipulate the valuation of shares for repayment purposes, the amount will be determined by three experts or a specialised company. The experts or specialised company must be nominated from a six- or three-person list, respectively, by the board of directors or, if there is none, by the officers, and chosen by the GM (by majority approval); each share shall carry one vote, independent of type or class.

33. In which circumstances can dividends be distributed among shareholders? Is it possible to exclude or limit the right of certain shareholders to dividends? Does a certain portion of the profits need to be set aside in a reserve fund where it cannot be distributed to the shareholders? Are advances on dividends allowed and, if so, under which circumstances? Can advances on dividends be reclaimed by the company?

The company may only pay dividends from the year-end net profits, the accrued profits and the profit reserves. Advances on dividends are not allowed.

Without prejudice to criminal prosecution as applicable, the management and audit committee members shall be jointly liable for reimbursement to the company of the amount distributed as dividends in breach of the foregoing rule.

The shareholders shall not be required to repay the dividends received in good faith. Bad faith is held to occur when dividends are distributed without preparation of a balance sheet or otherwise than in accordance with the results it discloses.

Any GM resolution or by-laws provision that excludes the right of any shareholder to the dividends is void. Nevertheless, the right to dividends is not specific to a certain percentage of the profits. Therefore, different classes of shares may have distinct dividend related rights.

Before any other use, five per cent of the year-end net profit shall be set aside to a legal reserve, which may not exceed 20 per cent of the capital stock. The legal reserve is intended to secure the capital stock and may only be utilised to offset losses or to increase the capital stock.

In the case of limited companies, the articles of association may allow the disproportional distribution of profits.

34. What are the rights of shareholders in the case of an issue of new stock (increase of the company's corporate capital) (pre-emption rights)?

The shareholders have pre-emptive rights in the subscription for a capital increase in proportion to the number of shares they own.

The by-laws or a GM will establish a period of not less than 30 days within which the pre-emptive right may be exercised.

The by-laws of a listed company authorising capital increases may provide for the issuance – without granting the existing shareholders the pre-emptive rights, or with a term for the exercise of such rights shorter than 30 days – of shares, debentures convertible into shares or subscription warrants, provided that these securities are placed by means of: (i) a sale in a stock exchange or public subscription, or (ii) by exchange for shares in a public tender offer for the acquisition of corporate control.

The issue price in a capital increase must be fixed, without unjustified dilution in the equity interests held by existing shareholders, even if they have pre-emptive rights of, considering, alternatively or jointly, the following criteria:

- the company's income forecast;
- the net equity value of the shares; and/or
- the price of its shares on the stock exchange or organised over-the-counter market, a premium or discount being permitted in accordance with market conditions.

35. May minority shareholders ban or limit the company's capital structure in any manner?
No.

36. Which are the financial assistance prohibitions in force?
Limitations to financial assistance are related to thin capitalisation rules (please refer to question 2).

37. Apart from publicly listed companies, in which cases (if any) are shareholders obligated to obtain an authorisation from, or provide information to, a public authority about events that have an impact on their stock interest in the company?
Apart from publicly listed companies, there are no events in which the shareholders are obligated to obtain any authorisation or provide any information about impact on their stock interest in a company, except for antitrust authorisation (when applicable).

SHAREHOLDERS' RIGHTS IN THE CASE OF EXTRAORDINARY TRANSACTIONS AND/OR WINDING-UP
38. What rights are available to shareholders in the case of a sale of all or a substantial portion of the company's assets? In the case of a merger or de-merger?
With respect to the sale of company assets, the Corporation Law provides that the board of directors of a company shall, unless otherwise provided in its by-laws, decide on the disposal of any fixed assets, as well as on any encumbrance or lien created in respect to any asset, and on in rem collaterals granted for the benefit of third parties.

In the merger and de-merger scenarios, the dissenting shareholder shall have the right to withdraw from the company against repayment of its shares (please refer to question 32 above).

39. Which rights are available to shareholders in the case of conversion of the company into a European Company (SE) or into another type of company?
A change in the corporate type of a company requires the unanimous consent of the shareholders, unless otherwise prescribed in the by-laws or articles of association. When the by-laws provide for a smaller quorum, the dissenting shareholder shall have the right to withdraw from the company (please refer to question 32 above). Please note that the withdrawal right upon a change of corporate type may be previously waived by the shareholders in the by-laws of the company.

40. Which rights are available to shareholders of a company in liquidation?

Neither the by-laws nor the GM may deprive a shareholder of its right to participate in the assets of the company in the case of winding-up. Prior to completing the liquidation and after all creditors have been paid, the shareholders' GM may decide on the apportionment of the remaining assets among the shareholders. With the approval of the shareholders representing 90 per cent of the shares of the company, the GM may determine special conditions for the apportionment of the remaining assets by attributing assets to the shareholders at book value or at another value established by the GM.

41. Can shareholders cause the liquidation of the company? How?

In addition to the events of a court order and a decision of competent governmental authorities, a company shall be dissolved:
(i)   when its period of duration terminates;
(ii) in the cases provided in the by-laws;
(iii) by resolution of a GM;
(iv) if there remains one single shareholder (as certified at an annual GM) and at least two shareholders are not in place until the annual GM of the following year; and
(v) by cancellation of its authorisation to operate, by operation of law.

If the by-laws are silent, a GM (or the board of directors, if any) shall establish the liquidation mechanisms and appoint the liquidator and the audit committee to serve during the period of liquidation. The liquidator may be removed at any time by the body that had appointed him.

COMPANY GROUPS

42. Is the concept of 'group' recognised as such under specific legislation? What are the implications?

The Corporation Law provides that the controlling company and its controlled companies may form a group by an agreement to combine resources or efforts to achieve their respective purposes or to participate in joint activities or undertakings. Additionally, Brazilian labour laws provide that companies under common control or management may be considered a group and may be held jointly liable for labour and social security matters.

43. Does a controlling company have any particular duties *vis-à-vis* its controlled company shareholders?

Among others, the controlling shareholder must use its controlling power to make the company accomplish its purpose and perform its social role, and shall have duties towards the other shareholders of the company, respecting and defending their rights and interests.

44. What are the rights of company shareholders when the controlling company puts in place actions and/or transactions that can be prejudicial to the shareholders?

The company's shareholders may sue the controlling shareholder for damages caused by acts performed in abuse of its power (please refer to question 6).

45. What are the limitations, if any, to the possibility of owning reciprocal stock interests in companies?

As a general rule, the Corporation Law prohibits cross-holdings between a company and its affiliates or controlled companies. However, such a prohibition shall not apply to the cases in which a certain company holds equity interests in another under the conditions on which the law authorises acquisition of its own shares (please refer to question 31 above).

When cross-holdings derive from a merger, consolidation or spin-off, or from acquisition by the company of a controlling interest in another company, this fact shall be mentioned in the reports and financial statements of both companies and shall be eliminated within one year; in the case of affiliates, unless otherwise agreed, the shares or quotas acquired most recently or, when acquired on the same date, those representing a lesser percentage of the capital stock, shall be disposed of.

The managers of a company may be held civilly and criminally liable for the acquisition of shares or quotas resulting in cross-holdings in breach of the law.

Chile

Cariola Diez Perez-Cotapos & Compañía Limitada
Francisco Javier Illanes, Pedro Lluch & Carolina Flisfisch

BASIC INFORMATION ON THE TYPES OF LIMITED LIABILITY COMPANIES AND ON THE RIGHTS OF SHAREHOLDERS
1. What types of companies enjoy limited liability? If more than one, which ones have shareholders, ie holders of share certificates? Which one is the most common? Which one is mostly used by foreign investors?
The companies that enjoy limited liability are:
- Corporations (*sociedad anónima*), a company incorporated by at least two shareholders, owning shares, which is governed by Law 18,046 on Corporations (the Corporations Law), Decree 587 of 1982, that approves the Corporations Regulations (the Corporations Regulations), and Law 18,046 about Market Securities Law (the Securities Law), as applicable;
- Corporation by shares (*sociedad por acciones*)(SPA), is a company incorporated by at least one shareholder, owning shares, which is governed by the applicable provisions of the Commercial Code. The shareholders may freely agree in the company's by-laws their rights and liabilities, the management regime and other agreements. Otherwise, they are governed by the rules for non-listed corporations; and
- limited liability company (*sociedad de responsabilidad limitada*) - a company incorporated by two or more partners (owners of interest rights), which is governed by Law 3,918.

The companies indicated in the first and second points have shareholders. The most common companies are those indicated in the first and third points, both for local and foreign investors. The SPA is unusual under local law, as they were only recently created.

2. Are there minimum capital requirements and/or thin capitalisation rules in force?
No, there are not.

3. Describe the types of shares that can be issued by a company and the different rights that they attribute to their owners, as well as any other financial instruments (bonds or other) and other instruments of a participatory nature in the company's capital that can also be issued by the company.
A company may issue different classes of shares, ie, common shares or preferred shares. The common shares grant the same rights to all of the shareholders. The preferred shares grant some privileges or preferences

to their holders, with respect to the holders of common shares. The shareholders of a given preferred class of shares have the same rights.

A company may issue debt securities convertible into shares. The most common debt securities are bonds. The securities that grant future rights over the shares of a company shall be offered at least once, to the company's shareholders on a pro rata basis. This preferential right of the shareholders may be waived and may be transferred.

4. Can a company have only one shareholder and still enjoy limited liability?
The SPA may have one shareholder. The corporations (on a temporary basis and in certain events) may have one shareholder and still enjoy limited liability.

5. Are the rights of shareholders the same in any type of company?
Not necessarily. The shareholders of an SPA may freely regulate their rights in the company's by-laws. In cases where the by-laws do not cover them, an SPA's shareholders' rights will be governed by the laws and rules applicable to corporations.

6. What are the basic rights of any shareholder? Describe briefly the rights of minority shareholders and indicate which thresholds, if any, are required to allow the minority shareholders to exercise any such rights.
The basic rights of any shareholder are:
* ownership over their shares, which comprises the right freely to transfer and encumber the same, and not to be deprived of their ownership, unless by judicial order or expropriation;
* not to be deprived of their quota in the company's capital, which is expressed in the pre-emptive right to subscribe to shares in the case of a capital increase;
* to the profits of the company, amounting to the proportion stated in the by-laws in the case of non-listed companies, and amounting to at least 30 per cent of the annual profits in the case of listed companies;
* to speak and vote in the shareholders' meetings;
* to be informed about the company's activities;
* to exercise their judicial rights in order to challenge any act of the company, such as the agreements of the board of directors or the shareholders' general meeting (GM), or others; and
* to withdraw from the company in the event of circumstances provided by the Corporations Law.

The main legal rights of minority shareholders are the following:
* shareholders who represent at least 10 per cent of the issued voting shares may request the board of directors to call for a GM, and in the case of non-listed corporations, if the board does not call a GM when it has to, the shareholders who represent 10 per cent of the issued voting shares may directly call one;

- shareholders who represent at least five per cent of the issued voting shares may, on behalf and for the benefit of the company, claim indemnity against whoever may be liable, for any damage or loss caused to the company's equity, as a result of a breach of the Corporations Law, the corporations regulations, the company's by-laws, the regulations provided by the board of directors pursuant to the law, and the regulations issued by the local National Commission of Securities and Insurance (the 'superintendence' or SVS);
- shareholders of non-listed companies who represent at least 20 per cent of the issued voting shares may judicially request the dissolution of the company in some events; and
- some GM matters require the approval by a supermajority of two-thirds of the voting stock of the company, ie, the transformation or merger of the corporation or its split-up into two or more companies, the amendment of the corporation's duration term, the early dissolution of the corporation, the reduction of the number of board members and the manner in which the profits are distributed, among others.

7. Do all shareholders enjoy the same rights or can some shareholders be attributed specific rights, whether by reason of the particular class of stock owned or other? Are such rights generally provided for at the level of the company's by-laws and/or in shareholders' agreements?

The general rule is that all shareholders enjoy the same legal rights. However, the company's by-laws may provide the existence of particular classes of shares whose holders may be attributed some specific preferences or rights. The existence of classes of shares shall be provided in the company's by-laws (whether at the time of the incorporation of the company or through a later amendment) and shall have the duration of a given period of time.

8. May the rights of shareholders, generally speaking, be limited, modified, suppressed or waived in any way? If so, how? Are such modifications or limitations provided for in the company's by-laws and/or in shareholders' agreements?

The rights of shareholders may be limited, modified, suppressed or waived in the company's by-laws and/or in shareholders' agreements, provided that they are not deemed to be public law or non-waivable (ie, the right to receive dividends; the right to receive payments of capital reductions).

GENERAL MEETING OF SHAREHOLDERS (GM) AND VOTING RIGHTS

9. Which decisions are reserved to the competence of the GM?

Shareholders may meet in annual or extraordinary GMs.

The following decisions are reserved to the competence of annual GMs:

- the review of the company's situation and the reports of the account inspectors or external auditors, and the approval or rejection of the

annual report, balance sheet, financial statements and financial statements submitted by the corporation's managers or liquidators;
- the distribution of profits of each financial year and, especially, dividend distribution;
- the election or revocation of the regular and alternate board members, liquidators and management supervisors; and
- in general, any other subject of corporate interest that is not reserved to the competence of extraordinary GMs.

The following decisions are reserved to the competence of extraordinary GMs:
- the company's dissolution;
- the company's transformation, merger or split-up, and the amendment of its by-laws;
- the issuing of bonds or debentures convertible into shares;
- the transfer of 50 per cent or more of the company's assets, or the making or amendment of any business plan that contemplates the transfer of assets that exceeds this percentage; the transfer of 50 per cent or more of the assets of a subsidiary, provided the subsidiary represents at least 20 per cent of the assets of the relevant company, as well as any transfer of the shares that entails that the controlling company loses its control;
- the granting of real or personal securities to secure third parties' obligations, except if those are subsidiaries, in which case the approval of the board of directors shall be sufficient; and
- any other subjects that, pursuant to the law or the by-laws, are reserved to the competence of a GM.

The meetings dealing with matters outlined in the first to the fourth points listed above, shall be held before a notary public.

10. How does a shareholder participate in a GM? Are there any limitations to having a minimum number of shares? May a shareholder delegate attendance to another shareholder or to the board? May a shareholder obtain assistance from the courts or any other governmental body to intervene in a GM or to cause one to be held in some particular cases?

A shareholder may only participate in a GM if their shares are registered in the company's shareholder registry at the time of the GM. In the case of listed corporations, a shareholder may participate and exercise their right to vote only if their shares are registered in the shareholder registry at least five days before the relevant GM is held. If the company has issued shares that do not give their holders the right to vote, the shareholders may attend the GM and only exercise their right to speak. There are no limitations on the minimum number of shares owned to be allowed to participate in a GM.

Shareholders may participate in a GM acting personally or represented by another person, who may be another shareholder (provided it is an individual) or a third party. The relevant proxy shall be granted by the shareholder in writing for the total number of shares they (the shareholder) holds. The attendance cannot be delegated to the board of directors.

A representative of the SVS may participate in any listed company GM. If any dispute arises regarding the validity of any power of attorney filed by a shareholder's delegate to participate in a listed or non-listed corporation's GM, the dispute may be taken to the courts or arbitration.

Shareholders of listed corporations may obtain assistance from the SVS to call a GM. Also, in the case of listed and non-listed corporations, the shareholders that represent at least 10 per cent of the issued voting shares may request the board of directors to call for a GM.

11. May a GM be called and held at the request of any shareholder? Is there a threshold regarding the percentage of the stock interest owned in the company that may entitle a shareholder to such a right?

GMs are called by the company's board of directors. Shareholders representing 10 per cent of the issued voting shares may request the board of directors to call for a GM. In the case of non-listed corporations, if the board of directors has not called a GM when it should have, shareholders representing at least 10 per cent of the issued voting shares may call the GM directly by means of publishing a notice in a national newspaper stating the date and time at which the GM will be held and the matters that will be submitted to the shareholders. In the case of listed corporations, the SVS may also request the board of directors to call for a GM or directly call a GM in cases where it deems it necessary.

Also, the shareholders may validly hold a GM without the prior call of the board of directors, provided all the issued voting shares attend the relevant GM.

12. May a shareholder bring up an issue to be resolved upon and put it to a vote if it is not included on the agenda? May a shareholder require more information from the GM and/or the board concerning the agenda of the GM, to be put in a better position to exercise their vote?

A shareholder may bring up an issue to be resolved upon and put it to a vote in a GM if it was not included on the agenda, provided the GM is attended by all of the voting shares issued by the company. During the GM, the shareholders may request more information from the GM and the board of directors, concerning the matters that are being submitted to the shareholders.

13. May a GM be held by telecommunication means and/or by correspondence (ie by written consent)?

A GM may not be held by telecommunication means and/or by correspondence. However, the SVS may authorise listed corporations to establish and implement systems allowing shareholders to issue their votes remotely, as long as these systems properly guarantee the shareholders' rights and a normal voting process.

14. Are voting rights always proportionate to the stock held by each shareholder or can they vary by share class?

Voting rights are generally proportionate to the shares held by each shareholder and each shareholder shall have one vote for each share they hold or represent. The by-laws of a company may contemplate the existence of preferred shares with limited voting rights or without voting rights (except for some limited matters that require the unanimous vote of shareholders). Notwithstanding, it is expressly forbidden to establish classes of shares with multiple voting rights.

15. Are there non-voting shares? Is there a maximum percentage of capital represented by non-voting shares?

The by-laws of a company may contemplate a series of preferred shares without voting rights, or with a limited right to vote. The preferences must have a fixed duration. Non-voting shares or shares with a limited right to vote shall not be computed to calculate the quorum to hold a GM or for reaching agreements in a GM. In cases where there are preferred non-voting (or limited voting) shares, such shares shall acquire full voting rights if the company fails to fulfil the preferences granted in their favour, and shall maintain the right until the preferences are fully honoured. The Corporations Law does not contemplate a maximum percentage of capital that can be represented by non-voting shares.

16. Can shareholders group their shares in order to exercise their voting rights (eg by trust, shareholders' agreements or otherwise)?

When exercising the voting rights in an election carried out in a GM, shareholders may accumulate their votes in favour of a single person, or instead group their votes as they deem convenient.

17. Under what circumstances can a shareholder challenge the resolutions adopted by the GM? Are there thresholds concerning the stock interest owned to be able to bring such a claim?

As a general rule, shareholders may not challenge *per se* the resolutions adopted by the GM, unless said resolutions directly breach the Corporations Law, the regulations law, the company's by-laws, the regulations provided by the board of directors pursuant to the law and the regulations issued by the superintendence, and only if said breach causes damage to the company or any other person.

Consequently, any damage or loss caused to the company's equity as a result of said breach shall give a shareholder or a group of shareholders representing at least five per cent of the shares issued by the company, or any of the members of the board of directors, the right to claim indemnity against whoever may be liable, on behalf of the company and for the company's benefit.

18. What are the terms and procedures to challenge a resolution of the GM?

Any controversy that may arise between the shareholders or between the shareholders and the corporation or its management, whether during the corporation's term or during its liquidation, must be subject to arbitration. Unless otherwise stated, the rules and procedures for said arbitration shall be those applicable to the arbitrator *ex aequo et bono*.

SHAREHOLDERS' RIGHTS VERSUS DIRECTORS AND DUTIES OF OTHER CORPORATE BODIES IN THE COMPANY

19. What is the procedure for the appointment/replacement/ revocation of directors and of statutory auditors, if any?

The company's by-laws must establish a fixed number of board members and a period for the duration in their position as directors, which cannot exceed three years. The board shall be completely renovated at the end of each period, and board members may be re-elected indefinitely. The election of the members of the board must take place in a GM, where shareholders may accumulate their votes in favour of a single person, or instead group and/ or distribute their votes as they deem convenient. The candidates with the highest number of votes are elected to be a member of the board.

In the event of the vacancy of a director from their position as a member of the board, the complete board of directors must be renewed in the following annual GM to be held, and, in the meantime, the board may appoint a substitute for the vacant position.

The board of directors may only be revoked completely by an annual or extraordinary GM. The individual or collective revocation of one or more of its members is not allowed.

The annual GMs of non-listed corporations must name two regular and two alternate account inspectors, or a firm of independent external auditors each year, which shall examine the accounts, inventory, balance sheet and other financial statements, unless the shareholders have provided in the by-laws a different means of control for the company. In the case of listed corporations, the annual GM must appoint an external auditing company. These agreements shall be adopted by the absolute majority of the voting shares present or represented in the relevant GM.

20. May shareholders challenge the resolutions of the board of directors? Is there a minimum percentage of capital required to challenge a board resolution?

As a general rule, shareholders may not challenge *per se* the resolutions adopted by the board of directors, unless said resolutions directly breach the Corporations Law, the corporations regulations, the company's by-laws, the regulations provided by the board of directors pursuant to the law, or the regulations issued by the superintendence, and only if that breach causes damage to the company or any other person.

Consequently, any damage or loss caused to the company's equity as a result of said breach shall give a shareholder or a group of shareholders representing at least five per cent of the shares issued by the company, or any of the members of the board of directors, the right to claim indemnity against whoever may be liable, on behalf of the company and for the company's benefit. In any event, the shareholders, through a resolution of a shareholders' meeting, may pass a resolution overruling the board's decision.

21. Are shareholders entitled to bring a legal action against the directors of the company? In which circumstances? Please describe briefly the principles of directors' liability.

Any damage or loss caused to the company's capital as a result of an act of a director or a board of directors' resolution that breaches the Corporations Law, the corporations regulations, the company's by-laws, the regulations provided by the board of directors pursuant to law, or the regulations issued by the SVS, shall give a shareholder or a group of shareholders representing at least five per cent of the shares issued by the company, or any of the members of the board of directors, the right to claim indemnity against whoever may be liable, on behalf of the company and for the company's benefit.

Members of the board of directors must exercise their duties and functions with the diligence that people normally use in their own affairs and businesses, and shall be jointly liable for any damage caused to the company and the shareholders for any fraudulent or negligent actions. Any provision in the company's by-laws or any resolution adopted by a GM that aims to mitigate, release or restrict the liability of the board members shall be null and void.

22. What are the rights in connection with transactions where the directors have a conflict of interest situation?

A non-listed corporation may exclusively enter into contracts or agreements that involve significant amounts (defined in the Corporations Law) in which one or more of the board members has an interest, directly or indirectly, when such transactions are previously acknowledged and approved by the board, and meet conditions similar to those usually prevailing in the market, unless the by-laws authorise the execution of said transactions without the compliance of these conditions.

The violation of the aforementioned rule shall not affect the transaction's validity, but in addition to the relevant administrative penalties that might be applicable, and the corresponding criminal penalties, it shall grant the company, the shareholders or any third parties interested, the right to claim indemnity for the damage caused.

INFORMATION RIGHTS ON THE COMPANY'S BUSINESS

23. What information may be requested by the shareholders from the board concerning the general state of the company's business or any specific transaction? Are information rights different depending on the number of shares owned? Are shareholders entitled to receive written information before, during or after the GM about the meeting agenda and to what extent? Is it possible for a shareholder to obtain a copy of the minutes of the GM?

Information rights are not different depending on the number of shares owned by a shareholder. The board of directors must provide the shareholders and the public in general with sufficient, trustworthy, reliable and timely information, which the law and, if applicable, the SVS may determine in connection with the corporations' legal, economic and financial situation. If the failure to fulfil this obligation causes damage to the corporation, shareholders or third parties, the infringing board member shall be jointly liable for the damage caused.

For listed corporations, the board must send a citation by post to each shareholder at least 15 days in advance of the date set for holding the GM, which must contain a reference to the agenda, as well as indicate how to obtain complete copies of the documents that sustain each of the options that shall be put up to a vote and make available such information on the company website.

During the 15-day period preceding the date set for holding the annual GM, the company shall make available to its shareholders in its corporate offices the annual report, the balance sheets, the inventories, the corporate books and the reports of the account inspectors or external auditors, of the company and its subsidiaries. Listed companies must also make available on their website the annual reports and the audited financial statements. Notwithstanding, the board may approve – with the vote of three-quarters of the directors – that some documents about pending negotiations, the disclosure of which would damage the company's interests, be kept private. Shareholders of non-listed corporations may only have access to minutes of the meetings of the GM during the aforementioned period. A listed corporation must upload on its website and make available to the shareholders the minutes of the most recent shareholders' meeting.

24. Do shareholders have the right/duty to resolve in the GM upon matters which were not on the agenda?

A shareholder may not bring up an issue to be resolved upon at a GM if it was not included in the agenda, unless the GM is attended by all the voting shares issued by the company.

25. Are shareholders entitled to inspect the corporate books and/or any other corporate or accounting documents? To what extent? Can they do it through external counsel or advisors?

The annual report, balance sheet, inventory, minutes, books and reports of the external auditors and, if applicable, of the account inspectors, must be available to the shareholders for their examination at the corporation's management office during a 15-day period prior to the date set for the holding of the annual GM. The shareholders may only examine the documents within the aforementioned period and are not allowed to request this information outside the indicated timeframe.

Although it has not been expressly provided, it is understood and accepted that shareholders are entitled to inspect the corporate books through external counsel or advisors, provided said counsel or advisors evidence proper and sufficient power of attorney.

SHAREHOLDERS' AGREEMENTS

26. Are shareholders' agreements validly enforceable? What are their typical contents and term of duration? Are they enforceable by or against third parties and, if so, to what extent?

Private agreements between shareholders are validly enforceable. They usually refer to two main matters: the transfer of shares (for example, right of first offer, right of first refusal, tag-along, drag-along, prohibition on encumbrances, etc), and corporate governance (for example, the approval of business plans, the election of board members, consultation prior to a GM, protection to minority shareholders, etc). The parties are free to set the duration of these shareholders' agreements, which may even be indefinite.

Shareholders' agreements are enforceable against third parties. In cases where shareholders' agreements refer to the transfer of shares, the agreements must be deposited in the company and placed at the disposal of the rest of the shareholders and any interested third party, and a reference of the same must be made in the company's shareholders' registry. In cases in which a transfer of shares takes place with an infringement of a shareholders' agreement, the third party who purchased the relevant shares is subject to a claim by the complying party, who could request the revocation of said transfer.

There may be a question regarding the responsibility of the company that is a party to a shareholders' agreement, due to its obligation to perform the transfer of shares regardless of any issue in connection with it.

27. Do shareholders' agreements have to be disclosed to the public or registered in any public registry?

Shareholders' agreements that refer to the transfer of shares must be deposited in the company and placed at the disposal of the rest of the shareholders and any interested third party, and reference shall be made to it in the company's shareholders' registry. If the foregoing requirements are not fulfilled, the relevant agreement cannot be opposed to *bona fide* third parties.

ECONOMIC RIGHTS AND RIGHTS OVER THE STOCK

28. Is the stock always freely transferable? Are there any legal limitations? Are there any restrictions on contractual limitations?

The stock is always freely transferable. Companies cannot condition, prevent or obstruct the transfer of shares, and shall be obliged to register any transfers submitted to them, provided that they comply with the formalities specified in the corporations regulations.

The by-laws of non-listed corporations may have provisions restricting the free transfer of shares. Listed corporations cannot do so. Also, shareholders of listed and non-listed corporations may agree certain restrictions or limitations for the transfer of shares in shareholders' agreements.

29. Are shareholders entitled to pledge their stock?

Shareholders are entitled freely to pledge their stock. The exercise of the right to vote and the right to exercise the pre-emptive rights for pledged shares shall correspond to the pledgor, unless otherwise provided in the pledge agreement.

30. Are there financial assistance issues to be considered and other prohibitions to be evaluated in the context of a leveraged buyout transaction?

There are no specific rules regarding financial assistance issues. Notwithstanding, there are some restrictions for the financial support rendered by a subsidiary in favour of its holding company. Any security granted by a subsidiary must have a benefit for the latter (it may be an economic benefit, such as the payment of a guarantee fee).

The granting of securities by a holding company to its subsidiary only requires the board's approval, while the granting of securities by the subsidiary to its holding company requires the approval of two-thirds of the voting issued shares in an extraordinary GM.

31. May a company buy back its own stock and, if so, under what circumstances and subject to which limitations?

Companies may only acquire and hold shares of their own issuance when the acquisition:

(i)   results from the exercise of shareholders' legal right to withdraw from the company;
(ii) results from the merger with another company, which is a shareholder of the surviving company;
(iii) enables the carrying out of a by-law amendment to reduce capital, when the current market price of the shares is lower than the redemption value, which must be proportionately paid to shareholders; and
(iv) allows the fulfilling of a resolution adopted by an extraordinary GM to acquire the shares issued thereby, under certain conditions.

While the shares are held by the corporation, they shall not be computed to establish the quorum in the shareholders' meetings and they shall not have the right to vote, to payment of dividends or preference in the subscription of capital increases.

The shares acquired in accordance with the provisions in (i) and (ii) above shall be sold on a stock exchange within a maximum period of one year, starting from their acquisition, and the non-fulfilment of this provision shall cause the capital to be reduced *ipso facto*.

In the case of companies whose shares are publicly traded, the companies may acquire and hold shares of their own issuance under the following copulative conditions:

(i)   that it is agreed in an extraordinary GM by two-thirds of the voting shares issued;
(ii) the acquisition may only be made up to the amount of the retained earnings; and
(iii) if the company has classes of shares, the acquisition offer must be made in proportion to the number of shares of each class that is publicly traded.

The shareholders' GMs called to consider the acquisition of shares of their own issuance must give an opinion about the maximum amount or percentage to be acquired, the purpose and the duration of the programme, which may not exceed five years, as well as the minimum and maximum price to be paid for the relevant shares. In any case, the shareholders' GM may delegate to the board of directors the setting of the acquisition price. Once the programme to acquire and hold shares of its own issuance is approved in the shareholders' GM, the corporation may not keep shares of its own issuance in its portfolio that represent more than five per cent of its subscribed and paid-in shares. Any resulting excess must be sold within a period of 90 days of the acquisition date that would have generated such excess, notwithstanding the liabilities of the corporation's board members and managers.

Only shares that are fully paid and free of any liens, encumbrances and prohibitions may be acquired through this procedure.

32. Is there a legal right to withdraw from the company and if so, under what circumstances? How is the shareholders' stock valued and paid in such a case?

Shareholders are entitled to withdraw from the company in the event that a shareholders' meeting approves and adopts any of the following matters:

(i) the corporation's transformation;

(ii) the corporation's merger;

(iii) the sale of 50 per cent or more of the assets of the corporation, as well as the transfer of 50 per cent or more of the assets of its subsidiary, provided said subsidiary represents at least 20 per cent of the assets of the company;

(iv) the granting of securities to secure third parties' obligations that exceed 50 per cent of the corporation's assets, unless said third party is a subsidiary;

(v) creating preferences for a class of shares or the increase, reduction or extension of already established preferences, in which event only the dissenting shareholders of the affected series shall have the right to withdraw;

(vi) the validation and amendment of the nullity caused by irregularities of procedure in the company's incorporation, and

(vii) any other event established in law or the by-laws, if applicable.

Notwithstanding, in the event that the corporation has been declared bankrupt, the right to withdraw shall be suspended until outstanding debts that existed at the time the right was generated have been paid.

Withdrawing shareholders shall be paid for the value of their shares. The price to be paid by the corporation to withdrawing shareholders shall be, in non-listed corporations, the book value of the shares, and in listed corporations, the market value of the shares.

The right to withdraw shall be exercised by the dissenting shareholder within 30 days from the date of the shareholders' meeting that adopted the relevant resolution. The price of the shares shall be paid without any

surcharge within 60 days following the date of the shareholders' meeting.
If the price is not paid within said timeframe, the price shall be adjusted by
inflation and shall accrue average interest.

33. In which circumstances can dividends be distributed among shareholders? Is it possible to exclude or limit the right of certain shareholders to dividends? Does a certain portion of the profits need to be set aside in a reserve fund where it cannot be distributed to the shareholders? Are advances on dividends allowed and, if so, under which circumstances? Can advances on dividends be reclaimed by the company?

Dividends shall be paid exclusively from the net earnings of the relevant
financial year, or retained earnings from past balances approved by a
shareholders' meeting. Notwithstanding, in cases where the corporation has
accumulated losses, the financial year's earnings shall be used first to absorb
such losses. If the financial year should have losses, they shall be absorbed
by retained earnings, if there are any.

Unless otherwise unanimously agreed by the voting shares in the relevant
annual shareholders' meeting, listed corporations shall annually distribute
to their shareholders a cash dividend of at least 30 per cent of the net
earnings of the financial year in proportion to the number of shares held by
each shareholder or in the proportion established in the by-laws if there are
preferred shares. For non-listed corporations, the distribution shall be carried
out as provided in the by-laws or, in default of a by-law provision, according
to the rule just mentioned. However, the board of directors may, under the
personal responsibility of the board members concurring with the relevant
resolution, distribute provisional dividends during the financial year to be
charged to the earnings thereof, provided there are no accumulated losses.

There is no legal obligation to set aside a certain portion of the profits in a
reserve fund without distributing it to the shareholders.

34. What are the rights of shareholders in the case of an issue of new stock (increase of the company's corporate capital) (pre-emption rights)?

In the case of an issue of new stock due to the increase of the company's
capital, the options to underwrite said shares or debentures convertible into
shares of the issuing corporation, or of any other securities that grant future
rights over those shares, shall be offered at least once, preferentially, to the
shareholders in proportion to the shares they hold. It is a legal pre-emptive
right.

This right may be waived and transferred, and must be exercised or
transferred within a period of 30 days of the publishing of the option in the
manner and conditions determined in the Corporations Law.

35. May minority shareholders ban or limit the company's capital structure in any manner?

No.

36. Which are the financial assistance prohibitions in force?

Chilean law does not have specific rules regarding financial assistance issues. However, every agreement is required to have a valid cause or consideration. Therefore, the financial support granted by a subsidiary in favour of its holding company, requires a cause, whether a direct benefit for said subsidiary, the payment of a guarantee fee, or other similar benefit.

In addition, the granting of security by a subsidiary to its holding company requires the approval of two-thirds of the voting issued shares in an extraordinary GM. The granting of security by a holding company to its subsidiary only requires the board's approval.

37. Apart from publicly listed companies, in which cases (if any) are shareholders obligated to obtain an authorisation from, or provide information to, a public authority about events that have an impact on their stock interest in the company?

Prior to the reduction of a company's equity or its dissolution, shareholders are obligated to obtain an authorisation from the Internal Revenue Service.

Also, regarding some regulated industries (eg, telecommunications, media), prior to the change of control or merger of a company, or in the case of a transfer of shares, the shareholders must obtain the authorisation of the antitrust authority, and/or have some information obligations with the relevant authorities.

SHAREHOLDERS' RIGHTS IN THE CASE OF EXTRAORDINARY TRANSACTIONS AND/OR WINDING-UP

38. What rights are available to shareholders in the case of a sale of all or a substantial proportion of the company's assets? In the case of a merger or de-merger?

The sale of 50 per cent or more of the company's assets, as well as the transfer of 50 per cent or more of the assets of its subsidiary, provided said subsidiary represents at least 20 per cent of the assets of the company, shall grant to dissenting shareholders the right to withdraw from the company. The same right to withdraw is granted to dissenting shareholders in the event of a merger or de-merger.

39. Which rights are available to shareholders in the case of conversion of the company into a European Company (SE) or into another type of company?

The conversion of the corporation into any other type of company shall also grant to dissenting shareholders the right to withdraw from the company.

40. Which rights are available to shareholders of a company in liquidation?

A dissolved company shall survive as a company for the purposes of its liquidation, and its by-laws shall be fully effective. During its liquidation, the company may only execute acts and enter into contracts for the sole purpose of facilitating the liquidation, and under no circumstances may it continue with its line of business. Apart from the foregoing, shareholders of a company in liquidation maintain all their rights as if the company was still valid and in force.

41. Can shareholders cause the liquidation of the company? How?
Shareholders may cause the winding-up of the company, provided it is agreed in an extraordinary shareholders' meeting with the favourable vote of two-thirds of the voting shares.

Also, shareholders of a non-listed company that represent at least 20 per cent of the voting shares, may request to the relevant court to wind up the company in cases where they consider there is cause, such as a serious infringement of the laws or the regulations that damage the shareholders or the company, bankruptcy of the company, fraudulent management or other situation of the same seriousness.

COMPANY GROUPS
42. Is the concept of 'group' recognised as such under specific legislation? What are the implications?
The concept of 'group' is recognised under the securities law, under the definition of 'business group'. The securities law defines 'business group' as a whole, consisting of entities that present links in their properties, management or debt liabilities, which allows the assumption that the financial or economic performance of the group's members is guided by the common interests of the group or is subordinated to them, or there exists a common financial risk in the debts granted to them or in the acquisition of the securities issued. The same law provides that some entities are deemed to form part of a group, such as:
(i)   a company and its controller;
(ii) all the companies that have a common controller and the controller; and
(iii) any entity determined by the SVS pursuant to some criteria provided in the law.

The main implication for the entities that form part of a business group is that listed companies have certain information obligations with the SVS. Likewise, every entity belonging to the same business group of a listed company that carries out relevant commercial activities with it, shall inform the company that they both have the same controller.

Also, according to the securities law the entities that form part of a business group are considered 'related parties', so the legal and regulatory obligations applicable to the latter also apply to the entity members of the business group.

43. Does a controlling company have any particular duties *vis-à-vis* its controlled company shareholders?
Chilean regulations do not contemplate particular duties *vis-à-vis* a controlling company's controlled company shareholders. However, there is a general legal obligation on the shareholder to exercise their rights with due

respect to the rights of the company and the rights of the other shareholders of the company.

44. What are the rights of company shareholders when the controlling company puts in place actions and/or transactions that can be prejudicial to the shareholders?

There are no specific rights. However, shareholders that represent at least five per cent of the voting shares issued, or any director of the company may, on behalf and for the benefit of the company, claim indemnity against whoever may be liable, for any damage or loss in the company's equity as a result of a breach of the Corporations Law, the corporations regulations, the company's by-laws, the regulations provided by the board of directors pursuant to the law, and the regulations issued by the superintendence.

45. What are the limitations, if any, to the possibility of owning reciprocal stock interests in companies?

Wholly- or partially-owned subsidiaries cannot have, whether directly or indirectly, reciprocal stock interests in their stock interest, nor in the stock interest of their holding company. However, if said reciprocal stock interests occur due to an incorporation, merger, division or acquisition of the control of a corporation, such a circumstance shall be stated in the relevant annual reports and end in the term of one year counted from the relevant event.

People's Republic of China

Fangda Partners Chuanjie Zhou
Kirkland & Ellis International LLP XY Li, David Patrick
Eich, Chuan Li, Mark Horvick, Jing Li & Daniel Wang

BASIC INFORMATION ON THE TYPES OF LIMITED LIABILITY COMPANIES AND ON THE RIGHTS OF SHAREHOLDERS

1. What types of companies enjoy limited liability? If more than one, which ones have shareholders, ie holders of share certificates? Which one is the most common? Which one is mostly used by foreign investors?

Two types of company established within the People's Republic of China (PRC) enjoy limited liability, the limited liability company (LLC) and the company limited by shares (CLS). Both LLCs and CLSs have shareholders and are commonly used, although LLCs, including wholly foreign owned enterprises (WFOEs), equity joint ventures (EJVs) and cooperative joint ventures (CJVs) (as discussed below), are most commonly used by foreign investors.

A company with at least 25 per cent foreign investment is in a distinct category of PRC legal entity called a foreign-invested enterprise (FIE). Although there are several types of FIE, an FIE is typically either a WFOE or a joint venture.

WFOEs

A WFOE is an enterprise the entire equity capital of which is owned by one or more foreign investors. It is a Chinese legal entity formed as an LLC.

Joint ventures

An entity owned partly by a Chinese entity or entities, and usually not less than 25 per cent by one or more foreign investors, is a joint venture, of which there are two basic forms: an EJV and a CJV. Each of an EJV and a CJV is a PRC legal entity, customarily in the form of an LLC created by one or more Chinese entities and one or more foreign investors. Under PRC law, a CJV also can be formed as a non-legal person partnership; however, most existing CJVs have been formed as LLCs.

Other foreign investment entities

In addition to typical WFOE and joint venture structures, there are two special forms of FIE: the foreign-invested holding company (FIHC) and the foreign-invested company limited by shares (FICLS).

An FIHC is an LLC authorised to hold equity in other FIEs. As discussed below, PRC law generally defines an LLC as a company whose shareholders' liability to the company is limited to their subscribed registered capital. In an FICLS, the shareholders' liability to the company is instead based on the relative number of shares held by each shareholder. An FICLS is the only type of FIE that can be listed directly on a stock exchange in China.

2. Are there minimum capital requirements and/or thin capitalisation rules in force?
Minimum capital requirements
The capital structure of a standard FIE is divided into two components: registered capital and total investment. Registered capital is the amount of equity contributed to the company. In general, an investor's ownership interest in a company is determined by the proportion of the registered capital to which it contributes. The registered capital of a PRC company must be fully paid, although payments may be made in instalments. The minimum registered capital requirements of the companies described above can be summarised as follows:

- LLC: generally, RMB 30,000 subject to certain exceptions (eg, in the case of a sole shareholder LLC: RMB 100,000; in the case of a WFOE LLC, however, the threshold is often raised to more than $100,000, the specific amount of which may vary from city to city).
- CLS: RMB 5 million.
- FIHC: $30 million.
- FICLS: RMB 30 million.

Higher minimum capital requirements also may apply to companies within certain regulated industries, such as banking, insurance and telecommunications.

Thin capitalisation rules and debt/equity ratios
In addition to minimum capital requirements, foreign-invested LLCs (including WFOEs and JVs) have maximum permitted debt-to-equity (expressed as minimum equity-to-debt) ratios based upon the total investment of the company. The total investment of a company is the total amount of funding available to the company from both equity and debt of any kind (including bank loans and shareholder loans). That is, an entity generally may borrow foreign debt only to the extent of the difference between its total investment and registered capital. PRC laws generally impose the following requirements on the ratio of the total investment to the registered capital of a foreign-invested LLC.

Total investment	Registered capital
$3 million or less	At least 70 per cent of the total investment
Between $3 million and $10 million	Minimum of $2.1 million, and at least 50 per cent of the total investment
Between $10 million and $30 million	Minimum of $5 million, and at least 40 per cent of the total investment
Over $30 million	Minimum of $12 million, and at least one-third of the total investment

The general rules described above notwithstanding, there is no 'total investment' concept for an FICLS and its offshore borrowing is subject to the approval of applicable PRC governmental authorities on a case-by-case basis. In addition, there is no 'total investment' concept for an FIHC. Generally, though, an FIHC may borrow up to six times its registered capital.

The maximum debt-to-equity ratios may vary for companies under certain circumstances, such as an FIE involved in real estate. In addition, if the total investment is relatively large (eg, exceeding $30 million), upon approval by relevant governmental authorities, the debt-to-equity ratio may be greater than 3:1.

3.   Describe the types of shares that can be issued by a company and the different rights that they attribute to their owners, as well as any other financial instruments (bonds or other) and other instruments of a participatory nature in the company's capital that can also be issued by the company.

Types of shares

Under PRC law, there is only one type of share: the 'ordinary' or 'common' share. In a CJV, however, certain shareholders' rights may by contract be structured differently from the respective proportions of such shareholders' capital contributions (eg, enhanced voting rights including veto rights, preferential distributions, etc). As such, with some limitations, it is possible to effect some preferences among shareholders of the same class of shares in a CJV.

Shareholder loans

Shareholder loans from foreign investors, which are subject to certain governmental registrations and the maximum debt-to-equity ratios noted above, are relatively common in the PRC. Subject to applicable approvals, such loans may be converted into registered capital of an FIE. Generally, individual PRC shareholders are not allowed to make loans to FIEs due to financial regulation restrictions. In addition, under PRC law, PRC entities other than commercial banks and other authorised financial institutions are not permitted to lend directly to a borrower and instead must effect such a loan via an intermediary such as a commercial bank or other authorised financial institution in the form of an 'entrusted loan'.

Corporate bonds

In practice, the PRC corporate bond market remains underdeveloped. Significant regulatory approvals are required for the issuance of corporate bonds, and the issuer must satisfy various criteria including the maximum permitted debt-to-equity ratios, which has made corporate bond issuances by FIEs very rare to date.

4. Can a company have only one shareholder and still enjoy limited liability?

Yes, but the sole shareholder may be held jointly and severally liable for the company's debts if the shareholder fails to prove that the company's assets are separate from and independent of the shareholder's own assets.

5. Are the rights of shareholders the same in any type of company?

Shareholders of each type of company generally share the same types of rights. In a CJV, however, shareholders may contractually vary their rights. In addition, for foreign-invested LLCs (ie, EJVs and CJVs) there are no shareholder meetings and an action taken by the board is the highest authority of the company. In a WFOE, CLS, FIHC or FICLS, the highest authority is an action taken at a general meeting of the shareholders (GM).

6. What are the basic rights of any shareholder? Describe briefly the rights of minority shareholders and indicate which thresholds, if any, are required to allow the minority shareholders to exercise any such rights.

The basic rights of shareholders are as follows:

- to attend and vote at meetings (except for EJVs and CJVs, which do not have shareholder meetings);
- to have access to the company's governance documents, shareholder meeting minutes, board resolutions and financial reports, etc;
- to receive dividends declared by the company;
- to receive a distribution in a liquidation after certain priority payments and creditors have been paid; and
- pre-emptive rights on new issuances (in the case of LLCs).

EJVs and CJVs

In a foreign-invested LLC (ie, an EJV or a CJV), certain decisions require approval by unanimous consent of the directors. Because in an EJV or a CJV board appointment rights generally are proportionate to an investor's relative investment and thus a significant minority investor typically is entitled to a board seat, a minority investor customarily has de facto veto rights over certain material matters requiring unanimous board approval, such as:

- an amendment of the articles;
- a liquidation;
- an increase or decrease of registered capital;
- a merger or spinoff;

- a pledge of assets (in the case of a CJV); and
- other matters as set forth in the articles of association or otherwise agreed to by the shareholders.

WFOEs, CLSs, FIHCs and FICLSs

In a WFOE, CLS, FIHC or FICLS, the highest authority is an action taken at a GM. In these entities, certain decisions require passing a resolution supported by at least two-thirds of the votes of the shareholders. Such decisions include:

- an amendment of the articles;
- a liquidation;
- an increase or decrease of registered capital;
- a merger or spinoff;
- a change of corporate form; and
- other matters as set forth in the articles of association or otherwise agreed to by the shareholders.

7. Do all shareholders enjoy the same rights or can some shareholders be attributed specific rights, whether by reason of the particular class of stock owned or other? Are such rights generally provided for at the level of the company's by-laws and/or in shareholders' agreements?

Shareholder rights are provided in the company's articles of association. Shareholders also may enter into a shareholders' agreement, however, to agree how they will vote on specified matters (see question 25). PRC companies only have one class of shares. EJVs and CLSs generally cannot provide a shareholder with specific rights disproportionate to the percentage of shares owned by such holder, but CJVs can contractually alter rights that shareholders otherwise have in the articles and at law.

8. May the rights of shareholders, generally speaking, be limited, modified, suppressed or waived in any way? If so, how? Are such modifications or limitations provided for in the company's by-laws and/or in shareholders' agreements?

See question 6.

Generally, the rights of shareholders in unlisted companies can be limited, modified, suppressed or waived by express agreement set forth in the company's articles of association or the shareholders' agreement, unless PRC law provides otherwise.

It is difficult to limit, modify, suppress or waive listed companies' shareholders' rights.

GENERAL MEETING OF SHAREHOLDERS (GM) AND VOTING RIGHTS

9. Which decisions are reserved to the competence of the GM?

In a JV, the board of directors is the highest authority of the company, and has the power to make all major decisions affecting the company. In an LLC (except for an EJV or a CJV), CLS and certain other types of company, the decisions listed below are required to be taken at a GM (or by unanimous written consent of the company's shareholders):

- adoption of operational guidelines and investment plans;
- election of directors and supervisors and matters relating to their compensation;
- approving reports of the board of directors;
- approving reports of the board of supervisors or the supervisor(s);
- approving annual financial budget and related plans;
- approving profit distribution plans and loss recovery plans;
- an increase or decrease of registered capital (ie, issuances, redemptions, etc);
- issuance of corporate bonds;
- a sale of the company, spinoff, change of company form, dissolution or liquidation;
- an amendment to the articles of association; and
- other decisions as specified in the articles of association.

EJVs and CJVs do not have GMs.

10. How does a shareholder participate in a GM? Are there any limitations to having a minimum number of shares? May a shareholder delegate attendance to another shareholder or to the board? May a shareholder obtain assistance from the courts or any other governmental body to intervene in a GM or to cause one to be held in some particular cases?

Any shareholder is entitled to participate in a GM (in companies that have GMs) and it is required that shareholders be given at least: (i) 15 days' notice in the case of an LLC or for an interim GM of a CLS; and (ii) 20 days' notice in the case of a regular GM of a CLS, before any shareholders' meeting, unless otherwise specified in the articles of association or agreed by the shareholders.

A shareholder may entrust an agent as proxy to attend a GM.

There is no specific right of a shareholder to request court or governmental assistance to intervene or cause meetings. Any shareholder that individually (or collectively with others) holds at least 1 per cent of a company's shares for at least 180 consecutive days prior to the action, however, may initiate proceedings against the directors (including proceedings to cause meetings).

EJVs and CJVs do not have GMs.

11. May a GM be called and held at the request of any shareholder? Is there a threshold regarding the percentage of the stock interest owned in the company that may entitle a shareholder to such a right?

No. Only a shareholder that individually (or collectively with others) holds at least 10 per cent of the shares of the company is entitled to call a GM.

12. May a shareholder bring up an issue to be resolved upon and put it to a vote if it is not included on the agenda? May a shareholder require more information from the GM and/or the board concerning the agenda of the GM, to be put in a better position to exercise their vote?
In companies that have GMs, if a shareholder individually (or collectively with others) holds at least three per cent of the shares of the company, the shareholder has the right to submit a proposal for a resolution in the GM. There is no statutory right for a shareholder to request additional information to be provided in the agenda in order to be more informed about how to exercise its vote.

EJVs and CJVs do not have GMs.

13. May a GM be held by telecommunication means and/or by correspondence (ie by written consent)?
If permitted by the company's articles of association, a GM may be held telephonically. In addition, it is possible to pass resolutions by unanimous written consent of all of the shareholders.

14. Are voting rights always proportionate to the stock held by each shareholder or can they vary by share class?
Except in an EJV or CJV, voting rights must be exercised in proportion to capital contributions unless otherwise provided in the articles of association of an LLC. There is only one class of shares in PRC companies. In an EJV or CJV, however, because it does not have shareholder meetings and the highest authority is its board – the seats of which are allocated by reference to a shareholder's proportionate equity interest – voting rights may deviate slightly from such equity interest.

15. Are there non-voting shares? Is there a maximum percentage of capital represented by non-voting shares?
There is only one class of shares in PRC companies. All shares are voting except for company shares held by the company.

16. Can shareholders group their shares in order to exercise their voting rights (eg, by trust, shareholders' agreement or otherwise)?
Yes. In a listed CLS, shareholders that group their voting rights are deemed to be acting in concert and their shareholdings are calculated on a consolidated basis, which may trigger certain disclosure requirements or temporary purchase and sale restrictions, depending on the size of the group's shareholdings.

17. Under what circumstances can a shareholder challenge the resolutions adopted by the GM? Are there thresholds concerning the stock interest owned to be able to bring such a claim?
If the procedure for calling a GM, the manner of voting or the matter voted upon violates any law or regulation or the company's articles of association, any shareholder may request the court to revoke any resulting resolutions

adopted. In addition, any shareholder having a right to call a GM can call a subsequent meeting to vote to revoke any earlier resolution violating any law or regulation or the company's articles of association.

EJVs and CJVs do not have GMs.

18. What are the terms and procedures to challenge a resolution of the GM?

To challenge a resolution at a GM for a CLS, a shareholder must request a court to revoke the resolution within 60 days following the date on which the resolution was made. The court may, upon the company's request, require the challenging shareholder(s) to provide appropriate collateral or bond in respect of the claim.

If the resolution relates to any company alteration (eg, a change to the articles, increases or reductions in capital, etc) which has been completed, once the court declares the resolution null and void or revokes the resolution, the company must take actions necessary to apply for a revocation of the registration of the alteration. If the challenge relates to a third-party action, damages would be an appropriate remedy (see questions 42 and 43).

EJVs and CJVs do not have GMs.

SHAREHOLDERS' RIGHTS VERSUS DIRECTORS AND DUTIES OF OTHER CORPORATE BODIES IN THE COMPANY

19. What is the procedure for the appointment/replacement/ revocation of directors and of statutory auditors, if any?

For the appointment, replacement or revocation of directors, a shareholder resolution is required.

There is no concept of statutory auditors under PRC law. If a company plans to appoint or replace its auditors, either a shareholder or a board resolution is required, in respect of which the auditors are permitted to state their opinion to the board or shareholders in advance of the vote on the proposed replacement or revocation.

20. May shareholders challenge the resolutions of the board of directors? Is there a minimum percentage of capital required to challenge a board resolution?

Yes, shareholders may challenge resolutions of the board of directors in a manner similar to challenges to a resolution at a GM as discussed in question 18. To challenge a board resolution, a shareholder must request a court to revoke the resolution within 60 days after the date on which it was made. In such event, a court may, at the company's request, require the challenging shareholder(s) to provide appropriate collateral or bond in respect of the claim.

If the resolution relates to any company alteration (eg, a change to the articles, increases or reductions in capital, etc) which has been completed, once the court declares the resolution null and void or revokes the resolution, the company must take actions necessary to apply for a revocation of the registration of the alteration. If the challenge relates to a third-party action, damages would be an appropriate remedy (see question 21).

21. Are shareholders entitled to bring a legal action against the directors of the company? In which circumstances? Please describe briefly the principles of directors' liability.

Shareholder actions against directors

Any shareholder (or, in the case of a CLS, any shareholder individually (or collectively with others) holding at least one per cent of the company's shares for at least 180 consecutive days prior to the action) may initiate proceedings against the director(s) for violation of any law or applicable regulation or the company's articles of association during the course of duty, if any loss is caused to the company. A shareholder should initially pursue such action via the board of supervisors or supervisor(s) of the company, as the case may be, and may take such action directly in its own name if the board of supervisors or the supervisor(s) refuses to initiate the proceeding after receiving a request from the shareholder or fails to initiate the proceeding within 30 days after receiving a request from the shareholder or in the case of an emergency. In addition, a shareholder may initiate a court action against a director for violating any law, regulation or the company's articles of association, if such violation causes damages to any shareholder.

Director liability

Generally, a director's civil liability is as follows:

* If a director causes damages and losses to the company by: (i) violating laws, administrative regulations or the articles of association of the company when discharging their duties; or (ii) misusing the director's related-party relationship to prejudice the company's interests, the director is required to indemnify the company for the damages and losses suffered by the company.
* If a director breaches their duties of loyalty (see question 22), any income generated therefrom must be returned to the company.
* For a CLS, its directors, excluding those expressly rejecting such resolutions as recorded in relevant meeting minutes, are liable for any board resolution that violates applicable law, administrative regulations or the articles of association or the shareholder resolutions of the company. Although this rule is applicable specifically to CLSs, it is likely the same or a similar principle would be applied to LLCs.
* If the company becomes bankrupt due to the breach of the duty of loyalty or the duty of care of a director, the director is required to assume the relevant civil liabilities of the company.

22. What are the rights in connection with transactions where the directors have a conflict of interest situation?

A director will be liable to a company for any loss caused to the company arising from the director taking advantage of a related-party transaction with the company. In addition, the directors of listed PRC companies are not permitted to vote on transactions in which they have an interest (or to vote on such transactions on behalf of any other directors).

Furthermore, a director of a PRC company is subject to the following duties of loyalty:

- not to misuse any related-party relationship to prejudice interests of the company (the related-party relationship refers to the relationship between directors of a PRC company and enterprises directly or indirectly controlled by them, and any other relationship that may lead to the transfer of or damage to any interests of the company; a state-owned enterprise (SOE), however, will not be considered to have a related-party relationship to another SOE solely because they are both controlled by the state);
- not to abuse their powers to take any bribe or other illegal gains, or misappropriate properties or funds of the company;
- not to deposit any of the company's funds into an account in their or any other person's name;
- without prior consent of the shareholders or the board, not to lend the company's funds to any other person or to provide any guarantee with the company's assets which violates the articles of association of the company;
- without prior consent of the shareholders, not to enter into any contract or arrangement with the company which violates the articles of association of the company;
- without prior consent of the shareholders, not to seek business opportunities belonging to the company for themselves or any other person by taking advantage of their powers, and not to carry out, for their own or others, any businesses which are the same type as those of the company;
- not to take any commission from transactions between the company and a third party;
- not to disclose confidential information about the company; and
- not to conduct other activities which are in breach of their duty of loyalty.

INFORMATION RIGHTS ON THE COMPANY'S BUSINESS

23. What information may be requested by the shareholders from the board concerning the general state of the company's business or any specific transaction? Are information rights different depending on the number of shares owned? Are shareholders entitled to receive written information before, during or after the GM about the meeting agenda and to what extent? Is it possible for a shareholder to obtain a copy of the minutes of the GM?

Information rights

All shareholders have statutory information rights (eg, the right to review and copy the articles of association, board and shareholder minutes and resolutions and accounting records of the company). If a shareholder makes a request to review the accounting records of the company, it must submit a written request stating its reasons. If the company believes that the shareholder has improper motives and may impair the legitimate interests of the company, it may reject the request within 15 days of receipt and state the reasons. Upon rejection, the shareholder may appeal to a court.

Meeting agendas
A written meeting agenda must be delivered by the company to all shareholders at least 15 days in advance of the GM in the case of an LLC and 20 days in advance for the regular meetings of a CLS (unless otherwise provided in the articles of association).

24. Do shareholders have the right/duty to resolve in the GM upon matters which were not on the agenda?
Generally, no. A shareholder individually (or collectively with others) holding three per cent or more of the shares of the CLS, however, may put forward a written interim proposal to the board of directors 10 days before a GM is held. The board of directors shall then notify other shareholders within two days and submit the interim proposal to the meeting of the GM for deliberation. For LLCs that have GMs, there is a recent court ruling suggesting that shareholders may decide matters outside of the proposed agenda.

25. Are shareholders entitled to inspect the corporate books and/or any other corporate or accounting documents? To what extent? Can they do it through external counsel or advisors?
All shareholders have statutory information rights (eg, the right to review and copy the articles of association, board and shareholder minutes and resolutions and accounting records of the company). Such rights have historically been viewed as personal to the shareholder and thus may not be exercised through external counsel or advisors without consent of the company. However, certain PRC courts have recently ruled that shareholders can designate an accounting firm to review such records.

SHAREHOLDERS' AGREEMENTS
26. Are shareholders' agreements validly enforceable? What are their typical contents and term of duration? Are they enforceable by or against third parties and, if so, to what extent?
Shareholders' agreements generally are enforceable. The shareholders' agreement of an FIE, however, will not be effective and enforceable unless it has been approved by the applicable authorities. Typical terms include those common in shareholders' agreements in other jurisdictions, such as voting arrangements regarding directors, transfer restrictions, rights of first offer and refusal, tag-along and drag-along provisions, put and call options, information rights and pre-emptive rights. The exercise of some of these rights (particularly put and call options, tag-along and drag-along rights), however, is subject to further approval of the applicable authorities, thus making specific performance administratively burdensome to achieve in practice.

A shareholders' agreement is not required to have a fixed term and will typically survive perpetually subject to termination upon specific events (eg,

IPO, change of control, disposition of applicable shares, etc).

27. Do shareholders' agreements have to be disclosed to the public or registered in any public registry?

Generally, shareholders' agreements do not have to be disclosed under the current PRC company registration regulations. A shareholders' agreement for an FIE (ie, a joint venture agreement), however, can only become effective and enforceable upon the approval of the PRC Ministry of Commerce or its local counterparts (where applicable). Generally, the shareholders' agreement is not required to be disclosed to the company registration authority in connection with the registration of a company. Accordingly, such agreements would not be obtainable through public records. However, certain information such as the parties' names, percentage holdings and registered capital amounts, would likely be obtainable through public records. In addition, as a matter of local practice, certain local company registration authorities may require the disclosure of a copy of the joint venture agreement (ie, the shareholders' agreement) in the case of a joint venture in connection with the company registration process.

ECONOMIC RIGHTS AND RIGHTS OVER THE STOCK
28. Is the stock always freely transferable? Are there any legal limitations? Are there any restrictions on contractual limitations?

Generally, stock is freely transferable. In an EJV or CJV, however, a transfer requires relevant PRC governmental approval and shareholders have the veto rights described in question 6 as well as a statutory right of first refusal on transfers. In the case of a transfer of equity interest in an EJV or CVJ held by a PRC SOE, such a transfer would be subject to regulatory control applicable to the transfer of state-owned assets, including a state-owned assets appraisal, confirmation of the appraisal results by, or filing thereof with, the relevant state-owned assets supervisory authority and the transfer of the equity interest via a public bidding process on a recognised equity exchange. For purely domestic LLCs, shareholders have a right of first refusal on transfers, and failure to exercise this right of first refusal would be deemed to be consent to the transfer to a third party.

In addition, upon a company being listed on a PRC stock exchange, shares issued prior to the listing are subject to a statutory lock-up ranging from one to three years. Generally, there are no restrictions on contractual limitations of stock transfers of shares in a CLS.

29. Are shareholders entitled to pledge their stock?

Generally, shareholders are entitled to pledge their stock. Shareholders of an FIE, however, may not pledge such shares without governmental approval.

30. Are there financial assistance issues to be considered and other prohibitions to be evaluated in the context of a leveraged buyout transaction?

As a result of restrictions on debt-to-equity ratios and other regulations regarding the use of target assets to support debt (eg, foreign exchange controls, banking regulations and state-owned asset regulation), leveraged buyouts are uncommon in the PRC. In the context of a global leveraged buyout of a target of which there is a PRC subsidiary, however, the shares of an FIE may be pledged with governmental approval. Such a subsidiary FIE's assets cannot be pledged for third-party debt (ie, its direct or indirect parent's debt) and an FIE cannot be a guarantor of third-party debt without governmental approval, which is rarely granted.

31. May a company buy back its own stock and, if so, under what circumstances and subject to which limitations?

Generally, an LLC may buy back its stock by decreasing its registered capital subject to the veto rights discussed in question 6. In addition, if an LLC is also an FIE, such a buyback requires governmental approval.

A CLS may only purchase its own shares in the following circumstances:
- to decrease the registered capital of the company;
- to merge with and into another company holding shares of the CLS;
- in connection with an award to its employees of company shares; or
- if it is requested by any shareholder to purchase their shares because the shareholder objects to the company's resolution on a merger or split-up.

32. Is there a legal right to withdraw from the company and, if so, under what circumstances? How is the shareholders' stock valued and paid in such a case?

Yes, subject to the terms of the articles of association and any shareholders' agreement, a shareholder may withdraw via a decrease of registered capital or a transfer of its equity interests. In certain instances, such actions require governmental approval and are subject to the veto rights of other shareholders described in question 6.

Although the valuation of the withdrawing shareholder's equity is generally within the discretion of the parties (the selling company's shareholder and the buying or redeeming company), such withdrawals typically require governmental approval in the context of an FIE, which may encounter difficulty if the valuation is not at fair market value (even if the terms of the articles of association or shareholders' agreement provide otherwise) due to concerns over tax evasion. If the payment for such shares involves payment into or out of China, it may be subject to certain foreign exchange approvals or clearance.

33. In which circumstances can dividends be distributed among shareholders? Is it possible to exclude or limit the right of certain shareholders to dividends? Does a certain portion of the profits need to be set aside in a reserve fund where it cannot be distributed to the shareholders? Are advances on dividends allowed and, if so, under which circumstances? Can advances on dividends be reclaimed by the company?

Dividends may be distributed only once annually out of the after-tax profits of the company (and no dividends can be paid until prior losses have been made up for). Moreover, PRC companies are required to retain at least 10 per cent of their after-tax profits on an annual basis as a mandatory 'reserve fund' until such funds exceed at least 50 per cent of their registered capital, an issue often referred to as 'trapped cash'.

Generally, all shareholders are entitled to participate in dividends pro rata. In a CJV, however, shareholders may contractually alter their dividend rights with governmental approval.

Generally, advances on dividends are not allowed. A foreign investor in a CJV, however, may receive advances on the return of its capital investment in the CJV under certain scenarios and with governmental approval.

34. What are the rights of shareholders in the case of an issue of new stock (increase of the company's corporate capital) (pre-emption rights)?

Shareholders of an LLC have statutory pre-emption rights unless the shareholders' agreement specifies otherwise.

Shareholders of a CLS do not have statutory pre-emption rights, though such rights are frequently provided in the company's articles of association or shareholders' agreement.

35. May minority shareholders ban or limit the company's capital structure in any manner?

A minority shareholder of an EJV or a CJV can veto the increase, decrease or transfer of registered capital by exercising its statutory veto rights as discussed in question 6.

36. Which are the financial assistance prohibitions in force?

See questions 2 and 29.

37. Apart from publicly listed companies, in which cases (if any) are shareholders obligated to obtain an authorisation from, or provide information to, a public authority about events that have an impact on their stock interest in the company?

Generally, none. PRC law imposes certain foreign exchange controls, however, which may require shareholders to report certain actions to relevant governmental authorities in order to repatriate funds into and out of the PRC.

SHAREHOLDERS' RIGHTS IN THE CASE OF EXTRAORDINARY TRANSACTIONS AND/OR WINDING-UP

38. What rights are available to shareholders in the case of a sale of all or a substantial portion of the company's assets? In the case of a merger or de-merger?

In FIEs, shareholders have veto rights over mergers and other transfers of registered capital. In a CLS, a shareholder who objects to a merger or split may demand that the company repurchase its shares. PRC law does not provide veto rights over sales of substantially all of a company's assets, although such veto rights would frequently be provided in a company's articles of association or shareholders' agreement.

39. Which rights are available to shareholders in the case of conversion of the company into a European Company (SE) or into another type of company?
PRC laws do not permit a Chinese company to be converted into a European company or any other foreign company.

An LLC could be converted into a CLS and vice versa, however, provided that the mandatory shareholder resolution is obtained and other criteria are met. The change of corporate form of an FIE will be subject to governmental approvals and also may be subject to the veto rights as described in question 6.

40. Which rights are available to shareholders of a company in liquidation?
After paying liquidation expenses and creditors, the remaining assets are distributed on a pro rata basis to each shareholder based on its holdings (or, in a CJV, as otherwise contractually agreed).

Liquidations, however, are also subject to the veto rights described in question 6.

41. Can shareholders cause the liquidation of the company? How?
Generally, liquidation is subject to approval by shareholders holding at least two-thirds of the shareholder votes. However, in the case of an EJV or a CJV, liquidation would also be subject to the terms of any shareholders' agreement and the unanimous approval of the company's board of directors.

If a company meets any serious difficulty in its operations or management causing the interests of the shareholders to be severely prejudiced if the company continues to exist and the difficulty cannot be solved by other means, however, shareholders holding at least 10 per cent of the shareholder votes may petition the court to dissolve the company.

COMPANY GROUPS
42. Is the concept of 'group' recognised as such under specific legislation? What are the implications?
Although 'companies group' is a defined term under the PRC laws, a company group is not recognised as an independent company or other legal entity. Historically, establishing a 'companies group' entitled the group to establish a financial company to provide financial support services within the group. Currently, other forms of companies (such as an FIHC) are allowed to establish a financial services company upon satisfaction of certain criteria.

43. Does a controlling company have any particular duties *vis-à-vis* its controlled company shareholders?
A controlling company in its capacity as controlling shareholder is liable

to the extent of any loss caused to the company by taking advantage of its affiliated relationship. In addition, it may not make decisions that harm the company or other shareholders' legitimate interests when exercising its voting rights.

44. What are the rights of company shareholders when the controlling company puts in place actions and/or transactions that can be prejudicial to the shareholders?
See question 42.

45. What are the limitations, if any, to the possibility of owning reciprocal stock interests in companies?
There are no clear rules governing the ownership of reciprocal stock interests by affiliated companies.

Colombia

Cárdenas & Cárdenas Abogados Dario Cárdenas

BASIC INFORMATION ON THE TYPES OF LIMITED LIABILITY COMPANIES AND ON THE RIGHTS OF SHAREHOLDERS
1. What types of companies enjoy limited liability? If more than one, which ones have shareholders, ie holders of share certificates? Which one is the most common? Which one is mostly used by foreign investors?

Companies with limited liability partners or shareholders and unlimited limited liability partners or shareholders (*Sociedades en Comandita*) (*SenC*), stock corporations (*Sociedades Anónimas*) (SA), limited liability companies (*Sociedades de Responsabilidad Limitada*) (SRL), simplified stock corporations (*Sociedad por Acciones Simplificada*) (SAS) enjoy limited liability in general.

There are some exceptions to the abovementioned limited liability general rule as follows:

SAS
The corporate entity or veil is disregarded when the corporation is used to defraud the law or to the detriment of third parties. The shareholder(s) as well as the administrators involved in the fraud are jointly liable for the obligations derived from the fraud and for any damages caused. (Article 42 of Law 1258 of 2008.)

SA/SAS/SRL/SenC/branches of foreign companies
A parent or controlling company that leads a direct or indirect subsidiary into insolvency or liquidation proceedings has a secondary liability for the subsidiary's obligations. This is provided the parent's actions were taken for its own benefit and to the detriment of the subsidiary. Nevertheless, it is assumed in law that, because of the control by the parent company, the insolvency is the result of those actions unless it is otherwise evidenced. (Article 61 of law 1116 of 2006.)

SRL/SenC
In an SRL/SenC, however, partners are jointly liable for the company's tax and labour obligations as follows:
*   the company's taxes depending on: (i) each of the partners' number of quotas (a pro rata); and (ii) the period of time they have been partners (Articles 13 and 794 of the Tax Code); and
*   the company's labour obligations up to the amount of each partner's quotas (Article 36 of the Labor Code).

SenC by shares /SAS/SA

These have shareholders (ie, holders of share certificates).

The most common companies are SRLs and SASs.

Foreign investors most commonly use SRLs, SASs, SAs and branches of foreign companies.

In addition to the above types of limited liability companies branches of foreign companies are established in Colombia to do permanent business. The home office is liable for the obligations of the branch.

2. Are there minimum capital requirements and/or thin capitalisation rules in force?

There are no minimum capital requirements. Losses that reduce the net worth of a company below 50 per cent of its capital may lead to dissolution and liquidation of the company. (Article 457 of the Code of Commerce and, with respect to SASs, Article 34 of Law 1258 of 2008.)

3. Describe the types of shares that can be issued by a company and the different rights that they attribute to their owners, as well as any other financial instruments (bonds or other) and other instruments of a participatory nature in the company's capital that can also be issued by the company.

The different types of shares may be:

*   Shares with a preferential dividend and without voting rights, approved at a shareholders' meeting or by a board of directors, as the case may be. These shares cannot represent more than 50 per cent of the subscribed capital and they are issued at nominal or par value (Article 61 Law 222 of 1995).
*   Shares with a privilege consisting of a preferential right to the reimbursement in the event of a liquidation of up to their nominal value (Article 381 of the Code of Commerce).
*   Shares with a preferential right to a percentage of the profits which may or may not be cumulative for up to five years (Article 381 of the Code of Commerce).
*   Shares with any other preference of an economic nature (Article 381 of the Code of Commerce).
    The above privileges may be agreed in the articles of incorporation and by-laws or at any time with the approval of a shareholders' meeting.
*   Bonds and bonds that are convertible into shares.
*   Shares to compensate labour, services, industrial commercial secrets or technical assistance. These shares grant the right to attend a shareholders' meeting with the right to speak but not to vote. (Article 137, 138, 139 and 380 of the Colombian Code of Commerce.)
*   In the case of an SAS, there may be other kinds of shares in addition to the ones mentioned, such as shares with an annual fixed dividend and payment shares (meaning shares delivered to creditors of the company in payment of their credits) (Article 10 of Law 1258 of 2008).
*   There is the possibility of having different minimum and/or maximum

types of capital (Article 9 Law 1258 of 2008).
- Pursuant to Article 1.1.2.5 of Resolution 400 issued by the Colombian Financial Superintendency (Resolution 400), securities (including shares and bonds) public offerings must be authorised by the said Superintendency. As per Article 1.2.1.1 of Resolution 400, a public offering is defined as an offering with the purpose of subscribing, selling or acquiring securities, issued in series or blocks, which grant their owners economic, voting and transfer rights, or are representative of warehoused property, addressed at: (i) indeterminate persons, or (ii) 100 or more determined persons.
- An offering is not deemed public, however, when the offering is: (i) in the case of shares or convertible bonds, addressed to fewer than 500 shareholders of the issuer; (ii) required to comply with an order of capitalisation of a competent authority, aimed only at shareholders of the issuer; or (iii) required to comply with an order of competent authority to capitalise liabilities recognised in an insolvency proceeding, disregarding the number of persons the offering is aimed at.

4. Can a company have only one shareholder and still enjoy limited liability?
Yes. Only SASs offer the possibility to have one shareholder and still enjoy limited liability, except in the event of fraud as indicated above (Article 1 Law 1258 of 2008).

5. Are the rights of shareholders the same in any type of company?
The rights of shareholders are basically the same in any type of company.

6. What are the basic rights of any shareholder? Can any such rights be modified or even suppressed and if so, how? Describe briefly the rights of minority shareholders and indicate which thresholds, if any, are required to allow the minority shareholders to exercise any such rights.
The basic rights of any shareholder are (Article 379 of the Code of Commerce):
- to participate in shareholders' meetings and voting;
- to receive a proportional part of dividends;
- to transfer freely the shares unless there is a preferential right in favour of the company or the other shareholders;
- to inspect freely the company´s books and records within 15 working days prior to an ordinary GM whereby the annual financial statements are reviewed. This is provided, however, that in no case this right will include the possibility of inspecting documents containing industrial secrets or data that may be used against the company (see Article 48 of Law 222 of 1995); and
- to receive their proportional share of the company's assets upon liquidation of the company, once debts with third parties are paid.
  None of these rights can be modified or even be suppressed.

Minority shareholders are protected when electing the board of directors by a system called 'electoral quotient'. This electoral quotient shall be determined by dividing the total number of the valid votes issued by the number of people to be elected. The scrutiny begins with the list of those who have obtained the largest number of votes, proceeding in descending order. From each list there shall be elected as many names as the times the quotient can be obtained in the number of votes obtained by the list, and if there are positions to be filled, they shall correspond to the highest residues, scrutinising them in the same descending order. In the case of a tie in the residues, the outcome will be decided by a draw.

This system is mandatory for types of companies with a board of directors except for SASs in which case it is optional (Article 197 of the Code of Commerce).

In SRLs any by-law amendment requires the favourable vote of at least 70 per cent of the partners.

In an SA at least 70 per cent of the votes of the shareholders attending the meeting is required to decide that the issuance of new shares be made without a preferential right in favour of all shareholders (number 5, Article 420 of the Code of Commerce).

Furthermore, at least 78 per cent of the votes of the shares in all companies, except for an SAS, is needed in order prevent the distribution of profits among the shareholders. Otherwise, at least 50 per cent or 70 per cent, as the case may be, must be distributed if the legal reserve and other reserves exceed 100 per cent of the subscribed capital (Articles 155 and 454 of the Code of Commerce). In the case of an SAS, the provisions of Articles 155 and 454 of the Code of Commerce are not applicable unless they are included in the by-laws of the company. Payment of dividends shall be made in cash. Dividends, however, may be paid with shares of the company if the GM so decides with a favourable vote by 80 per cent of the shares represented at the meeting (Article 455 of the Code of Commerce).

Minority shareholders can also be protected in the by-laws of the companies requiring unanimous or high voting quorums.

7. Do all shareholders enjoy the same rights or can some shareholders be attributed specific rights, whether by reason of the particular class of stock owned or other? Are such rights generally provided for at the level of the company's by-laws and/or in shareholders' agreements?

All shareholders enjoy basically the same rights unless their shares have specific rights as indicated in question 3 above. In an SAS, however, the shares can have different voting rights depending on the type of shares involved, the type being an indicator of whether the shares will have a single vote or multiple ones (Article 11 of Law 1258 of 2008). A shareholder's rights are provided at the level of the law and the company's by-laws. In an SAS, it is possible when electing the board of directors that the shareholders' votes are divided (Article 23 of Law 1258 of 2008).

8. May the rights of shareholders, generally speaking, be limited, modified, suppressed or waived in any way? If so, how? Are such modifications or limitations provided for in the company's by-laws and/or in shareholders' agreements?

Basic shareholders' rights cannot be modified or even suppressed, nor can minority rights be limited. Without prejudice to the above, by-laws may determine a quorum for adopting decisions, depending on their equity participation in the company (Article 379 of the Code of Commerce).

GENERAL MEETING OF SHAREHOLDERS (GM) AND VOTING RIGHTS

9. Which decisions are reserved to the competence of the GM?

The following are the decisions reserved to the competence of the GM (Articles 187 and 420 of the Code of Commerce):

- to study and approve amendments to the by-laws;
- to examine the fiscal auditor's report;
- to examine, approve or disapprove the annual financial statements at the end of each fiscal year;
- to distribute the company's profits;
- to elect board members and the fiscal auditor, determine their remunerations and freely remove them;
- to approve or disapprove the management report;
- to adopt, in general, all the measures necessary for the compliance with the by-laws and the common interest of the shareholders;
- to set up occasional reserves; and
- all other functions stipulated in the by-laws or in the law.

10. How does a shareholder participate in a GM? Are there any limitations to having a minimum number of shares? May a shareholder delegate attendance to another shareholder or to the board? May a shareholder obtain assistance from the courts or any other governmental body to intervene in a GM or to cause one to be held in some particular cases?

The shareholder participates in a GM directly or by appointing an attorney (Article 184 of the Code of Commerce). There are no limitations to the number of shares owned. A shareholder may delegate attendance to another shareholder but not to the board of directors. A plural number of shareholders may request the assistance of the Superintendency of Companies (*Superintendencia de Sociedades*) to call a meeting, provided that they have one-fifth of the shares of the company (Article 423 of the Code of Commerce.)

11. May a GM be called and held at the request of any shareholder? Is there a threshold regarding the percentage of the stock interest owned in the company that may entitle a shareholder to such a right?

See above.

12. May a shareholder bring up an issue to be resolved upon and put it to a vote if it is not included on the agenda? May a shareholder require more information from the GM and/or the board concerning the agenda of the GM, to be put in a better position to exercise their vote?

The shareholder may bring up an issue to be resolved upon and put it to a vote if it is not included on the agenda provided it is at the annual ordinary GM (Article 182 of the Code of Commerce). This is not possible at an extraordinary GM (Article 425 of the Code of Commerce).

A shareholder may obtain more information concerning the agenda of the GM when inspecting the company's books and records within 15 working days prior to the annual ordinary shareholders' meeting. Otherwise, additional information may be requested by the shareholder, but they may be turned down on the grounds of confidentiality (Article 48 of Law 222 of 1995).

13. May a GM be held by telecommunication means and/or by correspondence (ie by written consent)?

A GM may be held by telecommunication means or by written consent (Articles 19 and 20 of Law 222 of 1995).

14. Are voting rights always proportionate to the stock held by each shareholder or can they vary by a share class?

Voting rights are always proportionate to the stock held by each shareholder except in an SAS where there is the possibility of having shares with a multiple vote (Article 11 of Law 1258 of 2008). There can also be shares without a vote or a preferential dividend.

15. Are there non-voting shares? Is there a maximum percentage of capital represented by non-voting shares?

As indicated above, shares with a preferential dividend and without voting rights may be approved at a shareholders' meeting or a board of directors, as the case may be. These shares cannot represent more than 50 per cent of the subscribed capital and they are issued at nominal or par value (Article 61 Law 222 of 1995).

16. Can shareholders group their shares in order to exercise their voting rights (eg, by trust, shareholders' agreement or otherwise)?

Two or more shareholders that are not administrators of the company may enter into agreements to vote in a certain manner at shareholders' meetings. These agreements need to be recorded with the company (Article 70 of Law 222 of 1995). In an SAS it is also possible to have shareholders' agreements that are not limited to voting matters only, but deal with any other matter related to the company that it is legal (Article 24 of Law 1258 of 2008).

17. Under what circumstances can a shareholder challenge the resolutions adopted by the GM? Are there thresholds concerning the stock interest owned to be able to bring such a claim?

A shareholder can challenge the resolutions adopted by a GM when such resolutions are contrary to the by-laws and the applicable law. There are no thresholds concerning the stock interest owned to be able to bring such a claim (Article 191 of the Code of Commerce).

18. What are the terms and procedures to challenge a resolution of the GM?

There is a term of two months following the meeting date in which to challenge the resolutions (Article 191 of the Code of Commerce). If the resolutions relate to matters that should be registered in the commercial registry of the relevant chamber of commerce, the two-month period is counted from the day of their registration (Article 191 of the Code of Commerce). The challenge is filed with the courts (Article 194 of the Code of Commerce) or the Superintendency of Companies, as the case may be (Article 137 of Law 446 of 1998).

If requested by the plaintiff, a suspension of the challenged resolution may be granted by the court if it considers such suspension necessary to prevent serious damages and the plaintiff presents a bond in the amount estimated by the court (Article 421 of the Civil Procedure Code as amended by Decree 2282 of 1989).

SHAREHOLDERS' RIGHTS VERSUS DIRECTORS AND DUTIES OF OTHER CORPORATE BODIES IN THE COMPANY

19. What is the procedure for the appointment/replacement/revocation of directors and of statutory auditors, if any?

A GM is required for the appointment/replacement/revocation of directors and of statutory auditors (Articles 187 and 420 of the Code of Commerce).

20. May shareholders challenge the resolutions of the board of directors? Is there a minimum percentage of capital required to challenge a board resolution?

A shareholder may challenge the resolutions adopted by the board of directors when such resolutions are contrary to the by-laws and the applicable law. There are no thresholds concerning the stock interest owned to be able to bring such a claim (Article 191 of the Code of Commerce and Article 421 of the Civil Procedure Code as amended by Decree 2282 of 1989).

There is a term of two months following the meeting date in which to challenge the resolutions (Article 191 of the Code of Commerce). If the resolutions relate to matters that should be registered in the commercial registry of the relevant chamber of commerce, the two-month period is counted from the day of their registration (Article 191 of the Code of Commerce). The challenge is filed with the courts (Article 194 of the Code of Commerce) or the Superintendency of Companies, as the case may be (Article 137 of Law 446 of 1998).

If requested by the plaintiff, a suspension of the challenged resolution may be granted by the court if it considers such a suspension necessary to prevent serious damages and the plaintiff presents a bond in the amount estimated by the court (Article 421 of the Civil Procedure Code as amended by Decree 2282 of 1989).

21. Are shareholders entitled to bring a legal action against the directors of the company? In which circumstances? Please describe briefly the principles of directors' liability.

Shareholders may decide at a shareholders' meeting to start a legal action against the administrators of the company. The shareholders' meeting to decide on such legal action needs to be called by at least 20 per cent of the shareholders of the company; the decisions must be adopted by a minimum of 50 per cent plus one share and will involve the removal of the administrator(s). If the action is not started in the following three months, the action may be started by any administrator, the statutory auditor or any of the shareholders. Creditors that represent a least 50 per cent of the extraordinary debt of the company may proceed with the legal action provided the net worth, or patrimony, of the company is not enough to pay their debts (Article 25 of the Law 222 of 1995).

The grounds for initiating legal action against the administrators are the non-fulfillment of the administrators' duties as defined in the law and in the by-laws, which basically are as follows (Article 23 of Law 222 of 1995):

- to make the necessary efforts to lead the company into performing its corporate purpose satisfactorily;
- to follow up on the compliance by the company of its by-laws and applicable legal provisions;
- to permit that the statutory auditor be allowed to perform their duties;
- to keep the commercial and industrial information of the company confidential;
- to abstain from using any privileged information;
- to treat equally all shareholders and allow them their inspection rights; and
- to abstain from participating in any activities that may create a conflict of interest with their role as director, unless authorised by a shareholders' meeting. The latter's authorisation can only be given if doing so is not contrary to the interests of the company.

22. What are the rights in connection with transactions where the directors have a conflict of interest situation?

The administrators will be jointly liable and without any limit for any damages to the company, the shareholders or third parties caused by their gross negligence or negligence. Directors that did not have any knowledge of the action (or omission) taken to the detriment of the company and the shareholders, or that have voted against it, will not be liable, provided the decision (or omission) was made without their consent (Article 200 of the Code of Commerce as amended by Article 24 of Law 222 of 1995).

INFORMATION RIGHTS ON THE COMPANY'S BUSINESS

23. What information may be requested by the shareholders from the board concerning the general state of the company's business or any specific transaction? Are information rights different depending on the number of shares owned? Are shareholders entitled to receive written information before, during or after the GM about the meeting agenda and to what extent? Is it possible for a shareholder to obtain a copy of the minutes of the GM?

Every year at the ordinary GM the administrators (board of directors and legal representative or manager) must present a management report including a statement of how the company has been performing and its economic, administrative and legal situation. In addition, the report must describe the most important events that have taken place after 31 December of the prior year, make a forecast on how the company will behave, list any transactions by the company with shareholders and administrators, and confirm that the intellectual property and copyright regulations are being complied with by the company. (Article 47 of Law 222 of 1995 as amended by Article 1 of Law 602 of 2000.)

The following information will be included, attached to the management report (Article 446 of the Code of Commerce):

- salaries and fees paid;
- payments to external advisors;
- donations;
- advertising and public relation expenses;
- investments that the company may have abroad and any debts in foreign currency; and
- investments in companies abroad or in Colombia.

The information rights are the same regardless of the number of shares owned as this information is presented to all shareholders at the ordinary annual GM. Shareholders are entitled to receive notice of the meeting being called, inviting them to attend and informing them that the management report, the statutory auditor's report, the prior year financial statements and the proposed distribution of profits, if any, are available at the company's offices for them to review, together with the books and records of the company as indicated above (Article 446 of the Code of Commerce). In all cases, copies of the aforementioned information are required to be available to the shareholders at the meeting and the shareholders may obtain a copy of the meeting of the GM.

24. Do shareholders have the right/duty to resolve in the GM upon matters which were not on the agenda?

Shareholders have the right to resolve in the GM upon the matters which were not on the agenda of the annual ordinary shareholders´ meeting. At extraordinary shareholders' meetings, shareholders representing 70 per cent of the shares may decide to resolve other matters not included on the agenda.

25. Are shareholders entitled to inspect the corporate books and/or any other corporate or accounting documents? To what extent? Can they do it through external counsel or advisors?

The shareholders may freely inspect the company's books and records within 15 working days prior to the ordinary GM whereby the annual financial statements are reviewed. This is provided, however, that in no case this right will include the possibility of inspecting documents containing industrial secrets or data that may be used against the company (Article 48 of Law 222 of 1995).

Shareholders may do the inspection through external counsel or an advisor authorised by the shareholders, but under no circumstances may it lead to an external auditor (Superintendency of Companies Letter Number 220-21510 of 29 May 2001).

In the case of extraordinary GMs, the shareholders will have the right to receive notice in writing at a prior date (the term of the advance period being stated in the by-laws), indicating the purpose of the meeting.

SHAREHOLDERS' AGREEMENTS

26. Are shareholders' agreements validly enforceable? What are their typical contents and term of duration? Are they enforceable by or against their parties and, if so, to what extent?

Two or more shareholders that are not administrators of the company may enter into agreements to vote in a certain manner at shareholders' meetings. These agreements need to be recorded with the company (Article 70 of Law 222 of 1995). In an SAS it is also possible to have shareholders' agreements that are not limited to voting matters only, but cover any other matter relating to the company that it is legal (Article 24 of Law 1258 of 2008). The typical term of duration is the same as the duration of the company or at the moment when one or all parties are no longer shareholders. In an SAS, the permitted term of duration is 10 years, extendable, by the unanimous decision of its parties, for periods that may not exceed 10 years each.

The shareholders' agreement may include a provision that one of the parties of the agreement or a third party may represent all in GMs. This provision will be enforceable provided the agreement is in writing and a copy of it is delivered to the company.

In an SAS, the shareholders' agreement will be abided by the company when a copy of the agreement has been delivered to the company. The president of the shareholders' meeting will not take into account any vote that is in contradiction to the shareholders' agreement that has been deposited. In an SAS, the shareholders – those party to the shareholders' agreement – must indicate when filing it with the company the person who will represent them to receive information or to supply it when requested.

27. Do shareholders' agreements have to be disclosed to the public or registered in any public registry?

There is no requirement that a shareholders' agreement be disclosed to the public or registered in any public registry.

ECONOMIC RIGHTS AND RIGHTS OVER THE STOCK

28. Is the stock always freely transferable? Are there any legal limitations? Are there any restrictions or contractual limitations?

Stock is freely transferrable unless it is agreed in the by-laws that there is a preferential right when transferring stock in favour of the other shareholders. Shares that have been pledged cannot be transferred without the authorisation of the pledgee (Article 403 of the Code of Commerce.) In an SAS, it may be agreed in the by-laws that the shares cannot be transferred for a period not exceeding 10 years, extendable for an additional period of 10 years by a unanimous vote of the shareholders (Article 13 of Law 1258 of 2008). Furthermore, in the by-laws of an SAS it may be agreed that the negotiation of shares in general, or of one of the different kinds of shares that may exist, requires the prior approval of a GM. Shares and any other securities that the SAS may issue cannot be registered in the National Registry of Securities and Issuers nor be transacted on a stock exchange (Article 4 of Law 1258 of 2008).

29. Are shareholders entitled to pledge their stock?

Shares may be pledged or given in usufruct (Article 410 of the Code of Commerce).

30. Are there financial assistance issues to be considered and other prohibitions to be evaluated in the context of a leverage buyout transaction?

In evaluating a leveraged buyout transaction, the question of if there is a preferential right or a first refusal right in transferring the shares should be taken into account, or if any approval is required.

31. May a company buy back its own stock and, if so, under what circumstances and subject to which limitations?

Companies may acquire back their own stock, but may take the necessary funds from profits only (Article 396 of the Code of Commerce).

32. Is there a legal right to withdraw from the company and, if so, under what circumstances? How is the shareholders' stock valued and paid in such a case?

Shareholders are entitled to withdraw from the company. The right to withdraw takes place with respect to absent or dissident shareholders when, in the event of the transformation or conversion merger or spin-off (the merger), the shareholders end up with more liability or if there is some detriment to their patrimony. In the case of a withdrawal, the shares of the absent or dissident shareholder will be offered to the other shareholders. If the shares are not purchased by the other shareholders, the company may buy them provided there are sufficient profits or reserves created for such a purpose. Otherwise, the shareholders will have the right to be reimbursed the value of the shares by the company. If there is no agreement on the purchase price or the amount of the reimbursement, experts will determine the price or the amount to be reimbursed (Articles 12, 14, 15 and 16 of Law 222 of 1995).

33. In which circumstances can dividends be distributed among shareholders? Is it possible to exclude or limit the right of certain shareholders to dividends? Does a certain portion of the profits need to be set aside in a reserve fund where it cannot be distributed to the shareholders? Are advances on dividends allowed and, if so, under which circumstances? Can advances on dividends be reclaimed by the company?

Dividends can be distributed among shareholders by the decision of the shareholders at a GM, provided they are supported by accurate financial statements after having set aside the legal reserve, any reserves required by the by-laws and any occasional reserve, as well as the relevant allocation for the payment of taxes (Article 451 of the Code of Commerce). The right of certain shareholders to dividends may be limited as a consequence of shares issued with an economic privilege (Article 381 of the Code of Commerce and, in the case of an SAS, Article 10 of Law 1258 of 2008).

Companies shall set aside a legal reserve amounting to at least 50 per cent of the subscribed capital made up by 10 per cent of the net profits of each exercise. When this reserve reaches above 50 per cent, the company shall not be obliged to continue to carry this 10 per cent of net profits. If the reserve decreases, the same 10 per cent of the profits should again be set aside until the reserve amounts to 50 per cent (Article 452 of the Code of Commerce).

Advances on dividends are not allowed.

34. What are the rights of shareholders in the case of an issue of new stock (increase of the company's corporate capital) (pre-emption rights)?

Shareholders are entitled to a preferential subscription on any new issue of shares amounting to a number proportional to those shares owned (Article 388 of the Code of Commerce).

35. May minority shareholders ban or limit the company's capital structure in any manner?

Minority shareholders may ban a capital increase or decrease, but such actions require the favourable vote of a high enough number of shareholders to make the vote of the minority shareholders necessary.

36. Which are the financial assistance prohibitions in force?

There is no appropriate answer to this question.

37. Apart from publicly listed companies, in which cases (if any) are shareholders obligated to obtain an authorisation from, or provide information to, a public authority about events that have an impact on their stock interest in the company?

Shareholders of non-publicly listed companies are not obligated to obtain an authorisation from, or provide information to, a public authority about events that have an impact on their stock interest in the company unless criminal matters may be involved.

SHAREHOLDERS' RIGHTS IN THE CASE OF EXTRAORDINARY TRANSACTIONS AND/OR WINDING-UP
38. What rights are available to shareholders in the case of a sale of all or a substantial portion of all of the company's assets? In the case of a merger or de-merger?
In the case of a sale or disposition of the company's assets, the shareholders' rights remain the same, on the understanding that the company will have the proceeds of the sale. In the case of a merger or de-merger, the absent or dissident shareholders will have the withdrawal right mentioned in answer to question 32 above. In an SAS, when the intention is to sell assets and liabilities that represent 50 per cent or more of the net worth, it will be understood to be a global sale of assets. The global sale of assets requires the prior approval of a GM, granted with the favourable vote of one or more shareholders who represent at least 50 per cent plus one share of the shares present at the meeting. This sale or disposition will grant the withdrawal right in favour of the shareholders who are absent or dissident if there is detriment to the patrimony (Article 32 of Law 1258 of 2008).

39. Which rights are available to shareholders in the case of conversion of the company into a European Company (SE) or into another type of company?
In the case of a transformation or conversion of the company, the absent or dissident shareholders will have the withdrawal right mentioned in question 30 above.

40. Which rights are available to shareholders of a company in liquidation?
The shareholders of a company in liquidation have basically the same rights as the shareholders of a company in good standing, as well as the right to receive a proportion (depending on the number of each shareholder's shares) of the assets left after payment of all debts to third parties (Articles 225 and 379 of the Code of Commerce).

41. Can shareholders cause the liquidation of the company? How?
The shareholders at a GM with the quorum required may take the decision to dissolve the company and to place it in liquidation (number 1 of Article 187 of the Code of Commerce).

COMPANY GROUPS
42. Is the concept of 'group' recognised as such under specific legislation? What are the implications?
There is a 'group of companies' when, in addition to a subordination link, there is unity of purpose and direction (Article 28 of Law 222 of 1995). The

implications of having a group of companies basically are:

- at the annual ordinary GMs of the controlling and controlled companies a special report should be presented by the administrators of each of the companies on the economic relationships existing between the controlling and the controlled companies (Article 29 of Law 222 of 1995);
- the group of companies should be registered with the chamber of commerce in the domicile of the controlled companies (Article 30 of Law 222 of 1995); and
- every 30 June at the latest, the controlling company of any group of companies registered as such before the corresponding chamber of commerce, must file their consolidated financial information before the Colombian tax authorities (Article 631-1 of the Tax Code). Failure to comply with this obligation can trigger penalties of up to COP$368,325,000 (€538,000 approximately).

43. Does a controlling company have any particular duties *vis-à-vis* its controlled company shareholders?

A parent or controlling company that leads a direct or indirect subsidiary into insolvency or liquidation proceedings has a secondary liability for the subsidiary's obligations. This is provided the parent's actions were taken for its own benefit and to the detriment of the subsidiary. Nevertheless, it is assumed by law that the insolvency, because of the control by the parent company, is the result of such actions unless it is otherwise evidenced (Article 61 of law 1116 of 2006).

44. What are the rights of company shareholders when the controlling company puts in place actions and/or transactions that can be prejudicial to the shareholders?

The rights of company shareholders, where the controlling company puts in place actions and/or transactions that could be prejudicial to the business of the company and, therefore, of its shareholders, are basically:

(i) the minority rights mentioned above;
(ii) the legal action against the administrators, mentioned in question 21 above; and
(iii) to challenge the decisions of the GM and the board of directors, mentioned in questions 17 and 18 above.

45. What are the limitations, if any, to the possibility of owning reciprocal stock interests in companies?

Subordinated companies may not have any title shares in companies that control them (Article 262 of the Code of Commerce).

Czech Republic

Havel & Holásek Michael Mullen & Jan Koval

BASIC INFORMATION ON THE TYPES OF LIMITED LIABILITY COMPANIES AND ON THE RIGHTS OF SHAREHOLDERS

1. What types of companies enjoy limited liability? If more than one, which ones have shareholders, ie holders of share certificates? Which one is the most common? Which one is mostly used by foreign investors?

There are two main types of companies enjoying limited liability in the Czech Republic, namely limited liability companies and joint stock companies. Only the shareholders of a joint stock company are holders of share certificates. The shareholders of a limited liability company have legal title to ownership interests which are not in certificated form. The most common type of company in the Czech Republic is a limited liability company because of the relatively low capital requirements and fewer administratively burdensome corporate rules. Joint stock companies are more demanding in terms of corporate administration and minimum registered capital requirements and are generally preferred by larger groups of investors.

2. Are there minimum capital requirements and/or thin capitalisation rules in force?

The minimum registered capital of a limited liability company is CZK 200,000 (approx €7,700). The minimum registered capital of a joint stock company is CZK 2,000,000 (approx €77,000) if the company is formed through a private placement and CZK 20,000,000 (approx €770,000) if the company is formed by a public share offer.

Thin capitalisation rules in the Czech Republic now apply only to transactions between related parties, whereas only an amount not exceeding four times the equity capital of the borrower can be acknowledged as tax expenditure from the debt interest.

3. Describe the types of shares that can be issued by a company and the different rights that they attribute to their owners, as well as any other financial instruments (bonds or other) and other instruments of a participatory nature in the company's capital that can also be issued by the company.

A joint stock company may issue:
(i) registered or bearer shares;
(ii) certificated or uncertificated shares; and
(iii) ordinary or priority shares.

Registered shares can be transferred through endorsement and delivery; their transferability may be limited by the company's by-laws. It is not common to enter share transfer restrictions on the share certificates themselves. Bearer shares can be transferred simply by delivery and they cannot be burdened by share transfer restrictions. Certificated shares may be physically held by the shareholders, while uncertificated shares are registered with a central depositary. Priority shares (unlike ordinary shares) may be connected with a priority right to dividends or a liquidation share. The joint stock company's by-laws may allow for non-voting shares. Joint stock companies may also issue convertible and priority bonds, provided that the general meeting (GM) of the company decides on the conditional increase of the registered capital of the company. Convertible bonds allow for the exchange of bonds for shares and priority bonds allow for a priority right to subscribe for new shares. Czech limited liability companies do not issue shares or bonds.

4. Can a company have only one shareholder and still enjoy limited liability?

Both limited liability companies and joint stock companies can have only one shareholder and still enjoy limited liability. However, as a general principle, under Czech law a limited liability company having only one shareholder may not be the sole shareholder of a Czech limited liability company. Despite pending discussions on cross-border application of this rule, the Czech courts, supported by certain reputable commentators on Czech law, currently seem to apply this rule to foreign entities in the form of a limited liability company and to sole shareholders of Czech limited liability companies as well. The shareholders of a limited liability company bear liability for the company's obligations up to the aggregate unpaid subscription price of the shares. Similarly, shareholders of a joint stock company are not liable for the obligations of the company and are only liable to the company to the extent of their unpaid subscription price.

5. Are the rights of shareholders the same in any type of company?

The shareholders in both limited liability companies and joint stock companies generally enjoy the same basic rights, such as the rights to: participate in the company's profit; participate in the liquidation remainder of the company; vote at the GM of the company; and obtain relevant information regarding the company, among others. Some of these rights may, however, be limited or excluded. The by-laws of a limited liability company may, for example, allow some shareholders a higher profit share and/or liquidation share than the others. In a joint stock company such provision of the company's by-laws would be invalid; on the other hand a joint stock company may issue priority shares connected with priority rights to dividends or liquidation shares in favour of their holders. The aggregate nominal value of such priority shares may not exceed one-half of the company's registered capital. There is, however, a difference between the rights of minority shareholders in a limited liability company, who can only cause the convocation of the GM of the company, and the rights of minority shareholders in a joint stock company, who have a wider range of rights (see below). On the other hand, the majority shareholders of a joint stock company may under conditions specified by law squeeze-out the minority shareholders.

6. What are the basic rights of any shareholder? Describe briefly the rights of minority shareholders and indicate which thresholds, if any, are required to allow the minority shareholders to exercise any such rights.

As described above, the basic rights of the shareholders are the rights to: participate in the company's profit; participate in the liquidation remainder of the company; vote at the GM of the company; obtain relevant information regarding the company; inspect corporate books and records; and transfer their shares. While minority shareholders of a limited liability company, ie shareholders having in aggregate at least a 10 per cent participation in the registered capital of the company, can only cause the convocation of the GM of the company, minority shareholders in a joint stock company, ie the shareholders having in aggregate at least a 5 per cent participation in the registered capital of a company with registered capital equal to or lower than CZK 100,000,000 (approx €3,800,000), and the shareholders having in aggregate at least a three per cent participation in the registered capital of a company with registered capital higher than CZK 100,000,000 (approx €3,800,000), can cause the convocation of the GM of the company and propose its agenda, request the board of directors to file an action against shareholders who are in delay with payment of the subscription price of the shares, request the supervisory board to review the indicated acts of the board of directors, and require the supervisory board to claim damages caused to the company by a member of the board of directors, among others. On the other hand each shareholder of a limited liability company is entitled to file, on behalf of the company, an action against the directors who caused damage to the company.

7. Do all shareholders enjoy the same rights or can some shareholders be attributed specific rights, whether by reason of the particular class of stock owned or other? Are such rights generally provided for at the level of the company's by-laws and/or in shareholders' agreements?

All shareholders generally enjoy the same rights; however the Czech Commercial Code allows for exceptions to this rule. As mentioned previously, a joint stock company may issue priority shares connected with a priority right to dividends or liquidation shares. In a limited liability company such priority rights could be agreed in the company's by-laws. Other differences between the rights of individual shareholders may be agreed in the company's by-laws or shareholders' agreements. More complicated and often confidential arrangements between the shareholders, such as rights of first refusal, drag-along rights, tag-along rights, option rights, lock-up rights and other similar restrictions, are typically contained only in the shareholders' agreements because the company's by-laws must be filed with the commercial register and are publicly available.

8. May the rights of shareholders, generally speaking, be limited, modified, suppressed or waived in any way? If so, how? Are such modifications or limitations provided for in the company's by-laws and/or in shareholders' agreements?

The Czech Commercial Code allows the shareholders in certain cases to agree on the limitation, modification or exclusion of certain rights of all or individual shareholders. There are, however, certain rights, such as the right to be present at the GM, the right to transfer the shares or the right to participate in the company's profit that cannot be completely excluded by agreement of the shareholders. As mentioned above, more complicated and confidential arrangements are typically contained in the shareholders' agreements.

GENERAL MEETING OF SHAREHOLDERS (GM) AND VOTING RIGHTS

9. Which decisions are reserved to the competence of the GM?

The Czech Commercial Code contains an explicit list of decisions reserved to the GM separately for a limited liability company and a joint stock company. In both types of companies the GM decides on:

(i) changes to the company's by-laws;
(ii) increase and decrease of the registered capital;
(iii) appointment and recall of the members of the corporate bodies (except for cases where the members of the board of directors are appointed and recalled in accordance with the company's by-laws by the supervisory board) and their remuneration;
(iv) liquidation of the company, appointment and recall of a liquidator and their remuneration; and
(v) merger, de-merger, transfer of assets to a shareholder and conversion of legal form of the company.

The GM also approves:
(i) the company's financial statements;
(ii) agreements on the transfer or lease of the company's enterprise or its part, and pledge agreements in respect of the company's enterprise or its part;
(iii) controlling agreements, agreements on profit transfer, and agreements on silent partnership; and
(iv) pre-incorporation acts performed by the company founders prior to the registration of the company in the commercial register.

The GM may decide on other matters specified by law or the company's by-laws. The GM of a joint stock company may not decide on matters other than those specified by law or by-laws. The GM of a limited liability company may not decide on those matters that fall within the authority of other corporate bodies.

10. How does a shareholder participate in a GM? Are there any limitations to having a minimum number of shares? May a shareholder delegate attendance to another shareholder or to the board? May a shareholder obtain assistance from the courts or any other governmental body to intervene in a GM or to cause one to be held in some particular cases?

Each shareholder has a right to be present at the GM, either in person or through a proxy. There are no limitations on having a minimum number of shares in this respect. The shareholders generally also have the right to vote at the GM. However, the voting rights may be excluded in certain cases or for certain shareholders (eg, a shareholder is not entitled to vote at the GM if they are in delay with payment of their contribution, if the GM decides on their non-monetary contribution, if they hold priority shares without voting rights, etc). A shareholder can delegate attendance to another shareholder or a member of the board of directors. Minority shareholders of a joint stock company may request a court to authorise them to convoke the GM of the company if the board of directors fails to do so despite a legitimate request of the minority shareholders. Minority shareholders of a limited liability company may in the same situation convoke the GM of the company even without such authorisation of the court. Finally, shareholders of both joint stock companies and limited liability companies may ask the court to declare the invalidity of the GM.

11. May a GM be called and held at the request of any shareholder? Is there a threshold regarding the percentage of the stock interest owned in the company that may entitle a shareholder to such a right?

The convocation of the GM is generally carried out by the corporate bodies of the company. The executive directors of a limited liability company are obliged to convoke the GM upon the request of the shareholders having in aggregate at least a 10 per cent participation in the registered capital. The board of directors of a joint stock company is obliged to convoke the GM upon the request of the shareholders having in aggregate at least a five per cent participation in the registered capital of a company with registered capital equal to or lower than CZK 100,000,000 (approx €3,800,000) and upon the request of the shareholders having in aggregate at least a three per cent participation in the registered capital of a company with registered capital higher than CZK 100,000,000 (approx €3,800,000). Notwithstanding the foregoing, the GM of both limited liability companies and joint stock companies must be convened at least once a year.

12. May a shareholder bring up an issue to be resolved upon and put it to a vote if it is not included on the agenda? May a shareholder require more information from the GM and/or the board, concerning the agenda of the GM, to be put in a better position to exercise their vote?

The agenda of a GM is generally contained in the invitation sent to the shareholders in advance. While at the GM of a limited liability company the matters not listed in the invitation can only be discussed if all the shareholders are present; at the GM of a joint stock company, such matters may be discussed despite the absence of one or more shareholders, but cannot be decided if all the shareholders are not present. As mentioned previously, the minority shareholders of joint stock companies may require the board of directors to convoke the GM in order to discuss the matters proposed by them. The shareholders have the right to ask for explanations and to receive answers to questions about matters concerning the company in respect of the agenda of the GM, unless the disclosure of such information could cause detriment to the company or would be subject to trade secrets or would otherwise negatively impact the company. Should the board of directors refuse to provide the requested information due to the reasons above, it may only be provided to the shareholders if the supervisory board approves it. If the supervisory board does not approve the disclosure of the requested information, the shareholders may ask the competent court to order the disclosure of the information.

13. May a GM be held by telecommunication means and/or by correspondence (ie by written consent)?
A GM of a limited liability company cannot be held by means of electronic communication. Nevertheless, the shareholders may adopt the resolutions in writing outside the GM. The GM of a joint stock company can be held by means of electronic communication. The conditions for voting by means of electronic communication have to be set up in such a manner that allows the company to verify the identity of the shareholder. The by-laws of a joint stock company may also allow correspondence voting, voting by means of a handover of votes before or during the actual GM, so that the shareholders do not have to participate personally at the GM.

14. Are voting rights always proportionate to the stock held by each shareholder or can they vary by share class?
The voting rights of shareholders of a limited liability company are generally proportionate to the shares held by them. However, the shareholders may agree on different rules in the company's by-laws, including the possibility to grant one vote to each shareholder, irrespective of their investment contributions into the company's registered capital. In a joint stock company, the number of votes attached to each share and the method of voting at the GM has to be stipulated in the company's by-laws. Apart from that, the by-laws must contain the information on the number of votes pertaining to a share of a particular nominal value, if the company issued shares in different nominal values.

15. Are there non-voting shares? Is there a maximum percentage of capital represented by non-voting shares?
As mentioned previously, a joint stock company may issue priority shares connected with the priority right to the dividends and liquidation share. The company's by-laws may then stipulate that the voting rights are not attached to the priority shares in order to balance the rights of their holders with the

rights of the holders of the other type of shares. The total nominal value of the priority shares may not exceed one-half of the registered (share) capital.

16. Can shareholders group their shares in order to exercise their voting rights (eg, by trust, shareholders' agreement or otherwise)?

There are no limitations on the grouping of the shares by the shareholders in order to exercise their voting rights. The only limitations set forth by the Czech Commercial Code in respect of the exercise of the shareholders' voting rights are those concerning certain undertakings of the shareholders vis-à-vis the company. In particular, any agreements containing the shareholder's undertaking to:

(i)   follow instructions given by the company or any of its corporate bodies on how to vote;

(ii) vote for proposals submitted by the company's bodies; and

(iii) use their voting right in a predetermined manner or not vote, in exchange for advantages granted to them by the company would be invalid.

17. Under what circumstances can a shareholder challenge the resolutions adopted by the GM? Are there thresholds concerning the stock interest owned to be able to bring such a claim?

Each shareholder of the company may ask the competent court to nullify a resolution of the GM, should the resolution be contrary to the statutory provisions, or the company's by-laws. However, the court shall not nullify a resolution of the GM if:

(i)   a violation of the statutory provisions or the by-laws resulted only in a minor violation of the rights of the persons claiming the nullity or of other persons, or if such a violation did not have any significant legal consequences;

(ii) the declaration of the nullity of a resolution adopted by the GM would essentially interfere with third party rights acquired in good faith;

(iii) the registration of a merger, transfer of business assets, division or conversion of legal form in the Commercial Register was permitted; or

(iv) a declaration of the nullity of a resolution adopted by the GM is sought only on the grounds that the GM was convened contrary to the law, or the company's by-laws, by the person who convened the GM or who participated in its convening, or if all the shareholders were present at a GM convened contrary to the law, or if those shareholders who were not present at the GM subsequently expressed their consent for the GM's resolution.

Apart from the shareholders, the members of the supervisory board, members of the board of directors or executive directors, the liquidator and the insolvency trustee are also entitled to file a petition to nullify a resolution of the GM.

18. What are the terms and procedures to challenge a resolution of the GM?

The right to challenge a resolution of the GM shall lapse if it is not asserted within three months of the day the GM is held, or, if the GM was not properly convened, within three months of the day when the shareholder (or other person entitled to assert such a right) could have learned about the holding of the GM, but no later than one year after the day when the GM was held. Should the reason for a complaint be an allegation that the resolution was not adopted by the GM because it was not voted on, or that the content of the contested resolution does not correspond to the resolution adopted by the GM, such a complaint can be filed within three months of the day when the petitioner learned of the contested resolution, but no later than one year after the day of the holding or alleged holding of the GM.

SHAREHOLDERS' RIGHTS VERSUS DIRECTORS AND DUTIES OF OTHER CORPORATE BODIES IN THE COMPANY
19. What is the procedure for the appointment/replacement/ revocation of directors and of statutory auditors, if any?
The executive directors of a limited liability company are appointed and recalled by the GM of the company. The members of the board of directors of a joint stock company are appointed and recalled either by the GM of the company or by the company's supervisory board if it is set forth in the company's by-laws. A limited liability company does not have to establish a supervisory board, but if established the members of the supervisory board are appointed and recalled by the GM of the company. Similarly, the members of a supervisory board of a joint stock company (as a mandatory corporate body) are appointed and recalled by the GM of the company, however if such a joint stock company has more than 50 employees, one-third of the members of the supervisory body are appointed by the company's employees. The statutory auditors are generally appointed and revoked by the GM or supervisory board of the company.

20. May shareholders challenge the resolutions of the board of directors? Is there a minimum percentage of capital required to challenge a board resolution?
Shareholders do not have any special right to challenge the resolutions of the board of directors. However, they may file a court petition against the members of the board of directors who caused damage to the company by acting or deciding in contradiction with the law or the company's by-laws. The shareholders of a limited liability company may file a court petition and the shareholders of a joint stock company may request the supervisory board to examine the board's resolution and/or to file a court petition against the responsible members of the board. In a limited liability company there are no minimum thresholds for exercising such a right; in a joint stock company such a right may be exercised by shareholders that together have at least a minority share (ie three per cent or five per cent of the company's registered capital).

21. Are shareholders entitled to bring a legal action against the directors of the company? In which circumstances? Please describe briefly the principles of directors' liability.

In a limited liability company each shareholder is entitled to file a complaint on behalf of the company for compensation for damage against the executive officer who is liable to the company for the damage caused. In a joint stock company, the resolutions of the board of directors are controlled by the company's supervisory board. At the request of the minority shareholders, the supervisory board must examine the performance of the board of directors in the matters raised in the request and must assert any right to compensation for damage (damages) which the company has against a member of the board of directors. Should the supervisory board fail to comply with a request by the minority shareholders without undue delay, such shareholders may assert the right to damages on behalf of the company.

The directors of a company are liable for any damage caused to the company by a breach of their duties as members of the company's statutory body. The presumptions of liability are in general:

(i)   a breach of an obligation (statutory or contractual) by the director;
(ii) the existence of damage;
(iii) a causal connection between the breach of the obligation and the existence of damage; and
(iv) the non-existence of a circumstance excluding the liability.

The directors who breached their duties and caused damage to the company are obliged to compensate for such damage, where the damage generally includes the actual damage and a profit loss. The directors who breached their duties and caused damage to the company are liable jointly and severally. The liability of the directors may not be limited or excluded, either by the company's by-laws or by an agreement between the company and the director. The directors may also be held liable for committing a crime while executing their offices.

22. What are the rights in connection with transactions where the directors have a conflict of interest situation?

Unless the by-laws or a resolution of the GM impose further restrictions, a member of the board of directors may not:

(i)   carry out a business activity in an identical or similar line of business to that of the company or enter into business relations with the company;
(ii) act as an intermediary for other persons in transactions with the company;
(iii) participate in the business activity of another entity (partnership) as a partner with unlimited liability or as a person controlling other persons engaged in an identical or similar line of business activity; or
(iv) act as, or be a member of, the statutory organ of another legal entity engaged in an identical or similar line of business to that of the company, unless that legal entity is a holding-type group.

If a member of the board of directors violates such restrictions, the affected company may demand that the member surrenders to the company

any benefit gained from the transaction by which they violated the prohibition, or that they transfer the corresponding rights to the company. This shall not affect the right of the company to claim damages.

INFORMATION RIGHTS ON THE COMPANY'S BUSINESS

23. What information may be requested by the shareholders from the board concerning the general state of the company's business or any specific transaction? Are information rights different depending on the number of shares owned? Are shareholders entitled to receive written information before, during or after the GM about the meeting agenda and to what extent? Is it possible for a shareholder to obtain a copy of the minutes of the GM?

As mentioned previously, the shareholders have the right to ask for explanations and to receive answers to questions about matters concerning the company, unless the disclosure of such information could cause detriment to the company, would be subject to trade secrets or would otherwise negatively impact the company. Should the board of directors refuse to give the requested information due to the above reasons, it may only be provided to the shareholders if the supervisory board approves doing so. If the supervisory board does not approve the disclosure of the requested information, the shareholders may ask the competent court to order the disclosure of the information. The information right is given to each shareholder. The agenda of the GM must be specified in the invitation to the GM. Any shareholder may ask the board of directors for a copy or abstract of the minutes of a GM held during the company's existence.

24. Do shareholders have the right/duty to resolve in the GM upon matters which were not on the agenda?

Generally, the shareholders do not have the right to resolve in the GM on matters which were not on the agenda. However, with the consent and in the presence of all shareholders, the GM may decide on matters not placed on the proposed agenda.

25. Are shareholders entitled to inspect the corporate books and/or any other corporate or accounting documents? To what extent? Can they do it through external counsel or advisors?

Shareholders of a limited liability company have the right to inspect corporate and accounting documents and to demand a copy of the financial statements. The right to information is restricted to the documents of the company which do not contain information subject to commercial secrets or a confidentiality clause. The shareholder of a limited liability company may empower an auditor or a tax advisor to inspect the accounting documents. However, this far-reaching information right relating to corporate books and accounting documents does not apply to joint stock companies. The shareholders of a joint stock company only have information rights regarding the state of the company and can only exercise them within the GM.

SHAREHOLDERS' AGREEMENTS
26. Are shareholders' agreements validly enforceable? What are their typical contents and term of duration? Are they enforceable by or against third parties and, if so, to what extent?
It is a very common practice that shareholders enter into shareholders' agreements in order to set out their rights and obligations as shareholders within the existence of the company, as well as rights and obligations related to the individual or joint exit from the company. The shareholders' agreements are validly enforceable, provided that their content is not contrary to the mandatory provisions of the Czech Commercial Code or other laws. The shareholders' agreements typically contain provisions regarding the character and amount of initial and eventual future contributions to the registered or equity capital of the company, nature of the company's business, governance of the company, control of the company and the rights of minority shareholders, manner of distribution of profit and payment of loss, limitation of transferability of shares and rules for individual or joint exit of the shareholders from the company (eg pre-emption rights, tag-along and drag-along rights, put options and call option rights, etc), competition and arbitration clauses, and the like. The shareholders' agreements are typically concluded for the time of the shareholders' presence in the company and are effective only among the contractual parties and their legal successors and not *vis-à-vis* the third parties.

27. Do shareholders' agreements have to be disclosed to the public or registered in any public registry?
Contrary to the company's constitutional documents containing general information on the company, the company's founders and their contributions, the amount of the registered capital, the scope of the business of the company, the manner of acting on behalf of the company and other basic information; shareholders' agreements containing more detailed and often confidential information, do not have to be disclosed to the public or registered in any public registries.

ECONOMIC RIGHTS AND RIGHTS OVER THE STOCK
28. Is the stock always freely transferable? Are there any legal limitations? Are there any restrictions on contractual limitations?
The transferability of shares in a limited liability company or a joint stock company with registered shares may be limited. The transfer of shares may be conditional upon approval of the GM or other corporate bodies of the company; by the rights of other shareholders such as pre-emptive rights/rights of first refusal, option rights, etc; or by other conditions such as the minimum purchase price or selected purchasers. If the transfer of shares is conditional upon approval of the GM or another corporate body, the absence of such approval could in most cases cause ineffectiveness of the transfer, while failing to meet the other conditions, such as pre-emptive rights, option rights, or other conditions contained in the constitutional documents could cause invalidity of the transfer. Should the conditions of the transfer be contained

only in a shareholders' agreement and not in the constitutional documents of the company, the failure to meet such conditions would most likely not cause the invalidity or ineffectiveness of the transfer but the responsibility of the shareholder who breached the conditions *vis-à-vis* the other shareholders of the company. The transferability of bearer shares of a joint stock company may not be excluded nor limited.

29. Are shareholders entitled to pledge their stock?
The shareholders are generally entitled to pledge their shares, on the basis of a written agreement, in both limited liability and joint stock companies. The right to pledge the shares may be subject, however, to the prior consent of a company's corporate body.

30. Are there financial assistance issues to be considered and other prohibitions to be evaluated in the context of a leveraged buyout transaction?
The regulation of financial assistance in the Czech Republic, including provision of security by a company for the purpose of acquisition of shares in the same company is based on, but not identical to, Directive 77/91/EC. Provision of financial assistance must be permitted in the company's by-laws and approved by the company's GM in advance. The financial assistance may only be provided on an arm's length basis. The board of directors of the company must verify whether the borrower will be able to fulfil its obligations and prepare a report which:
(i) justifies the provision of financial assistance together with its benefits and risks to the company;
(ii) states the terms of the financial assistance;
(iii) states the conclusions of the verification of the financial capacity of the borrower; and
(iv) justifies why the financial assistance is in the interest of the company.

The company must create a special reserve fund in the amount of the financial assistance. The financial assistance must not cause immediate insolvency of the company. Agreements concluded in breach of the statutory prohibition will be null and void (*ab initio*) and any security established on their basis will not legally exist. While the procedure is in principle feasible, we have so far advised caution, primarily for the following reasons: (i) there are many ambiguities and technical defects in the language of the regulation which therefore lends itself to varying interpretations; and (ii) the regulation entrusts a number of responsibilities to the judgement of the board of directors, who may not be comfortable with the attendant liability risk.

31. May a company buy back its own stock and, if so, under what circumstances and subject to which limitations?
A joint stock company may in general buy back its own shares if:
(i) the GM approves it;
(ii) such an act does not cause a decrease of the equity capital under the amount specified by the Czech Commercial Code;

(iii) such an act does not cause insolvency of the company; and
(iv) the company has sources for the creation of a special reserve fund (if required by law).

In some cases a joint stock company may acquire its own shares without having to meet the above conditions (eg the company acquires the shares for the purpose of decreasing the registered capital; the company acquires the shares as a legal successor entering into all rights of the previous owner of the shares; the company acquires the shares on the basis of a decision of a court in connection with the protection of minority shareholders, etc). However, in no case may the company hold its own shares for a period exceeding five years. A limited liability company may not buy back its own shares on the basis of a transfer agreement, although it may acquire its own shares in another way (eg, as a universal legal successor of the previous owner of the share).

32. Is there a legal right to withdraw from the company and, if so, under what circumstances? How is the shareholders' stock valued and paid in such a case?

According to Czech law, the shareholders may not in general withdraw from the company on the basis of a unilateral act, except for some cases related to the company's transformations resulting in the change of the legal form of the company, provided that the shareholder who wishes to withdraw from the company voted against such a transformation at the GM approving the transformation. The shareholder withdrawing from the company is entitled to a 'settlement share', the amount of which is calculated:
(i)   on the basis of an appraisal issued by a court-appointed appraiser;
(ii) on the basis of information contained in the company's accounts; or
(iii) in another way stipulated in the project of transformation or in the company's articles of association, depending on the character of the transformation and legal form of the company prior to and after the transformation.

Moreover, each shareholder of a limited liability company is entitled to file a petition with the court for termination of their participation in the company if they cannot reasonably be required to remain in the company any longer. In such a case the shareholder is entitled to a settlement share calculated on the basis of:
(i)   an appraisal issued by a court-appointed appraiser;
(ii) on the basis of information contained in the company's accounts; or
(iii) in another way stipulated in the company's articles of association.

33. In which circumstances can dividends be distributed among shareholders? Is it possible to exclude or limit the right of certain shareholders to dividends? Does a certain portion of the profits need to be set aside in a reserve fund where it cannot be distributed to the shareholders? Are advances on dividends allowed and, if so, under which circumstances? Can advances on dividends be reclaimed by the company?

Dividends can be distributed among the shareholders only on the basis of the approval of the GM on distribution of profit, taking into account the company's financial results. According to the Czech Commercial Code a company may not distribute the profit if the company's equity capital, as stated in ordinary or extraordinary accounts, is or, due to the distribution of profit, would be lower than the registered capital of the company, increased by: (i) the subscribed nominal value of shares, if the company's shares were subscribed in order to increase its registered capital, and the new registered capital was not entered in the Commercial Register at the day when the ordinary or extraordinary financial statements were drawn up; and (ii) the portion of the reserve or reserve funds which, under the law and its statutes, the company may not use for payment to shareholders.

Each shareholder is entitled to a portion of the profit approved for distribution among the shareholders (profit share). The amount of the profit share is generally determined on the basis of the proportion of shares held by the shareholders. While the by-laws of a limited liability company may stipulate a different manner for determination of the amount of the profit share for individual shareholders, for a joint stock company such proportionality is mandatory, unless the company had issued priority shares connected with the priority right regarding the profit share. It is a prevalent legal opinion that the right of the shareholders to a profit share generally may not be excluded. Advances on dividends are not allowed under Czech law.

The amount of a profit share may only be determined after appropriate financial means have been allocated to top up the reserve fund. A reserve fund is formed mandatorily by both limited liability companies and joint stock companies from the net profit; in limited liability companies the amount of the reserve fund must eventually be at least 10 per cent of the company's registered capital and in joint stock companies at least 20 per cent of the company's registered capital.

34. What are the rights of shareholders in the case of an issue of new stock (increase of the company's corporate capital) (pre-emption rights)?

Each shareholder of a joint stock company has a pre-emptive right to subscribe for a part of the company's new shares, if these are intended to increase registered capital, in proportion to their portion of the existing registered capital, provided that such shares are to be subscribed by monetary contributions. Shareholders' pre-emptive rights may not be restricted or eliminated in the by-laws. A resolution of the GM to increase registered capital may only restrict or exclude pre-emptive rights if there is a serious reason to do so on the part of the company. Pre-emptive rights may only be restricted to the same extent for all shareholders. Pre-emptive rights may only be excluded for all shareholders.

Similarly, each shareholder of a limited liability company has a priority (preferential) right to participate in the increase of registered capital if such capital is increased by monetary investment contributions, namely by committing themselves to increasing their investment contributions. Such commitment may be undertaken by each shareholder in proportion to their shares, unless the articles of association provide otherwise. The priority right of shareholders to participate in an increase of the registered capital may be excluded by the articles of association.

35. May minority shareholders ban or limit the company's capital structure in any manner?

The influence of the shareholders on the company's capital structure is to a great extent dependant on the company's by-laws in which the manner of adoption of certain resolutions might be adjusted in accordance with the agreement between the shareholders themselves. If there is no such special agreement within the by-laws, general provisions of the Czech Commercial Code shall apply. For instance, the voting on the decision to increase or reduce registered capital needs a two-thirds majority of votes at the company's GM. The minority shareholders might thus limit such a resolution only when the number of their votes exceeds one-third altogether.

36. Which are the financial assistance prohibitions in force?

Financial assistance for the purpose of acquisition of shares of the same company is generally permitted under Czech law, provided that the company's by-laws allow it and subject to the conditions specified above in connection with leverage buyouts:

(i)   the financial assistance is provided at arm's length;
(ii) the board of directors of the company verifies whether the borrower will be able to fulfil its obligations and prepares a report which justifies the provision of financial assistance together with its benefits and risks to the company, states the terms of the financial assistance, states the conclusions of the verification of the financial capacity of the borrower and justifies why the financial assistance is in the interest of the company;
(iii) the company creates a special reserve fund in the amount of the financial assistance; and
(iv) the financial assistance does not cause immediate insolvency of the company.

37. Apart from publicly listed companies, in which cases (if any) are shareholders obligated to obtain an authorisation from, or provide information to, a public authority about events that have an impact on their stock interest in the company?

The shareholders are not obligated to obtain any authorisation or provide any information to a public authority about events that have impacted their stock interest in the company.

SHAREHOLDERS' RIGHTS IN THE CASE OF EXTRAORDINARY TRANSACTIONS AND/OR WINDING-UP

38. What rights are available to shareholders in the case of a sale of all or a substantial portion of the company's assets? In the case of a merger or de-merger?

A sale of a company's assets in the ordinary course of business generally falls within the day-to-day transactions and therefore does not imply any special rights for the company shareholders, except for a general right of the shareholders to claim damages caused to the company. However, the sale of the company's assets may be limited by the company's by-laws or, in the case of transactions between related parties, by the Czech Commercial Code. On the other hand, a sale of the company's enterprise or part of the enterprise is subject to the approval of the GM. In addition, large transactions out of the ordinary course of business of a joint stock company (with the value exceeding one-third of the company's equity capital) require the approval of the company's supervisory board. Special rules apply for transactions between related parties, where any transfers of assets in a value of at least 10 per cent of the company's registered capital to a related party should be evaluated by a court-appointed appraiser, unless such transactions fall within the ordinary course of business or meet certain other criteria specified by law.

In the case of a merger or de-merger, the basic rights of shareholders include:

(i)   information rights related to the merger/de-merger process itself (the shareholders are mainly authorised to be informed on the content of the merger/de-merger project and the respective financial statements of the participating companies);

(ii) the right to attend the GM which passes a resolution on the merger/de-merger; and

(iii) the rights arising from the fact that the exchange rate regarding the shares is not appropriate (supplementary payments).

39. Which rights are available to shareholders in the case of conversion of the company into a European Company (SE) or into another type of company?

By virtue of the process of conversion, the company does not cease to exist; only the internal matters of the company are subject to a change, as well as the position of its shareholders. In this regard, it can be concluded that the rights of shareholders in the case of conversion of the company into an SE or another type of company are very similar to those granted to shareholders within the national merger process.

40. Which rights are available to shareholders of a company in liquidation?

In the case of liquidation of a company, each shareholder is entitled to a portion of the liquidation remainder (liquidation share). The amount of the liquidation share is generally determined on the basis of the proportion of shares held by the shareholders. While the by-laws of a limited liability company may stipulate a different manner for determination of the amount of the liquidation share for individual shareholders, for a joint stock company such proportionality is mandatory, unless the company had issued priority shares connected with the priority right regarding the liquidation share.

Any shareholder who disapproves of the proposal of the company's liquidator for distributing the liquidation remainder may ask the court to review the amount of the liquidation share to be paid to such a shareholder according to the liquidator's proposal. This right has to be asserted within three months of the day when the proposal for distributing the liquidation remainder was discussed by the shareholders or the relevant corporate body of the company.

41. Can shareholders cause the liquidation of the company? How?
The shareholders may generally cause the winding-up of the company either by agreeing on the winding-up of the company (or by voting at the GM of the company provided that the required majority of votes is reached) or by asking the relevant commercial court to decide on the winding-up of the company. The court may decide on the winding-up of a company in cases specified by the Czech Commercial Code (eg, no GM has been held for two years, the company has not carried out any activity in the last two years, the company is unable to carry out activity due to insurmountable conflicts between its shareholders, etc). The winding-up of the company in the above cases is followed by a liquidation process which ends up with the distribution of the liquidation remainder (if any) to the shareholders and the removal of the company from the commercial register.

COMPANY GROUPS
42. Is the concept of 'group' recognised as such under specific legislation? What are the implications?
The concept of 'group' and its implications are described by the Czech Commercial Code primarily in a subsection titled 'business groupings', which specifies terms such as concerted conduct, controlling and controlled persons, and describes the relations between the controlling and controlled persons in a contractual and factual concern (holding). The basic provisions set forth that in the case of a contractual holding, ie if a controlling and controlled person enter into a controlling contract (or a contract on a profit transfer), and the controlled person's trading results in a loss, the controlling person shall have to settle such a loss if it cannot be settled from the controlled person's reserve fund or other disposable resources. In a factual holding, the controlling person may not exert their influence to force through the adoption of a measure or the conclusion of an agreement which may cause a property detriment to the controlled person, unless the controlling person remedies such detriment. Should the controlling person in a factual holding require a controlled person to adopt such a measure without remedying the detriment, the controlling person shall compensate for the damage. The obligation to provide such compensation shall not arise, however, if such a measure is adopted by a person that is not a controlled person acting with all due managerial care.

43. Does a controlling company have any particular duties *vis-à-vis* its controlled company shareholders?
The character of duties of a controlling company *vis-à-vis* its controlled company shareholders depends on the character of the arrangement

between the controlling and controlled persons. In a factual holding, the statutory body of the controlled person is obliged to prepare a detailed report on relations between the controlling and controlled person, and each shareholder is, subject to the conditions specified by law, entitled to ask a relevant court to appoint an expert to review such a report. In a contractual holding the controlling contract (or a contract on a profit transfer) must contain an undertaking towards 'outside shareholders' declaring that a contract will be concluded to transfer their shares for a consideration adequate to the value of such shares.

44. What are the rights of company shareholders when the controlling company puts in place actions and/or transactions that can be prejudicial to the shareholders?
In addition to the controlling person's obligation to compensate the controlled person in a factual holding specified above, the controlling person shall also compensate any damage suffered by the shareholders of such a controlled person, and it shall do so separately from the obligation to compensate damage to the controlled person.

45. What are the limitations, if any, to the possibility of owning reciprocal stock interests in companies?
According to Czech law, the controlled companies may not gain participation in their controlling persons on the basis of a concluded contract. However, obtaining such participation may be the result of certain legal transactions allowed by law. If such a situation occurs, the company is obliged to alienate such gained participation within the period of time stated by law.

Denmark

Gorrissen Federspiel Niels Heering & Niels Bang

BASIC INFORMATION ON THE TYPES OF LIMITED LIABILITY COMPANIES AND ON THE RIGHTS OF SHAREHOLDERS

1.   What types of companies enjoy limited liability? If more than one, which ones have shareholders, ie holders of share certificates? Which one is the most common? Which one is mostly used by foreign investors?

The new Danish Companies Act (CA) entered into force on 1 March 2010. The CA offers three types of companies where the shareholders' liability is limited to the funds paid for the shares: The private limited company (*anpartsselskab* or ApS), the public limited company (*aktieselskab* or A/S) and the limited partnership company (*partnerselskabor* P/S). All three company types have shareholders and issue shares (the shareholders may decide that the company shall issue share certificates, but it is not a necessity).

The rules of the CA applicable to the A/S apply mutatis mutandis to the P/S. The P/S is rarely used and will not be mentioned further in the following.

The ApS and the A/S are equally common and used to the same extent by foreign investors. The ApS was intended as the most common corporate entity in Denmark to achieve limited shareholder liability for small enterprises. The ApS has also been used by large international groups, particularly in the form of holding companies, as the ApS is eligible to elect entity classification under the US tax rules in CFR 301.7701-1ff (known as the 'check-the-box' regulations) and thereby electing transparency for US tax purposes. This possibility has, however, been restricted significantly by recent Danish tax legislation. The statutory company law requirements applicable to the ApS are not strict and permit a high degree of flexibility in the drafting of the by-laws. The A/S is the other important corporate entity offering limited shareholder liability in Denmark. The advantage of the A/S is that it has access to capital markets and therefore greater scope for raising funds to finance its business activities. However, as this could result in a large number of shareholders, its governance structure is stricter than that of the ApS.

A company may adopt a management structure: (i) where the company is managed by a board of directors, which must appoint an executive board to be responsible for the day-to-day management of the company; or (ii) where the company is managed by an executive board. In A/S companies, the executive board must be appointed by a supervisory board that oversees the executive board. At present, almost no companies have chosen the structure with a supervisory board, and, consequently, in the following, reference is made to the board of directors. The term 'management' covers both members of the board and the executive board.

2. Are there minimum capital requirements and/or thin capitalisation rules in force?

An A/S must have a minimum share capital corresponding to DKK 500,000, and an ApS must have a minimum share capital corresponding to DKK 80,000. An amount equal to 25 per cent of the share capital, but not less than DKK 80,000, must be paid up at all times. Where a premium is fixed, it must be fully paid up, notwithstanding that part of the share capital is not paid up. Payment must be made on each individual share. However, where all or part of the share capital is paid up by way of noncash contributions, the entire share capital must be paid up.

If a Danish company has a debt/equity ratio exceeding 4:1, the possibility to deduct related party interest expenses relating to the debt that exceeds 4:1 are partly limited for tax purposes unless it can be demonstrated that the intra-group loan has been entered at arm's length.

3. Describe the types of shares that can be issued by a company and the different rights that they attribute to their owners, as well as any other financial instruments (bonds or other) and other instruments of a participatory nature in the company's capital that can also be issued by the company.

The rights of a shareholder under the CA subsist regardless of whether their shares are fully paid up. If a shareholder has failed to duly comply with the central governing body's request for payment of the amount outstanding on a share, the shareholder may not exercise the voting rights attaching to any part of its shareholding in the company at general meetings of shareholders (GM) and its shares will be considered unrepresented at GMs until the amount has been paid to and registered by the company.

All shares carry equal rights. However, the by-laws of a company may provide that the company must have different share classes, in which case the articles must specify the different characteristics and size of each class.

All shares carry voting rights. However, the by-laws may provide that certain shares carry no voting rights, and that the voting power of certain shares differs from that of the other shares. Non-voting shares only carry a right of representation if so provided by the by-laws.

A company may issue par value shares or non-par value shares, or any combination of such shares. Non-par value shares have no nominal value. Each non-par value share represents an equal amount of the share capital.

Shares are freely transferable and non-redeemable, unless otherwise provided by statute. Shares may be registered in the names of the holders. The by-laws may include restrictions on the transferability of registered shares, or rules on their redemption. Shares may also be issued to bearer.

No purchaser of a registered share may exercise the rights conferred on that purchaser as a shareholder unless and until the purchaser has been registered in the register of shareholders or has given notice of its acquisition of the shares to the company and established good title to them. However, this does not apply to the right to receive dividends and other distributions, or to the right to subscribe for new shares issued in connection with a capital increase.

The GM may resolve to issue convertible debt instruments or warrants if it also resolves at the same time to increase the capital as required. The resolution passed by the GM must specify the terms of the issue, including the maximum amount of the capital increase that may be subscribed on the basis of the security and the class to which the new shares will belong. Finally, the GM may resolve to raise loans against the issue of debt instruments carrying interest, the amount of which depends in whole or in part on the dividend paid on the company's shares, or on the profit for the year.

4. Can a company have only one shareholder and still enjoy limited liability?
Yes.

5. Are the rights of shareholders the same in any type of company?
Because the ApS is designed for small businesses with few shareholders, the rights of shareholders in an ApS are to some extent more far-reaching than those of shareholders in an A/S.

6. What are the basic rights of any shareholder? Can any such rights be modified or even suppressed and if so, how? Describe briefly the rights of minority shareholders and indicate which thresholds, if any, are required to allow the minority shareholders to exercise any such rights.
All shareholders are entitled to attend and speak at GMs. In A/S companies whose shares are admitted to trading on a regulated market, a shareholder's right to attend a GM and to vote on their shares must, however, be determined on the basis of the shares held by the shareholder one week before the date of the GM (the date of registration). The by-laws of an A/S company may, furthermore, provide that shareholders are required to notify the company that they will attend a GM no later than three days before the date of the meeting.

All shareholders are entitled nominate specific issues for inclusion on the agenda for an annual GM. In an A/S, shareholders must submit a written request to the board in order to nominate a specific issue for consideration at the annual GM. Shareholders are entitled to have their nominated issues included on the agenda for the GM where their request is received at least six weeks before the date of the meeting. If the request is received less than six weeks before the date of the GM, the board must decide whether the request has been made with enough time for the issues to be included on the agenda. In ApS companies, any shareholder can request an extraordinary GM.

The most important minority shareholder rights are the following.
Shareholders < 10 per cent of share capital and voting rights
*   any proposed resolution to change the principle of all shares carrying

equal rights, or increase shareholder obligations to the company, requires the unanimous agreement of all shareholders;
- for A/S companies, shareholders that hold five per cent of the share capital can request an extraordinary GM;
- any proposed resolution to increase the share capital at a price below market value in favour of certain existing shareholders requires the unanimous agreement of all shareholders;
- any proposed resolution to decrease the share capital at a price above market value in favour of certain shareholders requires the unanimous agreement of all shareholders;
- any proposed resolution to decrease the share capital directed at certain shareholders requires the agreement of the shareholders in question;
- a minority shareholder may require redemption if more than 90 per cent of share capital and voting rights are owned by one shareholder.

Shareholders > 10 per cent but < 25 per cent of share capital and voting rights

The following proposed resolutions to amend the by-laws must be passed by at least nine-tenths of the votes cast as well as at least nine-tenths of the share capital represented at the GM:
- resolutions to reduce shareholder rights to receive dividends or distribution of the company's assets;
- resolutions to restrict the transferability of the shares or increase existing restrictions;
- resolutions to require shareholders to redeem their shares on equal terms, except on dissolution of the company or in case of redemption in accordance with the CA;
- resolutions whereby shareholder rights to exercise voting rights in respect of their own or other shareholders' shares is restricted to a specific part of the votes or the voting share capital;
- resolutions to hold GMs in a language other than Danish, Swedish, Norwegian or English without providing for simultaneous interpretation to and from Danish for all participants.

Furthermore,
- where any shareholders in a company have wilfully contributed to passing a resolution by the GM that is clearly likely to give certain shareholders or others an undue advantage over other shareholders or the company, or have otherwise abused the influence that they have over the company or contributed to a contravention of the CA or the company's by-laws, the court may, upon request from shareholders representing no less than one-tenth of the share capital, order that the company be dissolved if special grounds exist because of the duration of the abuse or other circumstances; and
- shareholders holding no less than one-tenth of the capital may elect an additional auditor to participate in the audit together with the other auditor(s).

7.   Do all shareholders enjoy the same rights or can some shareholders be attributed specific rights, whether by reason of the particular class of stock owned or other? Are such rights generally provided for at the level of the company's by-laws and/or in shareholders' agreements?

All shares carry equal rights. However, the by-laws of a company may provide that the company must have different share classes, in which case the by-laws must specify the different characteristics and size of each class.

8.   May the rights of shareholders, generally speaking, be limited, modified or waived in any way? If so, are such modifications or limitations provided for in the company's by-laws and/or in shareholders' agreements?

Resolutions made by shareholders at a GM can, in general, be passed without complying with the rules on form and notice provided by the CA, provided that a resolution to that effect is passed by unanimous agreement, and rules that provide for passing such resolutions are set out in the by-laws. Where shareholders holding more than 10 per cent of the share capital so request, GMs must be held by physical attendance. However, the shareholders of state-owned companies and companies whose shares are admitted to trading on a regulated market in an EU or EEA member state may not pass resolutions without complying with the rules on form and notice provided by the CA. This also applies to companies whose GMs must be open to the press by virtue of statute or an executive order.

GENERAL MEETING OF SHAREHOLDERS (GM) AND VOTING RIGHTS

9. Which decisions are reserved to the competence of the GM?

The GM is omnipotent and may decide on any matter, which is not explicitly made a sole competence of the board. Matters reserved for the GM are amendments of the by-laws, election of the board and auditor and approval of the annual report.

10. How does a shareholder participate in a GM? Are there any limitations to having a minimum number of shares? May a shareholder delegate attendance to another shareholder or to the board? May a shareholder obtain assistance from the courts or any other governmental body to intervene in a GM or to cause one to be held in some particular cases?

Any shareholder may attend a GM – electronically in case of an electronic GM or physically in case of a physical GM. Furthermore, any shareholder may vote by letter, email or other written instrument or attend by proxy to any person or to the board.

GMs must be convened and organised by the board. If the company has a board, or if the board fails to convene a GM required to be held by statute, by the by-laws or by a resolution of the company at a GM, such GM must be convened by the Danish Commerce and Companies Agency (CCA) upon request from a member of the company's board, the auditor elected by the GM, if any, or a shareholder. The CCA may determine the agenda for the GM.

11. May a GM be called and held at the request of any shareholder? Is there a threshold regarding the percentage of the stock interest owned in the company that may entitle a shareholder to such a right?

In an ApS, any shareholder can request an extraordinary GM. Extraordinary GMs to consider specific issues must be convened within two weeks of receipt of a request to such effect. In an A/S, shareholders that hold five per cent of the share capital or any smaller fraction of the capital provided in the by-laws, as well as shareholders that are specifically authorised under the by-laws, can request an extraordinary GM in writing. Extraordinary GMs to consider specific issues must be convened within two weeks of receipt of a request to such effect.

12. May a shareholder bring up an issue to be resolved upon and put it to a vote if it is not included on the agenda? May a shareholder require more information from the GM and/or the board concerning the agenda of the GM to be put in a better position to exercise its vote?

Any matter which is not on the agenda can only be determined by the GM if all of the shareholders consent. However, at any time the annual GM can pass resolutions to be passed at annual GMs under the CA or the by-laws, and resolutions to convene extraordinary GMs to consider specific issues.

On information rights, see question 23 below.

13. May a GM be held by telecommunication means and/or by correspondence (ie by written consent)?

Unless otherwise provided by the company's by-laws, the board may determine that in addition to a right to physically attend GMs, shareholders may be given the right to attend electronically, including using electronic voting that does not require physical attendance at the meeting, so that the GM will be partly electronic.

Furthermore, the GM may resolve to hold GMs electronically without any opportunity for parties to physically attend, so that the meeting is held by electronic means alone. A resolution to that effect must explain how electronic media can be used to attend the GM.

Finally, the shareholders may resolve - either ad hoc or in general - to hold GMs by written resolution.

14. Are voting rights always proportionate to the stock held by each shareholder or can they vary by share class?

The by-laws may provide that the voting power of certain shares differs from that of the other shares. There are no limitations to such voting differences.

15. Are there non-voting shares? Is there a maximum percentage of capital represented by non-voting shares?

The by-laws may provide that certain shares carry no voting rights. At least one share must carry voting rights. Treasury shares do not carry voting rights.

16. Can shareholders group their shares in order to exercise their voting rights (eg, by trust, shareholders' agreement or otherwise?

Yes, by agreement.

17. Under what circumstances can a shareholder challenge the resolutions adopted by the GM? Are there thresholds concerning the stock interest owned to be able to bring such a claim?

Legal proceedings can be instituted by a shareholder if a resolution passed by the GM has not been lawfully passed or is contrary to the CA or to the company's by-laws.

18. What are the terms and procedures to challenge a resolution of the GM?

Except in certain specific situations listed in the CA, legal proceedings must be instituted no later than three months after the date of the resolution, or the resolution will be deemed to be valid.

If the court finds that the resolution has not been lawfully passed or is contrary to the CA or to the company's by-laws, it must be amended or declared invalid by a court ruling. However, the resolution may only be amended if a claim is made to such effect and the court is able to establish the proper contents of the resolution. The ruling of the court also applies to shareholders who have not instituted proceedings.

In addition, a resolution of the GM, which is required to be filed for registration with the CCA, may be challenged if anyone asserts that the registration is detrimental to them. The question of deregistration is to be determined by the courts. Such legal proceedings must be commenced against the company within six months from the date of publication of the registration in the CCA's IT system. The court will send a transcript of the judgment to the CCA for publication of the outcome of the case in the agency's IT system.

SHAREHOLDERS' RIGHTS VERSUS DIRECTORS AND DUTIES OF OTHER CORPORATE BODIES IN THE COMPANY

19. What is the procedure for the appointment/replacement/ revocation of directors and of statutory auditors, if any?

Directors

The majority of the directors must be elected by the GM. Such resolution may be passed by a simple majority of votes. Before holding elections, A/S companies must provide information on managerial posts held by the candidates in other commercial enterprises, except for posts held in the company's own wholly owned subsidiaries. The shareholders may deviate from this information requirement by unanimous decision.

The directors elected by the GM hold office in the period specified in the by-laws. The directors' term of office expires with the closing of an annual GM held no later than four years after their election.

Directors may resign at any time. Notice of resignation must be given to the board of the company and, if the director has not been elected by the GM, also to the appointing party. Directors may be removed at any time by the electing or appointing party.

If there is no alternate director to replace the director, the other members of the board must arrange for the election of a new director to replace the resigning director during the remainder of their term of office. However, if the election is to be held at the GM, it may be postponed until the next annual GM, provided that the remaining directors can form a quorum.

Auditors

If a company is subject to audit obligations under the Danish Financial Statements Act or any other statute, the GM must elect one or more approved auditors. Such resolution may be passed by a simple majority of votes.

Auditors may be removed by the party that appointed them. An auditor elected to audit the company's financial statements may only be removed before their term of office expires if such removal is based on reasonable grounds. If an auditor elected by the GM resigns or is removed from office, or if an auditor's appointment is otherwise terminated before the auditor's term of office expires, the auditor must notify the CCA to such effect as soon as possible. The notice must be accompanied by an adequate account of the reason for the termination if this took place before expiry of the auditor's term. In companies whose securities are admitted to trading on a regulated market, an auditor elected by the GM must also notify the market of his resignation or removal as soon as possible in accordance with the provisions of the Danish Securities Trading Act.

The board must cause a new auditor to be elected as soon as possible. An extraordinary GM must be convened to elect a new auditor no later than two weeks after the company has been notified of the resignation or removal. However, in state-owned companies and companies whose securities are admitted to trading on a regulated market, the GM must be convened no later than eight days after the company has been notified of the resignation or removal.

20. May shareholders challenge the resolutions of the board of directors? Is there a minimum percentage of capital required to challenge a board resolution?

Members of management must comply with resolutions passed by the GM, unless that resolution is invalid or contravenes the law or the company's by-laws.

Furthermore, a resolution of the board, which is required to be filed for registration with the CCA, may be challenged if anyone asserts that the registration of the resolution is detrimental to them. The question of deregistration is to be determined by the courts. Such legal proceedings must be commenced against the company within six months from the date of publication of the registration in the CCA's IT system. The court will send a transcript of the judgment to the CCA for publication of the outcome of the case in the agency's IT system.

Otherwise, shareholders may not challenge the contents of board resolutions, but members of management who, in the performance of their duties, have intentionally or negligently caused damage to the company and/or shareholders are liable to pay damages.

21. Are shareholders entitled to bring a legal action against the directors of the company? In which circumstances? Please describe briefly the principles of directors' liability

Shareholders or the company may bring legal action against the management if management have breached their duties under the CA and/or if members of management, in the performance of their duties, have intentionally or negligently caused damage to the company and/or shareholders. Any resolution that the company should take legal action against its members of management must be passed by the GM.

22. What are the rights in connection with transactions where the directors have a conflict of interest situation?

No member of management may participate in the transaction of business that involves any agreement between the company and that member, or legal proceedings against that member, or the transaction of business that involves any agreement between the company and a third party, or legal proceedings against a third party, if the member has a material interest in such business and that material interest could conflict with the interests of the company. Shareholders may bring legal action against the relevant directors, see question 21.

INFORMATION RIGHTS ON THE COMPANY'S BUSINESS

23. What information may be requested by the shareholders from the board concerning the general state of the company's business or any specific transaction? Are information rights different depending on the number of shares owned? Are shareholders entitled to receive written information before, during or after the GM about the meeting agenda and to what extent? Is it possible for a shareholder to obtain a copy of the minutes of the meetings of the GM?

Upon request from a shareholder and when deemed by the board not to cause any significant detriment to the company, the company's management must disclose to the GM the information at hand about all matters of importance to the assessment of the annual report and the company's position in general, or to any proposed resolution put forward for vote at the GM.

If the answer to a request requires information that is not at hand at the GM, such information must be made available to the shareholders no later than two weeks after the meeting and must also be sent to any shareholder upon request. The board may resolve that shareholders can ask questions about agenda items or documents, etc to be used for the GM, subject to a time limit stipulated in the by-laws.

For A/S companies whose shares are admitted to trading on a regulated market and state-owned A/S companies, the disclosure requirement also applies to questions submitted in writing by a shareholder within the three months prior to the GM. The answer may be given in writing, in which case both the question and answer must be made available to the shareholders at the beginning of the GM. No answer is required to be provided if the shareholder is not represented at the GM. Any questions that are the same may be answered together. Questions will be deemed to be answered if the relevant information is made available on the company's website in the form of a 'question and answer' feature.

No later than two weeks after a GM, the minutes of the meeting or a certified copy of the minutes must be made available to the shareholders.

24. Do shareholders have the right/duty to resolve in the GM upon matters which were not on the agenda?
Shareholders may resolve upon a matter which was not on the agenda, provided that all shareholders agree to do so.

25. Are shareholders entitled to inspect the corporate books and/or any other corporate or accounting documents? To what extent? Can they do it through external counsel or advisors?
In ApS companies, the register of shareholders must be kept available for inspection by all shareholders. In A/S companies, the register of shareholders must only be kept available for inspection by the shareholders if provided for in the by-laws.

The company must keep a register of large shareholders (above five per cent). Such register is publicly available. Anyone may inspect and obtain copies of documents, including minutes of meetings and annual reports, which must be filed with the CCA.

In connection with a GM, the documents relevant for the agenda, including documents required by the CA to be produced in respect of the items on the agenda, must be made available to the shareholders.

Any shareholder may, at the annual GM or at a GM whose agenda includes such issues, submit a proposal for scrutiny of the company's formation, of any specific matter relating to the administration of the company, or of certain financial statements. If the proposal is adopted by a simple majority of votes, the GM must elect one or more scrutinisers. If the proposal is not adopted, but shareholders representing 25 per cent of the share capital vote in favour of the proposal, any shareholder may, no later than four weeks after the GM, request that scrutinisers be appointed by the bankruptcy court with jurisdiction over the place where the company's registered office is situated.

SHAREHOLDERS' AGREEMENTS
26. Are shareholders' agreements validly enforceable? What are their typical contents and term of duration? Are they enforceable by or against third parties and, if so, to what extent?
According to the CA, which entered into force on 1 March 2010,

shareholders' agreements are not binding on the company, or with regard to resolutions passed at GMs from a company law perspective. A shareholders' agreement is, however, legally binding among its parties as contract law. In order to enforce the agreement in case of breach, the non-breaching party must initiate legal proceedings.

The typical areas covered by a shareholders' agreement are restrictions on and other rules governing share transfers, appointment of directors and majority requirements for material decisions. Normally, shareholders' agreements cannot be terminated unless in case of material breach. Only upon transfer of its shares will a party be released from its obligations under the agreement.

27. Do shareholders' agreements have to be disclosed to the public or registered in any public registry?
No, unless it concerns a listed company.

ECONOMIC RIGHTS AND RIGHTS OVER THE STOCK
28. Is the stock always freely transferable? Are there any legal limitations? Are there any restrictions on contractual limitations?
Shares are freely transferable, unless otherwise provided by statute. According to the CA, the by-laws may include restrictions on the transferability of registered shares. Typical limitations are pre-emptive rights and consent to sale. There are no restrictions on contractual limitations.

29. Are shareholders entitled to pledge their stock?
Shareholders are entitled to pledge their stock unless otherwise stipulated in the by-laws or a shareholders' agreement. A Danish company may not, directly or indirectly, advance funds, make loans or provide security for a third party's acquisition of the limited liability company's shares or shares in its parent company, unless such financial assistance has been approved in advance of the GM. A shareholders' pledge of stock in the target company as security for acquisition debt is not covered by the financial assistance prohibition because the stock is not the property of the target company, but of the shareholder.

30. Are there financial issues to be considered and other prohibitions to be evaluated in the context of a leveraged buyout transaction?
A company may not, directly or indirectly, advance funds, make loans or provide security for a third party's acquisition of the limited liability company's shares or shares in its parent company (financial assistance), except if the following requirements are satisfied:
• the board must ensure that any third party receiving financial assistance is credit rated;
• the board must present a written report to the GM, including information about: (i) the reason for the proposed financial assistance; (ii) the company's interest in entering into the transaction; (iii) the conditions on which the transaction is entered into; (iv) the

consequences of the transaction for the company's liquidity and solvency; and (v) the price to be paid by the third party for the shares;

- the GM must approve the financial assistance by the same majority of votes that is required to amend the by-laws;
- the report presented to the GM must be filed with the CCA within two weeks after the date of approval by the GM;
- the total financial assistance granted by the company may at no time exceed what is reasonable having regard to the company's financial position. If the company is a parent company, the aggregate financial assistance may not exceed what is reasonable having regard to the group's financial position;
- the company may only use funds that can be distributed as dividends; and
- the financial assistance must be granted at arm's length.

31. May a company buy back its own stock and, if so, under what circumstances and subject to which limitations?

Companies may only acquire their own shares if they are fully paid up. The shares may be acquired both in ownership and by way of security. If a limited liability company acquires its own shares for consideration, such consideration may only consist of:

(i) distributable reserves, which are amounts stated as retained earnings in the company's latest adopted financial statements, and reserves that are distributable under statute or the company's by-laws, less retained earnings;

(ii) profit for the current financial year if such profit has not been distributed, appropriated or tied up; and

(iii) any distributable reserves created or released in the current financial year.

The company's holding of its own shares must be disregarded when assessing whether the company satisfies the minimum capital requirements (see section 2 above).

An acquisition of a company's own shares for consideration cannot proceed without the board obtaining authority from the GM (except where the acquisition is necessary in order to avoid significant and imminent detriment to the company).

Notwithstanding the above, and without the said limitations being applicable, companies may, directly or indirectly, acquire their own shares: (i) in connection with a reduction of the share capital; (ii) in connection with a transfer of assets by merger, de-merger or other universal succession; (iii) in satisfaction of a statutory takeover obligation of the company; and (iv) in connection with the purchase of fully paid-up shares in a forced sale for the satisfaction of a claim held by the company.

32. Is there a legal right to withdraw from the company and, if so, under what circumstances? How is the shareholders' stock valued and paid in such a case?

Shareholders do not have a general right to withdraw from a company. A shareholder is entitled to transfer its shares to the company in the following instances:

- if the by-laws include provisions on redemption and the shareholder qualifies for such redemption according to the terms stated in the by-laws;
- where a shareholder holds more than nine-tenths of the shares in a company and a corresponding share of the votes, each minority shareholder of the company may demand redemption by that shareholder;
- shareholders who have opposed certain far-reaching amendments to the by-laws referred to in the CA at the GM may demand that their shares be redeemed by making a written request to such effect no later than four weeks after the date of the GM;
- in connection with a cross-border merger, the shareholders in the non-surviving companies who opposed the merger at the GM may demand redemption of their shares by the company by making a written request to this effect no later than four weeks after the date of the GM; and
- in connection with a cross-border de-merger, the shareholders in the transferor company who opposed the de-merger at the GM may demand redemption of their shares by the company by making a written request to this effect no later than four weeks after the date of the GM.

The company must buy the shareholder's shares at a price corresponding to the value of the shares, which, in the absence of agreement, must be determined by experts appointed by the court with jurisdiction over the place where the company's registered office is situated.

33. In which circumstances can dividends be distributed among shareholders? Is it possible to exclude or limit the right of certain shareholders to dividends? Does a certain portion of the profits need to be set aside in a reserve fund where it cannot be distributed to the shareholders? Are advances on dividends allowed and, if so, under what circumstances? Can advances on dividends be reclaimed by the company?

Dividends may be paid as dividends based on the latest adopted financial statements or as extraordinary dividends. Advances on dividends are not allowed.

Dividends based on the latest adopted financial statements

The GM must decide how to distribute, by dividend, the amount available for distribution as recorded in the financial statements. The GM cannot decide to distribute dividends of a higher amount than that proposed or accepted by the company's board. Dividends may only be distributed out of distributable reserves, which are amounts stated as retained earnings in the company's latest adopted financial statements, and reserves that are distributable under statute or the company's by-laws, less retained earnings.

Extraordinary dividends

The GM, or the board upon authorisation by the GM, may decide to distribute extraordinary dividends after the company has presented at least one ordinary annual report. The GM cannot decide to distribute extraordinary dividends of a higher amount than that proposed or accepted by the company's board. Extraordinary dividends may only be made up of:

(i) the amounts eligible as dividends based on the latest adopted financial statements;
(ii) profit for the current financial year up to the date of the resolution on distribution if such profit has not been distributed, appropriated or tied up; and
(iii) any distributable reserves created or released in the current financial year.

Exclusion or limitation of the right of certain shareholders to dividends

All shares carry equal rights in respect of dividends. However, the by-laws of a company may provide that the company must have different share classes, in which case the right to dividends may be limited or excluded in one or more share classes.

34. What are the rights of shareholders in the case of an issue of new stock (increase of the company's corporate capital) (pre-emption rights)?

In the event of a cash increase of the share capital, shareholders are entitled to subscribe for new shares in proportion to their existing shareholdings (pre-emption right). The GM may resolve (by at least two-thirds of the votes cast as well as at least two-thirds of the share capital represented at the GM the same majority of votes) to depart from the said pre-emption rights for the benefit of any other persons.

If there are different share classes, it may be stipulated in the by-laws that holders of the same class of shares have a priority right to subscribe for shares within their own share class. In this case, holders of shares of other classes may exercise their pre-emption rights only after such subscription.

35. May minority shareholders ban or limit the company's capital structure in any manner?

See question 6 above.

36. Which are the financial assistance prohibitions in force? Financing of purchase of own shares.

A company may not, directly nor indirectly, advance funds, make loans or provide security for a third party's acquisition of the company's shares or shares in its parent company, except where certain requirements on approval by the GM, reasonableness of the resolution, a report by the board, credit rating of any third party receiving financial assistance and arm's length terms are satisfied. Specific exemptions apply to employees of the company and banks.

Financial assistance to parent companies, shareholders, members of management and others

A company cannot, directly or indirectly, advance funds, make loans or provide security to its shareholders or members of the management. The same applies in relation to shareholders or members of management in the company's parent company or businesses other than parent companies that control the company. This also applies to persons who, by marriage or lineal consanguinity, are related to a person falling within the first or second sentence or who have other close affiliations to such person.

Notwithstanding the above prohibition, a company may grant financial assistance:

- for the purpose of financing any purchase of its own shares if permitted under one of the exemptions mentioned above;
- for the obligations of Danish and certain foreign parent companies (EU, EEA and OECD countries rated in classification 0 or 1); and
- for the purpose of usual business transactions.

37. Apart from publicly listed companies, in which cases (if any) are shareholders obligated to obtain an authorisation from, or provide information to, a public authority about events that have an impact on their stock interest in the company?

Any amendment of the by-laws must be filed with the CCA. An acquisition or sale of shares must be reported to the Danish tax authorities.

SHAREHOLDERS'RIGHTS IN THE CASE OF EXTRAORDINARY TRANSACTIONS AND/OR WINDING-UP

38. What rights are available to shareholders in the case of a sale of all or a substantial portion of the company's assets? In case of a merger or de-merger?

Sale of assets

A sale of the company's assets is only a matter for the GM if, upon the sale, an amendment to the company's objects are required. If so, the GM must approve the transfer by at least two-thirds of the votes cast as well as at least two-thirds of the share capital represented at the GM.

Merger

The shareholders in a non-surviving company may claim compensation from the company if the consideration offered for the shares in the non-surviving company is not fair and reasonable, and if they have made a reservation to this effect at the GM at which the merger resolution was passed.

De-merger

The shareholders in the transferor company may claim compensation from the company if the consideration offered for the shares in the transferor company is not fair and reasonable, and if they have made a reservation to this effect at the GM at which the resolution to implement the de-merger was passed.

39. Which rights are available to shareholders in the case of conversion of the company into a European Company (SE) or into another type of company?

When an SE is formed by merger, shareholders who opposed the merger at the GM are entitled to demand that the company redeems their shares at a price equivalent to the value of the shares.

Opposing shareholders cannot require redemption in connection with conversion of an ApS to an A/S or the opposite.

40. Which rights are available to shareholders of a company in liquidation?

The GM elects one or more liquidators to liquidate the company. Shareholders holding at least 25 per cent of the share capital are entitled to elect a liquidator at the GM who will liquidate the company together with other liquidators elected by the GM.

41. Can shareholders cause the liquidation of the company? How?

If all shareholders agree, a company that has paid all creditors may be dissolved by the company's shareholders making a declaration to the CCA that all debts, whether due or not, have been paid and that it has been resolved to dissolve the company.

Otherwise, a resolution on voluntarily dissolution by liquidation must be passed by the GM by at least two-thirds of the votes cast as well as at least two-thirds of the share capital represented at the GM.

GROUP COMPANIES

42. Is the concept of 'group' recognised as such under specific legislation? What are the implications?

A group is defined in the CA as 'a parent company and its subsidiaries', a parent company being a limited liability company controlling one or more subsidiaries. The CA does not contain a set of rules particularly designed for the legal aspects of groups. The CA does refer to groups in certain of its articles, which are, however, applicable to and designed for a company's activities.

The board of a Danish parent company must notify the board of a subsidiary as soon as any group relationship has been established. The board of a Danish subsidiary must provide the parent company with such information as is necessary to assess the group's position and the results from its activities.

The Danish rules on financial assistance allow for group lending in respect of certain parent companies, see above question 34.

43. Does a controlling company have particular duties *vis-à-vis* its controlled company shareholders?

No.

44. What are the rights of company shareholders when the controlling company puts in place actions and or transactions that can be prejudicial to the business of the shareholders?
None, unless any such rights (eg, redemption rights) appear in the by-laws.

45. What are the limitations, if any, to the possibility of owning reciprocal stock interests in companies?
When reciprocal stock interests reach a level where either one or both companies become the parent company of the other, the limitations regarding subsidiaries' acquisition of shares in parent companies will apply. A subsidiary's acquisition of shares in its parent company is subject to the restrictions regarding treasury shares according to which a company's holding of its own shares must be disregarded when assessing whether the company satisfies the minimum capital requirements (see question 2 above). In other words, the ownership can never exceed the share capital minus the required minimum capital.

France

Jeantet Associés Yvon Dréano

BASIC INFORMATION ON THE TYPES OF LIMITED LIABILITY COMPANIES AND ON THE RIGHTS OF SHAREHOLDERS
1.   What types of companies enjoy limited liability? If more than one, which ones have shareholders, ie holders of share certificates? Which one is the most common? Which one is mostly used by foreign investors?
Companies having the form of either an SARL (*société à responsabilité limitée*) or of a stock company (*société par action:* SA, *société anonyme*, SAS, *société par actions simplifiée*, or SCA, *société en commandite par actions*) enjoy limited liability. Liability of their shareholders may not exceed their respective contribution to the share capital.

According to recent statistics, the type of company which is mostly used in France is the SARL. The SAS, which was created in 1994 as a simplified form of the SA, has become the second mostly used company form in France. Through its flexibility in its organisation, the SAS has become an alternative to the SARL and SA and might be the form favoured by foreign investors.

2.   Are there minimum capital requirements and/or thin capitalisation rules in force?
A minimum capital of €37,000 is required for SA and SCA, either listed or not. There are no minimum capital requirements for SAS and SARL companies.

The French tax code (*Code général des impôts*) provides for a thin capitalisation rule which restrains deductibility of interest on loans granted by shareholders or related companies (ie either controlling the borrower, owning directly or indirectly at least 50 per cent of the dividend or voting rights of the borrower or companies controlled or owned by the same company as the borrower). The amount of interest should not exceed simultaneously the following three thresholds:
(i)   the debt-equity ratio, including loans granted by related companies should not exceed 1.5;
(ii) the amount of interest, increased by the provision for depreciation, due to related companies should not exceed 25 per cent of the current profits of the borrowing company; and
(iii) the interest received from related companies should not exceed the interest due to related companies.
When the amount of interest paid by the borrowing company to related

companies exceeds simultaneously the three conditions above, the part of interest which exceeds the highest limit of these three conditions is not deductible. As an exception, if the exceeding part of the interest amounts to less than €150,000, it is deductible.

3.   Describe the types of shares that can be issued by a company and the different rights that they attribute to their owners, as well as any other financial instruments (bonds or other) and other instruments of participatory nature in the company's capital that can also be issued by the company.

Stock companies may issue ordinary shares, which grant to their owners political rights (such as voting and information rights) and financial rights (dividend and liquidation rights) proportionally to their shareholding.

Stock companies may also issue preferred shares (*actions de préférence*) which may depart from the proportionality rule of ordinary shares by granting particular rights to their owners (such as double-voting rights, prior access to information, or priority dividend rights).

In addition, stock companies may issue other financial instruments, such as bonds or securities giving access to capital. These financial instruments mainly consist of equity warrants (*bons de souscription d'actions* – BSA), bonds (obligations), bonds redeemable in shares (*obligations remboursables en actions* – ORA), share convertible bonds (*obligations convertibles en actions* – OCA) and bonds with attached equity warrants (*obligations à bons de souscription d'actions* – OBSA).

An SARL cannot issue any preferred shares or financial instruments. Furthermore, SASs and SARLs are not allowed to offer their shares to the public.

4.   Can a company have only one shareholder and still enjoy limited liability?

Both the SAS (in the form of a *société par actions simplifiée unipersonnelle* – SASU) and the SARL (*entreprise unipersonnelle à responsabilité limitée* – EURL) may have only one shareholder and still enjoy limited liability.

5.   Are the rights of shareholders the same in any type of company?

The basic rights of shareholders are similar in any type of company, subject to preferred shares which may be issued by stock companies only and may grant specific rights to their holders.

6.   What are the basic rights of any shareholder? Describe briefly the rights of minority shareholders and indicate which thresholds, if any, are required to allow the minority shareholders to exercise any such rights.

The basic rights of shareholders consist of political and financial rights. Political rights mainly refer to the right to vote in general meetings (GM), information rights, rights to act in justice in order to defend the shareholder's or the company's interests. Financial rights include the right to receive dividends or part of the remaining assets of the company upon its liquidation. Such rights may not be amended or suppressed, subject to preferred shares which may grant specific rights to theirs holders.

In some circumstances, shareholders may be temporarily deprived of their voting rights. For example, a shareholder will be temporarily deprived of its voting rights when it is involved in a regulated agreement (*convention réglementée*) which is submitted to the shareholders for approval.

In addition, some rights are subject to thresholds. For instance the right for the shareholder to request from the court the appointment of an expert to report on a specific management operation requires a minimum shareholding of five per cent.

7.   Do all shareholders enjoy the same rights or can some shareholders be attributed specific rights, whether by reason of the particular class of stock owned or other? Are such rights generally provided for at the level of the company's by-laws and/or in shareholders' agreements?

Holders of ordinary shares all enjoy the same rights. In addition to ordinary shares, stock companies may issue preferred shares which attribute to their owners additional rights. A wide range of rights, either political or financial, may be granted to the holders of these preferred shares, such as a preferred dividend (*dividende préciputaire*) or a double voting right.

Rights attached to preferred shares must be included in the by-laws. An extraordinary meeting of the shareholders is required to create such a category of shares.

The shareholders may also agree in shareholders' agreements to provide specific rights to some shareholders (for example: pre-emptive rights, prior approval in the event of share transfers), it being specified that said rights may not be enforceable against third parties.

8.   May the rights of shareholders, generally speaking, be limited, modified or waived in any way? If so, are such modifications or limitations provided for in the company's by-laws and/or in shareholders' agreements?

Any modifications or limitations to the shareholders' rights require their prior agreement as such amendments need to be authorised by a shareholders' meeting. Modifications or limitations will have to be included in the by-laws in order to be enforceable to all shareholders. A shareholders' agreement may contain provisions which might limit or modify the rights of their signatories. However, such provisions may only be enforceable against signatories of the shareholders' agreements and thus only regulate their contractual relationships.

Certain limitations are legally prohibited. For example, the dividend right may not be totally cancelled for a shareholder. Furthermore, preferred shares without voting rights may not represent more than 50 per cent of the share capital of a stock company (25 per cent in listed companies).

GENERAL MEETING OF SHAREHOLDERS (GM) AND VOTING RIGHTS

9. Which decisions are reserved to the competence of the GM?

For SA, SCA and SARLs, the GM is always competent for the approval of the financial statements, which has to take place on a yearly basis. In addition, the GM enjoys a reserved competence for some specific decisions listed in the Commercial Code. As such, the GM will have to state over the allocation of the resulting profits, the appointment or the removal of board members and statutory auditors, the final approval of agreements between the company and its board members. These decisions are qualified as ordinary decisions and require simple majority. A reinforced majority is required for so-called extraordinary decisions, which mainly cover amendments to the by-laws, increase or reduction of capital. The change of the nationality of the company or an increase in the shareholders' commitments will require a unanimous vote of the shareholders.

For SAS companies, French law provides that the following decisions are reserved to the competence of the GM: approval of financial statements; increase or reduction of capital; capital amortisation; mergers; spin-offs; liquidation; appointment of statutory auditors; and amendment of the by-laws. Besides these decisions, the by-laws may add other decisions reserved to the competence of the GM.

10. How does a shareholder participate in a GM? Are there any limitations to having a minimum number of shares? May a shareholder delegate attendance to another shareholder or to the board? May a shareholder obtain assistance from the courts or any other governmental body to intervene in a GM or to cause one to be held in some particular cases?

Any shareholder may participate in any GM regardless the number of shares it owns. However, the by-laws may require that a shareholder intending to attend a GM be recorded in the company's book up to three days prior to the date of the GM.

Shareholders are convened to the GM by the company's board. A meeting notice has to be addressed to them by mail. For listed companies, this meeting notice also has to be published in the official bulletin (*bulletin des annonces légales et officielles* – BALO).

Shareholders may delegate attendance through a proxy either to another shareholder or to their spouse. If a proxy is granted without specifying any proxy-holder, the chairman of the GM is deemed to be empowered to vote on behalf of the shareholder having granted the proxy. Such a proxy is only valid for a specific GM.

A shareholder may decide to be assisted by a bailiff (*huissier*) in order to officially establish the content of the GM. In practice, the shareholder has to request a prior authorisation from the court allowing the bailiff to attend the GM. The court decision appointing the bailiff has to be motivated by serious cause.

11. May a GM be called and held at the request of any shareholder? Is there a threshold regarding the percentage of the stock interest owned in the company that may entitle a shareholder to such a right?
In an SA or an SCA, if the GM has not been convened by the board of directors, one or several shareholders representing at least five per cent of the shareholding, may request the judicial appointment of a representative (*mandataire désigné en justice*) with a view to convening a GM; the request has to comply with the company's corporate interest and shall not be justified solely by the interest of the shareholders. This right can also be exercised by a duly registered shareholders' association in listed companies, in which case the five per cent threshold progressively declines when the company's share capital is higher than €750,000.

In an SAS, the by-laws freely determine the convocation rules of shareholders and may therefore provide the shareholders with a right to convene a GM, either subject to a capital threshold or not.

In an SARL, the managing director (*gérant*) must call a meeting on request of one of more shareholders representing either half of the registered capital or one-quarter of the shareholders representing 25 per cent of the registered capital.

12. May a shareholder bring up an issue to be resolved upon and put it to a vote if it is not included on the agenda? May a shareholder require more information from the GM and/or the board concerning the agenda of the GM to be put in a better position to exercise their vote?
Prior to the GM, shareholders of an SA representing at least five per cent of the capital may request the submission of a resolution to the vote of the GM. The board of directors is bound to include this resolution on the agenda of the GM. The requested five per cent threshold declines when the company's capital is higher than €750,000.

During the GM, shareholders may only debate issues provided for by the agenda, except for the revocation of board members which may be brought up in the course of the GM. Shareholders are however free to amend the content of resolutions submitted to their vote, as the power of the GM is not limited to the sole rejection or approval of the draft resolutions.

Prior to a GM, shareholders have access to financial and governance documents, which are listed in the Commercial Code (see question 23). During the GM, shareholders are free to ask questions or request further explanation of the documentation which is submitted to them at the GM.

13. May a GM be held by telecommunication means and/or by correspondence (ie by written consent)?
Regardless of the form of the company, a GM may be held by videoconference if so provided in the by-laws. A shareholder may also vote by correspondence.

The by-laws of SARL and SAS companies may allow the shareholders to adopt resolutions through a written consultation (not possible in SAs and SCAs). In such a case, the draft resolutions have to be sent to the shareholders who are asked either to accept or to reject them. Such a written consultation cannot be used for the approval of the financial statements for which a GM must be held.

14. Are voting rights always proportionate to the stock held by each shareholder or can they vary by share class?

As a general rule, one share gives rise to one vote. However, preferred shares may challenge this proportionality rule by creating classes of shares which either are deprived of any voting right or enjoy double-voting rights. By-laws may also provide that a double-voting right may be granted to shareholders holding their shares for more than two years, provided that the shares are registered in the company's book.

15. Are there non-voting shares? Is there a maximum percentage of capital represented by non-voting shares?

Preferred shares may be issued without any voting rights. Non-voting shares cannot represent more than half of the share capital in non-listed companies and more than a quarter of the share capital in listed companies.

16. Can shareholders group their shares in order to exercise their voting rights (eg by trust, shareholders' agreement or otherwise)?

Shareholders of listed companies may group themselves into a specific 'association' which will be in charge of representing their interests. As such, the Commercial Code provides that this association will be entitled to exercise some rights originally devoted to the individual shareholders who joined the association.

For instance, the association is entitled to raise questions to the management prior to the shareholders' ordinary general meeting or to require more detailed information from the company. Nevertheless, shareholders still exercise their voting rights on an individual basis at shareholders' meetings since there are no legal provisions which enable delegation of these rights to a shareholders' association.

The Commercial Code requires a minimum share capital in order to be able to set up such an association: if the share capital amounts to less than €750,000, the association must represent at least five per cent of the shareholding. The requested five per cent shareholding decreases progressively if the share capital exceeds €750,000. Furthermore, the shares pooled in this association have to be registered in the shareholders' registers for at least two years.

17. Under what circumstances can a shareholder challenge the resolutions adopted by the GM? Are there thresholds concerning the stock interest owned to be able to bring such a claim?

Any shareholder may challenge a resolution adopted by the GM if it contravenes any compulsory provision of the Commercial Code. The breach of any competence or majority rule, the violation of the regulation related to the issuance of securities giving access to the capital or the absence of

statutory auditors for the approval of financial accounts are some examples
of such compulsory provision.

Furthermore, French case law has granted minority shareholders the
right to challenge resolutions if they bring sufficient evidence that these
resolutions have been voted exclusively in the interest of the majority
shareholders and against the company's interests (*abus de majorité*).

There are no thresholds required to bring such a claim.

18. What are the terms and procedures to challenge a resolution of the GM?

A resolution of the GM may be challenged before court within three years.
In some cases provided by the Commercial Code, the court must declare the
resolution null and void if it contravenes compulsory legal provisions. For
instance, the violation of majority or competence rules in SAs causes the
nullity of the GM. Otherwise, in some limited cases, the Commercial Code
leaves it up to the court to decide whether or not the resolution should be
declared null and void. For instance, the violation of convocation terms or
of shareholders' information duties may be declared null and void if the
court considers it necessary.

SHAREHOLDERS' RIGHTS VERSUS DIRECTORS AND DUTIES OF OTHER CORPORATE BODIES IN THE COMPANY

19. What is the procedure for the appointment/replacement/ revocation of directors and of statutory auditors, if any?

The directors (*administrateurs*) of an SA and the manager of an SARL are
appointed and dismissed by the shareholders. The managing director
(*directeur général*) of an SA is appointed by the board of directors. In SCAs,
the members of the supervisory board (*conseil de surveillance*) are appointed
by the limited partners (*commanditaires*, which liability is limited) and
the manager is appointed and dismissed by the shareholders with the
unanimous vote of the general partners (ie the *commandités* which liability
is unlimited and which shares cannot be freely transferred). The rules
regarding the appointment of the chairman (*president*) of the SAS are freely
decided in the by-laws.

Concerning the board of directors in SAs and the supervisory board in
SCAs, the replacement of a resigning member can be made by the other
members. This co-optation has to be confirmed following GM.

Except for SARL, in which the revocation of the manager may only occur
for cause, revocation of directors of an SA or members of the supervisory
board of an SCA is free and may happen at any time at the request of the
GM. Specific rules restraining the free revocation may be included however
in the by-laws for the chairman of the SAS. If the by-laws of an SCA do
not provide for revocation provisions, the manager of an SCA may only be
revoked by court decision.

When a justification is requested either by a legal provision or by the by-laws,
damages may be due to a director revoked without any cause. Further, even
when no justification is requested, a dismissed director may claim for damages if

it demonstrates that the circumstances of its revocation were persecutory.

Statutory auditors are appointed by shareholders for six years. Revocation before the term of their office requires the authorisation of the judge who will check whether this request is based on a just cause.

20. May shareholders challenge the resolutions of the board of directors? Is there a minimum percentage of capital required to challenge a board resolution?

According to French case law, shareholders may challenge the resolutions of the board of directors. Such an action may occur for a violation of any legal provision or a breach of the by-laws. No minimum percentage of capital is required to challenge a board resolution.

21. Are shareholders entitled to bring a legal action against the directors of the company? In which circumstances? Please describe briefly the principles of directors' liability.

Shareholders are entitled to bring legal action against directors of the company for any matters relating to their individual shareholder's interest. If the plaintiff argues that its personal interest has been violated, it has to evidence that the damage resulting from the director's negligence differs from the company's damage and from the other shareholders' damage. This condition may prove to be difficult to meet for a shareholder, as the suffered damage is often shared with all shareholders or with the company itself.

Shareholders are also entitled to undertake legal actions in the name of the company in order to engage the liability of directors. In such a case, any compensation granted by the court will benefit the company.

Legal action may be brought by shareholders against a director who committed negligence, either through a violation of a legal provision, a breach of the by-laws or a deliberate or negligent misconduct (*faute de gestion*). French case law also considers that directors can be sued by shareholders where they would not comply with their duty of loyalty towards the company or the shareholders.

22. What are the rights in connection with transactions where the directors have a conflict of interest situation?

Transactions involving (directly or indirectly) directors constitute 'regulated agreements' (*conventions réglementées*). In SA and SCA companies, such an agreement is subject to the prior approval of the board of directors or supervisory board. Subsequently, this agreement has also to be submitted to the GM for ratification. French law does not provide for any prior approval in SARL and SAS, but the relevant agreement has to be submitted to the shareholders for ratification.

Shareholders may refuse to ratify the agreement already executed between the company and any of its directors. In such a case, the agreement remains valid but the director involved in the transaction, and as the case may be the board which authorised it, shall be held liable for any damage caused to the company as a result of said agreement.

In addition, the Commercial Code lists some agreements which cannot be signed between the directors and the company (*conventions interdites*). For instance, directors cannot benefit from any loan, advance or guarantee from the company, even with prior approval. Such an agreement would be declared null and void.

INFORMATION RIGHTS ON THE COMPANY'S BUSINESS
23. What information may be requested by the shareholders from the board concerning the general state of the company's business or any specific transaction? Are information rights different depending on the number of shares owned? Are shareholders entitled to receive written information before, during or after the GM about the meeting agenda and to what extent? Is it possible for a shareholder to obtain a copy of the minutes of the GM?
Upon request, shareholders of SAs and limited partners of SCAs are entitled to have access to corporate documents relating to the situation of the company. Documents which have to be made available to shareholders are listed in the Commercial Code and include for example the financial accounts, the management reports and the minutes of the shareholders' meetings from the last three financial years. These documents have to be consulted at the company's headquarters and shareholders are entitled to take copies of these documents. In addition to this permanent information right, the Commercial Code grants a specific right of information to shareholders prior to a GM; shareholders may request the communication of documents listed by the Commercial Code, including but not limited to the agenda of the GM, the financial accounts, the draft resolutions and the management's and statutory auditors' reports. A minimum shareholding is not required to exercise these rights. However, an addition right is granted to one or more shareholders representing more than five per cent of the capital, who may ask the court to appoint an expert in order to make a report on a specific management operation.

General partners of SCAs may obtain communication of the corporate books and registers twice a year and may ask written questions on the company.

In SASs, shareholders' information has to be defined in the by-laws.

In SARLs, the management has to deliver to the shareholders a list of the inventory, the financial accounts, the management report and a draft of the resolutions to be submitted to the ordinary annual shareholders' meeting. A report and the draft of the resolutions have to be made available to the shareholders prior to any extraordinary meeting. Shareholders are entitled to ask questions to the management which have to be answered during the shareholders' meeting.

24. Do shareholders have the right/duty to resolve in the GM upon matters which were not on the agenda?
During the GM, shareholders may only debate issues provided by the agenda, except for the revocation of board members in SAs, the manager in an SARL and members of the supervisory board in SCAs, which may be

brought up during the GM. Shareholders are also free to amend the content of the resolutions which are submitted to their vote.

25. Are shareholders entitled to inspect the corporate books and/or any other corporate or accounting documents? To what extent? Can they do it through external counsel or advisors?

Pursuant to their permanent right of information, shareholders are entitled to review the register of the shareholders' meetings and the financial accounts for the last three financial years.

This review may only take place at the corporate office of the company. Any shareholder can exercise this right at any time, and may be assisted by an expert, provided that this expert is duly registered on a list held at the clerk office of the court. Shareholders may take a copy of the any documents consulted (except for the list of inventory in the SARL).

SHAREHOLDERS' AGREEMENTS

26. Are shareholders' agreements validly enforceable? What are their typical contents and term of duration? Are they enforceable by or against third parties and if so, to what extent?

Shareholders' agreements are validly enforceable against their signatories. The infringement of a provision of the shareholders' agreement by a party may result in the payment of damages to the co-contracting party, or in the termination of the agreement. Specific performance has been allowed by French case law in very few cases, such as, for example, in the case of a breach of a pre-emptive right when the third party who acquired the shares in violation of such a right was aware of the existence of said right and of the willingness of the beneficiary to exercise this right.

Shareholders' agreements may contain a wide range of provisions, which relate to the governance (for example: prior consultation before a board meeting or a GM), or the shares held by the parties to the shareholders' agreement (tag-along, drag-along or pre-emptive rights).

There is no typical term applying to shareholders' agreements. However, duration should be specified in the agreement so as not to be considered as an undetermined contract, which may be terminated at any time by one of the parties.

Under French law, the effects of a shareholders' agreement are limited to the signing parties as a matter of principle. Therefore, third parties shall not be held liable for a breach of a provision of the shareholders' agreements. However, French case law provides for a few exceptions in case of bad faith of the third party.

27. Do shareholders' agreements have to be disclosed to the public or registered in any public registry?

Except for listed companies, shareholders' agreements need neither to be disclosed to the public nor to be registered in any public registry.

If the agreement relates to more than 0.5 per cent of the shareholding or the voting rights of a listed company, the provisions of this agreement concerning pre-emptive rights, puts or calls have to be communicated to the company and to the French stock exchange authority (*Autorité des Marchés Financiers* – AMF) within five days following its signature. Such information is then disclosed to the public. If the parties fail to disclose this information, the related provisions of the shareholders' agreement are suspended.

ECONOMIC RIGHTS AND RIGHTS OVER THE STOCK
28. Is the stock always freely transferable? Are there any legal limitations? Are there any restrictions on contractual limitations?
Except for companies having the form of SARL, where the law provides that prior approval of the other shareholders is requested for any transfer of shares to third parties, stock is freely transferable.

Nevertheless, it is possible to restrain the transfers of shares in the by-laws of any company by submitting them to a prior approval procedure, an inalienability period (which shall not exceed 10 years), or by granting a pre-emptive right to the other shareholders.

In some cases, a shareholder might also be deterred from transferring its shares in order to benefit from a specific legal provision. For example, a shareholder who has been granted free shares (*actions gratuites*) must keep these shares for a minimum period of two years. A similar obligation is requested for shares granted to employees in the scope of profit sharing plans, as these shares are not disposable for a period of five years.

29. Are shareholders entitled to pledge their stock?
Shareholders are entitled to pledge their stock except for SARLs in which the prior approval of the other shareholders is required.

For other company forms, pledges may be submitted to the procedure applicable to transfers of shares to third parties.

30. Are there financial assistance issues to be considered and other prohibitions to be evaluated in the context of a leveraged buyout transaction?
Pursuant to the Commercial Code, it is forbidden for a company (SA, SCA or SAS) to grant a financial advance, a loan or a security in order to finance the subscription or the purchase of its own shares by a third party (such a prohibition does not apply to SARLs) (see question 36).

In addition to the financial assistance issue, the directors shall always comply with the corporate interest of the company and may not misuse its assets or credits.

31. May companies buy back their own stock and, if so, under what circumstances and subject to which limitations?
Companies are authorised to buy back their own shares under restrictive conditions.

Such a buy back is authorised in the event of a capital reduction not caused by losses. The repurchased shares will have to be cancelled immediately. In some restricted cases, the company is authorised to buy back its own shares without cancelling them. This concerns shares purchased in order to grant them to managers or employees. The company may also hold temporarily some of its own shares following a merger, a spin-off or a court decision. Listed companies are entitled to acquire their own shares in order to improve the management of its equity or to enhance the market liquidity.

In any case, the buy back of shares should not exceed the total amount of 10 per cent of the shareholding. In addition, voting, dividend and stock purchase rights are suspended for these shares as long as they are owned by the company itself.

32. Is there a legal right to withdraw from the company and if so, under what circumstances? How is the shareholders' stock valued and paid in such a case?

There is no right of withdrawal for shareholders in SA, SCA, SARL or SASs. There is an exception provided by the Commercial Code concerning companies with a variable capital (*capital variable*), in which shareholders are entitled to withdraw from the company when they consider it appropriate. In such a case, the valuation and repayment rules of the shares shall be specified in the by-laws of the company (in the case of disagreement, an expert is to be appointed to assess the value). There have been ongoing discussions at the French Parliament in order to generalise this right to all companies, but no reform has been undertaken yet.

The most natural way for a shareholder to withdraw from the company consists in the transfer of their shares.

33. In which circumstances can dividends be distributed among shareholders? Is it possible to exclude or limit the right of certain shareholders to dividends? Does a certain portion of the profits need to be set aside in a reserve fund where it cannot be distributed to the shareholders? Are advances on dividends allowed and, if so, under which circumstances? Can advances on dividends be reclaimed by the company?

The GM may decide to distribute dividends to shareholders after the approval of the financial accounts provided that the company has made a net profit. The GM may also decide to distribute an interim dividend (*acompte sur dividende*) before the accounts are approved, provided that a profit is stated by a statutory auditor since the last approved accounts.
As a matter of principle, shareholders have a right to dividends proportional to their shareholding. This rule might be amended by the creation of preferred shares with specific dividend rights (*actions de préférence*). As such, a priority dividend (*dividende préciputaire*) may be granted to holders of preferred shares. In any case, the dividend right cannot be totally cancelled for a shareholder.

The GM enjoys substantial freedom as regards the amount of dividends where there is a profit. However, it is required by law to constitute a reserve, which should amount to 10 per cent of the share capital. Each year, at least five per cent of profits must be allocated to this mandatory reserve until this level of 10 per cent is reached. Furthermore, by-laws may require the constitution of additional statutory reserves. Rules concerning its level and its allocation should be respected by the GM. Any dividend distributed in violation of these provisions would be considered to be fictive and directors may face criminal actions.

34. What are the rights of shareholders in the case of an issue of new stock (increase of the company's corporate capital)(pre-emption rights)?

For any increase of the company's share capital, shareholders are granted a preferred subscription right (*droit preferentiel de souscription*) on the newly issued shares in proportion to their respective shareholding.

The GM may decide to withdraw this preferred subscription right when the shareholders decide upon the capital increase. Such a deliberation needs to be unequivocally approved by a specific resolution.

If the issuance is made with preferred subscription rights, shareholders may renounce their individual right either in favour of determined persons or without indication of a beneficiary. Such waiver has to be duly notified to the company. This preferred subscription right is freely negotiable and may therefore be assigned by its holder.

Shareholders also have a preferred subscription right for any issuance of securities giving access to the capital, as the exercise of such securities may lead to a dilution of their shareholding.

35. May minority shareholders ban or limit the company's capital structure in any manner?

Minority shareholders may have some impact on the company's capital structure in so far as a share capital increase or decrease requires the approval of 66.66 per cent of the voting rights (SARL and SAS by-laws may also provide a higher percentage).

36. Which are the financial assistance prohibitions in force?

Pursuant to the Commercial Code, it is forbidden for a company (SA, SCA or SAS) to grant a financial advance, a loan or a security in order to finance the subscription or the purchase of its own shares by a third party (such prohibition does not apply to an SARL).

Directors who have agreed to grant such financial assistance are subject to criminal prosecution for a maximum amount of €9,000.

Furthermore, even if such a remedy is not provided by the applicable legal provision, contracts signed in violation of this provision may be declared null and void by the court.

37. Apart from publicly listed companies, in which cases (if any) are shareholders obligated to obtain an authorisation from, or provide information to, a public authority about events that have an impact on their stock interest in the company?

Transfers of controlling interest in a company may be subject to mandatory merger control and therefore may have to be authorised by either the

French competition authority (*Autorité de la Concurrence*) or the European Commission, depending on the thresholds applicable.

The prior authorisation of the French Minister of Economy is required for investments made in sectors defined by the French Monetary Code as 'sensitive' (including but not limited to gambling, research-development activities in weapon or nuclear industries, etc). Such an authorisation is required for any operation which enables a non-EU investor to hold directly or indirectly one-third of the share capital of a French company carrying out such an activity. For EU investors, such an authorisation is requested for any operation leading to a change of control of the French entity.

In any other sector, investments by non-EU investors which would lead to a change of control of a French company need to be declared to the Ministry of Economy upon completion.

In addition, prior approval may have to be obtained in some regulated activities. For instance, the authorisation of the *Autorité de Contrôle Prudentiel* (ACP) is required for any transaction which would result in the change of control or the crossing of certain thresholds determined by law, in the share capital of French financial institutions, including insurance companies.

SHAREHOLDERS' RIGHTS IN CASE OF EXTRAORDINARY TRANSACTIONS AND/OR WINDING-UP
38. What rights are available to shareholders in the case of a sale of all or a substantial portion of all of the company's assets? In case of a merger or de-merger?
The sale of all or substantially all of the company's assets (which would entail a change of the corporate purposes of the company) and any merger or de-merger are subject to the prior approval of the GM of both companies involved in the operation and therefore are submitted to the shareholders' vote.

The majority required for such an operation is the one applicable for amendments of by-laws and depends on the companies' form. If the operation involves SAs or SASs, some specific rules will have to be complied with: in particular, managers have to prepare a report on the envisioned operation which has to be submitted to the shareholders with the draft of the merger agreement and the report of the auditors appointed for the operation.

If the merger or de-merger leads to an increase in the shareholders' financial commitment, a unanimous vote from the GM is then required. The same rules apply to a spin-off, where the contribution agreement has to be approved by the shareholders of both companies involved.

39. Which rights are available to shareholders in the case of conversion of the company into a European Company (SE) or into another type of company?
The conversion of a company into another form (being an SE or not) leads to amendment of the by-laws and is therefore subject to the prior approval of the shareholders, the majority required being the one for extraordinary shareholders' meetings; in addition, some provisions (pre-emptive right, inalienability) may require a unanimous vote.

Furthermore, shareholders are granted a specific information right since an auditor has to be appointed by the commercial court in order to prepare a report on the conversion of the company. The auditor is asked to give an evaluation of the company's assets which is to be made available to the shareholders at least eight days before the GM. The shareholders have to give their opinion on said evaluation.

40. Which rights are available to shareholders of a company in liquidation?

In the event of a voluntary liquidation (*liquidation à l'amiable*), shareholders have the right to a portion of the company's liquidation distribution (*boni de liquidation*). This liquidation distribution is made of the assets which would be left once the third party claims are paid and share capital is redeemed. This liquidation distribution is distributed among shareholders in consideration of their respective shareholding. Nevertheless, it is possible to establish other rules for distribution in the by-laws which unequivocally depart from proportionality.

In the event of a liquidation decided by a court (*liquidation judiciaire*), shareholders do not manage the liquidation process and are not entitled to vote on the liquidation plan. As the case may be, remaining assets will be distributed among shareholders once all creditors have been reimbursed.

41. Can shareholders cause the liquidation of the company? How?

Shareholders may collectively, at any time, decide upon the winding-up of the company. This decision has to be taken pursuant to the rules applicable to the amendment of the by-laws. However, said winding up should not harm minority shareholders' interests or should not be done with fraudulent intent. In such a case, shareholders may be liable for any damages caused to either minority shareholders or third parties.

Shareholders may individually request the judicial winding-up of the company before the Commercial Court. The plaintiff will then have to bring evidence of serious cause which justifies such a decision. The non-performance of its duties by a shareholder or a serious dissension among shareholders may lead the jurisdiction to wind-up the company, provided these events paralyse the running of the business of the company.

COMPANY GROUPS
42. Is the concept of 'group' recognised as such under specific legislation? What are the implications?

There is no legal concept of group under French law. As such, the group is not considered as a legal entity (*personne morale*).

However, various fields of French law (commercial law, labour law, antitrust law or tax law) take into consideration the existence of a control that a company may own towards one or several entities; the control is defined by the Commercial Code and includes, in particular, a situation where a shareholder owns, directly or indirectly, more than 50 per cent of the voting rights or when it owns the power to appoint or revoke the majority of the members of the board of directors.

Furthermore, French case law may take into account the existence of a group of companies in some specific situations; for example, the company's commitments towards its group (eg under a cash-pooling agreement) may be considered as valid provided that a group interest (*intérêt de groupe*) could be evidenced through certain tests defined by French case law. Demonstrating the existence of such a group interest needs to be reviewed on a case-by-case basis.

43. Does a controlling company have any particular duties *vis-à-vis* its controlled company shareholders?

Except for misuse of majority, a holding company does not have to comply with any particular duties towards its controlled company shareholders.

44. What are the rights of company shareholders when the controlling company puts in place actions and/or transactions that can be prejudicial to the shareholders?

The majority shareholders (which control the group) shall comply with the controlled company's particular interests within the group. On this basis, the shareholders of a controlled company may bring legal actions against the controlling company if they believe that the controlling company misused its rights derived from its majority position. For example, a cash management agreement among the companies within the group (*convention de gestion de trésorerie*) may be challenged if it appears that this agreement has been entered into without any consideration for the relevant subsidiary.

In addition, agreements between an SA or an SCA and one of its shareholders holding more than 10 per cent of the share capital is considered as a regulated agreement (*convention réglementée*) and is therefore subject to the prior approval of the board of directors or supervisory board of the controlled company and the ratification of the shareholders.

45. What are the limitations, if any, to the possibility of owning reciprocal stock interests in companies?

Reciprocal shareholding is strictly regulated for SA, SCA and SASs. Such companies cannot hold more than 10 per cent of the share capital of a company which would be one of its own shareholders. If such a situation happens, companies have to regularise this situation within one year. If the companies fail to reach an agreement and do not comply with the 10 per cent limitation, the company having the lowest shareholding in the other must withdraw its investment. Voting rights of the shares involved in the reciprocal shareholding are suspended.

The author wishes to extend special thanks to associate Alexandre Schaff for his contribution to the preparation of this chapter.

Germany

Noerr LLP Dr Ingo Theusinger

BASIC INFORMATION ON THE TYPES OF CORPORATIONS WITH LIMITED LIABILITY COMPANIES AND ON THE RIGHTS OF SHAREHOLDERS

1. What types of companies enjoy limited liability? If more than one, which ones have shareholders, ie holders of share certificates? Which one is the most common? Which one is mostly used by foreign investors?

Mainly, two types of corporations are used for entrepreneurial purposes, which enjoy limited liability: the *Aktiengesellschaft* (AG), equivalent to the anglo-saxon public limited company (plc) and the *Gesellschaft mit beschränkter Haftung* (GmbH), equivalent to the anglo-saxon private limited company (Ltd). Both companies have shareholders. Their fundamental difference, however, is defined by the possibility of publicly trading AG shares at stock exchanges, whilst GmbH shares have to be transferred through private, notarially certified legal acts. However, non-listed companies in the legal form of an AG also exist. The GmbH is the legal form most commonly used since, compared with the AG, a GmbH is less rigidly regulated by the legislator, who left the determination of shareholder relationships to a large extent up to the GmbH's articles of association. Furthermore, it is far easier for shareholders to exercise their influence on management compared to the relatively independently operating executive board of the AG. Hence, from a corporate law perspective, foreign investors mostly use the GmbH. Furthermore, there are two commonly used types of partnerships enjoying limited liability: the *Gesellschaft mit beschränkter Haftung and Compagnie Kommanditgesellschaft* (GmbH and Co KG) and the *Kommanditgesellschaft auf Aktien* (KGaA), which are mainly used for tax purposes. Because of the general focus of this evaluation, the following will concentrate on the AG and the GmbH.

2. Are there minimum capital requirements and/or thin capitalisation rules in force?

For the AG, the minimal capitalisation amounts to €50,000; for the GmbH, the minimum capital required is €25,000. Once a GmbH has been founded, all assets necessary to cover the statutory capital may not be paid out to its shareholders. In an AG, none of the company's assets necessary to cover the entire equity may be paid out. Hence, the capitalisation rules of the GmbH are significantly more liberal than those applying to the AG. Under German corporate law, there are no thin capitalisation rules beside the described minimum equity requirements.

3. Describe the types of shares that can be issued by a company and the different rights that they attribute to their owners, as well as any other financial instruments (bonds or other) and other instruments of a participatory nature in the company's capital that can also be issued by the company.

With respect to the GmbH, the Limited Liabilities Companies Act (GmbHG) does not differ between specific share types. The GmbH shareholders are free to agree on specific rights including, but not limited to, restrictions on transferability and provisions regarding preference shares. Preference shares usually have preferred rights for dividends, but no voting rights. Regarding financial instruments, German law accepts all major financial instruments which are internationally common. There are no specific limitations on using such instruments for financing purposes.

4. Can a company have only one shareholder and still enjoy limited liability?

Yes, the number of shareholders has no impact on the limitation of liability.

5. Are the rights of shareholders the same in any type of company?

The rights of shareholders are basically identical, regardless of the type of company. However, there are differences because of the company structure. Typically, the shareholders of a GmbH know each other and also the management of the GmbH. Mostly, the shareholder structure persists for many years. Instead, the shareholder circle of an AG is generally larger, volatile and anonymous. The German legislator therefore restricted the rights of shareholders of an AG basically to those foreseen in the German Stock Corporation Act (AktG). Shareholders of a GmbH however, are less restricted. Further, the rights differ in that the management of the AG acts independently from its shareholders while the GmbH shareholders may issue binding orders. Publicly listed AGs are subject to German capital market law, containing *inter alia* information duties when shareholders own a specific amount of the share capital of the listed company.

6. What are the basic rights of any shareholder? Describe briefly the rights of minority shareholders and indicate which thresholds, if any, are required to allow the minority shareholders to exercise any such rights.

Shareholders' rights in incorporated companies can be divided into administrative rights (*Verwaltungsrechte*) and asset rights (*Vermögensrechte*). Administrative rights govern the extent to which shareholders may influence management decisions, which information they may request and for which measures their assent is required. Asset rights on the other hand entitle shareholders to participate in company profits. The most important administrative rights are the right to vote (*Stimmrecht*), to receive information (*Informationsrecht*) and to challenge shareholders' resolutions (*Klagebefugnis*).

Another basic and *prima facie* self-evident right of shareholders is the right to remain in the company. In a GmbH, this right remains in principle untouched. In AGs however (both listed and non-listed), German law knows the concept of 'squeeze-out', which generally allows for a majority shareholder holding 95 per cent of the share capital to force the remaining shareholder(s) out of the company. Furthermore, a squeeze out is possible in a takeover scenario: upon ownership of 95 per cent of the share capital, the buyer can acquire the outstanding five per cent of the share capital per court decision. Both cases are subject to compensatory payments.

In both the AG and GmbH, certain substantial decisions by the general meeting (GM) require qualified majorities of votes representing three-quarters of the company's share capital. These resolutions include: amendments to the articles of association; changes to the stated capital; the issuing of profit participation rights or convertible bonds; the conclusion of domination and/or profit transfer agreements; and the sale of all, or almost all, assets. Therefore, 25 per cent of the share capital plus one share constitute a blocking minority (*Sperrminorität*) with respect to fundamental decisions as described above.

As pointed out, shareholders' rights are more deeply regulated in the AG, while legislation leaves the determination of shareholders' rights in the GmbH largely to the articles of association. In both a GmbH and an AG, shareholders have the administrative right to challenge resolutions of the shareholders' meeting. Since the right to challenge resolutions is only codified in the AktG, the provisions of which accordingly apply to GmbH resolutions. This right is very similar in both legal forms. Apart from that, it is difficult to make general comparative statements about shareholders' rights in a GmbH and an AG as the GmbH shareholders' rights are subject to a much larger extent to the articles of association and thus vary considerably between different companies.

7.   Do all shareholders enjoy the same rights or can some shareholders be attributed specific rights, whether by reason of the particular class of stock owned or other? Are such rights generally provided for at the level of the company's by-laws and/or in shareholders' agreements?

In principle, all shareholders enjoy the same rights. However, shareholders' rights may be constituted in a way that deviates from the usual form. In an AG, the best examples are non-voting preference shares (*stimmrechtslose Vorzugsaktien*), which in principle allow for higher dividends at the price of the loss of voting rights. At the same time, it is not possible to link more than one vote to an AG share. In a GmbH, by contrast, both asset and administrative rights are subject to a much larger extent to the articles of association. Hence, the structure of shares held by different shareholders can theoretically be very complex. For instance, one GmbH shareholder could be entitled to a blocking right which entitles them to prevent specific or all shareholders' resolutions passed without their consent.

8. May the rights of shareholders, generally speaking, be limited, modified, suppressed or waived in any way? If so, how? Are such modifications or limitations provided for in the company's by-laws and/or in shareholders' agreements?

In general, shareholder's rights can be modified. Some vital rights, however, may not be affected by the articles of association or shareholders' agreements. For instance, the general fiduciary duty (*allgemeine Treuepflicht*) of all shareholders towards each others' shareholder rights, even their core rights, cannot be waived. This legal institute has not been explicitly codified in the Codes but is generally accepted by German case law. It is commonly used to guarantee shareholder behaviour in the company's interest.

However, within a GmbH, shareholders can take more liberties to define and curb their individual rights. For instance, GmbH by-laws may grant each individual shareholder the right to call a shareholders' meeting at any time. AG shareholders are not affected by non-competition provisions applicable to other legal forms such as the GmbH. Important differences also exist with regard to information rights concerning accounts and balance statements. GmbH shareholders may request such information at any time, AG shareholders may – principally – only do so during a GM and when it is relevant to the GM's agenda.

GENERAL MEETING OF SHAREHOLDERS (GM) AND VOTING RIGHTS

9. Which decisions are reserved to the competence of the GM?

In general, in all corporations, shareholders may not have an intrinsic right to run the company. This is exclusively the task of the managing director (GmbH) or the executive board (AG). Exemptions are ruled by German case law, for instance, if management plans to shift business operations to activities that are not reconcilable with the company's statutory purpose as provided in the articles of association. In order to perform such measures, the managing director or the executive board respectively require the assent of the GM. Also, despite the formal separation between shareholding and management, there are vast differences in the possibilities of shareholders to influence management decisions. Whereas AG shareholders have almost no possibility to challenge management decisions outside the GM, the GM of a GmbH may issue direct binding orders to the managing director. In a GmbH, therefore, all decisions may in practice be reserved to the GM's competence. In AGs on the other hand, only decisions with a substantial impact on shareholders' rights such as elections of supervisory board members, appointing auditors, amendments to by-laws, changes to the capital structure etc are subject to GM resolutions. Further, management decisions only require the assent of the GM if the executive board requests it. It is obliged to request this assent if a management decision affects business operations so crucially that shareholder interests are directly and substantially affected.

10. How does a shareholder participate in a GM? Are there any limitations to having a minimum number of shares? May a shareholder delegate attendance to another shareholder or to the board? May a shareholder obtain assistance from the courts or any other governmental body to intervene in a GM or to cause one to be held in some particular cases?

Generally, shareholders participate through personal attendance and casting their votes in the GM. As participation is one of the most central rights of corporate membership, any shareholder may participate in the GM. This even holds for shareholders with non-voting shares. Upon attendance of one shareholder, there is no minimum limitation for attendance. Shareholders do not necessarily have to be present in person at a GM. They may grant power of attorney to a third person (eg another shareholder). Recent changes in the AktG enable companies to let shareholders participate online in the GM but the GM itself cannot be virtually held.

In principle, shareholders may delegate their voting rights to the members of the management board. However, in certain circumstances, they are not allowed to vote, eg on resolutions about their exoneration.

A court may intervene in a GM by granting an interim injunction banning certain shareholders from voting.

11. May a GM be called and held at the request of any shareholder? Is there a threshold regarding the percentage of the stock interest owned in the company that may entitle a shareholder to such a right?

In a GmbH, shareholders holding 10 per cent of the shares may demand that a shareholders' meeting be called. The articles of association, however, may state different thresholds for shareholder minorities to be able to call a GM. In an AG, a minority of five per cent of the share capital is sufficient to provide the same right.

12. May a shareholder bring up an issue to be resolved upon and put it to a vote if it is not included on the agenda? May a shareholder require more information from the GM and/or the board, concerning the agenda of the GM, to be put in a better position to exercise their vote?

Concerning the AG, there is a procedure set forth in the AktG, which allows for a minority of shareholders (holding at least €500,000 or five per cent of the share capital) to claim that a certain issue be included on the agenda before the GM is held. Shareholders are entitled to request information relevant to the issue currently being discussed at any time during the GM. Any information may be withheld if it contains company secrets or pertains to taxes, accounting methods, or if it has been provided to every shareholder for at least the last seven days before the GM on the company website. Regarding the GmbH, shareholders representing 10 per cent of the share capital are entitled to put an issue on the agenda. When all shareholders of the company are present in the GM and agree, they can resolve upon newly raised issues.

13. May a GM be held by telecommunication means and/or by correspondence (ie by written consent)?

With respect to the AG, the shareholders are generally required to physically attend the GM. More recently, the AktG has allowed, exceptionally, voting in written form or online voting at the discretion of a by-law provision or authorisation of the executive board. Participation via telephone is not permitted.

In principle, the same applies to the shareholders of a GmbH. In general, personal attendance at the GM is required. However, the shareholder can adjust such a principle. If all shareholders agree, they may waive the requirement of personal attendance by resolution in writing to the issue at hand or to accepting votes in writing. Further, the articles of association of a GmbH may allow any form of resolution, for instance by telephone conference. But, resolutions regarding core topics of the company, for example, the agreement on a domination agreement, need to be resolved in front of a notary in an ordinary GM with at least one shareholder present and representing the other shareholders.

14. Are voting rights always proportionate to the stock held by each shareholder or can they vary by share class?

The basic principle in both legal forms is 'one share, one vote'. However, this principle may be differently modified for AGs and GmbHs. In an AG, it is possible to issue non-voting preference shares; which usually yield higher dividends up to 50 per cent of the share capital.

By contrast, it is not permitted to issue multiple-vote shares (*Mehrstimmrechtsaktien*) in AGs. GmbHs on the other hand are far more liberal in devising their own shareholder rights, which may differ considerably between shareholders. Shares may entitle shareholders to more or less than one vote per share and may also entitle them to different proportions of the company's profit.

15. Are there non-voting shares? Is there a maximum percentage of capital represented by non-voting shares?

In an AG there are non-voting shares (*stimmrechtslose Vorzugsaktien*), which allow for higher dividends at the price of the loss of voting rights. Non-voting shares may only constitute up to 50 per cent of the share capital. In a GmbH, the GM generally has more liberties to set up share classes and to link votes to individual shares. Hence, there may well be non-voting shares. These shares are not subject to any percentage restrictions.

16. Can shareholders group their shares in order to exercise their voting rights (eg, by trust, shareholders' agreement or otherwise)?

There are no limitations regarding the GmbH. In principle, the same applies for the AG. Shareholders may also use each others' shares by borrowing and lending them. However, shareholders of an AG will have to observe notification duties, eg stated by takeover law when crossing certain thresholds, the lowest of which being three per cent of the share capital for listed companies.

17. Under what circumstances can a shareholder challenge the resolutions adopted by the GM? Are there thresholds concerning the stock interest owned to be able to bring such a claim?

All legal provisions governing the challenging of resolutions are stated in the AktG. In principle, they also apply to the GmbH.

Shareholders can challenge all resolutions adopted by the GM on the grounds of formal or material violations of the law or the articles of association. In general, there are no thresholds concerning the stock interest owned to be entitled to claim. Expressly for the AG, the legislator has indirectly introduced such a threshold. To minimise the risk of shareholders prolonging resolutions of the GM which need to be registered with the Commercial Register by – abusing – the possibility to challenge shareholder resolutions before the court, the company itself can initiate a request for registration (*Freigabeverfahren*). Shareholders with shares below a threshold of €1,000 of the share capital cannot object to this request.

18. What are the terms and procedures to challenge a resolution of the GM?

With respect to the AG, the codified term to challenge a resolution is one month. The defendant of such a claim would be the company itself. Only a shareholder who attended the shareholders' meeting and objected to an incorrect procedure or a material violation is entitled to claim. The executive board (*Vorstand*) and the advisory board (*Aufsichtsrat*) are also entitled to claim under specific requirements. The GmbHG does not contain similar rulings. Therefore, the principles of the AktG apply in general, as long as the articles of association of the GmbH do not state anything different.

SHAREHOLDERS' RIGHTS VERSUS DIRECTORS AND DUTIES OF OTHER CORPORATE BODIES IN THE COMPANY

19. What is the procedure for the appointment/replacement/ revocation of directors and of statutory auditors, if any?

To understand the procedure, it is important to know the main institutions of a GmbH and an AG: in the GmbH, there are the managing director(s) as the executing management and the GM as the forum of shareholders. In the AG, there is the executive board as the executing management, the GM as the forum of shareholders and, additionally, the supervisory board supervising the executive board. The GM of the GmbH appoints its managing directors (*Geschäftsführer*). The GM of an AG appoints its supervisory board which nominates the executive board. Upon a certain number of employees (500), the supervisory board becomes also mandatory for the GmbH. The number of supervisory board members and its composition depend on the amount of the share capital and the number of employees respectively. Upon a specific number of employees, the supervisory board must also comprise representatives of the employees.

While the GmbHG does not contain any time limit with respect to the term of office, the AktG states that the terms of office for the executive board as well as for the supervisory board are five years at the maximum. Revocation and replacements are in principle resolved by the GM and the supervisory board respectively. The annual auditor of an AG is appointed by the GM.

20. May shareholders challenge the resolutions of the board of directors? Is there a minimum percentage of capital required to challenge a board resolution?

In a GmbH, shareholders may issue direct orders to the managing directors. The GM could also revoke actions by the managing directors upon violation of internal orders. To challenge decisions taken by the managing directors, only a simple majority is required, unless the company's by-laws state a higher capital majority. With respect to third parties, such post-revocations are not effective because the managing directors of a GmbH represent their company – *vis-à-vis* third parties – without limitations. In an AG, the executive board is independent from shareholders while running the operating business. It is, however, possible for AG shareholders to bring legal action against the company on the grounds that the executive board failed to request the assent of the GM for a crucial decision (see question 9). If this is successful, the executive board is subsequently obliged to let the GM decide about the decision in question. Hence, the decision is blocked until the voting of the GM.

21. Are shareholders entitled to bring a legal action against the directors of the company? In which circumstances? Please describe briefly the principles of directors' liability.

Basically, the management is only liable to the company. In general, there is no direct liability of the management to its shareholders. Exemptions are made in the case of tort law.

Benchmarks for directors' liabilities to the company are the contractual and statutory duties as well as the comparison to the standard of care of a prudent business man. This obviously does not include failure of the company due to reasons that are subject to entrepreneurial risk.

The AktG lists cases in which directors and/or supervisory board members are personally liable (section 93 AktG). Although, the GmbHG Code does not contain such a listing, the underlying principles of the codified cases within the AktG also apply to the GmbH. However, the AktG explicitly codifies that the shareholder majority may request an extraordinary audit (*Sonderprüfung*) of specific circumstances. If the majority of shareholders decline such a request, a court can install an extraordinary auditor by request of a specific minority (holding €100,000 or at least one percentage of the share capital).

22. What are the rights in connection with transactions where the directors have a conflict of interest situation?

Generally, the fact that a director acts in conflict of interest does not affect the validity of the transaction. Such a managing director acting in bad faith is subject to tort claims. In the case of collusion, meaning that the other party knows about the conflict of interest, the transaction could be void.

INFORMATION RIGHTS ON THE COMPANY'S BUSINESS

23. What information may be requested by the shareholders from the board concerning the general state of the company's business or any specific transaction? Are information rights different depending on the number of shares owned? Are shareholders entitled to receive written information before, during or after the GM about the meeting agenda and to what extent? Is it possible for a shareholder to obtain a copy of the minutes of the GM?

The information rights of shareholders of a GmbH and an AG differ. According to the GmbHG, any shareholder may at any time demand information from the managing director about the company's general state as well as insight into the commercial books. Managing directors may only refuse to acquiesce to such a request if there is reason to believe that the shareholder will use the information to the disadvantage of the company. Unlike many other provisions of the GmbHG, these information rights are mandatory and inalienable.

In an AG, shareholders have far more limited information rights. They are basically confined to the agenda of the GM. Shareholders may only ask questions that are relevant to form an opinion on the agenda topic at hand and receive oral information. The determination of what is relevant to a certain topic depends on the circumstances of the individual case. Under specific circumstances, eg capital increase excluding pre-emption rights), the shareholders receive written reports on the agenda topics. Many legal procedures, by which the GM's resolutions are challenged, revolve around whether the chairman of the supervisory board was right to refuse to answer a question by a shareholder. The standard by which the relevance of such questions is measured is the 'point of view of an objectively thinking shareholder'. Where a shareholder has been informed in their function as a shareholder outside the GM, the information given to the single shareholder must be given to all shareholders.

Shareholders of an AG may obtain a copy of the minutes, which have to be handed to the commercial register, after the GM.

24. Do shareholders have the right/duty to resolve in the GM upon matters which were not on the agenda?

In general, the shareholders have no right/duty to resolve in the GM upon matters which were not on agenda. One exemption is commonly accepted for topics in a direct context to the listed ones. Such matters may also be resolved if all shareholders are present or legally represented at the GM (*Vollversammlung*), they are then free to differ from the agenda if they decide to do so.

25. Are shareholders entitled to inspect the corporate books and/or any other corporate or accounting documents? To what extent? Can they do it through external counsel or advisors?

GmbH shareholders may fully inspect the corporate books and other documents upon request (see question 23). In an AG, this is not the case.

Shareholders' information rights are generally confined to those in relation to specific agenda topics. In a group structure, however, the mother company is in principle entitled to request information from its group companies necessary for the group accounting.

While the shareholders of a GmbH are entitled to be advised by an external counsel or adviser while inspecting the corporate books, the shareholders of an AG are only entitled to an extraordinary audit upon specific requirements.

SHAREHOLDERS' AGREEMENTS
26. Are shareholders' agreements validly enforceable? What are their typical contents and term of duration? Are they enforceable by or against third parties and, if so, to what extent?
Shareholders' agreements are subject to the same legal rules as any other contractual agreement. As long as they are legally valid, they are enforceable just like any other contract. They may, however, not be valid if they contradict fundamental principles of corporate law. *Vis-à-vis* or by third parties, shareholders' agreements are only enforceable if they are explicitly included in the contract with the third party. Typically, a shareholders' agreement contains provisions regarding the envisaged economic development of the company, financing provisions and deals with the coordination of voting rights.

27. Do shareholders' agreements have to be disclosed to the public or registered in any public registry?
In principle, there is no such obligation for any company. However, in connection with capital increases, the commercial register may request relevant documents to clarify whether the shareholders' payment obligations under corporate law have been fulfilled.

ECONOMIC RIGHTS AND RIGHTS OVER THE STOCK
28. Is the stock always freely transferable? Are there any legal limitations? Are there any restrictions on contractual limitations?
In principle, all stock is freely transferable. However, in a GmbH and an AG, there are different procedural rules to be obeyed. Most notably, shares in a GmbH can only be transferred by a notarially certified written agreement, whereas AG shares can be freely traded on or outside the capital market. However, in both an AG and a GmbH, transferability of shares can be restricted by the articles of association (*Vinkulierung*). Beside that restriction on transferability within the articles of association, the shareholders may also agree on a contractual restriction. A breach of the shareholders' agreement would actually only entitle a tort claim while an incorporated restriction actually prevents the transfer of shares.

29. Are shareholders entitled to pledge their stock?
Yes, as long as their shares are not subject to restricted transferability.

30. Are there financial assistance issues to be considered and other prohibitions to be evaluated in the context of a leveraged buyout transaction?

The general provision prohibiting financial assistance for AGs is section 71a *et seq* AktG, which transposes Article 23 of the EC Capital Directive into German law (see question 36). The GmbHG knows no equivalent provisions to section 71a AktG. Therefore, financial assistance is subject only to section 30 GmbHG, which prohibits any payments of assets necessary to cover the company's share capital. In the context of a leveraged buyout transaction, the management board of the target company needs to diligently consider whether the financing measures requested from the buyer are in the best interest of the company, especially in view of their own obligations.

31. May a company buy back its own stock and, if so, under what circumstances and subject to which limitations?

With respect to the AG: the general concept is that all shares are held by shareholders and not by the company itself. However, the legislator has codified exemptions generally allowing the buy-back of the company's stock by the company itself – so called own shares (*eigene Aktien*) – subject to tight restrictions. Typically, the GM empowers the executive board to buy own shares up to an amount of 10 per cent of the share capital. With respect to the GmbH, acquiring own stock is only restricted in that only shares which are fully paid in can be repurchased by the company.

32. Is there a legal right to withdraw from the company and, if so, under what circumstances? How is the shareholders' stock valued and paid in such a case?

In an AG, shareholders can sell their shares at their own discretion, unless they own registered shares with limited transferability. In a GmbH, usually the assent of the GM is required to transfer shares, since shares are usually subject to restricted transferability set out in the articles of association. In an extreme situation, shareholders may have the right to extraordinarily cancel their company membership at any time if they have an important reason to do so. Typically, it is only the case when under no circumstances the shareholders can be expected to remain in the company. Shareholders are then pecuniary compensated for their shares out of non-equity bound assets. The value of shares is determined according to their real value and not according to their nominal value.

33. In which circumstances can dividends be distributed among shareholders? Is it possible to exclude or limit the right of certain shareholders to dividends? Does a certain portion of the profits need to be set aside in a reserve fund where it cannot be distributed to the shareholders? Are advances on dividends allowed and, if so, under which circumstances? Can advances on dividends be reclaimed by the company?

Shareholders are in principle entitled to balance sheet profits as codified or as set out in the articles of association. Basically, all shareholders are entitled to a profit relative to their participation in the share capital. The AktG allows different rulings as long as they are incorporated in the articles of association. In an AG, these provisions have to distinguish between annual balance sheets drawn up by the GM on the one hand and the executive and the supervisory board on the other hand. In any case, a certain portion of the profits needs to be set aside (*gesetzliche Rücklage*). In principle, advances on dividends are only permitted in the GmbH. This is because in AGs no equity-bound assets may be paid out to shareholders. In a GmbH it is important to consider that only assets in excess of the capital stock may be paid out to shareholders because assets bound by share capital may never be paid out to shareholders. Shareholders are free to agree that they or specific shareholders are not entitled to dividends. Such exclusion may also be incorporated into the articles of association upon approval of the respective shareholder.

34. What are the rights of shareholders in the case of an issue of new stock (increase of the company's corporate capital) (pre-emption rights)?

In order to prevent the dilution of capital and voting rights, shareholders have pre-emption rights to new stocks or rights to receive new stock issued by the company, eg shares, convertible bonds and options. If these rights are unlawfully excluded, such resolutions may be challenged by the shareholders.

35. May minority shareholders ban or limit the company's capital structure in any manner?

Alterations to the stated capital structure require in most cases 75 per cent of the votes cast. Hence, shareholders holding more than 25 per cent of the shares may in principle block changes to the stated capital structure. However, they may be forced by their general fiduciary duty to vote for changes to the stated capital structure if the company's survival is at risk if the changes proposed are not passed.

36. Which are the financial assistance prohibitions in force?

Particular financial assistance prohibitions only apply to AGs, not to GmbHs. Article 23 of the EC Capital Directive has been transposed into German law by section 71a *et seq* AktG. Financial assistance given by an AG to third parties acquiring company shares is prohibited. This provision, just like Article 23 of the EC Capital Directive, has the purpose of curbing leveraged buyout transactions financed by the target company itself. With respect to the GmbH, it is generally prohibited to pay back GmbH shareholders using the company's share capital or assets. This rule does not apply as long as the company is entitled to an intrinsic and enforceable claim against its shareholders which is as valuable as the assets paid out.

37. Apart from publicly listed companies, in which cases (if any) are shareholders obligated to obtain an authorisation from, or provide information to, a public authority about events that have an impact on their stock interest in the company?

The answer depends on the facts of each individual case. Competition law may oblige the company and the shareholders to provide information to, and sometimes obtain an authorisation from, the respective competition authority. Furthermore, upon individual indication of facts proving money laundering, banks especially are obliged to inform authorities. In individual cases in which national interests may be affected by a foreign investment of or in a company, official approval may be requested.

SHAREHOLDERS' RIGHTS IN THE CASE OF EXTRAORDINARY TRANSACTIONS AND/OR WINDING-UP

38. What rights are available to shareholders in the case of a sale of all or a substantial portion of the company's assets? In the case of a merger or de-merger?

If a company plans to sell all or a substantive amount of the company's assets, shareholders representing at least 75 per cent of the company's capital have to agree to it. In the case of a merger or a de-merger, a minimum of 75 per cent of voting shares have to agree. Therefore, the shareholders are basically protected against winding-up scenarios. Furthermore, shareholders may challenge such resolutions about their compensation in front of the courts.

39. Which rights are available to shareholders in the case of conversion of the company into a European Company (SE) or into another type of company?

The SE is to a vast extent subject to the SE Regulation, which leaves shareholders' rights during the foundation of SEs largely up to national legislation. Thus, the conversion of a German AG into an SE is governed by German conversion law. According to section 240 UmwG (Transformation Act), votes representing three-quarters of the company's share capital are required to convert an AG into an SE, unless a higher threshold is defined by the articles of association. All shareholders, whose assent is required for the transfer of any share, have to agree to the conversion. After the conversion has been resolved and registered with the commercial register, shareholders may swap their AG shares for SE shares according to general provisions.

Within one month of the conversion resolution, shareholders may also bring legal action to challenge the resolution's validity, sections 195, 198 UmwG. This is in turn subject to the registration procedure of sections 16 III UmwG, 198 III UmwG. Furthermore, all shareholders who have objected to the conversion resolution have to be offered a cash settlement for turning in their shares, section 207 UmwG.

40. Which rights are available to shareholders of a company in liquidation?

Shareholders are entitled to all leftover assets of the liquidated company after all creditors' claims have been settled and all claims of the company have been converted into assets.

41. Can shareholders cause liquidation of the company? How?
Companies can be liquidated by their shareholders by way of an enactment to dissolve the company, which is then followed automatically by liquidation. In order to resolve the dissolution of the company, a 75 per cent majority vote is required in both the AG and the GmbH.

COMPANY GROUPS
42. Is the concept of a 'group' recognised as such under specific legislation? What are the implications?
The AktG contains provisions regarding the group or *Konzern*, which exists if one company dominates one or more companies directly or indirectly. Such domination and therefore the group structure can be based on the mere factual holding of the majority of shares (*faktischer Konzern*) or on a domination agreement by which one company agrees to be dominated by the other (*Vertragskonzern*). If the influence is just factual, the AktG contains just some provisions regarding reporting duties and the duty of the dominating entity to compensate for damages suffered by the influence. However, in a factual group the management of the dominated entity is not obliged to follow prejudicial requests. In a contractual group the management is generally obliged to follow such instructions, because the domination entity balances the loss potentially suffered by such measures.

43. Does a controlling company have any particular duties *vis-à-vis* its controlled company shareholders?
Upon a domination agreement, the controlling entity has specific duties to the dominated entity. It is obliged to pay an adequate compensation to the rest of the shareholders of the dominated entity on a yearly basis. Further, the dominating entity is entitled to purchase the outstanding shares for an adequate price if the shareholder wants to sell. Under no circumstances, is any shareholder entitled to destroy the business of the entity (*existenzvernichtender Eingriff*).

44. What are the rights of company shareholders when the controlling company puts in place actions and/or transactions that can be prejudicial to the shareholders?
In principle, shareholders have no right to prevent such an influence. In theory, they are protected by special damage claims of their company against the dominating entity. In practice, such claims are difficult to prove.

45. What are the limitations, if any, to the possibility of owning reciprocal stock interests in companies?
The holding of reciprocal stock interest is generally allowed. Restrictions are codified for a structure under which the AG holds indirectly a major interest in a company which itself holds a major interest in the AG itself. Regarding the GmbH, reciprocal share interest is also possible.

Greece

Karatzas & Partners Christina Faitakis

BASIC INFORMATION ON THE TYPES OF LIMITED LIABILITY COMPANIES AND ON THE RIGHTS OF SHAREHOLDERS

1. What types of companies enjoy limited liability? If more than one, which ones have shareholders, ie holders of share certificates? Which one is the most common? Which one is mostly used by foreign investors?

In Greece there exist two types of companies which enjoy limited liability: the *societe anonyme* (SA) and the limited liability company (EPE). From the two types only a shareholder of an SA holds share certificates either in paper form for non-listed SAs or in the form of dematerialised entries in the Central Depositary Service of the Athens Exchange (ATHEX) for listed SAs. The SA is the most common type used by both local and foreign investors and the only type of Greek company whose shares can be listed. Therefore this report will be limited to this type of Greek company and any reference to 'company' hereafter shall refer to the SA type. The Greek SA is primarily regulated by codified law 2190/1920 as amended from time to time including a recent amendment to transpose to Greek law the Directive 2007/36/EC regarding the protection of listed companies' shareholders (the 2010 amendment). Listed companies are regulated additionally by special laws regarding corporate governance, insider trading and disclosure requirements. Bonds issuances are regulated by special law 3156/2003 in combination with the codified law 2190/1920.

2. Are there minimum capital requirements and/or thin capitalisation rules in force?

The general rule is that an SA is required to have a minimum share capital of €60,000. Certain types of SAs, such as banks, insurance companies, investment companies, airline companies etc, are required to have a higher initial share capital. In addition a minimum share capital of €3 million on a consolidated basis is required for an SA to get listed. At any time if the company's own funds (ie share capital and share capital reserves plus retained earnings minus losses carried forward) fall below half of the nominal share capital, then the board of directors is obliged to convene a shareholders' meeting to resolve on the company's future. In addition, if the own funds fall below one-tenth of the share capital then anyone having a legitimate interest can request the court to dissolve the company.

3. Describe the types of shares that can be issued by a company and the different rights that they attribute to their owners, as well as any other financial instruments (bonds or other) and other instruments of a participatory nature in the company's capital that can also be issued by the company.

An SA can issue registered or bearer shares. Certain companies are by law required to issue registered shares due to the type of business, eg banks, insurance companies and utilities companies.

Shares can be: (a) ordinary shares which give all shareholders' rights to the holder; or (b) preference shares with or without voting rights, attributing special preferential financial rights such as the right to collect dividends first, preference to the proceeds post-liquidation, fixed dividend, interest, the right to participate in profits earned from a specific activity (tracking shares) or any other benefit of a financial nature. Preferred shares may be issued as (mandatory or not) convertible into common shares. Companies are allowed to issue redeemable shares.

A company may issue common bonds, convertible bonds, exchangeable bonds or bonds which give the right to the bondholders to participate in the company's profits but, unless converted to shares, do not form part of the share capital. It must be noted that the articles of association cannot create any class of shares other than those provided by law.

4. Can a company have only one shareholder and still enjoy limited liability?

Yes.

5. Are the rights of shareholders the same in any type of company?

There are not different types of SAs.

6. What are the basic rights of any shareholder? Describe briefly the rights of minority shareholders and indicate which thresholds, if any, are required to allow the minority shareholders to exercise any such rights.

A shareholder of an SA has financial rights (such as the right to collect dividends, pre-emption rights or the right to receive any balance of assets after completion of liquidation); participation rights (such as the voting right, the right to appoint directly a number of the members of the board or the right of information); and ancillary rights.

On minority rights one should distinguish between blocking minority and other minority rights. Blocking minority is 33.1 per cent of the paid-up share capital as certain decisions of the GM require increased quorum and majority, ie two-thirds of shareholders present and a two-thirds majority vote. In listed companies though, due to the high free float requirements and also the low ordinary quorum (20 per cent of the paid-up share capital), shareholders holding 10-15 per cent may prove in practice a blocking minority.

Other minority rights under Greek law provide that upon request by shareholders representing one-twentieth of the paid-up share capital:

(i)   the board of directors is obliged to convene an extraordinary GM to be held within 45 days from the service of the request;

(ii) the board of directors is obliged to add supplemental items in the forthcoming GM's agenda;

(iii) the chairman of the GM is obliged to allow one postponement of the adoption of resolutions in disputes by the general assembly provided an adjourned meeting is convened within 30 days to resolve upon the relevant issues;

(iv) the resolution of any matter included on the agenda for the general assembly must be adopted by a roll call;

(v) the board of directors must disclose to the annual general assembly any amounts or any other benefits granted that were distributed to the directors, the senior management or to the employees during the course of the last two years and any agreements concluded between the company and such persons; and

(vi) the board of directors must add as an item of the agenda any additional item to be discussed at a GM, provided such a request is received by the board of directors 15 days prior to the relevant GM.

Any shareholder can request five days before the GM that specific information on the business of the company is presented by the board of directors in the GM, if such information is necessary to assess the items of the agenda.

Shareholders representing one-twentieth of the company's paid-up share capital have the right to request a competent court to order an investigation of the company if it is believed that actions taken by the board of directors or otherwise violated applicable law, the articles of association or the resolutions of the GM.

Shareholders representing one-fifth of the company's paid-up share capital have the right to request a competent court to review the company's operations, when it is believed that the company is not properly managed. Finally, any shareholders may request the board of directors to provide, at a general assembly of shareholders, additional specific information regarding the company's business for the purposes of better assessing the matters to be discussed thereat, provided such a request is submitted five days prior to the relevant session. The board of directors may refuse to provide such information on material grounds recorded in the minutes of the GM.

Minority shareholders may be given the right to appoint board members (see question 20), request that actions be brought against members of the board (see question 22) or block or oppose certain transactions (see questions 31 and 44).

7. Do all shareholders enjoy the same rights or can some shareholders be attributed specific rights, whether by reason of the particular class of stock owned or other? Are such rights generally provided for at the level of the company's by-laws and/or in shareholders' agreements?

The principle of equality of shareholders had been supported strongly by legal writing and jurisprudence in Greece and after the recent amendment (in 2010) of the Greek law on SAs the principle of equality of shareholders became an explicit provision of law. Notwithstanding the above, differences may exist or specific privileges can be awarded to different classes of stock, eg preferred shares may be issued without voting rights, tracking shares may be limited to collect only part of the dividend; but the principle of equality should be respected within the same class of shares.

Holders of preferred shares without voting rights are allowed to participate in GMs but such shares are not accounted for in the quorum required while they enjoy the same information rights as all other shareholders.

8. May the rights of shareholders, generally speaking, be limited, modified, suppressed or waived in any way? If so, how? Are such modifications or limitations provided for in the company's by-laws and/or in shareholders' agreements?

The general rule is that participation shareholders' rights cannot be limited, modified, suppressed or waived. Financial rights though, can be waived or limited not *a priori* or *de facto* but only if a decision of an increased majority of the shareholders, as the case may be, is adopted. Namely pre-emption rights or rights to dividends can be waived by an increased quorum and increased majority resolution of a GM.

Therefore any alteration or limitation of shareholders' rights should be decided on an *ad hoc* basis and any such provision in the company's articles of association would not be acceptable as it would violate the equality principle and the freedom of the shareholder. It can be said though, that articles of association can 'regulate' the exercise of shareholders' rights indirectly, by adopting increased quorums and majorities in the decision-making processes.

Shareholders' agreements can provide for special arrangements as to the exercise of the parties' shareholders' rights but such arrangements are binding only between the parties; they are not binding or enforceable upon the company or any third party. As a consequence, any exercise of a right in breach of shareholders' agreements will only create compensation claims against the breaching shareholder. We note, however, that shareholders' agreements can be contrary to the *bonos mores* principle of general law and therefore void if they constrain excessively the freedom of the contracting shareholder.

GENERAL MEETING OF SHAREHOLDERS (GM) AND VOTING RIGHTS

9. Which decisions are reserved to the competence of the GM?

The GM is the supreme corporate body of the SA. Its resolutions are binding on the board of directors and executive officers as well as all shareholders, including those absent from the GM and those dissenting. The GM is the only body competent to decide on the below issues:

- extension of the company's term, merger, de-merger, conversion or dissolution;
- any amendment of the articles of association;

- increase or reduction of the share capital (except for increases resolved by the board of directors by virtue of limited and specific authorisation of the statutes);
- the issuance of convertible bonds or bonds which grant the right to their holders to participate in the profits of the company;
- election of the members of the board of directors, expect for members appointed directly by (a) shareholder(s) by virtue of a specific provision in the articles of association;
- the appointment of auditors and liquidators;
- the distribution of annual profits;
- the approval of the annual financial statements; and
- the release of the board of directors and auditors from liability upon approval of the financial statements.

In principle decisions are adopted by a simple quorum (20 per cent of the paid-up share capital present or represented at the meeting). If a simple quorum is not achieved, the GM convenes again within 20 days of the date of the previous meeting. At the subsequent assembly, the GM is in quorum and decides lawfully on all items of the initial agenda irrespective of the paid-up share capital present or represented.

Exceptionally resolutions such as:

(i)   a change in the purpose of the company;
(ii)   a change of the nationality of the company;
(iii)   an increase in the obligations of shareholders;
(iv)   an increase of the share capital, if such increase is not effected pursuant to a decision of the board of directors in accordance with the articles of association of the company, or imposed by law or made after a capitalisation of reserves;
(v)   a reduction of the share capital;
(vi)   a decision to merge, de-merge or convert to another type of company;
(vii)   the extension of the duration or dissolution of the company;
(viii) the issuance of a convertible bond loan, if this issuance is not made pursuant to a decision of the board of directors in accordance with the articles of association, or a bond loan which gives the bondholders the right to participate in the profits;
(ix)   the granting or renewal of the power of the board of directors to increase the share capital or issue convertible bond loans; and
(x)   the alteration of the method of distribution of profits, require an increased quorum (two-thirds of the paid-up share capital to be present either in person or by proxy).

In the event that an increased quorum is not achieved, the GM is adjourned and the required quorum at the subsequent GM is reduced to 50 per cent of the paid-up share capital to be present. If such a threshold is not met, the GM is adjourned for a second time and in the re-assembled GM the minimum quorum is one-third of the paid-up share capital for non-listed companies and one-fifth for listed companies.

The articles of association may provide for any additional issues to be referred to the competency of the GM or to be resolved by an increased quorum or majority. Additionally the articles of association may increase (but not decrease) the required quorum and majorities.

10. How does a shareholder participate in a GM? Are there any limitations to having a minimum number of shares? May a shareholder delegate attendance to another shareholder or to the board? May a shareholder obtain assistance from the courts or any other governmental body to intervene in a GM or to cause one to be held in some particular cases?

Every shareholder, even if holding one share, has the right to participate in the GM but only holders of voting shares are allowed to vote.

Shareholders are invited at least 20 days before the scheduled meeting by way of an invitation published in the official government's gazette and in one general and one financial newspaper. Listed SAs are obliged to publish such an invitation in the daily bulletin of the ATHEX and their internet site.

In non-listed companies, lawful participation in the GM presupposes that the shareholder deposits its shares either with a credit institution or with the Loans and Consignment Fund or to the company's treasury at least five days prior to the scheduled meeting.

In listed companies, the recent 2010 amendment has introduced the concept of record date for shareholders to be allowed to participate in the GM. The record date is set as the fifth day before the GM and the authority who keeps the shareholder record (in Greece the ATHEX) issues the relevant shareholders' certificate to be sent to the company on the third day before the meeting. For adjourned and re-assembled meetings the record date is the fourth day before the meeting and the relevant certificate has to be sent to the company on the third day before the meeting.

The board of directors is responsible for confirming the eligibility of shareholders to participate in the GM. For this purpose it draws and publishes 48 hours before the meeting (or 24 hours for listed companies) the list of the shareholders who can lawfully participate in the GM. It should be mentioned though that if shareholders failed to follow the above described procedures in a timely manner to legalise their right to participate, then the GM may allow them to participate by a special decision during the meeting but before the discussion of the items on the agenda.

Proxy voting is allowed. Legal entities have the right to appoint up to three persons to represent them in the GM.

It has been accepted by jurisprudence and legal writing that if a shareholder is illegally deprived of the right to participate in the GM (eg the board of directors did not or refuses to include the shareholder in the shareholders' list), then the shareholder is entitled to request, by way of an interim measures procedure, the court to order the company to accept its participation.

11. May a GM be called and held at the request of any shareholder? Is there a threshold regarding the percentage of the stock interest owned in the company that may entitle a shareholder to such a right?

The general principle is that the board of directors convenes the GM. The annual (ordinary) GM is convened by the board of directors and is held within six months after the end of each financial year to decide upon the approval of the financial statements; the discharge of the board of directors' members and of the auditors from liability; and the election of auditors for the financial year to come. The board of directors may also convene an extraordinary GM when and as it deems necessary. Shareholders holding one-twentieth of the company's paid-up share capital have the right to request the board of directors to convene a GM within 45 days after delivery of the request. If the GM is not convened by the board of directors within 20 days of the aforementioned request, the meeting will be held by the applicant shareholders at the expense of the company, with an interim measures decision of the One-Member Court of First Instance with jurisdiction over the seat of the company. Moreover the statutory auditors are entitled to request the chairman to convene an extraordinary GM within 10 days of the notification of such a request.

12. May a shareholder bring up an issue to be resolved upon and put it to a vote if it is not included on the agenda? May a shareholder require more information from the GM and/or the board, concerning the agenda of the GM, to be put in a better position to exercise their vote?
Shareholders holding one-twentieth of the company's stock have the right to request the board of directors to include additional items on the agenda of a GM. The board of directors is obliged to register the additional items if the request is submitted at least 15 days before the GM. The additional items must be published or announced at least seven days before the GM.

13. May a GM be held by telecommunication means and/or by correspondence (ie by written consent)?
The law allows the articles of association of a non-listed company to provide for distant voting by mail. The agenda and voting sheets are sent to shareholders who then have to return the voting sheets to the company at least two days before the GM.

The 2010 amendment also allowed for distant participation in listed companies' GMs either by email or by regular mail following a provision in the articles of association provided that the articles of association include such an option.

Secondary legislation is expected in order for GMs to be held by way of teleconference both in listed and non-listed companies.

14. Are voting rights always proportionate to the stock held by each shareholder or can they vary by share class?
Voting rights are always proportionate to the stock held.

15. Are there non-voting shares? Is there a maximum percentage of capital represented by non-voting shares?
Only preferred shares can be issued without voting rights. There is no maximum percentage or threshold for the issuance of non-voting shares.

16. Can shareholders group their shares in order to exercise their voting rights (eg, by trust, shareholders' agreement or otherwise)?

The notion of trust is not recognised by Greek law.

There are no explicit provisions of law allowing shareholders to act and vote in concert but it has been the prevailing view in Greek legal writing and in the case law on the matter that agreements as to the manner of voting shares are valid. The validity of voting contracts is based on the principle of freedom of contract, which is enshrined in Article 361 of the Greek Civil Code and forms the basic principle of the Greek law of obligations. According to this principle an agreement is valid unless there is a rule of law rendering such an agreement invalid. There is no rule of Greek law prohibiting voting contracts in general or agreements to act in concert and therefore such agreements are in principle valid.

17. Under what circumstances can a shareholder challenge the resolutions adopted by the GM? Are there thresholds concerning the stock interest owned to be able to bring such a claim?

A shareholder can challenge the resolutions of the GM if the resolution is:

(a) void because there was no legal convocation or the contents of the decision violate the law or the company's articles of association;

(b) is voidable because it was adopted in violation of the law and the company's articles of association; or

(c) is voidable because the information rights of the minority shareholders were violated or the resolution was passed by the majority shareholder in an abusive exercise of its right.

There is no percentage threshold to request the court to recognise the nullity of a void decision.

Voidable decisions may be challenged by any shareholder holding two-hundredths of the paid-up share capital if such a shareholder was not present in the GM or was opposed to the decision process. A resolution may be challenged by the shareholders for violation of the minority rights of information who requested the information and hold one-twentieth of the paid-up share capital.

18. What are the terms and procedures to challenge a resolution of the GM?

To challenge voidable decisions an action against the company must be brought before a court within three months from the publication or submission to the company's registry of the relevant minutes. Actions to proclaim the null decisions must be initiated within a year from such a submission. Interim measures can be sought to suspend temporarily the application of the contested resolutions until a decision is issued by the court.

SHAREHOLDERS' RIGHTS VERSUS DIRECTORS AND DUTIES OF OTHER CORPORATE BODIES IN THE COMPANY

19. What is the procedure for the appointment/replacement/revocation of directors and of statutory auditors, if any?

The members of the board of directors are elected by the GM following a proposal of the chairman of the meeting. An election by way of a list of candidates is also possible if the articles of association provide for such a procedure. Members from each list are appointed pro rata to the votes each list receives which might be proven detrimental to the minority shareholders. Alternatively, the articles of association may give to a specific and named shareholder the right to appoint members of the board of directors not exceeding one-third of the total number to be elected.

Only directors appointed by way of a direct appointment can be removed from their office and be replaced by others either at any time by their appointees or by a court decision following a petition of shareholders representing one-tenth of the company's stock, if serious reason exists in respect of the director.

Statutory auditors are appointed by each annual GM for the subsequent financial year and cannot be revoked or replaced during the financial year unless there are serious grounds of professional integrity or if they resign.

20. May shareholders challenge the resolutions of the board of directors? Is there a minimum percentage of capital required to challenge a board resolution?

Unlike the provisions of annulment of GM decisions, there are no specific rules in Greek law for the right to challenge a board of directors' decision. As a consequence both legal writing and jurisprudence have accepted that the provisions of law regarding the void or voidability of a GM decision should apply by analogy to the decisions of the board of directors and its potential challenge.

The prevailing opinion is that the shareholders have no right to intervene in the way the board of directors runs the business of the company. Such control is exercised in each annual shareholders' meeting when shareholders are required to approve the annual financial statements, part of which is the annual report of the board of directors, and to release the members of the board from any liability regarding their management. On the contrary it has been broadly accepted that a decision of the board of directors which violates the law, or a decision of the GM or the articles of association of the company (eg a decision adopted without the legal quorum and majority) is invalid and therefore can be challenged. Any person, including any shareholder, having a legitimate interest may request the court to proclaim the invalidity of such a decision by way of a lawsuit. Also interim measures may be sought to suspend the enforceability of such a decision until the decision on the main lawsuit.

21. Are shareholders entitled to bring a legal action against the directors of the company? In which circumstances? Please describe briefly the principles of directors' liability.

According to the prevailing legal writing and case law, a shareholder can sue the directors of the company only if the shareholder suffered direct damages. Mismanagement is considered to cause a direct damage to the company rather than its shareholders and derivative actions are not recognised in Greek law so there are very limited grounds for a shareholder to bring an action against the directors or the management. As a consequence, actions against the members of the board are initiated primarily by the company by virtue of a GM decision if shareholders holding one-tenth of the paid-up share capital file such a request to the board of directors or to the liquidators (if the company is in liquidation). The board of directors and the liquidators are obliged to initiate proceedings.

According to general principles of Greek corporate law, the members of the board of directors are liable towards the company for every damage or loss of profit suffered by the company as a result of their actions or omissions which do not comply with their duties as prescribed in the articles of association of the company, the law and, most importantly, the best interests of the company. According to the 'business-judgement-rule' concept introduced in 2007 in Greek law, directors are released from such liability if they prove that they have acted solely:

(i)   in good faith;
(ii) on the basis of sufficient information; and
(iii) in the best interests of the company without involving self-interest (duty of loyalty).

In addition, directors shall not be held liable towards the company for decisions taken after the relevant explicit approval thereof by a lawfully convened GM. The board of directors is also collectively liable for the accuracy of the company's financial statements. In listed companies the board of directors is additionally liable for the accuracy of the information provided within its annual report on the corporate governance rules applied by the company.

An important aspect of the business-judgement-rule is the duty of directors to protect creditors from transacting with an insolvent company, ie directors bear a personal and direct liability towards third-party creditors in the event that: (i) they have not filed for bankruptcy within 15 days from the date that the company has been in a permanent and general cessation of payments; and (ii) they have not taken every individually possible action or measure for the purposes of the adoption and implementation of the necessary corporate resolution to submit the company to bankruptcy.

22. What are the rights in connection with transactions where the directors have a conflict of interest situation?

According to the law the members of the board of directors and any person having delegate powers to represent and manage the company are explicitly prohibited to act against the company's interest. Moreover each member of the board and each person having delegate powers to represent and manage the company, must state in a timely manner to the board of directors any personal benefit arising from the company's business or any event of a conflict of interest with the company or any affiliate or subsidiary thereof. It is evident that such provisions if violated create a liability of the persons named therein and the company will have the right to claim damages.

Moreover members of the board of directors and high management are not allowed to conduct parallel business to that of the company without a prior approval by the GM. Transactions of the company with its board of directors are subject to the same limitations and prior GM approval as applied to controlling shareholders (see question 44).

INFORMATION RIGHTS ON THE COMPANY'S BUSINESS
23. What information may be requested by the shareholders from the board concerning the general state of the company's business or any specific transaction? Are information rights different depending on the number of shares owned? Are shareholders entitled to receive written information before, during or after the GM about the meeting agenda and to what extent? Is it possible for a shareholder to obtain a copy of the minutes of the GM?
Any shareholder has the right to request 10 days before the annual GM, a copy of the annual financial statements.

For details on information rights please see question 6.

Detailed minutes are drawn on each GM. Shareholders are allowed to request information during the meeting on each item under discussion.

Listed companies are obliged either to publish on the company's website before each GM or to send by mail to any shareholder requesting so the agenda, any documents to be provided in the GM, the opinion and the proposal of the board of directors on each item of the agenda. Moreover if an amendment to the articles of association is proposed, then the company must provide on the company's website the proposed amendments.

Listed companies are additionally subject to the capital markets regulations regarding market abuse, insider trading and obligations to inform the public on any substantial transaction that affects the company's business. The minutes of each GM are submitted to the company's registry with the competent regulator, from which any shareholder has the right to obtain a copy.

24. Do shareholders have the right/duty to resolve in the GM upon matters which were not on the agenda?
A matter can be added for discussion in the GM only if shareholders holding 100 per cent of the paid-up share capital are present and no shareholder objects to such discussion.

25. Are shareholders entitled to inspect the corporate books and/or any other corporate or accounting documents? To what extent? Can they do it through external counsel or advisors?
Please see question 23.

SHAREHOLDERS' AGREEMENTS

26. Are shareholders' agreements validly enforceable? What are their typical contents and term of duration? Are they enforceable by or against third parties and, if so, to what extent?

Shareholders' agreements are acknowledged as valid agreements by virtue of Article 361 of the Civil Code, which safeguards the freedom of contract and allows the contracting parties to formulate the context of their obligations and of their cooperation.

Similarly to the international practice, such agreements are particularly common in Greece in cases of joint ventures and are considered to be indispensable for the functioning of the company. It is very common that through the shareholders' agreement minority shareholder(s) secure participation in the board of directors with rights of veto, increased quorum and majority in the GM for the adoption of certain resolutions. Moreover parties regulate in such agreements exit rights, call or put option over shares, or pre-emption rights, an obligation to vote in a certain way, to manage the company in a certain way, to give certain information, prohibition to acquire shares beyond a certain percentage etc.

It must be noted at the outset that shareholders' agreements in general operate at a different level from company law, as they merely create obligations among the parties and do not directly affect the relevant company operation, thus being governed only by the law of obligations. As a consequence they create *inter partes* obligations and are not binding upon third parties. Notwithstanding the above, legal writing and recent case law have accepted that shareholders' agreements between all shareholders of the same company do have a direct impact on the company's acts and resolutions as it is unethical for a shareholder to invoke company law in order to 'lawfully' violate the shareholders' agreement. It is not uncommon though insofar as permitted by corporate law to construct the company's articles of association to reflect shareholders' agreements, in which case such shareholders' arrangements become mandatory and obtain an *erga omnes* effect to the extent incorporated in the company's articles of association. As an example, one should mention that it is explicitly permitted to include in the company's articles of association first refusal rights regarding the transfer of shares.

27. Do shareholders' agreements have to be disclosed to the public or registered in any public registry?

No such obligation exists, with the exception of the requirements of the Prospectus Regulation for listed companies whereby shareholders have to state whether such agreements exist.

ECONOMIC RIGHTS AND RIGHTS OVER THE STOCK

28. Is the stock always freely transferable? Are there any legal limitations? Are there any restrictions on contractual limitations?

The shares are freely transferable. Limitations to transfer may be imposed either contractually or by provisions in the articles of association. Such limitations to transfer company stock may not result in an absolute prohibition of transfer.

29. Are shareholders entitled to pledge their stock?
Pledge over shares is permitted unless the articles of association have explicitly prohibited such a right.

30. Are there financial assistance issues to be considered and other prohibitions to be evaluated in the context of a leveraged buyout transaction?
A company is not allowed to provide advances, loans or guarantees to any person or entity for the purpose of acquiring the company's shares or shares of the mother company unless:
(i)   a GM approves the transaction by an increased quorum and majority;
(ii) the board of directors submits a written statement to the GM on the reasons and the company's interest for the transaction to be approved, on the terms of the transaction and on the potential risks that the transaction entails for the viability and financial soundness of the company; and
(iii) the total financial assistance will not cause the company's own funds to fall below the share capital. As long as such financing is outstanding, the company is obliged to maintain an equal non-distributable reserve.

On upstream loans and guarantees see also question 37. Due to the above provisions, leveraged buyouts in Greece were consummated through the reverse merger of the target company.

31. May a company buy back its own stock and, if so, under what circumstances and subject to which limitations?
According to the law a company is allowed to buy back its shares (treasury shares) with the prior approval of the GM and for a period not exceeding 24 months. The total nominal value of the shares purchased, including shares previously acquired by the company and still held by it, as well as shares acquired by a person acting in their own name but on the company's behalf must not exceed one-tenth of the paid-up share capital of the company. The acquisition of shares, including shares which the company had already acquired and still holds or acquired on its behalf, must not result in a decrease of the own funds of the company to an amount lower than the amount of the paid-up share capital. Treasury shares may be held indefinitely.

The terms and conditions and the price range of the buy-back programme are defined by the GM. However, it is not required under Greek law to explicitly specify the purpose of the buy-back programme. Thus, and in view of the fact that according to Article 3 of Regulation 2273/2003 specific purposes pursuit by a buy-back programme are pre-requisites for a buy-back programme to fall within the scope of Regulation 2273/2003 and the safe harbour of Article 8 of Directive 2003/6/EC (the Market Abuse Directive), such information must be included in the minutes of the GM. Consequently in order for the buy-back programme to fall within the scope of Regulation 2273/2003 and the exemption of Article 8 of Directive 2003/6/EC, the sole purpose of that buy-back programme must be to reduce the capital of a company (in value or in number of shares) or to meet obligations arising from any of the following: debt financial instruments exchangeable into equity instruments; and/or employee share option programmes or other allocations of shares to employees of the company or of a connected undertaking.

Moreover in order to benefit from the buy-back exceptions of the Market Abuse Directive and EC Regulation 2273/2003, buy-back transactions must also fully comply with the pricing and disclosure requirements of the said EC Regulation, including in particular: (i) that the strike price shall not exceed the market price of the underlying share; and (ii) each single transaction is adequately disclosed to the market.

32. Is there a legal right to withdraw from the company and, if so, under what circumstances? How is the shareholders' stock valued and paid in such a case?

A shareholder of a non-listed company may petition the court to compel the company to buy all its shares, if it is detrimental to its own interests to remain in the company and, despite their opposite vote, the GM decided:
(i)   to change the nationality of the company;
(ii) to adopt a share transfer restriction in the company's articles of association; or
(iii) to change the company's scope of business.
The same right is granted to a shareholder if the board of directors refused or failed to approve the transfer of shares when the articles of association of the company provide for such a procedure. The price and the way of payment are determined by the court. The purchase price has to be fair and correspond to the real value of the participation. The court may request an independent valuation to be conducted for the price determination.

In both listed and non-listed companies a minority shareholder has a sell-out right if 95 per cent of the share capital of the company is held directly or indirectly by one shareholder. Such a right is exercised again by way of the same lawsuit described above but it is filed against the majority shareholder.

Sell-out rights are provided also for minority shareholders who did not participate in the selling process of the tender offer.

33. In which circumstances can dividends be distributed among shareholders? Is it possible to exclude or limit the right of certain shareholders to dividends? Does a certain portion of the profits need to be set aside in a reserve fund where it cannot be distributed to the shareholders? Are advances on dividends allowed and, if so, under which circumstances? Can advances on dividends be reclaimed by the company?

One-twentieth of net profits are allocated to a statutory reserve until this reserve equals at least half of the company's share capital. Once this requirement is satisfied, the allocation of further profits to the statutory reserve is not mandatory. The allocation of profits to the statutory reserve will again become mandatory if the reserve subsequently falls below half of the share capital.

Each company is required to pay a minimum dividend equal to at least 35 per cent of the unconsolidated profit, if any, after the deduction of the amount allocated to the aforementioned statutory reserve.

At the annual GM, a majority representing 65 per cent of the paid-up share capital may decide to distribute less than the minimum dividend required by Greek law. In such a case, the undistributed dividend has to be transferred to a special reserve which must, within four years following said GM, be distributed in the form of a share dividend. Alternatively, a majority representing 70 per cent of the company's paid-up share capital may vote to distribute an amount lower than the minimum mandatory dividend or not to pay any dividend at all without transferring the relevant amounts to a special reserve.

Subject to the provisions regulating a share capital decrease, no profits may be distributed to shareholders if at the end of the previous financial year, the company's total own funds are, or as a result of the said distribution will be, less than the share capital plus reserves, whose distribution is prohibited by law or the articles of association.

The distributable profits shall not exceed the profits for the last financial year on an unconsolidated basis net of tax, plus retained earnings and reserves the distribution of which is allowed (and has been approved by the annual GM), less any losses carried forward and any amounts required by law or the articles of association to be allocated towards the formation of reserves. The profits to be distributed are payable to the shareholders within two months from the approval of the annual financial statements by the annual GM. A shareholder's claim to a declared dividend is subject to a five-year statute of limitations, after which the dividend passes to the Greek state. The five-year period begins as of the end of the year during which its distribution was approved by the annual GM.

Advance dividends are allowed to be distributed following a board of directors' decision and a publication of a provisional accounting statement. Advance dividends cannot exceed half of the net profits shown on the accounting statement.

Any distribution to the shareholders may be reclaimed by the company if the distribution was illegal to the knowledge, or deemed knowledge of the shareholders who collected such payments.

34. What are the rights of shareholders in the case of an issue of new stock (increase of the company's corporate capital) (pre-emption rights)?

Each shareholder has pre-emption rights over new shares in every case of an increase in the share capital of a company other than by way of contribution in kind or convertible bonds. It exists in favour of the current shareholders at the time of issuance, *pro rata* to their participation in the already paid-up share capital.

The pre-emption right can be abolished or limited in relation to a specific capital increase under the following conditions: submission to the GM of a written report by the board of directors, explaining the reasons which make the said abolition or limitation necessary and justifying the proposed price for the issuance of the new shares; and resolution by the GM to this effect, with an increased quorum and majority.

35. May minority shareholders ban or limit the company's capital structure in any manner?
Minority shareholders holding more than one-third of the paid-up share capital present in the GM may block a share capital increase or decrease.

36. Which are the financial assistance prohibitions in force?
Under Greek corporate law a company is prohibited to grant loans to its shareholders, members of the board of directors, general managers or managers and up to third-degree relatives of them and to any entities controlled by the above. However, it is permitted to provide a guarantee and security for the benefit of such persons following an approval of the GM provided that:
(i)   shareholders representing one-tenth of the paid-up share capital or one-twentieth in the case of listed companies did not oppose the granting of the guarantee or security;
(ii) the guarantee or security serves the company's interest;
(iii) the company retains the right to claim against the obligors any amount that it will be required to pay; and
(iv) the beneficiary's claims are subordinated to the creditors of the company that exist at the time of the GM decision's publication.
  Please refer to question 31 for financial assistance prohibitions.

37. Apart from publicly listed companies, in which cases (if any) are shareholders obligated to obtain an authorisation from, or provide information to, a public authority about events that have an impact on their stock interest in the company?
There are no such obligations for non-listed companies.

SHAREHOLDERS' RIGHTS IN THE CASE OF EXTRAORDINARY TRANSACTIONS AND/OR WINDING-UP
38. What rights are available to shareholders in the case of a sale of all or a substantial portion of the company's assets? In the case of a merger or de-merger?
The sale of the company's assets fall in principle within the competence and day-to-day management of the board of directors, therefore there are no specific rights of the shareholders except if the board of directors acts to the detriment of the company's interest, in which case they have the right to challenge the decision as illegal (see question 20).

  A merger or a de-merger is resolved by a GM decision adopted by an increased quorum and majority. Shareholders of the converted company acquire shares in the surviving or new entity in accordance with the exchange ratio determined by the GM corroborated by the valuators and incorporated into the deed of conversion. If shareholders of the absorbed company contest the exchange ratio, they have a right to demand to be compensated by the surviving entity. Sell-out rights are granted to the minority shareholders of the de-merging company if they are not granted proportionally shares to the new company. Sell-out rights are also granted in a merger by way of acquisition.

39. Which rights are available to shareholders in the case of conversion of the company into a European Company (SE) or into another type of company?
The law that introduced the SE is very recent in Greece. Rights of minority shareholders in the SE do not differ substantially from the rights of minority shareholders in an SA and in certain cases the SE law refers such issues to the Greek corporate law. Sell-out rights are awarded to minority shareholders who opposed the conversion.

40. Which rights are available to shareholders of a company in liquidation?
Shareholders maintain all their rights during the process of the company's liquidation.

41. Can shareholders cause the liquidation of the company? How?
Shareholders may decide to liquidate the company by virtue of a decision of the GM adopted by an increased majority and quorum. Minority shareholders holding one-third of the paid-up share capital may request the court to order the liquidation of the company if for serious cause the continuation of the company is impossible.

COMPANY GROUPS
42. Is the concept of 'group' recognised as such under specific legislation? What are the implications?
The concept of 'group' as a separate entity is not recognised under Greek law. However, Greek law indirectly assumes the existence of a group in terms of providing for consolidated financial accounts or referring in various instances to the 'mother company', subsidiaries or affiliated companies.

43. Does a controlling company have any particular duties *vis-à-vis* its controlled company shareholders?
The controlling company may not enter into contracts with the controlled company without the previous approval of the GM. Such approval is not granted if minority shareholders holding one-third of the paid-up share capital oppose. Subsequent approval may be sought by the GM provided that minority shareholders holding one-twentieth of the paid-up share capital for non-listed companies or one-tenth for listed companies do not oppose.

As a general statement a controlling company has the obligations of any majority and/or controlling shareholder to serve the controlled company's interest and respect the minority shareholders.

44. What are the rights of company shareholders when the controlling company puts in place actions and/or transactions that can be prejudicial to the shareholders?

Shareholders have the same rights and remedies against a shareholder acting to the detriment of the company regardless of whether such a shareholder is a controlling company. (Please see questions 18 and 19.)

45. What are the limitations, if any, to the possibility of owning reciprocal stock interests in companies?

Under Greek law a controlled company may acquire shares of the controlling company only if the conditions for buy-back shares are followed (see question 31). Such shares are treated as treasury shares and therefore are deprived of the right to vote and collect dividends. As a consequence, owning reciprocal stock interests should be considered as not applicable or not beneficial under Greek law, as the subsidiary company holding shares of the parent company would not have any rights.

Hong Kong

Hong Kong

Deacons John Richardson & Alexander Que
Kirkland & Ellis International LLP Pierre-Luc Arsenault
& David Patrick Eich

BASIC INFORMATION ON THE TYPES OF LIMITED LIABILITY COMPANIES AND ON THE RIGHTS OF SHAREHOLDERS

1. What types of companies enjoy limited liability? If more than one, which ones have shareholders, ie holders of share certificates? Which one is the most common? Which one is mostly used by foreign investors?

The two types of companies enjoying limited liability are companies limited by shares (including private and public companies) and companies limited by guarantee.

Companies limited by shares – private companies

A private company is defined as a company that by its articles must:

*   restrict the right to transfer its shares;
*   limit the number of shareholders to 50, excluding employees and past employees; and
*   prohibit any invitation to the public to subscribe for shares or debentures in the company.

Companies limited by shares – public companies

Companies limited by shares which do not fulfil the requirements of a private company are considered to be public companies. Public companies may or may not be listed on The Stock Exchange of Hong Kong Limited.

Companies limited by guarantee

In companies limited by guarantee, the liability of the members is limited to an amount which they have agreed to contribute in the event of a liquidation.

Public and private companies have shareholders who hold share certificates. Companies limited by guarantee normally issue membership certificates to their members. Private companies are by far the most common type of limited liability companies and are the type of company most often used by a foreign investor.

2. Are there minimum capital requirements and/or thin capitalisation rules in force?

Except for regulated entities, such as, among others, authorised financial institutions, entities regulated under the Securities and Futures legislation, insurance companies and brokers, there is no minimum capital requirement. Companies outside regulated areas are often financed by a combination of share capital, shareholders' loans and outside financing.

Hong Kong has no thin capitalisation rules. However, as described in question 21, directors have fiduciary duties. Fiduciary duties may be violated if directors permit a company to be heavily financed other than by share capital, which could potentially put its business at risk if shareholders or lenders call in their loans.

3. Describe the types of shares that can be issued by a company and the different rights that they attribute to their owners, as well as any other financial instruments (bonds or other) and other instruments of a participatory nature in the company's capital that can also be issued by the company.

Hong Kong law is very flexible as to the types of shares and other securities that can be issued by a company. The rights attaching to the shares are normally set out in the articles. A brief description of the main types of shares and other securities is set out below.

Ordinary shares

Ordinary shares are by far the most common type of share issued by a company. Companies often issue only ordinary shares. Typically, holders of ordinary shares have equal rights (that is, rank *pari passu*), *pro rata* based on the numbers of shares owned by them, in respect of voting or receiving dividends or distributions in a liquidation.

Preference shares

Preference shares carry a preferential right to dividends and/or distributions in a liquidation ranking ahead of ordinary shares. The right to a dividend is normally a right to a fixed percentage of the nominal value of the shares and may or may not be cumulative (that is, if no dividend is declared in any year, the arrears may or may not be carried forward). Voting rights attached to preference shares may be different from those attached to ordinary shares and, in some cases, are exercisable only if the preference dividend is in arrears.

Non-voting shares

Non-voting shares have most of the rights attaching to ordinary shares, except that their holders are not entitled to vote at a general meeting (GM).

Deferred shares

Deferred shares enjoy limited rights to dividend ranking behind ordinary shares. They may be voting or non-voting shares.

Redeemable shares

Redeemable shares are by their terms redeemable at the option of the shareholder or the company according to the mechanism set out in the articles.

Debentures

Companies may issue debentures, which are debt instruments whose holder is a creditor of the company. In some cases, the holders of debentures will hold security over the company's assets. Debenture holders are creditors of the company and their rights to distributions essentially rank ahead of the rights of shareholders.

Convertible and exchangeable bonds

Convertible and exchangeable bonds are debt instruments issued by a company which carry an option to convert or exchange the bond into shares of the company (or in respect of exchangeable bonds into shares of another company) at an agreed price. In certain circumstances, conversion or exchange is mandatory. Prior to conversion or exchange, the bondholders are creditors of the company who rank ahead of shareholders in a distribution upon liquidation.

Share warrants

A warrant is an instrument issued by a company which entitles its holder to subscribe for shares in the company during a particular period and at a particular price. Warrants may confer rights on the warrant holders, but until such time as the warrant holders exercise their option to subscribe for shares, they are not shareholders.

4. Can a company have only one shareholder and still enjoy limited liability?

Yes.

5. Are the rights of shareholders the same in any type of company?

Most rights of shareholders are set out in the articles. As among shareholders holding shares of the same class, the rights of shareholders rank equally. The rights of shareholders in private companies, public companies and companies limited by guarantee are essentially of a similar type subject to the requirements in respect of private companies described in question 1.

6. What are the basic rights of any shareholder? Describe briefly the rights of minority shareholders and indicate which thresholds, if any, are required to allow the minority shareholders to exercise any such rights.

The basic rights of shareholders include rights:

- to vote at GMs;
- to receive dividends declared by the company;
- to receive the audited accounts with the directors' and auditors' report of the company and certain notices and circulars; and
- to receive a distribution in a liquidation after creditors have been paid.

As a general rule, decisions taken at GMs are passed by an 'ordinary resolution', which requires a majority of votes of shareholders attending and voting. Certain types of decisions need to be passed by a 'special resolution', which requires the support of at least 75 per cent of the votes of shareholders attending and voting. The most important matters which require a special resolution include:

- change of name;
- change to the memorandum or articles;
- authorise the giving of financial assistance for the acquisition of shares by unlisted companies;
- authorise the buy-back of shares;
- authorise a reduction in capital;
- sanction a variation of class rights; and
- winding-up or dormancy.

In addition, the support of a majority in the number of shareholders present at a meeting representing at least 75 per cent of the disinterested shares attending such a meeting is required to approve a scheme of arrangement between a company and its shareholders (which usually is done to give effect to a takeover).

In respec of a listed company, the number of votes cast against the resolution to approve a scheme of arrangement must not be more than 10 per cent of the votes attached to all disinterested shares. Similarly, a proposal to delist a listed company requires approval of at least 75 per cent of the votes attaching to securities held by holders voting at the meeting and the number of votes cast against the resolution shall be not more than 10 per cent of all the votes attaching to shares permitted to vote at the meeting. Controlling shareholders, directors and the chief executive of the listed company and their respective associates shall abstain from voting on any such resolution.

Accordingly, with the exceptions of a scheme of arrangement for a listed company or delisting, a minority shareholder who does not hold more than 25 per cent of the shares in a company has no veto right in respect of resolutions passed at GMs.

7. Do all shareholders enjoy the same rights or can some shareholders be attributed specific rights, whether by reason of the particular class of stock owned or other? Are such rights generally provided for at the level of the company's by-laws and/or in shareholders' agreements?
The rights of shareholders are set out in the articles and, as discussed in question 3, shares of different classes may have different rights.

It is also possible for shareholders to agree in a shareholders' agreement that, as among themselves, shareholders will exercise their rights in a certain way and shareholders' rights will be limited. As to the contents of shareholders' agreements, see question 26.

In respect of a listed company, the Rules Governing the Listing of Securities on The Stock Exchange of Hong Kong Limited (the Listing Rules) require that all holders of listed securities be treated fairly and equally, and generally the listed company cannot give rights to some but not all shareholders.

8. May the rights of shareholders, generally speaking, be limited, modified, suppressed or waived in any way? If so, how? Are such modifications or limitations provided for in the company's by-laws and/or in shareholders' agreements?

The rights of shareholders may be altered by amending the articles, which can be done by way of a special resolution. A variation of the rights of shareholders holding shares of a particular class is subject to further statutory protection in that it normally requires the passing of a resolution approved by written consent of the shareholders owning at least 75 per cent of the shares of such a class or by the passing of a special resolution of the holders of shares of that class.

As discussed in question 7, shareholders' agreements may contain agreements among shareholders as to the manner in which they will exercise their rights.

GENERAL MEETING OF SHAREHOLDERS (GM) AND VOTING RIGHTS

9. Which decisions are reserved to the competence of the GM?

The main decisions which have to be taken by the GM are as follows:

- appointment and removal of directors (although the articles may also provide that the directors themselves may appoint and remove directors);
- remuneration of directors (although often the GM will allow the board to set the remuneration of directors);
- appointment, removal and remuneration of auditors (this may also be done by the directors in the case of a casual vacancy);
- increase of share capital;
- certain disposals of fixed assets by listed companies (see question 38);
- approval of the annual directors' and auditors' reports and accounts;
- declaration of final dividends;
- authority of the directors to issue shares;
- schemes of arrangement or reconstruction; and
- matters requiring the passing of a special resolution (see question 6).

The articles normally reserve all decisions regarding the day-to-day running of the company's business to the directors. Exceptionally, however, the articles may confer additional approval rights on the GM.

In respect of listed companies, the Listing Rules provide that certain matters, such as 'connected transactions' and certain substantial acquisitions or dispositions, require shareholders' approval.

10. How does a shareholder participate in a GM? Are there any limitations to having a minimum number of shares? May a shareholder delegate attendance to another shareholder or to the board? May a shareholder obtain assistance from the courts or any other governmental body to intervene in a GM or to cause one to be held in some particular cases?

Shareholders who are individuals may attend a meeting in person or by proxy and shareholders who are companies may attend a meeting through a representative. The proxy may be any other person (whether or not another shareholder) and has the same right to speak at the meeting as the shareholder who appoints it. The procedures for appointing a proxy are normally set out in the company's articles. A notice calling a GM typically contains a specimen form of appointment of proxy, which normally is in the form required under the articles, and such a form must be delivered to the company within a period of not more than 48 hours before the time of the meeting.

A large proportion of shares in listed companies are held through a Central Clearing and Settlement System nominee. A shareholder holding shares in a listed company through such a nominee must ask that nominee to transfer the shares to it so that it may attend a meeting directly, appoint a corporate representative or proxy, or exercise other rights in respect of its shareholding.

If for any reason calling a meeting in the manner provided in the company's articles or under the Companies Ordinance (CO) is impracticable (see question 11 below), a court may order that a meeting be called and conducted in such a manner as the court deems fit. Courts have been reluctant to exercise this power.

11. May a GM be called and held at the request of any shareholder? Is there a threshold regarding the percentage of the stock interest owned in the company that may entitle a shareholder to such a right?

The CO allows shareholders holding five per cent or more of the capital of a company to require the directors to convene a GM. The articles may allow this power to be exercised by a lower percentage of shareholders. To exercise this right, the requisitioning shareholders must deliver a signed requisition stating the objects of the meeting. If the directors do not within 21 days from the deposit with the company of the requisition convene a GM, the requisitioning shareholders or half of them may themselves convene a GM.

Also, shareholders holding 2.5 per cent or more of the capital of a company or 50 shareholders holding shares on which an average of HK$2,000 per shareholder has been paid may requisition for a matter to be considered at the next annual GM.

In addition, the CO provides that, unless set forth otherwise in the articles, any two or more shareholders holding 10 per cent or more of the issued share capital of a company may call a GM. This power enables shareholders to convene a GM where the company has no directors.

12. May a shareholder bring up an issue to be resolved upon and put it to a vote if it is not included on the agenda? May a shareholder require more information from the GM and/or the board, concerning the agenda of the GM, to be put in a better position to exercise their vote?

In the case of meetings convened by shareholders, because the notice convening the GM has to contain the text of the proposed resolutions, the subject matter of the discussion is determined by the shareholders. Any shareholder attending a GM, whether convened by shareholders or by directors, may before the resolution is put to a vote seek information pertinent to the subject matter of the resolution to enable it to decide how to vote.

A listed company is required to provide all material information to shareholders no later than 10 business days before the date of the relevant GM.

13. May a GM be held by telecommunication means and/or by correspondence (ie by written consent)?

If permitted by the articles, a GM may be held by telecommunication means through which all participants are able to hear each other.

In addition, it is possible to pass resolutions by written consent of all of the shareholders of the company. When a resolution is passed in writing, the company must send a copy of the resolution to the auditors before or at the same time as the resolution is sent to shareholders for signature. A resolution removing an auditor or a director before the expiry of the period of its office must be taken at a GM.

The holding of GMs by telecommunication or by written resolution is likely to be impractical in the case of a listed company.

14. Are voting rights always proportionate to the stock held by each shareholder or can they vary by share class?

The voting rights of holders of shares of the same class are proportionate to the number of shares held by them. As among holders of shares of different classes, the voting rights may vary in accordance with the terms of the articles.

In the case of a listed company, the Listing Rules require that the voting power of the shares bears a reasonable relationship to the nominal value of such shares.

15. Are there non-voting shares? Is there a maximum percentage of capital represented by non-voting shares?

A company may issue non-voting shares. There is no limitation on the percentage of capital represented by non-voting shares.

16. Can shareholders group their shares in order to exercise their voting rights (eg, by trust, shareholders' agreement or otherwise)?

Shareholders may agree on the exercise of their voting rights. In respect of listed companies, however, such agreements may cause shareholders to:
- become concert parties under the Code on Mergers and Takeovers (the Code), in which case their shareholdings will be aggregated for the purpose of considering whether a mandatory general offer to the other shareholders to purchase their shares needs to be made by those concert parties (see question 38);
- become connected persons for the purpose of the Listing Rules, which may give rise to the requirement that the company issue a circular to shareholders or obtain their approval at a GM in respect of any transactions involving them; or
- become subject to disclosure requirements in respect of their interests in listed companies.

17. Under what circumstances can a shareholder challenge the resolutions adopted by the GM? Are there thresholds concerning the stock interest owned to be able to bring such a claim?

Generally, a validly passed resolution adopted by the GM is binding on minority shareholders, but there are a number of protections afforded to minorities:

- In the case of a private company which alters its memorandum, shareholders holding five per cent of the shares may apply for a court order to cancel the alteration. The application must be made within 28 days of the special resolution approving the change.

- Where class rights are varied, the holders of not less than 10 per cent of the shares of the relevant class may apply to court to have the variation set aside. The variation can then only have effect if confirmed by the court. The application must be made within 28 days of the passing of the resolution and the court will allow the application if it is satisfied that the variation would unfairly prejudice the shareholders of the relevant class.

- In the case where a resolution has been passed by a private company to approve a redemption or buy-back of shares out of capital, a shareholder who did not vote in favour of such a resolution may within five weeks of the resolution being passed apply to court for the cancellation of the resolution. On hearing the application, the court may make such orders as it deems fit, including cancelling or confirming the resolution or adjourning the proceedings in order to arrange for the purchase of the dissentient shareholders' interests or the protection of the dissentient shareholders' interests.

- Any shareholder may petition for a court order on the ground that the affairs of the company are being conducted in a manner which is unfairly prejudicial to the shareholders or part of the shareholders. Courts have broad jurisdiction to make an order, but will not make an order if it is apparent that the appropriate resolution is a sale of shares and that there is a mechanism for determining a fair price. Courts will also strike down a petition if a reasonable offer for the petitioner's shares is made and the petitioner declines the offer. If a court decides to grant the petition, it may make such orders as it deems fit, including orders regulating the affairs of the company; providing that certain shareholders or the company buy back shares held by other shareholders; or restraining the company from doing or continuing a particular act.

- A shareholder may also bring a statutory or common law derivative action for an order authorising proceedings to be brought on behalf of the company against such persons as the court deems fit; an order appointing a receiver or manager; or an order requiring the payment of damages to persons who have been unfairly prejudiced. These are actions brought by a shareholder on behalf of the company where the company is harmed by certain types of misfeasance and the company does not pursue its rights. Typically, the parties involved in the misfeasance are in control of the company. In the action, the company is a defendant and the court will grant the remedy sought to the company.

- A shareholder may apply for an order for the winding up of the company. There are a number of specific grounds for the making of a winding up order together with a residual ground of it being just and equitable that the company should be wound up. This includes failure of the main objects, carrying out a fraudulent or illegal business, failure of mutual trust and understanding among the shareholders and other reasons on the basis of which the court considers it to be just and equitable to wind up the company.

18. What are the terms and procedures to challenge a resolution of the GM?
See question 17.

SHAREHOLDERS' RIGHTS VERSUS DIRECTORS AND DUTIES OF OTHER CORPORATE BODIES IN THE COMPANY
19. What is the procedure for the appointment/replacement/ revocation of directors and of statutory auditors, if any?
The first directors of the company are normally appointed by the subscriber to the articles and, thereafter, the procedure for the appointment and removal of directors is as set out in the articles. Typically, directors are appointed for a term expiring at the next annual GM and may offer themselves for re-election at that meeting. The articles also normally provide that the board of directors itself is able to fill an occasional vacancy or to appoint an additional director. At an annual GM, the shareholders may refuse to reappoint a director.

In respect of listed companies, the Listing Rules provide that every director shall be subject to retirement by rotation at least once every three years.

Auditors are also normally appointed and removed at the annual GM.

20. May shareholders challenge the resolutions of the board of directors? Is there a minimum percentage of capital required to challenge a board resolution?
The articles normally vest the broad authority to run the day-to-day business of the company in the directors, and courts are reluctant to interfere in the day-to-day business of the company. In addition to the matters reserved to the competence of the GM set forth in question 9, the GM may by ordinary resolution intervene in a number of limited situations:
- where the board is unwilling or unable to act;
- where the board seeks approval for acts beyond its powers; or
- where the board seeks ratification of a breach of fiduciary duty (see question 21).

Any shareholder may also bring the unfair prejudice and derivative actions referred to in question 17.

21. Are shareholders entitled to bring a legal action against the directors of the company? In which circumstances? Please describe briefly the principles of directors' liability.

See questions 17 and 20. A shareholder who wishes to bring a legal action against the directors would probably need to do so through a derivative action enforcing the rights of the company against the particular director as described in question 17(e). The principal circumstance that could prompt such a derivative action is a breach of fiduciary duties. Directors' fiduciary duties are to:

- act in good faith and for the benefit of the company;
- exercise powers for a proper purpose and for the benefit of the shareholders as a whole;
- not delegate powers except with proper authorisation;
- exercise independent judgement;
- exercise care, skill and diligence;
- avoid conflicts between personal interests and interests of the company;
- not enter into transactions in which the directors have an interest except in compliance with the requirements of the law;
- not gain advantage from the position as a director; and
- not make unauthorised use of the company's property or information.

22. What are the rights in connection with transactions where the directors have a conflict of interest situation?

Where a director has a conflict of interest in relation to any transaction, it is required to disclose the interest to the board. If it fails to do so and the transaction is approved, then the resolution concerned may be set aside.

In addition, the company's articles typically provide for more detailed provisions regarding declarations of directors' interests, including whether or not the interested director may vote on the relevant matter and, if it does, whether its vote will be counted and whether it may be counted in a quorum.

Hong Kong law also restricts loans, guarantees, quasi loans and credit transactions between a company and its directors and their associates.

Under the Listing Rules, the articles of a listed company must provide that, subject to certain exceptions, a director shall not vote on any resolution approving any contract or arrangement in which it or any of its associates has a material interest, and shall not be counted in the quorum present at the board meeting. If any such transaction requires shareholders' approval, shareholders with a material interest in the transaction shall abstain from voting.

INFORMATION RIGHTS ON THE COMPANY'S BUSINESS

23. What information may be requested by the shareholders from the board concerning the general state of the company's business or any specific transaction? Are information rights different depending on the number of shares owned? Are shareholders entitled to receive written information before, during or after the GM about the meeting agenda and to what extent? Is it possible for a shareholder to obtain a copy of the minutes of the GM?

Generally, the information which shareholders are entitled to receive is

limited to:
- notices of GMs;
- the company's annual directors' and auditors' reports and accounts; and
- in respect of listed companies, circulars and other documents required to be provided to shareholders under the Listing Rules, which normally include information regarding connected transactions or substantial acquisitions or dispositions, changes to the memorandum and articles and other circulars in respect of the provision of further details regarding resolutions to be proposed at GMs.

All shareholders are entitled to this information regardless of the number of shares owned by them. Shareholders are not otherwise entitled to receive written information before, during or after the GM about the meeting agenda. In addition, listed companies are required to ensure equal dissemination of information to the market and are not allowed to selectively disclose price sensitive information to particular shareholders.

It is not possible for a shareholder to obtain a copy of the minutes of a GM (however, see question 25).

24. Do shareholders have the right/duty to resolve in the GM upon matters which were not on the agenda?
A GM may only pass resolutions which have been covered by the notice convening the GM, although minor amendments to the resolutions contained in the notice may be made to correct clerical errors.

25. Are shareholders entitled to inspect the corporate books and/or any other corporate or accounting documents? To what extent? Can they do it through external counsel or advisors?
Shareholders are not entitled to inspect the corporate books or any other corporate or accounting documents of a company. However:
- any shareholder may inspect the register of shareholders and obtain a copy on payment of a statutory fee;
- shareholders holding 2.5 per cent of the shareholdings of the company having the right to vote, shareholders holding share capital with a paid up amount of HK$100,000 or not fewer than five shareholders may apply to the court for an order allowing inspection of the records of the company. The inspection may be conducted by the persons applying to the court or someone on their behalf and they may make copies of the records unless the court orders otherwise. The court would only make the order if it is satisfied that the application is made in good faith and the inspection applied for is for a proper purpose;
- shareholders are entitled to receive the annual directors' and auditors' reports and accounts (see question 23(b)); and
- public companies and companies limited by guarantee are required to file their annual directors' and auditors' reports and accounts at the Companies Registry and once filed they are available for public inspection.

SHAREHOLDERS' AGREEMENTS

26. Are shareholders' agreements validly enforceable? What are their typical contents and term of duration? Are they enforceable by or against third parties and, if so, to what extent?

Shareholders' agreements are enforceable and frequently entered into in respect of arrangements among shareholders of joint ventures conducted through a company.

Typical provisions in shareholders' agreements include:

- rights to appoint and remove directors;
- pre-emptive rights in respect of the issue of new shares and the transfer of existing shares;
- provisions regarding the further financial requirements of the company;
- veto rights by particular shareholders or groups of shareholders in respect of certain reserved matters;
- put and call options in respect of shares;
- tag along rights;
- drag-along rights; and
- deadlock resolution provisions.

Shareholders' agreements may last indefinitely or be subject to termination on the occurrence of an event of default or certain other events, in which case the rights of the shareholders revert to their general statutory rights in the absence of a shareholders' agreement.

Shareholders' agreements are not enforceable by or against third parties.

27. Do shareholders' agreements have to be disclosed to the public or registered in any public registry?

Shareholders' agreements do not need to be disclosed to the public or registered in any public registry. However, if, as is customary, an agreement itself provides that certain of its provisions be replicated in the company's articles, then those changes will need to be passed by a special resolution, which will need to be filed at the Companies Registry. Once so filed, it will be available for public inspection.

ECONOMIC RIGHTS AND RIGHTS OVER THE STOCK

28. Is the stock always freely transferable? Are there any legal limitations? Are there any restrictions on contractual limitations?

Shares in a company are freely transferable by the shareholder, except as otherwise provided in the articles. The articles may provide that the directors have the authority to decline to register a transfer of shares either for one or more specific reasons or in their sole discretion, without specifying a reason. Consideration is being given to an amendment to the CO requiring directors to give a reason for declining registration of a transfer of shares. The directors' authority must be exercised *bona fide* in what the directors consider to be the best interests of the company.

As mentioned under question 1, one of the components of the definition of a private company is that the articles must restrict the shareholders from transferring their shares. Usually, the directors of a private company may, in their absolute discretion, decline to register any transfer of shares.

In the case of a listed company, shares have to be freely transferable in order for the company to meet the listing requirement that there be an open market in the securities.

In the case of a non-listed public company, the articles may provide that shares are transferable without restriction.

29. Are shareholders entitled to pledge their stock?

A shareholder may charge its shares either with a legal or, as is more customary, an equitable charge. In the case of a legal charge, the shareholder, as chargor, will transfer the legal title to the shares to the chargee. In the case of an equitable charge, the shareholder, as chargor, remains the registered owner of the shares, but deposits the share certificates with the chargee, usually with a signed undated instrument of transfer and in the case of private companies with undated directors' resignations and resolutions to give effect to the transfer of shares.

30. Are there financial assistance issues to be considered and other prohibitions to be evaluated in the context of a leveraged buyout transaction?

See question 36 for a summary of financial assistance prohibitions, which are relevant in the context of a leveraged buyout transaction.

Other relevant considerations include:

- variation of class rights discussed in question 8;
- Listing Rules requirements in respect of connected transactions or substantial acquisitions or dispositions discussed in question 9;
- directors' fiduciary duties discussed in question 21;
- share buy-backs discussed in question 31;
- dividend distributions discussed in question 33;
- issue of new shares discussed in question 34;
- disposals of fixed assets discussed in question 38; and
- the requirement that a reduction of capital be approved by special resolution and sanctioned by the court, the simplification of which is being given consideration.

31. May a company buy back its own stock and, if so, under what circumstances and subject to which limitations?

A company having a share capital may, if authorised to do so by its articles, issue shares that are to be redeemed at the option of either the company or the shareholders. Redeemable shares may only be issued if the company also has issued non-redeemable shares, and redeemable shares may be redeemed only if they are fully paid. With a few exceptions, the redemption price must be paid only out of distributable profits of the company or out of the proceeds of a fresh issue of shares made for the purposes of the redemption, and any premium payable on redemption must be paid out of distributable profits. The redemption will generally be effected on such terms and in such a manner as are set forth in the company's articles.

In addition, a company may buy back its own shares (including redeemable shares) if permitted by its articles so long as, after the purchase, the company's capital will still include some non-redeemable shares. As with a redemption, the price for the shares that are bought back must generally be paid out of distributable profits or the proceeds of a new issue of shares.

An unlisted company may buy back its own shares only pursuant to an agreement approved by a special resolution. Private companies may buy back shares out of capital subject to the following requirements:

- the payment out of capital is approved by a special resolution;
- the making by the directors of a statement specifying the permissible capital payment and confirming the solvency of the company;
- the preparation of an auditors' report confirming the accuracy of the directors' statement;
- the publication of a notice in the Hong Kong Government Gazette and a Chinese and English language newspaper; and
- the filing of the directors' statement and auditors' report at the Companies Registry.

Shareholders or creditors may apply to court for an order cancelling the special resolution whereupon the payment out of capital may not proceed. See question 17.

In the case of a listed company, the company may buy back its own shares:

- under a general offer to all shareholders or all shareholders holding a particular class of shares;
- as a market purchase of shares listed on a stock exchange; or
- otherwise when approved by the Securities and Futures Commission and a special resolution approved by disinterested shareholders holding 75 per cent of the shares attending and voting at a GM.

32. Is there a legal right to withdraw from the company and, if so, under what circumstances? How is the shareholders' stock valued and paid in such a case?

There is no general statutory right of withdrawal.

However, as discussed in question 31, a company may issue shares that are redeemable at the option of the shareholder, in which case the requirements with respect to the financing of a redemption described in question 31 are applicable. In the event that the company fails to redeem shares when required, the shareholder will not be entitled to collect damages, and the courts will not grant specific performance of the redemption if the company shows that it is unable to finance the purchase out of its distributable profits.

In respect of unfair prejudice actions discussed in question 17, a court may grant an order that certain shareholders purchase the shares held by other shareholders. In this case, the court will direct how the shares will be valued.

Shareholders' agreements may provide contractual methods which give shareholders the right to have their shares purchased on specified terms.

33. In which circumstances can dividends be distributed among shareholders? Is it possible to exclude or limit the right of certain shareholders to dividends? Does a certain portion of the profits need to be set aside in a reserve fund where it cannot be distributed to the shareholders? Are advances on dividends allowed and, if so, under which circumstances? Can advances on dividends be reclaimed by the company?

A company may only issue a dividend out of its distributable profits. A company's distributable profits for this purpose are its accumulated, realised profits less its accumulated, realised losses.

Amounts are required to be transferred to a reserve as follows:

- where shares are issued at a premium (that is, in excess of nominal value), then the amount of the premium is required to be credited to a share premium account; and
- where shares are redeemed or repurchased out of profits, then the amount of the share capital diminished is required to be credited to a capital redemption reserve.

Neither of these reserves may be distributed as dividends.

In addition, a listed company may only issue a dividend if, after the dividend, its net assets are equal to or greater than the total of its called-up share capital plus undistributable reserves. Undistributable reserves of a listed company include (in addition to the share premium account and capital redemption reserve):

- any revaluation reserve, which consists of the balance of unrealised profits less accumulated unrealised losses; and
- any other reserve that the company is prohibited from distributing under its articles.

In effect, therefore, a listed company cannot distribute its realised profits without first making good any excess of unrealised losses over unrealised profits.

As discussed under question 3, a company may issue deferred shares with limited rights to dividends or preference shares with preferential rights to dividends; in which case, relative to preference shares, ordinary shares' rights to dividends will be limited and, relative to deferred shares, ordinary shares' rights to dividends will be preferred.

Payment of dividends in advance of the generation of distributable profits is not permitted.

34. What are the rights of shareholders in the case of an issue of new stock (increase of the company's corporate capital) (pre-emption rights)?

The directors require approval by a GM to allot shares other than pro rata to existing shareholders. This gives shareholders a form of pre-emption right in the absence of approval by a GM.

Also, as indicated in question 26, shareholders' agreements can include a pre-emptive right to the effect that the company may not issue new shares unless it gives existing shareholders the right to purchase such shares pro rata to their existing respective shareholdings.

35. May minority shareholders ban or limit the company's capital structure in any manner?

The capital structure of a company, including the different classes of shares and the rights attaching to these classes of shares, is typically set forth in the company's articles. As discussed in question 6, a special resolution is required to reduce the share capital, buy back shares or amend a company's articles. See also question 8 in respect of the variation of class rights. Minority shareholders who do not own more than 25 per cent of the shares do not have a veto right on such matters.

36. Which are the financial assistance prohibitions in force?

As a general rule, it is not lawful for a company or any of its subsidiaries to give financial assistance, directly or indirectly, for the purpose of either the acquisition by another person of shares of the company before or at the same time as such acquisition is made, or the reduction or discharge of a liability incurred for the purpose of acquiring shares in the company after the acquisition is made.

The term 'financial assistance' is broadly defined to include assistance by way of a gift, guarantee, security, indemnity or loan. However, certain transactions are expressly exempted from the prohibition on giving financial assistance, including, among other exemptions:
- a dividend distribution;
- a distribution upon liquidation;
- the allotment of bonus shares;
- certain redemptions or repurchases of shares;
- lending money in the ordinary course of business of the company; and
- the provision of money for the purpose of enabling employees to purchase shares in the company.

For listed companies, there are some limitations on the availability of these exemptions.

Notwithstanding the foregoing, the restriction is not violated if a company has two or more purposes in giving the financial assistance and the principal purpose is not to give assistance for the acquisition of shares or the discharge of a liability incurred for the acquisition of shares, so long as the financial assistance is given in good faith in the interest of the company.

Notwithstanding the foregoing restrictions, financial assistance restrictions are relaxed in the case of an unlisted company. An unlisted company or its subsidiary may give financial assistance for the acquisition of the company's shares if the assistance does not reduce the company's net assets (or if it does, the assistance is given out of distributable profits) when it is supported by a special resolution and a majority of the company's directors issue a statement specifying, among several other matters, that there could be no ground on which it would be found that the company is unable to pay its debts.

The financial assistance rules are currently under review and may in the medium term be abolished or streamlined.

37. Apart from publicly listed companies, in which cases (if any) are shareholders obligated to obtain an authorisation from, or provide information to, a public authority about events that have an impact on their stock interest in the company?

Except for regulated entities or entities holding particular government licences, there is no general requirement to obtain any governmental or regulatory approval for a transfer of shares.

SHAREHOLDERS' RIGHTS IN THE CASE OF EXTRAORDINARY TRANSACTIONS AND/OR WINDING-UP

38. What rights are available to shareholders in the case of a sale of all or a substantial portion of the company's assets? In the case of a merger or de-merger?

A listed company or a member of a listed group is subject to a statutory restriction on the disposal of fixed assets save to the extent approved in a GM. The restriction covers disposals of fixed assets where the consideration for a disposal (including the consideration for any disposals in the four months preceding the disposal) exceeds 33 per cent of the value of all fixed assets of the company as per the latest audited balance sheet laid before the company in a GM.

Also, listed companies are subject to restrictions in the Listing Rules in respect of connected transactions and substantial transactions. These may require the preparation of a circular to shareholders and/or the approval of shareholders.

The Code regulates takeovers and mergers affecting public companies in Hong Kong. The Code takes effect when a person or group of persons acting in concert (see question 16) acquire shares representing 30 per cent or more of the voting rights of a company, or when a person or group of persons acting in concert who hold not less than 30 per cent and not more than 50 per cent of the voting rights of a company acquire an additional two per cent of the voting rights in any 12-month period. Such persons must make an offer to purchase the shares of all of the company's shareholders, under which all shareholders of the same class are to be treated in the same manner and shareholders holding different classes of equity must be treated comparably.

39. Which rights are available to shareholders in the case of conversion of the company into a European Company (SE) or into another type of company?

Hong Kong law does not permit a Hong Kong company to transfer its place of incorporation to any other jurisdiction.

40. Which rights are available to shareholders of a company in liquidation?

Upon a liquidation, the assets of a company will be applied first to repay the company's liabilities, and any assets left will be distributed to the shareholders in accordance with their rights and interests in the company as set forth in the company's articles. Shareholders of the company may also be required to contribute, upon a liquidation, any unpaid amount on their shares and, in the case of a company limited by guarantee, to the extent required to meet its obligations, any amount that they agreed would be contributed upon a liquidation.

The conduct of the liquidation is the responsibility of a liquidator. If the liquidation is ordered by a court, the liquidator will be appointed by the court and act under the court's direction. In a voluntary liquidation, if the directors certify that the company is solvent, the shareholders will have the right to appoint the liquidator; otherwise, the company's creditors will appoint the liquidator.

41. Can shareholders cause the liquidation of the company? How?

If the period during which the company is to exist according to the articles expires, or upon the occurrence of an event that would trigger the termination of the company under the articles or memorandum, the shareholders may pass a resolution in a GM that the company be liquidated. At any other time, the shareholders can pass a special resolution that the company be liquidated. The articles cannot restrict the right to voluntarily liquidate the company.

The shareholders may also petition the court for the winding up of the company on various grounds, including insolvency or the more general ground that it is just and equitable that the company be wound up.

COMPANY GROUPS

42. Is the concept of 'group' recognised as such under specific legislation? What are the implications?

Generally, the approach of Hong Kong law is to regard companies as being separate from their shareholders and not to pierce the corporate veil. Under this approach, companies which are part of a group remain regarded as independent legal entities.

In relation to the relationship between subsidiaries and holding companies, however, courts have been prepared to pierce the corporate veil under the following limited circumstances:

- where the corporate form has been used as a sham concealing true facts;
- where one company could be said to be an agent for another; and
- in the case of liability for tort, where an action has been permitted to proceed against the parent company where the damage occurred as a result of tortious activities of various subsidiaries.

Nevertheless, the general approach of not piercing the corporate veil is a robust one.

One statutory exception to regarding companies as independent entities is in respect of the preparation of group accounts. In this context, if a company has subsidiaries, group accounts dealing with the states of affairs and profit and loss of the company and its subsidiaries should be prepared and laid before the holding company in a GM. This requirement is not applicable where the company is a wholly owned subsidiary of another

company or where:
a) the preparation of group accounts is impracticable or of no real value to shareholders of the company;
b) the result would be misleading or harmful to the business of the company; or
c) the business of the company and of the subsidiary are so different that they cannot reasonably be treated as a single undertaking.

In respect of items (b) and (c), approval of the financial secretary is required if group accounts are not to be produced.

Hong Kong law also requires that a company and its subsidiaries have the same financial year unless the directors, in their opinion, deem that there are good reasons to have separate financial years.

For the purpose of this question (and question 45), a holding company is one of which another company is a subsidiary. A subsidiary is one which has its board of directors controlled by the holding company, where more than half of the share capital or voting power is controlled by the holding company or where a company is a subsidiary of another company which is itself a subsidiary.

43. Does a controlling company have any particular duties *vis-à-vis* its controlled company shareholders?
The general proposition of law is that shareholders do not have duties to the companies in which they hold shares, but the directors appointed by them have fiduciary duties owed to their company (see question 21). In addition, there is some very limited scope to argue that in certain circumstances the shareholders of a company may owe duties of a fiduciary type to the other shareholders of the company. The authorities, however, give rise to a strong presumption against finding any such duties.

44. What are the rights of company shareholders when the controlling company puts in place actions and/or transactions that can be prejudicial to the shareholders?
The rights of the shareholders in this case would be to bring an unfair prejudice action or a derivative action (see question 17).

45. What are the limitations, if any, to the possibility of owning reciprocal stock interests in companies?
It is possible for a company to hold shares in another company, but it is not possible (with certain exceptions) for a subsidiary to hold shares in its parent company.
The exceptions are:
*   shareholdings existing prior to 1984;
*   where the subsidiary is a personal representative or trustee or is holding shares by way of security;
*   where the company is already a shareholder of another company at the date when it becomes a subsidiary of that other company;
*   where the subsidiary is allotted shares through the exercise of

conversion rights of shares in its holding company;
* where the subsidiary acquires shares as a consequence of capitalisation of reserves or profits of the holding company.

Even when the exceptions apply, a subsidiary which is a shareholder of its holding company has no right to vote at GMs of the holding company.

Hungary

Lakatos, Köves & Partners Ügyvédi Iroda
Dr Pál Rahóty & Richard Lock

BASIC INFORMATION ON THE TYPES OF LIMITED LIABILITY COMPANIES AND ON THE RIGHTS OF SHAREHOLDERS

1. What types of companies enjoy limited liability? If more than one, which ones have shareholders, ie holders of share certificates? Which one is the most common? Which one is mostly used by foreign investors?

In Hungary: (a) the company limited by shares (*részvénytársaság* (Rt)), which may be either private (*Zártkörűen Működő Részvénytársaság* (Zrt)) or public (*Nyilvánosan Működő Részvénytársaság* (Nyrt)); and (b) the limited liability company (*korlátolt felelősségű társaság* (Kft)), enjoy limited liability. From January 2010, individual entrepreneurs may also choose to operate in an individual company form having limited liability (*korlátolt felelősségű egyéni cég* (Kfc)).

Only a company limited by shares, (a Zrt or Nyrt), has shareholders, and only such companies may issue shares.

Owners in a Kft hold 'quotas' and not shares. Each member may have one quota only, which embodies all that member's proportional rights and obligations *vis-á-vis* the Kft. Quotaholders are also referred to as members of a Kft. Unless the constitutive document of a Kft (articles of association) provides otherwise, the transfer of quotas to non-member third parties is subject to statutory pre-emption rights, the beneficiaries of which are any other member of the Kft, the Kft itself or a person appointed by the members' meeting (in that order). A Kft member's liability is limited to its initial investment and any other contributions required under the Kft's articles of association.

The Kft is the most common form of company in Hungary, and is often used for medium or large operating and holding companies. The Kft is also the most common type of company used by foreign investors. A Kft is a private company and is not entitled to raise its capital publicly.

2. Are there minimum capital requirements and/or thin capitalisation rules in force?

The minimum capital requirement is HUF 500,000 (about €1,800) for a Kft; HUF 5,000,000 (about €18,000) for a Zrt; and HUF 20,000,000 (about €72,000) for a Nyrt. There are thin capitalisation rules in force providing a maximum debt to equity ratio of 3:1. Thin capitalisation rules do not apply to debts owed to financial institutions.

3. Describe the types of shares that can be issued by a company and the different rights that they attribute to their owners, as well as any other financial instruments (bonds or other) and other instruments of a participatory nature in the company's capital that can also be issued by the company.

Shares

A company limited by shares, a Zrt or Nyrt, may issue: (i) ordinary shares; (ii) preference shares; (iii) employee shares; (iv) interest-bearing shares; and (v) redeemable shares.

A share may be either printed or dematerialised (electronic). Only authorised printing houses may print the shares, and the involvement of the Hungarian central depository and clearing house (KELER Zrt) is required for the creation of electronic shares. Ownership of printed shares is transferred by way of endorsing the share certificate; ownership of dematerialised shares is transferred by way of transferring the share to and crediting it on the securities account of the buyer.

Ordinary shares

The aggregate nominal value of the ordinary shares must exceed half of the share capital (ie the aggregate nominal value of all other shares, if issued, may not reach half of the share capital). As the name suggests these are the ordinary shares of the company limited by shares with no special rights or restrictions.

Preference shares

The preference shares give the shareholder greater rights than those who hold ordinary shares. The following preferences may be given:
- Preference related to dividends: holders of such shares receive their dividends first and/or in a higher amount than the ordinary shareholders from the annual dividends available for distribution, as defined in the articles of association.
- Preference related to voting rights: holders of such shares may exercise multiple voting rights to the extent defined in the articles of association. The voting rights attached to one such preference share, however, may not exceed 10 times the voting rights corresponding to the nominal value of the share (see also question 15 for non-voting shares). If the articles of association provide, the general meeting (GM) may pass a resolution on specific issues determined in the articles of association, upon the majority vote of preference shares related to voting rights.
- Preference related to liquidation proceeds: in the event the company limited by shares terminates without succession, preferred shareholders can have a prior entitlement before the ordinary shareholders from the assets to be distributed.
- Preference related to the appointment of board members or supervisory board members: holders of such shares may appoint up to one-third of members of the board and/or the supervisory board. Such shareholders

are also entitled to remove the members they have appointed. Preference shares related to the appointment of board members or supervisory board members can be issued only for Zrts.

- Preference related to pre-emption rights: the holder of such shares is granted the right of pre-emption for any type of shares of the private company limited by shares when offered for sale. Shares providing pre-emption rights cannot be issued for public companies limited by shares.

A company limited by shares may issue shares combining the aforementioned preference rights and it is also possible to issue preference shares carrying the right to exchange the preference share held to another type of preference share or ordinary share.

Employee shares

A company limited by shares cannot issue employee shares at foundation but only later in the event of a capital increase. Employee shares may be provided to full and part time employees at a discounted price or free of charge (in the first case, the capital is paid in fully or partly by employees, while in the latter case, the company pays in the full capital from the equity exceeding the share capital). Employee shares are transferable only among employees or (if provided by the articles of association) former employees of the company.

Interest-bearing shares

Interest-bearing shares up to 10 per cent of the share capital may be issued entitling their holders to a pre-determined rate of interest. No interest can be paid if, as a result of the payment, the equity would drop below the share capital.

Redeemable shares

Redeemable shares may be issued up to 10 per cent of the share capital providing a call option to the company limited by shares and/or a put option to the shareholder according to the terms outlined in the articles of association.

Other financial instruments

Convertible bonds

A company limited by shares may issue registered bonds up to half of its share capital, which shall be converted into shares at the request of the holder.

Bonds with subscription rights

A company limited by shares may issue registered bonds providing subscription rights to the holders, after shareholders, in a capital increase.

Quotas in limited liability companies do not qualify as financial instruments including securities. See question 1 for details.

4. Can a company have only one shareholder and still enjoy limited liability?

A Zrt can have one shareholder and still enjoy limited liability. If one shareholder acquires all the shares of a Nyrt then the company shall continue to operate as a Zrt.

A Kft can have a sole member and still enjoy limited liability.

5. Are the rights of shareholders the same in any type of company?

As a general principle, the rights of the shareholders or quota holders are the same unless the articles of association provide any specific restriction or limitation. The threshold to exercise minority rights (eg adding items to the agenda) is different between private and public companies limited by shares.

As regards a Kft, the membership rights attached to the quotas are the same unless the articles of association provide specific rights to particular quotas.

6. What are the basic rights of any shareholder? Describe briefly the rights of minority shareholders and indicate which thresholds, if any, are required to allow the minority shareholders to exercise any such rights.

The basic rights of shareholders are:
(i)   attending the GM;
(ii)   voting at the GM;
(iii) requesting information;
(iv) making remarks and proposals at the GM; and
(v)   receiving dividends.

Each shareholder may request the judicial supervision of a resolution passed by any corporate body on the ground that the resolution breaches the law or any provision of the articles of association.

Shareholders having five per cent of the voting rights both in Zrts and Nyrts may request the convening of the GM. The same applies to Kfts, where members having five per cent of the voting rights may request the convening of the members' meeting.

Shareholders of a Zrt having five per cent of voting rights and shareholders of a Nyrt having one per cent of the voting rights may add items to the agenda of the GM, and may request the appointment of an independent expert to examine the annual report of the company, any particular management action of the previous two years, and also whether a particular payment to a shareholder has been performed in line with the accounting and corporate regulations, including the specific requirement that the equity cannot decrease below the share capital as a result of the payment.

Any member of a Kft may add additional items to the agenda of the members' meeting for discussion purposes, if the new item is communicated to the other members at least three days prior to the members' meeting. Members of a Kft having five per cent of voting rights may request the appointment of an independent expert to examine the annual report of the company, and any particular management action of the previous two years.

7. Do all shareholders enjoy the same rights or can some shareholders be attributed specific rights, whether by reason of the particular class of stock owned or other? Are such rights generally provided for at the level of the company's by-laws and/or in shareholders' agreements?

As a general principle all shareholders enjoy the same rights. However, it is the articles of association, and not the shareholders' agreements, which may provide specific rights to particular classes of shares.

8. May the rights of shareholders, generally speaking, be limited, modified, suppressed or waived in any way? If so, how? Are such modifications or limitations provided for in the company's by-laws and/or in shareholders' agreements?

The rights of shareholders may be limited in the articles of association. See also question 26 re shareholders' agreements.

The articles of association may restrict or exclude voting rights attached to specific classes of shares, and at public companies limited by shares the voting rights which can be exercised by each shareholder or group of shareholders can be restricted.

GENERAL MEETING OF SHAREHOLDERS (GM) AND VOTING RIGHTS

9. Which decisions are reserved to the competence of the GM?

Companies limited by shares and the GM

The following decisions are reserved to the exclusive competence of the GM:
- approval and amendment of the articles of association;
- changing the operating form of the company;
- transformation or termination of the company without succession;
- appointment and removal of the members of the board of directors/ CEO, members of the supervisory board and the auditor, and deciding on their remuneration;
- approval of the annual report;
- paying interim dividends;
- converting printed shares into dematerialised shares;
- alteration of the rights attached to the various series of shares, and the conversion of categories or classes of shares;
- issuing convertible bonds or bonds with subscription rights;
- increase or decrease of the share capital;
- excluding the exercise of pre-emptive subscription rights; and
- decisions on all issues which are assigned to the competence of the GM by law or the articles of association.

In addition to the foregoing, at public companies limited by shares, the following decisions shall be made by the GM:
- decisions concerning the guidelines and framework for a long-term salary and incentive scheme for executives, supervisory board members and executive employees; and

- appointment of members of the audit board.

Decisions on issuing convertible bonds or bonds with subscription rights, or increasing the share capital may be delegated to the board of directors by the GM. The articles of association may provide the right to the supervisory board to appoint and remove the members of the board of directors and decide on their remuneration, and may entitle the board of directors to decide on paying interim dividends, if approved by the supervisory board.

Limited liability companies and the quota holders' meeting

The supreme body of a Kft is the quota holders' (or members') meeting. All quota holders are entitled to attend the quota holders' meeting and vote there unless the voting right attached to the particular quota holder's quota is restricted.

The following decisions are reserved to the exclusive competence of the quota holders' meeting:
- approval of the annual report;
- decision to pay interim dividends;
- order and repayment of supplementary capital contributions;
- exercising pre-emption rights concerning the quotas of the company on behalf of the company;
- designation of a person for the right to exercise pre-emption rights concerning the quotas of the company;
- granting consent for the transfer of any quota to a third person;
- in the event that the auction fails, adopting a decision concerning the quota;
- consent for the division of the quota, and order for the withdrawal of quotas;
- resolution for initiating the exclusion of a quota holder;
- election and removal of the managing director and the establishing of their remuneration;
- election and removal of supervisory board members and the establishing of their remuneration;
- election and removal of the auditor and the establishing of their remuneration;
- approval to conclude contracts which take place between the company and one of its quota holders, its managing director or their close relatives;
- enforcement of claims *vis-a-vis* members, managing directors, supervisory board members or the auditor;
- ordering the examination of the company's annual report, management and financial operations by an auditor;
- adopting a decision for the creation of a recognised group of companies and for the contents of the draft control contract, approval of the draft version of the control contract;
- decision on termination without succession or transformation of the company;
- any amendment of the articles of association;
- adopting a decision for the increase or reduction of the initial capital;
- in connection with any increase of the initial capital, preclusion of

preferential rights of quota holders;
- in connection with any increase of the initial capital, designation of the persons for the entitlement to exercise preferential rights;
- in connection with any increase of the initial capital or the exercise of preferential rights, a decision regarding any deviation from the percentage of quota holders' contributions to the company's capital; and
- in connection with any reduction of the initial capital, a decision regarding any deviation from the percentage of quota holders' contributions to the company's capital.

10. How does a shareholder participate in a GM? Are there any limitations to having a minimum number of shares? May a shareholder delegate attendance to another shareholder or to the board? May a shareholder obtain assistance from the courts or any other governmental body to intervene in a GM or to cause one to be held in some particular cases?

The shareholder may participate in a GM personally or by proxy. There is no limitation regarding the number of shares required to give the right to participate. The shareholder may delegate attendance to another shareholder but not to the board, except if the articles of association of a Zrt allow the delegation to the board. In the Nyrt, the board may act as the proxy of the shareholder if the shareholder determines in writing how the board shall vote in all agenda items.

Applying auto proxies is feasible under Hungarian law; in some Hungarian Nyrts, the Global Depositary Receipt (GDR) holders have provided auto proxies to the banks to represent them at the GM. If the banks do not receive an instruction on how to vote, they vote for the proposal of the board.

The quota holders in a Kft may participate in a quota holders' meeting personally or by a proxy. The quota holder may not delegate attendance to the members of the management and supervisory board and the auditor. The articles of association may not override this restriction.

The convening of the GM/quota holders' meeting may be requested from the court, if the board fails to convene in spite of the request.

11. May a GM be called and held at the request of any shareholder? Is there a threshold regarding the percentage of the stock interest owned in the company that may entitle a shareholder to such a right?

Shareholders and also quota holders having at least five per cent of the voting rights are entitled to request the board to convene the GM/quota holders' meeting, if the board fails to do so, the court convenes the GM/quota holders' meeting.

12. May a shareholder bring up an issue to be resolved upon and put it to a vote if it is not included on the agenda? May a shareholder require more information from the GM and/or the board, concerning the agenda of the GM, to be put in a better position to exercise their vote?

Shareholders having five per cent of the voting rights in a Zrt and shareholders having one per cent of the voting rights in a Nyrt may put an issue on the agenda before the GM within eight days from receiving or publishing the invitation to the GM.

Any quota holder in a Kft is entitled to request the discussion of an agenda item not included in the invitation to the quota holders' meeting, if they circulate to all members the new agenda item to be discussed at least three days before the quota holders' meeting.

Agenda points not included in the invitation may be included on the agenda of a GM/quota holders' meeting only if all shareholders/quota holders are present and agree to that.

A shareholder/quota holder may require more information from the GM/quota holders' meeting: when the agenda is discussed, the directors are obliged to provide to all shareholders the necessary information.

13. May a GM be held by telecommunication means and/or by correspondence (ie by written consent)?

If the articles of association so provide, a GM may be held by telecommunication means for both Zrts and Nyrts but holding a GM by correspondence is possible only for Zrts.

The quota holders' meeting of a Kft may also be held by telecommunication means and correspondence, if the articles of association so provide.

The articles of association may list matters which cannot be resolved at a GM held by telecommunication means.

If the GM/quota holders' meeting is held by correspondence then at least eight days shall be provided to the shareholders/quota holders to provide their votes in writing. In a Kft, the result of the voting shall be communicated by the managing director(s) to the quota holders in writing within eight days from receiving the last vote. In a Zrt, the result of the voting shall be assessed by the board of directors within three days from the deadline open for the shareholders to vote, and within a further three-day period the board of directors shall notify the shareholders in writing of the result of the voting.

14. Are voting rights always proportionate to the stock held by each shareholder or can they vary by share class?

Voting rights are generally proportionate to the stock held by each shareholder or quota holder unless the articles of association provide otherwise (ie voting preference share – see question 3.

15. Are there non-voting shares? Is there a maximum percentage of capital represented by non-voting shares?

Voting rights attached to some preference shares may be excluded or limited. Preference shares with no voting rights may be issued up to a maximum of 49 per cent of the share capital.

16. Can shareholders group their shares in order to exercise their voting rights (eg, by trust, shareholders' agreement or otherwise)?

The shareholders may agree on how to exercise their voting rights, but no such formal procedure exists under Hungarian law. There are some companies which regulate and/or restrict the operation of shareholder groups in their articles of association.

17. Under what circumstances can a shareholder challenge the resolutions adopted by the GM? Are there thresholds concerning the stock interest owned to be able to bring such a claim?

If the resolution violates the law or any provision of the articles of association then any shareholder can challenge the resolution before the court.

18. What are the terms and procedures to challenge a resolution of the GM?

The resolution may be challenged within 30 days from obtaining knowledge of the resolution passed but in any event within 90 days from passing the resolution; the latter deadline terminates the right to challenge the resolution before the court. The claim shall be launched against the company.

SHAREHOLDERS' RIGHTS VERSUS DIRECTORS AND DUTIES OF OTHER CORPORATE BODIES IN THE COMPANY

19. What is the procedure for the appointment/replacement/ revocation of directors and of statutory auditors, if any?

Generally the GM exercises such rights; however, in Zrts the articles of association may delegate these rights to the supervisory board.

The same applies to limited liability companies.

20. May shareholders challenge the resolutions of the board of directors? Is there a minimum percentage of capital required to challenge a board resolution?

Any shareholder/quota holder may challenge the resolution of the board of directors or managers before the court if the resolution violates the law or any provision of the articles of association.

21. Are shareholders entitled to bring a legal action against the directors of the company? In which circumstances? Please describe briefly the principles of directors' liability.

If the directors caused damage to the company by not acting with due care or violating the law, or the articles of association, or the resolution of the GM/quota holders' meeting, then the main rule is that shareholders/quota holders directly are not, but the company is, entitled to bring legal action against the directors. However, if a proposal put forward at a GM/quota holders' meeting for bringing such a legal action is refused, a legal action can be brought by shareholders having five per cent of the voting rights, on behalf of the company.

The risk of a legal action against the directors may be mitigated if the directors act strictly in line with the resolutions of the GM/quota holders' meeting, or in the case of sole shareholder/quota holder companies, if they insist on receiving instructions from the sole shareholder/quota holder in writing.

A further option to mitigate the risk of a legal action is if the directors are granted discharge. As a prerequisite, the articles of association of the company shall contain the possibility of exemption (granting discharge) according to which the management activity pursued by the directors in the previous year can be ratified by the GM/quota holders' meeting and the directors cannot be later challenged, unless the court decides subsequently that the exemption was based on false information.

The general principles of the directors' liability are that the directors shall perform the management duties with due care and diligence as generally expected from persons in such positions and give priority to the interests of the company. However, if the company faces the possibility of becoming insolvent, the director shall give priority to the creditors' interest. Determining the point at which the directors' priorities change can be difficult and depends upon a careful consideration of all the circumstances.

22. What are the rights in connection with transactions where the directors have a conflict of interest situation?

As a general rule, directors cannot be in a situation giving rise to a conflict of interest unless the articles of association or the GM authorises the conflict.

If the directors have a conflict of interest situation, the GM may call on the director to end the situation or may revoke the director. If any damage occurred as a result of the conflict of interest situation, the company may bring an action against the director.

INFORMATION RIGHTS ON THE COMPANY'S BUSINESS

23. What information may be requested by the shareholders from the board concerning the general state of the company's business or any specific transaction? Are information rights different depending on the number of shares owned? Are shareholders entitled to receive written information before, during or after the GM about the meeting agenda and to what extent? Is it possible for a shareholder to obtain a copy of the minutes of the GM?

Shareholders and quota holders may request any kind of information concerning the business of the company or any transaction. The information rights are not different depending on the number of shares owned. The limit to this is that directors are under a general obligation to preserve the interests and business secrets of the company.

The invitation to the meeting of the GM/quota holders' meeting shall include the agenda items (eg change to articles of association, appointment and reward of directors) but no detailed proposal relating to each item is required to be provided. Reports of the board and the supervisory board and the main data of the annual financial statements shall be disclosed to the shareholders/quota holders before the GM/quotaholders' meeting.

Shareholders/quota holders may request copies of the GM/quota holders' meeting minutes.

24. Do shareholders have the right/duty to resolve in the GM upon matters which were not on the agenda?

This is possible if all the shareholders/quota holders attend the GM/ quota holders' meeting and agree to resolve on matters not on the agenda circulated prior to the GM/quota holders' meeting.

25. Are shareholders entitled to inspect the corporate books and/or any other corporate or accounting documents? To what extent? Can they do it through external counsel or advisors?

Shareholders or quota holders are entitled to inspect the accounting and corporate documents, as long as it is without detriment to the business interests and secrets of the company, through themselves or external counsel or advisors as the representative of the shareholder/quota holder.

SHAREHOLDERS' AGREEMENTS

26. Are shareholders' agreements validly enforceable? What are their typical contents and term of duration? Are they enforceable by or against third parties and, if so, to what extent?

Shareholders' agreements are enforceable on a civil law basis as the Hungarian corporate law regime does not regulate shareholders' or quota holders' agreements. Provisions that are not in line with mandatory corporate law provisions may not be enforceable in a corporate law context, and their validity may be disputed from a civil law perspective too. Shareholders' agreements generally cover issues not included in the articles of association such as option rights and delegating board members. Shareholders' agreements cannot be enforced by or against third parties.

27. Do shareholders' agreements have to be disclosed to the public or registered in any public registry?

Nyrts have to disclose shareholders' agreements (if they are aware of them).

ECONOMIC RIGHTS AND RIGHTS OVER THE STOCK

28. Is the stock always freely transferable? Are there any legal limitations? Are there any restrictions on contractual limitations?

Shares are freely transferable unless the articles of association provide any limitation on Zrts. A typical limitation can be when the approval of the board is required for the transfer. Transfer limitations need to be made apparent on the shares.

The transfer of quotas in Kfts is subject to statutory pre-emption rights unless the articles of association exclude that (see also question 1).

There is no specific restriction on contractual limitations.

29. Are shareholders entitled to pledge their stock?

Both the shareholders and quota holders are entitled to pledge their stock.

30. Are there financial assistance issues to be considered and other prohibitions to be evaluated in the context of a leveraged buyout transaction?

Hungarian law prohibits a target company limited by shares providing loans, security or meeting financial obligations before due in order that a third party buyer may acquire its shares. The prohibition does not apply to transactions for the acquisition of shares by employees or their organisations and transactions constituting the general business of banks.

31. May a company buy back its own stock and, if so, under what circumstances and subject to which limitations?

Broadly speaking, a company may buy back shares only if its financial position otherwise makes the company able to pay dividend according to the accounting rules and the GM approves the buyback. Shares bought back shall be ignored when the quorum is determined and at voting.

Hungarian law provides for some exceptions when there is no need for the approval of the GM to acquire shares, such as when the acquisition of the shares is in connection with the transformation of the company, the settlement of any claim of the company in a judicial or non-judicial procedure, or acceptance of any security for a claim. However, in these exceptional cases, Hungarian law sets the requirement of either selling or redeeming (with a simultaneous capital decrease) shares so acquired exceeding 10 per cent of the share capital within three years from the acquisition.

A Kft may acquire its own quota if all the conditions under which the Kft may be entitled to pay dividend are satisfied. Any such acquired quota shall be alienated within one year of purchase, provided to the members of the Kft free of charge or redeemed in a simultaneous capital decrease unless the articles of association provide otherwise. No voting rights and dividends are attached to such quotas held by the company.

32. Is there a legal right to withdraw from the company and, if so, under what circumstances? How is the shareholders' stock valued and paid in such a case?

Shareholders are not entitled to withdraw from the company. However, if the company merges with another company or transforms into another type of company, shareholders may elect to depart and be bought out.

33. In which circumstances can dividends be distributed among shareholders? Is it possible to exclude or limit the right of certain shareholders to dividends? Does a certain portion of the profits need to be set aside in a reserve fund where it cannot be distributed to the shareholders? Are advances on dividends allowed and, if so, under which circumstances? Can advances on dividends be reclaimed by the company?

Dividends can be distributed to shareholders if:

(i) the company has sufficient funds from the taxed profit or from the taxed profit supplemented with available profit reserves;

(ii) following the distribution of dividends the equity still reaches the share capital; and

(iii) the GM resolves on the distribution.

It is not possible to exclude or limit the right of certain shareholders to dividends unless particular share rights are defined in the articles. There is no requirement that a certain portion of the profits needs to be set aside in a reserve fund.

If the articles of association allow, the GM/quota holders' meeting may pass a resolution on paying advances on dividends between the approval of two consecutive annual reports if:

- according to the interim balance sheet prepared for this purpose, the company has funds sufficient to cover such advances on dividends;
- such payments do not exceed the amount of profits earned after the closing of the books of the financial year to which the last annual report pertains, or the amount supplemented with the available profit reserves;
- the payments of such advances on dividends do not result in the company's equity capital dropping below its share capital; and
- the shareholders/quota holders agree to repay the advances on dividends in the event of any subsequent reason not making possible the payment of dividends under the Hungarian relevant legal provisions (ie the final year end accounts do not justify the payment).

The company may reclaim the advances on dividends if it turns out after the payment that the company is not in a position to pay dividends according to the Hungarian rules.

34. What are the rights of shareholders in the case of an issue of new stock (increase of the company's corporate capital) (pre-emption rights)?

The shareholders may subscribe for the new stock and they have priority rights if the articles of association so provide.

The quota holders in a Kft have priority rights unless either the articles of association or the resolution on the capital increase exclude that.

35. May minority shareholders ban or limit the company's capital structure in any manner?

A GM resolution passed with a three-quarters majority of the votes of the shareholders present is required for a capital decrease.

36. Which are the financial assistance prohibitions in force?

Please see question 28.

There is no express prohibition of financial assistance in the case of the acquisition of quotas in a Kft.

37. Apart from publicly listed companies, in which cases (if any) are shareholders obligated to obtain an authorisation from, or provide information to, a public authority about events that have an impact on their stock interest in the company?

If a shareholder of a Zrt or a quota holder of a Kft acquires directly or indirectly 75 per cent of the voting rights (ie acquisition of qualified influence), the court of registration shall be notified within 15 days of the acquisition.

When there is a change to the stock interest in companies operating in a regulated business sector (eg banking, energy), the authorisation from the relevant regulator may need to be obtained (eg if certain thresholds are passed).

For example in the banking sector, the approval of the Hungarian Financial Supervisory Authority is required for the acquisition of qualified influence (see definition below) in a financial institution and for the increase of the influence exceeding the 20 per cent, 33 per cent and 50 per cent thresholds. Qualified influence can be acquired either directly or indirectly and it covers the following:

- having 10 per cent of voting rights;
- having the right to appoint or withdraw at least 20 per cent of the board of directors and supervisory board members; or
- having significant influence on the operation of the company on the basis of the articles of association or an agreement.

SHAREHOLDERS' RIGHTS IN THE CASE OF EXTRAORDINARY TRANSACTIONS AND/OR WINDING-UP

38. What rights are available to shareholders in the case of a sale of all or a substantial portion of the company's assets? In the case of a merger or de-merger?

Shareholders may request the GM to contract with an auditor to inspect the sale. If the GM rejects the proposal, shareholders having five per cent of the voting rights may request the court to order the inspection.

In the case of a merger or de-merger, the shareholder may decide to participate in the successor company. If the shareholder chooses not to be a shareholder of the successor company, then the shareholder can request that it be bought out and a settlement needs to be made proportionately to the shareholder's contribution in the share capital.

39. Which rights are available to shareholders in the case of conversion of the company into a European Company (SE) or into another type of company?

Shareholders have the same right as in the case of a merger or de-merger; they may choose not to participate in the new type of company.

40. Which rights are available to shareholders of a company in liquidation?

Shareholders may exercise their right to information and they are entitled to the repayment of the nominal value of their shares after all other creditors have been satisfied, and their proportionate shares of any remaining balance.

41. Can shareholders cause the liquidation of the company? How?
Shareholders may pass a resolution on the liquidation with a three-quarters majority.

COMPANY GROUPS
42. Is the concept of 'group' recognised as such under specific legislation? What are the implications?
The concept of a group of companies is recognised under Hungarian corporate law. The controlling company is required to prepare consolidated annual reports according to the accounting provisions and the controlling and the controlled company may enter into a control contract and this fact needs to be registered with the court of registration. Alternatively, in the absence of a control contract and registration as a recognised group, the controlling company and the controlled company may be regarded as constituting a group if they operate in cooperation under a common business strategy for at least three consecutive years ensuring the predictable and balanced allocation of advantages and drawbacks stemming from operating as a group.

Operating as a group implies that the controlling company and its management may instruct the management of the controlled company and pass a resolution binding on the controlled company. The controlling company may be entitled to appoint and revoke the management and supervisory board members of the controlled company, and determine their remuneration. The members of the management and supervisory board of the controlling company may be appointed to be also the members of the management and supervisory board of the controlled company.

43. Does a controlling company have any particular duties *vis-à-vis* its controlled company shareholders?
The control contract shall include provisions ensuring the predictable and balanced allocation of advantages and drawbacks stemming from operating as a group in order to protect the minority shareholders of the controlled company. Hungarian corporate law does not prescribe such provisions as obligatory, it only gives examples such as the commitments of the controlling company to cover the losses of the controlled company, or supplement the dividends of the shareholders, or exchange the shares, or participate in the reorganisation of the controlled company in the case of a future insolvency. After publishing the decision on operating as a group, the minority shareholders of the controlled private company limited by shares may request the controlling company to purchase their shares at market price but not lower than the value proportionate to the nominal value of the shares from the equity capital.

44. What are the rights of company shareholders when the controlling company puts in place actions and/or transactions that can be prejudicial to the shareholders?

Shareholders of the controlled company having five per cent of the voting rights may request:

(i)   information;

(ii) the convention of the GM of the controlling company; or

(iii) an order from the court of registration mandating an expert to inspect the actions and transactions in order to establish whether they infringe the law or the control contract.

Upon the request of the shareholders or the management of the controlled company, the court of registration may:

(i)   call the controlling company to meet the obligations assumed in the control contract;

(ii) prohibit the operation as a recognised group; or

(iii) apply any action allowed in a so-called judicial supervisory procedure, eg notifying the controlling company to restore the lawful operation, imposing a fine, annulling resolutions infringing the law, appointing a commissioner to supervise the operation and eliminating the company by deleting it from the corporate registry.

45. What are the limitations, if any, to the possibility of owning reciprocal stock interests in companies?

Generally, there are no such limitations. However, if a public company limited by shares acquires control of 25 per cent or more of the voting rights in another company limited by shares or in a limited liability company, henceforward the company limited by shares or the limited liability company shall not be entitled to acquire the shares of the public company limited by shares. Any share in the public company limited by shares acquired previously by such a company shall be alienated within 60 days of the acquisition of control by the public company limited by shares. Failure to comply with this obligation results in the restriction on the exercise of voting rights attached to the shares of the public company limited by shares.

India

Dua Associates Neeraj Kumar, Sanjeev Kaul, Abhinav Rastogi & Jay Badola

BASIC INFORMATION ON THE TYPES OF LIMITED LIABILITY COMPANIES AND ON THE RIGHTS OF SHAREHOLDERS

1. What types of companies enjoy limited liability? If more than one, which ones have shareholders, ie holders of share certificates? Which one is the most common? Which one is mostly used by foreign investors?

There are two types of companies that enjoy limited liability under the Companies Act 1956 (the Act):

- private company (which restricts transfer of shares, restricts number of members, prohibits an invitation to the public to subscribe for any shares/debentures and prohibits the invitation and acceptance of deposits); and
- public company (a company which is not a private company).

The liability of members of a company may be limited by shares or limited by guarantee. In the case of companies limited by shares, the liability is limited to the amount for the time being remaining unpaid on the nominal amount of shares. In the case of companies limited by guarantee and with no share capital, liability is limited to the amount the member has undertaken to contribute to the assets of the company in the event of its being wound up. In the case of companies limited by guarantee and having share capital, liability includes sums remaining unpaid on shares in addition to the amount guaranteed by the member.

The members/shareholders of companies with share capital hold share certificates.

The most common type of company is a private company. Foreign investors mostly prefer to organise their investments/ventures in India as private companies, because private companies enjoy certain privileges/exemptions which are not available to public companies. However, a private company which is a subsidiary of a public company does not enjoy the same privileges and rights as are available to a private company simpliciter. An Indian private company that is a subsidiary of a foreign body corporate, which if incorporated in India would be a public company within the meaning of the Act, will not be deemed to be a subsidiary of a public company in case the entire share capital of the private company is held by one or more bodies corporate incorporated outside India. If any portion of the share capital is held by one or more individuals or by an Indian company, however small the fraction of the shareholding may be, the private company will be treated as a subsidiary of a public company.

A private company shall have a minimum of two shareholders and two directors, whereas a public company shall have a minimum of seven shareholders and three directors.

In terms of section 179 of the Income-tax Act 1961, directors of a private company may under certain circumstances be held liable in respect of recovery of tax due to the company.

2. Are there minimum capital requirements and/or thin capitalisation rules in force?

Yes. The minimum paid-up capital requirement for a private company is INR 100,000 and for a public company is INR 500,000.

3. Describe the types of shares that can be issued by a company and the different rights that they attribute to their owners, as well as any other financial instruments (bonds or other) and other instruments of a participatory nature in the company's capital that can also be issued by the company.

A public company can issue two types of share capital, namely preference share capital and equity share capital.

Preference share capital carries a preferential right to dividends and the repayment of paid-up capital on winding up.

Equity share capital can be of two types: (i) with voting rights; and (ii) with differential rights as to dividend, voting or otherwise.

A private company may issue the above or any other kind of share capital and on terms that it thinks fit. However, as a practice and being mindful of the scheme of the Act, private companies ordinarily restrict their share capital to the aforesaid two types of share capital.

Public companies listed on any recognised stock exchange in India (listed companies) are required under their listing agreements not to issue shares in any manner which may confer on any person superior rights as to voting or dividend *vis-à-vis* the rights on equity shares that are already listed.

Other financial instruments of a participatory nature are convertible debentures (debentures include bonds and any other securities of a company, whether constituting a charge on the assets of the company or not) and warrants. Participatory rights would arise only upon their conversion.

Preference shares or debentures allotted to a foreign investor need to be compulsorily convertible into equity shares to qualify as foreign direct investment (FDI) and to avoid implications under the Reserve Bank of India (RBI)'s guidelines on external commercial borrowing (ECB).

4. Can a company have only one shareholder and still enjoy limited liability?

The Act does not permit a 'one shareholder company'. As stated above, a public company is to have a minimum of seven shareholders and a private company at least two shareholders. Every shareholder who is cognisant of the fact that the company is carrying on business for more than six months with fewer than the mandatory minimum shall be severally liable for the payment of the whole debts of the company contracted during that time and may be severally sued for them.

5.   Are the rights of shareholders the same in any type of company?

Generally, rights attached to the shares are the same in any type of company, unless the company has issued shares with differential rights. The articles of association of a company (Articles) may provide for additional rights to a specific shareholder/shareholders' group provided such rights do not conflict with the provisions of the Act.

6.   What are the basic rights of any shareholder? Describe briefly the rights of minority shareholders and indicate which thresholds, if any, are required to allow the minority shareholders to exercise any such rights.

Basic rights of any shareholder are to:
- attend and vote on resolutions at general meetings (GMs);
- receive copies of the annual report, notice of a GM, declared dividends;
- inspect documents such as the register of members and the minutes of a GM; and
- appoint proxies/authorised representatives for representing the concerned shareholder at any GM.

For rights of minority shareholders, please see response to question 7.

7.   Do all shareholders enjoy the same rights or can some shareholders be attributed specific rights, whether by reason of the particular class of stock owned or other? Are such rights generally provided for at the level of the company's by-laws and/or in shareholders' agreements?

Please see responses to questions 3 and 5.

Additionally, shareholders holding a certain threshold percentage of shares enjoy certain rights and they are:

I.   Shareholder(s) holding at least 10 per cent and up to 25 per cent in the equity share capital/total voting power of a company:
- may call for an extraordinary general meeting of the company (EGM) on requisition;
- may block the holding of an annual general meeting (AGM) or EGM at shorter notice. In the case of an AGM, consent of all shareholders entitled to vote is required for calling such a meeting at shorter notice, and in the case of an EGM, the consent of shareholders holding not less than 95 per cent of the paid-up share capital is required for calling such a meeting at short notice;
- may make an application to the Company Law Board (CLB) for investigating the affairs of the company;
- has the right to apply to the CLB for the prevention of oppression and mismanagement; and

- has the ability to make any application to the CLB alleging that the affairs of the company are being conducted either in a manner which is oppressive to any of its members or in a manner which is prejudicial to the interests of the company or to public interest for seeking an order from the central government to make appointments of such number of persons as directors of the company in order to prevent the affairs of company from being conducted in the said manner.

II. Shareholder(s) holding more than 25 per cent and less than 75 per cent in the equity share capital/total voting power has, in addition to the rights mentioned in point I above, the ability to block any resolution required to be passed as a special resolution at any GM.

III. Shareholder(s) holding more than 50 per cent and less than 75 per cent in the equity share capital/total voting power has, in addition to the rights mentioned in point II above, the ability to pass any resolution (other than a special resolution) required to be passed at any GM.

IV. Shareholder(s) holding 75 per cent or more in the equity share capital/total voting power has (have), in addition to the rights mentioned in point III above, the ability to pass any resolution (including a special resolution) at any GM.

Further, Articles may give additional right(s) to shareholder(s) over and above as provided under the Act subject to such rights being not inconsistent with the provisions of the Act. It should also be mentioned that under the Act certain rights accrue to the shareholders of a company if their number exceeds the prescribed number (eg, as outlined under section 235 (dealing with investigation of the affairs of a company) and section 399 (dealing with right to apply to the CLB for relief in cases of oppression or mismanagement) of the Act).

8. May the rights of shareholders, generally speaking, be limited, modified, suppressed or waived in any way? If so, how? Are such modifications or limitations provided for in the company's by-laws and/or in shareholders' agreements?

The rights of shareholders under the Act cannot be limited or modified or suppressed by a company. However, rights being proprietary in nature can be waived by a shareholder under contractual arrangements between shareholders. Ordinarily, pursuant to contractual arrangements, additional rights (such as a right of presence for constituting a valid quorum at meetings of the board of directors of the company (board) or GM, an affirmative vote on certain reserved matters at board and/or shareholders' level, to nominate directors on the board) can be made available to a shareholder and such rights can be modified or waived. Any such understanding should be reflected in the Articles to make such rights binding on the company to the extent possible and permissible, being mindful of the provisions of the Act.

Just for information, in the case of listed companies such rights would need to be in consonance with the requirements under the listing agreements and any consequences carefully examined with respect to the Securities and Exchange Board of India (Substantial Acquisition of Shares and Takeovers) Regulations 1997, (Takeover Regulations) and other applicable stock market security laws. Further, in the case of listed companies some of the additional contractual rights that may be agreed inter se shareholder(s) groups are not reflected in the Articles for a variety of reasons, including a possible challenge to their legal enforceability, dependency on other shareholders for their support to the relevant resolutions, etc.

GENERAL MEETING OF SHAREHOLDERS (GM) AND VOTING RIGHTS
9. Which decisions are reserved to the competence of the GM?
There are a number of matters prescribed under the Act reserved for decisions to the competence of the GM. Below is an illustrative list of matters that, under the Act, require ordinary resolution (that is, where votes cast in favour of the resolution are greater in number than the votes cast against the resolution):

i.	To issue shares at a discount.
ii.	To issue further shares without pre-emptive rights to non-members with central government approval.**
iii.	If authorised by the Articles, to alter share capital that is to: increase its authorised share capital; consolidate and divide all or any of its share capital into shares of larger amount than the existing shares; convert all or any of the fully paid-up shares into stock and reconvert that stock into fully paid-up shares of any denomination; sub-divide shares into shares of smaller amount; cancel shares not taken or agreed to be taken by any person.
iv.	For: (a) the consideration of balance-sheets and reports of the board of directors and auditors; (b) the declaration of dividend; (c) the appointment of directors in place of those retiring; and (d) the appointment of and fixing of remuneration of auditors. These matters are reserved to the competence of an AGM as ordinary business.†
v.	To appoint another auditor in place of a retiring auditor.
vi.	To fill the casual vacancy of an auditor caused by resignation.
vii.	To remove the statutory auditors.
viii.	To fill the vacancy caused by the retirement of director at an AGM.*
ix.	To appoint a managing director or full-time director.*
x.	To authorise the board to: sell, lease or dispose of any or whole of the undertaking of the company; and borrow money (except a temporary loan) exceeding the aggregate of the paid-up capital of the company and its free reserves.*
xi.	To fix the remuneration of directors including a full-time director or managing director.*
xii.	To appoint a liquidator and to fix the remuneration, in a members' voluntary winding-up.

* Not applicable to a private company unless it is a subsidiary of a public company.
** Not applicable to a private company simpliciter, ie, a private company which is not a subsidiary of a public company.
† AGM/GM can transact any other business as required under the Act or the Articles and such business is termed as special business requiring an explanatory statement to be annexed to the notice convening the AGM/GM.

An illustrative list of matters under the Act requiring special resolution (that is, votes cast in favour of the resolution are not less than three times the number of the votes, if any, cast against the resolution):

i.	To alter the objects clause in the memorandum of association of a company or to change the place of its registered office from one state to another.
ii.	To change the name of a company.
iii.	To alter the Articles.
iv.	To buy back its own shares or other specified securities, subject to compliance with the conditions/ requirements prescribed.
v.	To issue further shares without pre-emptive rights to non-members or to convert loans or debentures into shares.***
vi.	To reduce the share capital.
vii.	To approve a variation of rights of special classes of shares.
viii.	To commence any new line of business.***
ix.	To request the government to investigate the affairs of the company and to appoint inspectors for the purpose.
x.	To fix the remuneration of directors, where the Articles require such resolution.***
xi.	To authorise payment of remuneration by way of a commission to a director who is neither in the whole-time employment of the company nor a managing director on the basis of a percentage of net profits, if their remuneration does not include anything by way of monthly payment.***
xii.	To approve the holding of an office or place of profit under the company or its subsidiary in certain cases.
xiii.	To make loans and investments, provide guarantee or security in excess of the prescribed limits.***
xiv.	To wind up the company voluntarily..

***Not applicable to a private company simpliciter, ie, a private company which is not a subsidiary of a public company.

10. How does a shareholder participate in a GM? Are there any limitations to having a minimum number of shares? May a shareholder delegate attendance to another shareholder or to the board? May a shareholder obtain assistance from the courts or any other governmental body to intervene in a GM or to cause one to be held in some particular cases?

A shareholder attending a GM (either by themselves or through proxy or, in the case of a body corporate shareholder, through an authorised representative/their proxy) can participate in voting by way of a show of hands or at a poll, as the case may be. We may add that in the case of a public company a proxy is not entitled to vote except on a poll unless the Articles provide otherwise. Further, in the case of listed companies, certain prescribed matters are required to be voted by way of a postal ballot by shareholders.

There are no limitations to having a minimum number of shares for participating in a GM.

A body corporate shareholder can designate any person including a director on the board to represent it as its authorised representative. An individual shareholder can appoint any person including a director on the board as their proxy.

Any shareholder may apply to the CLB for a direction to call or direct the calling of an AGM, if the same has not been held as per the Act. A shareholder may also make such an application in respect of any other GM.

A shareholder may also obtain relief from a civil court, the CLB or the central government, if they are able to show to the court/CLB/central government a serious case of detriment being caused to their interest, to the company's interest or to the public interest. Such intervention may, in appropriate cases, be granted by way of immediate order, which may even extend to injuncting the holding of any meeting (whether a GM or a board meeting), directing that the meeting refrain from considering certain agenda items or directing that, while certain agenda items may be discussed and agreed, the decision taken will not be implemented by the company until allowed by the court/CLB/central government.

11. May a GM be called and held at the request of any shareholder? Is there a threshold regarding the percentage of the stock interest owned in the company that may entitle a shareholder to such a right?

A shareholder cannot call and hold an AGM by themselves. However, in the case of a company having a share capital, any shareholder(s) holding at least one-tenth of the paid-up capital carrying voting rights or, in the case of a company without share capital, one-tenth of the total voting power, may requisition the board to call an EGM. If the board does not within 21 days from the date of deposit of a valid requisition in regard to any matter, proceed duly to call an EGM for the consideration of those matters on a day not later than 45 days from the date of the deposit of the requisition, the meeting may be called amongst others by the requisitionists themselves.

12. May a shareholder bring up an issue to be resolved upon and put it to a vote if it is not included on the agenda? May a shareholder require more information from the GM and/or the board concerning the agenda of the GM, to be put in a better position to exercise their vote?

A shareholder cannot bring up an issue to be resolved upon and put it to a vote at the GM if it was not included in the agenda/notice convening the GM. However, subject to the provisions of the Act (section 188), shareholders not being less than the specified number or not holding less than the specified voting power are entitled to make a requsition to the company to circulate to all the members of the company: a resolution to be moved at an AGM; or a statement with respect to the matter referred to in any resolution proposed to be passed at a GM.

Under the Act, notice convening a GM is required to be accompanied with an explanatory statement in respect of any special business detailing all the material facts and information relevant to the proposed resolution. A shareholder may, before a meeting, request more information that would make them better placed to vote. Such requested information must be material and pertinent to the proposed resolution. Any resolution that is passed on insufficient disclosure of material information in a notice may be held invalid.

13. May a GM be held by telecommunication means and/or by correspondence (ie by written consent)?
A GM cannot be held by telecommunication means and/or by correspondence. However, as aforesaid, in the case of listed companies certain prescribed matters are required to be voted by way of a postal ballot.

14. Are voting rights always proportionate to the stock held by each shareholder or can they vary by share class?
On a poll voting rights on equity shares are always proportionate to the stock held by each shareholder, unless a company has issued equity shares with differential rights as to voting and dividends. Each shareholder is entitled to one vote, on a show of hands.

15. Are there non-voting shares? Is there a maximum percentage of capital represented by non-voting shares?
Under the Act a public company cannot issue any capital which is non-voting. However, it would appear that a private company in addition to having voting equity share capital may also issue a separate class of shares having no voting rights.

16. Can shareholders group their shares in order to exercise their voting rights (eg, by trust, shareholders' agreement or otherwise)?
Voting/pooling agreements between shareholder groups are not unknown to Indian company law. However, the use of proxies is far more common.

17. Under what circumstances can a shareholder challenge the resolutions adopted by the GM? Are there thresholds concerning the stock interest owned to be able to bring such a claim?
A shareholder may challenge the resolution adopted by the GM by showing that the same would be detrimental to the interests of the company, its shareholders or to the public. The courts and CLB, through a long line of decisions, have delineated the circumstances in which such powers may be invoked by a shareholder, and the general rule is that it is not each and every non-observance of company law, failure to comply with required procedures, or even a stray illegality that would give rise to such circumstances. It is only where the complainant shareholder shows that the affairs of the company are being conducted in a manner oppressive to any shareholder, that is, in a manner that shows consistent conduct on behalf of the majority which is harsh, burdensome and wrong towards the complaining shareholders, that the court/CLB/central government may intervene. Though company

law requires that shareholders approaching the CLB with such a complaint need to be not less than 100 members of the company in number or not less than one-tenth of the total number of its members (whichever is less), or members holding not less than one-tenth of the issued share capital of the company, there is a power that permits such an application even where the thresholds outlined are not met. In any case there is no threshold of this kind for a shareholder seeking to approach a civil court.

18. What are the terms and procedures to challenge a resolution of the GM?

Although no specific time frame is prescribed for approaching the court/ CLB, shareholders are advised to make their complaints without undue delay and preferably before the next GM. The procedure might entail filing a civil case or making a complaint by way of petition to one or other authority. It is usual that an application for urgent interim orders be made at the time of such filing, prior notice of which should be served on the company and the opposite party. Such applications are heard in a relatively short period, that is to say within a week of their being filed, and at the hearing an interim order may or may not be passed. Thereafter such matters follow the usual litigation procedures such as the filing of reply by the opposite party, rejoinder by the complaining petitioner and other interim application as necessary. While the civil court holds a full trial the procedure followed by the CLB is summary and matters are almost always heard on affidavits. It should also be mentioned that the jurisdiction of the CLB is discretionary as is the jurisdiction of the civil court entertaining a suit for specific relief and, therefore, at times courts have a tendency to leave matters to be decided by the majority of the shareholders in a court-supervised GM rather than by adjudication.

SHAREHOLDERS' RIGHTS VERSUS DIRECTORS AND DUTIES OF OTHER CORPORATE BODIES IN THE COMPANY

19. What is the procedure for the appointment/replacement/ revocation of directors and of statutory auditors, if any?

Directors – appointment/replacement

In a public company, directors are appointed by shareholders in a GM. Unless Articles provide for the retirement of all directors at every AGM, not less than two-thirds of the total number of directors shall be persons whose period of office is liable to determination by retirement by rotation. One-third of such of the directors who for the time being are liable to retire by rotation shall retire from office at every AGM. Retiring directors are eligible to seek re-appointment. Casual vacancies in the office of director (due to death, resignation, or disqualification, etc) can, subject to the provisions of the Articles, be filled in by the board at its meeting.

In a private company, directors are appointed or replaced according to the terms of the Articles.

Additionally and subject to the Articles, in both private and public companies, the board may appoint:

- additional directors to hold office up to the date of the next AGM; and
- alternate directors, to hold office in place of an original director during their absence for at least three months from the state in which board meetings are ordinarily held.

Directors – revocation

The office of a director shall become vacant on the happening of any of the events specifically prescribed under the Act. In the case of a private company simpliciter Articles can provide for additional grounds for vacation of the office of the director (eg withdrawal of nomination by the nominating shareholder).

Further, the company can remove a director by an ordinary resolution pursuant to receipt from a shareholder of a special notice of a resolution to remove a director. The Act provides for an elaborate process to be complied with in relation to removal of a director.

Auditors – appointment/replacement/revocation

Auditors of a company (other than a government company) are appointed by the shareholders in the AGM and hold office as such until the conclusion of the next AGM. If the retiring auditor is not to be re-appointed, a special notice is required for the appointment of a new auditor. Vacancies in the office of auditors due to resignation are filled at a GM and any other casual vacancy may be filled by the board. Auditors appointed in a GM may be removed before the expiry of their term only by the company in a GM after obtaining the previous approval of the central government. Where no auditors are appointed or re-appointed at an AGM, the central government may appoint a person to fill the vacancy.

The first auditors of the company can be appointed by the board within one month of the date of the registration of the company, failing which the first auditors are to be appointed by the company in the GM.

20. May shareholders challenge the resolutions of the board of directors? Is there a minimum percentage of capital required to challenge a board resolution?

Generally if the board has passed resolutions in compliance with the Act and which are not ultra vires the memorandum of association of the company or the Articles, it is difficult to challenge such resolutions and the courts in India are reluctant to interfere with the management decisions taken in the best judgement of the directors unless it can be proved that the directors acted mala fide or for their personal aggrandisement to the detriment of the company or acted in an oppressive manner with ulterior motive. Please also refer to the response to question 17, which to a greater extent applies here as well.

21. Are shareholders entitled to bring a legal action against the directors of the company? In which circumstances? Please describe briefly the principles of directors' liability.

Directors of the company have a fiduciary duty to the company and do not have such a duty to an individual shareholder. Under exceptional circumstances the shareholders may approach the civil court to lodge and prove a case to show that wrongdoers are in control of the company. In this regard, Indian law follows the rules of English law whereby shareholders in certain extreme circumstances acquire or derive the right to protect the interest of the company against its management. Instances of such actions are, however, rare.

Under the Act the ultimate control and management of the company vests with the board of directors. Directors are therefore liable for offences of companies under various statutes. In other words, therefore, directors are vicariously liable for an offence committed by a company merely by virtue of holding such office. Vicarious liability can be either civil liability or criminal liability. In India directors being vicariously held for civil liability is extremely rare and this arises only either in exceptional cases where there is widespread damage to the public at large by gross acts of negligence of the company, or under some direct and indirect tax statutes where a director of a private limited company is personally liable for arrears of tax payable by the company under certain circumstances. As for criminal liability, this arises as and when a company commits an offence under the offences and penalties chapter in any statute applicable to the company and since the company cannot face imprisonment, it is the directors who are impleaded as co-accused and, if the offence is proved at trial, it is the directors who normally face the punishment. It may be noted, however, that the offences committed by the company are mostly bailable offences. However, before the actual prosecution or trial commences most statutes provide for an opportunity for the company to justify the impugned action and, therefore, the directors are rarely taken by surprise. Since the criminal justice system follows the principle of culpability only if *mens rea* (criminal intent) is established, non-working directors do get an opportunity to defend themselves and seek discharge on the grounds that they were not concerned or involved with the day-to-day management of the company and the events that led to the offence.

It is possible, depending on the facts, for a director to be personally liable for a criminal offence if the offence is directly attributed to a culpable or negligent act which results in a crime under the Indian Penal Code, which is the general criminal statute that defines crime and prescribes punishment.

22. What are the rights in connection with transactions where the directors have a conflict of interest situation?

Various provisions contained in the Act aim to strengthen corporate governance measures. To mention a few, board sanction and/or central government approval is required for certain kinds of contracts in which a director is interested (section 297), disclosure to the board of the nature of interest or concern felt by directors in any contract or arrangement entered into or to be entered into by the company (section 299); an interested director is not to participate or vote in board proceedings (section 300); directors and their relatives are not to hold office or a place of profit in the company (section 314).

Additionally, in the case of listed companies, the listing agreement with the stock exchanges requires among other things a company to make various disclosures, which include disclosures to the audit committee with respect to related party transactions, transactions not in the normal course of business and material transactions which are not on an arm's-length basis.

INFORMATION RIGHTS ON THE COMPANY'S BUSINESS

23. What information may be requested by the shareholders from the board concerning the general state of the company's business or any specific transaction? Are information rights different depending on the number of shares owned? Are shareholders entitled to receive written information before, during or after the GM about the meeting agenda and to what extent? Is it possible for a shareholder to obtain a copy of the minutes of the GM?

The shareholders under the Act are entitled to receive all the relevant material and information concerning matters which require approval of the shareholders (please see response to question 9) at a GM. Such information is provided in the explanatory statement annexed to the notice convening the GM or the resolution to be approved by postal ballot. Further, shareholders are also entitled to receive copies of the annual report prior to their approval and adoption at the AGM. Listed companies are also required to make various disclosures to the stock exchanges including in relation to price-sensitive information, events having a bearing on the financial performance and state of affairs of the company, etc. Further, should a shareholder require more information on any matter requiring shareholder approval they can approach the company for the same.

The right to receive the documents and information as above is not linked to or dependent upon the number of shares owned. Any clarification or more information on the matters can be sought before or during the meeting. Any shareholder is entitled to be furnished with a copy of the minutes of a GM within seven days of their request in that respect to the company.

24. Do shareholders have the right/duty to resolve in the GM upon matters which were not on the agenda?

Please see response to question 12.

25. Are shareholders entitled to inspect the corporate books and/or any other corporate or accounting documents? To what extent? Can they do it through external counsel or advisors?

Shareholders are not entitled to inspect the account books and other books and papers of a company. However, they can inspect and take extracts of certain statutory registers and returns such as registers of members, loans and investments, directors, charges, etc. Such inspections can be made subject to any reasonable restrictions as to the timing and duration of the inspection as the Article may provide. The inspection can be made through external counsel or advisors.

SHAREHOLDERS' AGREEMENTS

26. Are shareholders' agreements validly enforceable? What are their typical contents and term of duration? Are they enforceable by or against third parties and, if so, to what extent?

Shareholders' agreements are enforceable as between the contracting shareholders. However, for the contracting shareholders to enforce the relevant provisions of the shareholders' agreement against the joint venture company (eg, a right of a contracting shareholder to nominate representatives on the board of the joint venture company) care should be taken to ensure that the relevant provisions of such agreement are reflected in the Articles. It is important to remember that: the provisions of the Act have effect notwithstanding anything to the contrary contained in any such agreement; and any provision contained in such an agreement shall, to the extent to which it is repugnant to the provisions of the Act, become or be void, as the case may be.

Typical contents of shareholders' agreements pertain or relate to the management of a joint venture company, constitution and composition of its board, conduct of and proceedings at the board meetings and GM, increase in and future induction of share capital, provision on transfer of shares, exit options, assignment, non-compete and non-solicitation and the usual provisions such as arbitration, confidentiality, termination, etc. In view of the provisions of the Act providing for free transferability of the shares of public companies the enforceability of provisions for right of first refusal, tag- and drag-along rights is questionable but on the other hand restrictions on the transfer of shares are necessarily required to be provided in the Articles in the case of a private company. It may be added that conflicting judgements have been pronounced by the High Courts of different states on the enforceability of the right of first refusal in respect of shares of a public limited company.

The term of shareholders' agreements is the period for which the contracting shareholders continue to hold their respective shareholdings in the company and upon exit of any of the parties (or when such shareholding falls below a stated minimum) the shareholders' agreement comes to an end. Further, it is also usual to address the consequences upon change in control of any party in the shareholders' agreement.

Apart from a few situations third parties cannot intervene or complain against agreements between shareholders. The FDI policy of the government of India provides that prior approval of the government would be required for new proposals for foreign investment and technical collaboration in cases where the foreign investor has an existing joint venture or technology transfer or trade mark agreement in the 'same' field in India as on 12 January 2005. If the existing Indian partner does not provide a no-objection the partner has a right to oppose the foreign investor's second joint venture with another person.

Any person complaining against a shareholders' agreement should be able to show that the action complained about is beyond the powers of the company and causes sufficient detriment to themselves, the company or the public interest, as to call for the intervention of a court.

27. Do shareholders' agreements have to be disclosed to the public or registered in any public registry?

Shareholders' agreements are, generally, not required to be disclosed to the public or registered in any public registry. However, under the FDI policy of the government of India there are certain sectors where there is a cap on FDI (such as defence, telecommunication, insurance etc), the *inter se* agreements between shareholders are required to be disclosed to the approving authority. The approving authority will consider such *inter se* agreements for determining ownership and control when considering the case for granting approval for foreign investment.

ECONOMIC RIGHTS AND RIGHTS OVER THE STOCK

28. Is the stock always freely transferable? Are there any legal limitations? Are there any restrictions on contractual limitations?

As per the Act, the shares/stock in a private company are not freely transferable and transfer is governed by restrictions contained in the Articles.

As per the Act, shares in a public company are freely transferable. Any provision in the Articles restricting such free transfer will be *ultra vires* and not enforceable.

Please also see response to question 26.

29. Are shareholders entitled to pledge their stock?

Shareholders are entitled to pledge their stock and shares. In the case of shareholders who are resident outside India, prior permission of the RBI is required for them to pledge their shares held in an Indian company.

In the case of listed companies the promoters are required to disclose details of shares pledged by them in accordance with the listing agreement and the Takeover Regulations.

30. Are there financial assistance issues to be considered and other prohibitions to be evaluated in the context of a leveraged buyout transaction?

In the context of a leveraged buyout transaction, assuming that the question relates to borrowing and leverage from persons resident outside India by an Indian corporation for the acquisition of shares and involves the pledge of such shares as collateral for the borrowed funds, utilisation of such borrowed funds (being ECB) is not permitted for on-lending or investment in the capital market or acquiring a company (or a part of one) in India by a corporation.

31. May a company buy back its own stock and, if so, under what circumstances and subject to which limitations?

Yes, a company may purchase its own shares (buyback) out of
(i) its free reserves;
(ii) securities premium account; or
(iii) proceeds of any shares or other specified securities.

No buyback is permitted by a company unless among others the following requirements are met:
- the buyback is authorised by its Articles;
- a special resolution is passed in the GM authorising the buyback. However, for a buyback of up to 10 per cent of the total paid-up equity capital and free reserves only a board resolution is required;
- the buyback is equal to or less than 25 per cent of the total paid-up capital and free reserves of the company, provided that the buyback of equity shares in any financial year does not exceed 25 per cent of its total paid-up equity capital in that financial year;
- the ratio of debt owed by the company is not more than twice the capital and its free reserves after such a buyback;
- all the shares for a buyback are fully paid up; and
- the buyback of the shares with respect to companies other than listed companies is in accordance with the Private Limited Company and Unlisted Public Limited Company (Buyback of Securities) Rules 1999.

A company cannot buy back its shares if, among other things, a default by the company in the repayment of a deposit or interest payable thereon, the redemption of debentures or preference shares or the payment of a dividend to any shareholder or the repayment of any term loan or interest payable thereon to any financial institution or bank, is subsisting.

32. Is there a legal right to withdraw from the company and, if so, under what circumstances? How is the shareholders' stock valued and paid in such a case?

Yes, shareholders can withdraw from the company by selling their shareholding or shares. Shares of a private company can be transferred subject to restrictions in the Articles. Shares of a public company are freely transferable.

The transfer of shares under the automatic route by way of sale from a person resident in India to a person resident outside India and *vice versa* requires compliance with the pricing guidelines prescribed by the RBI. The transfer of shares otherwise than by way of sale or at a price not in consonance with such pricing guidelines requires regulatory approvals.

33. In which circumstances can dividends be distributed among shareholders? Is it possible to exclude or limit the right of certain shareholders to dividends? Does a certain portion of the profits need to be set aside in a reserve fund where it cannot be distributed to the shareholders? Are advances on dividends allowed and, if so, under which circumstances? Can advances on dividends be reclaimed by the company?

A dividend can be distributed by a company out of its distributable profits, having been arrived at in accordance with the Act. Subject to prescribed rules, in the event of the inadequacy or absence of profits in any year, the dividend can be declared out of the accumulated profits transferred to the reserves.

A company cannot exclude or limit the right of certain shareholders to the dividends to which they are entitled.

Where a proposed dividend exceeds 10 per cent, 12.5 per cent, 15 per cent or 20 per cent of the paid-up capital of a company, then at least 2.5 per cent, five per cent, 7.5 per cent or 10 per cent respectively of current profits are to be transferred to the reserves. A company can voluntarily transfer to reserves a percentage higher than 10 per cent subject to the prescribed conditions.

Advances on dividends are not allowed.

34. What are the rights of shareholders in the case of an issue of new stock (increase of the company's corporate capital) (pre-emption rights)?

The rights of shareholders in the case of an issue of new stock by a private company are governed by its Articles. The Articles ordinarily provide for pre-emptive rights in respect of a further issue of capital.

In the case of public companies where at any time after the expiry of two years from the formation of a company or at any time after the expiry of one year from the allotment of shares made for the first time after its formation, whichever is earlier, further issue of shares is proposed, the new shares need to be first offered to the existing shareholders in proportion to their shareholding in the company prior to such issue. However, further or new shares may be offered to any person(s) on a preferential allotment basis if the necessary special resolution to that effect is passed at the GM; or failing which an ordinary resolution is passed at the GM and the same is then approved by the central government.

35. May minority shareholders ban or limit the company's capital structure in any manner?

Minority shareholders acting by way of derivative action may occasionally get a court to restrain issuance of further capital or hold such issuance invalid or in abeyance if they are able to show that wrongdoers are in control of the company. Such orders are considered extreme and may be granted where shareholding has been unjustifiably created. Further, a minority holding more than 25 per cent of the equity shareholding in a company can block a special resolution of the company to increase share capital by way of preferential allotment.

36. Which are the financial assistance prohibitions in force?

With regard to prohibitions in force on financial assistance for the purchase or subscription of shares in an Indian company, the Act inter alia provides that no public company, or private company that is a subsidiary of a public company, can give, directly or indirectly, any financial assistance (by means of a loan, guarantee, the provision of security or otherwise) for the purpose of or in connection with a purchase or subscription made or to be made by any person of or for any shares in the company or in its holding company. However, the above prohibition is not applicable in certain specified cases.

37. Apart from publicly listed companies, in which cases (if any) are shareholders obligated to obtain an authorisation from, or provide information to, a public authority about events that have an impact on their stock interest in the company?

A shareholder is not obligated to obtain an authorisation from, or provide information to, a public authority about events that have an impact on their stock interest in the company.

SHAREHOLDERS' RIGHTS IN THE CASE OF EXTRAORDINARY TRANSACTIONS AND/OR WINDING-UP

38. What rights are available to shareholders in the case of a sale of all or a substantial portion of the company's assets? In the case of a merger or de-merger?

The board is empowered to sell the assets of the company. However, in the case of a public company, or a private company that is a subsidiary of a public company, shareholders' prior consent at a GM is required for the board to sell, lease or otherwise dispose of the whole, or substantially the whole, of the undertaking of the company and the shareholders may give such consent subject to conditions.

Shareholders have a right to vote on and approve a scheme of arrangement involving a merger or de-merger. A scheme of arrangement involving a merger or de-merger can be implemented only if sanctioned by the relevant court(s). Before a scheme is sanctioned by the court(s), the scheme is required to be approved by the shareholders at the court-convened meetings of shareholders or class of shareholders and, where required, of the creditors or class of creditors, as the case may be. Such approval must be by a majority in number representing three-fourths in value of the creditors, or class of creditors, or members or class of members as the case may be, present and voting either in person or by proxy, at such meeting(s). Once the court sanctions the scheme it becomes binding on all the creditors, all the creditors of the class, all the members or all the members of the class, as the case may be, and also on the company.

39. Which rights are available to shareholders in the case of conversion of the company into a European Company (SE) or into another type of company?

In India there is no concept of an SE. Under the Act it is possible to convert a public company into a private company and *vice versa* subject to necessary compliances with the relevant provisions. Such conversion also requires a special resolution to be passed at the GM.

40. Which rights are available to shareholders of a company in liquidation?

The principal right of shareholders in liquidation (whether members' or creditors' voluntary winding-up or winding-up by the court) is to receive surplus assets of the company according to their right and interests in the company after having applied, subject to preferential payments, the assets

of the company in satisfaction of its liabilities. The other rights in the case
of members' voluntary winding-up include the right to appoint and fix the
remuneration of the liquidator and to fill any such vacancy; and the right to
be called to a GM by the liquidator, in cases where the winding-up continues
for more than a year.

41. Can shareholders cause the liquidation of the company? How?
Yes, shareholders can cause the winding-up/liquidation of the company *inter
alia* by:
* passing an ordinary resolution in a GM requiring the company to be
  wound up voluntarily: (i) on expiry of the period fixed for the duration
  of the company in the Articles; or (ii) on the occurrence of an event
  which the Articles provide that the company is to be dissolved;
* passing a special resolution in a GM that the company be wound up: (i)
  voluntarily; or (ii) by the court; and
* making an application to the court on just and equitable grounds. Such
  grounds could be oppression, mismanagement, where the substratum of
  the company has gone etc. The court may order winding up only if an
  alternative remedy is not available.

COMPANY GROUPS
42. Is the concept of 'group' recognised as such under specific legislation? What are the implications?
Yes, the concept of 'group' companies is recognised under specific
legislations, eg, under the Competition Act 2002, the Companies Act 1956,
the Income-tax Act 1961, the Takeover Regulations and the Securities and
Exchange Board of India (Prohibition of Insider Trading) Regulations 1992
(Insider Regulations).

Briefly speaking the concept of group assumes significance for certain
purposes such as:
* The Competition Act 2002, in relation to determining anti-competitive
  agreements and abuse of dominant position and implications
  thereunder. The concept of group would also assume significance in
  relation to combinations including mergers and acquisitions once their
  provisions are notified for being implemented.
* The Companies Act 1956, in relation to the preparation of consolidated
  financial statements and restrictions on the acquisition of certain shares
  under certain specified circumstances.
* The Income-tax Act 1961, in relation to transfer pricing.
* The Takeover Regulations, in relation to making disclosures and availing
  of an exemption from a public announcement/offer for the *inter se*
  transfer of shares of a listed company amongst group of companies,
  provided certain prescribed conditions are fulfilled, and for determining
  persons acting in concert, promoter groups, an acquirer etc.
* The Insider Regulations, in relation to making disclosures and
  determining whether a person is deemed to be a connected person for
  the definition of 'insider', who is reasonably expected to have access to

unpublished, price-sensitive information in respect of the securities of a company.

43. Does a controlling company have any particular duties *vis-à-vis* its controlled company shareholders?

The controlling company as a shareholder does not *per se* have any particular duties to the other shareholders of the controlled company. The general rule is that the controlling shareholder should not cause the conduct of the business and affairs of the company to be undertaken in a manner which is prejudicial to the interests of the controlled company or any of its other shareholders.

44. What are the rights of company shareholders when the controlling company puts in place actions and/or transactions that can be prejudicial to the shareholders?

Unless the Articles or inter se shareholders agreement(s) provide(s) for any restrictions on the actions and/or transactions that a company can or cannot undertake, the other shareholders do not have any rights when the controlling company puts in place actions and/or transactions in its controlled company that can be prejudicial to the business of the shareholders.

However, if the company shareholders can demonstrate acts of oppression/ mismanagement by the controlling shareholder that are also prejudicial to the interests of the controlled company or its shareholders or public interest, those shareholders can seek appropriate remedies as discussed in response to question 17.

45. What are the limitations, if any, to the possibility of owning reciprocal stock interests in companies?

Under the Act the only limitation to the possibility of owning reciprocal stock interests in companies is that a subsidiary cannot hold shares in or be a member of its holding company.

Israel

Goldfarb Levy Eran Meiri Tzafrir & Co
Ido Gonen & Michal Matthews

BASIC INFORMATION ON THE TYPES OF LIMITED LIABILITY COMPANIES AND ON THE RIGHTS OF THE SHAREHOLDERS

1. What types of companies enjoy limited liability? If more than one, which ones have shareholders, ie holders of share certificates? Which one is the most common? Which one is mostly used by foreign investors?

In Israel there is only one type of company that enjoys limited liability. Such a limited liability company is referred to as a 'Ltd' type company. It should be noted that partnerships can be comprised of partners having limited liability.

2. Are there minimum capital requirements and/or thin capitalisation rules in force?

Generally, there are no capital requirements in order to establish a company. The capital of a company may be composed of shares having certain par value (such par value can be minimal), or of shares having no par value, yet a company cannot be composed of both shares having par value and of shares having no par value. Certain companies, such as insurance companies and other financial institutions are required to hold minimal capital as a pre-requirement for their conduct of business and operations.

As to thin capitalisation, in general, under the 'lifting the corporate veil' doctrine, in exceptional circumstances where the court finds that a company has an unreasonable debt to equity ratio, it can place personal liability on the company's shareholders.

3. Describe the types of shares that can be issued by a company and the different rights that they attribute to their owners, as well as any other financial instruments (bonds or other) and other instruments of a participatory nature in the company's capital that can also be issued by the company.

The customary types of shares issued by a company are: ordinary shares; shares conferring the holders of them with preferred rights; shares conferring the holders of them with deferred rights; voting/non-voting shares; redeemable shares and management shares. Each type of share allows the holders of them equal rights.

The ordinary shares usually attribute to the holder the three following rights:

(i) the right to vote in respect of each ordinary share held by them;

(ii) the right to participate in dividend distributions; and

(iii) the right to participate in the company's asset distribution upon liquidation.

The preferred shares usually entitle the holders to preferential rights such as: veto rights, management rights, priority at dividend distribution and priority at distribution of the company's assets upon liquidation.

The law provides all shareholders with basic rights (as described in question 6 below). Other and additional rights (whether preferential or not) are usually referred to in shareholders' agreements/founders' agreements and/or the company's by-laws (referred to in Israel as 'articles of association'). In this matter it should be clarified that the articles of association of a company bind both the company and its shareholders, whereas shareholders' agreements/founders' agreements do not bind the company. This notwithstanding, shareholders' agreements/founders' agreements to which the company is also a party should be considered.

Additional financial instruments which companies usually issue are: notes, bonds, convertible bonds, convertible notes and options.

4.   Can a company have only one shareholder and still enjoy limited liability?

In Israel a company can have one shareholder and still enjoy limited liability.

5.   Are the rights of shareholders the same in any type of company?

As there is only one type of limited liability company in Israel, this question is not applicable.

6.   What are the basic rights of any shareholder? Describe briefly the rights of minority shareholders and indicate which thresholds, if any, are required to allow the minority shareholders to exercise any such rights.

The basic rights attributed to all shareholders in a company under the Companies Law (1999, effective from February 2000) (in the event there is only one class of shares) are:

- the right to receive certain information (as detailed in questions 23 and 24 below);
- the right to receive invitations and participate in shareholders' general meetings (GM);
- the right to demand the convening of a GM (as described in answers 10 and 11 below);
- the right not to be discriminated against;
- the right to file a derivative action on behalf of the company, and a class action against the company; and
- the right to require that certain matters will be included in the agenda of a GM (as described in question 12 below).

The aforementioned rights are basic rights attributed to shareholders in a company, whether such shareholders are minority shareholders or not, and other than the thresholds detailed in questions 10, 12 and 23 below, no threshold is required in order to allow the shareholders to exercise the aforementioned rights.

7. Do all shareholders enjoy the same rights or can some shareholders be attributed specific rights, whether by reason of the particular class of stock owned or other? Are such rights generally provided for at the level of the company's by-laws and/or in shareholders' agreements?

Shareholders of a company are not required to hold the same rights, yet shareholders within the same class must hold the same rights, meaning that companies can comprise shareholders holding different classes of shares, but within the same class of shares the rights of shareholders are the same.

The rights of shareholders are provided in the company's articles of association and in some cases also in founders' agreements/shareholders' agreements (it should be noted in this respect that only articles of association which were registered in the Israeli Registrar of Companies can be binding upon third parties, while founders' agreements/shareholders' agreements can only bind the parties to it).

8. May the rights of shareholders, generally speaking, be limited, modified, suppressed or waived in any way? If so, how? Are such modifications or limitations provided for in the company's by-laws and/or in shareholders' agreements?

The general principle is that the rights of the shareholders can be modified (and even suppressed) by a majority vote of a GM by the shareholders present at the GM, and the modification (and suppression) of rights granted to a certain class of shareholders requires the additional majority vote of shareholders of the same class of shares present at a class meeting. However, a higher majority can be required according to the company's articles of association, shareholders' agreements/founders' agreements or under certain provisions of applicable law. It should be noted that if the rights are established pursuant to a founders' agreement/shareholders' agreement, unless such agreement states otherwise, according to contract law principles the modification of such a right is subject to the consent of all the shareholders party to the founders' agreement/shareholders' agreement.

GENERAL MEETING OF SHAREHOLDERS (GM) AND VOTING RIGHTS

9. Which decisions are reserved to the competence of the GM?

The following decisions are decisions reserved to the competence of the GM (in both listed (publicly traded) and non-listed (private) companies):

- Modification of the company's articles of association.
- Determination that the company's board of directors is incapable of functioning or is incapable of exercising its powers, and therefore the GM is to assume the powers of the company's board of directors.

- Appointment of the company's auditor, and approval of its engagement terms and termination of it.
- Appointment of the company's external directors.
- Appointment of the company's directors, unless provided otherwise in the company's articles of association.
- Approval, under certain limitations and conditions, of an action done by an office holder of the company (as the term 'office holder' is defined in the Companies Law, ie, a director, general manager, chief business manager, deputy general manager, vice-general manager, any other person performing any of these positions in the company even if they hold a different title, and any other manager directly subordinated to the general manager of the company) which: (a) conflicts with the interests of their role in the company; or (b) competes with the company's business; or (c) was done while taking advantage of a business opportunity of the company, and other certain transactions of the company where the office holder has an interest.
- Approval of the company's engagement with a director with respect to the director's terms of office, including an exemption from liability, insurance and indemnification, as well as the company's engagement with a director with respect to other roles of that director in the company.
- Approval of certain private placements.
- In listed companies only: (1) approval of an extraordinary transaction (as the term 'extraordinary transaction' is defined in the Companies Law, ie: (i) a transaction not in a company's ordinary course of business; (ii) a transaction that is not undertaken in market conditions; and/or (iii) a transaction that is likely to substantially influence the profitability of a company, the company's properties or the company's liabilities) which has been entered into by the listed company and a controlling party of it (as the term 'control' is defined in the Israeli Securities Law of 1968, ie, the ability to direct the activity of a company, except for ability stemming only from being a director or holding another position in a company, and it is presumed that a person or entity is controlling a company if said person or entity holds at least half of: (i) the right to vote in the GM; or (ii) the right to appoint the directors or the general manager of that company, including a person or entity holding 25 per cent or more of the voting rights in the GM of the company if there is no other person/entity who holds more than 50 per cent of the voting rights in the company of the company); or (2) an extraordinary transaction (as the term is defined above) entered between the listed company and another person or entity which a controlling party (as the term is defined above) has personal interest in (as the term 'personal interest' is defined in the Companies Law, ie, a person's personal interest in an act or a transaction of the company, including, without limitation, the personal interest of said person's relative and of another entity in which said person or said person's relative is an interested party, excluding a personal interest that stems from the fact of holding shares in the company); or (3)

a private placement in which the controlling party (as the term is defined above) has personal interest in (as the term is defined above); or (4) the company's engagement with a controlling party (as the term is defined above) or with a relative, if that party is also an office holder (as such terms is defined in question 9 above) or an employee of the company with respect to the terms of condition of their employment terms.

- Approval of changes in the company's capitalisation.
- Approval of a merger of the company.

It should be noted that the company's articles of association and shareholders' agreements/founders' agreements can add additional decisions that are reserved to the competence of the GM (or are reserved to the competence of certain classes of shareholders).

10. How does a shareholder participate in a GM? Are there any limitations to having a minimum number of shares? May a shareholder delegate attendance to another shareholder or to the board? May a shareholder obtain assistance from the courts or any other governmental body to intervene in a GM or to cause one to be held in some particular cases?

In non-listed companies a shareholder has the right to receive an invitation to participate in the GM at least seven days before the date the GM convenes, and not more than 45 days before the GM convenes. However, the GM can resolve without convening and without an invitation if the decision is unanimously resolved upon by all shareholders.

In listed companies, notice of a GM is to be published in Israeli newspapers 21 days before the GM convenes, unless otherwise provided in the company's articles of association (in certain events where special decisions are to be resolved a 35-day prior notice is required).

A shareholder is not required to hold a minimum number of shares in order to participate in a GM.

Unless provided otherwise in the company's articles of association, shareholders may vote on their own or by proxy (who may be a member of the company's board of directors). In listed companies, with respect to certain decisions, shareholders may also vote by a deed of vote in which they state their way of voting (for, against or abstention).

Shareholders are entitled to apply to a competent court and request that the court rule the convening of an annual meeting in the event an annual meeting did not take place (in principle, every company is required to hold an annual meeting not later than 15 months after the preceding GM, yet, non-listed companies, under certain circumstances, are exempted from this requirement to conduct an annual meeting unless a shareholder or a director has requested an annual meeting be convened).

In addition, where a GM cannot actually be convened or cannot be conducted in the manner set out in the company's articles of association or in the Companies Law, a shareholder entitled to vote at a GM may apply to a competent court and request that the court rule the convening of a GM and the manner by which the GM is to be conducted.

11. May a GM be called and held at the request of any shareholder? Is there a threshold regarding the percentage of the stock interest owned in the company that may entitle a shareholder to such a right?

In non-listed companies, upon the request of one or more shareholders holding at least 10 per cent of the company's share capital and at least one per cent of the company's voting rights, or holding 10 per cent of the company's voting rights, the company's board of directors is required to convene a special GM.

In listed companies, upon the request of one or more shareholders holding at least five per cent of the company's share capital and at least one per cent of the company's voting rights, or holding five per cent of the company's voting rights ('requesting shareholder' or 'requesting shareholders'), the company's board of directors is required to convene a special GM. In the event the board of directors does not convene a special GM despite the fact that it was requested as provided above, the requesting shareholder or the shareholders holding more than 50 per cent of the voting rights held by the requesting shareholders are entitled to convene a meeting.

12. May a shareholder bring up an issue to be resolved upon and put it to a vote if it is not included on the agenda? May a shareholder require more information from the GM and/or the board, concerning the agenda of the GM, to be put in a better position to exercise their vote?

In principle, the agenda of the general meeting is determined by the board of directors and only matters included in the agenda can be resolved upon at the GM. However, shareholders holding more than one per cent of the voting rights may request the board of directors to add an additional matter to be resolved in a future GM. Such matters should be only those which are subject to the authority of the GM.

In non-listed companies, shareholders have the right to receive from the company information that is required for passing resolutions on the GM's agenda.

In listed and non-listed companies, shareholders have the right to receive from the company information with respect to the agenda of the GM, provided that such information pertains to a resolution concerning any of the matters referred to in the sixth to ninth points listed in question 9 above.

13. May a GM be held by telecommunication means and/or by correspondence (ie by written consent)?

A GM may be held by telecommunication means, provided that all shareholders participating in the general meeting can hear one another.

As to written consents, in non-listed companies a shareholder is entitled to vote in writing if the company's articles of association allow voting in such a manner. In listed companies, with respect to certain matters required according to the Companies Law, a shareholder is entitled to vote by a deed of vote in which they state their way of voting (for, against or abstention) and request the company to send the other shareholders in the company a statement of position on behalf of the voting shareholder. In response, the board of directors may send its own statement of position to the voting shareholders.

14. Are voting rights always proportionate to the stock held by each shareholder or can they vary by share class?

The voting power in a company may vary by classes of shares. In the event the company's share capital consists of only one class of shares, the voting rights are proportionate to the number of shares held by any shareholder.

15. Are there non-voting shares? Is there a maximum percentage of capital represented by non-voting shares?

A company may issue non-voting shares. There is no maximum percentage of capital which can be represented by non-voting shares.

16. Can shareholders group their shares in order to exercise their voting rights (eg, by trust, shareholders' agreement or otherwise)?

Generally, shareholders may group their shares to exercise their voting rights. In listed companies there are certain thresholds which cannot be crossed by shareholders joining their voting power unless a tender offer is made.

17. Under what circumstances can a shareholder challenge the resolutions adopted by the GM? Are there thresholds concerning the stock interest owned to be able to bring such a claim?

Any shareholder may challenge, before a competent court, resolutions adopted by the GM if the GM was not convened or directed in accordance with the provisions of the company's articles of association or according to law. This notwithstanding, a shareholder cannot request to cancel a resolution due to a default in the timing or in the place of conduct of the GM if such shareholder attended the GM despite the default. In addition, shareholders can challenge resolutions of the GM before a competent court, if a resolution discriminates against a shareholder or if a resolution was made in breach of the shareholders' obligation to act in good faith and in a customary manner and avoid exploitation of power.

18. What are the terms and procedures to challenge a resolution of the GM?

In order to challenge a resolution made by the GM, a shareholder must address a competent court.

SHAREHOLDERS' RIGHTS VERSUS DIRECTORS AND DUTIES OF OTHER CORRPORATE BODIES IN THE COMPANY

19. What is the procedure for the appointment/replacement/revocation of directors and of statutory auditors, if any?

Directors

Unless provided otherwise in the company's articles of association, the GM is authorised to appoint, replace and revoke the position of the directors of the company.

Auditors

The auditors are appointed at the annual meeting by a regular majority (50 per cent of the voting power represented at the annual meeting) for a period of one year (ie, until the next annual meeting). However, if the company's articles of association permit, the GM can appoint an auditor for a longer period, provided that the period will not extend beyond the end of the third annual meeting following the one in which the auditor was appointed.

In non-listed companies which do not conduct annual meetings (as described in question 10 above), auditors can be appointed to serve as auditors of a company until the completion of a single act of audit, or if the company's articles of association permit, until the completion of three acts of audit.

In newly incorporated companies, and until the convening of an annual meeting, the board of directors is required to appoint the auditor.

In addition to the foregoing, where the position of an auditor becomes vacant, the board of directors is required to convene a special GM for the appointment of the auditor.

20. May shareholders challenge the resolutions of the board of directors? Is there a minimum percentage of capital required to challenge a board resolution?

Shareholders may challenge resolutions of the board of directors before a competent court as described in question 21 below.

There is no minimum percentage of capital required in order to challenge a board resolution.

21. Are shareholders entitled to bring a legal action against the directors of the company? In which circumstances? Please describe briefly the principles of directors' liability.

Shareholders can address a competent court, either by a direct or by a derivative claim, and bring a legal action against a director upon the following circumstances:

- the director acted in a manner discriminating to the shareholders;
- the director breached their fiduciary duty towards the company;
- the director breached their duty of care towards the company; and
- the director acted in bad faith.

In general, a director owes duty of care towards the company (which is a legal obligation derived from tort), as well as fiduciary duty towards the company, which includes, among others, the obligation:

(i) to act in good faith and for the benefit of the company;
(ii) to refrain from any act involving a conflict of interest between the fulfilment of their role in the company and the fulfilment of any other role or their own personal affairs;
(iii) to refrain from any act involving competition with the business of the

company;

(iv) to refrain from taking advantage of a business opportunity of the company with the aim of obtaining a benefit for themselves or for any other person;

(v) to disclose all information to the company and to provide the company with all documents relating to the company that were obtained by them in virtue of their position in the company.

In addition, the Companies Law requires a director to act with the standard of proficiency in which a reasonable director, in the same circumstances, would act. This obligation includes taking reasonable steps, in view of the circumstances of each case, to obtain information regarding the business worthiness of an act submitted for their approval or of an act done by them by virtue of their position, and to obtain all other pertinent information regarding such acts.

22. What are the rights in connection with transactions where the directors have a conflict of interest situation?

In principle, a transaction in which the directors had a conflict of interest constitutes a breach of the director's fiduciary duty, and thus can be challenged before a competent court. However, such a transaction can be approved by the competent organs provided that the directors had acted in good faith and had disclosed the essence of their personal interest.

INFORMATION RIGHTS ON THE COMPANY'S BUSINESS

23. What information may be requested by the shareholders from the board concerning the general state of the company's business or any specific transaction? Are information rights different depending on the number of shares owned? Are shareholders entitled to receive written information before, during or after the GM about the meeting agenda and to what extent? Is it possible for a shareholder to obtain a copy of the minutes of the GM?

Information can be requested by the shareholders from the board of directors according to the following rules:

Upon the demand of one or more shareholders holding at least 10 per cent of the voting power in the company, the board of directors will provide such a shareholder or shareholders with a statement verified by the company's auditor, containing full details of all payments made by the company to each of the directors of the company, and the company's payment obligations in relation to it, including retirement conditions with respect to each of the last three years in which the company had prepared financial statements; the amount must also include payments directors received in their capacity as office holders in a subsidiary of the company. However, where the board of directors finds that the demand was not made in good faith, it is entitled to refuse to comply.

Shareholders are entitled to require from the company any document in the company's possession, indicating the purpose of its use, in any of the following instances: in non-listed companies – a shareholder may require information from the company if such information is required for passing a resolution on the GM's agenda; in listed and non-listed companies – a shareholder may require information if such information pertains to a resolution referred to in the sixth to ninth points listed in question 9 above.

As to minutes of general meetings, a company is required to keep the minutes of the proceedings of the GM at its registered office for a period of seven years from the date of the meeting. The minutes are to be open for inspection by its shareholders, and a copy of the minutes is to be sent to any shareholder who so requests.

24. Do shareholders have the right/duty to resolve in the GM upon matters which were not on the agenda?

Unless permitted by the company's articles of association, shareholders may not resolve in a GM upon matters which were not included in the meeting agenda.

25. Are shareholders entitled to inspect the corporate books and/or any other corporate or accounting documents? To what extent? Can they do it through external counsel or advisors?

The shareholders of a company have a right to review and inspect the company's register of shareholders and the company's register of substantial shareholders, as well as any document which the company is required to file under law with the Israeli Registrar of Companies or with the Israeli Securities Authority, and which is available for public inspection.

In addition, every shareholder is entitled to receive from the company, at their request, a copy of the articles of association and, in a non-listed company, a copy of the financial reports and of the opinion of the auditor in respect to them.

SHAREHOLDERS' AGREEMENTS
26. Are shareholders' agreements validly enforceable? What are their typical contents and term of duration? Are they enforceable by or against third parties and, if so, to what extent?

In principle, shareholders' agreements are validly enforceable. A typical shareholders' agreement includes: rights with respect to the appointment of directors; obligations with respect to the financing of the company and dilution; resolutions which require a special vote; provisions regarding the transfer of shares (such as rights of first refusal, co-sale, tag-along and drag-along); and non-compete provisions. The duration of the shareholders' agreement is most often indefinite (so long as the parties to it are shareholders of the company) or is terminated upon a decrease in holding of certain parties.

Shareholders' agreements are not enforceable by and against third parties, as they usually constitute a contractual obligation only upon the parties to it. Yet, since a company's articles of association is public, had the provisions of the shareholders' agreement been included in the company's articles of association, then under certain circumstances third parties may rely on such provisions.

27. Do shareholders' agreements have to be disclosed to the public or registered in any public registry?

Public disclosure in Israel is generally done by submission of a document to the Israeli Registrar of Companies or, if the company is a listed a company, by filing a report with the Israel Securities Authority (ISA).

Shareholders' agreements in non-listed companies are not required to be submitted to the Israeli Registrar of Companies.

As to listed companies, the general rules are as follows: if an interested party is party to a shareholders' agreement (as the term 'interested party' is defined in the Companies Law, ie a person holding at least five per cent of a company's share capital or its voting rights, a person who has the authority to appoint one or more directors or the general manager, or a person acting as a director or a general manager of the company) then such a shareholders' agreement does not have to be submitted to the ISA, but the joint holding of the parties to it has to be reported. If a controlling shareholder (as the term 'controlling shareholder' is defined in the ninth point listed in question 9 above) is a party to a shareholders' agreement, then such an agreement is required to be reported to the ISA. A shareholders' agreement pursuant to which a party to it becomes an interested party requires the parties to report their becoming interested parties, although the content of the agreement need not necessarily be reported.

ECONOMIC RIGHTS AND RIGHTS OVER THE STOCK
28. Is the stock always freely transferable? Are there any legal limitations? Are there any restrictions on contractual limitations?

The basic presumption under the Companies Law is that stock is transferrable. However, different restrictions on transfer of shares can be imposed under the company's articles of association or under shareholders' agreement/founders' agreement, such as: prohibition on share transfer, rights of first refusal, tag-along rights, drag-along rights and so on.

29. Are shareholders entitled to pledge their stock?

Generally, shareholders are entitled to pledge their shares, unless otherwise provided in the company's articles of association or in the shareholders' agreement/founders' agreement.

30. Are there financial assistance issues to be considered and other prohibitions to be evaluated in the context of a leveraged buyout transaction?

In Israel leveraged buyouts are subject to the profit and ability-to-pay criteria detailed in question 31 below.

31. May a company buy back its own stock and, if so, under what circumstances and subject to which limitations?

Companies that conform to the following criteria can buy back the company's shares:

Profit criteria

The buyback will be done from the company's profits, as the term 'profits' is defined in the Companies Law, ie, the balance of surplus or the surplus (defined as sums included in a company's equity originating from the net profits of the company, as determined according to accepted accounting rules, and other sums included in the equity under accepted accounting rules, other than share capital or premiums that are to be considered surplus) accumulated over the past two years, whichever is the greater, in accordance with the latest adjusted financial reports (defined as financial reports adjusted to the index, or financial reports that replace or will replace such reports, in accordance with accepted accounting procedures), audited or surveyed and prepared by the company, provided that the date in respect of which such reports were prepared is no earlier than six months prior to the date of buyback.

The ability-to-pay criteria

According to this criteria there should be no reasonable suspicion that the buyback of shares by the company might deprive the company of its ability to pay its existing and anticipated debts when due.

It should be noted that the aforementioned criteria are the general rule and that there are specific regulations which determine presumptions as to the company's conformance with the ability-to-pay criteria, and exemptions or alleviations regarding the adjustment of the financial reports.

32. Is there a legal right to withdraw from the company and, if so, under what circumstances? How is the shareholders' stock valued and paid in such a case?

The Companies Law does not refer to withdrawal by shareholders. According to the Companies Law withdrawal is done by the company and not by shareholders by the issuance of redeemable shares. Such redemption is not subject to profit criteria or the ability-to-pay criteria (as described in question 31 above), provided that the company included in its articles of association a provision permitting the company to issue securities subject to redemption. It should be noted, shares redeemed by the company will not be regarded as part of the company's equity unless the right to redeem is limited to the event of winding-up after payment of the debts of the company to its creditors.

The circumstances in which the shareholder will have the right to demand that the company buy back its shares and the price for them, is usually regulated in the underlying agreements between the company and the shareholders or in the company's articles of association. Redemption under such circumstances is subject to the profit criteria and the ability-to-pay criteria (as described in question 31 above).

33. In which circumstances can dividends be distributed among shareholders? Is it possible to exclude or limit the right of certain shareholders to dividends? Does a certain portion of the profits need to be set aside in a reserve fund where it cannot be distributed to the shareholders? Are advances on dividends allowed and, if so, under which circumstances? Can advances on dividends be reclaimed by the company?

In order to distribute the dividend the company must conform to the profit criteria and the ability-to-pay criteria (as described in question 31 above). In addition, a resolution regarding the distribution must be passed by the company's board of directors, and, if so provided in the company's articles of association, also by the GM. A company may, notwithstanding, determine in its articles of association that the resolution will be passed in one of the following ways:

(i)   by the GM, after receiving the recommendation of the board of directors. In such a case the GM may accept the recommendation or reduce the amount of dividend to be distributed, but it may not increase the amount of dividend to be distributed; or

(ii) by the board of directors of the company, after the GM has determined the maximum amount of the distribution of dividend; or

(iii) in such other manner as may be determined in the articles of association, provided that the board of directors is given a proper opportunity to determine, before the distribution is affected, that the distribution of the dividend is not a prohibited distribution.

In light of the governing principle according to which shareholders of the same class are entitled to the same rights, it is only possible to limit the rights of a class of shareholders to receive dividends. Limitation of distribution of dividends from certain shareholders while other shareholders who belong to the same class receive dividends is prohibited.

34. What are the rights of shareholders in the case of an issue of new stock (increase of the company's corporate capital) (pre-emption rights)?

In many companies, issuance of new stock is subject to pre-emptive rights referred to in the company's articles of association or in a founders' agreement/shareholders' agreement, according to which the existing shareholders have the right to purchase the shares issued by the company in priority to issuance to a third party in order to maintain their percentage of holdings in the company.

In non-listed companies where the articles of association do not refer to a pre-emptive provision, the law provides that in a company which has only one class of shares, new issued securities will be first offered to the shareholders of the company in accordance with the proportion of each shareholder's holding of the issued share capital, and only upon the refusal of the shareholder to purchase the shares (which must be done no later than the final date of the offer) the company may offer a third party the shares.

35. May minority shareholders ban or limit the company's capital structure in any manner?

There is no specific provision regarding the minority shareholders' right to ban or limit the company's capital structure, yet as part of the minority shareholders' right not to be discriminated against, minority shareholders might seek limitations with respect to the company's capital structure.

36. Which are the financial assistance prohibitions in force?

See question 30 above.

37. Apart from publicly listed companies, in which cases (if any) are shareholders obligated to obtain an authorisation from, or provide information to, a public authority about events that have an impact on their stock interest in the company?

According to the Companies Law, non-listed companies are required to report to the Israeli Registrar of Companies with respect to the transfer of stock held by shareholders or the issuance of it to them by the company. Under certain circumstances shareholders are required to receive authorisation from the antitrust authorities with respect to events that have an impact of their stock interest in the company.

SHAREHOLDERS' RIGHTS IN THE CASE OF EXTRAORDINARY TRANSACTIONS AND/OR WINDING-UP

38. What rights are available to shareholders in the case of a sale of all or a substantial portion of the company's assets? In the case of a merger or de-merger?

Sale of the company's assets is usually subject to the board of directors' approval (unless provided otherwise in the company's articles of association or in the founders' agreement/shareholders' agreement), and thus shareholders usually do not have special rights deriving out of the sale of assets unless the company's articles of association or shareholders' agreement/founders' agreement determine otherwise. Mergers and de-mergers are generally subject to the approval of the board of directors and the approval of the company's GM (as the required majority is dependent on the type of transaction). The rights available to shareholders in mergers and de-mergers are determined in the underlying merger/de-merger agreements and they can vary from rights to receive a consideration to a right to receive shares in other companies etc.

39. Which rights are available to shareholders in the case of conversion of the company into a European Company (SE) or into another type of company?

Since an SE is a body created by the European Union and governed by European Community law directly applicable in all European member states, the question is not applicable to Israeli companies.

40. Which rights are available to shareholders of a company in liquidation?

In a liquidation procedure that is implemented by the courts (as opposed to liquidation procedures that are implemented by shareholders or debt holders), the basic right available to the shareholders is the right to receive the surplus of the company's assets (after distribution to the company's creditors). Other rights provided to shareholders during a liquidation procedure are as follows:

(i)   the right to apply to court and object to the liquidation proceeding;
(ii) the right to apply to court and request the convening of a GM or a class meeting in order for them to resolve on a significant matter affecting the shareholders (or the class of shareholders) rights;
(iii) shareholders holding more than 10 per cent of the company's share capital may apply to court and request the convening of shareholders or of classes of shareholder in any matter;
(iv) a right to vote with respect to the identity of the liquidator; and
(v)   a right to apply to court with respect to any question arising out of the liquidation.

41. Can shareholders cause the liquidation of the company? How?

Liquidation by the shareholders up can be implemented by a GM with the vote of shareholders holding at least 75 per cent of the company's share capital, provided that the company is not insolvent (in the event the company is insolvent then the shareholders can vote in favour of a liquidation, yet the proceeding will be controlled by the creditors of the company, including the appointment of the liquidator), and following a statement of the board of directors of the company regarding the company's ability to pay its debts (which is not required when the company is insolvent). After the GM resolves with respect to the company's liquidation, the GM is required to appoint a liquidator. The latter will be responsible for the liquidation procedure and will have to submit to the GM at the end of the procedure a report detailing the manner in which the liquidation proceeding was implemented and what has been done with the company's assets.

COMPANY GROUPS

42. Is the concept of 'group' recognised as such under specific legislation? What are the implications?

The concept of 'group' is mainly recognised under the legislation that refers to the public disclosure of a company's activity. The implications are generally severe public disclosure obligations.

43. Does a controlling company have any particular duties *vis-à-vis* its controlled company shareholders?

Other than the general duty of loyalty, which applies to all shareholders exercising their rights and powers in a company, and according to which shareholders should exercise their rights in good faith and in a customary manner and avoid exploiting their power and discriminating other shareholders ('duty of loyalty'), holding companies that are considered a controlling party (as the term 'control' is defined in the ninth point listed in question 9 above) have an additional duty of fairness towards the company ('duty of fairness').

44. What are the rights of company shareholders when the controlling company puts in place actions and/or transactions that can be prejudicial to the shareholders?

The rights available to the shareholders if a controlling company (as the term 'control' is defined in the ninth point listed in question 9 above) puts in place actions and transactions that are prejudicial to its shareholders are as follows:

(i) in the event that a shareholder was discriminated against by the controlling company, the shareholder discriminated against may apply to the court and request the court to instruct with respect to the necessary actions to be taken for the removal or prevention of the discrimination; and

(ii) in the event the controlling company breaches its duty of care a shareholder can apply to court on the grounds of a breach of contract and request to implement its rights under contract law.

45. What are the limitations, if any, to the possibility of owning reciprocal stock interests in companies?

In general, owning reciprocal stock interests in companies is a permitted action. However, a subsidiary or another corporation controlled by a parent company (as the term 'control' is defined in the ninth point of question 9 above), may purchase shares (or other securities convertible into shares) of the parent company to the same extent as the parent company may affect dividend distributions (as explained in question 33 above), and where a share of a certain parent company was purchased by a subsidiary or by another corporation controlled by the parent company, the share will not bear any voting rights for so long as the share is owned by the subsidiary or by the other corporation controlled by a parent company.

Italy

CBA Studio Legale e Tributario Alessandro Varrenti

BASIC INFORMATION ON THE TYPES OF LIMITED LIABILITY COMPANIES AND ON THE RIGHTS OF SHAREHOLDERS
1.   What types of companies enjoy limited liability? If more than one, which ones have shareholders, ie holders of share certificates? Which one is the most common? Which one is mostly used by foreign investors?
Italian corporate law contemplates:
(i)   limited liability companies (Srl);
(ii) joint stock companies (SpA); and
(iii) limited partnerships (SapA).

In Srls and SpAs, the liability of stockholders is limited to the amount of their contribution to the company. In SapAs, there are two kinds of partners: (i) limited, who enjoy limited liability status; and (ii) general, with whom rests the management of the company and who are unlimitedly and jointly liable for the company's obligations.

Statistics indicate that Srls are the most commonly used type of companies, as a sign of reflection of the Italian economy, which is rather fragmented and principally features small and medium enterprises. SpAs are usually used in relation to bigger enterprises, when larger capitals and more flexibility in the circulation of shares are required. The governance structure of SpAs is more complex and, as such, it intrinsically offers a better protection to minority shareholders (see, eg, the presence of a board of statutory auditors, as it is described below in further detail). Foreign investors traditionally seem to favour the use of SpAs; save for the initial phase of an acquisition, where an Srl type of vehicle is most often used. We are deliberately omitting to address limited partnerships, considering the rather scarce use of such a form of company.

2.   Are there minimum capital requirements and/or thin capitalisation rules in force?
The minimum capital required is €10,000 for an Srl and €120,000 for an SpA (Articles 2327 and 2463 respectively of the Civil Code (the Code).

The thin capitalisation rule was introduced by Legislative Decree 344/2003, but was then repealed in 2008 and replaced by a new mechanism of deductibility of passive interest (Article 96 of the Income Tax Act).

3. Describe the types of shares that can be issued by a company and the different rights that they attribute to their owners, as well as any other financial instruments (bonds or other) and other instruments of a participatory nature in the company's capital that can also be issued by the company.

The general rule is that all shares must have the same value and grant to the shareholders the same rights (ordinary shares). However, if permitted by the by-laws, special classes of shares can be issued to grant additional administrative or patrimonial rights (Article 2348, paragraph 2, the Code), such as:

- privileged shares, which may grant privileged rights with respect to, eg, dividend distributions or the liquidation of the company's assets;
- shares with limited or non-voting rights;
- shares in favour of employees (stock options);
- enjoyment shares (usually without voting rights), which are issued in the case of reduction of the corporate capital and are attributed to the shareholders whose shares were reimbursed upon the reduction of the capital to temper the possible damages of having repaid the ordinary shares at nominal value;
- performance shares, whose holders, in addition to a monetary contribution, are obligated to perform certain activities in favour of the company. These shares must be registered and cannot be transferred without the directors' consent;
- tracking shares, that grant patrimonial rights depending on the company's economic results in certain business areas operated by the company;
- redeemable shares, which can be repurchased by the company or other shareholders; and
- saving shares (without voting rights), which can be issued only by publicly listed companies.

As regards other equity instruments, the Code expressly contemplates the issuance of convertible bonds and of the so-called participation securities (Article 2346, paragraph 6). These instruments are issued in exchange for the provision of work or services to shareholders or even third parties and incorporate patrimonial rights which are generally connected to the economic results of the company, as well as some administrative rights (except for the voting right in the general meeting (GM), which is excluded) as determined by the by-laws. In addition, practice has given rise to other kinds of instruments, such as reverse convertible bonds, where the option to convert the bonds pertains to the issuer.

No shares are issued by an Srl, where the corporate capital is represented by quotas. Holders of the quotas are hereafter referred to as 'stockholders'.

4. Can a company have only one shareholder and still enjoy limited liability?

SpA and Srl companies can indeed have only one shareholder and still enjoy limited liability, either at the time of the company's incorporation or at any

time thereafter. In such a case, the company is subject to certain specific disclosure obligations. However, the benefit of limited liability is prejudiced if (Articles 2325, paragraph 2 and 2462, paragraph 2, the Code):
- the company becomes insolvent; and
- the contributions were not made in compliance with the law, or the disclosure obligations are not in compliance with the law.

In these cases, the sole shareholder is liable, without limitation, for the company's obligations which arose during the time when the company's stock was owned by only one person.

5. Are the rights of shareholders the same in any type of company?
The rights of the shareholders of the two forms of companies examined in this chapter are not necessarily the same (see question 6 below).

6. What are the basic rights of any shareholder? Describe briefly the rights of minority shareholders and indicate which thresholds, if any, are required to allow the minority shareholders to exercise any such rights.
Generally speaking, the rights afforded to shareholders are: (i) patrimonial rights, such as the right to receive dividends, the right to be attributed a proportional part of the company's assets at the time when the company is wound up, pre-emptive rights in the case of issue of new stock (and, for SpAs, also in the case of issue of convertible bonds) and the right to withdraw from the company; and (ii) administrative rights, such as the right to participate and vote in GMs and to challenge its resolutions, and information rights regarding the conduct of the company.

Minority shareholders in SpAs, enjoy, inter alia, the following rights:
- shareholders who own at least 10 per cent of the corporate capital have the right to request that the GM is convened and to set out the meeting's agenda (Article 2367, the Code);
- shareholders who represent at least one-third of the overall corporate capital at any GM have the right to request that the meeting is postponed for a maximum of five days if they are not sufficiently informed about the agenda of the meeting (Article 2374, the Code);
- shareholders who represent at least five per cent of voting shares in respect to a resolution of the GM can challenge such a resolution (the threshold is 0.1 per cent in the case of 'open companies', as defined in the resolution 11971/99 of the Stock Exchange Commission (Consob)) (Article 2377, the Code);
- shareholders who own at least 10 per cent of the overall corporate capital (or five per cent in the case of open companies) have the right to file a complaint with the court to report any 'grounded suspicions' about serious irregularities in the management of the company (Article 2409, the Code);
- any shareholder has the right to file complaints with the board of statutory auditors (BSA) concerning the management of the company.

In such a case the BSA shall give notice thereof to the GM in its yearly report. However, if the complaint is brought up by the shareholders who represent at least five per cent of the corporate capital (or two per cent in the case of open companies) (these thresholds can be lower if the by-laws so provide) the BSA shall investigate the matters brought to its attention and report its findings and conclusions to the GM (Article 2408, the Code). Furthermore, any shareholder has the right to challenge any board resolution that 'is in breach of their rights' (Article 2388, the Code);

- shareholders who represent at least 20 per cent of the corporate capital can sue directors for their liability (Article 2393-*bis* of the Code). This threshold can be changed by the company's by-laws, but in no case can it exceed one-third. In open companies, the threshold is 2.5 per cent (or less, if it is so provided in the by-laws); and
- shareholders who represent at least 20 per cent of the corporate capital (or five per cent in the case of open companies) can veto any waiver and/or settlement of the company's liability action against directors (Article 2393, paragraph 6, the Code).

The principal rights of minority stockholders in Srl companies are the following:

- stockholders who own at least one-third of the corporate capital have the right to submit specific matters to the approval of the GM, even if they would not usually fall within the GM's competence (Article 2479, paragraph 1, the Code);
- stockholders who own at least one-third of the corporate capital have the right to cause a resolution to be adopted by the GM, rather than by means of written consultation or written consent (Article 2479, paragraph 4, the Code);
- any stockholder (as long as they are not, at the same time, a director) has the right to be informed about the conduct of the company's business and to inspect the corporate books and any documents 'concerning the management of the company' (Article 2476, paragraph 2, the Code);
- any stockholder has the right to sue the company's directors for their liability and demand their provisional revocation (Article 2476, paragraph 3, the Code). The liability action can only be waived or settled by the stockholders who represent at least two-thirds of the capital, provided that such a waiver or settlement is not vetoed by as many stockholders as those who represent 10 per cent of the entire capital of the company (Article 2476, paragraph 5, the Code); and
- where the company has a BSA, the same provisions described above concerning SpAs shall apply.

7.   Do all shareholders enjoy the same rights or can some shareholders be attributed specific rights, whether by reason of the particular class of stock owned or other? Are such rights generally provided for at the level of the company's by-laws and/or in shareholders' agreements?

SpAs can issue various classes of shares different from ordinary ones, to incorporate different types of rights (see also question 3 above).

As regards Srls, stockholders' rights are proportional to the quota owned. On principle, quotas are attributed to stockholders in proportion to the value of their contributions, although the by-laws can establish different attribution criteria (Article 2468 of the Code).

8.   May the rights of shareholders, generally speaking, be limited, modified, suppressed or waived in any way? If so, how? Are such modifications or limitations provided for in the company's by-laws and/or in shareholders' agreements?

The company's by-laws and shareholders' agreements can limit, modify, suppress or waive certain rights, and can establish some specific rights in favour of this or that shareholder, subject to the respect of mandatory legal provisions. In some cases, the extent to which the rights may be limited or modified is set forth by the law (eg, limitations to the transferability of the stock, see question 28 below).

GENERAL MEETING OF SHAREHOLDERS (GM) AND VOTING RIGHTS

9.   Which decisions are reserved to the competence of the GM?

In SpAs, GMs are ordinary or extraordinary. The following matters are reserved to the competence of ordinary GMs in companies which do not have a supervisory board (Article 2364, the Code):

- approval of the yearly financial statement;
- appointment and revocation of directors, BSA members and the person in charge of accountancy control, if any;
- determination of the directors' and BSA members' fees;
- decision on the liability of directors and members of the BSA;
- decision on other matters reserved to its competence by the law or the by-laws; and
- approval of the GM's internal rules, if any.

Where the company has a supervisory board, the ordinary GM appoints and revokes its members and determines their fees (if not provided for in the by-laws), resolves upon their liability, as well as upon the distribution of profits. It also appoints the accountancy auditor (Article 2364-*bis*, the Code).

The extraordinary GM resolves, *inter alia*, on the following matters (Articles 2365 and 2349, paragraph 2, the Code):

- modifications to the deed of incorporation and the by-laws;
- appointment, replacement and revocation of liquidators and determination of their powers; and
- issuance of shares or other financial instruments in favour of employees

of the company or of controlled companies.

As regards Srls, stockholders' decisions need not always be formally adopted by the GM. A GM's resolution is mandatorily required only if:

(i) the by-laws do not contemplate alternative methods of decision (ie written consultation or written consent);

(ii) the decisions concern the modification of the by-laws or the performance of activities which give rise to a substantial modification of the company's purpose or the stockholders' rights; or

(iii) the stockholders who represent at least one-third of the corporate capital so require.

Unlike SpAs, in Srls, there is no formal distinction between an ordinary and extraordinary GM. However, certain resolutions shall be adopted by a larger majority of votes than others.

The following matters must be decided by the stockholders' meeting (Article 2479 of the Code):

- approval of the financial statement and profit distributions;
- appointment of directors and BSA members, if any;
- amendment of the by-laws;
- decision to carry out activities which give rise to a substantial modification of the company's purpose or the stockholders' rights; and
- other matters submitted to the stockholders' decision pursuant to the by-laws or by one or more directors or stockholders that represent at least one-third of the corporate capital.

10. How does a shareholder participate in a GM? Are there any limitations to having a minimum number of shares? May a shareholder delegate attendance to another shareholder or to the board? May a shareholder obtain assistance from the courts or any other governmental body to intervene in a GM or to cause one to be held in some particular cases?

Any shareholder is entitled to participate in the GM, without any limitation as to the number of the shares or the entity of the quota owned, with the exception of the holders of some specific classes of shares (such as saving shares) who cannot participate in the GM.

Shareholders can participate in the GM personally or by proxy, which can be attributed to another shareholder or to a third person, if the by-laws should not so prohibit (proxies cannot be given, *inter alia*, to board of directors and BSA members and/or to employees of the company or of its controlled companies, nor to controlled companies).

As regards SpAs, the form and contents of the proxy are disciplined by the Code (Article 2372). A proxy must be granted in writing, the name of the proxy cannot be left blank and it can be revoked at any time, notwithstanding any agreement to the contrary.

One or more shareholders can request courts to convene the GM when the corporate bodies of the company do not comply with a legitimate request by the shareholders to convene the meeting. In addition, a GM can be convened upon a court's order when the court ascertains the existence of serious irregularities in the management of the company, following the request of the shareholders that represent at least 10 per cent of the corporate capital of the company (five per cent in open companies).

No specific legal provisions allow the stockholders of an Srl to request the court to convene the GM and the prevailing case law excludes the existence of such a right.

11. May a GM be called and held at the request of any shareholder? Is there a threshold regarding the percentage of the stock interest owned in the company that may entitle a shareholder to such a right?

In SpAs, shareholders who represent at least 10 per cent of the corporate capital (or a lower percentage, if provided for in the by-laws) have the right to request the GM to be convened. This right cannot be exercised by the shareholders where the law provides that the GM shall adopt a resolution based on the directors' proposal or on a project or report drawn up by the directors (Article 2367, the Code).

The Code does not contain any specific provisions concerning the calling of a GM at the request of stockholders of limited liability companies. According to the prevailing case law and to most legal scholars, the right to call a GM shall be attributed to the same persons who, pursuant to Article 2479, paragraph 1, are entitled to submit certain matters to the stockholders' decision (ie the directors of the company and the stockholders that represent at least one-third of the corporate capital).

12. May a shareholder bring up an issue to be resolved upon and put it to a vote if it is not included on the agenda? May a shareholder require more information from the GM and/or the board, concerning the agenda of the GM, to be put in a better position to exercise their vote?

The only time a shareholder is allowed to bring up for discussion an issue that is not included in the agenda is in the 'totalitarian' GM. In SpAs, a totalitarian GM is validly constituted when it is attended by the entire corporate capital and by the majority of the board and supervisory board members (Article 2366, paragraph 4, the Code). In Srls, the entire corporate capital, as well as all directors and BSA members shall be represented in, or informed about, the totalitarian GM (Article 2479-*bis*, paragraph 5, the Code).

In both cases, however, no resolution can be adopted by the GM if any of the participants should so object.

The Code does not contain any express provision concerning the adjournment of the GM in Srl companies. It has been held in some cases that Article 2374 of the Code might be applicable to limited liability companies by way of analogy (see, eg, Tribunal of Milan, 25 August 2006). This position is, however, criticised by many, based on the argument that in Srls the stockholders have broad information rights which would render unjustified the recourse to such a remedy.

13. May a GM be held by telecommunication means and/or by correspondence (ie by written consent)?

In SpAs, the shareholders can participate in the GM by telecommunication means and can also vote by correspondence if it is so permitted by the by-laws (Article 2370, paragraph 4, the Code).

As indicated in question 9, in Srls written consultation and written consent are alternative resolution methods. Certain decisions must be, however, mandatorily adopted by a GM. In such a case, the Code does not contain specific provisions allowing for the stockholders to participate in the meeting by telecommunication means or to vote by correspondence. Most scholars believe that this possibility applies in full to Srls by way of analogy, while others contend that the by-laws of Srls can only contemplate the possibility of holding the GM by telecommunication means, not the possibility of voting by correspondence.

14. Are voting rights always proportionate to the stock held by each shareholder or can they vary by share class?

Voting rights are not necessarily proportionate to the stock held by each shareholder, although some rights are indeed proportionate to the percentage of stock owned as indicated in questions 3 and 7 above. Rights (including voting rights) may vary based on each class of shares. In addition, the by-laws of companies which are not 'open' can provide that, depending on the number of shares held by the same shareholder, the voting rights can be subject to a maximum limit or that the weight of the shareholder's vote can be gradually reduced in proportion to the quantity of the shares owned. Shares with multiple votes are prohibited (Article 2351, paragraph 4, the Code). For Srls see question 15 below.

15. Are there non-voting shares? Is there a maximum percentage of capital represented by non-voting shares?

SpA by-laws may provide the right to issue non-voting shares, shares with voting rights limited to certain specific matters or subject to the occurrence of certain conditions, provided that the overall amount of such shares does not exceed 50 per cent of the corporate capital (Article 2351, paragraph 2, the Code).

The vote of each stockholder of an Srl shall be proportionate to the quota owned (Article 2479, paragraph 5, the Code). This provision is mandatory and cannot be derogated (Article 2479, paragraph 5, the Code).

16. Can shareholders group their shares in order to exercise their voting rights (eg, by trust, shareholders' agreement or otherwise)?

By means of a shareholders' agreement, shareholders of both types of companies can group up their stock to exercise their voting rights. As regards the duration and the publicity of such agreements, see questions 26 and 27 below.

17. Under what circumstances can a shareholder challenge the resolutions adopted by the GM? Are there thresholds concerning the stock interest owned to be able to bring such a claim?

As regards SpAs, GM resolutions which were not adopted in compliance with the law or the by-laws can be challenged by the shareholders (who were either absent or in dissent) who own at least five per cent (0.1 per cent in open companies) of the corporate capital, within 90 days from the date on which they were adopted or filed with the Companies' Register (Article 2377, the Code). Resolutions falling under the cases of nullity contemplated in Article 2379 of the Code can be challenged by any interested person (even if not a shareholder), within three years from the date when they are recorded in the company's book or are filed with the Companies' Register. No time limit applies if the resolution modifies the corporate purpose by rendering it unlawful or impossible (Article 2379).

In Srls, stockholders' decisions which were not adopted in compliance with the law or the by-laws or were adopted with a decisive vote of a stockholder who is in a conflict of interest situation can be challenged by any dissenting stockholder, within 90 days from the date on which they were recorded in the company's books. The decisions concerning unlawful or impossible matters and those which were adopted in a complete absence of information to the stockholders can be challenged by any interested person within three years from the date when they were recorded in the company's books (Article 2479-ter, the Code).

18. What are the terms and procedures to challenge a resolution of the GM?

As regards terms, see question 17. In respect to both types of companies, the claim is submitted by means of a writ of summons to the court of the place where the company has its registered office. Simultaneously upon filing the law suit, the plaintiff has the right to demand that a temporary restraining order is issued to suspend the enforceability of the resolution that is being challenged.

SHAREHOLDERS' RIGHTS VERSUS DIRECTORS AND DUTIES OF OTHER CORPORATE BODIES IN THE COMPANY

19. What is the procedure for the appointment/replacement/revocation of directors and of statutory auditors, if any?

In both types of companies, the initial directors and BSA members (if present in Srls) are appointed in the by-laws (Article 2328, the Code). Thereafter, they are appointed by the GM (in Srls they can also be appointed by written consultation or written consent).

In SpAs, directors can be revoked by the GM at any time and for any reason, save for their right to claim damages when the revocation is made without just cause. Members of the BSA can be revoked only for just cause, by a resolution to be approved also by the court.

If during the period when the board of directors is in office one or more directors cease from their post, they are replaced by the remaining directors by means of a resolution to be approved by the BSA, provided that the majority of the board still consists of the directors appointed by the GM. Should this not be the case, the GM shall be convened immediately.

If a member of the BSA ceases their office, they shall be replaced by a deputy statutory auditor (two deputy statutory auditors are appointed together with the board) until the following GM, which shall provide for the integration of the board.

In respect to Srls, there are no specific legal provisions concerning the revocation and replacement of directors. Therefore, it is advisable to insert in the by-laws specific provisions governing these aspects. In addition, the BSA must not necessarily be appointed in Srls, except when the corporate capital exceeds €120,000, or in some other cases set forth in the Code or by the law (Article 2477 of the Code).

20. May shareholders challenge the resolutions of the board of directors? Is there a minimum percentage of capital required to challenge a board resolution?

SpA shareholders who represent at least five per cent of the corporate capital (0.1 per cent in open companies) have the right to challenge resolutions of the board of directors, but only when such resolutions are in breach of their rights (Article 2388 of the Code).

On the contrary, stockholders of Srl companies cannot challenge board of directors' resolutions.

21. Are shareholders entitled to bring a legal action against the directors of the company? In which circumstances? Please describe briefly the principles of directors' liability.

Under Article 2392 of the Code, directors of SpAs are liable *vis-à-vis* the company for any damages suffered as a consequence of their breach of:
- the fiduciary duty;
- conflict of interest rules;
- the obligation to act in an informed manner; or
- obligations and prohibitions provided for by applicable laws or the by-laws.

In these cases, the liability action can be exercised following a resolution of the ordinary GM or exercised directly by the shareholders that represent at least 20 per cent of the corporate capital (2.5 per cent in open companies). The action is subject to a statute of limitations period of five years from the termination of the interested director from their office. When the action is resolved upon by the GM by the favourable vote of at least five per cent of the corporate capital, the directors are revoked from their office (Article 2393, the Code).

The directors of Srls are liable *vis-à-vis* the company for damages arising from a breach of their duties under applicable law or provided by the by-laws. A liability action can be exercised by each stockholder who can demand that the court revokes provisionally by way of urgency the directors in the case of serious irregularities. The stockholders who intentionally approved or authorised the directors' actions are jointly liable with the directors (Article 2476, the Code).

In both types of companies, any shareholder (or third party) who was directly damaged by the directors' negligence or misconduct can sue personally the directors for the repayment of damages.

22. What are the rights in connections with transactions where the directors have a conflict of interest situation?

The shareholders of both types of companies do not have the right to challenge directly the resolutions adopted, or the transactions carried out by directors in a conflict of interest situation. In both cases, however, if damages arise from such conduct, the shareholders have the right to institute a liability action against any such directors (see question 21).

INFORMATION RIGHTS ON THE COMPANY'S BUSINESS
23. What information may be requested by the shareholders from the board concerning the general state of the company's business or any specific transaction? Are information rights different depending on the number of shares owned? Are shareholders entitled to receive written information before, during or after the GM about the meeting agenda and to what extent? Is it possible for a shareholder to obtain a copy of the minutes of the GM?

Shareholders of SpAs have the right to inspect, and obtain an extract from, the shareholders' book and the book of the GM minutes (Article 2422, the Code). They can also inspect the draft financial statement 15 days prior to its approval (Article 2429, paragraph 3, the Code).

Information rights of the stockholders of Srls are broader, because they are often personally involved in the business of the company. They have the right to: (i) obtain information on the management of the company and inspect all the relevant documents; and (ii) access most of the company's corporate books. In the exercise of these rights, the stockholders can be assisted by third party experts (Article 2476, paragraph 2, the Code). According to prevailing case law, stockholders can obtain extracts, and even entire copies, of the documents which they have the right to access (see, eg, Tribunal of Milan, 22 April 1993 and 30 March 1993).

These rights pertain to any shareholder, regardless of the quantity of stock owned.

In the notice of call of the GM, the shareholders must be informed about the matters which will be discussed. The notice of call can be somewhat brief, provided that it shall be clear, unambiguous and specific (see, eg, Supreme Court no. 23269/2005, 21232/2004).

24. Do shareholders have the right/duty to resolve in the GM upon matters which were not on the agenda?

Except for the case of the totalitarian meeting (see question 12), the GM cannot validly resolve upon any matter which was not indicated in the agenda. It is, however, competent to resolve upon matters which are accessory or consequent to those indicated in the agenda (see, eg, Supreme Court no. 21232/2004, 13019/1995).

25. Are shareholders entitled to inspect the corporate books and/or any other corporate or accounting documents? To what extent? Can they do it through external counsel or advisors?

See question 23.

SHAREHOLDERS' AGREEMENTS

26. Are shareholders' agreements validly enforceable? What are their typical contents and term of duration? Are they enforceable by or against third parties and, if so, to what extent?

Shareholders' agreements are validly enforceable between the parties, but not against good faith third parties. The Code (Article 2341-*bis*) expressly governs shareholders' agreements in SpAs concerning:

(i)   the exercise of voting rights in such companies or in companies that are subject to the parent company's direction and coordination;
(ii) limitations to the transfer of the shares of such companies or of their controlled companies; or
(iii) the exercise of a dominating influence on such companies.

Their validity cannot exceed five years (three years in listed companies) and they are renewable. If the duration is undetermined, any party to it can withdraw upon a six-month prior notice.

Although the Code does not contain any specific provisions concerning agreements of this type in Srl companies, there is no doubt about their legitimacy. Where an Srl controls an SpA, Article 2341-bis of the Code applies (and, therefore, the stockholders' agreements are subject to the above limits of duration). In other cases, the provisions of the Code are generally considered not applicable to Srls and, as a consequence, the stockholders' agreements are not subject to the above time limits. However, also in the case of Srls, stockholders have the right to withdraw from the stockholders' agreements which have an unlimited duration.

27. Do shareholders' agreements have to be disclosed to the public or registered in any public registry?

Only agreements relating to open companies are subject to disclosure obligations. Their existence shall be communicated to the company's board of directors and recalled prior to each GM. The communication shall be recorded in the minutes of the GM and filed with the Companies' Register.

In the case of a breach of the disclosure obligations, the shareholders who are parties to the agreement cannot validly exercise their voting rights, and the resolutions adopted with their determining vote can be challenged.

Publicly listed companies are subject to more rigorous disclosure obligations (Article 2341-*ter*, the Code).

ECONOMIC RIGHTS AND RIGHTS OVER THE STOCK

28. Is the stock always freely transferable? Are there any legal limitations? Are there any restrictions on contractual limitations?

In general, the stock of both types of companies is freely transferable, unless its transferability is limited by the law, by the by-laws or by a shareholders' agreement, if any (in this case, the limitation is enforceable only against the parties to the agreement).

Legal limitations to the transferability of the shares apply in rather exceptional cases. The most relevant concerns the purchase of the company's own shares (see below in question 31).

As regards registered and dematerialised shares of SpAs, their circulation can be subject to certain conditions or can even be excluded completely by the by-laws (the exclusion cannot exceed five years). The provisions of the by-laws which subject the transfer of the shares to the discretionary approval of the corporate bodies or other shareholders are valid only if they establish the obligation of the company or the other shareholders to purchase such shares or the right of the transferring shareholder to withdraw from the company (Article 2355-*bis*, the Code).

In Srls, the by-laws can exclude the right of the stockholders to transfer the quota or subject it to the discretionary approval of the corporate bodies, other stockholders or third parties. In these cases, as well as in the case in which the approval is subject to such conditions and limits that render the transfer of the quota following the stockholder's death *de facto* impossible, stockholders have the right to withdraw from the company. The by-laws can provide for a term not exceeding two years during which the right of withdrawal cannot be exercised.

29. Are shareholders entitled to pledge their stock?

Unless it is otherwise provided in the by-laws or the shareholders' agreements, the company's stock can be validly pledged. In such a case and unless it is otherwise provided, the voting rights shall be exercised by the pledgee. On the contrary, the exercise of the pre-emptive right (if any) pertains to the pledgor (Article 2352 of the Code).

30. Are there financial assistance issues to be considered and other prohibitions to be evaluated in the context of a leveraged buyout transaction?

As regards financial assistance rules in general, please refer to question 36 below.

Merger leveraged buyout (Mlbo) transactions are specifically governed by Article 2501-bis of the Code. An Mlbo is defined therein as a merger between two companies, one of which incurred debt for the purchase of the other, where, as a result of the merger the assets of the target become a generic security for the reimbursement of the debt. This kind of transaction is legitimate only when it is carried out in compliance with the following formal and substantial requirements:

(i) the merger project indicates the financial resources necessary to the company resulting from the merger to repay the debt;

(ii) the board report outlines the reasons underlying the transaction and it contains a sound economic and financial plan with the indication of the financial resources and the description of the purposes of the transaction;

(iii) the appraisals' report confirms that the indications contained in the board report are reasonable; and

(iv) a report by an auditing company of the target or the purchaser is attached to the merger project.

31. May a company buy back its own stock and, if so, under what circumstances and subject to which limitations?

An SpA can purchase its treasury stock only if it is authorised by the GM and within the limits of the distributable profits and of any available reserve funds reported in the last duly approved financial statement. Only shares that are fully paid up can be repurchased by the company (Article 2357, the Code). As regards open companies, treasury stock can be purchased within the limits of 20 per cent of the corporate capital.

Srls are not allowed to purchase treasury stock (Article 2474, the Code).

32. Is there a legal right to withdraw from the company and, if so, under what circumstances? How is the shareholders' stock valued and paid in such a case?

In SpAs, shareholders who did not approve the following resolutions of the GM (because they were absent, dissented or abstained from voting) have the right to withdraw from the company by operation of law (Article 2437, the Code):

a) significant change of the corporate purpose;

b) reorganisation of the company;

c) transfer of the company's registered office abroad;

d) revocation of the winding-up;

e) suppression of one or more causes of withdrawal set forth in the by-laws;

f) suppression of the right to withdraw following the approval by the GM of the resolution which: (i) extends the terms of duration of the company; or (ii) introduces or removes restrictions to the circulation of the shares;

g) modification of the criteria of determination of the value of the shares in the case of withdrawal;

h) modification of voting and patrimonial rights;

i) extension of the duration of the company; or

j) introduction or removal of restrictions to the circulation of the shares.

The right of withdrawal in the cases under letters a) to h) cannot be excluded by the by-laws. On the contrary, by-laws can suppress the right of withdrawal in the cases under letters i) and j).

The law provides for other cases in which the shareholders can withdraw from the company, such as when the duration of the company is unlimited, an arbitration clause is introduced in the by-laws or suppressed, etc.

According to Article 2437-bis of the Code, the value of the shares shall be determined taking into account the company's assets and its prospective profits, as well as (if available) the shares' market value. Shares listed on stock exchanges are valued exclusively on the basis of the average closing prices in the previous six months. The by-laws can provide for different evaluation methods, which, however, shall be fair *vis-à-vis* the withdrawing shareholder in those cases when the cause of withdrawal cannot be suppressed by the by-laws. In other cases, the evaluation criteria can also be determined in the by-laws in such a way as to discourage the shareholders from withdrawing from the company.

Under Article 2473 of the Code, in Srls, the right of withdrawal can be exercised, inter alia, by those stockholders who dissent with a resolution concerning:

- the change of the corporate purpose and type of the company;
- a merger or de-merger project;
- the revocation of liquidation proceedings;
- the transfer of the registered office abroad;
- the exclusion of one or more cases of withdrawal set forth in the by-laws; or
- transactions which give rise to a substantial amendment of special rights granted to the stockholders in respect to the management of the company and profit distribution.

Stockholders also have the right to withdraw from companies which have an unlimited duration, as well as in other cases set forth by applicable laws.

The value of the quota shall be determined in proportion to the company's assets, to be appraised based on their market value. Where there is disagreement, the quota shall be valued by an expert appointed by the court.

33. In which circumstances can dividends be distributed among shareholders? Is it possible to exclude or limit the right of certain shareholders to dividends? Does a certain portion of the profits need to be set aside in a reserve fund where it cannot be distributed to the shareholders? Are advances on dividends allowed and, if so, under which circumstances? Can advances on dividends be reclaimed by the company?

Distributions of dividends shall be approved by the same resolution of the GM which approves the company's financial statement. Only profits which were actually achieved and are reported in a duly approved financial statement can be distributed. Where there are losses, dividends cannot be distributed until the capital is reintegrated or reduced accordingly (Article 2433, the Code).

Five per cent of the annual net profits shall be set aside in a statutory reserve fund, until such a fund is filled up with an amount equal to 20 per cent of the corporate capital (Article 2430, the Code).

Provisions contained in the by-laws or other agreements pursuant to which one or more shareholders are completely excluded from sharing profit and/or losses of the company are null and void (Article 2265, the Code). The right of certain shareholders to dividends can be limited by issuing special classes of shares.

If permitted by the by-laws, advances on dividends can be distributed in companies where the financial statement is audited by a registered auditing company, provided that the audit results are positive, and however subject to the quantitative limits set forth in the Code. Advances on dividends cannot be distributed when there are losses resulting from the last approved financial statement (Article 2433-*bis* of the Code).

34. What are the rights of shareholders in the case of an issue of new stock (increase of the company's corporate capital) (pre-emption rights)?

In the case of issue of new stock or convertible bonds, existing shareholders have the right to subscribe the newly issued stock in proportion to the shares and/or convertible bonds owned (pre-emption rights). The GM can limit or exclude the pre-emption rights in the interest of the company, if it should be so resolved by the shareholders who represent at least half of the corporate capital (Article 2441, the Code).

Also in Srls, stockholders have the right to subscribe newly issued stock in proportion to the quotas owned. If permitted by the by-laws, newly-issued stock can be offered to third parties. However, in such a case the stockholders who dissent with such a decision have the right to withdraw from the company (Article 2481-*bis* of the Code).

35. May minority shareholders ban or limit the company's capital structure in any manner?

Minority shareholders have on principle no right to limit the capital structure of the company in the absence of, eg, veto rights concerning the sale of stock to third parties. Minority shareholders have nonetheless the right to pre-empt their shares so that at any given issue of new stock their shareholding interest is not diluted (Article 2441, the Code), and they have the additional right to challenge frivolous or intentionally dilutive resolutions by the majority shareholders to issue new stock in the company. This latter right falls into the larger category of rights to challenge ordinary GM resolutions (see question 17 above).

36. Which are the financial assistance prohibitions in force?

An SpA is not allowed to grant loans or provide guarantees for the purchase or subscription of its own shares, unless certain conditions are satisfied, such as, inter alia (Articles 2357-2358, the Code):

- the transaction is authorised by the extraordinary GM;
- at least 30 days prior to the GM, the directors file with the company's offices a report describing the transaction and certify that it will be carried out at arm's-length;
- the GM's resolution and the report is filed with the Companies' Register; and
- the total amount of the loans and guarantees does not exceed the dividends distributable and the reserves available resulting from the last financial statement.

The company is not allowed (even indirectly) to accept its treasury stock as a security.

Srls cannot grant loans or provide guarantees for the purchase or subscription of their treasury stock, nor can they accept their stock as a guarantee (Article 2474, the Code).

37. Apart from publicly listed companies, in which cases (if any) are shareholders obligated to obtain an authorisation from, or provide information to, a public authority about events that have an impact on their stock interest in the company?

Pursuant to the Italian Antitrust rules (Law 287/90), entities that participate in a concentration transaction shall submit a prior notice of it to the Antitrust Authority, where their yearly turnover exceeds certain thresholds. The Antitrust Authority can start an investigation proceeding within 30 days from the receipt of the notice and, in such a case, it can order the companies in question to postpone the completion of the transaction.

The Consolidated Banking Act (Legislative Decree no. 385/1993) and the Consolidated Finance Act (Legislative Decree no. 58/1998) govern certain cases in which the purchase of the shares in banks, investment companies (and other entities) is subject to the authorisation of the Bank of Italy. The purpose of such an authorisation is to ensure that the new shareholder satisfies certain requirements set forth by the law.

SHAREHOLDERS' RIGHTS IN THE CASE OF EXTRAORDINARY TRANSACTIONS AND/OR WINDING-UP

38. What rights are available to shareholders in the case of a sale of all or a substantial portion of the company's assets? In the case of a merger or de-merger?

There are no specific provisions safeguarding shareholders in the case of a sale of the company's assets. However, where the consequence of such a transaction should be a substantial change in the company's corporate purpose, the dissenting shareholders shall have the right to withdraw from the company (Article 2437, the Code).

In the case of a merger or de-merger, the shareholders have the following rights (Articles 2501 *et seq* of the Code):
* to challenge the resolution of a merger or de-merger, in compliance with the provisions governing the challenge by the shareholders of the GM resolutions; and
* to be attributed the stock of the new company which results from the merger, in proportion to the entity of their previous stock. They may also obtain a monetary adjustment which cannot, however, exceed 10 per cent of the par value of the shares of SpAs (in the case of a merger, the limit of 10 per cent is not applicable to limited liability companies).

In addition, stockholders of Srls have the right to withdraw from the company in the case of a merger or de-merger (Article 2473, the Code).

39. Which rights are available to shareholders in the case of conversion of the company into a European Company (SE) or into another type of company?

Statistics indicate that no SE companies seem to have been incorporated in Italy so far. Pursuant to the EC Regulation no. 2157/2001, an SE can be created, inter alia, by the conversion of an SpA incorporated under the laws of an EU member state, if it has had a subsidiary governed by the laws of another member state for at least two years. The project of conversion and the by-laws of the SE shall be approved by the GM, with the majorities set forth in Article 7 of EC Directive 78/855. No other specific provisions concerning the conversion of an SpA into an SE are contained in the above Regulation. Therefore, Italian legal provisions concerning homogeneous conversion (see below) shall apply.

In the case of the conversion of an SpA or an Srl into one of the types of companies without limited liability ('personal companies'), the relevant GM resolution shall be adopted with the majorities necessary for the amendment of the by-laws and it shall be approved by all the shareholders who become unlimitedly liable (such an unlimited liability also applies to the company's obligations which arose prior to its conversion).

The conversion of a personal company into an SpA or an Srl shall have to be approved by the majority of the stockholders. Dissenting or absent stockholders have the right to withdraw.

The conversion of an Srl into an SpA, or vice versa ('homogeneous conversion'), shall be resolved upon by the GM.

In any case, each shareholder has the right to be attributed stock in the new company in proportion to their shares/quotas.

40. Which rights are available to shareholders of a company in liquidation?

The GM (in SpAs, the extraordinary GM) can appoint liquidators, revoke them for just cause and resolve upon the manner in which the winding-up shall take place. When the winding-up procedure is completed, the liquidators shall draw up the final financial statement, which shall be approved by all shareholders (Article 2487, the Code). Each shareholder has the right to challenge such a financial statement before the court, within 90 days from their deposit with the Companies' Register. Shareholders have the right to be attributed the proceeds resulting from the sale of the company's assets. If the by-laws or a resolution of the GM provide so, the shareholders' stakes can be liquidated in kind.

A winding-up procedure can be revoked at any time by the GM (in SpA companies by the extraordinary GM), subject to the prior elimination of the cause of winding-up. The revocation is effective upon expiration of 60 days from the date of filing the resolution with the Companies' Register (Article 2487-*ter* of the Code).

41. Can shareholders cause the liquidation of the company? How?

The GM (in SpAs, the extraordinary GM) can resolve upon the liquidation of the company. According to the case law, a resolution of winding-up which was fraudulently adopted in pursuit of interests other than those of the company or with the purpose of damaging minority shareholders can be challenged by such shareholders and declared null and void by the court for abuse or excess of power (Supreme Court no. 4923/1995, 3535/1990).

COMPANY GROUPS
42. Is the concept of 'group' recognised as such under specific legislation? What are the implications?
Italian law does not recognise the concept of 'group' as such. However, Articles 2497 *et seq* of the Code contain some specific rules concerning the liability and publicity requirements of the companies which exercise direction and coordination activity over their subsidiaries.

43. Does a controlling company have any particular duties *vis-à-vis* its controlled company shareholders?
Pursuant to the rules indicated above in question 42, the company that exercises direction and coordination activity over another company shall be liable *vis-à-vis* the shareholders of the latter for the prejudice to its profitability and value of the stock, when the controlling company acts in its own or in third parties' interest, in breach of the principles of correct corporate and entrepreneurial governance.

44. What are the rights of company shareholders when the controlling company puts in place actions and/or transactions that can be prejudicial to the shareholders?
Shareholders have the right to bring a legal action for the damages mentioned in question 43 against the controlling company and other subjects who contributed to cause the damage (such as, eg, directors and managers), as well as against those who intentionally benefited from the damaging event (Article 2497, the Code).

45. What are the limitations, if any, to the possibility of owning reciprocal stock interests in companies?
A subsidiary company can purchase the stock of its parent (controlling) company only within the limits of the distributable profits and available reserves reported in the last duly approved financial statement. In no case can the par value of such stock exceed 10 per cent of the corporate capital of the controlling company (taking into account also the stock owned by the same controlling company and by its subsidiaries). A controlled company cannot exercise voting rights in the GM of its parent (controlling) company (Article 2359-*bis*, the Code).

A controlled company cannot subscribe the stock of the controlling company (Article 2359-*quinques*, the Code). The reciprocal subscription of shares between companies is also forbidden (Article 2360 of the Code).

Japan

Nagashima Ohno & Tsunematsu Tsuyoshi Shimizu

BASIC INFORMATION ON THE TYPES OF LIMITED LIABILITY COMPANIES AND ON THE RIGHTS OF SHAREHOLDERS

1.   What types of companies enjoy limited liability? If more than one, which ones have shareholders, ie holders of share certificates? Which one is the most common? Which one is mostly used by foreign investors?

The Companies Act (CA) provides for four types of companies that may be used on a for-profit basis:
(i)   a stock company (*kabushiki kaisha*);
(ii) a general partnership company (*goumei kaisha*);
(iii) a limited partnership company (*goushi kaisha*); and
(iv) a limited liability company (*goudou kaisha*).

Among these four types of companies, all equity holders of a stock company and a limited liability company may enjoy the benefit of limited liability. No equity holders of a general partnership company may enjoy the benefit of limited liability, and only one or more equity holders of a limited partnership company specified in its articles of incorporation as a limited liability member (as opposed to an unlimited liability member) may enjoy the benefit of limited liability. Of these four entity types, only a stock company may issue shares to its equity holders, ie, shareholders.

Stock companies are much more common than limited liability companies. There are approximately 2.5 million stock companies in existence in Japan as of the date of writing, and they vary from major listed companies to small private companies, such as wholly owned subsidiaries and family-owned businesses. Stock companies are also the most widely used entity type by foreign investors.

On the other hand, the limited liability company is a type of entity newly introduced in 2006 under the CA. Although the number of limited liability companies is still relatively small, it is increasing.

2.   Are there minimum capital requirements and/or thin capitalisation rules in force?

Neither a stock company nor a limited liability company is subject to any minimum capital requirements or thin capitalisation rules under the CA. Before the CA came into effect in May 2006, a stock company was required to maintain capital in an amount not less than 10 million Japanese yen. However, the minimum capital requirement was abolished when the CA came into effect. Technically speaking, both a stock company and a limited liability company may be incorporated with an amount of capital of only one Japanese yen under the current law.

It should be noted, however, that minimum capital requirements apply under certain regulations when a company operates the relevant regulated business(es).

3. Describe the types of shares that can be issued by a company and the different rights that they attribute to their owners, as well as any other financial instruments (bonds or other) and other instruments of a participatory nature in the company's capital that can also be issued by the company.

A stock company may issue classes of shares, if so provided in its articles of incorporation, that have different rights in terms of the following:
(i) distribution of dividends;
(ii) distribution of residual assets;
(iii) voting rights that may be exercised at a general meeting of shareholders (GM);
(iv) whether a transfer of the class of shares is subject to the approval of the company;
(v) whether shareholders of the class of shares may require the company to acquire their shares;
(vi) whether the company may acquire the class of shares from the shareholders in certain prescribed cases;
(vii) whether the company may acquire the class of shares from the shareholders if so resolved at a GM;
(viii) whether a resolution at a meeting of the class shareholders is required in addition to a resolution by a GM or the board of directors, as applicable (ie, whether a meeting of the class shareholders has a veto); and
(ix) whether one or more of the directors and/or statutory auditors (*kansayaku*) may be appointed by a resolution at a meeting of the class shareholders.

Item (ix) is applicable only to a 'closed company' without committees. (A closed company is a stock company all of the shares of which are subject to the approval of the company under its articles of incorporation when they are transferred. A stock company that is not a closed company is called an 'open company' whether or not it is listed on a stock exchange.) The terms of each class of shares are required to be provided for in the company's articles of incorporation.

A stock company may also issue stock acquisition rights (*shinkabu yoyaku ken*) to any person. A holder of a stock acquisition right may obtain shares of the company by exercising the right in accordance with the terms and conditions decided by the company when the right was issued to the holder. Stock acquisition rights are typically used for stock options granted to directors and employees and as convertible bonds in combination with corporate bonds.

A stock company may also issue corporate bonds.

4. Can a company have only one shareholder and still enjoy limited liability?

A stock company with only one shareholder is legitimate under the CA. In fact, there are many stock companies in Japan that are wholly owned by their respective parent companies or a natural person.

A company with one shareholder may still enjoy the benefit of limited liability. However, it should be noted that, in quite limited cases, the theory of 'piercing the corporate veil' may be applicable. Cases where the courts have applied the theory are generally classified into two types, although in both types the shareholder's full control over the company in question is required: (i) cases where, based on the facts taken as a whole, the company is deemed to have no substance as an individual legal entity (eg, no GM or board meeting is held, the company does not conduct operations independently from the shareholder and the assets of the company are commingled with those of the parent company); and (ii) cases where the company's corporate veil is deemed to be abused by the shareholder for illegal or inappropriate purposes.

5. Are the rights of shareholders the same in any type of company?

If the articles of incorporation of a stock company provide for any classes of shares, shareholders of the class of shares have the rights as set forth in the articles of incorporation, see question 3.

In addition, the CA provides for some rights that may be exercised by a shareholder. Some of these rights may be exercised by any shareholder, but some may be exercised only by a shareholder (or combination of shareholders) who satisfies certain shareholding thresholds (eg, holding a certain number or percentage of shares, and/or duration of the shareholding). Such rights and thresholds vary depending on, among other factors, whether the company has a statutory auditor and whether the company is a closed company or an open company.

6. What are the basic rights of any shareholder? Describe briefly the rights of minority shareholders and indicate which thresholds, if any, are required to allow the minority shareholders to exercise any such rights.

The basic rights of shareholders are:
(i)   the right to receive dividends;
(ii) the right to receive residual assets; and
(iii) the right to vote at a GM.

Such rights are granted to all shareholders even if the company's articles of incorporation do not so provide. These basic rights may be modified or even eliminated if so provided in the company's articles of incorporation, except that it is not permissible to eliminate both (i) and (ii) above with respect to the same class of shares.

As mentioned in question 5, the CA provides for some rights that may be exercised by a shareholder, some of which may be exercised by any shareholder and some only by a shareholder (or combination of shareholders) who satisfies certain shareholding thresholds. Such thresholds vary depending on the rights. For example, in the case of a stock company with a board of directors, holding one per cent or more of the voting rights held by all the shareholders of the company or 300 voting rights or more (or in the case of an open company, continuous holding of said percentage or number of voting rights for the preceding six months) is required to demand that the directors include in the agenda of a GM an agendum proposed by the shareholder. In addition, holding three per cent or more of the voting rights held by all the shareholders of the company (or in the case of an open company, continuous holding of said percentage of the voting rights for the preceding six months) is required to demand that the directors convene a GM and, upon obtaining the permission of the court, to convene such a GM itself if the directors nevertheless fail to do so without delay.

7.   Do all shareholders enjoy the same rights or can some shareholders be attributed specific rights, whether by reason of the particular class of stock owned or other? Are such rights generally provided for at the level of the company's by-laws and/or in shareholders' agreements?
A stock company may issue classes of shares that have different rights from each other in terms of items (i) through (ix) set forth in question 3 if so provided in its articles of incorporation. Various other rights may be provided for in a shareholders' agreement, but it is generally understood that the enforceability of a shareholders' agreement is limited. See question 26.

8.   May the rights of shareholders, generally speaking, be limited, modified, suppressed or waived in any way? If so, how? Are such modifications or limitations provided for in the company's by-laws and/or in shareholders' agreements?
As mentioned in question 6, each shareholder has:
(i)   the right to receive dividends;
(ii) the right to receive residual assets; and
(iii) the right to vote at a GM.
    However, such rights may be limited, modified or eliminated if so provided in the company's articles of incorporation except that it is not permissible to eliminate both (i) and (ii) above with respect to the same class of shares.
    On the other hand, the rights granted to shareholders by the CA (see questions 5 and 6) may not generally be limited, modified (except for modifications to the thresholds with respect to the rights by so providing in the articles of incorporation as specifically permitted under the CA) or eliminated.
    Shareholders sometimes agree to limit, modify or eliminate the rights granted to them by entering into a shareholders' agreement. However, it is generally understood that the enforceability of a shareholders' agreement is limited. See question 26.

GENERAL MEETING OF SHAREHOLDERS (GM) AND VOTING RIGHTS

9. Which decisions are reserved to the competence of the GM?

Under the CA, a stock company may have a board of directors if so provided in its articles of incorporation. Certain types of stock companies, such as an open company, are required under the CA to have a board of directors by providing so in their articles of incorporation. In practice, many stock companies have a board of directors irrespective of whether it is required under the CA.

In the case of a stock company with a board of directors, only those matters specified in the CA and the company's articles of incorporation may be resolved at a GM. Those matters specified in the CA include, but are not limited to:

(i)   election of directors, statutory auditors and accounting auditors (*kaikei kansanin*), removal of directors and accounting auditors, payment of remuneration to directors and statutory auditors, approval of financial statements and distribution of dividends;

(ii) removal of statutory auditors, issuance of shares by closed companies, capital reductions, reverse stock splits, amendments to the articles of incorporation, sale of all businesses or any material business of the company, dissolution of the company and approval of a merger agreement, a share exchange (*kabushiki koukan*) agreement and a de-merger agreement; and

(iii) amendments to the articles of incorporation by an open company to become a closed company.

Generally, the matters specified in the CA may not be decided by a board of directors alone.

The matters set forth in item (i) above must be resolved by an ordinary resolution, ie, a resolution by a majority of the voting rights held by the shareholders present (in person, by voting ballot or by proxy) at the GM where shareholders holding more than half of the voting rights held by all the shareholders entitled to vote are present. The matters set forth in item (ii) above must be resolved by an extraordinary resolution, ie, a resolution by two-thirds or more of the voting rights held by the shareholders present (in person, by voting ballot or by proxy) at the GM where shareholders holding more than half of the voting rights held by all the shareholders entitled to vote are present. The matters set forth in item (iii) above must be resolved by a special resolution, ie, a resolution by the affirmative vote by half or more of all the shareholders entitled to vote (by head count) and two-thirds or more of the voting rights held by all the shareholders entitled to vote. It should be noted that the quorum and voting requirements of each resolution mentioned above may be modified by the company's articles of incorporation to the extent permitted by the CA.

In the case of a stock company without a board of directors, any and all matters related to the company may be resolved at a GM while the CA specifies the matters that must be resolved at a GM (ie, those that may not be decided by a board of directors alone). Such matters include broader matters than those that may be resolved at a GM in the case of a stock company with a board of directors.

10. How does a shareholder participate in a GM? Are there any limitations to having a minimum number of shares? May a shareholder delegate attendance to another shareholder or to the board? May a shareholder obtain assistance from the courts or any other governmental body to intervene in a GM or to cause one to be held in some particular cases?

A shareholder may participate in a GM either in person or by proxy (as explained below). A shareholder may also participate by a written or electromagnetic voting ballot if the board of directors (or the directors in the case of a stock company without a board of directors) determines to adopt such means. If the company has 1,000 or more shareholders with voting rights, the board of directors must generally determine to adopt a written voting ballot.

A stock company may provide in its articles of incorporation that a certain prescribed number of voting shares constitutes a unit (*tangen*). If this unit system is adopted, one unit (instead of one share) is granted one vote under the CA, and thus, shareholders must have at least the prescribed number of voting shares to participate in and vote at a GM.

A shareholder may appoint a proxy and have such a proxy attend the GM and vote on the shareholder's behalf. The CA does not provide for any qualification for a proxy (however, most listed companies provide in their articles of incorporation that a proxy must be a shareholder of the company).

As explained in more detail in question 11, a shareholder who satisfies certain shareholding thresholds may request to convene a GM. In addition, any shareholder (or combination of shareholders) who holds one per cent or more of the voting rights held by all the shareholders of the company with voting rights (or, in the case of an open company, has continuously held said percentage of the voting rights for the preceding six months) may require that the court appoint an inspector to investigate the procedures for convening a GM and for the adoption of resolutions at it.

11. May a GM be called and held at the request of any shareholder? Is there a threshold regarding the percentage of the stock interest owned in the company that may entitle a shareholder to such a right?

Any shareholder (or combination of shareholders) who holds three per cent or more of the voting rights held by all the shareholders of the company (or, in the case of an open company, has continuously held said percentage of the voting rights for the preceding six months) may request that the directors convene a GM by giving notice to the directors of the agenda and the reason for convening such a GM. In addition, if the directors fail to convene the GM without delay following the above request or fail to give notice to shareholders to convene a GM to be held within eight weeks following the above request, the requesting shareholder may, upon obtaining the permission of the court, convene a GM itself.

12. May a shareholder bring up an issue to be resolved upon and put it to a vote if it is not included on the agenda? May a shareholder require more information from the GM and/or the board, concerning the agenda of the GM, to be put in a better position to exercise their vote?

In the case of a stock company without a board of directors, any shareholder entitled to vote at a GM may: (i) require that the directors include in the agenda of the GM an agendum (as opposed to a specific resolution) proposed by the shareholder; and/or (ii) require not later than eight weeks prior to the GM that all shareholders be provided with a summary of the specific resolution that the shareholder intends to propose at the GM relating to an agendum of the GM.

In the case of a stock company with a board of directors, any shareholder (or combination of shareholders) entitled to vote at a GM who holds one per cent or more of the voting rights held by all the shareholders of the company or 300 voting rights or more (or, in the case of a open company, has continuously held said percentage or number of the voting rights for the preceding six months) may require items (i) and/or (ii) above not later than eight weeks prior to the GM.

In addition, irrespective of whether in the case of a stock company with or without a board of directors, each shareholder entitled to vote at a GM may propose a specific resolution at the GM relating to the agenda already submitted to the GM (eg, an amendment to the specific resolution already submitted to the GM by the management).

Each shareholder entitled to vote at a GM also has the right to inquire of directors and statutory auditors at a GM as to any matters to be resolved or reported at the GM.

13. May a GM be held by telecommunication means and/or by correspondence (ie by written consent)?

A GM may be held by telecommunication means (eg, the telephone conference system) as far as such means ensure interactive and timely communication among the shareholders attending the GM.

The CA provides that if a director or a shareholder of the company proposes a matter to be resolved at a GM and all of the shareholders entitled to vote on the matter agree to the matter in writing or by electromagnetic means, the matter is deemed to be resolved without holding an actual meeting.

14. Are voting rights always proportionate to the stock held by each shareholder or can they vary by share class?

Under the CA, a stock company may issue non-voting shares as a class of shares. On the other hand, a share with multiple voting rights may not be issued. Thus, each shareholder of voting shares has votes in proportion to the number of its voting shares.

As explained in question 10, a stock company may provide in its articles of incorporation that a certain prescribed number of voting shares constitutes a unit (tangen). If this unit system is adopted, one unit (instead of one share) is granted one vote under the CA. The number of voting shares that constitutes a unit may be different for each class of shares. Thus, if the articles of incorporation provide that a unit of class A shares consists of 100 shares and a unit of class B shares consists of 200 shares, it essentially means that a shareholder of class A shares has twice as many votes as a shareholder of class B shares even though each shareholder may own an equal number of shares. However, it is arguable that provisions of the articles of incorporation providing for such units are not permissible if they are provided primarily for the purpose of substantiating multiple voting rights.

15. Are there non-voting shares? Is there a maximum percentage of capital represented by non-voting shares?

A stock company may issue non-voting shares as a class of shares by providing so in its articles of incorporation. The articles of incorporation may provide that: (i) the relevant class of shares does not have voting rights with respect to any and all matters to be resolved at a GM; or (ii) the relevant class of shares has voting rights with respect to some (but not all) of the matters to be resolved at a GM.

In the case of an open company, if the number of issued and existing non-voting shares (including both types of shares as set forth in items (i) and (ii) above) exceeds half the number of all the issued and existing shares of the company, the company must immediately undertake procedures necessary to make the former number not more than half the latter number (eg, cancel some non-voting shares or issue some voting shares).

16. Can shareholders group their shares in order to exercise their voting rights (eg, by trust, shareholders' agreement or otherwise)?

In order to, among other purposes, uniformly exercise their voting rights, shareholders may generally group their shares (shares as a whole as opposed to merely voting rights) in a trust. However, such entrustment may be deemed invalid in the exceptional cases where the entrustment is deemed to be made to unfairly restrict minority shareholders' voting rights.

In addition, shareholders may uniformly exercise their voting rights by entering into a shareholders' agreement. However, it is generally understood that the enforceability of a shareholders' agreement is limited. See question 26.

17. Under what circumstances can a shareholder challenge the resolutions adopted by the GM? Are there thresholds concerning the stock interest owned to be able to bring such a claim?

Any shareholder may bring an action to rescind a resolution of a GM for the reason that:
(i)   the resolution was adopted through convocation or resolution procedures in violation of any law or regulation or the articles of incorporation or in a grossly unfair manner;
(ii) the resolution is in violation of the articles of incorporation in substance; or
(iii) the grossly unfair resolution was adopted with the affirmative vote of an

interested shareholder.

In addition, any shareholder may challenge the existence of any resolution of a GM, whether in or outside the court, for the reason that a failure of procedures necessary to adopt such a resolution is material and therefore its substance as a resolution should not be recognised. Any shareholder may also challenge the effectiveness of any resolution of a GM, whether in or outside the court, for the reason that the resolution is in violation of any law or regulation in substance.

18. What are the terms and procedures to challenge a resolution of the GM?

In order to rescind a resolution of a GM for a reason mentioned in question 17, a shareholder must bring an action within three months following the date of the resolution.

Any shareholder may bring an action to confirm the non-existence or nullification of any resolution of a GM for the reasons mentioned in question 17. There is no time limitation to bring such actions. A shareholder may even challenge the existence or effectiveness of the resolution outside the court, but once the non-existence or nullification of the resolution is decided by the court, the decision will be final *vis-à-vis* any third party.

SHAREHOLDERS' RIGHTS VERSUS DIRECTORS AND DUTIES OF OTHER CORPORATE BODIES IN THE COMPANY

19. What is the procedure for the appointment/replacement/revocation of directors and of statutory auditors, if any?

Directors and statutory auditors may be appointed by an ordinary resolution of a GM (see question 9). If the company desires to remove any director or statutory auditor in the middle of its term, an ordinary resolution of a GM is required in the case of a director and an extraordinary resolution of a GM is required in the case of a statutory auditor (see question 9). If the removal is without cause, the removed director or statutory auditor may demand indemnity from the company for the damages caused by the removal (typically, the amount of remuneration that would have been paid by the company for the remaining term of the director's or statutory auditor's office).

20. May shareholders challenge the resolutions of the board of directors? Is there a minimum percentage of capital required to challenge a board resolution?

Any shareholder may challenge the resolutions of the board of directors if the resolutions or any procedures to adopt such resolutions are in violation of any law or regulation or the articles of incorporation. There is no minimum shareholding requirement for such a challenge.

21. Are shareholders entitled to bring a legal action against the directors of the company? In which circumstances? Please describe briefly the principles of directors' liability.

In principle, directors are required to indemnify the company against damages caused by any breach of duty as directors where the breach is committed with intent or negligence.

Any shareholder (or, in the case of an open company, any shareholder who has held at least one share continuously for the preceding six months) may demand that the company institute an action against the directors to establish their liability to the company, and if the company does not bring such an action within 60 days after the date on which the demand is made, the shareholder itself may bring such an action against the directors on behalf of the company (ie, a derivative action).

A shareholder may also demand indemnity from a director who intentionally breaches its duties or is grossly negligent in performing its duties as a director for damages incurred by the shareholder itself (as opposed to the company) arising as a result of such a breach.

In addition, any shareholder (or, in the case of an open company, any shareholder who has held at least one share continuously for the preceding six months) may demand that a director cease and desist from any act or potential action that is in violation of any law or regulation or the articles of incorporation and that may cause irreparable damage to the company.

22. What are the rights in connection with transactions where the directors have a conflict of interest situation?

If a director is deemed to have breached its duty of care in performing its duties as a director because of a conflict of interest with the company, any shareholder (or, in the case of an open company, any shareholder who has held at least one share continuously for the preceding six months) may demand that the company institute an action against the director to establish the director's liability to the company, and if the company does not bring such an action within 60 days after the date on which the demand is made, the shareholder may bring a derivative action against the director. In addition, any shareholder may bring an action against the director to require indemnity for the damages incurred by the shareholder itself. See question 21.

Moreover, if the transaction at issue is subject to approval by the board of directors and the approval is made by a board meeting in which the interested director in question participates, a shareholder may challenge the board resolution since no interested director may participate in any board resolution under the CA.

INFORMATION RIGHTS ON THE COMPANY'S BUSINESS
23. What information may be requested by the shareholders from the board concerning the general state of the company's business or any specific transaction? Are information rights different depending on the number of shares owned? Are shareholders entitled to receive written information before, during or after the GM about the meeting agenda and to what extent? Is it possible for a shareholder to obtain a copy of the minutes of the GM?

Under the CA, a director of a stock company must submit the company's business reports and financial statements to an annual GM for reporting and approval purposes as applicable. In the case of a stock company with a board of directors, when a written notice to convene an annual GM is sent to each shareholder entitled to vote, a director must provide those documents to each such shareholder regardless of the number of shares owned by it. (In addition, if the company is a listed company or other company subject to the Financial Instruments and Exchange Act, it must prepare and file an annual securities report that generally includes more detailed information than that included in the business report and financial statements required under the CA, as well as a quarterly or semi-annual securities report (whichever is applicable) under the Financial Instruments and Exchange Act.)

Each shareholder entitled to vote at a GM also has the right to inquire of directors and statutory auditors at the GM as to any matters to be resolved or reported at the GM. As business reports and financial statements must be reported and/or approved (as applicable) at an annual GM, a shareholder may at such a GM, as a matter of practice, inquire of directors and statutory auditors as to a broad scope of matters related to the company.

A director of a stock company with a board of directors must send to each shareholder entitled to vote at a GM a convocation notice setting forth the agenda of the GM in writing or, with the consent of the shareholder, by electromagnetic means. However, although a director of a stock company without a board of directors must also provide a convocation notice to each shareholder entitled to vote at a GM, the notice need not be given in writing or by electromagnetic means and need not set forth the agenda.

Each shareholder may demand that the minutes of GMs be disclosed and that the shareholder be permitted to make handwritten copies (as opposed to photocopies) of the contents.

24. Do shareholders have the right/duty to resolve in the GM upon matters which were not on the agenda?

As explained in question 12, each shareholder entitled to vote at a GM in the case of a stock company without a board of directors, and a shareholder entitled to vote who meets the shareholding thresholds set forth in question 12 in the case of a stock company with a board of directors, may: (i) require that a director include in the agenda of the GM an agendum (as opposed to a specific resolution) proposed by the shareholder; and/or (ii) require that all shareholders be provided with a summary of the specific resolution that the shareholder intends to propose at the GM relating to an agendum of the GM. In addition, irrespective of whether in the case of a stock company with or without a board of directors, each shareholder entitled to vote at a GM may propose a specific resolution at the GM relating to the agenda already submitted to the GM (eg, an amendment to a specific resolution already submitted to the GM by the management).

25. Are shareholders entitled to inspect the corporate books and/or any other corporate or accounting documents? To what extent? Can they do it through external counsel or advisors?

A shareholder may inspect the corporate books and other corporate and accounting documents of the company although it may be required to satisfy certain shareholding thresholds and other applicable requirements depending on the documents to be inspected. For example, any shareholder may request disclosure of the articles of incorporation, the shareholders' registry, minutes of a GM, business reports and financial statements of the company. In addition, any shareholder may, upon obtaining permission from the court in the case of a stock company with a statutory auditor or committees, request disclosure of minutes of meetings of the board of directors if necessary to exercise its rights as a shareholder. Any shareholder (or combination of shareholders) who holds three per cent or more of the voting rights or issued shares (excluding treasury shares) held by all the shareholders of the company may request disclosure of accounting books and related documents of the company, provided it state the reason for the request.

A shareholder may exercise such an inspection right itself or through any person (including external counsel and advisors) who formally represents them.

SHAREHOLDERS' AGREEMENTS
26. Are shareholders' agreements validly enforceable? What are their typical contents and term of duration? Are they enforceable by or against third parties and, if so, to what extent?
Shareholders' agreements typically provide for, among other things, nomination of directors, statutory auditors and other officers from each shareholder, veto power, the right to inspect corporate and accounting documents and other rights of minority shareholders, restrictions on the transfer of shares, and the term and termination of the agreement. The term of shareholders' agreements varies on a case-by-case basis, and some agreements continue until the shareholders agree otherwise.

A shareholders' agreement is, in general, validly enforceable between or among the shareholders who are parties to the agreement. However, the dominant view is that it is not enforceable *vis-à-vis* the company. According to the dominant view, supposing that one shareholder exercises its voting rights with respect to a certain matter without the consent of the other shareholders: although it is subject to the consent of the other shareholders under the shareholders' agreement, assuming there is no restriction under the articles of incorporation, the vote will still be counted as a valid vote (although the breaching shareholder must indemnify the other shareholders against the damages caused by the breach under the shareholders' agreement).

In addition, a shareholders' agreement is not generally enforceable by or against third parties (including shareholders who are not parties to the agreement).

27. Do shareholders' agreements have to be disclosed to the public or registered in any public registry?
There is no requirement to disclose a shareholders' agreement under Japanese law merely because it is a shareholders' agreement.

ECONOMIC RIGHTS AND RIGHTS OVER THE STOCK
28. Is the stock always freely transferable? Are there any legal limitations? Are there any restrictions on contractual limitations?
In general, shares are freely transferable under the CA. However, the articles of incorporation may provide that no share nor any class of shares issued by a stock company may be transferred without the approval of the company (more precisely, in such a case, the transfer is invalid *vis-à-vis* the company although it is valid between the transferor and the transferee). In such cases, furthermore, unless otherwise provided for in the articles of incorporation, the approval must be made by the board of directors in the case of a stock company with a board of directors or by an ordinary resolution of a GM in the case of a stock company without a board of directors.

Two or more shareholders may enter into a shareholders' agreement that restricts the transfer of shares by each party. The discussion on the enforceability of a shareholders' agreement in question 26 is also generally applicable in this situation.

29. Are shareholders entitled to pledge their stock?
Shareholders may pledge their shares. However, if the articles of incorporation of the company provide that no share nor any class of shares to which the pledged shares belong may be transferred without the approval of the company (see question 28), the acquisition of the shares as a result of the exercise of the pledge is also subject to the approval of the company. Thus, a pledgee should ensure that there is no provision in the company's articles of incorporation that requires such approval of the company.

30. Are there financial assistance issues to be considered and other prohibitions to be evaluated in the context of a leveraged buyout transaction?
Although there is no provision under Japanese law that specifically prohibits 'financial assistance', there are some rules under the CA that should be considered in the context of a leveraged buyout transaction. See question 36.

31. May a company buy back its own stock and, if so, under what circumstances and subject to which limitations?
A stock company may buy back its shares from a shareholder who agrees to sell the shares if the buyback is approved by a GM and the company has sufficient 'distributable surplus' (see question 33) to consummate the purchase. If the buyback is offered to all shareholders, the approval of the GM may be resolved by an ordinary resolution; but if the buyback is offered to any specific shareholders, the approval must be resolved by an extraordinary resolution. However, with respect to a stock company with a board of directors, the buyback through the open market or through a self-tender offer may be approved by the board of directors alone if so provided in the articles of incorporation. In addition, with respect to certain types of stock companies, the buyback may be approved by the board of directors alone if so provided in the articles of incorporation and the latest financial

statements were audited without the statutory auditors or the accounting auditor raising any issues in their audit reports.

A stock company may buy back its shares from a shareholder if the put option or the call option provided for in the articles of incorporation with respect to all of the shares or any class of shares is exercised by the shareholder or the company (as the case may be). The company must pay the purchase price to the shareholder at the specific price set forth in the articles of incorporation (or the price calculated in accordance with the rules therein).

Furthermore, the CA provides that a shareholder may have the company purchase its shares in certain exceptional cases. See question 32.

32. Is there a legal right to withdraw from the company and, if so, under what circumstances? How is the shareholders' stock valued and paid in such a case?

A shareholder does not have a right to withdraw from the company except in some limited cases.

An exceptional case is where a shareholder may exercise its right of dissent and have the company purchase its shares at a 'fair price' when the company is to implement a merger, de-merger, share exchange (*kabushiki-koukan*) or other similar transactions. In this case, the purchase price of the shares to be purchased by the company is first negotiated between the company and the dissenting shareholder. If no agreement is reached between the parties within a certain period, however, either party may file a petition for a court order to decide the fair price of the shares.

Another exceptional case is where the articles of incorporation provide that all of the shares or any class of shares have put options exercisable by the shareholders. In this case, the shareholders may withdraw from the company by exercising such put options. The company must pay the purchase price to the shareholders at the specific price set forth in the articles of incorporation (or the price calculated in accordance with the rules therein).

33. In which circumstances can dividends be distributed among shareholders? Is it possible to exclude or limit the right of certain shareholders to dividends? Does a certain portion of the profits need to be set aside in a reserve fund where it cannot be distributed to the shareholders? Are advances on dividends allowed and, if so, under which circumstances? Can advances on dividends be reclaimed by the company?

A stock company may distribute dividends to its shareholders if this is approved by an ordinary resolution of a GM. However, certain types of stock companies may distribute dividends by the approval of the board of directors alone if so provided in the articles of incorporation and the latest financial statements were audited without the statutory auditors or the accounting auditor raising any issues in their audit reports.

The dividends must be distributed among shareholders on a *pro rata* basis in accordance with their respective shareholding ratios. However, shareholders of any class of shares (eg, preferred shares and inferior shares in terms of dividends) may be treated otherwise in accordance with the articles of incor

The total amount of dividends may not exceed the amount of 'distributable surplus' (*bunpai-kanougaku*) of the company as of the date when the dividends are made. Roughly speaking, the amount of distributable surplus is the aggregate of: (i) the amount of the capital surplus (*shihon jyouyokin*) less the capital reserve (*shihon junbikin*); and (ii) the amount of the profit surplus (*rieki jyouyokin*) less the profit reserve (*rieki junbikin*). The aggregate amount of the capital reserve and the profit reserve is supposed to be not less than one-quarter of the amount of capital.

Shareholders have no right to actually receive dividends prior to the effective date of the distribution resolved at the GM (or by the board of directors as applicable). Apart from dividends, the company may consider providing funds to any party (including a shareholder) at its discretion if there is a business reason for doing so. However, one should be cautious that such provision of funds to any specific shareholder may conflict with the principle of shareholder equality under the CA.

34. What are the rights of shareholders in the case of an issue of new stock (increase of the company's corporate capital) (pre-emption rights?)?

In the case of a closed company, a stock company may not issue shares (other than the issuance of shares to existing shareholders on a *pro rata* basis in accordance with their respective shareholding ratios) unless it is approved by an extraordinary resolution of a GM. In other words, existing shareholders have pre-emptive rights except as otherwise resolved by an extraordinary resolution of a GM.

In the case of an open company, an issuance of shares may generally be approved by the board of directors alone, and an extraordinary resolution of a GM is required only when the issue price is 'particularly favourable' to the subscribers of the issued shares.

It should be noted that, unless the total number of authorised shares set forth in the articles of incorporation is amended in advance by an extraordinary resolution of a GM, the company may not issue shares when the total number of issued and outstanding shares after the issuance would exceed the total number of authorised shares set forth in the articles of incorporation. In addition, in the case of an open company, the total number of authorised shares set forth in the articles of incorporation may not be increased to a number exceeding four times the total number of shares then issued and outstanding.

35. May minority shareholders ban or limit the company's capital structure in any manner?

A shareholder may demand that the company cease an issuance of shares that will be made in violation of any law or regulation or the articles of incorporation of the company or in a grossly unfair manner, if the shareholder will likely be adversely affected by such issuance. Although the CA does not specify in which situations an issuance of shares is deemed to be made 'in a grossly unfair manner', it is generally understood from court precedents that if the main purpose of the issuance is to maintain the existing management's control over the company by issuing shares to a specific person on the management side (and thereby decreasing the shareholding ratio of the hostile acquirer), such issuance is deemed to be made in a grossly unfair manner.

In addition, as explained in question 34, an issuance of shares may be subject to the approval of a GM. If any issuance that is grossly unfair in substance (eg, an issuance at a grossly unfair price) is approved at a GM because of the affirmative vote of an interested shareholder, any of the other shareholders may bring an action to rescind the resolution of the GM. See question 17.

36. Which are the financial assistance prohibitions in force?
There is no provision under Japanese law that specifically prohibits 'financial assistance'. However, in certain cases, a director may be deemed to breach its duty of care as a director and be liable for any damages to the company and/or shareholders arising from such financial assistance (see question 21). In addition, a stock company may not provide any person with any benefit (including, but not limited to, financial assistance) in connection with the exercise of shareholders' rights by such a person under the CA. This prohibition should be noted because providing financial assistance to purchase the company's shares may be deemed to be made 'in connection with the exercise of shareholders' rights' under certain circumstances, such as the company's management assisting a party on the management's side in purchasing the company's shares so as to secure the management's control over the company as against an acquirer.

37. Apart from publicly listed companies, in which cases (if any) are shareholders obligated to obtain an authorisation from, or provide information to, a public authority about events that have an impact on their stock interest in the company?
There is no such requirement under Japanese law.

SHAREHOLDERS' RIGHTS IN THE CASE OF EXTRAORDINARY TRANSACTIONS AND/OR WINDING-UP
38. What rights are available to shareholders in the case of a sale of all or a substantial portion of the company's assets? In the case of a merger or de-merger?
Generally, in the case where all businesses or any material business of the company are sold or a merger, de-merger, share exchange (*kabushiki koukan*) or any other similar transaction is implemented, the agreement of such transactions must be approved in advance by an extraordinary resolution of a GM. If any such transaction that is grossly unfair in substance (eg, the amount of consideration is grossly unfair) is approved at a GM because of the

affirmative vote of an interested shareholder, any of the other shareholders may bring an action to rescind the resolution of the GM. See question 17.

In addition, any shareholder who objects to the transaction may dissent and have the company purchase its shares at a fair price. The fair price of the shares is first negotiated between the company and the dissenting shareholder, but if no agreement is reached between the parties within a certain period, either party may file a petition for a court order to decide the fair price.

39. Which rights are available to shareholders in the case of conversion of the company into a European Company (SE) or into another type of company?

A stock company incorporated under the Japanese CA may be converted into any of the other three types of companies available under the CA (see question 1). However, there is no way to convert a Japanese stock company into a European Company (SE).

A conversion of a stock company to another type of company is subject to the consent of all shareholders of the company. If any shareholder objects to the conversion, such conversion will not take effect.

40. Which rights are available to shareholders of a company in liquidation?

A liquidating company must first fully pay its debts owed both to those creditors who have within a certain period made notification to the company of their status as a creditor as well as to other creditors known to the company. Once such debts are fully paid, shareholders are then entitled to receive a distribution of any residual assets of the company on a *pro rata* basis in accordance with their respective shareholding ratios. Shareholders of any class of shares (eg, preferred shares and inferior shares in terms of residual assets) may, however, be treated otherwise in accordance with the articles of incorporation.

Shareholders may bring a legal action against a liquidator of the liquidating company substantially in the same manner as a legal action against a director. See question 21.

41. Can shareholders cause the liquidation of the company? How?

A stock company may be dissolved if approved by an extraordinary resolution of a GM (and must be liquidated thereafter). In addition, any shareholder (or combination of shareholders) who holds 10 per cent or more of the voting rights or issued shares (excluding treasury shares) held by all the shareholders of the company may bring an action to dissolve the company under certain limited situations. Such situations are, however, quite exceptional.

COMPANY GROUPS
42. Is the concept of 'group' recognised as such under specific legislation? What are the implications?

Under the CA (as opposed to the Financial Instruments and Exchange Act applicable to a listed company), the concept of 'group' (as opposed to the concepts of 'parent company' and 'subsidiary') is not recognised except in quite limited contexts, such as in the preparation of consolidated financial statements (which are only available to companies with an accounting auditor) and decisions to establish internal control systems.

43. Does a controlling company have any particular duties *vis-à-vis* its controlled company shareholders?

Under the CA, a controlling company has no particular duties *vis-à-vis* the shareholders of its controlled company. However, whether or not the CA should be amended with a view to addressing this issue might be raised as a subject for consideration by the Japanese legislature in the future.

44. What are the rights of company shareholders when the controlling company puts in place actions and/or transactions that can be prejudicial to the shareholders?

If any action or transaction of the company that is prejudicial to the other shareholders of the company is resolved at a GM with the affirmative vote of the controlling company, any of the other shareholders may bring an action to rescind the resolution of the GM. See question 17. If any such action or transaction is resolved by the board of directors in which any interested director (eg, a director dispatched to the company from the controlling company) participates, any of the other shareholders may challenge the effectiveness of the board resolution. See question 22.

In any event, any of the other shareholders (or, in the case of an open company, any of such shareholders who have held at least one share continuously for the preceding six months) may bring a derivative action against directors of the company seeking indemnification against damages incurred by the company if the directors' participation in the action/ transaction or failure to supervise the other directors' participation in the action/transaction is considered to be a breach of the directors' duty of care (including duty of loyalty) that was committed with intent or negligence. Any of the other shareholders may also bring an action against directors of the company seeking indemnification against the damages incurred by the shareholder itself if such a breach was committed with intent or gross negligence. See question 21.

45. What are the limitations, if any, to the possibility of owning reciprocal stock interests in companies?

Under the CA, company A has no voting rights with respect to company B shares held by company A if company B and its subsidiaries own in aggregate not less than one-quarter of all the voting rights of company A. The CA restricts the ownership of reciprocal stock interests indirectly through this restriction on voting rights.

Luxembourg

Oostvogels Pfister Feyten Stef Oostvogels

BASIC INFORMATION ON THE TYPES OF LIMITED LIABILITY COMPANIES AND ON THE RIGHTS OF SHAREHOLDERS

1. What types of companies enjoy limited liability? If more than one, which ones have shareholders, ie holders of share certificates? Which one is the most common? Which one is mostly used by foreign investors?

As a principle, the liability of shareholders in a *société anonyme* (SA) (a public limited liability company), a *société Européenne* (SE) (a European company, a derivative of the SA form) and a *société à responsabilité limitée* (Sarl) (a private limited liability company) is limited to their respective capital subscription.

In a *société en commandite simple* (SCS) (a limited partnership) or a *société en commandite par actions* (SCA) (a partnership limited by shares), limited partners (*associés commanditaires*) normally enjoy a limited liability while the general partner (*associé gérant commandité*) is jointly and severally liable for all obligations of the company.

The liability of the members of a *société coopérative* (SCoop) (a cooperative society) can be organised through its articles and they may commit themselves jointly and severally or just severally, indefinitely or up to a specific amount.

All of the above have 'shareholders'.

The most commonly used forms are the SA, Sarl and SCA. Each form offers legal personality, limited liability, qualifies for the important participation exemption and constitutes a preferred choice for holding and finance structures.

The SA is generally the preferred choice for flexibility and the free transferability of shares. The Sarl and SCA are commonly used by US investors when seeking check-the-box for US tax purposes.

The SCA also offers full discretionary management control of the company in favour of the general partner(s).

2. Are there minimum capital requirements and/or thin capitalisation rules in force?

The Company Act imposes the following minimum capital requirements:
- SA: €30,986.69 (often rounded to €31,000);
- Sarl: €12,394.68 (often rounded to €12,500);
- SCA: €30,986.69 (often rounded to €31,000);
- SE: €120,000;
- SCS: no minimum requirements; and

- SCoop: no minimum requirements.

Although no formal thin capitalisation rules are imposed, it is generally accepted that, for tax purposes, a debt-equity ratio of 85/15 should serve as a reference. This ratio is influenced by the particularities of a given investment structure, the terms and conditions of the debt and equity instruments and also by possible guarantees. International tax practice has developed certain guidelines in this respect.

For certain regulated activities, the minimum capital requirements have been raised. This applies, among others, to activities governed by the law on the financial sector as well as for investment fund structures.

3. Describe the types of shares that can be issued by a company and the different rights that they attribute to their owners, as well as any other financial instruments (bonds or other) and other instruments of a participatory nature in the company's capital that can also be issued by the company.

The Company Act defines certain equity and debt instruments. Additional ones have been developed based on the principle of contractual freedom, a cornerstone of the Company Act.

Contractual freedom is, however, tempered by mandatory provisions and provisions of public policy. In particular Article 1855 of the Civil Code (leonine clause) provides an important limitation: an agreement that allocates all profits to one of the shareholders will be null and void. The same applies to a provision that exempts sums or effects contributed by one or more of the shareholders from contribution to losses generated by the company.

The following instruments are frequently used:
- bearer shares;
- registered shares;
- limited shares;
- unlimited shares;
- shares with associated pre-emptive rights;
- shares with associated nomination rights;
- ordinary shares;
- founder shares or profit parts;
- amortisation shares;
- profit shares;
- bonus shares;
- non-voting shares;
- preference or priority shares;
- redeemable shares;
- tracking shares;
- alphabet shares;
- bonds;
- convertible bonds;
- preferred equity certificates; and
- warrants or subscription rights.

Parties have great autonomy in determining the rights and obligations attached to the above instruments, provided public policy rules and mandatory provisions are respected.

4. Can a company have only one shareholder and still enjoy limited liability?

The SA and Sarl can be construed as single shareholder companies and enjoy limited liability.

5. Are the rights of shareholders the same in any type of company?

The terms 'share(s)' and 'shareholders(s)' are used in a generic sense in this document.

Different company forms issue different types of membership rights. The rights and obligations of Sarl shareholders are fundamentally different from those of an SA. The rights and obligations of unlimited shareholders in an SCA are also fundamentally different from those of an SA/Sarl. Differences relate, among others, to the transferability of shares, equal treatment of shareholders and limitation of liability.

Shareholders' rights in the SCA are calculated on those established for the SA, however, with important differences for unlimited shares. The same applies to the SE.

6. What are the basic rights of any shareholder? Describe briefly the rights of minority shareholders and indicate which thresholds, if any, are required to allow the minority shareholders to exercise any such rights.

There are two main categories of rights, namely:
Membership rights

Rights to:
* information;
* attend shareholders' meetings, to partake in the shareholders' deliberations and to vote; and
* request the dissolution of the company.

Economic rights

Rights to:
* obtain repayment of the contribution; and
* share profits.

Certain rights derive from public policy rules and cannot be modified, suppressed or restricted. Others can be restricted under strict conditions.

Shareholders' rights derive from the law and from the articles of association. Excluding those companies established under a private agreement, any amendment to the articles requires a resolution of an extraordinary general shareholders' meeting (EGM) held before a notary public. One notorious exception exists for the SA and SCA, where the management body can be authorised by the shareholders' meeting to increase the share capital within the limits of the so called 'authorised capital'.

For minority shareholders of an SA, SCA or SE, those holding:

- more than one-third of the share capital may block any amendment to the articles of association;
- more than one-third of the shares in a particular class of shares may block any amendment to the rights and obligations of said class of shares;
- at least 25 per cent of the share capital may dissolve the company in the event the losses exceed three-quarters of the company's share capital;
- at least 20 per cent of the share capital may request the court to appoint an *ad hoc* auditor to verify the company's books and accounts;
- at least five per cent of share capital may request an auditor report on a contribution in kind that otherwise would be exempt from such a report; and
- any shareholder, without regard to the number of shares held, may consult 15 days prior to the statutory general shareholders' meeting:
  (i)   the annual accounts;
  (ii) the portfolio held by the company;
  (iii) the list of shareholders that have not paid-in their commitments;
  (iv) the report of the board or the supervisory board; and
  (v)   the report of the statutory auditor or the independent auditor.

For minority shareholders of a Sarl, those holding:

- more than 25 per cent of the company's share capital may block the transfer *inter vivos* of shares to non-members;
- more than 25 per cent of the company's shares owned by the survivors may block the transfer, by reason of death, of shares to non-members; and
- more than 25 per cent of the company's share capital, or collectively representing the majority of shareholders, may block any amendment to the articles.

Each shareholder of a Sarl has access to the communication of the inventory, the balance sheet and the report of the advisory board.

Shareholders of the SA, SCA, or Sarl, irrespective of the size of their participation, may further block any change of nationality of the company as well as the increase of the shareholders' commitments.

7.   Do all shareholders enjoy the same rights or can some shareholders be attributed specific rights, whether by reason of the particular class of stock owned or other? Are such rights generally provided for at the level of the company's by-laws and/or in shareholders' agreements?

All shareholders do not necessarily enjoy the same rights.

With an SCS or SCA, management is, for instance, exclusively reserved for the unlimited partners.

Different rights and obligations can result from: (a) the law; (b) articles of association; or (c) private agreements.

The Company Act provides, among others, for certain specific preferential rights for holders of non-voting shares in an SA.

Different classes of shares with different rights can be created, however, public policy provisions must be respected at all times.

Certain shareholders can be attributed specific rights under private contract.

8. May the rights of shareholders, generally speaking, be limited, modified, suppressed or waived in any way? If so, how? Are such modifications or limitations provided for in the company's by-laws and/or in shareholders' agreements?

With the exception of public policy rights, rights can be limited, restricted, altered or modified contractually. A shareholder can waive their rights under certain conditions.

To ensure their opposability, it is often recommended to insert modifications or limitations in the company's articles. Sometimes, however, parties prefer not to for reasons of confidentiality. Another reason for not inserting certain provisions in the articles is that when shareholders' agreements in a Luxembourg company are governed by foreign legislation, problems of interpretation and applicability could occur.

GENERAL MEETING OF SHAREHOLDERS (GM) AND VOTING RIGHTS

For the purpose of the following questions, only those rules applicable to the SA and Sarl are covered. Rules applicable to other types of companies are often inspired by them.

9. Which decisions are reserved to the competence of the GM?

The following matters are reserved for the GM:

- amendments to the articles, with an exception for the SA for the increase of share capital within the limits of the authorised capital;
- authorisation of the board of directors of an SA to proceed to a capital increase or a quasi contribution;
- appointment and removal of directors and auditors, with an exception for the appointment of replacement directors in an SA in the event of a vacancy or the appointment of auditors with respect to regulated entities;
- approval of annual accounts, allocation of profits and losses (with an exception for the payment of advances on dividends by the board), discharge to directors, statutory auditors, liquidators and auditors to the liquidation;
- initiation of the *actio mandati*; and
- amendments to the capital structure, dissolutions, liquidations, mergers, de-mergers, etc.

10. How does a shareholder participate in a GM? Are there any limitations to having a minimum number of shares? May a shareholder delegate attendance to another shareholder or to the board? May a shareholder obtain assistance from the courts or any other governmental body to intervene in a GM or to cause one to be held in some particular cases?

The articles contain provisions governing proceedings at GMs and the formalities necessary for admission. In the absence of such provisions, appointments are made and resolutions are adopted in accordance with the rules of deliberating assemblies.

Every shareholder is entitled to vote personally or via proxy. Generally, they can attend the GM in person or grant a power of attorney to a third party.

Notwithstanding any contrary provisions, shareholders are entitled to take part in the deliberation with a number of votes equal to that of shares in possession.

The exercise of voting rights attached to shares in respect of which calls have not been paid, are suspended until such time as those calls which have been duly made and are payable, are paid. Voting rights may also be suspended in situations such as cross-participations or when the company holds its own shares.

11. May a GM be called and held at the request of any shareholder? Is there a threshold regarding the percentage of the stock interest owned in the company that may entitle a shareholder to such a right?

For the SA, GMs are convened by the board of directors, the management board, the supervisory board or the statutory auditors. They must call the GM so that it is held within a period of one month if shareholders representing at least 10 per cent of the share capital so require.

For the Sarl, GMs are convened by the directors (*gérants*), failing which by the supervisory board, if it exists, failing which by members representing more than half the share capital of the company.

12. May a shareholder bring up an issue to be resolved upon and put it to a vote if it is not included on the agenda? May a shareholder require more information from the GM and/or the board, concerning the agenda of the GM, to be put in a better position to exercise their vote?

The convening notice must contain the meeting agenda.

The GM may deliberate on all items on the agenda. Also, matters that are only briefly summarised on the agenda can be discussed to the extent that shareholders can appreciate the interest and importance of the meeting and that directors are duly informed about the issues which they might be invited to explain or comment on.

The customary agenda item 'miscellaneous' cannot cover any additional matters but only communications or accessory remarks. Additional items can only be added to the agenda following the formalities and notice periods as required for the convening of the meeting itself. If all shareholders are present or represented they can, however, waive this requirement. Urgent items can be added to the agenda only in certain situations. Importantly, the Luxembourg court will not necessarily declare null and void the resolution voted by the GM regarding an item that was not on the meeting agenda. Many factors including the importance of the matter, urgency, any conflicts between shareholders or the possibility for certain shareholders to overturn the outcome of the vote should such shareholders have been informed in advance of the relevant agenda point or should an absent shareholder be present, will be taken into consideration by the court.

The company should provide the legally required information in advance of a GM. If this is inadequately detailed, the board may provide additional information, upon the request of shareholders.

Shareholders have the right to put questions to the board and the statutory auditors. They have a fundamental right to try to influence the outcome of the decision making process at the GM. Questions must be related to the agenda or to the board report or to that of the statutory auditors. Any refusal to answer a question could result in a professional liability to the extent there are no valid justifications.

13. May a GM be held by telecommunication means and/or by correspondence (ie by written consent)?

In an SA, the Company Act expressly provides the possibility to attend a GM via means of telecommunication provided the articles authorise it, and:
(i) the telecommunication enables the identification of the attending shareholder;
(ii) each shareholder can hear and speak to each other; and
(iii) there is a continuous broadcasting of the deliberations.

Shareholders may vote by correspondence provided that the articles authorise it, and that the form expresses the sense of the vote for each resolution to be made.

Whether the GM of an SA can be held by correspondence is a more debated subject. Some believe that resolutions taken would not be valid as there has been no real deliberation or meeting. Legal practice has shown, however, that the board can take circular resolutions. This has become accepted practice over the years.

For a Sarl, the holding of GMs is not obligatory where the number of members does not exceed 25. The Company Act expressly provides for written resolutions in such cases. Moreover, the articles frequently provide that meetings can be held by modern means of telecommunication.

14. Are voting rights always proportionate to the stock held by each shareholder or can they vary by share class?

Every shareholder, notwithstanding any clause to the contrary, can take part in the deliberations with a number of votes equal to the number of shares held. All shares have equal value and, with the exception of non-voting shares, each share has one vote. A draft law is pending which, among others, introduces multiple voting shares.

15. Are there non-voting shares? Is there a maximum percentage of capital represented by non-voting shares?

An SA and SCA can issue non-voting shares. They must not represent more than half of the corporate capital and must confer the right to a preferential and cumulative dividend and the right to a preferential reimbursement of the contribution.

In specific circumstances, non-voting shares can gain voting rights.

A Sarl cannot issue non-voting shares.

16. Can shareholders group their shares in order to exercise their voting rights (eg, by trust, shareholders' agreement or otherwise)?

No specific rules exist on the grouping of shares. Shareholders can, however, exercise their rights in application of a voting agreement or contribute their shares to a trust in view of the joint execution of the shareholders' rights and obligations by the trustee.

Provided mandatory legal provisions and public policy rules are respected, such agreements will be legal, valid, binding and enforceable. For questions regarding specific performance, reference is made to question 26 below.

17. Under what circumstances can a shareholder challenge the resolutions adopted by the GM? Are there thresholds concerning the stock interest owned to be able to bring such a claim?

A distinction must be made between resolutions that amend the articles of association and those that do not.

Resolutions amending the articles may only be declared void in the event:
(a) the minutes have not been drawn up in notarised form;
(b) the capital contributions and the amount of capital subscribed for are not stated in the event of a capital increase; and
(c) the corporate object as amended is unlawful or contrary to public policy.

Resolutions that do not amend the articles may be declared void in application of the general principles of common law. A distinction must be made here between a breach that is sanctioned by either absolute nullity or relative nullity.

Provisions sanctioned by a relative nullity tend to protect specific interests. Only those persons that the law intends to protect may avail of such relative nullity. The right to claim a relative nullity is extinguished by the acceptance or confirmation of the underlying act.

A resolution in breach of a provision that is sanctioned by an absolute nullity can be challenged by any person that has an interest. This nullity cannot be extinguished by the acceptance or confirmation.

Each shareholder has an individual right to claim the nullity. Where the court declares the resolution or the GM itself null and void, such decision has retroactive effect. However, an irregularity is not automatically resolved in the decision or the meeting being declared null and void. The courts require that the irregularity has had a deciding influence on the vote.

18. What are the terms and procedures to challenge a resolution of the GM?

The principle is that actions against companies are prescribed after the same period as those against individuals. Thus, a breach that is sanctioned by an absolute nullity is prescribed after 30 years and a breach that is sanctioned by a relative nullity is prescribed after 10 years.

Certain actions prescribe after five years. This is the case for actions for the avoidance of the incorporation of an SA, Sarl, SCA or SCoop, when such action is based on the failure to enact the incorporation deed in notarial form, the absence of denomination, of corporate object clause, of specification of the contributions or of the subscribed capital.

Actions for the avoidance of a merger, division or transfer of professional assets prescribe after six months.

The district court hears all actions in this respect.

SHAREHOLDERS' RIGHTS VERSUS DIRECTORS AND DUTIES OF OTHER CORPORATE BODIES IN THE COMPANY

19. What is the procedure for the appointment/replacement/ revocation of directors and of statutory auditors, if any?

This will differ according to the corporate form.

In an SA, directors and auditors are appointed by the GM. There are two important exceptions to this rule:

* With vacancy of the office of a director appointed by the GM, the remaining directors may, unless the articles provide differently, fill the vacancy on a provisional basis. In such circumstances, the next GM makes the permanent appointment.
* The law of the financial sector provides that, in certain entities, the board of directors and not the shareholders must appoint the independent auditor. In certain areas, it is necessary to obtain a *nihil obstat* from the prudential supervisor before appointing, replacing or revoking any directors and/or auditors.

Directors and auditors can generally be revoked *ad nutum*, without delay and without cause. They can be appointed for a period not exceeding six years.

The rules are similar in the Sarl, however, directors must be appointed by the shareholders, either in the constitutive or subsequent instrument for a limited or undetermined period. Unless otherwise provided for in the articles, they may be removed, regardless of the method of their appointment, for legitimate reasons only. Where a director is appointed in the constitutive instrument, an amendment of the articles may be required.

In an SCA, the general partner cannot be revoked.

20. May shareholders challenge the resolutions of the board of directors? Is there a minimum percentage of capital required to challenge a board resolution?

The board of directors is an organ of the company. The company acts through its board. The members of the board are appointed by the GM and not by individual shareholders. These members have a fiduciary duty *vis-à-vis* the company and not *vis-à-vis* individual shareholders. It is, therefore, a matter for the GM and not for individual shareholders to action the *actio mandati*. Decisions validly taken by the board cannot be challenged by the GM as these decisions are attributed to the company itself. The *actio mandati* only tends to offer damages.

The board has the power to do anything necessary or useful to realise the corporate object. For unlimited companies, the sole limit is the corporate object. For limited companies also, actions *ultra vires* will, in principle, be opposable to the company. Individual shareholders can challenge resolutions of the board of directors under the same conditions as can third parties, to the extent that such shareholders have an individual interest that is separate to that as a shareholder.

Any action by an individual shareholder or third party against a resolution must be brought against the company.

21. Are shareholders entitled to bring a legal action against the directors of the company? In which circumstances? Please describe briefly the principles of directors' liability.

Directors are liable to the company for a breach of fiduciary duties and management wrongs. They are also liable to the company and third parties for a breach of the articles and a breach of the Company Act. Liability in this respect is joint and several.

Only the company can bring a claim based on the *actio mandati*. Also, once the directors have obtained a valid discharge by the GM, it is no longer possible for the company to action the *actio mandati*.

A claim based on a breach of the articles of association or of the Company Act can be brought by both the company and any third parties, including individual shareholders.

Individual shareholders, including minority shareholders, can base a claim on the general tort provisions of the Civil Code. They must evidence a personal prejudice that is distinct from the prejudice of the company and other shareholders.

22. What are the rights in connection with transactions where the directors have a conflict of interest situation?

Any director with an interest in a transaction submitted for approval to the board of directors conflicting with that of the company, is obliged to advise the board and to make a record of their statement and include it in the minutes of the meeting. They cannot take part in these deliberations.

At the next following GM, before any other resolution is put to a vote, a special report is made on any transactions where the interest conflicts with that of the company.

The above does not apply: (a) where the decision of the board of directors or of the director relate to standard transactions concluded at arm's length; or (b) where the company has a sole director, in which case a mention must be made in the minutes of the transactions of a conflicting interest made between the company and its director.

While the law does not define the concept of conflicting interest, the interest must be of a financial or economic nature. It must be substantial and must be opposed or conflicting.

The law does not prohibit or sanction the conflicted transaction itself but only sets forth the conditions to avoid the company suffering any damages. As a result, the transaction itself made in violation of the conflict of interest procedure will not be void.

INFORMATION RIGHTS ON THE COMPANY'S BUSINESS
23. What information may be requested by the shareholders from the board concerning the general state of the company's business or any specific transaction? Are information rights different depending on the number of shares owned? Are shareholders entitled to receive written information before, during or after the GM about the meeting agenda and to what extent? Is it possible for a shareholder to obtain a copy of the minutes of the GM?

Information is a fundamental right of all shareholders, irrespective of the level of their participation.

Shareholders are invited to all GMs. The convening notices must include a detailed meeting agenda. They have the right to ask any questions that are related to the meeting agenda or to any of the reports tabled at the meeting.

For the statutory GM, shareholders of an SA can inspect at the registered office of the company 15 days before the meeting:

(i) the annual accounts;

(ii) any detail of the company's portfolio;

(iii) the list of shareholders who have not paid up their shares;

(iv) the report of the board of directors or management board and the remarks of the supervisory board; and

(v) the report of the statutory auditor or independent auditor.

Also, the annual accounts, the report of the statutory auditor or independent auditor and the report of the board of directors or management board are addressed to all registered shareholders together with the convening notice.

Specific reports must also be made available to shareholders such as when the resolutions limit or restrict preferential subscription rights.

Shareholders in a Sarl are entitled to receive a copy of the balance sheet and profit and loss accounts for review and approval.

Furthermore, shareholders may ask questions at the GM. Such questions are addressed to the directors and/or auditors, however, such persons are not obliged to reveal confidential or sensitive information.

Shareholders are entitled to obtain a copy of the minutes of the GM.

24. Do shareholders have the right/duty to resolve in the GM upon matters which were not on the agenda?

The GM may deliberate on all items on the agenda. Also, matters that are only briefly summarised on the agenda can be discussed to the extent that shareholders can appreciate the interest and importance of the meeting and that directors are duly informed about the issues on which they might be invited to explain or comment.

The customary agenda item, 'miscellaneous' cannot cover any additional matters but only communications or accessory remarks.

Additional items can only be added to the agenda following the formalities and notice periods as required for the convening of the meeting itself. If all shareholders are present or represented they can, however, waive this requirement. Urgent items can be added to the agenda only in certain situations. Importantly, the Luxembourg court will not necessarily declare null and void the resolution voted by the GM regarding an item that was not on the meeting agenda. Many factors including the importance of the matter, urgency, any conflicts between shareholders or the possibility for certain shareholders to overturn the outcome of the vote should such shareholder have been informed in advance of the relevant agenda point or should an absent shareholder be present, will be taken into consideration by the court.

25. Are shareholders entitled to inspect the corporate books and/or any other corporate or accounting documents? To what extent? Can they do it through external counsel or advisors?

Shareholders are not entitled to inspect the corporate books or any corporate or accounting documents. In exceptional circumstances, upon application by shareholders representing at least 20 per cent of the company's share capital, the district court may appoint one or more *ad hoc* auditors with the duty to examine the books and accounts of the company. Further, shareholders' agreements often create a right to information in favour of certain shareholders that goes beyond what is legally required.

SHAREHOLDERS' AGREEMENTS

26. Are shareholders' agreements validly enforceable? What are their typical contents and term of duration? Are they enforceable by or against third parties and, if so, to what extent?

The purpose of a shareholders' agreement is typically to:
- organise a joint venture;
- implement an investment strategy;
- guarantee funding for investment projects;
- organise distribution of profits;
- bring stability to the company's ownership structure;
- offer protection to minority shareholders, comfort to majority shareholders and avoid deadlocks; and
- plan family inheritance.

Most shareholders' agreements will thus cover the following items:
- funding and additional funding;
- management and control of the company and its subsidiaries;
- transferability of shares;
- dividend policy;
- repartition of profits;
- right of information;
- non-compete and non-solicitation;
- confidentiality; and
- exit strategy.

Shareholders' agreements compliant with the applicable legal provisions (mandatory and public policy rules) will be legal, valid, binding and enforceable.

Shareholders' agreements must have a limited term. The purpose of the agreement is to influence its term. Generally, such a term will not exceed 10 years.

Whether a breach will result in damages or whether specific performance can be obtained will depend on factual circumstances.

Interlocutory proceedings (*procedures en référé*) can be instituted to obtain either provisional remedies (*mesures conservatoires*) or repair measures (*mesure de remise en état*). Provided the contractual obligations of the obliging party are sufficiently clear and detailed and that the rights of the other party are not seriously contested, the interim judge (*juge de référé*) could order such a party, under penalty if necessary, to execute its obligations or alternatively substitute itself for such a party and order that the judgment will be rendered in lieu of the relevant legal act.

The rule of privacy of contracts has several exceptions:
(i)   the clause for the benefit of a third party;
(ii) direct action;
(iii) indirect or oblique action (Article 1166 of the Civil Code); and
(iv) paulian action (Article 1167 of the Civil Code).

27. Do shareholders' agreements have to be disclosed to the public or registered in any public registry?

There is no obligation to disclose the existence or content of shareholders' agreements, except in application of transparency legislation and for listed companies.

Often, however, the company's articles of association contain a reference to a shareholders' agreement.

ECONOMIC RIGHTS AND RIGHTS OVER THE STOCK

28. Is the stock always freely transferable? Are there any legal limitations? Are there any restrictions on contractual limitations?

The transferability of shares differs according to the company type.

Shares in an SA are, in principle, fully transferable. The transfer of shares is valid only after the final incorporation of the company.

A limitation on the transferability of shares can, however, result from the articles of association or from the shareholders' agreements. Such limitations may not have the effect of making a shareholder a prisoner of their shares. A complete prohibition on the transferability of shares must be justified by a specific corporate interest and must be limited in time. The most commonly used share transfer restrictions are lock-up periods, prior consent clauses, right of first refusal clauses, pre-emptive rights, drag-along and tag-along rights, call and put options, etc.

Shares in a Sarl, a closed-type of company, are less easily transferable to non-members. Shares in a Sarl may not be transferred *inter vivos* to non-shareholders unless shareholders representing at least three-quarters of the corporate capital have agreed it in a general meeting. The threshold for this approval can be increased (contractually or in the articles) but not lowered.

29. Are shareholders entitled to pledge their stock?

The Company Act does not impose restrictions on the pledge of shares. Often, they are imposed under the articles or under a shareholders' agreement.

Also transfer restrictions could complicate the execution and enforcement of a pledge. Further, the pledge over unlimited shares in an SCA brings additional complexity.

Finally, financial assistance rules and bankruptcy and insolvency legislation can also restrict the possibility to pledge shares. Entities that are supervised by the Luxembourg regulatory body, the *Commission de Surveillance du Secteur Financier* (CSSF), must also bear in mind restrictions applicable to regulated entities.

30. Are there financial assistance issues to be considered and other prohibitions to be evaluated in the context of a leveraged buyout transaction?

Limitations on financial assistance were introduced with respect to the SA in 1983 but were relaxed in 2009. They do not apply to the Sarl.

See question 36 for further details.

In leveraged buyout (LBO) transactions, the financial assistance rules must be carefully observed as these rules are of public policy and can result in the finance and security agreement or any related agreement being declared null and void. Also, restrictions on the acquisition by the company of its own shares, redemption of shares, cross-participations and capital decrease must be taken into consideration when structuring LBO transactions.

31. May a company buy back its own stock and, if so, under what circumstances and subject to which limitations?

The Company Act only regulates the buy back of the company's shares of an SA.

The company can:
- issue redeemable shares;
- purchase its (ordinary) shares; and
- amortise shares, cancel them and replace them with bonus shares.

The issue of redeemable shares is strictly regulated and must be authorised by the articles before the redeemable shares are subscribed for. The shares must be fully paid-up and the terms and conditions for the redemption must be laid down in the articles. Also, the redemption can only be made by using sums available for distribution or the proceeds of a new issue and a special reserve which cannot be distributed to the shareholders must be created.

Besides the special case of redeemable shares, the company can acquire its own shares under certain conditions. The GM must authorise and determine the terms and conditions of the transaction. The acquisition may not have the effect of reducing the net assets below the sums available for distribution. The Company Act provides for a number of exemptions.

32. Is there a legal right to withdraw from the company and, if so, under what circumstances? How is the shareholders' stock valuated and paid in such a case?

A shareholder has the right to remain a shareholder of the company. There is no corollary right for a shareholder to withdraw from the company. Rules applicable to the cooperative company constitute a notorious exception in that it can include in its constitutive instrument rules organising the withdrawal of a shareholder.

Generally, any withdrawal, if not specially organised in the articles or in a shareholders' agreement, will be negotiated between parties. In certain situations, a shareholder could initiate procedures to obtain the dissolution of the company resulting in the disappearance of the company itself. This does not constitute a withdrawal of the shareholder. Also, the rights established under public takeover legislation do not constitute a right of withdrawal.

Bill 5730, filed in 2007, contains proposals to introduce mechanisms for a squeeze-out, a withdrawal and a redemption. Pending approval of these proposals, current applicable legal provisions do not offer a right to withdraw.

33. In which circumstances can dividends be distributed among shareholders? Is it possible to exclude or limit the right of certain shareholders to dividends? Does a certain portion of the profits need to be set aside in a reserve fund where it cannot be distributed to the shareholders? Are advances on dividends allowed and, if so, under which circumstances? Can advances on dividends be reclaimed by the company?

In an SA, no distribution of dividends may be made when – on the closing date of the last financial year – the net assets are, or following such a dividend distribution would become, lower than the amount of the subscribed capital plus the reserves which may not be distributed under law or by virtue of the articles. The amount of a distribution to shareholders may not exceed the amount of the profits at the end of the last fiscal year plus any profits carried forward and any amounts drawn from reserves which are available for that purpose, less any losses carried forward and sums to be placed in reserve in accordance with law or the articles.

In a Sarl, dividends may only be distributed to the extent that they correspond to profits actually earned.

In principle, the decision to distribute dividends is taken by the statutory GM, after the fiscal year has been closed, the annual accounts approved and the result allocated. However, shareholders could opt for an ordinary GM to distribute dividends or, to the extent this has been foreseen by the articles, the board of directors could decide to pay advances on dividends. Payment of such advances is subject to strict conditions for the SA. The Company Act does not provide any guidance for payment of advances on dividends by a Sarl. It is generally accepted that the latter company, to the extent it is permitted under its articles of association, is entitled to make such payments. In the Sarl, any dividend distributed that does not correspond to profits actually earned, including any advances on dividends, can be reclaimed. In the SA, advances on dividends cannot be reclaimed but will be deemed to have been paid on account of the next dividend.

Five per cent of the net profits must be allocated each year to the creation of a legal reserve. Such an allocation will no longer be compulsory when the legal reserve has reached an amount equal to 10 per cent of the company's share capital, but is again compulsory if the reserve falls below 10 per cent. The articles of association can provide for additional profit reservations and allocations to special reserves that are not available for dividend distribution. Certain companies even provide in their articles of association that all profits will be capitalised and no dividends will be distributed. The funds allocated to the legal reserve or to any special reserve that has been declared unavailable, cannot be subsequently distributed.

In principle, all shareholders are treated equally when it comes to dividend distributions, however, it is possible to create different classes of shares with unequal profit allocations. It is also possible for a shareholder to waive their rights at the moment dividends are distributed.

34. What are the rights of shareholders in the case of an issue of new stock (increase of the company's corporate capital) (pre-emption rights)?

Shareholders in an SA benefit, in principle, from a preferential subscription right. However, this only applies to shares subscribed for in cash and not to those subscribed for by contribution in kind. This preferential right is proportional to the participation of each shareholder. Exceptionally, the preferential subscription right may be limited or withdrawn, to be decided by the general shareholders' meeting or by the board of directors.

Shareholders in a Sarl do not benefit from a preferential subscription right in proportion to their participation. The Sarl can issue new shares to existing shareholders in such proportions as it deems fit or, with the approval of at least three-quarters of the share capital, to non-shareholders. As the issue of new stock entails an amendment of the articles, the resolution must be approved by majority shareholders representing three-quarters of the company's share capital.

35. May minority shareholders ban or limit the company's capital structure in any manner?

Minority shareholders can ban or limit the company's capital structure to the extent they dispose of minority blockage participation. The SA requires a two-thirds majority vote of the shareholders present or represented to amend its articles of association and the Sarl requires a resolution approved upon by a majority of shareholders representing three-quarters of the company's share capital. Resolutions that amend the rights of a specific class of shares need the required majority in the relevant class of shares.

The same principles apply to the issue of debt instruments convertible into shares.

36. Which are the financial assistance prohibitions in force?
The Company Act provides that a company may, directly or indirectly, advance funds or make loans or provide security, with a view to the acquisition of its shares by a third party, subject to certain conditions. The transaction must take place under the responsibility of the board of directors or of the management board, be made at market conditions, and be submitted to the GM for prior approval. The board of directors or the management board must present a detailed written report to the GM. This report is made public and filed with the company registry. The aggregate amount of financial assistance is limited and a reserve, unavailable for distribution, is recorded on the balance sheet.

The Company Act provides for some specific exemptions to the above rules, in particular for investment funds, banks and financial institutions and for employee plans.

37. Apart from publicly listed companies, in which cases (if any) are shareholders obligated to obtain an authorisation from, or provide information to, a public authority about events that have an impact on their stock interest in the company?
Shareholders must inform and grant information to the CSSF in application of the 2006 public takeover offer legislation.

Also, the CSSF must grant a prior approval in the event the company is a regulated entity in application of the law on the 1993 financial sector. Similar rules may apply to other regulated activities such as insurance activities.

Further, the tax authorities must also be provided with information on events that might influence the level of participation required for a tax exemption.

SHAREHOLDERS' RIGHTS IN THE CASE OF EXTRAORDINARY TRANSACTIONS AND/OR WINDING-UP
38. What rights are available to shareholders in the case of a sale of all or a substantial portion of the company's assets? In the case of a merger or de-merger?
Even if the board of directors disposes of extensive powers, shareholders can still retort. Firstly, the powers of the board are limited to actions necessary or useful to realise the company's corporate object. The sale of all or a substantial portion of the company's assets does not necessarily fit with this limitation and potentially qualifies as a management wrong, a breach of fiduciary duties or a breach of the articles. The GM could refuse to grant discharge and even decide to launch the *actio mandati* against the directors.

Separately, in the event shareholders are sufficiently informed in advance of an upcoming transaction, they could remove the directors from office *ad nutum*.

Further, individual shareholders who have suffered a personal and distinct prejudice from that suffered by the company as a result of the sale of assets, have the right to request reparations and may sue the directors separately.

Important events such as a merger or a de-merger give rise to certain specific rights and even require the active intervention of the shareholders.

The draft terms of the merger must be approved by the GM after having examined the merger report established by the board of directors or the management board. In addition, the merger project must be the object of an examination and report by an expert. The shareholders can unanimously waive the intervention of such an expert. The decision of the GM requires that the conditions as to quorum and majority laid down for the amendment of the articles are fulfilled. Such conditions must be met in each class of shares. For certain corporate forms, the approval by all shareholders is required.

Each shareholder has access to the terms of the merger, the merger report and the report of the expert in addition to some further general financial information.

Under certain strict conditions, it is possible to proceed to a merger without the approval of the GM. Also, a simplified procedure exists for situations where a company is acquired by another company which holds: (i) 100 per cent; or (ii) 90 per cent or more of the shares of the other entity.

Specific rules can apply to certain types of companies. For closed-companies such as the Sarl, conditions similar to those applicable to the sale of shares to non-shareholders will apply to a merger by absorption.

The rules applicable to de-mergers are largely inspired by the rules applicable to mergers.

Certain other transactions such as:

(i)   the contribution of part of a company's assets to another company;
(ii) the contribution of a branch of activity;
(iii) the contribution of a generality of assets and liabilities; or
(iv) the sale of assets, branches of activity or generalities of assets and liabilities, can be voluntarily submitted to the rules applicable to the de-merger.

39. Which rights are available to shareholders in the case of conversion of the company into a European Company (SE) or into another type of company?

With a conversion, a company takes another corporate form and the respective rights of the shareholders are modified. In this respect, there are formalities to be strictly followed to protect their rights.

Each type of commercial company other than the SE can be transformed into a company taking the form of one of the other types of commercial company other than the SE.

An SA governed by Luxembourg law may be transformed into an SE if, for at least two years, the SA has a subsidiary company governed by the law of another member state of the European Economic Area. An SE, having its registered office in the Grand-Duchy of Luxembourg, may be transformed into an SA governed by Luxembourg law.

The above transformations do not entail dissolution of the company nor create a new legal person. The decision to transform is taken by the GM according to set conditions and in the form provided for in the amendments to the articles.

The Company Act further provides that the provisions regarding the establishment of an SA apply to the transformation of another type of company into an SA. The transformation of an SE into an SA or vice versa is more complex and requires the preparation and publication of a transformation project, the intervention of independent auditors and must have approval of the GM for the transformation project and the articles of the SA.

40. Which rights are available to shareholders of a company in liquidation?

After its dissolution, the company will be deemed to exist for liquidation purposes only. The liquidator replaces the board of directors but the GM remains in place.

The GM has the powers to appoint and dismiss the liquidator(s), hear the liquidator's report(s) and the auditor's report(s) and vote on the liquidation accounts and distributions. The GM retains all other powers but these powers will be restricted by the fact that the company now only exists for its liquidation. The liquidator must convene the GM to obtain authorisation to continue certain activities such as the company's industrial and commercial activity, to borrow moneys to pay the debts, issue negotiable instruments, mortgage and pledge the assets, dispose of its immovable property, even by private contract, and to contribute the company's assets to other companies.

Before the liquidation process closes, the liquidator convenes a GM to approve how the liquidation has been carried out.

The shareholders themselves can normally exercise their rights at the GM and otherwise.

41. Can shareholders cause the liquidation of the company? How?

A voluntary liquidation can be organised if the company is solvent and can settle all its debts. The cause for opening a voluntary liquidation can be that the corporate object of the company has no further relevance, that the company's assets were sold or that the company is dormant and has to be deregistered.

The company is dissolved and put into liquidation by resolution of the extraordinary general shareholders' meeting held before a notary public. A liquidator must be appointed and their powers must be determined. When the liquidation is completed, the liquidator convenes a second shareholders' meeting in order to present their report and the liquidation accounts, and to appoint an auditor to the liquidation. A third GM will finally hear the audit report, approve the liquidation accounts and close the liquidation process.

An application for dissolution of the company can be filed with the district court by shareholders or directors in the event of a serious disagreement between shareholders. Such a request must be justified and the requesting party must prove that a serious disagreement exists which will jeopardise the implementation of the corporate object of the company or the company itself.

COMPANY GROUPS

42. Is the concept of 'group' recognised as such under specific legislation? What are the implications?

A group of companies can be defined as a number of companies that are linked one to the other notwithstanding the fact that each of them maintains its proper legal existence, and one (the parent company) exercises control over each of the other entities (the subsidiaries) and imposes a common policy.

This definition is contradictory in itself in that the parent company exercises control and imposes a common policy and, at the same time, each individual group company remains an independent legal entity.

The concept of a group is not formally recognised as there is no formal or coordinated legislation on group companies. Different areas of law, however, directly or indirectly deal with the issue. This is particularly the case for:

(i)   the Company Act which deals with group companies on different occasions, eg the section on consolidated accounts refers to the group concept but uses a different terminology ('a larger body of undertakings');

(ii) the law of 1999 on domiciliation of companies (this law provides for an exemption for companies that are part of the same 'group');

(iii) the law of 1993 on the financial sector (specific exemptions are available for 'group' companies which mean these entities can provide certain services without the need of a prior authorisation from the minister); and

(iv) the tax legislation (the concept of fiscal consolidation (*intégration fiscale*)).

Finally, legal doctrine accepts that the concept of corporate interest can be perceived differently when a company is integrated into a group. The concept of group interest adds to the concept of corporate interest in such cases. The concept of group interest has been built on French jurisprudence. A group requires that there is an integrated and coordinated approach, not just a common shareholder.

43. Does a controlling company have any particular duties *vis-à-vis* its controlled company shareholders?

Providing the holding company exercises its rights and obligations as a shareholder and does not abuse its majority position, it has no specific duties *vis-à-vis* its controlled company shareholders. The situation could be different in the event the controlling company has interfered in the business of its subsidiary or has made credit facilities available under certain conditions, particularly in insolvency situations.

44. What are the rights of company shareholders when the controlling company puts in place actions and/or transactions that can be prejudicial to the shareholders?

When a controlling shareholder puts in place actions and/or transactions which prejudice the business of the company or other shareholders, such actions and/or transactions could be qualified as abusive. An action or transaction can constitute an abuse of majority when it is contrary to the company's interest and, at the same time, especially favours the majority shareholder or especially penalises the minority shareholders. Such actions or transactions must be taken with the sole intention to favour or to penalise.

Minority shareholders can either ask the courts to declare the relevant action or transaction null and void or try to obtain damages.

45. What are the limitations, if any, to the possibility of owning reciprocal stock interests in companies?

The subscription, acquisition or holding of shares in an SA by another company in which the SA directly or indirectly holds a majority of the voting rights or on which it can directly or indirectly exercise a dominant influence is regarded as having been effected by the SA itself. This means that the transaction must obtain the prior approval of the GM which determines the terms and conditions of the acquisition, and that the transaction may not result in the net assets of the company falling below the distributable amounts. In addition, the company may only acquire shares that have been entirely paid up.

Where the cross participation is held indirectly, those restrictions will not apply. However, where the voting rights attached to the shares in the SA are held by the other company, they will then be suspended.

There are no comparable restrictions applicable to the Sarl.

Mexico

Basham Ringe Y Correa, S.C. Daniel Antonio del Rio
Loaiza & Amilcar Garcia Cortes

BASIC INFORMATION ON THE TYPES OF LIMITED LIABILITY COMPANIES AND ON THE RIGHTS OF SHAREHOLDERS

1. What types of companies enjoy limited liability? If more than one, which ones have shareholders, ie holders of share certificates? Which one is the most common? Which one is mostly used by foreign investors?

Under Mexican law, there are only two kinds of companies that enjoy limited liability, the stock corporation or *sociedad anónima* and the limited liability company or *sociedad de responsabilidad limitada*.

The *sociedad anónima* is the most accepted structure in the business field (by national and foreign investors) and operates under a company name and is formed exclusively by stockholders whose liability is limited to paying for their shares as capital contributions.

The corporate name selected is followed by the initials 'SA', or the words *Sociedad Anónima*.

The limited liability company or *sociedad de responsabilidad limitada* is considered as a partnership for United States tax purposes and is formed by members whose obligations are limited to the payment of their contributions to capital, but in which capital contributions are not represented by negotiable certificates (shares), whether 'registered' or 'bearer.' After the stock corporation (SA), this is the structure most commonly used by national and foreign investors.

The commercial name of a limited liability company is followed by the phrase *Sociedad de Responsabilidad Limitada*, or its abbreviation, S de RL.

On the other hand, the new Securities Market Law effective as of 28 June 2006, introduced a new type of corporation known as *sociedad anónima promotora de inversión* (SAPI). This type of corporation can be incorporated as a SAPI or as an SA which later adopts the quality of a SAPI and is not supervised by the National Banking of Securities Commission unless it subscribes values in the National Registry of Securities, in which case it will become a listed company known as a *sociedades anónimas promotoras de inversión bursátil* (SAPIB).

The corporate name selected is followed by the initials PI (*Promotora de Inversión*). Such companies are usual among investors, considering the benefits they provide, their possible wider range of rights that can be granted to shareholders and their structural flexibility compared with a regular SA.

2. Are there minimum capital requirements and/or thin capitalisation rules in force?

Minimum capital requirements are applicable under Mexican law which provides that an SA's and a SAPI's capital stock may not be less than $50,000 (fifty thousand pesos 00/100 Mexican Cy) and as for the S de RL the capital of the company may never be less than $3,000 (three thousand pesos 00/100 Cy).

Thin capitalisation rules are in force under Mexican law. If the total debt of a corporation exceeds three times the amount of the stockholders' equity, interest paid in connection with such debts may not be deducted under the Income Tax Law.

3. Describe the types of shares that can be issued by a company and the different rights that they attribute to their owners, as well as any other financial instruments (bonds or other) and other instruments of a participatory nature in the company's capital that can also be issued by the company.

The following are the kinds of shares that can be issued under Mexican law:

- Shares of common stock: typical shares issued by a Mexican company that grant to shareholders the same rights and obligations.
- Preferred shares: a special type of share which is entitled to receive dividends ahead of common shares, according to minimum percentage provided in law or as set forth in the by-laws of the company and which may or may not have voting rights.
- Limited voting shares: this type of share can only vote at extraordinary shareholders' meetings, at which among others, the following matters are discussed:
  (i) amendments to by-laws;
  (ii) dissolution;
  (iii) change of corporate purpose;
  (iv) extension of the term of the company;
  (v) change of company nationality;
  (vi) mergers;
  (vii) corporate conversions, etc.
- Unlimited voting shares: this type of share grants shareholders the right to exercise voting rights in any shareholders' meeting and regarding any matter.
- Non-assessable shares: shares fully paid by the subscribing shareholders or given to shareholders as a result of the capitalisation of stock premiums or other shareholder contributions.
- Assessable shares: shares which have not been paid in full by the subscribing shareholder(s).
- Neutral shares: shares issued by publicly held corporations to Mexican trust institutions and which are used by these institutions to issue, in turn, *certificados de participación ordinaria* that represent monetary rights (as opposed to corporate rights) derived from such shares

Under Mexican law there are certain instruments which are not properly shares, because they do not represent the capital stock, but grant a

shareholder rights such as the following:
- Founders' shares: type of securities covering the incorporators' share in the annual profits of an SA, payable after at least a five per cent dividend is paid to the holders of common stock. These types of shares are not included as part of capital stock nor entitle holders to participate in the management of the corporation.
- Performance stock: special kind of stock issued in exchange for services rendered to the company and entitling the holder to dividends.
- Treasury stock: stock that has been authorised but not yet issued and is not outstanding.
- Dividend certificates: special kind of stock issued in exchange for shares being redeemed by a company with the company's distributable profits and which is entitled to receive dividends second in line to non-redeemable shares, as set forth in by-laws of the corporation, and which may or may not have voting rights.

4.   Can a company have only one shareholder and still enjoy limited liability?
Mexican legislation requires a minimum of two shareholders.

5.   Are the rights of shareholders the same in any type of company?
There are general and basic rights applicable to all types of companies, however depending on the specific type of corporation, those rights may change between one type of company or another. The by-laws of Mexican companies may include special rights for shareholders (provided these do not contravene Mexican law).

6.   What are the basic rights of any shareholder? Can any such rights be modified or even suppressed and if so, how? Describe briefly the rights of minority shareholders and indicate which thresholds, if any, are required to allow the minority shareholders to exercise any such rights.
Basic rights for shareholders include the following:
   Property rights: these are economic and include the right to:
- make capital contributions;
- transmit the status of shareholder;
- receive benefits, which include the right to receive dividends;
- obtain the refund of capital contributions; and
- share in the distribution of capital upon liquidation.
   Corporate rights: these refer to the management of the company and include the following:
- right of first refusal;
- right to vote;
- right to designate directors or statutory examiners; and
- right to request an account from directors.
   The rights of minority shareholders in a Mexican corporation are granted either according to law or pursuant to the company's by-laws; the latter may

give additional rights and/or may reduce the threshold required to exercise such rights. Among minority rights established under Mexican law, the following are the most relevant:

- At least 22 per cent of the capital stock is required in order to appoint a member of the board of directors (or an examiner) when the company has three or more shareholders.
- 33 per cent of those present at a shareholders' meeting have the right to request a postponement of the resolution of an issue for three days without it being necessary to formally call a new meeting.
- 33 per cent of the capital stock may object to a resolution before a court, provided such shareholders voted against the resolution or did not attend the meeting. The claim to object to a resolution must be filed within the following 15 days as of the closure of the meeting, establishing which provision or the law or by-laws was violated.
- 33 per cent of the capital stock may request the Board of Directors to call a shareholders' meeting if no meeting has been held for two consecutive years or if in the meeting, the issues on the agenda of the annual meeting were not discussed.

With respect to a SAPI the Securities Market Law establishes the following minority rights:

- Shareholders with voting rights that individually or jointly represent 10 per cent of the capital stock can appoint a member of the Board of Directors and/or an Examiner.
- Shareholders with voting rights that individually or jointly represent 10 per cent of the capital stock can request the examiner or president of the Board of Directors at any time, to call upon a shareholders' meeting regarding issues related to their voting rights and can request to postpone the resolution of a meeting's issue with respect to which they feel uninformed.
- Shareholders with voting rights that individually or jointly represent 20 per cent of the capital stock can object to a resolution related to their voting rights taken in a General Meeting (GM).

7.   Do all shareholders enjoy the same rights or can some shareholders be attributed specific rights, whether by reason of the particular class of stock owned or other? Are such rights generally provided for at the level of the company's by-laws and/or in shareholders' agreements?

Shareholders can be given specific rights according to the class of stock they own. Such rights are provided through the company's by-laws (which are the legal rules recognised by law for the corporate governance of a company), however special rights may be agreed upon by shareholders in shareholders' agreements, whereby shareholders agree upon certain rules for the governance of the company including the class of stock that is going to be issued and the rights granted by such shares (although special rights shall also be included in by-laws).

8. May the rights of shareholders, generally speaking, be limited, modified or waived in any way? If so, are such modifications or limitations provided for in the company's by-laws and/or in shareholders' agreements?

Generally speaking, under Mexican law, it is possible to limit, amend and/or waive rights of shareholders. Limitation and amendment of rights must be expressly included in by-laws of the company, but may also (if applicable) be included in a shareholders' agreement.

Rights of shareholders may be waived in the by-laws of the company or through separate actions or documents whereby a shareholder expressly waives certain rights. A shareholder may waive its right of first refusal to subscribe for stock in a shareholders' meeting or a separate letter.

Nevertheless, limitations, waivers or amendments to the rights of shareholders cannot go beyond provisions set forth under Mexican law, ie, it is illegal to exclude a shareholder from all benefits of the company.

GENERAL MEETING OF SHAREHOLDERS (GM) AND VOTING RIGHTS

9. Which decisions are reserved to the competence of the GM?

General meetings in Mexico are classified as extraordinary or ordinary meetings and which resolve different matters, as follows.

Extraordinary meetings: reserved for decisions that entail an amendment to the company's by-laws, such as: renovation of term; increase or decrease in the capital stock; amendment to company nationality; mergers; issuance of preferred shares; among others.

Ordinary meetings: matters not reserved for extraordinary meetings.

10. How does a shareholder participate in a GM? Are there any limitations to having a minimum number of shares? May a shareholder delegate attendance to another shareholder or to the board? May a shareholder obtain assistance from the courts or any other governmental body to intervene in a GM or to cause one to be held in some particular cases?

A shareholder can either participate in a GM personally or through a legal representative authorised by means of a proxy signed before two witnesses.

There are no limitations regarding a minimum number of shares required for a shareholder to participate in a GM.

Shareholders can delegate attendance to another shareholder if they are constituted as the shareholder's legal representative, but cannot be represented by the directors or examiners of the company.

Mexican legislation does not foresee the possibility of a single shareholder obtaining assistance from the courts or from any government body to intervene in a meeting. Nevertheless it foresees the possibility of a meeting being called by the courts if shareholders which represent at least 33 per cent of the capital stock have asked the Board of Directors or Examiners to call upon a general shareholders' meeting and this has not been held within the 15 days following the request.

11. May a GM be called and held at the request of any shareholder? Is there a threshold regarding the percentage of the stock interest owned in the company that may entitle a shareholder to such a right?
As a general rule it is not possible for any shareholder to call for a meeting, unless:
* it holds at least 33 per cent of the capital stock of the company;
* a meeting has not been held for two consecutive years; or
* if shareholders' meetings held during such term have not discussed the approval of financial statements, the annual report of administrators and examiners, the appointment of directors and examiners and (if applicable) the fees for directors and examiners.

However, as an exception and with respect to the SAPI the only requirement, is to hold at least 10 per cent of the capital stock and such call must be related to their voting rights.

12. May a shareholder bring up an issue to be resolved upon and put it to a vote if it is not included on the agenda? May a shareholder require more information from the GM and/or the board concerning the agenda of the GM to be put in a better position to exercise their vote?
As a general rule, a shareholder may propose to the meeting the discussion of an issue not included in the agenda, but its inclusion must be approved by the shareholders' meeting. With respect to a SA or an S de RL a shareholder which represents at least 33 per cent of the capital stock can postpone the meeting with respect to the resolution of a certain issue of the agenda, if the shareholder considers that it does not have enough information to exercise its vote. With regards to a SAPI, only 10 per cent of the capital stock is required in order to postpone the resolution of an issue being discussed in a GM.

13. May a GM be held by telecommunication means and/or by correspondence? (ie by written consent)
According to Mexican legislation, a GM can be carried out by other means, but in order for its resolutions to be effective, the by-laws usually require such resolutions to be ratified in writing by the shareholders.

14. Are voting rights always proportionate to the stock held by each shareholder or can they vary by share class?
As a general rule, voting rights of a shareholder are proportionate to its share interest. Nevertheless, Mexican law allows the issuance of preference shares which may grant different voting rights compared to ordinary shares, by reason of the class of stock.

15. Are there non-voting shares? Is there a maximum percentage of capital represented by non-voting shares?
Non-voting shares are only available in publicly held companies and in SAPIs when set forth in the corporation's by-laws. There is no limitation to the minimum or maximum amount of capital represented by such shares.

16. Can shareholders group their shares in order to exercise their voting rights? (eg by trust, shareholders' agreement or otherwise)?
There is no concept of grouping of shares established in Mexican law. Nevertheless in practice shareholders may enter into a shareholders' agreement in order to be obliged to exercise their voting rights regarding a specific issue, in a certain way.

17. Under what circumstances can a shareholder challenge the resolutions adopted by the GM? Are there thresholds concerning the stock interest owned to be able to bring such a claim?
As a general rule, shareholders can object to a resolution adopted by the GM if they comply with the following requirements:

- the shareholder(s) must own a stock interest of at least 33 per cent;
- the claimant must not have attended the meeting or must have voted against the resolution; and
- the claim must state the section of the articles of incorporation or legal provision which was violated by the resolution and the explanation of the violation.

   As an exception and as for shareholders in a SAPI the threshold required in order to challenge a resolution adopted in a GM is of at least 20 per cent of the capital stock and the resolution being objected to must be related to the shareholders' voting rights.

18. What are the terms and procedures to challenge a resolution of the GM?
Claimants may object to a resolution of the GM by filing a claim with a Mexican court within the 15 days following the meeting in question, having the obligation to previously deposit their shares with a notary public or financial institution.

SHAREHOLDERS' RIGHTS VERSUS DIRECTORS AND DUTIES OF OTHER CORPORATE BODIES IN THE COMPANY.
19. What is the procedure for the appointment/replacement/ revocation of directors and of statutory auditors, if any?
The appointment of directors and statutory examiners must be done at the incorporation of the company or through a subsequent general ordinary shareholders' meeting. In both cases, the appointment is by majority vote unless agreed to contrary in the by-laws. The replacement and/or revocation of such appointments can be carried out through an ordinary shareholders' meeting in accordance with the requirements and conditions provided by the company's by-laws.

20. May shareholders challenge the resolutions of the board of directors? Is there a minimum percentage of capital required to challenge a board resolution?
Mexican law does not foresee such an action by shareholders.

21. Are shareholders entitled to bring a legal action against the directors of the company? In which circumstances? Please describe briefly the principles of directors' liability.

As a general rule, a legal action against the directors of a company must be filed with the prior approval of a shareholders' meeting, appointing the person empowered to file the action. As a general rule, shareholders that own at least 33 per cent of the capital stock have the right to directly bring a legal action against the directors of the company. However, regarding a SAPI, shareholders must represent at least 15 per cent of the capital stock in order to exercise such right.

Legal action against directors may be initiated when the director(s) have failed to comply with the company's by-laws or the law during their performance as directors of the company.

The principles of directors' liability, among others, are the rendering of accounts, complying with the company's purpose, assisting the corresponding meetings, looking out for and protecting the company's interests.

22. What are the rights in connection with transactions where the directors have a conflict of interest situation?

Directors are obliged to inform the rest of the directors if they have a conflict of interest with the company's own interests regarding any transaction and must refrain from any deliberation or resolution on the matter.

INFORMATION RIGHTS ON THE COMPANY'S BUSINESS

23. What information may be requested by the shareholders from the board concerning the general state of the company's business or any specific transaction? Are information rights different depending on the number of shares owned? Are shareholders entitled to receive written information before, during or after the GM about the meeting agenda and to what extent? Is it possible for a shareholder to obtain a copy of the minutes of the GM?

The board of directors has the obligation to file with a shareholders' meeting an annual report, which includes: a report of the company's general status with respect to its performance; the policies followed by the directors and the principal existing projects; a report which explains the principal policies followed in order to prepare the financial information; the financial standing of the company; the status of the company's operations during the last fiscal year; variations and updates with respect to the financial standing of the company; and their respective notes. Such report must be available to shareholders, regardless of the number of shares they own, at least 15 days prior to the meeting in which it will be discussed and they have the right to receive a copy of same. Shareholders can request any information they need, when the annual report from the directors is approved, including a copy of the minutes or any other specific transaction (provided that such transaction is within the scope of matters managed or approved by the board of directors).

24. Do shareholders have the right/duty to resolve in the GM upon matters which were not on the agenda?

Shareholders have the right to discuss and resolve in a GM an issue which was not part of the agenda, provided all shareholders or corresponding representatives assist in the meeting and agree upon such discussion.

25. Are shareholders entitled to inspect the corporate books and/or any other corporate or accounting documents? To what extent? Can they do it through external counsel or advisors?

Shareholders have the right to consult and/or inspect the corporate books that are at all times kept by the board of directors. They may inspect the corporate books through an external counsel or advisor if they have a power of attorney to do so.

SHAREHOLDERS' AGREEMENTS
26. Are shareholders' agreements validly enforceable? What are their typical contents and term of duration? Are they enforceable by or against third parties and, if so, to what extent?

The general rule is that shareholders' agreements are enforceable either when they are registered in a public registry, if legally required, or if such obligation is set forth in the company's by-laws. If registration is not legally required, such agreements will be enforceable and can be enforced against third parties.

The typical shareholders agreement is in force for as long as the company is in existence and the content usually deals with the following:
* new shareholders;
* legal quorums;
* amendments to the term of the company;
* appointment of the Board of Directors;
* attorneys-in-fact;
* capitalisation rules;
* constitution of the capital stock; and
* authority of the Board of Directors and of the GM.

With respect to a SAPI there are particular issues set forth in shareholders' agreements which include the following: rights and obligations regarding the purchase and sale of shares; and obligations to not develop commercial industries which compete with the corporation.

Due to the foregoing under Mexican law, such agreements can be enforceable against third parties if the agreements comply with the provisions set forth in the company's by-laws and with the applicable laws.

27. Do shareholders' agreements have to be disclosed to the public or registered in any public registry?

Only when there is a specific legal provision or if it is established in the by-laws must shareholders' agreements be disclosed to the public or be registered in a public registry.

ECONOMIC RIGHTS AND RIGHTS OVER THE STOCK
28. Is the stock always freely transferable? Are there any legal limitations? Are there any restrictions on contractual limitations?
In general terms, stock must be considered to be freely transferable unless agreed to the contrary in the by-laws or in another agreement (ie shareholders' agreement, pledge, etc). The company's by-laws may foresee that a transfer of shares may only be carried out with the board's previous authorisation.

29. Are shareholders entitled to pledge their stock?
Shareholders may pledge their stock unless the by-laws provide otherwise, or if there are previous agreements that limit such rights.

30. Are there financial assistance issues to be considered and other prohibitions to be evaluated in the context of a leveraged buyout transaction?
Financial assistance issues are not dealt with under Mexican law and therefore it must be understood that from a legal standpoint there are no financial assistance issues to be considered in this regard. Nevertheless, this kind of prohibition may have been agreed upon in the by-laws or a shareholders' agreement which will have to be taken into account regarding a leverage transaction.

31. May companies buy back their own stock and if so under what circumstances and subject to which limitations?
SAs and S de RLs may not buy back their own stock with the exception of an acquisition derived from a court decision with respect to loan payments of the company.

Nevertheless according to the Securities Market Law, a SAPI is allowed to buy back its own stock with prior agreement from the Board of Directors.

32. Is there a legal right to withdraw from the company, and if so, under what circumstances? How is the shareholders' stock valued and paid in such a case?
In certain cases, shareholders have the right to withdraw from the company, except when as a consequence, the capital stock is reduced to less than the minimum provided by law. Mexican law foresees the right of shareholders to withdraw from the company in the following cases:
- when shareholders vote against resolutions regarding certain matters;
- when shareholders vote against the liquidation of the company; and
- when against a shareholder's vote, a director is appointed who is a third party to the company.

The right may be exercised in accordance with the company's by-laws and if the by-laws of the company were amended without a unanimous vote and this results in an increase in the shareholder's obligations or a restriction on its rights. In such cases, shareholders have the right to obtain a refund of their shares, in proportion to the company's assets, according to the last approved balance sheet.

33. In which circumstances can dividends be distributed among shareholders? Is it possible to exclude or limit the right of certain shareholders to dividends? Does a certain portion of the profits need to be set aside in a reserve fund where it cannot be distributed to the shareholders? Are advances on dividends allowed and, if so, under which circumstances? Can advances on dividends be reclaimed by the company?

Dividends can be distributed among shareholders once a balance sheet showing profits has been approved in an ordinary shareholders' meeting and the distribution of profits is also approved by the shareholders. Dividends are paid either proportionally to their shareholding, as established in law, or otherwise according to the company's by-laws. Dividends may only be paid from profits. Such right can be limited, through the constitution of a series of shares which establish an order of precedence in the payment of dividends, but cannot exclude a shareholder from the right to receive dividends. As an exception, a SAPI may limit or widen shareholders' rights for dividends.

Moreover, pursuant to Mexican law a minimum of five per cent of the company's profits must be set aside each year in order to constitute a 'reserve fund' until such fund reaches an amount equal to 20 per cent of the capital of the company. The reserve cannot be distributed among shareholders and if for any reason it decreases, it must be reconstituted.

Mexican law does not foresee the possibility of paying advanced dividends, it only establishes the possibility of approving the payment of dividends until the corresponding financial statements which reflect a net profit have been approved.

34. What are the rights of shareholders in the case of an issue of new stock (increase of the company's corporate capital) (pre-emption rights)?

Shareholders have a pre-emptive right to subscribe to such shares in proportion to the number of shares they own, and as a general rule, this right must be exercised within 15 days following publication of notice of the issue of new stock in the official gazette of the company's domicile (or according to the procedure set forth in the by-laws of the company).

35. May minority shareholders ban or limit the company's capital structure in any manner?

In general terms, minority shareholders may not limit the company's capital structure provided that increases in the variable capital stock can take place without the approval of minorities, subject to any preferential right to acquire shares in the event of an increase in capital.

36. Which are the financial assistance prohibitions in force?

Mexican law does not deal with this issue. Nevertheless financial assistance prohibitions can be enforced through a shareholders' agreement or in the by-laws, requiring a certain number of contributions by shareholders from time to time.

The only obligatory contribution that has to be carried out by a shareholder in order to be considered as such is the initial capital contribution.

37. Apart from publicly listed companies, in which cases (if any) are shareholders obligated to obtain an authorisation from, or provide information to, a public authority about events that have an impact on their stock interest in the company?

Shareholders as such, have no obligation to obtain authorisations or provide information to Mexican authorities, with respect to any issue that implies an impact on their stock interest, but companies do have several obligations.

SHAREHOLDERS' RIGHTS IN CASE OF EXTRAORDINARY TRANSACTIONS AND/OR WINDING-UP

38. What rights are available to shareholders in the case of a sale of all or a substantial portion of the company's assets? In case of a merger or de-merger?

In general terms, there is no provision regarding an objection to a sale of the company's assets if this is carried out by the holder of powers of attorney for acts of ownership. Nevertheless, depending upon how the sale of assets is carried out, shareholders may be able to exercise certain rights and object to such sale, if it is not done pursuant to the company by-laws. If the majority of the capital of the company is against such sale, it will not be allowed to take place or if the sale took place against the shareholders' wishes, they have the right to file a claim against the Board of Directors or whoever was in charge of the transaction. In case of amendments to the by-laws derived from a merger, shareholders have the right to withdraw from the company.

39. Which rights are available to shareholders in the case of conversion of the company into a European Company (SE) or into another type of company?

In the case of amendment to the by-laws derived from a conversion of the company, shareholders have the right to withdraw from the company.

40. Which rights are available to shareholders of a company in liquidation?

A final balance sheet will be presented to shareholders for their approval which reflects the capital stock of the company. The same balance sheet, as well as the relevant papers and corporate books, will be available to shareholders who will have the right to present their claims to the liquidators within a term of 15 days. Once the final balance sheet is approved, shareholders have the right to receive payment of their respective interest in the capital of the company.

Shareholders may appoint and revoke the appointment of the liquidators who will be in charge of the company's liquidation.

41. Can shareholders cause the liquidation of the company? How?
Shareholders or partners may agree to the dissolution and liquidation of the
company through a meeting approving this.

COMPANY GROUPS
**42. Is the concept of 'group' recognised as such under specific
legislation? What are the implications?**
It is a group of companies organised under a direct or indirect capital
structure, in which a company maintains control over the other companies,
in which the companies maintain a common purpose and direction

**43. Does a controlling company have any particular duties *vis-à-vis*
its controlled company shareholders?**
In general terms, there are no specific obligations of the holding company in
regards to the controlled company's shareholders. However, indirectly, the
shareholders, by means of the company in which they own capital stock,
may, via the procedures provided in the by-laws of the controlled company
and in the General Corporations Law (such as shareholders' meetings or
Board of Directors' resolutions), exercise any minority's right established in
the General Corporations Law, if they have the legal percentages for each
right or determine that the controlled company votes in a certain way on
matters related to the holding company.

**44. What are the rights of company shareholders when the controlling
company puts in place actions and/or transactions that can be
prejudicial to the shareholders?**
Article 201 of the General Corporations Law establishes that a shareholder or
group of shareholders owning at least 33 per cent of the capital stock of the
company may legally oppose the prejudicial action or transaction, provided
that the same is derived from a previous shareholders' meeting.

**45. What are the limitations, if any, to the possibility of owning
reciprocal stock interests in companies?**
There are no limitations in this respect.

The Netherlands

Houthoff Buruma Michiel Pannekoek, Marleen van Uchelen, Ariane Smits, Yvon Tang, Angela van Lamsweerde & Maurits de Haan

BASIC INFORMATION ON THE TYPE OF LIMITED LIABILITY AND ON THE RIGHTS OF SHAREHOLDERS

1. What types of companies enjoy limited liability? If more than one, which ones have shareholders, ie holders of share certificates? Which one is the most common? Which one is mostly used by foreign investors?

Basically two types of limited liability companies exist: the *Besloten Vennootschap* or BV and the *Naamloze Vennootschap* or NV. Sometimes for tax purposes a Dutch cooperative organisation is used as an international holding entity. The cooperative organisation does not have shareholders. For the purposes of this chapter we do not touch upon the cooperative organisation and other legal entities in the Netherlands which are less commonly used in a business environment.

The BV is most commonly used. The NV is required to be used if its shares are to be tradable. However, one may also see NVs in the private domain. This is mostly historically driven or has an emotional background as an NV is associated with large companies.

The Dutch government is in the process of preparing a modernisation of the Dutch Civil Code (DCC) with respect to BVs. In general the provisions regarding BVs will become more flexible, ie fewer mandatory rules are included in the DCC which means that contractual deviation from many of the rules becomes possible. These new BV rules are still under discussion and it is anticipated that they will partly or entirely be implemented in 2011. For the purposes of this book reference is made to the various proposals for modernisation (as they stand at July 2010) as the New Act.

2. Are there minimum capital requirements and/or thin capitalisation rules in force?

The minimum capital required for the incorporation of a BV amounts to €18,000. The minimal capital required for the incorporation of an NV amounts to €45,000. Under the New Act the minimum capital requirement for the BV will be abolished. Financial institutions in Europe are subject to solvency requirements under supervision laws.

Under Dutch civil law there are no thin capitalisation rules in force. Under Dutch tax law thin capitalisation may result in the mitigation or loss of deductibility of interest payments.

3. Describe the types of shares that can be issued by a company and the different rights that they attribute to their owners, as well as any other financial instruments (bonds or other) and other instruments of a participatory nature in the company's capital that can also be issued by the company.

As a default rule, shares of the company are common shares, sharing equally in the rights and obligations. It is possible to deviate from this rule in the articles of association (the Articles).

Typically, alternative types of shares used are 'preference shares' or 'priority shares'. The DCC does not really define these types of shares and creating these shares is a matter of defining them in the Articles. In this respect one also sees letter shares (ie Share A, B, etc) with separate share premium and/or dividend reserves attached to them. Preference shares have a certain preference over common shares in respect of profit and/ or liquidation distributions. Such preference can for example be limited to the amount paid onto those shares and an annual – whether or not compounding – interest making them resemble a financial instrument. Priority shares have specific rights attached to them, for example, the right to make binding nominations for the appointment of board members.

Apart from various types of shares, other financial instruments available include bonds. As these merely have a contractual basis, they appear in various shapes and forms.

4. Can a company have only one shareholder and still enjoy limited liability?

Yes it can.

5. Are the rights of shareholders the same in any type of company?

Yes; there is no distinction between the basic rights of shareholders of a BV and an NV. Specific distinctions exist, the most relevant one is the right of the General Meeting of Shareholders (GM) of an NV to approve board resolutions resulting in an important change of the company's business.

6. What are the basic rights of any shareholder? Describe briefly the rights of minority shareholders and indicate which thresholds, if any, are required to allow the minority shareholders to exercise such rights.

The basic rights of a shareholder are the right to cast votes at a shareholders meeting and the right to receive dividends.

Any possible limitations on these rights are described below under 'voting rights' and 'economic rights'.

A basic rule of the DCC that affects and protects, (among others) shareholders, is that a company and the persons who by virtue of the law and the Articles are concerned with its organisation must, in such capacity, conduct themselves in relation to each other in accordance with the dictates of reasonableness and fairness; any rule which binds them by virtue of the law, custom, the Articles, by-laws or resolutions shall not be applicable to the extent that, given the circumstances, it is unacceptable according to the standards of reasonableness and fairness.

A more specific basic rule in respect of shareholders is the equality principle laid down in the DCC: save as otherwise provided in the Articles, all shares shall rank *pari passu* in proportion to their amount. A company must treat shareholders whose circumstances are equal, in the same manner.

7.   Do all shareholders enjoy the same rights or can some shareholders be attributed specific rights, whether by reason of the particular class of stock owned or other? Are such rights generally provided for at the level of the company's by-laws and/or shareholders' agreements?

As said above, a default rule of Dutch law is the equal treatment of shareholders whose circumstances are equal.

Both in the company's Articles as well as in shareholders' agreements specific rights can be attributed to specific shares. As current company law is not very flexible, one would generally see specific arrangements being dealt with in shareholders' agreements. Under the New Act, the laws governing BVs and its Articles will be more flexible and one would expect these arrangements to be addressed in the Articles more and more.

8.   May the rights of shareholders, generally speaking, be limited, modified or waived in any way? If so, are such modifications or limitations provided for in the company's by-laws and/or in shareholders' agreements?

Most rights can be modified or waived by shareholders. Particularly under the New Act, the DCC becomes more flexible and the possibility exists to adversely amend the rights of shareholders by way of amendment of the Articles. However, any such amendment of the Articles will require the consent of the relevant shareholders.

GENERAL MEETING OF SHAREHOLDERS (GM) AND VOTING RIGHTS

9.   Which decisions are reserved to the competence of the GM?

According to the DCC, any powers not conferred upon other corporate bodies (management board, supervisory board) shall be vested in the GM, within the limits set by the DCC and the Articles.

The DCC reserves certain decisions to the competence of the GM. The most important decisions are:
- to appoint and dismiss members of the management board and supervisory board (an exception applies to companies under the so-called large companies regime);
- to amend the Articles;
- to adopt the annual accounts;
- to dissolve, to convert, to legally merge and divide a company;
- to designate one or more other persons to represent the company in all matters in which it has a conflict of interest with one or more directors.

Under the New Act this right will no longer exist;
* to issue new shares and to exclude pre-emptive rights with respect to these shares, unless otherwise stipulated in the Articles;
* to reduce the company's capital.

In addition to the above decisions, with respect to NVs, resolutions of the management board relating to a significant change of the company's structure or identity, including any resolutions on major acquisitions or divestments are subject to the approval of the GM.

10. How does a shareholder participate in a GM? Are there any limitations to having a minimum number of shares? May a shareholder delegate attendance to another shareholder or to the board? May a shareholder obtain assistance from the courts or any other governmental body to intervene in a GM or to cause one to be held in some particular cases?

Every shareholder is entitled to attend and to address the GM and to exercise its voting rights at the GM.

There are no limitations on having a minimum number of shares.

A shareholder may delegate attendance by means of a written proxy granted to another shareholder or to a member of the board, but not to the company itself. The Articles may limit this delegation right.

Besides the right mentioned below in question 11, Dutch law does not provide for the possibility of shareholders to obtain assistance from the court or a governmental body to intervene in a GM or cause a GM to be held. In general, in particular cases, shareholders may start the special court procedure which opens the possibility that the Enterprise Chamber of the Amsterdam Court of Appeal (Enterprise Chamber) orders an inquiry into the affairs of the company (the Inquiry Procedure) referred to in questions 20 and 23.

11. May a GM be called and held at the request of any shareholder? Is there a threshold regarding the percentage of the stock interest owned in the company that may entitle a shareholder to such a right?

In some particular cases one or more shareholders, together representing at least 10 per cent of the issued share capital (or a lower percentage stipulated in the Articles), may on request be authorised by the court in interlocutory proceedings to convene a GM.

Under the New Act the threshold of 10 per cent will be decreased to one per cent of the issued share capital.

12. May a shareholder bring up an issue to be resolved upon and put it to a vote if it is not included on the agenda? May a shareholder require more information from the GM and/or the board concerning the agenda of the GM to be put in a better position to exercise its vote?

Shareholders holding at least one per cent of the issued share capital (or a lower percentage stipulated in the Articles) may request an item to be placed on the agenda of the GM provided that the company has received such request at least 30 days before the GM and the company does not have a serious interest that conflicts with the requested agenda item and which interest should prevail. For NVs the only possible two grounds for refusing a request to place an item on the agenda are 'reasonableness and fairness' and 'abuse of law'.

The agenda of the GM must include – by means of a general reference – all topics to be discussed during the GM. Shareholders may not bring up additional issues during the GM. Only one exception to this rule exists: valid resolutions may be passed in respect of matters not on the agenda if a resolution is passed unanimously at a GM at which the entire issued capital is present or represented. This exception does not apply where the company also has holders of depository receipts for shares which were issued with the cooperation of the company (depositary receipts) because holders of depositary receipts have the right to be present at the GM. The rights of holders of depositary receipts can also be granted to usufructuaries and pledgees.

Under the New Act, legally valid resolutions may be passed in respect of matters not included on the agenda in the notice convening the GM, if those entitled to attend the GM have unanimously assented to decision-making taking place.

The GM, as a corporate body, may require the management board to provide the GM with information. The management board must provide the information the GM requires, unless the company has a substantial interest which prevails. In addition, every individual shareholder has the right to ask questions at the GM and the management board must – to the extent possible – answer these questions. However individual shareholders or groups of shareholders do not have the right to be provided with information. As a general rule all shareholders must be treated equally.

13. May a GM be held by telecommunication means and/or by correspondence (ie by written consent)?

Yes, the Articles can stipulate that shareholders may attend a GM, address the GM and exercise voting rights by telecommunication means. As a general rule in Dutch case law, resolutions of the GM are the result of consultations between the shareholders. Moreover, the management board and supervisory board must be given the opportunity to give advice prior to the decisions. The DCC requires that all shareholders using telecommunication means can be identified by the management board, can follow the meeting directly and can exercise voting rights. The Articles usually include the specific conditions for the use of telecommunications means. Listed NVs are required to enable shareholders to submit their proxies electronically.

A GM can be held in writing, ie without holding a physical meeting, provided that:
(i) the Articles provide for this possibility;
(ii) only registered shares are issued;
(iii) no depositary receipts are issued nor ususfructuaries or pledges with similar rights exist; and
(iv) the resolutions are passed by unanimous vote of the shareholders entitled to vote.

In the case of written resolutions, the votes can be cast electronically, for instance by email. The Articles may exclude this possibility or may include specific conditions such as demanding an electronic passcode in order to identify the shareholder.

Under the New Act, resolutions may be adopted outside the GM provided that those entitled to attend the GM have unanimously assented to adopt resolutions outside the GM.

14. Are voting rights always proportionate to the stock held by each shareholder or can they vary by share class?

According to the DCC each shareholder shall have at least one vote. The DCC further provides that:

- if the authorised capital is divided into shares of an equal nominal amount, each shareholder may cast as many votes as it holds shares; and
- if the authorised capital is divided into shares of unequal nominal amounts, the number of votes of each shareholder shall equal the multiple of the nominal amount of the smallest share included in the aggregate nominal amount of its shares. Fractions of votes shall be disregarded.

The voting rights are linked to the nominal value of the shares. In other words: all shares shall rank *pari passu* in proportion to their nominal amount. It is not possible to determine that shares of a certain class (for instance class A shares) give the right to cast one vote and shares of another class (for instance class B shares) give the right to cast two votes if the nominal value is equal. As a general principle, a company must treat shareholders (and holders of depositary receipts) whose circumstances are equal, in the same manner. The DCC provides for the possibility of limiting the voting rights of a shareholder by means of a provision in the Articles. The following voting right ceilings are provided for in the DCC:

- the number of votes to be cast by the same shareholder can be limited in the Articles, provided that shareholders whose number of shares are equal can cast the same number of votes and the limitation is not more favourable for holders of a larger number of shares than for holders of a smaller number of shares (decreasing voting rights);
- provisions in deviation of those mentioned above may also be included in the Articles, provided that not more than six votes are conferred on any shareholder if the authorised capital is divided into 100 or more shares and not more than three votes, if the capital is divided into less than 100 shares (unequal voting rights or 'statutory limitation').

Under the New Act a flexible voting right will be introduced for shares in BVs. The decreasing voting rights and statutory limitation will cease to exist as soon as the New Act comes into force. This means that the Articles can provide for shares with more than one vote (without the voting right ceiling mentioned above). If the Articles are amended in order to include those shares with multiple voting rights, the resolution of the GM can only be taken with unanimous votes in a meeting in which the entire capital is present or represented. In this way minority shareholders will not be faced with new share proportions without their consent.

15. Are there non-voting shares? Is there a maximum percentage of capital represented by non-voting shares?

Under the current legislation non-voting shares do not exist.

Under the New Act a BV will be enabled to issue non-voting shares if the Articles provide for this right. There will not be a minimum percentage of capital represented by non-voting shares. However, a minimum of one share with a voting right is compulsory.

16. Can shareholders group their shares in order to exercise their voting rights (eg, by trust, shareholders' agreement or otherwise)?

Yes, they can. In principle, shareholders are permitted to enter into voting agreements. This is restricted by public order and in particular by written and unwritten mandatory law. Further reference is made to question 26.

Regarding listed NVs, it is important to note that shareholders 'acting in concert' together holding more than 30 per cent of the voting rights must make a public bid. Moreover, shareholders in a listed NV must notify the regulator in the event that their joint holding exceeds or falls below certain thresholds.

17. Under what circumstances can a shareholder challenge the resolutions adopted by the GM? Are there thresholds concerning the stock interest owned to be able to bring such a claim?

A resolution of any corporate body which is contrary to the law or the Articles is null and void, unless the law stipulates otherwise.

In general, anyone with a reasonable interest, including a shareholder, can challenge a resolution adopted by the GM if the resolution is contrary to: statutory provisions or provisions in the Articles regulating the passing of resolutions; the principles of reasonableness and fairness required under the DCC; and any by-laws.

There is no threshold concerning the stock interest owned.

18. What are the terms and procedures to challenge a resolution of the GM?

Annulment referred to under question 17 is effected by a decision of the district court of the legal person's residence upon the demand of a person who has a reasonable interest in the due performance of the obligation which has not been performed.

The right to institute such action lapses one year from the end of the day on which sufficient publicity of the resolution was given, or on which the interested party became aware of the resolution or was notified of it.

SHAREHOLDERS' RIGHTS WITH RESPECT TO DIRECTORS AND DUTIES OF OTHER CORPORATE BODIES IN THE COMPANY

19. What is the procedure for the appointment/replacement/ revocation of directors and of statutory auditors, if any?

In principle the DCC provides for a two-tier board structure. This consists of an obligatory management board which performs executive duties, as well as an (optional) supervisory board which advises and supervises the management board. The vast majority of Dutch (listed) companies have a two-tier board structure.

When certain requirements concerning the equity and the number of employees are met, the company qualifies as a 'large company', in which case it is obligatory to set up a supervisory board.

The managing directors shall initially be appointed in the deed of incorporation and thereafter by the GM, unless, pursuant to the DCC and as mentioned below, the appointment is made by the supervisory board. If the GM appoints a director, the Articles may provide that an appointment by the GM shall be made from a list of candidates containing the names of at least two persons for each vacancy to be filled ('binding nomination'). This binding nomination right can be granted to a corporate body, to persons such as holders of certain classes of shares and to third parties. However, the GM may at all times decide, by a resolution passed with a two-thirds majority of the votes cast representing more than 50 per cent of the issued capital, that such list shall not be binding.

Recently a new provision was added to the DCC according to which the proposal to appoint, suspend or remove a managing director will not be presented to the GM, before the works council has had the opportunity to form an opinion on the issue.

If the company is a large company, the supervisory board shall appoint the managing directors of the company; this power may not be limited by any binding list of candidates. The supervisory board shall not remove a director until the GM has been consulted on the intended removal.

Each managing director may, at any time, be suspended and removed by the body that appointed the director. The Articles may provide that the resolution to remove (dismiss) one or more directors is subject to a quorum. Such quorum may not exceed a two-thirds majority of the votes representing more than 50 per cent of the issued capital. In addition, directors may be dismissed or suspended by the Enterprise Chamber in the event that an investigative procedure in connection with mismanagement has been instigated.

The supervisory board is also empowered to suspend any managing director at any time, if the Articles do not provide otherwise. The suspension may be set aside by the GM at any time, unless the power to appoint the managing directors is vested in the supervisory board.

The members of the supervisory board who are not already appointed by the deed of incorporation shall be appointed by the GM. The Articles may provide that one or more supervisory directors, not exceeding one-third of the total number, shall be appointed by another corporate body. A supervisory director may be suspended and removed by the corporate body that has the power of appointment.

If the company is a large company, the supervisory directors shall be appointed by the GM on the nomination and proposal of the supervisory board, to the extent that they were not already appointed in the deed of incorporation. The supervisory board shall inform the GM and the works council of the nomination and proposal at the same time. The GM and the works council may recommend persons to the supervisory board. In general, the supervisory board shall nominate and propose persons recommended by the works council for one-third of the number of members of the supervisory board. In general, a supervisory board member of a large company shall resign no later than four years after its last appointment as a supervisory board member. Upon application, the Enterprise Chamber may remove a supervisory board member for dereliction of duties, for other important reasons, or on account of any significant change of circumstances, as a result of which the company may not reasonably be required to maintain them as a supervisory board member.

A supervisory board member may be suspended by the supervisory board. With an absolute majority of the votes cast representing not less than one-third of the issued capital, the GM may pass a motion of no confidence in the supervisory board.

Under the DCC there are no specific regulations in respect of the appointment, replacement or revocation of statutory auditors.

Under the New Act, the holder(s) of a specific class of shares (not just the GM) will be able to appoint managing directors directly.

20. May shareholders challenge the resolutions of the board of directors? Is there a minimum percentage of capital required to challenge a board resolution?

Reference is made to the answer to question 17 which also applies to a Board resolution.

Furthermore a shareholder may file a request with the Enterprise Chamber that an Inquiry Procedure shall be held. Such request can be made by, among others, one or more shareholders who represent at least 10 per cent of the issued capital or who are entitled to an amount in shares or depositary receipts issued for that with a nominal value of €225,000 or such lesser amount as provided by the Articles.

The Enterprise Chamber will grant a request for an Inquiry Procedure if there are reasonable grounds to assume mismanagement of the company. If the Inquiry Procedure leads to a decision that there has indeed been mismanagement of the company, the Enterprise Chamber may take a number of measures:

- the suspension or annulment of a resolution of the managing directors, the supervisory directors, the GM or any other constituent body of a legal person;
- the suspension or dismissal of one or more managing or supervisory directors;
- the temporary appointment of one or more managing or supervisory directors;
- the temporary derogation from such provisions in the Articles as shall be specified by the Enterprises Division;
- the temporary transfer of shares to a nominee; and

- the dissolution of the legal person.

At any stage of the Inquiry Procedure the Enterprise Chamber may order an immediate remedy upon request of one of the applicants. A great variety of remedies is permitted, including the abovementioned measures.

21. Are shareholders entitled to bring a legal action against the directors of the company? In which circumstances? Please describe briefly the principles of directors' liability.

Dutch law does not provide for specific rights for shareholders in respect of legal actions against directors. As a general rule, a breach of a contract with the company or a wrongful act against the company results in liability towards the company, not towards the shareholders. Shareholders have a claim in tort against a director only if the managing director commits a tort directly against a shareholder. In general, this would require the director to have committed a wrongful act causing damage to a shareholder (and not to the company). The burden of proof would lie with the shareholder.

According to a general principle of the DCC, the company and the individuals and legal entities related to the company must deal with each other in accordance with the principles of reasonableness and fairness. In the context of liability towards shareholders, this principle may also play a role in specifying the duties of directors in situations of disproportional harm to shareholders' interests.

By virtue of the DCC, a director is under an obligation towards the company of which it is a director, to perform the task assigned to it in a proper way. This is an obligation towards the company and generally shareholders are not able to hold a director liable based on this provision of the DCC.

Based on the DCC, each director is to be held jointly and severally liable to a bankruptcy estate for the amount of any liabilities which cannot be satisfied out of the liquidation proceeds, if: it is evident that the director has performed its duties improperly; and it may be assumed that this improper fulfilment of duties has been an important cause of the bankruptcy.

An individual director may avoid liability by proving it was not negligent.

A claim based on this provision can solely be filed by the trustee in a bankruptcy, whereby the trustee represents the interests of all creditors.

As set out in question 20, if certain conditions are met, a shareholder can file a request with the Enterprise Chamber to hold an Inquiry Procedure. The Enterprise Chamber will grant a request for an inquiry if there are reasonable grounds to assume mismanagement of the company. Further reference is made to question 20.

22. What are the rights in connection with transactions where the directors have a conflict of interest situation?

According to the DCC, in principle the supervisory board will represent the company in a conflict of interest. The Articles may provide otherwise. The GM is at all times authorised to designate one or more other persons for such purpose.

The shareholder does not have a specific right concerning the situation in which transactions have been made where the director has a conflict of interest; only the company is entitled to challenge the resolution. The shareholder does have the general rights as set out in questions 20 and 21.

According to the Dutch Corporate Governance Code applicable to listed NVs, a director shall refrain from decision-making if it has a direct or indirect personal interest that conflicts with the interests of the company.

The New Act states that the directors will, in the fulfilment of their duties, behave in the best interests of the company and affiliated companies. The New Act shall also provide for BVs that a director shall refrain from decision-making if it has a direct or indirect personal interest that conflicts with the interests of the company.

INFORMATION RIGHTS ON THE COMPANY'S BUSINESS
23. What information may be requested by the shareholders from the board concerning the general state of the company's business or any specific transaction? Are information rights different depending on the number of shares owned? Are shareholders entitled to receive written information before, during or after the GM about the meeting agenda and to what extent? Is it possible for a shareholder to obtain a copy of the minutes of the meeting of the GM?

The management board and the supervisory board are obliged to provide the GM with all information requested except in the event the company has a material interest in non-disclosure. This information right lies with the GM as a corporate body and generally not with the individual shareholders. All shareholders must be treated equally.

As indicated before in the answer to question 20, the DCC provides for the Inquiry Procedure upon request of an interested party if there are substantive reasons to doubt that the company is concluding the right policies.

The convocation of a GM should include the agenda for the meeting. The description of the items on the agenda should be in such form and detail that shareholders can determine whether it is of any interest to them. The convocation should be sent out ultimately 15 days prior to the GM. The statutory period for convening a GM of a listed NV was recently extended to 42 days. Listed NVs are required to post the following information on their website 42 days before the meeting:
(i)   the aggregate number of shares outstanding and relating voting rights;
(ii) notice of the meeting;
(iii) the documents and draft resolutions to be submitted to the meeting; and
(iv) if applicable a proxy form and a form enabling voting via email.

A listed NV can make its notice of a GM available on its website.

A request to put an item on the agenda, as described in question 12, can only be included as a voting item to the extent that the GM has the authority to pass resolutions on it. This means for instance that any items related to the strategy of the company cannot be included on the agenda as a voting item, as the authority on issues relating to the strategy are vested in the management board and, if available, the supervisory board. However, the item can be put on the agenda as a point of discussion.

The management board of the company must record the resolutions of the GM. These records shall be made available for inspection by shareholders at the office address of the company. Shareholders may on request obtain a copy or an extract of these records. Listed NVs must post the voting results of the GM on the company's website within 15 days after the GM.

24. Do shareholders have the right/duty to resolve in the GM upon matters which were not on the agenda?

As regards matters that were not on the agenda, the GM can only validly adopt a resolution by a unanimous vote in a meeting in which all shareholders are present or represented. Reference is made to question 12.

25. Are shareholders entitled to inspect the corporate books and/or any other corporate or accounting documents? To what extent? Can they do it through external counsel or advisors?

Shareholders do not have a specific right to inspect the books of the company apart from the information rights of the GM as described above in question 23.

Pursuant to the Inquiry Procedure, the Enterprise Chamber can, on the request of – among others – shareholders, give orders to a company to draw up its accounts in accordance with its specific instructions.

SHAREHOLDERS' AGREEMENTS
26. Are shareholders' agreements validly enforceable? What are their typical contents and term of duration? Are they enforceable by or against third parties and, if so, to what extent?

Shareholders may enter into shareholders' agreements which mainly concern the cooperation of the shareholders, the corporate governance of the company and the transfer of shares. Furthermore, typical provisions in the shareholders' agreement are specific provisions on transfer of shares and exit schemes. Other provisions concern standstill clauses, drag-along and tag-along clauses, a non-compete clause and arbitration schemes.

As shareholders' agreements may contain provisions on exercising one's right to vote, shareholders' agreements may be seen as voting agreements as well. In the DCC there is no specific provision relating to voting rights, but according to Dutch case law voting agreements may as such not be in violation with the DCC or any other rules contrary to the public mores. A shareholder should be able to pursue its own interest in exercising its voting rights, taking into account its own interest in the company, as well as the company's interest and the general principles of corporate law. The following rules can be derived from relevant case law and literature on this subject. A voting agreement pursuant to which a shareholder is under the obligation to vote in favour of a certain proposal where the proposal has been specifically described is allowed. Shareholders are allowed to have a meeting before the general meeting of the company and they are allowed to vote in the general meeting in accordance with the result of the prior meeting. Furthermore, it is a generally accepted principle that an agreement to always vote in accordance with the instruction of a third party or a fellow shareholder is unlawful if the circumstances are not fully foreseeable. A shareholder should at all times be able to form an independent opinion on a certain subject for which voting is necessary. Finally, it should be noted that the agreement may not have improper consequences, for instance if the purpose of the agreement is to evade the law.

In order to make sure that the shareholders vote in accordance with their commitments to each other the voting agreement may contain a penalty clause. Besides, the shareholder who thinks the other shareholder(s) shall not vote in accordance with their voting agreement has the possibility to ask for a mandatory injunction in interim injunction proceedings. Finally, an irrevocable power of attorney could be used to secure the fulfilment of the voting agreement. However, please note that the power of attorney should not have such a 'punitive' character (*inter alia* penalty clauses) that a shareholder is not able to vote according to its own insight any longer.

In practice, shareholders' agreements are entered into for a definite period of time. This period usually ends when only one shareholder holds 100 per cent of the shares. The shareholders' agreement shall terminate for a specific shareholder in the event that the shareholder no longer holds any shares in the company. Shareholders can agree that some provisions of the shareholders' agreement will remain in effect after the termination of the shareholders' agreement, such as a confidentiality clause.

If a shareholder breaches the provisions of the shareholders' agreement there is breach of contract with respect to the other shareholders. As the agreement is only effective between parties the agreement cannot be opposed to a bona fide third party.

27. Do shareholders' agreements have to be disclosed to the public or registered in any public registry?

Shareholders' agreements are not disclosed to the public nor are they registered in any public register, such as the Dutch trade register. However, the Articles could contain similar or even equal provisions to the shareholders' agreement. As the Articles have to be disclosed to the public, this will lead to publicity of the provisions laid down in the Articles.

ECONOMIC RIGHTS AND RIGHTS OVER THE STOCK

28. Is the stock always freely transferable? Are there any legal limitations? Are there any restrictions on contractual limitations?

The Articles of a BV must contain transfer restrictions. Generally a shareholder may only freely transfer one or more of its shares to close relatives or co-shareholders but many times the Articles also stipulate a transfer restriction in these cases.

There are two possible procedures to restrict the transfer of shares. According to the approval procedure, the shareholder requires the approval of a transfer by a corporate body of the company designated by the Articles (many times the GM is designated). According to the right of first refusal procedure the shareholder must first offer its shares to its co-shareholders. Such restriction may also provide that, if the co-shareholders do not accept the offer, the offer must be made to other prospective purchasers proposed by a corporate body of the company designated by the Articles.

A transfer restriction may not be such that it would render transferability impossible or exceedingly onerous.

In principle, the shares in an NV are freely transferable. Transferability of shares issued in bearer form cannot be limited. However, the Articles may restrict the transferability of registered shares. The Articles can state that transferability is subject to the approval of a body of the company or a third party. This right is broader than for a BV, because a third party can also have the right of approval. The Articles may also provide that a shareholder who wishes to dispose of one or more shares must first offer such shares to co-shareholders or to a third person to be designated by a corporate body.

Under the New Act, the Articles of a BV no longer have to include restriction clauses.

29. Are shareholders entitled to pledge their stock?
The stock in a BV can be pledged, unless the Articles provide otherwise. The same applies to registered shares in an NV.

The right to pledge bearer shares in an NV may not be restricted or excluded by the Articles.

30. Are there financial assistance issues to be considered and other prohibitions to be evaluated in the context of a leveraged buyout transaction?
Reference is made to the financial assistance prohibitions as set out in question 36.

31. May a company buy back its own stock and, if so, under what circumstances and subject to which limitations?
A company can only acquire shares in its capital that are fully paid up. If the shares are not fully paid up, the acquisition shall be invalid.

Furthermore, a company may only acquire fully paid-up shares in its own capital gratuitously or if:
- its net assets minus the acquisition price is not less than the sum of the paid and called-up part of its capital and the reserves which must be maintained by law or under the Articles;
- the Articles permit the acquisition; and
- the authorisation to acquire is granted by the GM or by another corporate body appointed to do so by the Articles or the GM.

For the BV an additional requirement exists – the nominal amount of the shares to be acquired and of the shares already held by the company and its subsidiaries is not more than 50 per cent of the issued capital.

Under the New Act a BV will have more opportunity to repurchase its own shares, but at least one voting share will have to be held by a party other than the BV or a subsidiary of the BV.

32. Is there a legal right to withdraw from the company and, if so, under what circumstances? How is the shareholders' stock valued and paid in such a case?

If the conditions of the DCC are met, the shareholder whose rights or interests are seriously prejudiced by the conduct of one or more co-shareholders to such an extent that the continuation of their shareholding can no longer in reasonableness be expected of them, they may institute proceedings against their co-shareholders, demanding that their shares shall be acquired in accordance with the DCC. The court shall appoint one or three experts to report in writing on the price of the shares. The experts shall prepare their report in accordance with the provisions in respect of the valuation of the shares in the provisions on the restriction on transfer. After the experts have issued their report, the court shall determine the price of the shares. However, it is important to note that this is a right of a shareholder *vis-à-vis* other shareholders, and thus not involving the company itself. Furthermore, it should be noted that this legal remedy is not commonly used mainly because of the long term of the procedure.

33. In which circumstances can dividends be distributed among shareholders? Is it possible to exclude or limit the right of certain shareholders to dividends? Does a certain portion of the profits need to be set aside in a reserve fund where it cannot be distributed to the shareholders? Are advances on dividends allowed and, if so, under which circumstances? Can advances on dividends be reclaimed by the company?

As a principle of the DCC, the profits shall accrue to the shareholders, unless the Articles provide otherwise. The Articles generally require a resolution of a corporate body, in most cases the GM, to appropriate profits (distribution and/or reservation). Sometimes the Articles stipulate that a prior resolution of another corporate body is required. The Articles of many listed NVs provide for the opportunity of the management board to resolve to reserve part of the profits before the GM may resolve on the appropriation of the (remaining) profits.

According to the DCC, a company may make distributions only to the extent that its net assets exceed the sum of the amount of the paid and called-up part of the capital and the reserves which must be maintained under the law or the Articles. The distribution of profits shall be made after the adoption of the annual accounts from which it appears that the same is permitted.

Interim distributions may only be made if permitted by the Articles and the above-mentioned requirement has been met as evidenced by an interim statement of assets and liabilities relating to the condition of such assets and liabilities on a date no earlier than the first day of the third month preceding the month in which the resolution to distribute is published.

If the company distributes profits contrary to the provision as mentioned above, the company may reclaim the amount paid as undue payment.

None of the shareholders may be wholly excluded from sharing in the profits. However, the fact that the shareholder has a right to a part of the profit does not mean that the profit has to be paid. The Articles may provide that profits to which holders of shares of a particular class are entitled shall be reserved in full or in part for their benefit.

The DCC does not contain a provision stating that a certain portion of the profits needs to be set aside in a reserve fund and can therefore not be distributed to the shareholders.

Under the New Act, the rules for making a dividend payment or a distribution from a reserve will be fundamentally changed for BVs. The basic principle will be that a BV is allowed to make a distribution, but on the condition that a BV will, following the distribution, continue to be able to pay its due and payable debts. A resolution of the GM to make a distribution will require the approval of the management board. The management board will have to refuse the requested approval if it knows, or should reasonably have anticipated, that the company will not be able to continue paying its due and payable debts after a distribution. Under the New Act shares without profit rights will be introduced.

34. What are the rights of shareholders in the event of an issue of new stock (increase of the company's corporate capital) (pre-emption rights)?

New shares are issued pursuant to a resolution of the GM, unless the Articles appoint another corporate body. The GM may delegate its right to resolve to issue new shares to another corporate body, for instance the management board.

With respect to NVs the GM can only delegate this right for a maximum period of five years. In the event that different classes of shares are issued and the rights of holders of a particular class of shares are prejudiced as a result of the new issuance, a resolution of the holders of the relevant class of shares is required prior to the resolution of the GM or – in case of delegation – the other corporate body.

According to the DCC a shareholder shall have a pre-emption right on any issue of shares *pro rata* to the aggregate amount of its shares, unless the Articles provide otherwise. However a shareholder shall not have a pre-emption right in respect of shares issued to employees of the company or of a group company. The pre-emption right may be restricted or excluded by a resolution of the GM, unless the Articles provide otherwise. The authority of the GM to exclude pre-emption rights can also be delegated to another corporate body. As far as an NV is concerned, if less than 50 per cent of the issued capital is represented at the GM, a majority of at least two-thirds of the votes cast shall be required for the resolution of the GM to exclude pre-emption rights or to delegate this authority.

Unless the Articles provide otherwise, holders of preference shares (meaning shares that only share in the profits for a certain percentage or only share in a liquidation surplus to a limited extent) do not have pre-emption rights with respect to other classes of shares. On the other hand, unless the Articles provide otherwise, holders of other classes of shares do not have pre-emption rights with respect to preference shares.

Finally, shareholders will also have a pre-emption right on the grant of rights to subscribe for shares (options/warrants).

Under the New Act one significant change is made: a provision is added that the holder of non-voting shares shall not have a right of pre-emption.

35. May minority shareholders ban or limit the company's capital structure in any manner?

The Articles of BVs and NVs must reflect the authorised capital, meaning the maximum capital for which new shares can be issued. Increasing or decreasing the authorised capital or introducing new classes of shares requires a resolution of the GM to change the company's Articles.

Any type of decision to be taken typically requires a simple majority of the votes. The Articles, however, may contain higher majority demands and/or a quorum, for example the demand that all or certain shareholders' resolutions require a 90 per cent majority of the votes cast. In such case the majority demand can have the effect of a veto right for anyone with a 10 per cent shareholding or more.

36. What are the financial assistance prohibitions in force?

A BV or NV and its subsidiaries may only grant loans to third parties for the purchase of shares in the relevant BV or NV in as far as certain conditions are met. These are stricter for the NV than for the BV. With regard to the BV, such a loan may be granted to the extent of the distributable reserves and in as far as the Articles do not provide otherwise. With regard to the NV, the most relevant conditions are that the loan is granted on fair market terms, that the granting of the loan will not lead to the value of the equity falling below the issued share capital plus the statutory reserves, and that a majority of the shareholders has approved of the grant in a meeting in which at least two-thirds of the outstanding share capital is represented. If depository receipts of shares have been issued, a majority is required of at least 95 per cent of the votes cast.

A BV or NV may not provide collateral, guarantee the price of its shares, act as surety or otherwise bind itself jointly and severally with or for third parties, for the purpose of the subscription or acquisition by third parties of shares in its own capital or of depositary receipts issued for it. This prohibition also extends to its subsidiaries.

Under the New Act, the limitations on financial assistance will be abolished. However, the Explanatory Memorandum to the New Act stipulates that the directors may be held liable as a result of the grant of financial assistance if the financial assistance qualifies as mismanagement or wrongful act. Under Dutch case law, a requirement for this liability is that the directors can be seriously blamed with regard to the damage resulting from the financial assistance.

37. Apart from publicly listed companies, in which cases (if any) are shareholders obligated to obtain an authorisation from, or provide information to, a public authority about events that have an impact on their stock interest in the company?

A shareholder requires a certificate of no objection from the Dutch Central Bank for holding, acquiring or increasing a direct or indirect participation of more than 10 per cent in, for example, a bank or insurance company.

Any amendment of the Articles, including the amendment of the authorised capital and/or the classes of shares, currently requires a certificate of no objection from the Ministry of Justice. However, recently a new act was adopted (Act on continuous screening of legal entities) as a consequence of which this certificate of no objection will no longer be required. This new act is likely to come into force in 2011.

SHAREHOLDERS' RIGHTS IN THE EVENT OF EXTRAORDINARY TRANSACTIONS AND WINDING-UP

38. What rights are available to shareholders in the event of a sale of all or a substantial portion of the company's assets? In case of a merger or de-merger?

The board of an NV needs the prior approval of the GM for a sale of the company's assets when this sale results in an important change in the identity of the company. No such statutory approval right exists with regard to the BV. The Articles may however provide for this.

Both the resolution to legally merge and to de-merge (by universal title of succession) is adopted by the GM. This applies to both NVs and BVs. In the case of simplified mergers (100 per cent parent company with a subsidiary company or two companies having the same 100 per cent parent company), the resolution of the acquiring company may be adopted by the management board, unless the Articles provide otherwise. The conditions for a resolution to amend the Articles apply equally to the resolution to merge or de-merge. This means that a normal majority of the GM is required, but the Articles may provide otherwise. However, if less than 50 per cent of the outstanding capital is represented in the GM, a two-thirds majority is required.

With regard to a merger: if different classes of shares have been issued and the rights of holders of a particular class of shares are prejudiced as a result of the merger, then this/these group(s) of shareholders must approve of the merger separately prior to or simultaneously with the approval of the merger by the GM.

39. Which rights are available to shareholders in the event of a conversion of the company into a European Company (SE) or into another type of company?

A BV can be converted into an NV and *vice versa*, but only an NV can be converted into an SE. The resolution to convert an NV into a BV or *vice versa* is adopted by the GM according to the procedure for an amendment of the Articles, which requires a normal majority (but the Articles can stipulate a higher majority) or a two-thirds majority if less than 50 per cent of the outstanding share capital is present or represented at the GM.

According to European law, an NV may only be converted into an SE if it has had a subsidiary that has been incorporated under the laws of another member state for at least two years. The proposal for conversion is adopted by the GM under the same conditions as the resolution to merge. Reference is made to question 38.

40. Which rights are available to shareholders of a company in liquidation?

If the liquidator has not been appointed by a judge (eg in the event of a voluntary liquidation) then the liquidator is appointed and dismissed by the body authorised to appoint the members of the board. In general, this is the GM. During the liquidation, the GM functions as usual, but everything the GM does (every resolution taken) must be done for the benefit of the liquidation.

If after the liquidation a positive balance remains, this balance is distributed to the shareholders *pro rata* to their shareholdings. The Articles, however, may provide otherwise.

41. Can shareholders cause the liquidation of the company? How?

Yes, the shareholders can resolve to dissolve the company, after which it will go into liquidation. No special majority is required, unless the Articles provide otherwise (the Articles require a qualified majority).

GROUP COMPANIES

42. Is the concept of group recognised as such under specific legislation? What are the implications?

The DCC defines a group as an economic unit in which legal persons and partnerships are united. Group companies are legal persons and partnerships that are united in one group. As a rule, subsidiaries belong to the group of their parent company. Two implications must be mentioned.

In principle, the head of a group must prepare consolidated accounts for the group as a whole.

The head of the group can issue a statement in which it declares itself jointly and severally liable for the liabilities of its subsidiaries. The result of such a statement is that a less strict regime with regard to the organisation of the annual accounts applies to the subsidiaries, provided, however, that the head of the group prepares consolidated accounts.

43. Does a controlling company have any particular duties *vis-à-vis* its controlled company shareholders?

A controlling company does not have any particular duties under the DCC. All shareholders must, however, conduct themselves in relation to each other in accordance with the principles of reasonableness and fairness, which means that besides their own interest, they have to consider the interests of the company and the other shareholders when acting. However, in general the shareholder may serve its own interest.

44. What are the rights of company shareholders when the controlling company puts in place actions and/or transactions than can be prejudicial to the business of the shareholders?

One of the options for the shareholder is to summon the controlling company before the court on the basis of a wrongful act. In such a case, the claiming shareholder will have to prove that a specific standard of care has been violated *vis-à-vis* them.

Another option is to request the Enterprise Chamber to order an inquiry with regard to the group (see the answer to question 23). However, very specific conditions will have to be met before the Enterprise Chamber will allow such inquiry.

45. What are the limitations, if any, to the possibility of owning reciprocal stock interests in companies?

Under Dutch law a subsidiary may not, on its own account, subscribe or cause the subscription of shares in the capital of a company. Subsidiaries may only acquire or cause the acquisition of such shares for their own account insofar as the company may itself acquire its own shares (see the answer to question 31 for the relevant requirements). As a company is considered a subsidiary if the holding company holds more than 50 per cent of the votes in the company, reciprocal interest in which at least one of the companies holds more than 50 per cent of the shares in the other company are subject to this restriction.

The New Act will introduce some new restrictions. The acquisition of shares by a subsidiary in its controlling company will be subject to the approval of the board of directors of the controlling company. Furthermore, the moment all shares in the controlling company are held by its subsidiaries, one share transfers to the joint directors of the controlling company by operation of law. As a consequence, it will not be possible to own reciprocal 100 per cent-interests.

For NVs an additional limitation applies: no vote may be cast by the company at a GM in respect of a share belonging to the company or its subsidiary, which means that if NV A holds a majority interest in company B and company B holds shares in NV A, company B may not vote on these shares, as it is considered a subsidiary of NV A.

Poland

Noerr Arkadiusz Ruminski, Marta Szczepanik
& Krzysztof Banaszek

BASIC INFORMATION ON THE TYPES OF LIMITED LIABILITY COMPANIES AND ON THE RIGHS OF SHAREHOLDERS

1. What types of companies enjoy limited liability? If more than one, which ones have shareholders, ie holders of share certificates? Which one is the most common? Which one is mostly used by foreign investors?

Under Polish law there are two types of commercial companies in which shareholders enjoy limited liability: limited liability companies (LLC) and joint stock companies (JSC) and three types of partnerships: limited partnerships, limited joint stock partnerships and professional partnerships.

In limited partnerships and limited joint stock partnerships at least one natural or legal person enjoys limited liability (the limited partner in limited partnerships and shareholder in limited joint stock partnerships), while the other partners are liable for the obligations of the partnership without limitation. The limited partner is liable to the creditors of the partnership only up to the amount set out in the articles of association; the maximum liability threshold is reduced by the amount the limited partner effectively contributed to the capital of the limited partnership.

In professional partnerships a partner is not liable for the obligations of the partnership which arise in connection with the pursuit by the remaining partners of the profession, or for obligations of the partnership which result from acts or omissions of persons employed who have been guided by another partner while providing services connected with the object of activity of the partnership.

LLCs and JSCs constitute capital companies incorporated by shareholders who are not liable for the company's obligations. The most common type of commercial company in Poland is the LLC. It is also the company most frequently chosen by foreign investors.

A form of limited joint stock partnership is in practice rarely used in Poland. The purpose of a professional partnership is to pursue certain statutory prescribed professions.

Our further analysis is limited to the regulations pertaining to LLCs and JSCs.

2. Are there minimum capital requirements and/or thin capitalisation rules in force?

The minimum share capital of an LLC in Poland shall be PLN 5,000 and of a JSC PLN 100,000.

The tax deductibility of interest payments in Poland is restricted by thin capitalisation rules where the amount of loan financing from a shareholder or shareholders (holding more than 25 per cent of the share capital) exceeds a multiple of three times the level of the share capital. Interest on loans is disallowed to the extent that the debt of the company towards a shareholder or shareholders exceeds the ratio of three times the share capital of the company as of the day of the interest payment.

3. Describe the types of shares that can be issued by a company and the different rights that they attribute to their owners, as well as any other financial instruments (bonds or other) and other instruments of a participatory nature in the company's capital that can also be issued by the company.

The following apply in relation to JSCs:

Bearer shares

These kinds of shares are the most common in economic practice, especially in listed companies because the transfer of rights incorporated in them can be exercised more easily than in other types of shares (eg registered shares). In order to dispose of a bearer share it is sufficient to transfer the possession of the share certificate by execution of an agreement between the seller and buyer. Whereas the transfer of registered shares must be effected by way of a written declaration either in the share certificate or in a separate instrument and requires the transfer of possession. Bearer share certificates may not be issued before full payment of the corresponding capital contribution.

Registered shares

Rights incorporated in registered shares are attached to a specific person or persons mentioned in the share certificate. The Polish Commercial Companies Code (*kodeks spółek handlowych*) (KSH) stipulates in which cases the issue of registered shares is mandatory:
(i) shares for in-kind-contributions shall remain registered shares until the date of approval by earliest ordinary general meeting (GM) of the financial report for the financial year in which such shares have been paid for;
(ii) shares with special rights attached to them (preference shares) shall be registered shares, with the exception of non-voting shares; and
(iii) shares carrying the obligation to provide recurrent non-pecuniary performance can be issued only as registered shares.

Registered depositary certificates

The shareholder of a listed company who holds dematerialised shares is entitled to a registered depositary certificate. Registered depositary certificates are not to be issued by the company itself but by the entity operating the securities account in accordance with the provisions on trading with financial instruments.

Registered promoter certificates
The company may issue registered promoter certificates as remuneration for the services provided upon creation of the company. This document gives the right to participate in the division of profits of the company within the limits stipulated in the articles of association, after the minimum amount of dividends stipulated in the articles of association has been deducted for the benefit of the shareholders.

Registered temporary certificates
As outlined above, bearer share certificates may not be issued before the payment of the share capital is made; therefore, the company shall issue registered temporary certificates as proof of partial payment.

Preference shares
A JSC may also issue preference shares with special rights attached to them; such rights are to be identified in articles of association. Such special privileges may be granted to:
(i)   voting rights (maximum two votes per share);
(ii) profit participation (maximum 1.5 of the dividend due for one share); or
(iii) participation in the division of assets in case of liquidation of the company.
The articles of association may render special privileges conditional on additional services being provided towards the company, lapse of time or satisfaction of a condition. Furthermore, it is worth mentioning that the shareholder may execute the special rights attached to the preference share after the end of the financial year during which it made the contribution towards the share capital in full.

Bonds
If the articles of association so provide, the company may issue convertible bonds entitling the bondholder to demand the conversion of a bond into shares of the issuer.

In contrast to a JSC, an LLC may issue only preference shares (voting rights – maximum three votes per share; profit participation – maximum 1.5 of the dividend due for one share) and non-convertible bonds.

4.   Can a company have only one shareholder and still enjoy limited liability?
Yes.

5.   Are the rights of shareholders the same in any type of company?
The rights of shareholders in LLCs and JSCs differ in many respects, since an LLC has many characteristics that are typical for a partnership, including: a statutory right to control vested in each shareholder; stronger rights for shareholders of an LLC to impose restrictions regarding transfer and encumbrance of their shares; and the possibility to limit or exclude the joining of the company by the heirs in place of a deccased shareholder.

6. What are the basic rights of any shareholder? Describe briefly the rights of minority shareholders and indicate which thresholds, if any, are required to allow the minority shareholders to exercise any such rights.

With reference to an LLC, all shareholders have following basic rights:

- the right to participate in the profits specified in the annual financial report and allocated under resolution of the GM for division;
- a pre-emptive right, if not limited by the articles of association or shareholders' resolution;
- a right to participate in the GM;
- voting right;
- control rights; and
- a right to file a writ in an action for redress of damage caused to the company (this shall also apply to a JSC).

Apart from the abovementioned rights of all shareholders, the KSH provides for a set of rights that vest upon minority shareholders. Under the KSH, a minority shareholder is defined as representing at least one-tenth of the share capital. These additional rights are:

- the right to request an extraordinary GM to be convened; and
- the right to request certain matters to be placed on the agenda of the next GM.

(In the above two cases the articles of association may grant the said rights to shareholders representing less than one-tenth of the share capital.)

- a right to request the registry court to authorise shareholders to call a GM; and
- a right to request the registry court to appoint a party authorised to review the financial reports for the purpose of examining the accounts and operations of the company.

Concerning JSCs, all shareholders have the following basic rights:

- the right to participate in the profits declared in the financial report, audited by an auditor, which have been designated by the GM for distribution to the shareholders; and
- the right to participate in the GM.

KSH distinguishes between the right of participation in a GM of a non-listed JSC and a listed JSC. In the case of a non-listed JSC, those entitled by registered shares and temporary certificates, as well as the pledges and usufructuaries which carry voting rights, may participate in the GM if they were registered at least one week prior to the date of the GM. Whereas the right of the abovementioned persons to participate in the GM of a listed JSC is determined by the shares held by those persons 16 days prior to the GM (the 'record date').

The holders of bearer shares in a non-listed JSC have the right of participation in the GM provided that share certificates have been placed in the JSC at least one week prior to the holding of the GM and will not be collected before the its closure. Corresponding provisions apply in the case of listed JSCs with respect to the record date. In addition, there is:

- a right to information during the GM; and

- a pre-emptive right if not limited by articles of association or shareholders' resolution.

The following instruments ensure the protection of minority shareholders' rights:

- the right to request an extraordinary GM to be called. The applicable minority threshold is one-twentieth of the share capital;
- the right to request certain matters to be placed on the agenda of the next GM. Threshold applicable for minority as above.

(In the above two cases, articles of association may grant the rights to shareholders representing less than one-twentieth of the share capital.)

- the right to request the registry court to authorise shareholders to summon a GM (one-twentieth threshold applies);
- the right to request that the members of the supervisory board are elected by way of a vote in separate groups. This right strengthens the rights of minority shareholders, who represent at least one-fifth of the share capital, to supervise the activity of the JSC. This right can be exercised even if the articles of association provide for a different procedure for appointing the supervisory board;
- the right to request a forced purchase of shares of minority shareholders to be put on the agenda of the next GM.

7. Do all shareholders enjoy the same rights or can some shareholders be attributed specific rights, whether by reason of the particular class of stock owned or other? Are such rights generally provided for at the level of the company's by-laws and/or in shareholders' agreements?

A shareholder in an LLC or JSC can be granted specific benefits provided that these are specified in detail in the articles of association. The articles of association or statute may make the specific benefits conditional on the provisions of additional performance towards the company; lapse of time; or satisfaction of a condition. These special benefits are non-transferable and do not depend on the number or value of shares held by the privileged shareholder. In addition, shareholders may attribute special rights to themselves in shareholders' agreements. However, unlike special benefits laid down in the articles of association, shareholders' agreements are effective only between the parties to them.

8. May the rights of shareholders, generally speaking, be limited, modified, suppressed or waived in any way? If so, how? Are such modifications or limitations provided for in the company's by-laws and/or in shareholders' agreements?

The provisions of the KSH provide for the possibility of limitation of voting rights. In case of an LLC, the general rule is that each share of an equal nominal value shall carry one vote, unless the articles of association provide otherwise. Thus, voting rights may be limited only if the articles of association say so.

Articles of association of a JSC may also limit the voting rights, however, in this case the KSH provides for a minimum number of votes to enable the application of such limitation. This threshold has to exceed one-tenth of the total number of votes in order to limit voting rights. In addition to that, the limitation may apply only to the exercise of the voting right as to shares above the limit of the votes provided for in the articles.

Moreover, not only voting rights, but also other rights of shareholders of any kind may be limited, modified, suppressed or waived in shareholders' agreements. However, it has to be underlined that such agreements are effective only made *vis-à-vis* shareholders who are party to this agreement and cannot include provisions that aim to infringe or circumvent mandatory rules, or else they shall be null and void.

GENERAL MEETING OF SHAREHOLDERS (GM) AND VOTING RIGHTS

9. Which decisions are reserved to the competence of the GM?

Apart from the competences stipulated in the articles of association, the GM of an LLC and JSC:

- considers and approves the management board report on the operations of the company and the financial statements for the previous financial year;
- grants the approval for the performance of duties by the members of the company's governing bodies;
- decides upon claims for damages caused while establishing the company, managing it or exercising supervision;
- takes decisions concerning the enterprise or its organised part (its disposal, tenancy or creation of a limited right *in rem* over them);
- acquires and disposes of: real estate, the right of perpetual usufruct, a share in real estate (unless the articles of association provide otherwise);
- concludes a contract for management of a dependent company;
- decides upon the existence of the company in the event the balance sheet shows a loss exceeding the aggregate of supplementary and reserve capitals and half of the share capital in the LLC or one-third in a JSC;
- resolves upon division of profits or financing of losses (the articles of association of an LLC may provide otherwise);
- resolves upon dissolution of the company;
- amends the articles of association or the articles of association; and
- decides upon merger, division or transformation of the company.

Additionally the resolution of the GM in an LLC is required for the following matters:

- repayment of additional contributions;
- disposal of rights and undertaking of obligations to provide performance when the their value exceeds twice the amount of the share capital (unless the articles of association provide otherwise); and
- acquisition and disposal of real estate, a share in real estate, fixed assets the price of which exceeds one-fourth of the share capital and at the same time is not lower than PLN 50,000 if such a contract has not been envisaged in the articles of association and is concluded within two

years from registration of the company.

Additionally, in the case of a JSC, the resolution of GM is required in following cases:

- issue of convertible bonds or bonds with the right of priority and issue of subscription warrants in order to increase the share capital of the company;
- acquisition of the company's own shares which are to be offered for acquisition by current employees or persons previously employed in the company (affiliated company); and
- acquisition of any property the price of which exceeds one-tenth of the paid-in share capital, from the incorporator, the shareholder, the dominant company or a dependent company for the company or a dependent company or a co-operative if such a contract is concluded within two years from registration of the company (such resolution is to be adopted by a majority of two-thirds of the votes).

Please note that stipulations included in the articles of association concerning matters which require a shareholders' resolution not provided for in KSH has no legal effect upon third parties, but only an internal effect on the shareholders.

10. How does a shareholder participate in a GM? Are there any limitations to having a minimum number of shares? May a shareholder delegate attendance to another shareholder or to the board? May a shareholder obtain assistance from the courts or any other governmental body to intervene in a GM or to cause one to be held in some particular cases?

The articles of association of an LLC set out whether each shareholder may have only one or more shares. Should a shareholder be granted more than one share, all shares in the share capital are equal. There are no limitations as to the minimum number of shares. The shareholders may participate in the GM and exercise their voting rights by attorney-in-fact, who cannot be a member of the management board or an employee of the company. The articles of association or legal provisions may, however, rule out the delegation of attendance at a GM. If the GM is not convened within two weeks of the submission of a shareholders' request mentioned in question 11, the registry court summons the management board to make a representation and may subsequently authorise the said shareholders to convene an extraordinary GM.

In a JSC, one share carries one vote at the GM. The voting right arises as of the date the share is paid for in full (articles of association may, however, provide otherwise). The right may be limited in articles of association with respect to shareholders controlling more than one-fifth of the total number of votes in the company. If between shareholders a relationship of dominance or dependence exists, the articles of association may allow for cumulating of the votes held by these shareholders or, on the contrary, set out the rules for reduction of the votes. The votes attached to the shares of the dependent company or cooperative are added to the votes of the shareholders in the dominant company. There are no limitations regarding the minimum number of shares. The attendance at a GM of a JSC may be delegated to other persons, excluding the members of management board and employees. The registry court may also cause the GM to be held if it is not convened upon request. Such request may be submitted by a shareholder or shareholders representing one-twentieth of the votes.

There are no provisions allowing for the obtaining of assistance from any court or governmental body to intervene in a GM. However, a shareholder or shareholders owning at least one-tenth of the share capital in an LLC and one-twentieth in a JSC may request that certain matters be placed on the agenda of the next GM.

11. May a GM be called and held at the request of any shareholder? Is there a threshold regarding the percentage of the stock interest owned in the company that may entitle a shareholder to such a right?

The KSH vests minority shareholders of an LLC and JSC with the right to request an extraordinary GM to be called, as well as that certain matters be placed on the agenda of the next GM. Such request shall be submitted to the management board in writing, but in the case of a JSC it may be also submitted via email. The request to put certain issues on the agenda of the next GM shall be submitted to the management of an LLC not later than one month before the proposed date of the GM. For a non-listed JSC, requests must be made 14 days before and for a listed JSC 21 days before the GM.

If the extraordinary GM is not called within two weeks of the submission of the request by minority shareholders, the registry court may authorise shareholders who have submitted the request to call the extraordinary GM. The registry court is not bound by the request of the minority shareholders. Hence, it is within the court's discretion whether to authorise the minority shareholders to proceed with the extraordinary GM.

12. May a shareholder bring up an issue to be resolved upon and put it to a vote if it is not included on the agenda? May a shareholder require more information from the GM and/or the board concerning the agenda of the GM to be put in a better position to exercise their vote?

In both LLCs and JSCs a shareholder may put forward a proposal to adopt a matter not included on the agenda, but the matter may be put to a vote only if the entire share capital is represented at the GM and none of the shareholders has objected to adopting the resolution.

Since one of the fundamental rights of a shareholder is the right to be informed about the company's affairs, each shareholder may request such information from the management board, including information concerning the agenda of the GM.

13. May a GM be held by telecommunication means and/or by correspondence (ie by written consent)?

As a rule, the resolutions of shareholders in an LLC are adopted in the GM. Without holding a GM resolutions may be passed in the event all the shareholders expressing their consent in writing to the decision to be taken, or to a written vote. However, KSH specifies matters in relation to which a resolution can be adopted only by the GM. The ordinary GM shall be held within six months of the end of each financial year and have the following matters on its agenda:

- examination and approval of the report on the operations of the company and the financial report for the previous financial year;
- division of profits or financing of losses (if such power is not granted to other corporate body of an LLC); and
- approval for the performance of duties by the members of the company's governing bodies.

There are some matters with respect to which it is disputed whether they need to be subject to a GM or can also be resolved upon without holding a GM. These matters include:

- appointing and dismissing members of the management board;
- consent for the conclusion of a credit agreement, a loan agreement, a surety agreement or other similar agreement with a member of the management board, supervisory board, audit committee, a holder of the commercial power of attorney or a liquidator or for the benefit of any such person;
- granting as a dominant company, consent for the conclusion by the dependent company of an agreement with a member of the management board, a holder of the commercial power of attorney or a liquidator of the dominant company, in the event the dependent company does not have a supervisory board that shall primarily grant such consent;
- allocating the profits specified in the annual financial report for division;
- redemption of shares;
- adopting regulations of the supervisory board or auditing committee or authorising the auditing committee or supervisory board to adopt its own regulations;
- resolving upon the continued existence of the company if the balance sheet shows losses exceeding the aggregated supplementary and reserve capitals and half of the share capital;
- adopting a resolution where the costs of convening and holding the meeting shall be borne by the company;
- approving a balance sheet as at the opening of liquidation drawn up by the liquidators;
- approving the liquidation report; and
- merger, division and transformation of the company.

In a JSC all shareholders' resolutions shall be adopted by the GM.

14. Are voting rights always proportionate to the stock held by each shareholder or can they vary by share class?

In the case of preference shares concerning multiple voting rights one share in an LLC may carry up to three votes and in a JSC, two votes. However, such privileges do not apply to a listed JSC.

15. Are there non-voting shares? Is there a maximum percentage of capital represented by non-voting shares?

Provisions of the KSH give an explicit right to issue non-voting shares only with respect to a JSC. These non-voting rights may concern only preference shares relating to dividends. In practice non-voting rights are more attractive than 'normal' preference shares with respect to dividends because:

- they enjoy priority of satisfaction over the remaining shares;
- they may exceed the cap applying to 'normal' preference shares with respect to dividends (up to 1.5 times a non-preference share); and
- the articles of association may provide that the shareholder entitled under a non-voting share who has not been paid the dividends in their entirety or in part in a given financial year shall be entitled to a balance out of profits in the following years, not later, however, than the three following financial years.

Shareholders of an LLC may introduce non-voting shares into the articles of association. Polish law does not contain any express stipulations on maximum percentages of capital represented by non-voting shares.

16. Can shareholders group their shares in order to exercise their voting rights (eg, by trust, shareholders' agreement or otherwise)?

If there are shares with different rights attached to them, resolutions on amendments to the articles of association, reduction of the share capital and redemption of shares, which may affect the rights of the shareholders of a given class of shares, shall be mandatorily adopted by way of a separate vote in each of the groups (classes) of shares.

The shareholders representing at least one-fifth of the share capital may demand that the members of the supervisory board are elected by way of a vote in separate groups.

17. Under what circumstances can a shareholder challenge the resolutions adopted by the GM? Are there thresholds concerning the stock interest owned to be able to bring such a claim?

A GM's resolution can be challenged by a shareholder where the resolution contravenes law or contravenes the articles of association of an LLC/the articles of association of a JSC or the rules of equity and: harms the interests of the company; or is aimed at harming the shareholder.

The right to challenge a resolution is vested, irrespective of the stock interest owned, only in a shareholder who:

- voted against the resolution and, following its adoption, requested that its objection be recorded;
- was not allowed to participate in a GM without valid reason; or
- was not present at the GM in the event the GM was wrongly convened or the resolution concerned a matter not included on the agenda.

18. What are the terms and procedures to challenge a resolution of the GM?

A resolution of the shareholders in an LLC or JSC that is contrary to the law can be challenged through a suit brought against the company for declaration of invalidity of resolution.

An action for declaration of invalidity may be brought within six months from the date on which the shareholder received notice of the resolution, not later, however, than after three years in an LLC and two years in a non-listed JSC of the adoption of the resolution. In a listed JSC the term is 30 days after the resolution is announced, it cannot, however, be challenged later than within one year of its adoption.

An annulment of a resolution can be claimed in all companies within a month of the date on which the shareholder learned of the resolution, but not later than within six months from the adoption of the resolution in an LLC and non-listed JSC and three months in a listed JSC.

SHAREHOLDERS' RIGHTS VERSUS DIRECTORS AND DUTIES OF OTHER CORPORATE BODIES IN THE COMPANY

19. What is the procedure for the appointment/replacement/ revocation of directors and of statutory auditors, if any?

The members of the management board are appointed and dismissed in an LLC by a resolution of shareholders (unless the articles of association provide otherwise) adopted by an absolute majority of votes. In a JSC the appointment and revocation of members of the management board is the responsibility of the supervisory board which adopts resolutions by an absolute majority of votes, unless the articles of association provide otherwise, and where its meeting is attended by at least half of its members. The GM in a JSC is also entitled to revoke the members of the management board or suspend them from their activities by an absolute majority of votes. The articles of association can grant other entities or persons a right to appoint and/or revoke the members of the management board.

There is no legally prescribed procedure to appoint, replace or revoke the statutory auditors. The articles of association can stipulate that the auditors are to be appointed by the GM and this is the most common case in practice, unless legal provisions provide that the auditor shall be appointed by the registry court.

20. May shareholders challenge the resolutions of the board of directors? Is there a minimum percentage of capital required to challenge a board resolution?

Polish law does not envisage any specific procedure for challenging the resolutions of the management board. However, it seems that there are no legal impediments to challenge such resolutions by way of legal action for declaration of existence or non-existence of a legal relationship (pursuant to Article 189 Civil Procedure Code). A declaration action may be brought by any shareholder, irrespective of the stock interest owned, if the resolution contravenes the law, is aimed at its circumvention or is contrary to the rules of equity (principles of social interaction). A court may declare the non-existence of a resolution that satisfies one of the abovementioned conditions.

21. Are shareholders entitled to bring a legal action against the directors of the company? In which circumstances? Please describe briefly the principles of directors' liability.

In both LLCs and JSCs if the company does not bring an action for redress of damage caused to it within one year of the date on which the act causing the damage was discovered, each shareholder – and in a JSC additionally also a person who holds another title to participate in profits or division of assets – may file a lawsuit seeking redress of the damage caused to the company. The members of the management board are liable for causing damage to the company:

- in breach of the law through their fault while participating in the incorporation of a company; and
- by acts or omissions in breach of the law or the provisions of the articles of association, unless they are not at fault.

Furthermore, a member of the management board in a JSC is liable for causing damage to the company through:

- receipt of excessive benefits; and
- dissemination of false data.

Members of a management board are, in the course of performing their duties, obliged to exercise diligence characteristic of the professional nature of their activity. The assumption of duties of a member of the management board without special required knowledge can already be judged as lack of required diligence.

If the damage has been caused by several members of the management board jointly, they are liable for it jointly and severally. An important characteristic of director's liability is that the division of duties in Polish companies does not influence the liability of members of the management board. Such division of certain business areas between different members of the management board does not exclude liability against the company's creditors of one member of the management board for actions taken by another.

The members of the management board are also subject to criminal liability for the following reasons:

- acting to the detriment of the company;
- failing to file for bankruptcy of the company despite the existence of circumstances justifying it;
- announcing or submitting false data;
- allowing a company to acquire its own shares;
- unlawful issuance of certain documents;
- facilitating illegal vote or participation in it; or
- illegal issuance of shares in a JSC.

22. What are the rights in connection with transactions where the directors have a conflict of interest situation?

Where there exists a conflict between the interests of an LLC or a JSC and those of a member of the management board, their spouse, relatives or relations up to the second degree and persons with whom they have personal relations, the member of the management board shall withhold from deciding such matters and may request that this be recorded in the minutes. Furthermore, KSH provides for a special procedure pertaining to contracts between LLCs or JSCs and a member of the management board and in disputes with them. In such cases the company shall be represented by the supervisory board or an attorney in fact, appointed by the GM. Where the single shareholder is also the single member of the management board, an act in law between such shareholder and the company which it represents requires a notarial deed.

INFORMATION RIGHTS ON THE COMPANY'S BUSINESS
23. What information may be requested by the shareholders from the board concerning the general state of the company's business or any specific transaction? Are information rights different depending on the number of shares owned? Are shareholders entitled to receive written information before, during or after the GM about the meeting agenda and to what extent? Is it possible for a shareholder to obtain a copy of the minutes of the GM?
Each shareholder of an LLC, regardless of the number of shares owned, enjoys the right to control the affairs of the company. In order to exercise this right, it is at any time entitled to request explanations from the management board. All the information relating to the company's affairs, including those concerning any specific transactions, may be requested from the management board. The refusal to give explanations may take place solely if a justified concern exists that the shareholder may use them for purposes contrary to the interests of the company which may cause material damage to the company. A shareholder who has been refused explanations may apply to the court to oblige the members of the management board to provide the relevant information to the shareholder.

A GM is called by means of written notice that must specify a detailed agenda. Individual issues of the meeting agenda must be described precisely enough, so that they render it possible for the shareholder to discover what matters are to be discussed and voted upon. The shareholders may review the minutes and demand copies of the resolutions, certified by the management board.

The right to be informed in a JSC is also independent of the number of shares owned. All information concerning the company's affairs must be provided by the management board at shareholder's request. During the GM the management board is obliged to provide the shareholder with information, wherever this is required, so that a matter included on the agenda can be considered. In justified cases, the information may be disclosed in writing not later than within two weeks of the end of the GM. The disclosure of requested information may be refused solely where this could result in damage to the company, an affiliated company, a dependent company or cooperative or if this could expose a member of the management board to criminal, civil or administrative liability. A shareholder who has been refused explanations may apply to the court to oblige the members of the management board to provide relevant information to the shareholders.

JSC shareholders may receive written information about the meeting agenda prior to the GM only if all the shares issued by the company are registered shares. In other cases, the GM is convened by an announcement. Such written announcement also has to specify the meeting agenda in detail. The JSC shareholders may also review the minutes and obtain copies of the resolutions.

24. Do shareholders have the right/duty to resolve in the GM upon matters which were not on the agenda?

Matters not included on the agenda may be resolved upon only in the event that the entire capital is represented in the GM and none of those present has objected to the holding of the GM or the inclusion of particular matters on the agenda.

25. Are shareholders entitled to inspect the corporate books and/or any other corporate or accounting documents? To what extent? Can they do it through external counsel or advisors?

A manifestation of the abovementioned shareholders' right to control in an LLC is also their entitlement to inspect all the books and company documents and draw up a balance sheet for their use. The refusal to provide the books and documents for inspection may take place only in the cases specified under question 23. A shareholder who has been refused access to the documents may apply to the court to oblige the members of the management board.

A shareholder of a JSC has less access to information about the company and is entitled to inspect the corporate books and other corporate or accounting documents only when legal provisions provide it with such right (copies of the management board report on the operations of the company and of the financial report for the previous financial year, together with a copy of the supervisory board report and the opinion of the auditor shall be, upon request, provided to the shareholders).

SHAREHOLDERS' AGREEMENTS

26. Are shareholders' agreements validly enforceable? What are their typical contents and term of duration? Are they enforceable by or against third parties and, if so, to what extent?

Generally, shareholders' agreements are enforceable only between the parties to them. Hence, non-performance entails contract liability of the party in breach. This liability has only compensative character. It means that such liability does not execute the primary purpose of the agreement.

Such agreements typically concern rules on the disposal of shares, rules on the exercise of voting rights, division of dividends or coverage of losses. KSH explicitly provides for agreements pertaining to limitations concerning the disposition of the shares or a fraction of the shares in a JSC, stating that such limitation may not be stipulated for more than five years from the date of the agreement. Furthermore, KSH states with respect to a JSC that agreements creating pre-emption rights or other priority rights with respect to the acquisition of the shares or a fraction of the shares shall be allowed. In this case limitations concerning disposition of shares may not exist for more than 10 years from the date of the agreement. The above time-based limitations do not concern LLCs.

27. Do shareholders' agreements have to be disclosed to the public or registered in any public registry?
Shareholders' agreements neither have to be disclosed to the public, nor registered in public registry. However, Article 7 of the KSH rules that excerpts from the agreement for management of a dependent company or transfer of profits by such company with provisions on the liability of the dominant company for damage caused to the dependant company as a result of non-performance or improper performance of the agreement and on the liability of the dominant company for obligations of the dependent company towards its creditors, shall be filed in the registration file of the dependent company. If such is the case, the fact that the agreement does not regulate, or that it excludes liability of the dominant company, shall also be disclosed.

ECONOMIC RIGHTS AND RIGHTS OVER THE STOCK
28. Is the stock always freely transferable? Are there any legal limitations? Are there any restrictions on contractual limitations?
KSH prescribes two kinds of limitations regarding transfer of shares in a JSC. The first one is a prohibition on the transfer of the shares subscribed for in-kind contributions until the date of approval by the earliest ordinary GM of the financial report for the financial year in which such shares have been paid for. The second legal instrument limits the transfer of shares which carry the obligation to provide recurrent non-pecuniary performance. Such shares may be transferred only with the consent of the company.

Other restrictions on share transfer may result from the articles of association requiring the consent of the company for the transfer of shares, or other limitation on transferability. The transfer of shares without such consent is ineffective. However, this limitation concerns only the transfer of registered shares. It is widely acknowledged that a limitation on transferability of shares may not lead to an absolute ban on disposal. Such a clause would be ineffective as being against the nature of the JSC.

Finally, limitations can be created also by shareholders themselves in shareholders' agreements. It is noteworthy that limitations under shareholders' agreements, unlike limitations governed by articles of association, may also include bearer shares. Furthermore, under shareholders' agreements, transferability may be limited to wider extent.

The transferability of shares in an LLC may be confined by way of articles of association requiring the consent of the company for the transfer of shares or limiting the transferability in another way. The transfer of shares without such consent is ineffective.

29. Are shareholders entitled to pledge their stock?

Yes they are. The shares may be encumbered with ordinary pledges, registered pledges or financial collaterals. The articles of association may provide that pledging requires prior consent of the company or the shareholders.

30. Are there financial assistance issues to be considered and other prohibitions to be evaluated in the context of a leveraged buyout transaction?

There are no specific restrictions in respect to financial assistance in an LLC.

In a JSC, financial assistance is allowed if certain statutory conditions are fulfilled. It must be provided under 'fair market conditions'. This applies particularly to security interests established in favour of the company as well as interest received by it. Furthermore, the financing is to be preceded by verification of the financial condition of the debtor or any third party. There are, however, no guidelines as to the interpretation of this condition. A company may provide financial assistance only if it has previously established a reserve capital. The terms of assistance are to be laid down in a resolution of the GM that requires a qualified majority of two-thirds or a simple majority of at least half the share capital is present. The basis for the resolution shall be a written report of the management board.

31. May a company buy back its own stock and if so under what circumstances and subject to which limitations?

As a rule an LLC may not buy back its own stock. A company's own shares may, however, be acquired in the following situations:

- in the course of enforcement proceedings for satisfaction of company claims which may not be satisfied from other assets of the shareholder;
- for the purposes of redemption;
- in order to enable the shareholders of the company being acquired to take up shares (an aggregate nominal value may not exceed 10 per cent of the share capital); or
- after the division of the company, the acquiring company or the newly formed company may acquire its own shares for a total value not greater than 10 per cent of the share capital, upon the demand of a shareholder if the draft terms provide that the shareholders of the company being divided take up shares of the acquiring company or the newly formed company on less favourable terms than those existing in the company being divided.

A JSC may not acquire its own stock unless:

- an acquisition is effected in order to prevent major damage directly threatening the company and the total nominal value of the acquired shares does not exceed 20 per cent of the share capital of the company;
- shares are to be offered for acquisition by the employees or persons who have been employed in the company or an affiliated company for at least three years and the total nominal value of the acquired shares does not exceed 20 per cent of the share capital of the company;

- shares are acquired by a public company in order to meet the obligations arising under debt instruments convertible to shares;
- shares are acquired under general succession;
- fully paid up shares are acquired for value by a financial institution on the account of another entity for the purpose of resale;
- shares are acquired for the purpose of their redemption;
- fully paid up shares are acquired in the course of enforcement proceedings in order to satisfy company claims which could not be otherwise satisfied from the assets of the shareholder;
- fully paid up shares are acquired gratuitously and the total nominal value of the acquired shares does not exceed 20 per cent of the share capital of the company;
- shares are acquired by a financial institution on its own account for the purpose of resale, as authorised by the GM for a period not longer than one year. However, a financial institution shall not hold its own shares, acquired in accordance with this rule, of a total nominal value greater than five per cent of the share capital; or
- shares are acquired in other cases stipulated in the law (eg acquisition of own shares by the acquiring company or acquisition of own shares by the company participating in a division).

32. Is there a legal right to withdraw from the company and, if so, under what circumstances? How is the shareholders' stock valued and paid in such a case?

Polish law does not grant an LLC shareholder any special right to withdraw from the company.

In a JSC a shareholder or shareholders representing not more than five per cent of the share capital may request that the next GM resolves upon a forced purchase of their shares that can be accomplished by not more than five shareholders who jointly represent not less than 95 per cent of the share capital, each of whom holds not less than five per cent of the share capital. In such a vote, each share carries one vote, without privileges or limitations. The purchase price shall equal the value of the net assets per share, as stated in the financial report for the last financial year, minus the amount to be distributed among the shareholders. If the shareholder or company taking part in the purchase do not agree to the purchase price, they may apply to the registry court so that an auditor be appointed in order to determine the market price of the shares or a fair purchase price. The abovementioned provisions do not apply to listed companies, to companies in liquidation and to companies in bankruptcy, unless the resolution of the GM on a forced purchase of shares was adopted at least three months prior to the declaration of liquidation or bankruptcy. In the case of a listed JSC, a shareholder may demand that its shares be acquired by another shareholder who reaches or exceeds 90 per cent of the total vote in the company.

33. In which circumstances can dividends be distributed among shareholders? Is it possible to exclude or limit the right of certain shareholders to dividends? Does a certain portion of the profits need to be set aside in a reserve fund where it cannot be distributed to the shareholders? Are advances on dividends allowed and, if so, under which circumstances? Can advances on dividends be reclaimed by the company?

Dividends for a given financial year may be paid to the shareholders who held shares on the date of the resolution on division of profits. A shareholder is entitled to a share in the profits specified in the annual financial report and allocated under a resolution of the GM for division. In a JSC the financial report has to be additionally examined by an auditor. The articles of association cannot exclude the right of certain shareholders to dividends. That right in an LLC may, however, be limited in a way that privileged dividends enjoying satisfaction before the remaining shares will be granted to some shareholders.

The total profits are not to be fully divided among shareholders. According to the law or the articles of association, some of it is kept within the company to improve the company's cashflow or capital reserves for example. In a JSC at least eight per cent of the profits shall be transferred to the supplementary capital until it reaches at least one-third of the share capital. An advance on the expected dividends is allowed if the articles of association authorise the management board to make such payment and only where the company has sufficient funds for it. Advances may be paid only if the company's approved financial report for the previous financial year shows profits. In the event that a shareholder of an LLC received payment in breach of the law or the provisions of the articles of association, advances can be reclaimed by the company. In the case of a JSC it is disputed whether a *bona fide* shareholder is obliged to return advances received in breach of the law since legal provisions are unclear in this respect.

34. What are the rights of shareholders in the case of an issue of new stock (increase of the company's corporate capital) (pre-emption rights?)?

With regard to an LLC, unless the articles of association or resolution on the increase of the share capital provide otherwise, the existing shareholders shall have priority when subscribing for new shares in the increased share capital in proportion to their existing shares. The right of priority shall be exercised within a month from the date of the summons to exercise it.

In respect to JSCs, the shareholders shall have the right of priority when taking up the new shares in proportion to the number of shares they hold. Thus, this legal constriction differs from an LLC, as the priority right in a JSC is influenced by the number of shares and not by the proportion of shares as in the case of an LLC.

Another difference in comparison to LLCs lies in the modification of this right – if the interest of the company so requires, the GM may deprive the shareholder of the pre-emptive right, in whole or in part.

35. May minority shareholders ban or limit the company's capital structure in any manner?

As a general rule, the influence of shareholders on company matters like capital structure depends on the percentage of preference shares held or special rights attributed to a shareholder.

36. Which are the financial assistance prohibitions in force?

See question 30 above.

37. Apart from publicly listed companies, in which cases (if any) are shareholders obligated to obtain an authorisation from, or provide information to, a public authority about events that have an impact on their stock interest in the company?

Polish law imposes certain information and authorisation duties on shareholders of non-listed companies that can be divided into the following groups.

Companies of high importance

Transfers of shares in companies, which are of high importance for legal relations or economic development, may require a prior notification to special public authorities. Such requirements pertain to, *inter alia*, the banking, insurance, broadcasting and gambling sectors.

Control of concentrations

The intention of concentrations is basically subject to notification submitted to the President of the Office of Competition and Consumer Protection where the turnover of undertakings participating in the concentration in the financial year preceding the year of notification exceeds a certain value.

SHAREHOLDERS' RIGHTS IN THE CASE OF EXTRAORDINARY TRANSACTIONS AND/OR WINDING-UP

38. What rights are available to shareholders in the case of a sale of all or a substantial portion of the company's assets? In case of a merger or de-merger?

The rights of shareholders in LLCs and JSCs in the case of merger or de-merger are similar and can be summed up as follows:

Right to information

This privilege is realised by the right to inspect specific documents of merging/de-merging companies. These documents are, among others: the draft terms of merger/de-merger; financial reports and reports of the management boards on the activities of merging/de-merging companies for the three preceding financial years; and the opinion and report of the auditor if such opinion or report has been drawn up. The shareholders may request that copies of the above documents be made available to them on the premises of the company, free of charge.

Right to enjoy equivalent rights

In this case, persons who enjoyed special rights (specified in the KSH) in the company being acquired or in the companies merging by the formation of a new company/in the company being de-merged – like preference shares with respect to dividends – shall enjoy rights at least equivalent to those which they have hitherto enjoyed. However, these rights may be altered or abrogated by an agreement between those entitled and the acquiring company or the newly formed company.

The most important right in the case of a sale of all or a substantial portion of the company's assets is the right to request a forced purchase of shares (reverse squeeze-out), which applies only to non-listed or listed JSCs.

Non-listed JSC

A shareholder or shareholders representing not more than five per cent of the share capital may request that the agenda of the next GM includes the matter of adoption of a resolution on a forced purchase of their shares by not more than five shareholders who jointly represent not less than 95 per cent of the share capital, each of whom holds not less than five per cent of the share capital.

Listed JSC

A shareholder in a public company may demand that its shares be acquired by another shareholder who reaches or exceeds 90 per cent of the total vote in the company. Such a demand shall be made in writing within three months from the day on which the threshold has been reached or exceeded by such other shareholder.

39. Which rights are available to shareholders in the case of conversion of the company into a European Company (SE) or into another type of company?

In the conversion process, the shareholders are entitled to inspect the draft terms of transformation with attachments as well as the opinion of the auditor on the draft terms. Each shareholder may declare whether it wishes to participate in the transformed company and if not it has a claim for payment of an amount representing its shares in a company being transformed, in accordance with a financial report drawn up for the purposes of transformation. A shareholder who has objections with respect to reliability of valuation of the shares may lodge a request that a new valuation be made. If the request is not accommodated, it may bring an action for determination of share value.

A resolution approving the conversion of a capital company into another capital company or SE requires the support of at least three-quarters of the votes adopted, whereas at the GM, shareholders representing at least half of the share capital shall participate unless the articles of association provide for stricter requirements.

40. Which rights are available to shareholders of a company in liquidation?

Shareholders are entitled to participate in the division of the assets remaining after the creditors are satisfied or secured (in proportion to their shares) not earlier than after the end of one year from the date of the last announcement on the opening of liquidation and summoning of the creditors. Resolutions on additional contributions in an LLC may be adopted only with the consent of all shareholders. All other shareholders' rights remain unaltered.

41. Can shareholders cause the liquidation of the company? How?

The liquidation of an LLC and a JSC can be opened by shareholders' resolution on dissolution of the company. If the balance sheet drawn up by the management board shows a loss exceeding the aggregate of the supplementary and the reserve capitals and one-third of the share capital in a JSC (half of the share capital in an LLC), a resolution on the continued existence of the company shall be adopted.

In addition to the above, a shareholder of an LLC may request the company's dissolution by court in certain specified cases.

Please note that the articles of association may stipulate other reasons for dissolving the company.

COMPANY GROUPS

42. Is the concept of group recognised as such under specific legislation? What are the implications?

Companies form groups in the following most common situations:
- relationships of dominance;
- agreement for management of dependent company. The subject of this agreement concluded between the dominant and the dependent company is the management of the dependent company or a transfer of profits by such company; or
- tax capital group. Incorporated commercial law companies related by capital may also form groups for tax purposes on conditions laid down in the Corporate Income Tax Act. Tax capital groups may be formed exclusively by LLCs or JSCs whose seats are located in the territory of the Republic of Poland, providing, among others, that those companies have no arrears with respect to payment of taxes constituting revenues of the state budget.

43. Does a controlling company have any particular duties *vis-à-vis* its controlled company shareholders?

No it does not.

44. What are the rights of company shareholders when the controlling company puts in place actions and/or transactions that can be prejudicial to the shareholders?

Polish law does not provide for any specific safeguarding mechanism against prejudicial acts of a controlling company towards its shareholders. The management board of the controlled company is obliged to act in its interest and prevent any detriment to the company.

45. What are the limitations, if any, to the possibility of owning reciprocal stock interests in companies?

There are no such limitations.

Portugal

Gómez-Acebo & Pombo Teresa Baptista

BASIC INFORMATION ON THE TYPES OF LIMITED LIABILITY COMPANIES AND ON THE RIGHTS OF SHAREHOLDERS

1. What types of companies enjoy limited liability? If more than one, which ones have shareholders, ie holders of share certificates? Which one is the most common? Which one is mostly used by foreign investors?

Under the Portuguese Companies Code (*Código das Sociedades* Comerciais or CSC) the following companies enjoy limited liability: joint stock companies (*sociedades anónimas* or SA) and limited liability companies (*sociedades por quotas or Lda*).

According to the applicable legal provisions, the liability of the shareholders of an SA is limited to the number of shares each one holds. Therefore, the liability for paying the company's debts exceeding the number of shares held by the shareholders belongs to the company itself.

In the Lda, the ruling principle is that only the company's assets shall be liable for paying its debts. Notwithstanding that, it is possible that the company's by-laws set forth the liability of one or more shareholders for paying its debts. This liability shall be subject to certain limits:
(i) it can only be set up to a certain amount;
(ii) it shall be set as joint and/or ancillary of the company's liability;
(iii) it shall only cover the obligations undertaken by the company within the period the shareholder belongs to the company; and
(iv) it shall not be transferable by death of the shareholder.

In any case, unless otherwise provided, if the shareholder pays any debts of the company they have a right of recourse (*direito de regresso*) over the company in relation to the paid amount.

A final reference shall be made to the limited liability of a category of shareholders in a limited partnership (*sociedade em comandita* (SC)), which may be of two types: *sociedade em comandita simples* (SCS) or *sociedade em comandita por acções* (SCA).

In any SC the limited partners (*sócio comanditário*) shall only be liable for the amount of their entry in the company while the other category of partners (*sócios comanditados*), besides being liable for the amount of their entry in the company, shall also be liable for paying the company's debts, this liability being ancillary to the company's, together with the other partners.

The most common and also the most used by foreign investors are the Lda and the SA.

2. Are there minimum capital requirements and/or thin capitalisation rules in force?

The CSC sets forth minimum capital requirements which shall be met by the companies. According to the applicable provisions the Lda shall have a minimum share capital of €5,000 while the SA and the SCA shall have a minimum share capital of €50,000.

Thin capitalisation rules currently in place are not applicable to Portuguese or EU related parties. Hence, if the amount of shareholder loans in a company is considered to be excessive, interest deductions on the excess debt are disallowed for tax purposes. Shareholder debt is considered excessive if, at any moment, the amount owed to a related party exceeds twice the amount of the relevant participation in the company's shareholders' equity.

For calculation of the amount owed, all types of credits are taken into account, irrespective of the kind of remuneration agreed between the parties, including credits from commercial transactions at least six months overdue.

Interest deductions on excess debt will nevertheless be allowed if the company is able to provide evidence that the amount of debt is at arm's length, ie that the same amount of debt could have been obtained from independent and unrelated parties. However, interest deductions on excess debt shall never be allowed if the related party is resident in a country or territory blacklisted in Portugal.

3. Describe the types of shares that can be issued by a company and the different rights that they attribute to their owners, as well as any other financial instruments (bonds or other) and other instruments of a participatory nature in the company's capital that can also be issued by the company.

Unless otherwise provided, a company can issue nominative shares or bearer shares. The issuance of nominative shares is mandatory:

- while the shares are not fully released;
- when, according to the company's by-laws, the shares cannot be transferred without the company's consent or there is any other restriction on the transfer of shares; or
- in the case of shares the holder of which, according to the company's by-laws, has to make auxiliary contributions to the company.

Another distinction, which is independent from the one above, is between ordinary shares and non-voting preferred shares (please refer to question 15 below).

The CSC also sets forth the possibility of an SA, in certain circumstances, issuing bonds which, in the same issuance, assign equal credit rights. Bonds cannot be issued before the share capital is fully released or, at least, the shareholders which have not timely released their shares are put on default.

4. Can a company have only one shareholder and still enjoy limited liability?

Under the Portuguese Companies Code, it is possible to have both an Lda and an SA with a single shareholder.

In the Lda, the single shareholder shall be liable on the same terms as multiple shareholders of Ldas (please refer to question 1 above).

However, a sole shareholder of an SA will not enjoy limited liability on the terms enjoyed by multiple shareholders of SAs.

5. Are the rights of shareholders the same in any type of company?

Generally speaking, the rights of shareholders are the same in any type of company. The difference will lie in the terms of the execution of such rights, which may vary from company to company.

6. What are the basic rights of any shareholder? Describe briefly the rights of minority shareholders and indicate which thresholds, if any, are required to allow the minority shareholders to exercise any such rights.

The basic rights of any shareholder, under the CSC, are to:
- share in the profits;
- participate in shareholders' resolutions;
- be informed about the activity of the company, under the law and the contract;
- be appointed to the governing bodies of the company;
- a priority right in the case of share capital increase through cash contributions;
- challenge corporate resolutions and application for their suspension;
- require judicial investigation of the company;
- free transfer of shares within the limits of the law and the social contract;
- withdraw in the case of a merger or de-merger; and
- withdraw in the case of a decision to return to activity by the company after the resolution of winding-up.

Regarding minority shareholders in an SA, the relevant thresholds required to allow them to exercise any such rights vary in accordance with the concerned right. To this extent, besides the general principle which allows minority shareholders holding less than 10 per cent of the share capital to sell-out their shares in the case of a majority shareholder holding more than 90 per cent, it is possible to summarise the following rights assigned to them:
- opposition to the waiving by the company of the right to compensation or court settlement under litigation regarding civil liability for constitution, management or supervision of the company (holding at least 10 per cent of shares);
- require the management body to provide written information about the activity of the company (holding at least 10 per cent of shares);
- proposal for election of directors or members of the general council, if applicable, when provided for in the company by-laws (holding less than 20 per cent and more than 10 per cent of shares);
- designation of at least one director, when the shareholder has voted

against the winning proposal (holding at least 10 per cent of shares);

- application for a judicial disqualification of a director, based on a fair ground, when a general meeting (GM) to discuss the matter has not been convened (holding at least 10 per cent of shares);
- application for a judicial appointment of one effective and one substitute member to the supervisory board, in addition to the existing (holding at least 10 per cent of shares), since the shareholder has voted against the resolution adopted by the company;
- application for a judicial disqualification of the additional effective and substitute member of the supervisory board appointed by judicial decision mentioned on the previous point (it must be the same shareholder who has applied for the appointment, holding at least 10 per cent of shares);
- application to the court to appoint a special representative in the process regarding civil liability, if one has not been appointed by the company or if it is necessary to replace the existing one (holding at least five per cent of shares);
- application for an action for damages against directors in order to repair the damage caused to the company, when the company fails to do so (holding at least five per cent of shares);
- require information concerning the activity of the company (when holding at least one per cent of shares);
- receive preparatory documents of GMs by letter (holding at least one per cent of shares);
- constitute a group of shareholders in order to complete the minimum number of shares required to assign a voting right;
- require the convening of a GM (holding at least five per cent of shares);
- apply for a judicial convening of the GM when the application addressed to the company has been refused (holding at least five per cent of shares);
- require the inclusion of issues on the agenda of the GM (holding at least five per cent of shares); and
- apply for a judicial convening of a new GM when the application for inclusion of issues on the agenda has been accepted (holding at least five per cent of shares).

The rights assigned to minority shareholders in an SA regarding the convening and inclusion of issues in the agenda of a GM can be exercised by any shareholder of an Lda.

7. Do all shareholders enjoy the same rights or can some shareholders be attributed specific rights, whether by reason of the particular class of stock owned or other? Are such rights generally provided for at the level of the company's by-laws and/or in shareholders' agreements?
Usually, all shareholders have the same rights.

Notwithstanding this fact the shareholders of the Lda and the SA may enjoy special rights that may only be granted by the company by-laws.

Typical situations are: (i) shareholders owning non-voting preferred shares who shall not be entitled to vote on the company's resolutions; and (ii) a company that issues shares granting different rights to its shareholders, regarding the assignment of dividends and the distribution of assets in the case of liquidation.

8. May the rights of shareholders, generally speaking, be limited, modified, suppressed or waived in any way? If so, how? Are such modifications or limitations provided for in the company's by-laws and/or in shareholders' agreements?

Generally speaking, the rights of shareholders may be suspended in some situations determined by law, namely where the shareholder does not comply with their obligation of entry in the company's share capital.

On the other hand, unless otherwise provided by law or the company's by-laws, it is possible to suppress or limit special rights if the shareholder concerned gives their consent.

GENERAL MEETING OF SHAREHOLDERS (GM) AND VOTING RIGHTS
9. Which decisions are reserved to the competence of the GM?

The decisions reserved to the competence of the GM vary according to the type of company. As a general principle it is possible to say that the GM shall decide on the most relevant issues of the company while the day-to-day issues shall be dealt with by the management body.

In the Lda the GM shall decide on the following issues:

- provision of supplementary contributions (*prestações suplementares*) by the shareholders;
- any amendment or transfer of shares;
- exclusion of shareholders;
- discharge of directors or of members of the auditing body;
- approval of the management report and annual accounts, distribution of incomes and losses;
- disclaimer of directors, shareholders and members of the auditing body;
- amendment of the company's by-laws; and
- merger, de-merger, transformation, winding-up and return to activity of a liquidated company.

Unless otherwise provided by the company's by-laws the GM shall also decide on the following issues:

- appointment of directors and members of the auditing body;
- assignment or charge of real estate as well as assignment, charge and renting of establishment; and
- subscription or acquisition of shares in other companies and their assignment or charging.

Under the CSC, the GM of an SA has a residual competence. Indeed, apart from the annual approval of accounts, the GM shall decide on issues specifically assigned to it in the company's by-laws and on issues not assigned to the competence of the management body or to the auditing body. Usually, the SA's by-laws assign to the decision of the GM the same issues referred to above regarding the Lda.

10. How does a shareholder participate in a GM? Are there any limitations to having a minimum number of shares? May a shareholder delegate attendance to another shareholder or to the board? May a shareholder obtain assistance from the courts or any other governmental body to intervene in a GM or to cause one to be held in some particular cases?
All shareholders are entitled to participate in a GM, independently of the number of shares held, unless the by-laws state otherwise.

The number and type of shares are relevant to determine whether the shareholder has voting rights and, if so, how many votes they have.

Consequently, there may be shareholders with and without voting rights attending a GM.

Regardless of having voting rights, shareholders shall not be entitled to vote on issues referring to them, ie where there is a conflict of interest.

In terms of voluntary representation at the GM, while in an SA the general rule provides that the shareholder may be represented by anyone; in an Lda, they shall be represented, at least, by their spouse, ancestor, descendant or another shareholder. The company's by-laws may limit the possibility of representation in an SA but cannot exclude the representation by the shareholder's spouse, ancestor or descendant, by a director of the company or by another shareholder.

In the situations where a GM is not convened, despite being requested by shareholders duly empowered to that effect, the relevant shareholders may obtain assistance from the courts to cause one to be held. The same applies to the non-inclusion of issues on the agenda, where the concerned shareholder can request court assistance to determine the inclusion of these issues on the agenda.

11. May a GM be called and held at the request of any shareholder? Is there a threshold regarding the percentage of the stock interest owned in the company that may entitle a shareholder to such a right?
A GM of an Lda can be called and held at the request of any shareholder.

In the case of an SA the GM may be called and held at the request of any shareholder or a group of shareholders representing at least five per cent of the company's share capital.

12. May a shareholder bring up an issue to be resolved upon and put it to a vote if it is not included on the agenda? May a shareholder require more information from the GM and/or the board, concerning the agenda of the GM, to be put in a better position to exercise their vote?
The inclusion of issues on the agenda has to be requested prior to the day when the GM shall be held; otherwise the decision will be voidable, unless all shareholders are attending the meeting and agree to decide on the concerned issue.

The shareholder is entitled to require more information from the GM and/or the board concerning the agenda of the GM so that they may be in a better position to exercise their vote.

13. May a GM be held by telecommunication means and/or by correspondence (ie by written consent)?

Under the CSC the GM may be held by telecommunication means, unless otherwise provided by the company's by-laws. It is also possible that the shareholders take decisions through a written vote; in this case the decision shall be approved by all the shareholders.

14. Are voting rights always proportionate to the stock held by each shareholder or can they vary by share class?

Voting rights are proportionate to the stock held by each shareholder unless otherwise provided by the company's by-laws. Indeed, it is possible to make several shares correspond to one single vote, within certain limits set forth by law, and/or limit the number of votes issued by a shareholder to be taken into consideration.

Please refer to our answer below regarding the shares which do not grant voting rights to their holders.

15. Are there non-voting shares? Is there a maximum percentage of capital represented by non-voting shares?

Under the CSC there are non-voting preferred shares in the SA. Such shares, which cannot represent more than 50 per cent of the company's share capital, assign to their holders the right to a priority dividend, which cannot correspond to less than five per cent of their amount or similar.

This type of share shall not be considered for the determination of the share capital's representation, required by law or by the company's by-laws, regarding shareholders' decisions. Non-voting preferred shares also assign to their holders the same rights as ordinary shares do, except the voting right.

16. Can shareholders group their shares in order to exercise their voting rights (eg, by trust, shareholders' agreement or otherwise)?

Shareholders in an SA can group their shares to exercise their voting rights. It is also possible that shareholders holding few participation rights group their shares in order to reach the amount required for the exercise of voting rights. Usually this is not made in a formal way but it is possible to enter into shareholders' agreements to that effect.

17. Under what circumstances can a shareholder challenge the resolutions adopted by the GM? Are there thresholds concerning the stock interest owned to be able to bring such a claim?

A shareholder, regardless of the stock interest owned, can challenge the resolutions adopted by the GM in the following situations:
- they were against such a resolution, ie voted against it, and did not ratify it later;
- the resolution adopted is null or voidable, ie the formal requirements

were not met; or
- the resolution was adopted notwithstanding the fact that the information requested is missing.

18. What are the terms and procedures to challenge a resolution of the GM?

A resolution of the GM shall be challenged in the courts. In order to safeguard the useful effect of the court decision, and as it usually takes so long to be issued, it is possible to apply for a protective order determining the suspension of the company's resolutions.

The protective order shall be requested within 10 days after the resolution is taken or after the claimer knows it. After the request the company will be notified to contest.

While a decision regarding the protective order is pending, the company cannot implement the challenged resolution.

Since the validity of protective orders depends on the submission of the main claim, it is necessary to start the main proceedings within 30 days after the decision which determines the protective order.

SHAREHOLDERS' RIGHTS VERSUS DIRECTORS AND DUTIES OF OTHER CORPORATE BODIES IN THE COMPANY

19. What is the procedure for the appointment/replacement/ revocation of directors and of statutory auditors, if any?

The ruling principle is that the appointment/replacement/revocation of directors and of statutory auditors is made by the decision of the GM, unless the company's by-laws provide otherwise, in particular in respect of appointment and replacement.

20. May shareholders challenge the resolutions of the board of directors? Is there a minimum percentage of capital required to challenge a board resolution?

Shareholders with voting rights may challenge the resolutions of the board of directors, regardless of the share capital they hold, provided that such resolutions are harmful to the company, ie in the case of null or voidable resolutions.

21. Are shareholders entitled to bring a legal action against the directors of the company? In which circumstances? Please describe briefly the principles of directors' liability.

Shareholders representing at least five per cent (or two per cent in the case of companies whose shares are negotiated in a ruled market) of the company's share capital are entitled to bring legal actions against the directors of the company, requesting their condemnation to pay the company the damages caused to it whenever the company does not request it by itself.

The ruling principle in the Portuguese jurisdiction establishes that the directors shall be held liable before the company for all damages caused to it by actions or omissions derived from a breach of legal or contractual duties, unless the directors prove they are not guilty. This liability cannot be considered when the envisaged director was not present at the decision making or has voted against it. Directors cannot be held liable for implementing resolutions issued by the GM. By contrast, in companies with an auditing body the favourable opinion or consent of this body does not exempt the directors from their liability. In the SA the liability of the directors shall be guaranteed by collateral unless the GM agrees otherwise.

22. What are the rights in connection with transactions where the directors have a conflict of interest situation?
In transactions where the directors have a conflict of interest situation they are forbidden to vote on the relevant board resolution and shall inform the chairman or the other directors of the conflict of interest.

When there is a breach of that rule the shareholders may challenge the resolution adopted as it will be null or voidable.

INFORMATION RIGHTS ON THE COMPANY'S BUSINESS
23. What information may be requested by the shareholders from the board concerning the general state of the company's business or any specific transaction? Are information rights different depending on the number of shares owned? Are shareholders entitled to receive written information before, during or after the GM about the meeting agenda and to what extent? Is it possible for a shareholder to obtain a copy of the minutes of the GM?
The CSC establishes as a general principle that all shareholders are entitled to receive information regarding the company's business.

In the Lda all shareholders have this right, regardless of the amount of their quotas.

In the SA the extent of the right will vary, depending on the percentage of share capital held. Thus, shareholders representing at least one per cent of the company's share capital only have a minimum right to information, which allows them, when alleging a justified reason, to seek at the company's headquarters the management reports, financial statements, minutes, summons, presence lists, payments charts and similar documents. Shareholders holding shares corresponding to 10 per cent or more of the company's share capital can request written information from the board regarding corporate issues, which can only be refused in legitimate circumstances. Such information may refer to events which have already occurred or not. Once such information is provided to the applicant it shall be made available for all shareholders at the company's headquarters.

Information for preparation of the GM shall be made available for the shareholders' analysis at the company's headquarters within 15 days before the date of the relevant GM and shall also be sent to shareholders holding shares corresponding to at least one per cent of the share capital, at their request, within eight days. During the GM any shareholder can request further information regarding an issue to be voted on, so that they may be in a better position to vote; this may include written information whenever necessary.

Shareholders are also entitled to obtain a copy of the minutes of the GM.

The law also allows shareholders to group their shares in order to reach the minimum share capital required

24. Do shareholders have the right/duty to resolve in the GM upon matters which were not on the agenda?

Matters which were not on the agenda can only be decided if all shareholders give their consent.

25. Are shareholders entitled to inspect the corporate books and/or any other corporate or accounting documents? To what extent? Can they do it through external counsel or advisors?

Shareholders are entitled to inspect the corporate books or other accounting documents of the company at the company's headquarters or request the relevant information to be provided to them in writing. Such inspection shall be made by the shareholder itself, which can be assisted by an external accountant or other expert. In an SA this inspection can also be done by the person entitled to represent the shareholder at the GM.

SHAREHOLDERS' AGREEMENTS

26. Are shareholders' agreements validly enforceable? What are their typical contents and term of duration? Are they enforceable by or against third parties and, if so, to what extent?

Under the CSC shareholders are entitled to enter into parasocial agreements. These agreements, which may include all or only part of the shareholders, are enforceable between the parties and do not allow challenge of actions of the company or of the shareholders against the company. They can refer to the exercise of voting rights but not to the behaviour of interveners or other persons performing management or auditing functions.

Parasocial agreements by which a shareholder undertakes to vote in accordance with the instructions or proposals submitted by the company or by one of its bodies, or to use their voting right or not to vote, against the assignment of special advantages are null.

These agreements will have the duration agreed by the parties, under the limits of the law.

27. Do shareholders' agreements have to be disclosed to the public or registered in any public registry?

Shareholders' agreements typically do not have to be disclosed to the public nor registered in any public registry. They must be notified to the Portuguese Securities Commission if their purpose is to acquire, maintain or reinforce a qualified holding in an open-ended company.

ECONOMIC RIGHTS AND RIGHTS OVER THE STOCK

28. Is the stock always freely transferable? Are there any legal limitations? Are there any restrictions on contractual limitations?

The stock is freely transferable. The only limitations which may be set by law or by the company's by-laws are: to require the company's consent or to set a pre-emption right for the other shareholders. In certain circumstances where the company's consent is required the company is obliged to acquire the shares when it opposes the transmission.

29. Are shareholders entitled to pledge their stock?
Yes, shareholders are entitled to pledge their stock. The only limitation which can be set is the company reserving itself the right to amortise the shares in the case of a pledge.

30. Are there financial assistance issues to be considered and other prohibitions to be evaluated in the context of a leveraged buyout transaction?
A joint stock company may not grant loans or provide funds in any manner to a third party, so that the latter subscribes or acquires by any means shareholdings in the former. This prohibition is not applicable to ordinary banks nor other financial institutions and operations, or to staff buyouts or a company which is part of the same group. However, as a result of the relevant transaction or operation, the net assets of the company may not become inferior to the subscribed share capital and the legal or statutory reserves that may not be distributed. The agreements or unilateral acts breaching the aforementioned provisions are void.

31. May a company buy back its own stock and, if so, under what circumstances and subject to which limitations?
Companies may buy back their stock in some specific situations set forth by law. Companies are entitled to amortise their shares, ie buy them back in the case of a pledge by the shareholders or in other situations set by the company's by-laws. Such amortisation implies the extinction of the shares in the Lda and, when specially provided, in the SA; it is also possible to have amortisation with no extinction of shares in the SA.

Another situation where companies may buy back their stock is the selling of shares; indeed, it is quite common to have the companies reserving themselves a pre-emption right in this case. Companies have a duty to buy back their stock when they do not give their consent to an envisaged selling of shares by any shareholder, where such consent is required.

32. Is there a legal right to withdraw from the company and, if so, under what circumstances? How is the shareholders' stock valued and paid in such a case?
Shareholders are entitled to withdraw from the company in certain circumstances set by law or by the company's by-laws. The law provides for a general right of withdrawal from the company when the company has no fixed duration. When there is a duration fixed for the company's lifetime, shareholders can only withdraw from the company in the situations set by law or by the company's by-laws or when there is justified reason. This would be so when the shareholders have voted against a capital increase

operated by third parties, in the case of error, fraud, coercion or usury, of change of the corporate scope, of extension of the company's duration, of transfer of the company's head office abroad, of transformation of the company's type, of return to the activity of a dissolved company and in the case of a merger or de-merger when the shareholder showed their opposition. When there is justified reason for the exclusion of a shareholder, if the company does not decide to exclude them nor promote their judicial exclusion the other shareholders may withdraw from the company.

In the SA, the shareholders holding 10 per cent or less of the company's stock are also entitled to withdraw from the company when there is an acquisition of 90 per cent or more of this stock by a single shareholder. It is important to note that in this type of company the shareholders have a larger freedom to withdraw from the company than the other types.

In the case of withdrawal, the value of the shareholders' stock is usually determined as per the status of the company at the moment when the relevant decision is taken, by an accountant appointed by the parties or, in case of disagreement, by the court. The parties may also request a second evaluation in order to determine the value of the stock.

33. In which circumstances can dividends be distributed among shareholders? Is it possible to exclude or limit the right of certain shareholders to dividends? Does a certain portion of the profits need to be set aside in a reserve fund where it cannot be distributed to the shareholders? Are advances on dividends allowed and, if so, under which circumstances? Can advances on dividends be reclaimed by the company?

Under Portuguese jurisdiction dividends can be distributed among shareholders after deduction of the amounts assigned by the decision of the majority shareholders in pursuit of the corporate purpose. Unless otherwise provided in the company's by-laws or decided by more than three-quarters of the votes representing the share capital in a GM convened to that effect, half of the yearly distributable profits shall be distributed between the shareholders. The distribution of dividends shall also occur in the case of liquidation of the company or selling of shares by the company.

The right to dividends may be excluded or limited in the case of special rights in the SA, ie privileged shares which can assign their holders a different amount of dividends or a priority in the distribution or the dividend-right shares (*acções de fruição*), where the distribution of dividends shall only occur after the payment of the remaining categories of shares. The distribution of dividends may also be limited or excluded when all the shareholder's rights are suspended. However, any limitation or exclusion of distribution of dividends shall always be temporary.

As per the applicable legal provisions, it is mandatory to set aside at least 20 per cent of the company's net result for the legal reserve. The legal reserve shall correspond to, at least, one-fifth of the company's share capital. The amounts assigned for the legal reserve can only be used to cover losses which cannot be covered by the profits or by other reserves held by the company or included in the company's share capital.

Advances on dividends are allowed provided it is admitted in the company's by-laws and the following conditions are met:

(a) issuance of a decision from the board of directors, approved by the company's accountants;

(b) prior to the decision of the board of directors an interim balance stating the existence of enough amounts for payment of the advances shall be done, which shall be certified by the auditor;

(c) only one advance shall be done per year, and always on the second semester; and

(d) the amounts to be advanced shall not exceed half of those which should be distributed.

Advances on dividends can only be reclaimed by the company when they were irregular and the shareholders who received them knew of such irregularity.

34. What are the rights of shareholders in the case of an issue of new stock (increase of the company's corporate capital) (pre-emption rights)?

In the case of new stock, ie an increase of the company's corporate capital, the shareholders have pre-emption rights over third parties to acquire the new shares. This right grants the possibility of acquiring a number of shares up to the equivalent of the amount already held.

35. May minority shareholders ban or limit the company's capital structure in any manner?

Minority shareholders may ban or limit the company's capital structure by exercising minorities' rights, in particular through blocking minorities, ie by voting against any resolution of amendment of the capital structure (*minorias de bloqueio*).

36. Which are the financial assistance prohibitions in force?

Regarding financial assistance prohibitions, the CSC establishes that a company cannot grant loans or in any way provide funds or guarantees in order to allow a third party to acquire its own shares, otherwise these acts shall be void. This prohibition is not applicable to current transactions of banks or other financial entities or to transactions regarding the acquisition of shares by the company's staff or by the staff of a company in connection with it. Anyway, these transactions cannot make the net result of the company lower than the subscribed capital plus the reserves which, in accordance with the law or the company's by-laws, cannot be distributed.

37. Apart from publicly listed companies, in which cases (if any) are shareholders obligated to obtain an authorisation from, or provide information to, a public authority about events that have an impact on their stock interest in the company?

Apart from publicly listed companies shareholders are not obligated to obtain authorisation from nor provide information to any public authority about events with impact on their stock interest in the company.

SHAREHOLDERS' RIGHTS IN THE CASE OF EXTRAORDINARY TRANSACTIONS AND/OR WINDING-UP

38. What rights are available to shareholders in the case of a sale of all or a substantial portion of the company's assets? In the case of a merger or de-merger?

It must be noted that the shareholders have the information rights described in question 6 above, in particular the right to require the management body to provide written information about the activity of the company and receive by mail preparatory documents of GMs.

It should be taken into account whether the resolution to sell all or a substantial portion of the company's assets was taken by the GM or the management body of the company. In limited liability companies, the sale or encumbrance of immovable property or the sale, encumbrance or lease of establishments is subject to a resolution of the GM, unless the by-laws of the company provide otherwise. In the case of joint stock companies, the issue shall be, in principle, subject to a resolution of the board of directors.

When the relevant resolution was taken by the GM, the shareholder may challenge it where it was void or voidable, notably if they voted against the resolution and it breached the applicable legal provisions or the company's by-laws. The applicable requirements are referred to in question 17. When the decision to sell all or a substantial portion of the company's assets was taken by the management body, the shareholders may bring a legal action against the directors of the company who voted in favour of the resolution, as described in question 21, in particular if the sale breached the law or the company's by-laws and caused damage to the company. A shareholder may also challenge it where it was void or voidable, notably in the case of violation of the applicable laws or the by-laws of the company. The board of directors or the GM may declare void or voidable the relevant board of directors' resolution.

If provided in the company's by-laws, shareholders have the right to withdraw from the company if they did not approve the project of merger or de-merger. In consequence, the company will be obliged to acquire their shares or promote their acquisition by third parties, at an amount fixed as described in question 32.

39. Which rights are available to shareholders in the case of conversion of the company into a European Company (SE) or into another type of company?

In the case of conversion of the company into an SE or into another type of company, shareholders would be entitled to withdraw from the company if they did not approve the resolution of transformation. In consequence, the company will be obliged to acquire their shares or promote their acquisition by third parties, as mentioned in question 38.

40. Which rights are available to shareholders of a company in liquidation?

If a company is in liquidation its shareholders are entitled to share the company's assets, if any.

41. Can shareholders cause the liquidation of the company? How?

Shareholders may cause the liquidation of the company by deciding unanimously on its winding-up. Once the company's winding-up occurs it enters automatically into liquidation.

COMPANY GROUPS

42. Is the concept of 'group' recognised as such under specific legislation? What are the implications?

The CSC and other specific legislation, such as the laws of the Bank of Portugal and tax laws recognise the concept of 'group' as such. The main implications of recognition are:

(i)   the assignment of a management power to the controlling/parent company;

(ii) the obligation of consolidating accounts in some situations;

(iii) the taxation regime; and

(iv) the liability of the parent company for the debts and corporate losses of the dependent companies.

The consequences referred to in (i) and (iv) shall not be applicable to joint groups' agreements (*contratos de grupos paritários*).

43. Does a controlling company have any particular duties *vis-à-vis* its controlled company shareholders?

The controlling company is obliged, within a fixed deadline, to acquire the shares held by the shareholders of the controlled company, when they choose to withdraw from the company. It will also be responsible for paying to these shareholders the difference between the real profit and the highest of the following amounts: the average of the profits earned by the shareholders in the three years before the group agreement, calculated in percentage as per the share capital; or the profit which would be earned due to shares in the controlling company, if they were exchanged by shares of these shareholders.

44. What are the rights of company shareholders when the controlling company puts in place actions and/or transactions that can be prejudicial to the shareholders?

If the controlling company puts in place actions and/or transactions that can be prejudicial to the shareholders they can start legal proceedings for the suspension and/or cancellation of the relevant action or transaction and can also apply for the liability of the directors of the controlling company.

45. What are the limitations, if any, to the possibility of owning reciprocal stock interests in companies?

The possibility of owning reciprocal stock interests in companies will be subject to different limitations, according to the type of relation between the companies at stake, in particular in the case of reciprocal shareholdings' companies (*sociedades em relação de simples participação*) and companies in a controlling relationship (*sociedades em relação de domínio*).

Reciprocal shareholdings' companies are companies which hold at least 10 per cent of the share capital of each other and, for that reason, are obliged to inform the other about the amount of its shares really held. The company which has last made the communication of the amount of shares held cannot acquire new shares in the other company, under penalty that such an acquisition will be void and the exercise of the rights referred to these shares will be forbidden, except the right to sharing the result of the liquidation.

Companies in a controlling relationship are those where one (the dominant) can perform a dominant influence over the other (the dependent). This will occur when the dominant company:
(i) has a majority holding in the share capital of the dependent;
(ii) has more than half of the votes of the dependent; or
(iii) is entitled to appoint more than half of the members of the management or of the auditing body.

In this type of company, the dependent cannot acquire shares of the dominant – unless they are free acquisitions, acquisitions by adjudication in enforcement actions against debtors or acquisitions derived from the sharing of companies where the dependent holds shares – under penalty that such acquisitions will be void. This shall not apply in the case of stock exchange acquisitions with the limitations set forth by law.

Republic of Ireland

William Fry Bryan Bourke & Joanne Conlon

BASIC INFORMATION ON THE TYPES OF LIMITED LIABILITY COMPANIES AND ON THE RIGHTS OF SHAREHOLDERS
1. What types of companies enjoy limited liability? If more than one, which ones have shareholders, ie holders of share certificates? Which one is the most common? Which one is mostly used by foreign investors?

The most common forms of limited liability company in Ireland are the private company limited by shares and the public limited company (PLC). The other companies that have limited liability are private companies limited by guarantee having a share capital, public companies limited by guarantee not having a share capital (public guarantee companies) and *Societas Europeae* (SE). With the exception of public guarantee companies, each of these types of company has shareholders. Members of a public guarantee company guarantee to contribute a fixed amount to its assets on winding up.

2. Are there minimum capital requirements and/or thin capitalisation rules in force?

There are no minimum capital requirements for private companies, other than for credit institutions and investment firms which have minimum regulatory capital requirements. PLCs must have a minimum issued capital of just in excess of €38,000. An SE must have a minimum issued capital of €120,000.

3. Describe the types of shares that can be issued by a company and the different rights that they attribute to their owners, as well as any other financial instruments (bonds or other) and other instruments of a participatory nature in the company's capital that can also be issued by the company.

The main categories of shares are as follows:

- In most cases where 'shares' are referred to in this chapter, we refer to ordinary shares which are the most common class of shares, and usually carry the right to attend, speak and vote at general meetings, the right to participate in dividends declared, the right to a return of capital and to participate in surplus assets on a winding up.
- Most companies can also issue preference shares – these generally provide preferential rights in relation to the payment of dividends, the return of capital or voting rights. These rights are generally set out in the

company's constitutional documents (ie in its memorandum and articles of association).

- Redeemable shares, which often fall within the above categories, are liable at the option of the company or the shareholder to be redeemed. Strict conditions apply to the issue of redeemable shares and to their redemption. Instead of cancelling shares upon their redemption, a company may hold such shares as treasury shares, but no voting rights may be exercised, and no dividends are payable in respect of treasury shares.

Most Irish companies can also issue warrants and other debt instruments that are convertible into shares.

4.   Can a company have only one shareholder and still enjoy limited liability?

It is possible for private limited companies to have a single shareholder. All public companies must have a minimum of seven shareholders.

5.   Are the rights of shareholders the same in any type of company?

Under the Companies Acts 1963-2009 (Companies Acts), shareholders in private and public companies generally hold ordinary shares, and their shares have the same rights. The rights of shareholders in a particular company may be extended or limited by agreement or by the terms of the company's articles of association (articles). The shareholders of companies listed on the main market of the Irish Stock Exchange, or listed on another regulated market in the EU but having a registered office in Ireland, (listed companies) have certain additional rights under the Shareholders' Rights (Directive 2007/36/EC) Regulations 2009 (the Shareholders' Rights Regulations).

6.   What are the basic rights of any shareholder? Describe briefly the rights of minority shareholders and indicate which thresholds, if any, are required to allow the minority shareholders to exercise any such rights.

Unless otherwise provided in the articles, a shareholder has the right to attend, speak and vote at general meetings, to participate in dividends declared, to a return of capital and to participate in any surplus assets on a winding up. Under the Companies Acts, all shareholders have additional basic rights, including rights to:

- obtain a copy of the memorandum and articles of association and any resolution made by the company;
- receive each year a copy of the company's balance sheet and profit and loss account (with the directors' and auditors' reports on them);
- petition the court for relief where the affairs of the company are being conducted in a manner oppressive to them or any of the members, or in disregard of their interests as members; and
- inspect and obtain a copy of the company's statutory registers (ie registers of members, directors, directors' interests, etc)

There are additional rights based on the size of the shareholder's interest.

For example, where the shareholder holds 10 per cent or more of the issued share capital, it can requisition the holding of an extraordinary general meeting, demand a poll at a general meeting, and apply to the court for cancellation of a special resolution approving the giving of financial assistance for the purchase of the company's own shares. In addition, the shares of a member holding more than 10 per cent of the issued share capital of a public company listed on a regulated market cannot be compulsorily acquired in a takeover situation.

Where a shareholder holds 15 per cent or more of the issued share capital, it can apply in limited circumstances to the court to cancel an alteration of the provisions of the company's memorandum of association (memorandum) to which it objected. The shares of a member holding more than 20 per cent of the issued share capital of a private company or a public company cannot be compulsorily acquired in a takeover situation. Finally, where a shareholder holds more than 25 per cent of a company's issued share capital, it can veto a special resolution (see question 9 below for details of when special resolutions are required).

7.   Do all shareholders enjoy the same rights or can some shareholders be attributed specific rights, whether by reason of the particular class of stock owned or other? Are such rights generally provided for at the level of the company's by-laws and/or in shareholders' agreements?
Specific rights may be conferred on a particular shareholder or class of shares by the articles, by the terms of issue of the shares, or pursuant to a shareholders' agreement. A company may also have separate classes of shares in the company's capital to which specific rights are attached.

8.   May the rights of shareholders, generally speaking, be limited, modified, suppressed or waived in any way? If so, how? Are such modifications or limitations provided for in the company's by-laws and/or in shareholders' agreements?
In most cases, shareholders' rights may only be limited by agreement with those shareholders. In the absence of unanimous agreement, a special resolution (requiring the approval of the holder(s) of not less than 75 per cent of the ordinary shares in issue) would be required to alter the company's articles to seek to limit shareholders' rights. The memorandum and/or articles commonly contain a procedure for modifying rights attaching to shares/classes of shares. In the absence of such a provision, the modification may only be effected with the consent of the holders of 75 per cent in nominal value of the issued shares of the relevant class. The Companies Acts include provisions protecting minority shareholders from oppressive conduct which renders it difficult, in the absence of agreement, to limit a shareholder's rights.

GENERAL MEETING OF SHAREHOLDERS (GM) AND VOTING RIGHTS

9. Which decisions are reserved to the competence of the GM?

Companies must hold an annual general meeting (AGM) once in each calendar year. At each AGM, the directors must lay the annual financial statements and reports before the shareholders. The AGM also deals with any other 'ordinary business' specified in the articles, usually the appointment of an auditor, the declaration of dividends, and fixing the remuneration of the auditor and directors. All other business conducted at an AGM, and all business conducted at an extraordinary general meeting (EGM), is 'special business'.

Two types of resolution may be passed at GMs. An ordinary resolution is used for routine, non-contentious business, and requires the approval of the holder(s) of a simple majority of the ordinary shares in issue. Examples include approving the disposal of all or virtually all of a company's assets. Special resolutions require the approval of the holder(s) of not less than 75 per cent of the ordinary shares in issue, and are used for more fundamental issues such as amending the memorandum and articles, reducing the company's share capital (consequent upon a court sanction for such reduction), approving the giving of financial assistance in connection with a purchase/subscription for shares in the company, and approving a compromise or scheme of arrangement between the company and its creditors.

10. How does a shareholder participate in a GM? Are there any limitations to having a minimum number of shares? May a shareholder delegate attendance to another shareholder or to the board? May a shareholder obtain assistance from the courts or any other governmental body to intervene in a GM or to cause one to be held in some particular cases?

Shareholders' voting rights are governed by the articles and the terms of issue of the shares. Unless the articles provide otherwise, every member has one vote per ordinary share held. Generally speaking, on a show of hands every member present in person and every proxy has one vote. If a poll is called, in most cases every member has one vote for every ordinary share held. Only persons whose names are entered on the register of members are entitled to vote at GMs. Shareholders are entitled to appoint another person as their proxy to attend and vote at a GM. A proxy has the same right to speak and vote at the meeting as its appointer.

The Shareholders' Rights Regulations, which apply only to listed companies, provide for additional specific rights, including the right to ask questions about items on the GM agenda and, with some exceptions, to have the company answer those questions. Shareholders holding at least three per cent of voting rights in a listed company are entitled to put items on the agenda and to table resolutions at the GM, provided such request or draft resolution is provided to the company within a specified timeframe before the GM.

Private limited companies which have only one member are entitled to elect to dispense with the holding of AGMs under the European Communities (Single-Member Private Limited Companies) Regulations 1994. Where a single-member company does so elect, the powers which would otherwise be exercisable by the sole member at the AGM (eg the power to appoint the company's auditors) are instead exercisable by means of a written resolution of the sole member.

If a company fails to hold an AGM in any year (other than a single-member company which has elected to dispense with the holding of AGMs), the Director of Corporate Enforcement may, on the application of any shareholder, call or direct the calling of a GM. Under the Companies Acts, shareholders can requisition the holding of GMs in certain circumstances (see paragraph 11 below). The articles may also give additional rights to shareholders to call for the holding of a GM.

11. May a GM be called and held at the request of any shareholder? Is there a threshold regarding the percentage of the stock interest owned in the company that may entitle a shareholder to such a right?

Any shareholder(s) holding not less than 10 per cent (or, in the case of a listed company, five per cent) in aggregate of a company's issued shares or voting rights can requisition the directors to convene an EGM. If the directors do not, within 21 days from the date of such requisition, convene a GM, the requisitionists (or at least half of them) may themselves convene the GM.

12. May a shareholder bring up an issue to be resolved upon and put it to a vote if it is not included on the agenda? May a shareholder require more information from the GM and/or the board concerning the agenda of the GM, to be put in a better position to exercise their vote?

See question 10 above regarding the rights of shareholders of listed companies. Shareholders in other companies do not have similar statutory rights.

Adequate notice must be given of all business, particularly of special business, to be conducted at a GM. In the absence of unanimous shareholder consent, this requirement would prevent a shareholder from proposing new resolutions at a GM, as adequate notice would not have been given. At least 21 days' notice must be given of any special resolutions to be proposed at a GM, and the exact wording of each special resolution must be contained in the notice. Shorter notice periods apply in respect of ordinary resolutions.

The articles govern how GMs are conducted and will usually provide that the chairman may chair/administer the GM as it sees fit. The chairman may refuse to take questions from shareholders if it believes that they are not relevant or that it is not in the company's interests to answer them. However if the chairman does not give shareholders a reasonable opportunity to discuss a proposed resolution, it may render the substantive decision on the resolution void (*Wall v London and Northern Assets Corporation [1898] 2 Ch 469*).

13. May a GM be held by telecommunication means and/or by correspondence (ie by written consent)?

Since the introduction of the Shareholders' Rights Regulations, a listed company may provide for participation in a GM by electronic means, provided appropriate steps are taken to ensure identification of those taking part and security of the electronic communication.

The Companies Acts do not provide for shareholders of other forms of companies to attend a GM from separate locations by telecommunication means. However under draft terms for proposed new legislation, it is envisaged that the Companies Acts will be amended in the coming years to allow for the holding of a GM in two or more venues using technology.

A resolution in writing (other than one relating to the appointment or removal of an auditor, or the removal of a director) signed by all shareholders entitled to attend and vote on such a resolution at a GM is valid and effective.

14. Are voting rights always proportionate to the stock held by each shareholder or can they vary by the stock class?

Voting rights may be 'weighted' as between different shareholders, but it is more common for voting rights to be proportionate to the number or nominal value of the ordinary shares held. Unless the articles provide otherwise, every member has one vote per ordinary share held.

15. Are there non-voting shares? Is there a maximum percentage of capital represented by non-voting shares?

It is possible to have non-voting shares. Provided a company has some voting shares in issue, there is no limit on the percentage of capital which may be represented by non-voting shares.

16. Can shareholders group their shares in order to exercise their voting rights (eg by trust, shareholders' agreement or otherwise)?

Shareholders may vote as they see fit and in most cases are at liberty to contract with other shareholders and/or third parties to vote in a particular way, provided that they do not vote in a manner which perpetrates a fraud on the minority or which is oppressive.

Care does need to be exercised by shareholders in public listed companies which are subject to the rules of the Irish Takeover Panel, so as to ensure that no agreement entered into gives rise to a presumption that those parties are acting in concert.

17. Under what circumstances can a shareholder challenge the resolutions adopted by the GM? Are there thresholds concerning the stock interest owned to be able to bring such a claim?

If the notice issued by the company in respect of a GM is materially inadequate, shareholders may seek an injunction to restrain the holding of the meeting (*Jackson v Munster Bank (1884-85) 13 LR 118*), or a declaration that the resolutions passed at the GM are invalid. The court's jurisdiction is discretionary.

Shareholders may also apply to the court for the cancellation of certain special resolutions. For example, the holder(s) of not less than:

(a) 15 per cent in nominal value of the issued shares can apply for cancellation of an alteration to the company's memorandum;

(b) 10 per cent in nominal value of the issued shares can apply for cancellation of a resolution approving the giving of financial assistance for the purposes of, or in connection with, a purchase/subscription of or for shares; and

(c) five per cent in nominal value of the issued shares can apply for cancellation of a resolution approving the re-registration of a PLC as a private company.

In addition any member can petition the court for relief where the affairs of the company are being conducted in a manner oppressive to it or any of the members, or in disregard of their interests as members.

18. What are the terms and procedures to challenge a resolution of the GM?

A challenge referred to at question 17(a) above must be brought by petition to the court within 21 days of the resolution being passed. In the case of the challenges referred to at paragraph 17(b) and (c) above, a petition must be brought within 28 days of the resolution being passed. No time limit applies in the case of a petition for relief from oppression but, in practice, delay may prejudice a petition for relief.

SHAREHOLDERS' RIGHTS VERSUS DIRECTORS AND DUTIES OF OTHER CORPORATE BODIES IN THE COMPANY

19. What is the procedure for the appointment/replacement/ revocation of directors and of statutory auditors, if any?

Directors

The first directors are appointed at the time of the company's incorporation. Subsequent to incorporation, the procedures for appointment of directors are set out in the articles. In most cases shareholders may, by ordinary resolution, change the number of directors. Commonly the directors also have power to appoint additional directors, sometimes on a temporary basis.

Shareholders may by ordinary resolution remove a director from office. Extended notice is required for a meeting at which such a resolution is proposed. The director concerned is also entitled to make representations to the shareholders. If they are removed and if the director has a service contract, they may have a right to seek to avail of the remedies provided by unfair dismissals legislation, and/or to seek damages for breach of contract.

Standard-form articles provide for the retirement of directors 'by rotation' at each AGM, and for the election of directors to fill such vacated office(s). Such provisions are commonly disapplied by private companies. The articles may also provide for removal from office if the director is adjudged bankrupt, becomes of unsound mind or is convicted of an indictable offence.

Auditors

The first auditor of a company may be appointed by the directors at any time before the first AGM and, where that does not occur, the shareholders may appoint the first auditor by ordinary resolution. At each subsequent AGM the shareholders may appoint an auditor, by ordinary resolution, to hold office from the conclusion of that AGM until the conclusion of the next AGM.

20. May shareholders challenge the resolutions of the board of directors? Is there a minimum percentage of capital required to challenge a board resolution?

In most cases, management of the business of a company is delegated to the directors, except to the extent that the shareholders are required to exercise those powers under the Companies Acts. Having delegated their powers to the directors, it is not generally open to the shareholders to challenge decisions of the board. As long as they act within their powers and do not act oppressively or in disregard of shareholders' interests, directors may take decisions against the wishes of some or all of the shareholders (*Howard Smith v Amplol Petroleum Ltd (1974) AC 821*).

If shareholders wish to challenge the directors' decision, a special resolution may be passed amending the articles so as to enable the shareholders to assume responsibility for the relevant powers themselves. Alternatively, they may seek to remove some or all of the directors from office (see above).

21. Are shareholders entitled to bring a legal action against the directors of the company? In which circumstances? Please describe briefly the principles of directors' liability.

At common law, directors have fiduciary duties to the company of which they are directors. These include the duty to exercise skill, care and diligence in the discharge of their functions, and to act in the best interests of the company as a whole. Directors must not place their own interests, or those of persons connected with them, ahead of the company's interests and must avoid conflicts of interest. Directors must also take reasonable steps to prevent any breach of the Companies Acts and other legislation.

Where a director acts in breach of his/her duties, he/she may be liable for the losses caused to the company as a result of such breach. A director may also be made personally liable for the debts of a company being wound up or which is insolvent, if he/she has acted fraudulently or recklessly. Liability may also be imposed on directors if the company fails to keep proper books of account, or enters into certain loans, quasi-loans or credit transactions in favour of the directors.

If a company suffers damage as a result of any act or omission of a director, the cause of action lies with the company itself, and not with an individual shareholder (*Foss v Harbottle (1843) 2 Hare 461*). There are a limited number of circumstances in which a shareholder may be able to bring a 'derivative' action on behalf of the company, or to prove that a fiduciary relationship has been created between the directors and that shareholder. However, in such circumstances it would be more common for the shareholder to apply to the court for relief on the grounds that the powers of the directors are being exercised in an oppressive manner or in disregard of its interests.

22. What are the rights in connection with transactions where the directors have a conflict of interest situation?

At question 21, we highlighted the fact that directors have a fiduciary duty to the company to avoid conflicts of interest. Where a director breaches his/her fiduciary duty and makes a profit, he/she may have to recompense the company for that profit, and he/she may be liable for damages.

Where a director is interested in a contract or proposed contract with the company, he/she is generally required to disclose that interest to the other directors. Subject to certain statutory restrictions, the articles may allow the director to be interested in the contract, and to vote on the resolutions relating to that contract. If a director fails to disclose his/her interest in a contract, he/she will lose the protection of the articles and the contract will generally become voidable by the company. The director may also be liable to account for any profits made and for damages.

INFORMATION RIGHTS ON THE COMPANY'S BUSINESS

23. What information may be requested by the shareholders from the board concerning the general state of the company's business or any specific transaction? Are information rights different depending on the number of shares owned? Are shareholders entitled to receive written information before, during or after the GM about the meeting agenda and to what extent? Is it possible for a shareholder to obtain a copy of the minutes of the GM?

Unless otherwise provided in the articles or shareholders' agreement, shareholders (regardless of the number of shares held) are generally only entitled to inspect and/or receive a copy of the company's memorandum and articles, its statutory registers (eg register of members, directors, and directors' interests), and the minutes of all GMs. Shareholders are also generally entitled to receive a copy of the company's balance sheet and profit and loss account (with the directors' and auditors' reports thereon) prior to the company's AGM.

Shareholders also receive notice of each GM of the company (in the absence of any provisions to the contrary in the articles) containing details of any special business and the wording of any special resolution(s) proposed to be passed. The facts upon which shareholders will consider a resolution must also be accurately and fully represented in the notice of the GM.

The minutes of GMs are required to be kept at a company's registered office, and must be available for inspection by shareholders without charge. Shareholders must be furnished, on request, with a copy of any GM minutes within seven days of the request.

24. Do shareholders have the right/duty to resolve in the GM upon matters which were not on the agenda?

Shareholders do not have the right to resolve upon matters which were not set out in the notice of that GM, unless the shareholders unanimously agree otherwise. Shareholders do not have a duty to pass resolutions.

25. Are shareholders entitled to inspect the corporate books and/or any other corporate or accounting documents? To what extent? Can they do it through external counsel or advisors?

Shareholders are entitled to inspect the minutes of GMs and to receive copies of the company's annual accounts. Unless otherwise provided in the articles or shareholders' agreement, shareholders are not generally entitled to inspect minutes of the directors' meetings or the company's books of account.

SHAREHOLDERS' AGREEMENTS

26. Are shareholders' agreements validly enforceable? What are their typical contents and term of duration? Are they enforceable by or against third parties and, if so, to what extent?

Shareholders' agreements are enforceable in accordance with ordinary principles of contract law, and the normal remedies available for breach of contract will apply. The terms of a shareholders' agreement will only bind the parties to that agreement and, if provided for, their successors and assigns. Shareholders' agreements are generally not enforceable by or against other third parties unless those parties execute a deed of adherence to it.

Shareholders' agreements typically contain provisions to enhance the rights and powers (especially veto powers) of minority shareholders. They also deal with the governance and frequently contain restrictions on the transfer of shares and provide for shareholders' information rights. Shareholders' agreements often terminate where all, or a specified majority, of the shareholders agree that it be terminated, or where all of the shareholders (or their assignees) cease to hold any shares. The parties may also agree to termination in certain circumstances, eg where the company's shares are admitted to trading on a stock exchange.

27. Do shareholders' agreements have to be disclosed to the public or registered in any public registry?

There is no specific requirement for shareholders' agreements to be registered in the Companies Registration Office (CRO). However, if the effect of a shareholders' agreement is to amend or affect the interpretation of the articles, eg if the articles are only capable of interpretation by reference to the shareholders' agreement, then it should be registered in the CRO.

ECONOMIC RIGHTS AND RIGHTS OVER THE STOCK

28. Is the stock always freely transferable? Are there any legal limitations? Are there any restrictions on contractual limitations?

While shares in a PLC whose securities are listed on a recognised stock exchange are freely transferable, the rights of shareholders in private companies to transfer shares are more restricted. Under the Companies Acts, a private company cannot have more than 99 members and its shares may not be offered to the public. The directors of a private company are also empowered to decline to register any transfer of shares, subject to their duty to act *bona fide*. The articles may also contain specific pre-emption ('offer-round') or 'lock-in' restrictions on the transfer of shares.

29. Are shareholders entitled to pledge their stock?
In the absence of any restriction in the articles or shareholders' agreement, a shareholder will generally be entitled to pledge its shares. The enforceability of a pledge may be affected if the articles contain pre-emptive 'offer-round' rights or transfer approval restrictions.

30. Are there financial assistance issues to be considered and other prohibitions to be evaluated in the context of a leveraged buyout transaction?
It is unlawful for a company to give, directly or indirectly, financial assistance by any means for the purpose of, or in connection with, a purchase or subscription made or to be made of or for any shares in the company or in its holding company, unless the assistance comes within a list of specified exceptions. If a third party acquires shares using funding which is to be secured on the target company, the provision of that security will be voidable unless the company goes through a validation ('whitewash') procedure. This procedure allows the members of a private company (but not a PLC) to authorise the giving of the financial assistance if all, or a majority, of the directors of the company make a statutory declaration as to the solvency of the company. A director who makes this declaration without having reasonable grounds for his/her opinion as to the company's solvency is guilty of an offence. Where a company gives unlawful financial assistance, every officer of the company who is in default is also liable to prosecution.

31. May a company buy back its own stock and, if so, under what circumstances and subject to which limitations?
A company may, if authorised by its articles and sanctioned by the court, reduce its share capital by special resolution. A company may also be authorised by the court to purchase its own shares in a number of circumstances, eg as part of the relief granted to a minority shareholder where the company's affairs are being conducted in a manner oppressive to it.

A company may also, if authorised by its articles, purchase or redeem its own shares. Specific rules apply to such purchases/redemptions, including:
- shares can only be purchased or redeemed out of profits available for distribution or, subject to certain limitations, out of the proceeds of a fresh issue of shares;
- a company cannot purchase/redeem any of its shares under this procedure if, as a result of that purchase/redemption, the nominal value of the company's issued share capital which is not redeemable would be

less than one-tenth of the nominal value of its total issued share capital;

- a company cannot make an off-market purchase of its own shares, or enter into a contingent purchase contract in relation to its shares, unless it is authorised to do so in advance by special resolution of the company; and
- a company cannot make a market purchase or overseas market purchase of its own shares unless it is authorised to do so in advance by an ordinary resolution of the company, a copy of which is required to be filed in the CRO.

32. Is there a legal right to withdraw from the company and, if so, under what circumstances? How is the shareholders' stock valuated and paid in such a case?

A shareholder may withdraw from a company by transferring shares to another person in accordance with the articles. Where the other shareholders are given a right of pre-emption on the transfer of shares, the articles usually state how the consideration will be determined. Otherwise it is a matter for agreement between the parties.

Alternatively, the shareholder could surrender its shares, if permitted by the articles. No consideration is payable for the shares in such circumstances, and the shareholder remains liable for any amounts outstanding (ie not paid up) on its shares. This procedure is not commonly used.

If the shareholder's shares are redeemable or are converted into redeemable shares, the shareholder can exit by having its shares redeemed by the company. A company cannot convert shares into redeemable shares, or redeem any shares, if as a result of such conversion/redemption the nominal value of the issued share capital which is not redeemable would be less than one-tenth of the nominal value of the total issued share capital. Restrictions and limitations applicable to the purchase by a company of its own shares generally apply to the redemption of shares.

33. In which circumstances can dividends be distributed among shareholders? Is it possible to exclude or limit the right of certain shareholders to dividends? Does a certain portion of the profits need to be set aside in a reserve fund where it cannot be distributed to the shareholders? Are advances on dividends allowed and, if so, under which circumstances? Can advances on dividends be reclaimed by the company?

Dividends may only be declared and paid out of profits available for that purpose. A company's profits available for distribution are its accumulated realised profits, so far as not previously utilised by distribution or capitalisation, less its accumulated realised losses, so far as not previously written off in a reduction or reorganisation of capital.

In determining whether there has been a realised profit or realised loss, reference is made to the company's latest audited accounts and, if necessary and provided that certain conditions are met, to interim accounts properly prepared in accordance with the Companies Acts. In the case of a PLC, a distribution may only be made if at that time, the amount of its net assets is not less than the aggregate of its called-up share capital and undistributable reserves, provided that the distribution does not reduce the amount of its net assets to less than that aggregate.

The rights of certain shareholders to receive dividends may be excluded or limited under the articles or shareholders' agreement.

There is no mandatory requirement for any profits available for distribution to be applied to a reserve fund, although standard-form articles generally provide that the directors may, before recommending any dividend 'set aside out of the profits of the company such sums as they think proper as a reserve or reserves which shall, at the discretion of the directors, be applicable for any purpose to which the profits of the company may be properly applied'.

The Companies Acts do not provide for advances on dividends. However, if the articles provide, there is scope for the directors to pay such interim dividends as they believe are justified by the company's profits, and dividends may be paid in stages.

34. What are the rights of shareholders in the case of an issue of new stock (increase of the company's corporate capital) (pre-emption rights)?

The directors of a company may not allot relevant securities unless they are authorised to do so, either generally or in respect of a particular allotment, by the shareholders in a GM or by the articles. Such authority must state the maximum amount of securities that may be allotted, and must expire after five years unless renewed by the shareholders.

The Companies Acts grant pre-emptive rights to shareholders to the effect that where a company proposes to allot equity securities, it cannot allot those securities to any person unless it has first offered them to the existing shareholders in proportion to their existing shareholdings on the same or more favourable terms. These provisions are commonly excluded by the articles, either generally or by the substitution of a specific pre-emption right.

35. May minority shareholders ban or limit the company's capital structure in any manner?

Unless provided to the contrary in the articles or shareholders' agreement, a minority shareholder will not be able to prevent changes to the company's capital structure. Under standard-form articles, shareholders are generally entitled by ordinary resolution to subdivide or consolidate all or any of the company's share capital, or to cancel any shares which have not been taken or agreed to be taken by any person. Shareholders are generally also entitled, by special resolution, to reduce the company's share capital (including any capital redemption reserve fund or share premium account) in any manner provided such reduction is sanctioned by the court. In the absence of an express veto in the articles or shareholders' agreement, a minority shareholder will generally not be able to prevent the passing of such resolutions. However if the proposed restructuring of the company's capital prejudices the minority shareholder's interests, it may be able to apply for relief on the grounds that the restructuring is oppressive or in disregard of its interests.

36. Which are the financial assistance prohibitions in force?
We have dealt elsewhere with the prohibition on giving financial assistance.

37. Apart from publicly listed companies, in which cases (if any) are shareholders obligated to obtain an authorisation from, or provide information to, a public authority about events that have an impact on their stock interest in the company?
There are a variety of situations in which regulatory consent is required. Irish Competition Authority approval may be required where control of a company is acquired and certain financial thresholds are exceeded, or where there are particular competition concerns. Where a shareholding in a regulated entity (such as an insurance company, licensed credit institution, investment intermediary, investment manager, etc) is being acquired or disposed of then, depending on the percentage interest involved, the shareholder may be obliged to notify the Central Bank of Ireland.

SHAREHOLDERS' RIGHTS IN THE CASE OF EXTRAORDINARY TRANSACTIONS AND/OR WINDING-UP
38. What rights are available to shareholders in the case of a sale of all or a substantial portion of the company's assets? In the case of a merger or de-merger?
Where the power to dispose of assets has been delegated to the directors, then provided the directors are acting *bona fide* and in the interests of the company as a whole, the shareholders cannot prevent the sale of the company's assets. However it is generally accepted that the directors ought to seek shareholder approval if the proposed disposal involves all, or substantially all, of the company's assets. The articles and/or shareholders' agreement may also prevent the company from making a significant acquisition or disposal without shareholder approval.

In the case of a merger by takeover or a court-approved scheme of arrangement, dissenting members generally have standing in court to object to such merger. While the court has broad powers to make an order in such cases, courts have been reluctant to intervene in arms' length transactions which have broad shareholder acceptance.

Cross-border mergers are also permitted by the Cross-Border Mergers Directive (2005/56/EC), which is implemented in Ireland by the European Communities (Cross-Border Mergers) Regulations 2008. To fall within the scope of these Regulations, at least one of the merging companies must be an Irish company and at least one must be a company incorporated in another EEA state. Generally, the common draft terms of the merger require the approval of the shareholders of the Irish company by special resolution. A dissenting shareholder is entitled to have its shares bought by the successor company for cash at a price determined in accordance with the share exchange ratio set out in the common draft terms, without prejudice to the court's right to make any order necessary for the protection of the dissenting minority's interests.

The European Communities (Mergers and Divisions of Companies) Regulations 1987, which implemented the Third and Sixth Company Law Directives in Ireland, provide for the merger and division of PLCs in certain circumstances.

39. Which rights are available to shareholders in the case of conversion of the company into a European Company (SE) or into another type of company?

Under the European Communities (European Public Limited-Liability Company) Regulations 2007, where an Irish or foreign public limited liability company proposes to form an SE by merger under Article 2(1) of Council Regulation 2157/2001/EC, any member(s) holding in aggregate 10 per cent or more in nominal value of the issued share capital of the SE may apply to the court within 28 days to have the decision to merge annulled, or to require the SE to acquire for cash the securities of the shareholder(s) opposed to the merger. There is no equivalent provision for shareholders of private companies.

A special resolution is required where an unlimited liability company is converting to a company limited by shares or guarantee, and where a private company is converting to a PLC (or *vice versa*). Where a limited company is converting to an unlimited liability company, the written consent of all shareholders is required.

40. Which rights are available to shareholders of a company in liquidation?

On a winding up, shareholders are generally entitled to the return of their capital investment and to participate in the distribution of any surplus assets of the company after the creditors and expenses of the liquidator have been paid (unless the articles provide otherwise).

41. Can shareholders cause the liquidation of the company? How?

A solvent company may be wound up voluntarily if the shareholders resolve by special resolution that it be wound up. The notice of GM issued in respect of such resolution must be accompanied by a declaration made by all, or a majority, of the directors as to the company's solvency.

If a company is insolvent, the shareholders can resolve by ordinary resolution that the company cannot, by reason of its liabilities, continue its business and that it be wound up voluntarily.

Shareholders can also pass a special resolution to petition the court to compulsorily wind up the company. However because of the extent of the court's involvement in such a procedure, it tends to be a more costly way of winding up the company.

COMPANY GROUPS

42. Is the concept of 'group' recognised as such under specific legislation? What are the implications?

Under the Companies Acts, a company is a 'subsidiary' of another company if that other:

- is a member of it and controls the composition of its board of directors; or
- holds more than half in nominal value of its equity share capital or voting shares.

A company will also be a 'subsidiary' of another company if the first mentioned company is a subsidiary of any company which is that other's subsidiary. A company is deemed to be another's 'holding company' if, but only if, that other is its subsidiary.

Under the European Communities (Companies: Group Accounts) Regulations 1992, a 'parent undertaking' is required to prepare group accounts and to lay them before the AGM at the same time as its own annual accounts. A 'parent undertaking' is an undertaking that has one or more 'subsidiary undertakings'. The definition of a subsidiary undertaking is broader than the definition of a subsidiary under the Companies Acts, and extends to situations where one undertaking is entitled to exercise a 'dominant influence' over another undertaking's operating and financial policies. Different definitions of a 'group', 'subsidiary' and 'holding company' also apply under the provisions of the Taxes Consolidation Act 1997 and the Stamp Duties Consolidation Act 1999 relating to the availability of reliefs.

Irish law generally recognises the principle of the separate legal personality of each company (*Salomon v Salomon and Co [1897] AC 22*). The courts will generally recognise the separate legal personality of companies within a group, in the absence of exceptional circumstances. For instance if the affairs of the relevant companies have effectively been conducted and governed as if they are one and the same entity, eg without separate governance arrangements, then a court may be willing on an exceptional basis to make one group company liable for the debts of another. Under the Companies Acts, the court may also order one group company to contribute to the debts of another group company which is being wound up, if the court is satisfied that it is just and equitable to do so. Where two or more group companies are being wound up, the court may order that the companies are wound up together as if they were one company, such that their assets and liabilities are 'pooled'. In deciding whether it is just and equitable to make such contribution and/or pooling orders, the court has regard, among other factors, to the extent to which one company took part in the other's management and the extent to which the businesses of the companies were intermingled.

43. Does a controlling company have any particular duties *vis-à-vis* its controlled company shareholders?

Minority members are generally expected to submit to majority decisions, subject to any rights given to the minority under the articles or shareholders' agreement and provided that the company's affairs are not being conducted by the controlling company in a manner which is oppressive.

44. What are the rights of company shareholders when the controlling company puts in place actions and/or transactions that can be prejudicial the shareholders?

We have dealt elsewhere with the right of minority shareholders to seek relief where the affairs of the company are being conducted in a manner which is oppressive or in disregard of their interests as shareholders.

45. What are the limitations, if any, to the possibility of owning reciprocal stock interests in companies?

The principal limitation under the Companies Acts is that a body corporate cannot be a member of a company which is its holding company, unless:

- the consideration for the acquisition of such shares is provided for out of profits of the subsidiary available for distribution; and
- on the acquisition of the shares and for so long as the subsidiary holds them, the profits of the subsidiary available for distribution are restricted by a sum equal to the total cost of the shares acquired, and the shares are treated for the purposes of the holding company's consolidated accounts as treasury shares.

In addition, a subsidiary is not entitled to exercise any voting rights in respect of the shares held in its holding company, unless the subsidiary only holds those shares as a trustee or nominee. A contract for the acquisition by a subsidiary of shares in its holding company must be authorised by a special resolution of both companies in advance of them entering into such contract.

Russia

Noerr Yulia Solovykh & Dr Thomas Mundry

BASIC INFORMATION ON THE TYPES OF LIMITED LIABILITY COMPANIES AND ON THE RIGHTS OF SHAREHOLDERS
1. What types of companies enjoy limited liability? If more than one, which ones have shareholders, ie holders of share certificates? Which one is the most common? Which one is mostly used by foreign investors?

There are two main types of companies with limited liability in Russia – a so-called limited liability company (LLC) and a joint stock company (JSC) (both an LLC and an JSC is hereafter also referred to as a 'company'), which, in its turn, may be a closed joint stock company (CJSC) or an open joint stock company (OJSC).

Roughly speaking, OJSCs are 'public' companies, as their shares may be offered to an unlimited number of persons, including placement on stock exchanges. CJSCs are 'private' companies. They may not have more than 50 shareholders and may not publicly offer their shares. Their shareholders enjoy the right of first refusal if any shareholder intends to sell their shares to a third party.

Both CJSCs and LLCs are quite common and often used by foreign investors. An LLC is a simpler and more flexible corporate form, particularly in terms of its corporate governance. It is recommended for wholly owned subsidiaries and closely held joint ventures. A CJSC is more complicated and state-regulated, with many corporate procedures and formalities to be performed. This form is suitable for larger companies with a potential for corporate conflict – where a number of interests are present at shareholder (and management) level.

The capital of a JSC is split into shares, each of which (within the same category) confers on its holder the same volume of rights. A JSC's shares are qualified as securities and are subject to registration with a Russian authority for the securities market.

The capital of an LLC is not split into any units/stock. The share of each co-owner is determined by their individual ownership percentage of the company's capital with the relevant nominal value. The rights of the co-owners of an LLC may differ depending on the provisions of the company's charter.

A major corporate reform is currently underway in Russia to abolish the distinction between LLCs and CJSCs by merging them into one 'private' company type. The concept of OJSC will remain, subject to certain corrections, as that of a 'public' company.

2. Are there minimum capital requirements and/or thin capitalisation rules in force?

The minimum capital of a CJSC/LLC is 10,000 roubles (approximately €260), of an OJSC – 100,000 roubles (approximately €2,630).

If a company's capitalisation goes below its capital as set out in its by-laws as at the end of its second and each following financial year the company is obliged to decrease its capital. JSCs are given another year to improve their capitalisation before this requirement takes effect. A company whose capital goes below the minimum capital requirement must declare its liquidation. The company that does not respectively decrease its capital or declare its liquidation may be liquidated by a court order upon a claim of the Russian registration authority.

If the amount of the loans granted by shareholders exceeds the amount of the equity of a company by more than three times (if the company is a bank or leasing company: by more than 12.5 times) the profit tax deductibility of the interest to be paid under the shareholders' loans is limited.

3. Describe the types of shares that can be issued by a company and the different rights that they attribute to their owners, as well as any other financial instruments (bonds or other) and other instruments of a participatory nature in the company's capital that can also be issued by the company.

An LLC does not have 'stock' in the strict sense of this word. A JSC may issue two main types of shares: common and preferred.

Common shares give their holders the right to vote on all issues at general shareholders' meetings, to receive dividends and to obtain any distributions upon the JSC's liquidation. Preferred shares (which may not exceed 25 per cent of the share capital of the relevant JSC) confer on their holders the right to dividends and liquidation distributions, but voting rights apply only in exceptional circumstances. A JSC may issue different types of preferred shares (eg, with a different dividend entitlement), which must be provided for in its by-laws.

Companies may issue bonds. A bond gives the right to get back its nominal value (plus interest) or other property within a certain time.

A JSC may issue bonds that are convertible into its stock and 'issuer's options' (a financial instrument that gives its holder the right to buy the JSC's shares within a certain term and/or in certain circumstances at a pre-determined price).

4. Can a company have only one shareholder and still enjoy limited liability?

Companies may have only one shareholder. The company will still enjoy limited liability. However, there is a prohibition on the sole shareholder being a 'one-man company' itself.

5. Are the rights of shareholders the same in any type of company?

The basic rights of holders of 'common' shares of a JSC and shareholders of an LLC are very similar. The major differences are the following:

- the by-laws of an LLC may provide for an odd distribution of votes – in a JSC each share confers one vote (although the by-laws may limit the maximum number of votes given to one shareholder);
- all shareholders of an LLC enjoy all rights granted by law, while in a JSC exercising certain rights requires a certain minimum number of shares (see question 6); and
- individual shareholders of an LLC may enjoy additional rights, while the rights of each shareholder of a JSC are the same within the same category of the shares.

6. What are the basic rights of any shareholder? Describe briefly the rights of minority shareholders and indicate which thresholds, if any, are required to allow the minority shareholders to exercise any such rights.

The basic rights of any shareholder (except for holders of 'preferred' shares in JSCs) are participation in and voting at the company's general shareholders' meeting (GM), obtaining information on the company's activities and having access to the company's documents, and obtaining dividends and a portion of the company's assets at its liquidation.

The following rights are provided for minority shareholders in LLCs:

- each shareholder may introduce items in the agenda of a GM;
- holders of at least 10 per cent of the LLC's total votes may demand before a court the expulsion of a shareholder who grossly violates their duties or whose behaviour substantially impedes the LLC's activities;
- holders of at least 10 per cent of the LLC's total votes may demand the convocation of an extraordinary GM;
- each shareholder may block certain important decisions of a GM, particularly those that may affect their shareholding in the LLC (eg, liquidation or re-organisation of the LLC, granting of special rights to a shareholder, increase of the LLC's capital against a contribution of a certain shareholder or a third party); and
- holders of over one-third of the LLC's total votes may block some other important decisions of a GM (eg, amendment of the by-laws, increase or decrease of the LLC's capital).

The following rights are provided for minority shareholders in JSCs. Holders of:

- at least one per cent of the shares may review the list of persons entitled to participate in the next GM and to sue the JSC's officers for compensation for damage to the company inflicted by their wrongful actions;
- at least two per cent of the shares may introduce items in the agenda of a GM on certain issues and nominate members of the collective executive body (for both JSC and LLC hereafter referred to as 'collective executive body'), the general director (for both JSC and LLC hereafter referred to as 'general director'), the board of directors (which, in general has the function to supervise the collective executive body and/or the

general director) (for both JSC and LLC hereafter referred to as the 'board of directors') and other bodies;

- at least 10 per cent of the shares may demand the convocation of an extraordinary GM and determine the agenda of such a meeting, and demand a revision of the JSC's financial activities;
- at least 25 per cent of the shares have access to the JSC's internal documents; and
- more than 25 per cent of the shares may block important decisions of a GM (eg, amendment of the JSC's by-laws, increase or decrease of the JSC's capital).

There are further mechanisms for the protection of minority shareholders in companies.

7.   Do all shareholders enjoy the same rights or can some shareholders be attributed specific rights, whether by reason of the particular class of stock owned or other? Are such rights generally provided for at the level of the company's by-laws and/or in shareholders' agreements?

The shareholders of an LLC and the holders of common shares in a JSC enjoy the same rights. The by-laws of an LLC (but not that of a JSC) may grant additional rights to individual shareholders. With regard to the rights of the holders of preferred shares in a JSC please see question 3.

Shareholders' rights are generally provided for by law and to some extent by the company's by-laws. Under Russian law, shareholders' agreements may not grant any specific shareholders' rights or modify them. They may only determine the way in which such rights should be exercised (also see question 26). It is doubtful that a Russian court would recognise any additional shareholders' rights granted by a shareholders' agreement made under foreign law.

8.   May the rights of shareholders, generally speaking, be limited, modified, suppressed or waived in any way? If so, how? Are such modifications or limitations provided for in the company's by-laws and/or in shareholders' agreements?

Rights of shareholders can be limited, modified or suppressed only if the law explicitly allows this.

Some limitations/modifications may only be provided in the company's by-laws (eg, a prohibition on share transfers to third parties), some may be provided in a shareholders' agreement (see question 26).

GENERAL MEETING OF SHAREHOLDERS (GM) AND VOTING RIGHTS

9.   Which decisions are reserved to the competence of the GM?
The GM of the company decides on:
- changing the company's by-laws;
- appointing the company's internal auditor (or auditing committee);
- approval of the company's annual reports and annual balance sheets;

- distribution of profits to the shareholders;
- reorganisation and liquidation of the company, appointing a liquidation committee and approving liquidation balances;
- increase of the company's capital (in certain circumstances);
- appointing the general director (unless this is within the competence of the board of directors) and the members of the board of directors; and
- approving certain transactions entered into by the company (unless this is within the competence of the board of directors).

10. How does a shareholder participate in a GM? Are there any limitations to having a minimum number of shares? May a shareholder delegate attendance to another shareholder or to the board? May a shareholder obtain assistance from the courts or any other governmental body to intervene in a GM or to cause one to be held in some particular cases?

A shareholder in a company participates in a GM either personally or by proxy. There are no shareholding thresholds for participation in a GM.

There is no prohibition to delegate attendance at a GM to another shareholder or a member of the board of directors. However, such a delegation should be treated carefully, due to a possible conflict of interest between the two shareholders or, alternatively, the shareholder and the relevant member of the board of directors.

A shareholder, whose rights are violated at a GM may apply to a court to: (i) intervene in the GM by issuing a respective order and sending a court officer to attend the GM; and/or (ii) challenge the results of the GM that was conducted in violation of law.

A shareholder may further lodge a complaint with the police (or a public attorney) describing the violations of their rights, upon which the police may initiate criminal proceedings against the relevant officers of the company.

In a situation where, despite the lawful demand of a shareholder, a yearly or an extraordinary GM is not duly convened the shareholder(s) may petition the court to force the company to convene the GM.

11. May a GM be called and held at the request of any shareholder? Is there a threshold regarding the percentage of the stock interest owned in the company that may entitle a shareholder to such a right?

An extraordinary GM of the company may be called and held at the request of shareholders holding at least 10 per cent of the votes.

12. May a shareholder bring up an issue to be resolved upon and put it to a vote if it is not included on the agenda? May a shareholder require more information from the GM and/or the board concerning the agenda of the GM, to be put in a better position to exercise their vote?

Shareholders (see question 6 for further information on the required number of shares) have the right to make suggestions on or propose the agenda of a GM at the preparation stage of a GM. They may not do so in the process.

Russian law provides for the information and documents that need to be provided to the shareholders in preparation for a GM (annual reports and the auditor's opinions, draft changes to the by-laws, information on the nominated members of management bodies etc).

13. May a GM be held by telecommunication means and/or by correspondence (ie by written consent)?

A GM in an LLC may be held both by telecommunication means and correspondence, provided that the communication method allows a document exchange and ensures an authenticity of the messages sent and received. The yearly GM, which approves annual reports and annual balance sheets, may be held only by personal attendance.

A GM in a JSC may not be held by telecommunication means but may be held by correspondence, ie, ballot-sheet voting. Ballot-sheet voting is not allowed on:

- approval of the annual reports and annual accounts;
- distribution of profits (dividends) and losses of the company; and
- appointing the board of directors, the internal auditor (the auditing committee) and the external auditor.

14. Are voting rights always proportionate to the stock held by each shareholder or can they vary by share class?

See our comments on questions 5 and 6.

15. Are there non-voting shares? Is there a maximum percentage of capital represented by non-voting shares?

See our comments on question 3.

16. Can shareholders group their shares in order to exercise their voting rights (eg, by trust, shareholders' agreement or otherwise)?

It is expressly provided in the law that shareholders of the companies may enter into shareholders' agreements in which they agree to vote in a particular or an agreed way at GMs. However, as there is almost no court practice the legal basis for such voting arrangements is still uncertain.

17. Under what circumstances can a shareholder challenge the resolutions adopted by the GM? Are there thresholds concerning the stock interest owned to be able to bring such a claim?

Each shareholder of a company may challenge before a court a resolution adopted by the GM if:

(i) the resolution has been adopted with violations of the law and/or the company's by-laws (including procedural ones);
(ii) the shareholder did not take part in the relevant GM or voted against the resolution; and
(iii) the resolution violates the shareholder's rights and interests.

A shareholder's claim usually has a prospect of success if:

(i) the shareholder's votes could have affected the voting results at the GM,

had the shareholder participated in the meeting;
(ii) the violations of the law/the company's by-laws at the GM were
   significant; and
(iii) the resolution has resulted in losses to the shareholder.

18. What are the terms and procedures to challenge a resolution of the GM?

A resolution of the GM may be challenged before a court within three
months in a JSC and two months in an LLC, from the day when the
challenging shareholder was given (or should have been given) knowledge
of the adoption of the resolution and the circumstances that give cause for
challenging it.

The shareholder who wants to challenge a GM resolution must file a
claim with the Russian state court (*'arbitrazhny'* court) responsible at the
company's location, setting out their demand to avoid the GM resolution
and their reasoning, with reference to legal acts. The court is obliged
to review the claim within three months from the filing date, with the
possibility of extending the review up to six months in particularly
complicated cases.

SHAREHOLDERS' RIGHTS VERSUS DIRECTORS AND DUTIES OF OTHER CORPORATE BODIES IN THE COMPANY

19. What is the procedure for the appointment/replacement/revocation of directors and of statutory auditors, if any?

The members of the board of directors of a company are elected by the GM.

In a JSC the board of directors is necessarily elected by a cumulative vote.
Its powers continue until the next annual GM and automatically expire if
the next annual GM is not duly conducted at the right time.

The members of the collective executive body and the general director, as
well as the company's auditors, are appointed by either the GM or the board
of directors.

The appointment/removal requires a simple majority of votes.

20. May shareholders challenge the resolutions of the board of directors? Is there a minimum percentage of capital required to challenge a board resolution?

A shareholder may challenge a resolution of the board of directors of a
company, the collective executive body of a company or the general director
of an LLC before a Russian court if it: (i) was adopted in violation of the
law and/or the company's by-laws; and (ii) violates the rights and/or the
interests of the shareholder.

The court may refuse the shareholder's claim if: (i) the resolution has not
resulted in losses to either the company or the shareholder or other negative
consequences for them; and (ii) the violations of law/the company's by-laws
are insignificant.

The limitation period for challenging the resolutions of the respective
corporate bodies is three months in a JSC and two months in an LLC,

from the day when the shareholder learned (or should have learned) of the adoption of the resolution and the circumstances that gave cause for challenging it.

There is no minimum percentage of capital required to challenge a resolution of the respective corporate bodies.

21. Are shareholders entitled to bring a legal action against the directors of the company? In which circumstances? Please describe briefly the principles of directors' liability.

The general director and the members of the collective executive body and of the board of directors are liable to the company for the losses (including the direct loss and the loss of profits) incurred by the company as a result of their actions.

A shareholder (in a JSC, the shareholder(s) holding at least one per cent of the JSC's voting shares) may bring a legal action against the respective persons, to protect the company's interests, if:

- the losses are caused by the respective persons' actions;
- the respective persons have not acted in the interest of the company;
- the respective persons have not acted in good faith and reasonably; and
- the respective persons are at fault (ie, they have not exercised reasonable care as required by normal commercial practice).

The respective persons' liability is joint and several.

22. What are the rights in connection with transactions where the directors have a conflict of interest situation?

A transaction where a director has a conflict of interest requires the prior approval by the board of directors (by a majority of votes of the non-interested directors) or the GM (usually where the transaction value is two per cent of the balance value of the company's total assets or more).

A transaction not duly approved may be avoided by a court order upon a claim of the company or its shareholder. However, the court will turn down the claim if:

(i)   the voting of the relevant shareholder could not have affected the results of the voting at the GM that approved the transaction;

(ii) there is no evidence that the transaction has led to (or may lead to) losses or other negative consequences to the company or the shareholder; and

(iii) it is proved that the other party to the transaction did not know and should not have known of the lack of due approval of the transaction.

The limitation period for a court action is one year from the day when the company/shareholder learned (or should have learned) of the transaction and the lack of approval.

INFORMATION RIGHTS ON THE COMPANY'S BUSINESS

23. What information may be requested by the shareholders from the board concerning the general state of the company's business or any specific transaction? Are information rights different depending on the

number of shares owned? Are shareholders entitled to receive written information before, during or after the GM about the meeting agenda and to what extent? Is it possible for a shareholder to obtain a copy of the minutes of the GM?

Shareholders have the right of access to the company's general corporate documents (including by-laws), documents of title to its assets, the company's general accounting/financial documents, minutes of the meetings of the management bodies, court decisions and some other documents.

In a JSC, a 25 per cent shareholding is required to access the company's accounting documents and minutes of the meetings of the company's collective executive body. In an LLC all shareholders have equal access rights. The shareholders may review the documents in the company's offices or, at the shareholder's discretion, obtain copies of such documents.

Shareholders are further entitled to receive certain information and documents on the GM's agendas – within 20-30 days of the forthcoming GM, including a detailed agenda itself, the company's annual reports, the internal/external auditor's opinions, information on the proposed candidates to the management bodies, proposed changes to the company's by-laws.

24. Do shareholders have the right/duty to resolve in the GM upon matters which were not on the agenda?

Shareholders normally do not have the right/duty to resolve on the matters that were not on the GM agenda. A resolution of the GM thus adopted is void except for the following:

- The GM of an LLC may resolve on any matters if all the company's shareholders were present. Such resolution will have valid effect.
- In a JSC, if all shareholders were present and the GM went beyond its agenda the resolution would have legal effect but may be challenged by a shareholder who voted against it and whose rights/interests are impacted (also see questions 17 and 18).

25. Are shareholders entitled to inspect the corporate books and/or any other corporate or accounting documents? To what extent? Can they do it through external counsel or advisors?

Shareholders are entitled to inspect the company's corporate books and accounting documents (see question 23). This may be done through external counsel or advisors under a power of attorney.

SHAREHOLDERS' AGREEMENTS

26. Are shareholders' agreements validly enforceable? What are their typical contents and term of duration? Are they enforceable by or against third parties and, if so, to what extent?

Since 2009, Russian law contains express provisions on shareholders' agreements. Shareholders' agreements may, in particular, contain the following provisions:

- agreements on the exercise of their voting rights;

- assignment of shares upon, or non-assignment of shares until the occurrence of certain circumstances; and
- other agreements on actions regarding the management of the JSC or the activities, reorganisation or liquidation of the JSC.

In addition, for the JSC the following is provided (which in our view also applies to the LLC):

- voting of shareholders may not be bound to the instructions of a management body of the company;
- shareholder agreements may establish security for the performance of the obligations under the shareholders' agreement and civil liability for the non- or undue performance of such obligations; and
- shareholders' agreements have effect only in relation to the parties of the shareholders' agreement, not to third parties. A resolution of a management body of the respective company may not be held invalid on the basis of a breach of a shareholders' agreement.

Due to lack of practice with Russian law shareholders' agreements, it is not easy to summarise their typical contents and term of duration. Often the content is similar to the content of shareholders' agreements relating to companies under other jurisdictions.

As there is still no reliable court practice, it is not clear what provisions would be enforceable under Russian law and what would not. To avoid the risks under Russian law, many shareholders' agreements are made under foreign law, using offshore corporate structures. However, their enforceability in Russia is doubtful as, based on Russian law of conflicts, Russian courts consider Russian law as mandatorily applicable to shareholders' agreements. For example, in the OJSC *Megafon* and the CJSC *Russki* Standard *Strakhovanie* cases, Russian courts held the choice of non-Russian law for shareholders' agreements regarding Russian companies as invalid.

27. Do shareholders' agreements have to be disclosed to the public or registered in any public registry?

With regard to LLCs and CJSCs no public disclosure or public registration rules usually apply. There are some public disclosure and notification rules in relation to shareholders' agreements in OJSCs and CJSCs that are banks or which have publicly placed bonds or other securities.

ECONOMIC RIGHTS AND RIGHTS OVER THE STOCK
28. Is the stock always freely transferable? Are there any legal limitations? Are there any restrictions on contractual limitations?

In an OJSC stock is freely transferable subject to contractual limitations. In an LLC and a CJSC shareholders and, if the by-laws so provide, the respective company, enjoy the right of first refusal of the shares sold by other shareholders. However, as the right of first refusal applies only to share sales, it may be circumvented by transferring shares under a different contract – for example by a gift or a barter and exchange deal.

In an LLC some further limitations apply:

- shares may not be transferred until fully paid;

- if shares are sold at public sales they do not pass to the acquirer until all the company's shareholders give their consent;
- in the event of a charge on the shares, the company or the other shareholders may prevent the share transfer to a third party by paying out the actual value of such shares to the creditors; and
- the LLC's by-laws may provide for further limitations: eg, prohibition of share transfers to third parties, requirement of a prior consent.

Limitations of share transfers – both in JSCs and LLCs – may be provided for in shareholders' agreements. As Russian law on shareholders' agreements is new, there is no practice and no certainty with how far the contractual limitations may go. It is understood that shareholders may not completely waive their right to transfer shares.

29. Are shareholders entitled to pledge their stock?

Shareholders of a JSC are normally entitled to pledge their stock without restrictions.

Shareholders of an LLC may pledge their shares without restrictions only to other shareholders. Pledges of shares to third parties require the prior consent of a GM (which is taken by a majority of votes). An LLC's by-laws may prohibit share pledges to third parties altogether.

30. Are there financial assistance issues to be considered and other prohibitions to be evaluated in the context of a leveraged buyout transaction?

No.

31. May a company buy back its own stock and, if so, under what circumstances and subject to which limitations?

A JSC may buy back its own stock in the following circumstances:
- The GM (or the board of directors, as the case may be) decides that the JSC buys back a certain amount of its own stock; the JSC is then obliged to buy back the stock from any willing shareholder. This kind of buyback is subject to the following conditions:
  (i)   the JSC does not have capitalisation/solvency issues;
  (ii) the stock remaining in circulation upon the buyback is at least 90 per cent of the JSC's total issued stock;
  (iii) the JSC's share capital is fully paid;
  (iv) the JSC's net assets are sufficient; and
  (v)   the JSC has no outstanding obligations under the obligatory buyback upon the demand of a shareholder (see below and question 32 for more information).
- A shareholder so demands (see question 32 below).

An LLC may and is obliged to buy back its own shares in the following circumstances:
- a share transfer is intended/required but is prohibited by the LLC's by-laws or the required consent has not been granted (see question 28);
- a shareholder has demanded the buy back in events described in

question 32 below; or

- a shareholder is 'expelled' from the LLC by a court order upon the claim of other shareholders (in the event of a gross violation of their shareholder's duties or obstruction to the LLC's activities).

All these potential buyback scenarios in an LLC are subject to the following limitations: (i) only net assets may be used for the buyback; and (ii) the LLC should not have any solvency issues.

Another situation in which companies may buy back their own shares is when using their right of first refusal of the shares – see question 28 (this does not apply to OJSCs). Also, the non-paid shares in a company during its incorporation go over to the company, within a year of its incorporation (unless a shorter term applies).

32. Is there a legal right to withdraw from the company and, if so, under what circumstances? How is the shareholders' stock valued and paid in such a case?

A shareholder of a JSC may have their shares bought back by the company and thus withdraw in the event of:

(i)   the company's reorganisation;
(ii) the consummation by the company of a large transaction with a value exceeding 50 per cent of the JSC's total assets; or
(iii) the introduction of changes in the JSC's by-laws that restrict their rights – provided, in each case, that the shareholder voted against the relevant decision of the GM or did not participate in the GM.

The price is usually determined by the board of directors, but may not be less than the market price as determined by an independent expert or on the basis of the offering prices at a stock exchange (in relation to listed stock).

The shares may only be bought out providing the total consideration to all the shareholders in each relevant case of buyback will not exceed 10 per cent of the JSC's net assets.

In an LLC a shareholder may demand the buyback and thus withdraw:

- if the GM has approved a large transaction or has decided to increase the LLC's capital by additional contributions of all the LLC's shareholders, while the shareholder voted against this decision or did not participate in the GM; or
- (if allowed by the LLC's by-laws:) at their discretion, without cause, provided that as a result the LLC will not be left without shareholders.

The LLC must pay to the withdrawing shareholder the 'actual' value of their share, in cash or in assets. The 'actual' value is determined on the basis of the LLC's accounting reports for the last reporting period.

The payment of the 'actual' value is subject to the limitations described in question 31 above.

33. In which circumstances can dividends be distributed among shareholders? Is it possible to exclude or limit the right of certain shareholders to dividends? Does a certain portion of the profits need to be set aside in a reserve fund where it cannot be distributed to the

shareholders? Are advances on dividends allowed and, if so, under which circumstances? Can advances on dividends be reclaimed by the company?

Companies may distribute dividends if they have net profits.

A JSC may distribute dividends upon the end of each calendar quarter and the end of the financial year. An LLC may distribute profits once every quarter, every half year or every year.

Dividends may not be distributed if:
- the company's capital has not been fully paid;
- the company has not yet bought back the shares where it is obliged to do so (see questions 31 and 32);
- there are signs of the company's insolvency (bankruptcy); or
- the company's net assets are insufficient.

A JSC may not distribute dividends to a group of shareholders until it has distributed the dividends to those who, holding 'preferred' shares, have a preference on dividends.

In a JSC all shareholders holding the same 'type' of shares have the same rights to dividends, which cannot be limited or excluded in relation to individual shareholders.

The by-laws of an LLC may provide for distribution of dividends that is disproportionate to the shareholding. Certain shareholders may be limited in dividends or fully excluded for a certain period of time and/or in certain circumstances. However, an absolute exclusion from dividend payments is questionable.

A JSC must maintain a reserve fund of at least five per cent of the JSC's capital to cover the JSC's losses and, as the case may be, make other necessary payments. The JSC must make yearly payments into the reserve fund of at least five per cent of its net profits until the fund reaches the necessary amount. The net profits that are required for the reserve fund may not be distributed as dividends.

An LLC is not obliged to have a reserve fund.

Advances on dividends – both in JSC and LLC – are not allowed.

34. What are the rights of shareholders in the case of an issue of new stock (increase of the company's corporate capital) (pre-emption rights)?

With regard to JSCs:
- the stock distributed in a capital increase at the expense of the JSC's assets may be distributed only among the current shareholders and in proportion to their shareholdings;
- where, in a capital increase against new contributions, the new stock is being offered: (i) to third parties; or (ii) to shareholders but in a disproportionate manner, the shareholders who voted against the offering or did not participate in the GM have the right of first refusal of the new stock in proportion to their current shareholding; and
- shareholders of OJSCs have further rights in offerings by open subscription.

With regard to LLCs:

- in a capital increase at the expense of the LLC's assets the nominal value of the shares is increased without changes to the existing shareholding percentages; and
- if a GM has not decided on the capital increases by unanimous vote, each shareholder may contribute to the company's capital in the amount proportionate to their current shareholding; the shareholder who voted against the capital increase or did not participate in the GM may demand that the LLC buys back their share.

35. May minority shareholders ban or limit the company's capital structure in any manner?

Minority shareholders of the company may ban/limit the company's capital structure by:

- exercising their right of first refusal when shares are being sold to a third party (see question 28);
- exercising their rights granted during a capital increase (see question 34); and
- disapproving the sale of shares owned by the company itself to a third party or to the current shareholders in a disproportionate manner. In an LLC such sale requires the unanimous consent of all shareholders. In a JSC such sale may require approval by a majority of votes of the non-interested members of the board of directors or the non-interested shareholders at a GM (see question 22 for details).

In general (except, however, in the instance of the disapproval of a sale of shares owned by the OJSC), minority shareholders of OJSCs may not ban/limit the company's capital structure.

36. Which are the financial assistance prohibitions in force?

There are none.

37. Apart from publicly listed companies, in which cases (if any) are shareholders obligated to obtain an authorisation from, or provide information to, a public authority about events that have an impact on their stock interest in the company?

Such cases are as follows:

- the acquisition of shares which leads to the acquirer holding directly or indirectly over 25 per cent of the voting shares in an JSC or one-third of the shares in an LLC and any subsequent acquisitions may require the prior approval of, or notification to, the Russian antitrust authority – depending on the scale of businesses of the acquirer and the target and their position on the Russian market;
- the direct or indirect acquisition of shares in a so-called strategic Russian company (ie, a company with a strategic significance for the country's defence and state security) may require prior approval of, or notification to, the Russian competent authorities;
- if the shareholder is registered with the Russian tax inspectorate they

must notify the tax inspectorate of each direct acquisition of shares in a Russian company; and

- the shareholder of a JSC must notify the Russian Federal Service for the Financial Markets of the acquisition of five or more per cent of the voting shares in the JSC and each subsequent acquisition/transfer where their share in the JSC becomes more/less than five, 10, 15, 20, 25, 30, 50 or 75 per cent.

Shareholders that are Russian companies themselves are subject to further notification/publication requirements.

SHAREHOLDERS' RIGHTS IN THE CASE OF EXTRAORDINARY TRANSACTIONS AND/OR WINDING-UP

38. What rights are available to shareholders in the case of a sale of all or a substantial portion of the company's assets? In the case of a merger or de-merger?

The sale of all or a substantial amount of the company's assets qualifies as a 'large' transaction under Russian law.

Large transactions are subject to prior approval either by the board of directors or the GM, usually where the value of the transaction exceeds 50 per cent of the company's total assets. The shareholders may apply to a court to invalidate a large transaction that has not been duly approved (our comments to question 22 apply accordingly). Shareholders who voted against the large transaction at the GM or did not participate in the GM have the right to a buyback of their shares by the company (see question 32).

In the event of a merger/de-merger shareholders have the right to receive a share in the new company(ies) in proportion to their current shares; to be informed well in advance of the GM that will consider the merger/de-merger and make proposals on the GM's agenda; to challenge the transactions violating the terms of the merger/de-merger and to challenge the relevant resolutions of the company's management bodies.

In an LLC the decisions on the merger/de-merger are adopted by a GM by a unanimous vote of all the shareholders; in a JSC the shareholders who voted against the motion or did not participate in the GM have the right to a buyback of their shares by the company.

39. Which rights are available to shareholders in the case of conversion of the company into a European Company (SE) or into another type of company?

A company may not be converted into a European Company (SE).

Shareholders' rights in the event of a conversion of the company into a company of another type are basically the same as in the event of a merger/de-merger (see question 38).

40. Which rights are available to shareholders of a company in liquidation?

All shareholders of an LLC and the holders of voting shares in a JSC may receive a portion of the company's assets that remain after the settlements with the company's creditors. The holders of a JSC's preferred shares may receive the 'share liquidation values', which are determined by the by-laws of the respective JSC. Depending on the type of liquidation (ie, voluntary liquidation or liquidation within bankruptcy proceedings), the shareholders have different additional rights.

41. Can shareholders cause the liquidation of the company? How?

Shareholders may cause the company's liquidation by convening a GM with the company's liquidation on its agenda. In an LLC such a meeting may be convened by the owners of at least one-tenth of the total number of the shares; in the case of a JSC, those convening the meeting would need to own at least 10 per cent of the company's voting shares.

The decision to liquidate an LLC must be adopted in a GM by the unanimous vote of all shareholders. In a JSC such a decision requires a three-quarters majority of votes of the holders of the company's voting shares who participate in the meeting.

COMPANY GROUPS

42. Is the concept of 'group' recognised as such under specific legislation? What are the implications?

Under Russian law, companies belong to a 'group' if they are related to each other by direct or indirect majority shareholding. The concept of 'group' is primarily used in Russian antitrust law with regard to merger control, in order to determine market power. In Russian antitrust law, all companies belonging to one group are treated as one business unit, with the consequence that the market shares and assets of all companies belonging to a group are added up.

In addition, Russian law contains the concept of 'affiliated persons'. The affiliated persons of a company are its officers, as well as other companies of the same group and companies in which the company controls more than 20 per cent of the votes or *vice versa*. The concept of affiliated persons is used to determine conflicts of interest within a company particularly in relation to the company's transactions. Transactions with affiliated persons (the so-called interested-party transactions) require corporate approval before they are made (see question 22).

The company's affiliated persons are obliged to inform the company of their acquisition of voting shares in it. If the notice is not duly served the affiliated person is liable to the company for any incurred damage.

The company is obliged to store the information on its affiliated persons and, where required by law, provide/disclose it to public authorities and/or the public (the disclosure requirement mostly applies to public companies).

The Russian Civil Code contains the general provisions on subsidiaries and dependent businesses listed below:

- A holding company (according to Russian court practice, a company holding more than 50 per cent of the shares in another company (the subsidiary)) which has the right to give binding instructions to the subsidiary bears (together with the subsidiary) the joint liability for the obligations from all transactions into which the subsidiary enters upon such instructions. In the event of the bankruptcy of the subsidiary being caused by the fault of the holding company, the holding company (together with the subsidiary) bears joint liability for the obligations of the subsidiary.

- A company is deemed to be dependent on another company if that other company holds at least 20 per cent of the voting shares in a JSC or, in the case of an LLC, 20 per cent of the shares. A company that acquired more than 20 per cent of the voting shares in a JSC or 20 per cent of the shares in an LLC is obliged to publish notification of the acquisition.

43. Does a controlling company have any particular duties *vis-à-vis* its controlled company shareholders?

According to the Civil Code of the Russian Federation, the other shareholders of a subsidiary may claim compensation for damages which by its fault the holding company caused to its subsidiary.

44. What are the rights of company shareholders when the controlling company puts in place actions and/or transactions that can be prejudicial to the shareholders?

The company's shareholders may:

- block resolutions and actions of the company's management bodies by not approving an interested party or large transaction (see questions 22 and 38);
- block a GM's resolution where a unanimous vote or a qualified majority of votes is required;
- challenge the resolutions of the management bodies (see questions 17 and 20);
- bring a legal action against the company's officers (see question 21); and
- demand from the company the buyback of their shares and withdraw from the company (see questions 31 and 32).

45. What are the limitations, if any, to the possibility of owning reciprocal stock interests in companies?

Currently there are no such limitations.

Slovak Republic

Havel & Holásek Michael Mullen & Jan Koval

BASIC INFORMATION ON THE TYPES OF LIMITED LIABILITY COMPANIES AND ON THE RIGHTS OF SHAREHOLDERS

1. What types of companies enjoy limited liability? If more than one, which ones have shareholders, ie holders of share certificates? Which one is the most common? Which one is mostly used by foreign investors?

There are two main types of companies enjoying limited liability in the Slovak Republic, namely limited liability companies and joint stock companies. Only the shareholders of a joint stock company are holders of share certificates. The shareholders of a limited liability company are holders of ownership interests, which are not in certified form. The most common type of company in the Slovak Republic is a limited liability company because of the relatively low capital requirements and less-administratively burdensome corporate rules. Joint stock companies, which are more demanding in terms of corporate administration and minimum registered capital requirements are generally preferred by larger groups of investors.

2. Are there minimum capital requirements and/or thin capitalisation rules in force?

The minimum registered capital of a limited liability company is €5,000. The minimum registered capital of a joint stock company is €25,000. Thin capitalisation rules do not apply in the Slovak Republic.

3. Describe the types of shares that can be issued by a company and the different rights that they attribute to their owners, as well as any other financial instruments (bonds or other) and other instruments of a participatory nature in the company's capital that can also be issued by the company.

A joint stock company may issue
(i)   registered or bearer shares,
(ii) certified or uncertified shares, and
(iii) ordinary or priority shares.

Registered shares can be transferred through endorsement and delivery; their transferability may be limited by the company's by-laws. It is not common to enter share transfer restrictions on the share certificates themselves. Bearer shares can be transferred by contract according to the Securities Act and they cannot be burdened by share transfer restrictions. Certified shares may be physically held by the shareholders, while uncertified shares are registered with a central depositary. Priority shares (unlike ordinary shares) may be connected with a priority right to dividends or a liquidation share. The joint stock company's by-laws may allow for non-voting and voting shares rights. Joint stock companies may also issue convertible and priority bonds, provided that the general meeting of shareholders (GM) of the company decides on the conditional increase of the registered capital of the company. Convertible bonds allow for the exchange of bonds for shares and priority bonds allow for a priority right to subscribe for new shares. Slovak limited liability companies do not issue shares or bonds.

4. Can a company have only one shareholder and still enjoy limited liability?

Both limited liability companies and joint stock companies can only have one shareholder and still enjoy limited liability (the sole shareholder has to be a legal entity in a joint stock company). However, as a general principle, under Slovak law a limited liability company having only one shareholder may not be the sole shareholder of a Slovak limited liability company. This does not apply to foreign entities. The shareholders of a limited liability company bear liability for the company's obligations up to the aggregate unpaid subscription price of the shares. Similarly, shareholders of a joint stock company are not liable for the obligations of the company and are only liable to the company to the extent of their unpaid subscription price. In the Slovak legal system an individual can only be the sole shareholder in three limited liability companies.

5. Are the rights of shareholders the same in any type of company?

The shareholders in both limited liability companies and joint stock companies generally enjoy the same basic rights, such as the right to participate in the company's profit, the right to participate in the liquidation reminder of the company, the right to vote at the GM of the company and the right to obtain relevant information regarding the company, etc. Some of these rights may, however, be limited or excluded. The by-laws of a limited liability company may, for example, allow some shareholders to have a higher profit share and/or liquidation share than the others. In a joint stock company such a provision in the company's by-laws would be invalid; on the other hand, a joint stock company may issue priority shares connected with priority rights to dividends in favour of their holders. The aggregate nominal value of such priority shares may not exceed one-half of the company's registered capital. There is, however, a difference between the rights of minority shareholders in a limited liability company, who can only cause the convocation of a GM of the company, and the rights of minority shareholders in a joint stock company, who have a wider range of rights (see below). On the other hand, majority shareholders of a joint stock company may under conditions specified by law squeeze out the minority shareholders.

6. What are the basic rights of any shareholder? Describe briefly the rights of minority shareholders and indicate which thresholds, if any, are required to allow the minority shareholders to exercise any such rights.

As described above, the basic rights of the shareholders are: the right to participate in the company's profit, the right to participate in the liquidation remainder of the company, the right to vote at a GM of the company, the right to obtain relevant information regarding the company, the right to inspect corporate books and records and the right to transfer their shares. While minority shareholders of a limited liability company, ie shareholders having in aggregate at least a 10 per cent participation in the registered capital of the company) can only cause the convocation of a GM of the company, minority shareholders (a shareholder holding at least five per cent of the stocks) in a joint stock company can cause the convocation of a GM of the company and propose its agenda, request that the board of directors file an action against shareholders who are in delay with payment of the subscription price of the shares, request that the supervisory board review the indicated acts of the board of directors and require that the supervisory board claim damages caused to the company by a member of the board of directors, among others.

7. Do all shareholders enjoy the same rights or can some shareholders be attributed specific rights, whether by reason of the particular class of stock owned or other? Are such rights generally provided for at the level of the company's by-laws and/or in shareholders' agreements?

All shareholders generally enjoy the same rights; however, the Slovak Commercial Code allows for exceptions to this rule. As mentioned previously, a joint stock company may issue priority shares connected with a priority right to dividends. In a limited liability company such priority rights could be agreed in the company's by-laws. Other differences between the rights of individual shareholders may be of course agreed in the company's by-laws or shareholders' agreements. More complicated and often confidential arrangements between the shareholders such as rights of first refusal, drag-along rights, tag-along rights, option rights, lock-up rights and other similar restrictions are typically contained only in the shareholders' agreements because the company's by-laws must be filed with the commercial register and are publicly available.

8. May the rights of shareholders, generally speaking, be limited, modified, suppressed or waived in any way? If so, how? Are such modifications or limitations provided for in the company's by-laws and/or in shareholders' agreements?

The Slovak Commercial Code allows the shareholders in certain cases to agree in by-laws on the limitation, modification or exclusion of certain rights of all or individual shareholders. There are, however, certain rights, such as the right to be present at a GM, right to transfer the shares or right to participate in the company's profit, which cannot be completely excluded by agreement of the shareholders. As mentioned above, more complicated and confidential arrangements are typically contained in the shareholders' agreements.

GENERAL MEETING OF SHAREHOLDERS (GM) AND VOTING RIGHTS

9. Which decisions are reserved to the competence of the GM?

The Slovak Commercial Code contains a separate list of decisions reserved for the GM of a limited liability company and that of a joint stock company. In both types of companies a GM decides on:

(i) changes to the company's by-laws;
(ii) the increase and decrease of the registered capital;
(iii) the appointment and recall of the members of the corporate bodies (except for cases where the members of the board of directors are appointed and recalled in accordance with the company's by-laws by the supervisory board) and their remuneration;
(iv) the liquidation of the company, appointment and recall of a liquidator and their remuneration; and
(v) the merger, de-merger, transfer of assets to a shareholder and conversion of legal form of the company;

and approves:

(i) the company's financial statements;
(ii) the agreements on transfer or lease of the company's enterprise or its part, and the pledge agreements in respect of the company's enterprise or its part; and
(iii) the pre-incorporation acts performed by the company founders prior to the registration of the company in the commercial register.

A GM may decide on other matters specified by law or the company's by-law. The GM of a limited liability company may not decide on those matters that fall within the authority of other corporate bodies.

10. How does a shareholder participate in a GM? Are there any limitations to having a minimum number of shares? May a shareholder delegate attendance to another shareholder or to the board? May a shareholder obtain assistance from the courts or any other governmental body to intervene in a GM or to cause one to be held in some particular cases?

Each shareholder has a right to be present at a GM, either in person or through a proxy. There are no limitations on having a minimum number of shares in this respect. The shareholders generally also have the right to vote at a GM. However, the voting rights may be excluded in certain cases or for certain shareholders (eg a shareholder is not entitled to vote at a GM if the GM decides on their non-monetary contribution, if they hold priority shares without voting rights, etc). A shareholder can delegate attendance to another shareholder or a member of the board of directors. Minority shareholders of a joint stock company may request a court to authorise them to convoke a GM of the company if the board of directors fails to do so despite a legitimate request of the minority shareholders. Minority shareholders of a limited liability company may in the same situation convoke a GM of the company even without such authorisation of the court. Finally, shareholders of both joint stock companies and limited liability companies may ask the court to declare the invalidity of a GM.

11. May a GM be called and held at the request of any shareholder? Is there a threshold regarding the percentage of the stock interest owned in the company that may entitle a shareholder to such a right?

The convocation of a GM is generally carried out by the corporate bodies of the company. The executive directors of a limited liability company are obliged to convoke a GM upon the request of the shareholders having in aggregate at least a 10 per cent participation in the registered capital. The board of directors of a joint stock company is obliged to convoke a GM upon the request of the shareholders having in aggregate at least a five per cent participation in the registered capital of a company. Notwithstanding the foregoing, both limited liability companies and joint stock companies must convene a GM at least once a year.

12. May a shareholder bring up an issue to be resolved upon and put it to a vote if it is not included on the agenda? May a shareholder require more information from the GM and/or the board concerning the agenda of the GM, to be put in a better position to exercise their vote?

The agenda of a GM is generally contained in the invitation sent to the shareholders in advance. While at the GM of a limited liability company the matters not listed in the invitation can only be discussed if all the shareholders are present and agree with it, at the GM of a joint stock company such matters may be discussed but not decided unless all the shareholders are present. As mentioned previously, the minority shareholders of joint stock companies may require that the board of directors convoke the GM in order to discuss the matters proposed by them. The shareholders have the right to ask for explanations and to receive answers to questions about matters concerning the company in respect of the agenda of the GM, unless the disclosure of such information could cause detriment to the company or would be subject to trade secret protection. Should the board of directors refuse to provide the requested information due to the above reasons, it may only be provided to the shareholders if the supervisory board approves it. If the supervisory board does not approve the disclosure of the requested information, the shareholders may ask the competent court to order the disclosure of the information.

13. May a GM be held by telecommunication means and/or by correspondence (ie by written consent)?

A GM of a limited liability company cannot be held by means of electronic communication. Nevertheless, the shareholders may adopt the resolutions in writing outside the GM. The GM of a public joint stock company can be held by means of electronic communication. The conditions for voting by means of electronic communication have to be set up in such a manner that allows the company to verify the identity of the shareholder. The by-laws of a public joint stock company may also allow correspondence voting, voting by means of a handover of votes one day before the actual GM, so that the shareholders do not have to participate personally at the GM.

14. Are voting rights always proportionate to the stock held by each shareholder or can they vary by the stock class?

The voting rights of shareholders of a limited liability company are generally proportionate to the shares held by them. However, the shareholders may agree on different rules in the company's by-laws, including the possibility to grant one vote to each shareholder, irrespective of their investment contributions into the company's registered capital. In a joint stock company, the number of votes attached to each share and the method of voting at a GM has to be stipulated in the company's by-laws. Apart from that, the by-laws must contain the information on the number of votes pertaining to a share of a particular nominal value, if the company issued shares in different nominal values.

15. Are there non-voting shares? Is there a maximum percentage of capital represented by non-voting shares?

As mentioned previously, a joint stock company may issue priority shares connected with the priority right to the dividends. The company's by-law may then stipulate that the voting rights are not attached to the priority shares in order to balance the rights of their holders with the rights of the holders of the other type of shares. The total nominal value of the priority shares may not exceed one-half of the registered (share) capital.

16. Can shareholders group their shares in order to exercise their voting rights (eg by trust, shareholders' agreement or otherwise)?

There are no limitations on the grouping of the shares by the shareholders in order to exercise their voting rights. The only limitations set forth by the Slovak Commercial Code in respect of the exercise of the shareholders' voting rights are those concerning certain undertakings of the shareholders *vis-à-vis* the company. In particular, any agreements containing the shareholder's undertaking to:
(i) follow instructions given by the company or any of its corporate bodies on how to vote;
(ii) vote for proposals submitted by the company's bodies; and
(iii) use their voting right in a predetermined manner, or not to vote, in exchange for advantages granted to them by the company are not allowed.

17. Under what circumstances can a shareholder challenge the resolutions adopted by the GM? Are there thresholds concerning the stock interest owned to be able to bring such a claim?

Each shareholder of the company can ask the competent court to nullify a resolution of a GM, should such resolution be contrary to legal provisions or the company's by-laws. However, the court shall nullify a resolution of a GM contrary to the legal provisions or by-laws if the resolution might have resulted in the restriction of the rights of the demanding shareholder.

Apart from the shareholders, members of the supervisory board, members of the board of directors or executive directors, liquidators and insolvency trustees are also entitled to file a petition to nullify a resolution of a GM.

18. What are the terms and procedures to challenge a resolution of the GM?

The right to challenge a resolution of a GM shall lapse if it is not asserted within three months of the day the GM is held, or, if the GM was not properly convened, within three months of the day when the shareholder (or other person entitled to assert such right) could have learned about the holding of the GM.

SHAREHOLDERS' RIGHTS VERSUS DIRECTORS AND DUTIES OF OTHER CORPORATE BODIES IN THE COMPANY

19. What is the procedure for the appointment/replacement/ revocation of directors and of statutory auditors, if any?

The executive directors of a limited liability company are appointed and recalled by a GM of the company. The members of the board of directors of a joint stock company are appointed and recalled either by a GM of the company or by the company's supervisory board if it is set forth in the company's by-laws. A limited liability company does not have to establish a supervisory board, but, if established, the members of the supervisory board are appointed and recalled by a GM of the company. Similarly, the members of a supervisory board of a joint stock company (as a mandatory corporate body) are appointed and recalled by a GM of the company. However, if such joint stock company has more than 50 employees, one-third of the members of the supervisory body are appointed by the company's employees.
The statutory auditors are generally appointed and revoked by a GM or supervisory board of the company.

20. May shareholders challenge the resolutions of the board of directors? Is there a minimum percentage of capital required to challenge a board resolution?

Shareholders do not have any special right to challenge the resolutions of the board of directors. However, they may file a court petition against the members of the board of directors who caused damages to the company by acting or deciding in contradiction with the law or the company's by-laws. The shareholders of a limited liability company may file a court petition and shareholders of a joint stock company may request the supervisory board to examine the board's resolution and/or to file a court petition against the responsible members of the board. In a limited liability company there are no minimum thresholds for exercising such a right; in a joint stock company such a right may be exercised by shareholders that together have at least a minority share (ie five per cent of the company's registered capital).

21. Are shareholders entitled to bring a legal action against the directors of the company? In which circumstances? Please describe briefly the principles of directors' liability.

In a limited liability company each shareholder is entitled to file a complaint on behalf of the company for compensation of damage against the executive director who is liable to the company for the damage it caused. In a joint stock company, the resolutions of the board of directors are controlled by the company's supervisory board. At the request of the minority shareholders, the supervisory board shall examine the performance of the board of directors in the matters raised in the request and will assert any right to compensation for damages which the company has against a member of the board of directors. Should the supervisory board fail to comply with a request by the minority shareholders without undue delay, such shareholders may assert the right to damages on behalf of the company.

The directors of a company are liable for any damage caused to the company by breach of their duties as members of the company's statutory body. The presumptions of liability are in general:
(i)   a breach of an obligation (statutory or contractual) by the director;
(ii) the existence of damage;
(iii) a causal connection between the breach of the obligation and the existence of damage; and
(iv) the non-existence of a circumstance excluding the liability.
(The executive officer excludes their liability when providing evidence of acting with due professional care and good will, acting in compliance with the company's interests or executing a resolution of a GM.) The directors who breached their duties and caused damage to the company are obliged to compensate for such damage, where the damage generally includes the actual damage and a profit loss. The directors who breached their duties and caused damage to the company are liable jointly and severally. The liability of the directors may not be limited or excluded, either by the company's by-laws or by an agreement between the company and the director. The directors may also be held liable for committing a crime while executing their offices.

22. What are the rights in connection with transactions where the directors have a conflict of interest situation?

Unless the statutes or a resolution of a GM impose further restrictions, a member of the board of directors may not:
(i)   carry out a business activity in an identical or similar line of business to that of the company or enter into business relations with the company;
(ii) act as an intermediary for other persons in transactions with the company;
(iii) participate in the business activity of another entity (partnership) as a partner with unlimited liability or as a person controlling other persons engaged in an identical or similar line of business activity; or

(iv) act as, or be a member of, the statutory organ of another legal entity engaged in an identical or similar line of business to that of the company, unless such legal entity is a holding-type group.

If a member of the board of directors violates such restrictions, the affected company may demand that such member surrenders to the company any benefit gained from the transaction by which they violated the prohibition, or that they transfer the corresponding rights to the company. This shall not affect the right of the company to claim damages.

INFORMATION RIGHTS ON THE COMPANY'S BUSINESS

23. What information may be requested by the shareholders from the board concerning the general state of the company's business or any specific transaction? Are information rights different depending on the number of shares owned? Are shareholders entitled to receive written information before, during or after the GM about the meeting agenda and to what extent? Is it possible for a shareholder to obtain a copy of the minutes of the GM?

As mentioned previously, the shareholders have the right to ask for explanations and to receive answers to questions about matters concerning the company, unless the disclosure of such information could cause detriment to the company, would be subject to trade secret protection, or would otherwise negatively impact the company. Should the board of directors refuse to give the requested information due to the above reasons, it may only be provided to the shareholders if the supervisory board approves doing so. If the supervisory board does not approve the disclosure of the requested information, the shareholders may ask the competent court to order the disclosure of the information. The information right is given to each shareholder. The agenda of a GM must be specified in the invitation to the GM. Any shareholder may ask the board of directors for a copy or abstract of the minutes of a GM held during the company's existence.

24. Do shareholders have the right/duty to resolve in the GM upon matters which were not on the agenda?

The agenda of a GM shall be announced to the shareholders 15 days prior to the GM taking place. The GM may adopt resolutions beyond the announced programme only on the basis of the unilateral approval of all shareholders of inserting the additional issues to the programme of the GM. The programme of the GM of joint stock companies shall be announced 30 days ahead of time. Amendments to the programme are only allowed on the basis of the presence and unilateral approval of all the shareholders.

25. Are shareholders entitled to inspect the corporate books and/or any other corporate or accounting documents? To what extent? Can they do it through external counsel or advisors?

Shareholders of a limited liability company have the right to inspect corporate and accounting documents and to demand a copy of the financial statements. The right to information is restricted to the documents of the company which do not contain information subject to commercial secrets or a confidentiality clause. The shareholder of a limited liability company may empower an auditor or a tax adviser to inspect the accounting documents. However, this far-reaching information right related to corporate books and accounting document does not apply to joint stock companies. The shareholders of a joint stock company only have information rights regarding the state of the company and can only exercise them within a GM.

SHAREHOLDERS' AGREEMENTS
26. Are shareholders' agreements validly enforceable? What are their typical contents and term of duration? Are they enforceable by or against third parties and, if so, to what extent?
It is a very common practice that shareholders enter into shareholders' agreements in order to set out their rights and obligations as shareholders within the existence of the company, as well as rights and obligations related to the individual or joint exit from the company. The shareholders' agreements are validly enforceable, provided that their content is not contrary to the mandatory provisions of the Slovak Commercial Code or other laws. The shareholders' agreements typically contain provisions regarding the character and amount of initial and eventual future contributions to the registered or equity capital of the company, nature of the company's business, governance of the company, control of the company and the rights of minority shareholders, manner of distribution of profit and payment of loss, limitation of transferability of shares and rules for the individual or joint exit of the shareholders from the company (eg pre-emption rights, tag-along and drag-along rights, put options and call option rights, etc), competition and arbitration clauses, and the like. The shareholders' agreements are typically concluded for the time of the shareholders' presence in the company and are effective only among the contractual parties and their legal successors and not *vis-à-vis* the third parties.

27. Do shareholders' agreements have to be disclosed to the public or registered in any public registry?
Unlike the company's constitutional documents, which contain general information on the company, the company's founders and their contributions, the amount of the registered capital, scope of business of the company, manner of acting on behalf of the company and some other basic information, shareholders' agreements, which contain more detailed and often confidential information, do not have to be disclosed to the public or in any public registries.

ECONOMIC RIGHTS AND RIGHTS OVER THE STOCK
28. Is the stock always freely transferable? Are there any legal limitations? Are there any restrictions on contractual limitations?
The legal framework governing the transferability of the shares in a limited liability company comprises rules for the transfer of shares to the current shareholder and the transfer to a third party different from the current

shareholders. Transfer from a current shareholder to a different shareholder of the company is generally allowed unless the by-laws state otherwise. Nevertheless, the Commercial Code requires the approval of the GM of the company for the transfer. It is important to stress that provisions governing the transfer of shares are not strict, therefore parties can negotiate different conditions and the by-laws can generally exclude the transferability of shares to a different shareholder. Transfer to a third party needs to be specifically approved in the by-laws. Additional requirements, such as the approval of a GM, might be stipulated. The Commercial Code sets out the general rule that if the by-laws contain no provisions on the transferability of shares to a third party, or specifically exclude the transferability of shares to third parties, the shareholders are not allowed to transfer their shares to a third party. A common feature for both types of transfers is that the Commercial Code does not grant a pre-emptive right to the current shareholders. This right might be constituted by the by-laws. If the transfer is conditioned by the approval of a GM, the absence of such approval causes ineffectiveness of the transfer. The transferability of registered shares of a joint stock company may be limited, but not excluded.

29. Are shareholders entitled to pledge their stock?
Shareholders in both limited liability companies and joint stock companies may pledge their shares/stocks by contract. The pledge is established as of the day of registration in the Commercial/Pledge Registry administered by Central Securities Depository of the Slovak Republic. The by-laws of a limited liability company may subject the pledge of shares to approval of a GM. This does not apply when by-laws specifically exclude the transferability of shares. Under such circumstances the shareholder may not pledge their shares.

30. Are there financial assistance issues to be considered and other prohibitions to be evaluated in the context of a leveraged buyout transaction?
The shareholders are generally entitled to pledge their shares in both limited liability and joint stock companies. Financial assistance for the purpose of acquisition of shares of the same company is generally forbidden in the Slovak legal system. The Commercial Code contains a general prohibition of providing advance payments, loans, credits or guarantees to a third person who is obtaining the company's shares. The only acceptable form of financial assistance is to acquire monetary resources from a financial institution. The regulation of financial assistance in the Slovak Republic, including the provision of security by a company for the purpose of acquisition of shares in the same company, is based on, but not identical to, directive 77/91/EC.

31. May a company buy back its own stock and, if so, under what circumstances and subject to which limitations?
A joint stock company may in general buy back its own shares if:
(i)   a GM approves it. Such approval is not necessary if the imminent

damages are being parried;

(ii) the act does not cause a decrease of the equity capital to under the amount specified by the Slovak Commercial Code; and

(iii) the company has sources for the creation of a special reserve fund (if required by law).

The company can only acquire its own shares when the emission rate is fully paid. In some cases a joint stock company may acquire its own shares without having to meet the above conditions (eg the company acquires the shares for the purpose of decreasing the registered capital, the company acquires the shares as legal successor entering into all rights of the previous owner of the shares, the company acquires the shares on the basis of the decision of a court in connection with the protection of minority shareholders, etc). However, in no case may the company hold its own shares for a period exceeding three years. This does not apply if the amount of shares of all the company's own stocks acquired by the company, including stock acquired by a person acting on behalf of the company, does not exceed 10 per cent of the registered capital of the company. In case of failure to transfer its own shares in the above-mentioned period, the company must decrease its registered capital by the sum equal to the amount of its own shares. If the company fails to fulfil this duty, the court may order the liquidation of the company.

A limited liability company may not buy back its own shares on the basis of a transfer agreement, but it may acquire its own shares in another way (eg as a universal legal successor of the previous owner of the share).

32. Is there a legal right to withdraw from the company and, if so, under what circumstances? How is the shareholders' stock valuated and paid in such a case?

According to Slovak law, the shareholders may not in general withdraw from the company on the basis of a unilateral act, except for some cases related to the company's transformations resulting in the change of the legal form of the company, provided that the shareholder who wishes to withdraw from the company voted at the GM against such transformation. The shareholder withdrawing from the company is entitled to a 'settlement share', the amount of which is calculated:

(i) on the basis of an appraisal issued by a court-appointed appraiser;

(ii) on the basis of information contained in the company's accounts; or

(iii) in another way stipulated in the project of transformation or in the company's articles of association, depending on the character of the transformation and legal form of the company prior to and after the transformation.

Moreover, each shareholder of a limited liability company is entitled to file a petition with the court for termination of their participation in the company if they cannot reasonably be required to remain in the company any longer. In such cases the shareholder is entitled to a 'settlement share' calculated on the basis of:

(i) an appraisal issued by a court-appointed appraiser;

(ii) information contained in the company's accounts; or

(iii) in another way stipulated in the company's articles of association.

33. In which circumstances can dividends be distributed among shareholders? Is it possible to exclude or limit the right of certain shareholders to dividends? Does a certain portion of the profits need to be set aside in a reserve fund where it cannot be distributed to the shareholders? Are advances on dividends allowed and, if so, under which circumstances? Can advances on dividends be reclaimed by the company?

The shareholders are entitled to the distribution of profit, also known as dividends. Such distribution is subject to the GM's approval, which is granted on the basis of the financial results of the company. The dividends are distributed among the shareholders proportionally to the amount of shares. Such proportionality is mandatory, unless the company had issued priority shares connected with the priority right regarding the profit share. It is a prevalent legal opinion that the right of the shareholders to a profit share may not be generally excluded.

The by-laws of a limited liability company may stipulate a different procedure for determination of the amount of the profit share for individual shareholders. The amount of the profit share may only be determined after appropriate financial means have been allocated to top up the reserve fund. A reserve fund is mandatorily formed by each limited liability company or joint stock company from its net profit, whereas in limited liability companies the amount of the reserve fund must be eventually at least 10 per cent of the company's registered capital and in joint stock companies at least 20 per cent of the company's registered capital.

The company may not distribute the profit if the company's equity capital, as stated in its ordinary or extraordinary accounts, is or, due to the distribution of profit, would be lower than the registered capital of the company, increased by: (i) the subscribed nominal value of shares, if the company's shares were subscribed in order to increase its registered capital, and the new registered capital was not entered in the Commercial Register at the day when the ordinary or extraordinary financial statements were drawn up; and (ii) such portion of the reserve or reserve funds which, under the law and its statutes, the company may not use for payment to shareholders. The Slovak legal system does not allow any form of advances on dividends.

34. What are the rights of shareholders in the case of an issue of new stock (increase of the company's corporate capital) (pre-emption rights)?

Each shareholder of a limited liability company has a priority (preferential) right to participate in the increase of registered capital if such capital is increased by monetary investment contributions, namely by committing themselves to increase their investment contributions. Such commitment may be undertaken by each shareholder in proportion to their shares, unless the by-laws provide otherwise. The priority right of shareholders to participate in an increase of the registered capital may be excluded by the by-laws.

In the case of increasing the company's corporate capital by the issuing of new stock, each shareholder of a joint stock company has a pre-emptive right to subscribe for a part of the company's new shares. Provided that shares are to be subscribed by monetary contributions, the procedure is performed proportionally to the current shares. The pre-emptive right of the shareholders may not be excluded in general, although there is an exception which allows a GM to issue a resolution to increase the registered capital and which restricts or excludes pre-emptive rights if there is a serious reason to do so. The GM is obliged to present the proper explanation for the procedure mentioned herein, which considerably affects the rights of shareholders. If the GM decides on excluding or restricting pre-emptive rights, the decision may affect only the shareholders of a certain type of stocks. The restriction or exclusion does not have to be ordered for all shareholders equally.

35. May minority shareholders ban or limit the company's capital structure in any manner?
The influence of the shareholders on the company's capital structure is to a great extent dependant on the company's by-laws in which the manner of the adoption of a certain resolution might be adjusted in accordance with the agreement between the shareholders themselves. If there is no such special agreement within the by-laws, general provisions of the Slovak Commercial Code shall apply. For instance, the voting on the decision to increase or reduce registered capital needs a two-thirds majority of votes at the company's general meeting. The minority shareholders might thus limit such a resolution only when the number of their votes exceeds one-third altogether.

36. Which are the financial assistance prohibitions in force?
Financial assistance for the purpose of the acquisition of shares of the same company is generally forbidden in the Slovak legal system. The Commercial Code includes the general prohibition of providing advanced payments, loans, credits or guarantees to a third person that is obtaining the company's shares.

The only acceptable form of financial assistance is to acquire the monetary resources from a financial institution.

37. Apart from publicly listed companies, in which cases (if any) are shareholders obligated to obtain an authorisation from, or provide information to, a public authority about events that have an impact on their stock interest in the company?
There are no specific obligations on the shareholders regarding obtaining authorisation or providing information. Under certain circumstances this duty belongs to the company, but never to the shareholder.

SHAREHOLDERS' RIGHTS IN THE CASE OF EXTRAORDINARY TRANSACTIONS AND/OR WINDING-UP

38. What rights are available to shareholders in the case of a sale of all or a substantial portion of the company's assets? In the case of a merger or de-merger?

A sale of the company's assets in the Slovak Republic does not imply any special rights for the company shareholders, except for a general right of the shareholders to claim for damages caused to the company by the statutory organ. However, the sale of the company's assets may be limited by the company's by-laws or, in the case of transactions between related parties, by the Slovak Commercial Code, whereas where there is limited liability the sale of a company's enterprise or its part is subject to the approval of a GM. Special rules apply for transactions between related parties, where any transfers of assets of a value of at least 10 per cent of the company's registered capital to a related party should be evaluated by a court-appointed appraiser.

In the case of a merger, the basic rights of the shareholders of a limited liability company are:

(i) the right to attend the GM that will pass a resolution on the merger;
(ii) the right to information (a shareholder must be informed by the directors of all aspects of the merger in advance with respective documentation, which includes the right to obtain a copy of the project merger, financial statements of all the involved companies and the common merger agreement);
(iii) the right to require the auditor's revision of the intended merger; and
(iv) the right to withdraw from the company (provided that the shareholder who wishes to withdraw from the company voted at the GM against such transformation).

The shareholder withdrawing from the company is entitled to a settlement share.

39. Which rights are available to shareholders in the case of conversion of the company into a European Company (SE) or into another type of company?

By virtue of the process of conversion, the company does not cease to exist, but the internal matters of the company are subject to change, as is the position of its shareholders. In this regard, it can be concluded that the rights of shareholders in the case of a conversion of the company into an SE or another type of company are very similar to those granted to shareholders within the national merger process.

40. Which rights are available to shareholders of a company in liquidation?

In the case of the liquidation of a company, each shareholder is entitled to a portion of the liquidation remainder (liquidation share). The amount of the liquidation share is generally determined proportionally to the shares owned by the shareholders. The by-laws of a limited liability company may stipulate a different method for determination of the amount of the liquidation share for individual shareholders.

41. Can shareholders cause the liquidation of the company? How?

The shareholders may generally cause the winding-up of the company either by agreeing on the winding-up of the company (or by voting at a GM of the company provided that the required majority of votes is reached) or by asking the relevant commercial court to decide on the winding-up of the company.

The court may decide on the winding-up of a company in cases specified by the Slovak Commercial Code (eg where no GM has been held for a year, bodies of the company were not established within the three-month period, the company loses its authorisation to perform business activities etc). The winding-up of the company in the above cases is followed by a liquidation process, which ends up with the distribution of the liquidation remainder (if any) to the shareholders and the removal of the company from the commercial register.

COMPANY GROUPS

42. Is the concept of 'group' recognised as such under specific legislation? What are the implications?

The concept of 'group' and its implications are described in the Slovak Commercial Code by specifying the terms such as concerted conduct, controlling and controlled person, and describing the relations between the controlling and controlled persons. The basic provisions aim to regulate the conduct of the controlled and controlling person and to minimise the undesirable effects of the relationship. The controlling person is the enterprise that possesses the majority of the votes on the basis of holding a majority of the shares. The controlled person is therefore characterised as the opposite of the controlling person. The Slovak Commercial Code distinguishes concentration, which is defined as the connection of at least two enterprises or the acquiring of direct or indirect control over one or more enterprise or over part of the enterprise. The term 'contractual holding' is not defined in the Slovak Commercial Code and the legal provision for such an institute is absent as well. The term 'factual concern' (holding) is also not defined specifically within the Commercial Code.

43. Does a controlling company have any particular duties *vis-à-vis* its controlled company shareholders?

The character of duties of the controlling company is specified in several acts as a result of acquiring the controlling contribution of the shares carrying voting rights. A controlling contribution obliges the person to propose a takeover bid. Thirty-three per cent of the shares carrying the voting rights acquired by one subject are considered to be a controlling contribution according to the Security Act.

The Stock Exchange Act stipulates the obligation to inform the issuer of the contribution on the voting rights of the shareholders who reach, exceed, decrease or transfer stocks of the issuer that are listed on the regulated market over or under five per cent, 10 per cent, 15 per cent, 20 per cent, 25 per cent, 30 per cent, 50 per cent and 75 per cent.

44. What are the rights of company shareholders when the controlling company puts in place actions and/or transactions that can be prejudicial the shareholders?

In addition to the above the controlling person shall compensate any damage suffered by the shareholders of the controlled person, and it shall do so separately from the obligation to provide compensation for damage to the controlled person.

45. What are the limitations, if any, to the possibility of owning reciprocal stock interests in companies?

According to Slovak law, the controlled companies may not have participations in the controlling person. This does not apply in the case of acquiring the shares as an inheritance or acquiring all rights and obligations instead of the person who was the holder of shares.

Spain

Gómez-Acebo & Pombo Fernando de las Cuevas

BASIC INFORMATION ON THE TYPES OF LIMITED LIABILITY COMPANIES AND ON THE RIGHTS OF SHAREHOLDERS
1. What types of companies enjoy limited liability? If more than one, which ones have shareholders, ie holders of share certificates? Which one is the most common? Which one is mostly used by foreign investors?

Companies that enjoy limited liability are the following: public limited companies; limited liability companies; co-partnership companies; *sociedades agrarias de transformación*; mutual guarantee schemes; cooperatives; and mutual insurance associations. In public limited companies, shares can be represented by means of certificates or book entries and both are considered to be moveable securities. In contrast, shares cannot be thus represented in limited liability companies. The direct upshot of this is that share transfers are straightforward, since ownership is transferred by simply handing over the share certificate. The type of company most frequently used in Spanish law by both Spanish and foreign investors is the limited liability company.

2. Are there minimum capital requirements and/or thin capitalisation rules in force?

The Royal Legislative Decree 1/2010, dated 2 July 2010, by means of which the Capital Companies Act is passed (LSC) (Capital Companies Act) provides that the share capital of a public limited company shall not be less than €60,000. In contrast, a limited liability company must have a minimum share capital of €3,000. Accordingly, the LSC provides for thin capitalisation rules that require a company to be wound up when, as a result of losses, the value of the share capital falls to less than half, unless appropriate measures are taken to increase or reduce the capital, as required.

3. Describe the types of shares that can be issued by a company and the different rights that they attribute to their owners, as well as any other financial instruments (bonds or other) and other instruments of a participatory nature in the company's capital that can also be issued by the company.

According to the Spanish legal system, capital companies can issue ordinary or privileged shares or stock; the first are those that attribute to their owners the standard rights and obligations inherent in shareholder status while the second class of shares or stock are those that confer on individuals certain advantages in relation to the rights of the ordinary shares. The LSC allows privileges to be created on corporate rights with the exception of voting rights and pre-emption rights. This law also prohibits the issuance of shares that attribute the right to receive interest. By law, holders of ordinary shares will have the following rights: the right to receive a share in the profit; the right to share in capital resulting from the process of liquidation; pre-emption rights over new shares and convertible bonds; the right to information; the right to attend and vote at general meetings (GMs). With respect to privileged shares, the existence of so-called non-voting shares or stock and redeemable shares should be noted (see question 7). Lastly, the LSC foresees the possibility for a company to issue convertible bonds. These bonds incorporate a creditor's right in favour of those who subscribe them, granting them the option to choose to continue as creditors or to convert their bonds into shares within the time periods and pursuant to the conversion ratio established by the issuing company.

4. Can a company have only one shareholder and still enjoy limited liability?

The LSC provides for the possibility of creating a single member public limited company or limited liability company. It must, however, be taken into account that if a company becomes a single member company due to fortuitous circumstances, the legislation in question provides that the sole shareholder shall assume personal, unlimited and several liability for the company debts contracted during the period of sole proprietorship if such circumstances have not been recorded in the Commercial Registry within six months from becoming a single member company. Once single membership has been recorded, the sole shareholder shall not be liable for any corporate debts contracted thereafter.

5. Are the rights of shareholders the same in any type of company?

In general, shareholders enjoy the same rights in both public limited companies and limited liability companies, but there are some specific differences. Firstly, differences can be established in relation to basic rights, such as voting rights. Secondly, in public limited companies, the by-laws can also stipulate that a minimum number of shares must be held to permit attendance at a GM. Finally, in limited liability companies, in order to adopt corporate resolutions, it is possible to require that the majority of the capital must be present at the GM and also the favourable vote of a specific number of shareholders.

6. What are the basic rights of any shareholder? Describe briefly the rights of minority shareholders and indicate which thresholds, if any, are required to allow the minority shareholders to exercise any such rights.

Spanish commercial law clearly states that shareholders shall have at least the following rights:
(i)   the right to share in the company profit;
(ii) the right to share in capital resulting from the process of liquidation;
(iii) pre-emption rights over the issuance of new shares and convertible

bonds, or preferential acquisition rights over new shares in capital increases (excluding increases for the issuance of free shares);

(iv) voting rights;

(v) the right to information;

(vi) the right to attend GMs; and

(vii)the right to challenge corporate resolutions.

It is important to note that the minority shareholders who represent one per cent of the share capital may request the directors to appoint a notary to attend the GM. Similarly, those shareholders who represent five per cent of the share capital are entitled to:

(i) request the directors or a judge to convene an extraordinary general shareholders' meeting;

(ii) request the judge to suspend corporate resolutions that have been challenged;

(iii) challenge resolutions adopted by the board of directors that are null and void or voidable, or those adopted by any other corporate administration body;

(iv) request the appointment of an auditor in companies that are subject to external control; and

(v) object to the waiving and/or the reaching of a settlement in the case of a liability action against the directors.

Moreover, shareholders representing 20 per cent of the share capital are entitled to ask for government intervention to ensure the continuity of a company in dissolution. Lastly, shareholders who represent 25 per cent of the share capital may overrule the chairman's refusal to provide information required for the GM.

7.   Do all shareholders enjoy the same rights or can some shareholders be attributed specific rights, whether by reason of the particular class of stock owned or other? Are such rights generally provided for at the level of the company's by-laws and/or in shareholders agreements?

As explained above, the owners of non-voting shares or stock enjoy a number of privileges associated with the rights of ordinary shares. They are shares or stock that are characterised by attributing more economic rights to their owners in exchange for the suppression of their voting rights. The LSC has established a quantitative limit on the issuance of non-voting shares or stock, which can only be issued for a nominal amount that does not exceed half of the share capital, for limited liability companies, or half of the paid-in share capital, for public limited companies. The law recognises that in addition to all the rights inherent in their status as shareholders (with the exception of voting rights), the owners of these shares or stock also have the following rights:

(i) the right to receive a fixed or variable minimum annual dividend as established in the by-laws, and approved by the GM provided there is a profit to be distributed;

(ii) priority in receiving repayment of the amount paid up thereon, before any amount is paid out on the other shares in the event of the company's liquidation; and

(iii) the advantage of not being affected by capital reductions due to losses, provided the reduction does not exceed the nominal value of the remaining shares.

Another type of privileged shares are redeemable shares. These may only be issued by listed companies and are issued for their subsequent redemption by the company in predetermined conditions that must be stipulated in the by-laws. The issuance of these shares establishes a temporary corporate link between the shareholder and the company given that redemption leads to the restitution of the investment carried out. The LSC provides that these shares can be issued for an amount not exceeding one-quarter of the share capital.

8. May the rights of shareholders, generally speaking, be limited, modified, suppressed or waived in any way? If so, how? Are such modifications or limitations provided for in the company's by-laws and/or in shareholders agreements?

The LSC establishes that when it is in the company's interest, the GM, when deciding to carry out a capital increase, may agree upon the full or partial suppression of pre-emption rights. Similarly, in the case of listed companies the pre-emption rights of holders of non-voting shares can be excluded or limited. In general, a shareholder cannot be deprived of voting rights unless they hold non-voting shares or stock. There are, however, certain instances in which shareholders can be deprived of their voting right such as when payment of their called-up share capital in a public limited company is overdue. With respect to the right of attendance, the LSC establishes that the by-laws of public limited companies can limit the exercising of this right by requiring a minimum number of shares or by conditioning attendance on the prior identification of the shareholder. In limited liability companies, however, no limitations or conditions can be placed on this right. Lastly, it is important to note that the shareholders' right to information is a right that cannot be limited or excluded, both in the case of public limited companies and limited liability companies.

GENERAL MEETING OF SHAREHOLDERS (GM) AND VOTING RIGHTS

9. Which decisions are reserved to the competence of the GM?

The GM of shareholders is the competent body to adopt resolutions that enable the company to acquire certain goods, own shares or shares in the controlling company. It is also entitled to review the management of the company, to approve the annual accounts and pass resolutions on the allocation of profit and loss. The GM can also approve the company's liquidation balance sheet, appointments and dismissals of board members and exercise corporate liability action of other corporate bodies. The GM is also responsible for adopting resolutions to amend the by-laws or change the corporate structure. Lastly, the LSC confers on the GM the competence to pass the resolution to wind up the company.

10. How does a shareholder participate in a GM? Are there any limitations to having a minimum number of shares? May a shareholder delegate attendance to another shareholder or to the board? May a shareholder obtain assistance from the courts or any other governmental body to intervene in a GM or to cause one to be held in some particular cases?

The LSC provides that the by-laws of public limited companies may make the right to attend GMs conditional upon prior evidencing by the shareholder of their status as such, but under no circumstances may they prevent the exercise of such a right by the holders of registered shares and shares represented by means of book entries whose shares are entered in the relevant registers five days prior to the date on which the meeting is to be held, or by holders of bearer shares who, the same length of time in advance, have deposited their shares in the manner established in the by-laws or according to the law. In contrast to limited liability companies, in public limited companies the by-laws can require a minimum number of shares to be held to confer the right to attend, provided the required number does not exceed one-thousandth of the share capital. A shareholder who has the right of attendance may be represented at the GM by another person who does not have to be a shareholder. This power of representation can be limited in the by-laws. The LSC also foresees the 'public invitation to appoint as proxy for public limited companies'; by means of which the directors, the custodian institutions for the share certificates or the institutions responsible for the book entries register invite appointment of themselves or a third party as proxy. In certain cases, LSC provides that shareholders may request the Judge of First Instance of the town where the company's registered office is located to convene a GM of shareholders.

11. May a GM be called and held at the request of any shareholder? Is there a threshold regarding the percentage of the stock interest owned in the company that may entitle a shareholder to such a right?

The commercial law currently in force establishes that shareholders representing at least five per cent of the share capital are entitled to request the directors to convene a GM of shareholders.

12. May a shareholder bring up an issue to be resolved upon and put it to a vote if it is not included on the agenda? May a shareholder require more information from the GM and/or the board, concerning the agenda of the GM, to be put in a better position to exercise their vote?

In principle, only shareholders of a public limited company owning, at least, more than five per cent of the share capital may include one or more issue on the agenda of the GM. Apart from this case, a shareholder cannot bring up an issue that is not included on the agenda. However, when a GM takes the form of a universal meeting a shareholder may bring up any issue they choose. The issue of withdrawal of the directors can be brought up at any time, even when not included on the agenda. The shareholders' right to information can be exercised in writing, prior to (up to seven days earlier for public limited companies) the GM or verbally during the meeting. It merely allows the right to question given that initially only clarifications can be sought, or to information related to the items on the agenda. In the case of listed companies this right to information is broader, and not only comprises the items on the agenda, but also any issue included in the information provided by the company to the Spanish Securities and Exchange Commission (CNMV) since the date on which the last shareholders' meeting was held.

13. May a GM be held by telecommunication means and/or by correspondence (ie by written consent)?

The current legislation does not contemplate the possibility for GMs to be held by videoconference. However, most case law considers it legitimate for a GM to take place in this way when held in several different rooms that are linked by videoconference, and which are located in the registered offices (some scholars also sustain that GMs may be held out of rooms situated in different locations); provided the audiovisual media installed is adequate to effectively enable shareholders to participate and vote in real time on the items on the agenda, and provided there is no unfair discrimination when assigning the shareholders to different rooms. The Spanish legal system does not permit so-called virtual general meetings which occur when each shareholder is located in a different geographical area, but are linked by videoconference or any other media that allows, among others, for simultaneous communication and the instantaneous sending and receiving of documents, in order to control the shareholders' eligibility to attend. However, other scholars consider virtual universal GMs to be admissible considering that this type of meeting is valid irrespective of the place where it is held if all the shareholders are in agreement.

14. Are voting rights always proportionate to the stock held by each shareholder or can they vary by share class?

Whit regard to public limited companies, the LSC requires voting rights to be proportionate to the shares or stock held by each shareholder, given that cumulative voting is prohibited. However, this element of proportionality falls short to a certain extent since the LSC also provides that the by-laws of public limited companies may establish the number of votes that a single shareholder or companies belonging to a single group are entitled to cast. On the contrary, The LSC makes it clear that in principle each share of a limited liability company confers on its holder the right to cast one vote but the by-laws may provide for the issuance of cumulative voting shares/stock.

15. Are there non-voting shares? Is there a maximum percentage of capital represented by non-voting shares?

As explained above, Spanish law allows the issuance of non-voting shares or stock (see question 8).

16. Can shareholders group their shares in order to exercise their voting rights (eg, by trust, shareholders agreement or otherwise)?

The LSC provides that a shareholder may voluntarily limit its freedom to vote and be contractually bound, in conjunction with other shareholders, to vote at GMs in a specific sense. These are the so-called shareholders' syndicates or shareholders' agreements, which have full force in the internal relationships of those who are a party to them, but under no circumstances in relation to the company, therefore they cannot be enforced against the company. In the case of listed companies, these agreements must be communicated to both the company and the CNMV and the agreement must be published as a relevant fact.

17. Under what circumstances can a shareholder challenge the resolutions adopted by the GM? Are there thresholds concerning the stock interest owned to be able to bring such a claim?

According to the provisions of the LSC, the resolutions adopted by the GM can be challenged when they are contrary to the law, to the by-laws or when they are detrimental to the company's interests, to the benefit of one or several shareholders or third parties. Resolutions that are contrary to the law shall be null and void whilst the others will be voidable. Any shareholder, director, and any third party who proves a legitimate interest, is entitled to challenge the resolutions. In contrast, voidable resolutions may only be challenged by shareholders attending the GM whose opposition to the resolution was recorded in the minutes of the meeting, or by shareholders who did not attend the meeting and those who have been illegally deprived of voting, as well as directors.

18. What are the terms and procedures to challenge a resolution of the GM?

The term for challenging a resolution expires one year after the date on which it is adopted or from the date of its publication in the *Boletín Oficial del Registro Mercantil* (BORME) (Commercial Registry Official Gazette). Resolutions that, due to their cause or content, are contrary to public order are exempt from this rule. In the case of voidable resolutions, this expiry period is reduced to 40 days. With respect to the procedure, the LSC provides that the challenging of company resolutions shall be done according to the ordinary trial proceedings and provisions contained in the Spanish Civil Procedure Act.

SHAREHOLDERS' RIGHTS VERSUS DIRECTORS AND DUTIES OF OTHER CORPORATE BODIES IN THE COMPANY

19. What is the procedure for the appointment/replacement/revocation of directors and of statutory auditors, if any?

The first directors shall be appointed when the company is incorporated and shall be recorded in the deed of incorporation. Subsequent appointments are generally carried out by the GM. The LSC provides for two exceptions related to the appointment of members of the board of directors. Firstly, the law provides an optional system for the proportional representation of minorities on the board of directors. For this purpose, shares which are voluntarily pooled so that they constitute an amount of share capital greater than or equal to that which results from dividing the total share capital by the number of members of the board, shall have the right to appoint those which, exceeding whole fractions, result from the corresponding proportion. Secondly, the law contemplates the 'co-optation method' which is used to cover early vacancies on the board, granting this body the faculty to appoint, from amongst the shareholders, the persons who will provisionally fill the vacancies until the next GM. Auditors are generally appointed by the GM. However, if companies legally required to appoint an auditor have not appointed one within the mandatory period, the directors or any other shareholder shall resort to the Registrar who will appoint one.

20. May shareholders challenge the resolutions of the board of directors? Is there a minimum percentage of capital required to challenge a board resolution?

The legislation currently in force provides that directors and shareholders who represent five per cent of the share capital are entitled to challenge the resolutions of the board of directors, irrespective of the reason.

21. Are shareholders entitled to bring a legal action against the directors of the company? In which circumstances? Please describe briefly the principles of directors' liability.

There are two types of action pursuant to Spanish law: action for corporate liability and action for individual liability. The aim of corporate liability action is to seek compensation for damages suffered by a company as a result of the directors' negligent conduct. The company itself is initially responsible for bringing this action, and secondly the shareholders, as parties with an indirect interest in protecting the company's assets. In order to bring this action, the LSC requires that the shareholders represent at least five per cent of the share capital. In contrast to corporate liability action, individual liability action seeks to compensate the damages caused directly to the assets/patrimony of shareholders or third parties as a consequence of the directors' negligent conduct. Shareholders and third parties who suffer damages as a result of the directors' negligent conduct are entitled to bring this action. The directors are subject to a civil liability regime that seeks to compensate any pecuniary damages caused by their negligence. Their liability is linked to the damages caused due to conduct contrary to the law and the by-laws, and due to actions carried out without the diligence required in carrying out their obligations. Thus, failure to comply with the legally required level of diligence will give rise to the subsequent obligation to compensate for damages. The law provides that all the members of the administration body shall be jointly and severally liable for damages caused as a result of the detrimental action or resolution adopted. Those members who prove grounds for their exoneration will be exempt from liability. Lastly, it should be noted that not only does the law hold liable those who form part of the administration body but also any party who acts as a *de facto* director of the company.

22. What are the rights in connection with transactions where the directors have a conflict of interest situation?

The legislation currently in force requires that directors notify the board of directors of any direct or indirect conflict they may have with the company's interests. In the case of conflict, the director in question shall abstain from taking part in the transaction. Lastly, information on all the situations of conflicts of interests in which the company directors are involved will be included in the annual report.

INFORMATION RIGHTS ON THE COMPANY'S BUSINESS

23. What information may be requested by the shareholders from the board concerning the general state of the company's business or any specific transaction? Are information rights different depending on the number of shares owned? Are shareholders entitled to receive written information before, during or after the GM about the meeting agenda and to what extent? Is it possible for a shareholder to obtain a copy of the minutes of the GM?

Shareholders may request reports or clarifications concerning any of the items on the agenda of a GM, and in listed companies, as mentioned previously, they may request reports or clarifications about the information produced by the company since the last GM. This information right, as stated previously, may be exercised in writing, prior to the GM and/or verbally during the meeting. It is not an absolute right since it is not a mechanism for obstructing and paralysing the company's business. Neither does it enable an isolated shareholder to examine the accounts and the company books. It should be understood as a right to query, in the sense that a shareholder cannot ask for documents to be provided, but rather ask only for clarifications or information on particular items on the agenda. Although the information would in practice be requested and provided in print, the Spanish Securities Market Act (*Ley del Mercado de Valores*) (LMV) requires listed public limited companies to allow the exercising of the information right on technical, IT and telematic media, and they must therefore have a web page to allow the shareholders to exercise the information right in this manner. The LSC provides that shareholders shall have the right to freely and immediately obtain a copy of the relevant documents relating to the annual accounts, and the right in the more significant business transactions to examine the preliminary documents or to ask for the documents be sent to them. The Commercial Code establishes that those shareholders and persons who have attended the GM representing other shareholders have the right to obtain a certificate of the resolutions and minutes of the GM at any time.

24. Do shareholders have the right/duty to resolve in the GM upon matters which were not on the agenda?

Since items that are not included on the agenda cannot in principle be discussed at the GM, shareholders do not have the right or the duty to resolve upon those matters. Cases such as the withdrawal of directors and GMs in the form of a universal meeting are exempt from this general rule.

25. Are shareholders entitled to inspect the corporate books and/or any other corporate or accounting documents? To what extent? Can they do it through external counsel or advisors?

After the GM at which the annual accounts are to be approved has been convened, any shareholder may immediately obtain from the company, free of charge, the management report, the audit report and the documents that are to be submitted for approval by the GM. The shareholders can request the Registrar to appoint auditors when, in the case of companies required to submit their annual accounts for examination, the GM has failed to adopt a resolution to appoint them during the financial year to be audited, or when the appointed persons have not accepted their appointment or were unable to fulfil their obligations.

SHAREHOLDERS' AGREEMENTS

26. Are shareholders' agreements validly enforceable? What are their typical contents and term of duration? Are they enforceable by or against third parties and, if so, to what extent?

In the main, the regulations in force acknowledge the validity and legality of the shareholders' agreements provided they do not contravene the essential rules or principles of common law or commercial law. The LSC establishes that if these agreements are not included in the by-laws or in the deed of incorporation they will not be enforceable against the company. They are agreements therefore that are only enforceable at an internal level, ie between the parties, and failure to abide by them merely generates the typical consequences of a breach of contract. Even though the law makes no provision with respect to third parties, the majority of scholars are of the view that these agreements cannot be enforced against third parties. It is important to note that in the case of listed companies, the current legislation establishes that the agreement is not validly enforceable until it has been duly communicated, filed and published. The shareholders may decide the duration of the agreement but should they fail to do so, it shall be indefinite and termination of the agreement shall be governed by the rules applicable to contracts.

27. Do shareholders' agreements have to be disclosed to the public or registered in any public registry?

The legislation in force does not impose any obligation with respect to the publication or registration of shareholders' agreements except in the case of listed companies. The LMV establishes the obligation to immediately inform the CNMV and the company itself of the entering into, extension or amendment of a shareholders' agreement that affects any of the following: (i) the exercising of the voting rights in the GM of a listed public limited company; and/or (ii) the limitations or conditioning of the free transfer of shares or convertible bonds issued by this type of company. A copy of the clauses of the document in which the shareholders' agreement is recorded must be attached to the communication sent to the CNMV. When the listed company is an insurance company, a pension fund management company or a credit institution, the communication must also be sent to the competent supervisory bodies. Thereafter, the document recording the shareholders' agreement must be filed at the Commercial Registry corresponding to the company's registered offices. Finally, the shareholders' agreement must be published as a relevant fact. At the request of any of the interested parties, the CNMV may agree not to publish a shareholders' agreement or part of it and dispense with communicating it to the company itself. The CNMV's decision must be reasoned and must establish how long the agreement can be kept secret among the interested parties.

ECONOMIC RIGHTS AND RIGHTS OVER THE STOCK
28. Is the stock always freely transferable? Are there any legal limitations? Are there any restrictions on contractual limitations?
Given that shares or stock interests in public limited companies are movable securities, they are essentially transferable. The LSC establishes that the transfer of shares is free in principle but restrictions can be set on free transferability, provided such restrictions are applied to nominative shares and provided they are imposed expressly in accordance with the by-laws. The law also provides that the statutory restrictions that render shares practically non-transferable will be considered null and void, and that conditions can only be placed on their transferability when reference is made in the by-laws to the grounds for denying their transferral. Shares can be freely transferred in limited liability companies (unless otherwise stipulated in the by-laws) when carried out *inter vivos* between shareholders and in favour of a shareholder's spouse, ascendant or descendent or in favour of companies belonging to the same group as the transferor. For the rest of transfers *inter vivos* there is some restriction on free transferability since the law establishes pre-emption rights in favour of the other shareholders. The law also establishes that the statutory clauses whereby the transfer of shares *inter vivos* is made practically free, will be null and void. Clauses wherein a shareholder who offers all or part of their shares is obliged to transfer a different number of shares than those offered will also be null and void. Limited liability companies are allowed to voluntarily make their shares non-transferable provided the by-laws acknowledge the right of withdrawal. Neither shares nor stock interests can be transferred until the company or the capital increase resolution has been recorded at the Commercial Registry.

29. Are shareholders entitled to pledge their stock?
Shares in the form of securities can be pledged. To constitute the pledge, the essential pledge requirements established by common law must necessarily be met and are as follows:
(i) it is constituted to guarantee the fulfilment of a relevant obligation; (ii)

the pledged goods/property belongs to the pledgor;
(iii) the pledgor is entitled to freely dispose of their property and failing this, be legally empowered to do so;
(iv) the pledged property is placed in possession of the creditor or a third party, by common agreement; and
(v) the date of the pledge is recorded in a public document.

30. Are there financial assistance issues to be considered and other prohibitions to be evaluated in the context of a leveraged buyout transaction?

In Spain, the rules on financial assistance are more restrictive than those of other European countries. Without exception, a company may not advance funds, grant loans, extend guarantees nor provide any kind of financial assistance for the acquisition of its own shares or shares in its controlling company by third parties. Consequently, in leveraged buyouts (LBOs) it is necessary to create structures that do not contravene the prohibition against a company to provide financial assistance. In this respect, case law and the scarce number of court rulings in relation to this issue (specifically, the Ruling of Provincial Court of Madrid, dated 9 January 2007) consider that the merging of the newly incorporated company (Newco) and the target company after the acquisition, but prior to commencing repayment of the debt is the appropriate procedure in order to preclude the application of the financial assistance regulations, it being understood that a merger sufficiently protects the interests of parties that could be affected by these transactions (mainly shareholders and creditors). For this reason, forward and reverse merger LBOs have consistently been carried out in Spain on an almost exclusive basis as the means of accomplishing these transactions. In this respect, recently enacted Law 3/2009 regulates mergers carried out in the context of an LBO, specifying the information requirements and necessitating an independent expert's report to enable creditors and minority shareholders to be duly informed when exercising the rights to which they are legally entitled in a merger process. In our opinion, Law 3/2009 serves to ratify the assertion that a merger precludes the application of the Spanish regulations of prohibition against a company providing financial assistance.

31. May a company buy back its own stock and, if so, under what circumstances and subject to which limitations?

The LSC provides that a public limited company may acquire its own shares and those issued by its parent company provided the following three requirements are met. Firstly, that the share acquisition has been authorised by the company in a GM, by means of a resolution establishing the manner of acquisition, the maximum number of shares to be acquired, the minimum and maximum acquisition price and the duration of the authorisation, which shall not, under any circumstances, exceed five years. When shares in the controlling company are the object of the acquisition, the authorisation must also be granted by that company in a GM. When the object of the acquisition consists of shares that will be given directly to employees or directors of the company, or as a result of option rights held by them, the GM resolution must indicate that the authorisation is granted for that purpose. Secondly, that the acquisition, including the shares previously acquired by the company or person acting in their own name but on the company's behalf, and held in portfolio, does not result in the reduction of its net assets (*patrimonio neto*) to below the amount of share capital plus the mandatory legal reserves. Lastly, that the nominal value of the shares acquired directly or indirectly, added to the value of the shares already held by the acquiring company and its subsidiaries and, if applicable, the controlling company and its subsidiaries, does not exceed 20 per cent or, in the case of a listed company, 10 per cent of the paid-in share capital. The acquisition by the company of partially paid-in own shares shall be null and void, except when the acquisition is free of charge, and the acquisition of shares entailing the obligation to render ancillary services shall also be null and void. In the case of limited liability companies, the derivative acquisition of own shares is permitted where it forms part of the transfer of all outstanding shares, is a gift or is done in consequence of judicial execution to satisfy a judgment in favour of the company against the owner of the share. Derivative acquisition is also permitted when own shares are acquired in the execution of a resolution to reduce the share capital, adopted by the GM. In addition, it is also permitted when company shares or stock interests are acquired as provided in Article 109.3 LSC. Lastly, the LSC permits limited liability companies to acquire own stock when the acquisition has been authorised by the GM, when it is to be charged to company profit or freely available reserves and when its object is:

(i)   to acquire the shares of a shareholder who has withdrawn from or who has been expelled from the company;

(ii) to acquire the shares due to the application of a clause restricting their transfer; and

(iii) to acquire shares transferred *mortis causa*.

The acquired shares shall be redeemed within a period of three years.

32. Is there a legal right to withdraw from the company and, if so, under what circumstances? How is the shareholders' stock valued and paid in such a case?

The LSC regulates the right of the shareholders to withdraw from the company when certain legal or statutory causes concur (in the case of limited liability companies). Legal causes of withdrawal common to both public limited and limited liability companies:

(i)   the change of the corporate purpose;

(ii) extending or renewing the company;

(iii) the creation, modification or early cancellation of ancillary services, except as otherwise provided in the by-laws; and

(iv) the conversion of the company and the relocation of the registered offices abroad.

In a limited liability company, changing the share transfer regime also constitutes legal cause for withdrawal. In addition to the legal causes for withdrawal, the LSC provides that the by-laws may establish other causes for withdrawal. With respect to the valuation of a withdrawn shareholder's shares or stock, the legislation in force provides that they shall be reimbursed for the value that may be agreed between the withdrawn shareholder and the company. If the shareholder fails to reach an agreement with the company the Commercial Registry shall appoint an auditor who is not the company's auditor, to determine the reasonable value of the shares or stock.

33. In which circumstances can dividends be distributed among shareholders? Is it possible to exclude or limit the right of certain shareholders to dividends? Does a certain portion of the profits need to be set aside in a reserve fund where it cannot be distributed to the shareholders? Are advances on dividends allowed and, if so, under which circumstances? Can advances on dividends be reclaimed by the company?

The legislation in question establishes that once the conditions provided by the law and the by-laws have been met, dividends may only be distributed if charged to profit generated in that financial year or to freely disposable reserves, if the value of the company's net assets does not fall, or as a consequence of the dividend distribution is not reduced to less than the share capital. To these effects the profit attributed directly to shareholders' equity may not be directly or indirectly distributed. The legislation also imposes on companies the obligation to create a legal reserve, assigning to it an amount equal to at least 10 per cent of that year's profit, up to 20 per cent of the share capital. It should be taken into account that in addition to these reserves, the companies may also create statutory and voluntary reserves. Statutory reserves are constituted and governed by means of the by-laws, while the voluntary reserves are constituted by means of a resolution adopted at the GM and consequently the company may freely dispose of them.

34. What are the rights of shareholders in the case of an issue of new stock (increase of the company's corporate capital) (pre-emption rights)?

When there is a capital increase involving the issuance of new shares or stock, the shareholders have a pre-emption right to acquire new shares. This right is applicable to any capital increase by issuing new shares which entail monetary contributions. The value of the new shares or stock attributable to each shareholder must be proportionate to the nominal value of the shares they already own. Lastly, the company has to set a deadline to exercise this right that shall be no less than one month, and 15 days in the case of listed companies.

35. May minority shareholders ban or limit the company's capital structure in any manner?

In principle, statutory changes related to capital increases and decreases are adopted by the GM with a majority vote. Consequently, minority shareholders may not limit or prevent such changes from being carried out. However, when the increase is to be carried out by raising the nominal value the unanimous consent of the shareholders is necessarily required, except when the increase is charged in its entirety to company reserves or profit. Therefore, in this case, since the unanimous vote of the shareholders is required, the minority shareholders can limit or prevent the increase from taking place.

36. Which are the financial assistance prohibitions in force?

The company may not advance funds, grant loans, extend guarantees or provide any kind of financial assistance for the acquisition of its own shares or shares in its controlling company by third parties. This prohibition is not applicable to businesses intended to make it easier for the company employees to acquire shares in the company or shares in a group company.

Neither is the prohibition applicable to transactions carried out by banks or other credit institutions in the framework of ordinary transactions that are included in the corporate purpose, which are defrayed by charging them to the company's freely disposable assets. The company must set up a reserve in the shareholders' equity balance, equivalent to the sum of the credits recorded under assets.

37. Apart from publicly listed companies, in which cases (if any) are shareholders obligated to obtain an authorisation from, or provide information to, a public authority about events that have an impact on their stock interest in the company?

There are no cases in which the shareholders are obligated to obtain an authorisation from, or provide information to, a public authority about events that have an impact on their stock interest in the company.

SHAREHOLDERS' RIGHTS IN THE CASE OF EXTRAORDINARY TRANSACTIONS AND/OR WINDING-UP

38. What rights are available to shareholders in the case of a sale of all or a substantial portion of the company's assets? In the case of a merger or de-merger?

In cases of mergers and the total assignment of assets and liabilities, the shareholders have a right to information. With respect to mergers, when a GM is convened the directors have to make a series of documents available to the shareholders for examination, which include the joint merger project and merger reports from the directors of each of the companies. In both cases, the law requires the merger resolution or total assignment of the assets and liabilities to be communicated to the shareholders either by notifying each one of them individually or by publishing the announcement in the BORME and in a newspaper that is widely distributed in the province where the registered offices are located. Thus, in both cases the shareholders have the right to challenge the relevant resolution when the transaction has not been carried out in accordance with the applicable legal provisions. Lastly, in the case of intra-Community cross-border mergers the shareholders of the Spanish companies involved, who vote against the resolution in favour of the merger in which the resulting company will have its registered office in a different member state, may withdraw from the company pursuant to the provisions of the LSC.

39. Which rights are available to shareholders in the case of conversion of the company into a European Company (SE) or into another type of company?

In the case of the conversion of the company into another type of company, in principle the shareholders have a right to information. When convening the GM at which the conversion resolution is to be debated, the directors must make a series of documents available to the shareholders, such as the balance sheet of the company to be converted and a report on the significant changes in the net assets (*situación patrimonial*) that may subsequently take place. The adoption of the conversion resolution must also be communicated to the shareholders, either by notifying each one of them individually or by publishing the announcement in the BORME and in a newspaper that is widely distributed in the province where the registered offices are located. The law confers on the shareholders the right to challenge the conversion once it has been registered. This right may be exercised within a period of three months from the date on which the conversion was registered. It is also worth noting that shareholders who did not vote in favour of the resolution may withdraw from the company being converted, pursuant to the provisions of the LSC.

40. Which rights are available to shareholders of a company in liquidation?

In the case of a company in liquidation, shareholders have the right to information which consists of the liquidators periodically updating them on the status of the liquidation process. The final balance sheet approved by the GM must be published in the BORME and in a newspaper that is widely distributed in the province where the registered offices are located. The balance sheet can be challenged by any shareholder who considers it to be detrimental to him. Shareholders are also entitled to receive a share of the liquidation price based on their shares or stock interest in the share capital. Lastly, shareholders may bring a liability action against liquidators who have caused detriment through fraudulent or seriously negligent conduct when carrying out their duties.

41. Can shareholders cause the liquidation of the company? How?

The shareholders of a company cannot carry out its liquidation since that is a responsibility that corresponds to the liquidators. However, shareholders can trigger the winding-up of a company by adopting a resolution at the GM.

COMPANY GROUPS

42. Is the concept of 'group' recognised as such under specific legislation? What are the implications?

Article 42 of the Commercial Code contains a definition of the concept of 'group'. The most immediate consequence of this concept is that a controlling company of a group of companies is obligated to draw up consolidated annual accounts and a management report, in accordance with said Commercial Code.

43. Does a controlling company have any particular duties *vis-à-vis* its controlled company shareholders?

In Spain, the relationship between dependent and controlling companies is governed by the duty of loyalty. The controlling company shall therefore exercise its influence observing the corporate interest or common purpose and the legitimate interests of the rest of the shareholders. Consequently, the influence of the controlling company will not be acceptable (even when no detriment is caused to the dependant company) when it does not conform to the common corporate purpose established in the by-laws.

44. What are the rights of company shareholders when the controlling company puts in place actions and/or transactions that can be prejudicial to the shareholders?

Current legislation does not provide how shareholders should proceed when the controlling company carries out actions or transactions that may be detrimental to them.

45. What are the limitations, if any, to the possibility of owning reciprocal stock interests in companies?

Reciprocal holdings exceeding 10 per cent of the total capital of the companies involved may not be established. Banned reciprocal stock interests comprise not only direct stock in both companies, but also those that can be established indirectly, ie through subsidiaries. Any company that itself, or through its subsidiaries, holds more than 10 per cent of the capital of another company shall immediately communicate this circumstance to the investee company. The applicable legislation establishes the obligation to reduce such stock interests until they do not exceed the legal limits. The time period for reducing the stock interest is one year from the date of notification, except in the case of stock interests acquired in what are considered to be exceptional circumstances such as the legitimate acquisition of own stock, in which case the time period is extended to three years.

Switzerland

Lenz & Staehelin David Ledermann & Andreas Rötheli

BASIC INFORMATION ON THE TYPES OF LIMITED LIABILITY COMPANIES AND ON THE RIGHTS OF SHAREHOLDERS
1. What types of companies enjoy limited liability? If more than one, which ones have shareholders, ie, holders of share certificates? Which one is the most common? Which one is mostly used by foreign investors?

In Switzerland there are three types of companies which truly enjoy limited liability: the corporation limited by shares (*société anonyme* or SA/*Aktiengesellschaft* or AG) (the Corporation), the limited liability company (*société à responsabilité limitée* or Sàrl/*Gesellschaft mit beschränkter* Haftung or GmbH) (the LLC) and the Cooperative (*société coopérative*/Genossenschaft).

With a few notable exceptions, the Cooperative is nowadays rarely used in Switzerland to conduct profit-driven commercial activities as its capital and governance structure are generally ill-suited to this type of activity.

The Corporation and the LLC are the most common forms of limited liability companies in Switzerland. These forms are widely used across all industries to conduct all types of profit-driven commercial activities, from a pure holding activity to heavy industrial production.

The form of the Corporation is by far more prevalent than the form of the LLC. Due to a recent modernisation of the provisions of the Swiss code of obligations governing the LLC, this form of company is becoming more popular. Because its governance structure is simpler than the governance structure of the Corporation, Swiss subsidiaries of large international groups are increasingly being structured as LLCs.

Both the Corporation and the LLC have a stated capital divided in shares (for the Corporation) or in equity quotas (for the LLC), which will be referred to as the 'shares'.

2. Are there minimum capital requirements and/or thin capitalisation rules in force?

Swiss law requires the Corporation to have a minimum stated capital of CHF 100,000. At the time of incorporation, 20 per cent of the stated capital of a Corporation or CHF 50,000, whichever is higher, has to be paid up by the founders. There is no upper limit to the stated capital of a Corporation.

Swiss law requires the LLC to have a minimum stated capital of CHF 20,000. At the time of incorporation, 20 per cent of the stated capital of an LLC or CHF 20,000, whichever is higher, has to be paid up by the founders.

Swiss general corporate law does not provide for any thin capitalisation rules. On the other hand, Swiss tax authorities will deny the deductibility of interests paid by a company to its shareholders to the extent the company's debt equity ratio exceeds a certain level. Such ratio will depend on the type of assets composing the equity of the considered company. However, specific rules provide for minimum capital requirements to financial institutions such as banks, insurance companies and collective investment schemes. Minimum capital requirements also stem from Swiss listing rules.

3. Describe the types of shares that can be issued by a company and the different rights that they attribute to their owners, as well as any other financial instruments (bonds or other) and other instruments of a participatory nature in the company's capital that can also be issued by the company.

The Corporation may issue either bearer shares or registered shares. It is possible for a Corporation to have both types of shares outstanding at the same time. The shares issued by a Corporation have a par value. The minimum par value of a share is CHF 0.01.

Unless the articles of association provide otherwise, the voting rights attached to a share are proportional to the par value of such share. It is not possible to issue shares without voting rights. Each share grants to its holder a right to a portion of dividend and liquidation proceeds proportional to its par value. It is not possible to issue shares with absolutely no right to the dividend or liquidation proceeds. A Corporation may issue different classes of shares. Each class of shares can have a different par value. However, the par value of the class of shares with the highest par value cannot exceed 10 times the par value of the class of shares with the lowest par value. The articles of association of the Corporation can provide that each share, irrespective of its par value and its class, has only one vote (one share one vote). In such a case, the class of shares with the lowest par value will be considered as benefiting from a voting privilege since for a lower investment it will grant its holder with the same voting right as the higher par value class of shares. The rights and privileges attached to each class of shares are set forth in the articles of association of the company.

The most commonly granted privileges are preferred rights of dividend or preferred right of liquidation, but it is also possible to provide other types of rights and privileges such as a privilege on the first subscription on a future issuance of shares.

The Corporation can issue participation certificates and profit sharing certificates. Participation certificates have a par value and form part of the stated capital of the company. The holders of participation certificates are entitled to the financial rights and privileges set forth in the articles of association. Participation certificates have no voting rights and cannot be granted any of the social rights typically attached to shares. Because participation certificates can be granted the same financial rights as ordinary shares, they are oftentimes referred to as non-voting shares. It is possible to issue different classes of participation certificates.

Profit sharing certificates have no par value and do not form part of the stated capital of the company. The rights and privileges attached to the profit sharing certificates are set forth in the articles of association. Profit sharing certificates can only grant a right to a share of the dividend or liquidation proceeds or the right to subscribe new shares.

The Corporation may issue notes, bonds and other financial instruments such as options, warrants, etc.

Issuance of shares or bonds by a Corporation to the public requires that a prospectus be prepared in compliance with the relevant provisions of the Swiss Code of Obligations. Shares or bonds issued by a Corporation may be listed on an exchange in Switzerland or abroad.

An LLC may issue registered equity quotas. Equity quotas cannot be issued in the bearer form. The equity quotas issued by an LLC have a par value. The minimum par value per equity quota is CHF 100.

An LLC may issue different classes of equity quotas, as well as participation certificates and profit sharing certificates. The articles of association of the LLC set out the rights and privileges attached to the equity quotas, participation certificates and profit sharing certificates.

Equity quotas issued by an LLC cannot be listed on an exchange in Switzerland or abroad.

4.   Can a company have only one shareholder and still enjoy limited liability?

Both the Corporation and the LLC can have one single shareholder/quota holder and still enjoy limited liability. However, the corporate entity will be disregarded and the veil of limited liability pierced under certain circumstances where adherence to the fiction of separate corporate existence would only protect fraudulent conduct.

5.   Are the rights of shareholders the same in any type of company?

The rights of the shareholder of a Corporation and the rights of the quota holders of an LLC as set out in the relevant provisions of the Swiss Code of Obligations are substantially the same. The rights of the shareholders and the rights of the quota holders are however defined to a significant extent by the provisions of the articles of association of the considered company. Depending on the content of the articles of association, the rights of the shareholders may be significantly different from one Corporation to another.

6.   What are the basic rights of any shareholder? Describe briefly the rights of minority shareholders and indicate which thresholds, if any, are required to allow the minority shareholders to exercise any such rights.

The basic rights of any shareholder are the right to vote and the right to receive a share of the profit or liquidation proceeds. These two rights can be limited in the articles of association but can never be entirely suppressed.

Each shareholder has a right of first subscription with respect to any issuance of new shares by the company. Such right can only be limited or suppressed by a resolution of a qualified majority (two-thirds) of the shareholders and only if the company has a valid reason to do so. Financing new acquisitions or supporting employee stock option plans are examples of a valid reason where the right of first subscription of shareholders may be validly suppressed. Conversely, defending against a hostile tender offer is not considered as a justified ground for the suppression of the right of first subscription.

With respect to the right to be represented on the board, Swiss law provides that if there is more than one class of shares with regard to voting or property rights, the articles of association shall provide that each class of shareholder may elect at least one representative to the board of directors.

Each shareholder has a right to receive each year a copy of the audited accounts of the company, the management report of the board of directors and the audit report of the auditors. Each shareholder has in addition the right to ask questions during the shareholders' meeting to the board of directors and the auditor. Information requested by the shareholder has to be provided to the extent such information is necessary for the shareholder to exercise its rights. Information can be refused if it puts in jeopardy the business secrets of the company or other worthy interests of the company. A shareholder only has to consult the books and accounts of the company if expressly authorised to do so by the shareholders' meeting or the board of directors and only to the extent the business secrets of the company can be preserved at the same time.

If information or the consultation of the books and accounts are refused, the shareholder can request the competent court to decide whether its request has merit or not.

Each shareholder may propose to the shareholders' meeting to initiate a special audit to investigate specific facts provided: (i) such audit is necessary for such shareholder to exercise its rights; and (ii) the shareholder has already exercised its rights to obtain information and consult the books and accounts of the company.

If the shareholders' meeting refuses to institute a special audit, one or more shareholders representing at least 10 per cent of the stated capital or shares with an aggregate par value of at least CHF 2,000,000 may request a judge to appoint a special auditor within three months from the resolution of the shareholders' meeting refusing the special audit. The judge will appoint a special auditor if the applicants show that the company's organs have breached the law or the articles of association or have caused prejudice to the company or its shareholders.

Swiss corporate law provides very few specific rights for minority shareholders. Minority shareholders do not have the right to nominate a representative to the board of directors. Minority shareholders may request the board of directors to summon a shareholders' meeting and/or to add an item to the agenda of the meeting only if they represent at least 10 per cent of the stated capital or shares with an aggregate par value of CHF 1,000,000.

Furthermore, a shareholder may on certain conditions challenge resolutions passed by the GM, initiate derivative actions against directors and apply to court for the winding-up of the company.

7. Do all shareholders enjoy the same rights or can some shareholders be attributed specific rights, whether by reason of the particular class of stock owned or other? Are such rights generally provided for at the level of the company's by-laws and/or in shareholders' agreements?

As a rule all shareholders enjoy the same rights. It is, however, possible for the company to issue different classes of shares, which will grant its holders different rights. The rights attached to the different classes of shares will be set forth in the articles of association of the company. As a principle, shareholders of the same class have to be treated equally by the company. If there is a need to treat shareholders of the same class differently, then this is usually addressed by way of a shareholders' agreement among the interested parties.

8. May the rights of shareholders, generally speaking, be limited, modified, suppressed or waived in any way? If so, how? Are such modifications or limitations provided for in the company's by-laws and/or in shareholders' agreements?

The rights of shareholders may generally be limited, modified and even suppressed or waived. Such limitation, modification or suppression generally requires a resolution of the shareholders' meeting and an amendment to the articles of association of the company. Certain rights, such as the right to vote or the right to a portion of the profits or liquidation proceeds can be limited but not entirely suppressed. The right of first subscription may be limited or suppressed but only if there is a valid reason to do so. Certain rights, such as the right to participate in the shareholders' meeting, the right to information, the right to consult the books and accounts and the right to request a special audit may however not be limited or suppressed.

GENERAL MEETING OF SHAREHOLDERS (GM) AND VOTING RIGHTS

9. Which decisions are reserved to the competence of the GM?

The following decisions are reserved to the competence of the GM:
- adopting and amending the articles of association;
- appointing and removing the members of the board of directors and the auditors;
- approving the annual report and the consolidated financial statements;
- approving the annual financial statements and resolving on the distribution of dividends;
- voting the annual directors liability discharge;
- resolving on the following issues which are by law reserved to the shareholders' meeting: share capital increase; share capital reduction; limitation or suppression of the rights of first subscription; creation of extraordinary reserves; appointment of special auditor; dissolution of the corporation; and appointment and removal of liquidators.

10. How does a shareholder participate in a GM? Are there any limitations to having a minimum number of shares? May a shareholder delegate attendance to another shareholder or to the board? May a shareholder obtain assistance from the courts or any other governmental body to intervene in a GM or to cause one to be held in some particular cases?

The GM is summoned by the board of directors by sending to the shareholders a summons or publishing the same at least 20 days before the GM. The summons mentions the agenda of the meeting and the proposals of the board of directors for each item of the agenda.

When a Corporation has issued bearer shares, the shareholder will be admitted to the GM by either presenting its share certificates or a statement from its bank that the company's shares are held on its bank accounts. When shares are registered, only the shareholders registered on the company's share register at the date of the GM will be admitted to participate in the GM.

There is no limitation on having a minimum number of shares. The articles of association of the company can however provide that shareholders may not own more than a certain percentage of the stated capital of the company or that voting rights above a certain percentage will not be taken into consideration for the passing of resolutions of the GM.

A shareholder may grant a power of attorney to another person or entity to represent it at the GM. The articles of association can however restrict the right of a shareholder to be represented, by prohibiting such representation, by providing that only other shareholders can act as representative or by limiting the number of shares or shareholders that a representative can represent. Representation by depositary proxy such as banks and professional asset managers is also possible.

The board of directors may offer to the shareholders the possibility to grant a power of attorney to a member of the company's management to represent their shares. If the board of directors elects to do so, it has to offer to the shareholders the choice to designate an independent third party as their representative.

Minority shareholders representing at least 10 per cent of the stated capital or shares with an aggregate par value of CHF 1,000,000 may request the board of directors to summon a GM and/or to add an item to the agenda of the GM. If the board of directors fails to summon such GM promptly, the minority shareholders may request a court to summon such a GM.

11. May a GM be called and held at the request of any shareholder? Is there a threshold regarding the percentage of the stock interest owned in the company that may entitle a shareholder to such a right?

Only minority shareholders representing at least 10 per cent of the stated capital or shares with an aggregate par value of CHF 1,000,000 may request the board of directors to summon a GM.

12. May a shareholder bring up an issue to be resolved upon and put it to a vote if it is not included on the agenda? May a shareholder require more information from the GM and/or the board concerning the agenda of the GM to be put in a better position to exercise their vote?

No resolutions may be passed on items which have not been duly put on the agenda, with the exception of shareholders' motions for the convening of an extraordinary GM, the initiation of a special audit or the appointment of auditors. Motions proposed by shareholders during the GM which fall within the scope of agenda items can be validly resolved upon. In addition, any item upon which no formal resolution will be passed can be discussed at the GM even if it was not included on the agenda.

Only minority shareholders representing at least 10 per cent of the stated capital or shares with an aggregate par value of CHF 1,000,000 may request the board of directors to add an item to the agenda of a GM.

Each shareholder has the right to ask questions during the GM to the board of directors and the auditor. Information requested by the shareholder has to be provided to the extent such information is necessary for the shareholder to exercise its rights. Information can be refused if it puts in jeopardy the business secrets of the company or other worthy interests of the company. A shareholder only has the right to consult the books and accounts of the company if expressly authorised to do so by the shareholders' meeting or the board of directors and only to the extent the business secrets of the company can be preserved at the same time.

13. May a GM be held by telecommunication means and/or by correspondence (ie by written consent)?

Under Swiss law the GM can only be held physically. Attendance by videoconference, teleconference, or circular letter is not permitted.

14. Are voting rights always proportionate to the stock held by each shareholder or can they vary by share class?

By law the voting right attached to a share is proportional to the par value of such share. The articles of association can, however, provide that each share grants its holding with only the power to cast one vote (one share, one vote). The articles of association can also provide that the voting right of the shareholders is limited to a specific maximum percentage of the stated capital of the company. The articles of association can also provide that certain resolutions of the GM require a qualified majority of the voting rights or the approval of a certain class of share in addition to the general majority rule. At a minimum, each shareholder shall have at least one vote.

For certain resolutions of the GM, Swiss corporate law requires that the voting right be proportional to the par value of the shares present or represented at the GM. In particular, election of auditors, initiation of a special audit, resolution on the initiation of liability suit against the management or the auditor.

15. Are there non-voting shares? Is there a maximum percentage of capital represented by non-voting shares?

Swiss corporate law does not permit non voting shares. Corporations and LLCs can issue participation certificates. The holders of participation certificates have the same financial rights as the holders of shares (unless the articles of association state otherwise) but they have no voting rights. The articles of association can, however, grant certain social rights to the holders of participation certificates such as:

- the right to call a GM;
- the right to attend a GM;
- the right to information;
- the right to consult the books and accounts; and
- the right to make motions at the GM.

The holders of participation certificates shall have the right to challenge the resolutions of the GM that violate the law or the articles of association and to initiate liability suits against the organs of the company for breach of their fiduciary duties.

16. Can shareholders group their shares in order to exercise their voting rights (eg, by trust, shareholders' agreement or otherwise)?

Voting agreements are common in Switzerland and do not raise any issue with respect to privately held companies. With respect to publicly listed Corporations, a voting agreement will usually lead the parties to be considered as acting in concert and the shares held by such parties will be aggregated for the purpose of complying with disclosure requirements relating to substantial shareholdings. Such disclosure is required when a shareholder, or group of shareholders acting in concert, acquires or disposes of shares and thereby reaches, exceeds or falls below the limits of three, five, 10, 15, 20, 25, 33.3, 50 or 66.6 per cent of the voting rights of a Swiss Corporation listed in Switzerland.

17. Under what circumstances can a shareholder challenge the resolutions adopted by the GM? Are there thresholds concerning the stock interest owned to be able to bring such a claim?

Swiss corporate law makes a distinction between the resolutions of the GM which are void and the ones which are merely voidable.

Resolutions which are void can be challenged at any time by any shareholder. Resolutions which are only voidable can only be challenged within two months from the passing of the considered resolutions by shareholders who have not adhered to such resolutions.

There is no requirement for a minimum shareholding to challenges of GM resolutions which are void or voidable.

Under Swiss corporate law, a GM resolution is voidable if it:

- withdraws or limits the rights of a shareholder in violation of the law or the articles of association;
- withdraws or limits the rights of a shareholder without proper reason;
- favours a shareholder or discriminates against one in a manner which is

not justified by the company's purpose; or
- transforms the company into not-for-profit organisation without the consent of all shareholders.

Under Swiss corporate law, a GM resolution is void if it:
- withdraws or limits the shareholders' rights to participate in the GM, the minimum voting right, the right to sue, and other rights granted by mandatory provisions of law;
- limits the shareholder's rights of control over the company provided by law; or
- disregards the fundamental structures of the company or violates the provisions for the protection of the stated capital.

18. What are the terms and procedures to challenge a resolution of the GM?

The commercial court of the place of incorporation of the company has jurisdiction over shareholders' petitions challenging a resolution of the GM.

With respect to resolutions of the GM which are null and void, a shareholder can challenge the resolution at any time.

With respect to resolutions which are merely voidable, the shareholder has to challenge the resolution within two months from it being passed. To be entitled to take action, the shareholder shall not have voted in favour of the challenged resolution and shall have a legal sufficient interest to act. In particular, the plaintiff shall still be a shareholder at the time it initiates court proceedings to rescind the resolution of the GM.

In the event that the court decides in favour of the plaintiff, the resolution of the GM will be rescinded and such rescission will be binding on the plaintiff, the company and all the other shareholders of the company. In the event that the court decides in favour of the company, the court will decide at its discretion on the allocation of the costs of proceedings between the company and the plaintiff.

SHAREHOLDERS' RIGHTS VERSUS DIRECTORS AND DUTIES OF OTHER CORPORATE BODIES IN THE COMPANY

19. What is the procedure for the appointment/replacement/ revocation of directors and of statutory auditors, if any?

The directors and the statutory auditors are appointed, replaced and revoked by resolution of the GM. The board of directors will put the election, replacement or revocation of the directors and statutory auditors on the agenda of the GM and will outline the proposals of the board of directors in this respect.

It is customary for publicly listed companies and for large privately held companies to have a nomination committee whose task will be to make recommendations regarding vacancies to be filled on the board of directors or for the appointment/replacement of the statutory auditors.

The shareholders do not have to follow the recommendation of the nomination committee and may vote in favour of candidates which have not been vetted by the nomination committee.

The duration of a director's term is set forth in the articles of association but it shall never exceed six years. Directors can be re-elected, unless the articles of association provide otherwise. In publicly listed companies and large privately held companies, the usual term for a director is one year. It is, however, possible to provide for longer terms and create a staggered board.

The election, replacement and revocation of directors and statutory auditors usually requires only a majority resolution. The articles of association can however provide for a qualified majority.

20. May shareholders challenge the resolutions of the board of directors? Is there a minimum percentage of capital required to challenge a board resolution?

A shareholder may only challenge resolutions of the board of directors which are null and void, such as:

- any resolution withdrawing or limiting the rights of shareholders or directors which result from mandatory provisions of law;
- any resolution limiting the rights of shareholders or directors to control the company; and
- any resolution disregarding the fundamental structures of the company or violating the provisions protecting the stated capital of the company.

There is no minimum percentage of capital required to challenge a board resolution which is null and void.

21. Are shareholders entitled to bring a legal action against the directors of the company? In which circumstances? Please describe briefly the principles of directors' liability.

The directors of the company are liable to the company and the shareholders for any losses or damages resulting from the breach of their fiduciary duties. If such breach has caused a loss or damage only to the company, a shareholder can only bring a legal action for the indemnification of the company (derivative action). If the breach of fiduciary duty is causing a direct loss or damage to the shareholder (as opposed to an indirect damage resulting from the loss or damage suffered by the company), then such shareholder can bring a legal action against the breaching director and seek direct indemnification of its damage. The plaintiff will have to prove:

(i)   the breach of the director's fiduciary duties;
(ii) the damage suffered by the company or the shareholder itself;
(iii) the causation between the breach of fiduciary duty and the damage; and
(iv) that the breach is the result of a wilful action or negligence of the director.

If the board of directors has lawfully delegated the day-to-day business to a third party such as the management, the board is, however, exempt from liability provided that it can show that the management has been carefully selected, instructed and supervised.

22. What are the rights in connection with transactions where the directors have a conflict of interest situation?

The duty of a director is to always act in the interests of the company, including when they are in a conflict of interest situation. If the director fails to act in the interests of the company and favours their own interests over those of the company and thereby causes damage to the company, they will be liable towards the company for such damage. Any shareholder will have the right to bring a derivative action against such director and seek indemnification on behalf of the company. Swiss corporate law does not provide for specific provisions to address conflict of interest situations. There is in particular no legal requirement to abstain from attending meetings of the board or casting their vote at such meeting when in a conflict of interest situation. Swiss companies will often adopt internal regulations to set out the appropriate course of action for directors in a conflict of interest situation (such as disclosure, abstention from the meeting and abstention from voting).

INFORMATION RIGHTS ON THE COMPANY'S BUSINESS
23. What information may be requested by the shareholders from the board concerning the general state of the company's business or any specific transaction? Are information rights different depending on the number of shares owned? Are shareholders entitled to receive written information before, during or after the GM about the meeting agenda and to what extent? Is it possible for a shareholder to obtain a copy of the minutes of the GM?
Each shareholder has a right to receive each year a copy of the audited accounts of the company, the management report of the board of directors and the audit report of the auditors. Each shareholder has a right to obtain a copy of the minutes of the GMs. Each shareholder has in addition the right to ask questions during the shareholders' meeting to the board of directors and the auditor. Such questions may relate to the general state of the company's business or to a specific transaction. From a practical standpoint, it is advisable to communicate to the board of directors in advance the list of questions the shareholder intends to pose at the GM, so as to enable the board of directors to be ready to answer at the GM or to provide the shareholders with its answers ahead of the GM if the board of directors chooses to do so. The right of information of the shareholder is the same irrespective of the number of shares held.

Information requested by a shareholder has to be provided to the extent such information is necessary for such shareholder to exercise its rights. Information can be refused if it puts in jeopardy the business secrets of the company or other worthy interests of the company. A shareholder only has a right to consult the books and accounts of the company if it is expressly authorised to do so by the shareholders' meeting or by the board of directors and only to the extent the business secrets of the company can be preserved at the same time.

If information or the consultation of the books and accounts are refused, the shareholder can request the competent court to decide whether its request has merit or not.

24. Do shareholders have the right/duty to resolve in the GM upon matters which were not on the agenda?

No resolutions may be passed by the GM on items which have not been duly put on the agenda, with the exception of shareholders' motions for the convening of an extraordinary GM, the initiation of a special audit or the appointment of auditors. Motions proposed by shareholders during the GM which fall within the scope of agenda items can be validly resolved upon. In addition, any item upon which no formal resolution will be passed can be discussed at the GM even if it was not included on the agenda.

If all shareholders are present or represented at a GM, it is possible to resolve on an item which was not included on the agenda, provided all shareholders agree that a resolution be passed on such item.

25. Are shareholders entitled to inspect the corporate books and/or any other corporate or accounting documents? To what extent? Can they do it through external counsel or advisors?

A shareholder may only have the right to consult the books and accounts of the company if it is expressly authorised to do so by the shareholders' meeting or the board of directors, if such consultation is necessary for such shareholder to exercise its rights and only to the extent the business secrets of the company can be preserved at the same time.

Once a shareholder is granted the right to inspect corporate books and/or any other corporate or accounting documents, it may do so either directly or through its legal or financial advisers.

SHAREHOLDERS' AGREEMENTS

26. Are shareholders' agreements validly enforceable? What are their typical contents and term of duration? Are they enforceable by or against third parties and, if so, to what extent?

Shareholders' agreements are common in Switzerland and are enforceable against the shareholders who are parties to it. Shareholders' agreements are however not enforceable against third parties (such as other shareholders) who are not party to it.

Shareholders' agreements typically contain provisions regarding:
(i)   the composition of the board of directors;
(ii) decisions of the board of directors or the GM requiring qualified majority, the consent of a specific shareholder or board representative or subject to certain veto right;
(iii) right of pre-emption;
(iv) tag-along, drag-along and other change of control provisions; and
(v)   dividend policy and future financing, including anti-dilution protection.

Shareholders' agreements can also contain certain undertakings of one category of shareholders (eg founders) towards another (eg financial investors).

Shareholders' agreements governed by Swiss law usually provide for a fixed term with a mechanism of automatic renewal for further fixed term periods. It is not advisable to enter into a shareholders' agreement for an undetermined duration, as there is a risk that under Swiss law such agreement may be considered terminable at will by giving six months' written notice.

27. Do shareholders' agreements have to be disclosed to the public or registered in any public registry?

There is no requirement in Switzerland to disclose or register a shareholders' agreement entered into in relation to a privately held company.

With respect to publicly listed Corporations, a shareholders' agreement may lead the parties to be considered as acting in concert and the shares held by such parties will be aggregated for the purpose of complying with disclosure requirements relating to substantial shareholdings. Such disclosure is required when a shareholder or group of shareholders acting in concert acquires or disposes of shares and thereby reaches, exceeds or falls below the limits of three, five, 10, 15, 20, 25, 33.3, 50 or 66.6 per cent of the voting rights of a Swiss Corporation listed in Switzerland.

ECONOMIC RIGHTS AND RIGHTS OVER THE STOCK
28. Is the stock always freely transferable? Are there any legal limitations? Are there any restrictions on contractual limitations?

Bearer shares issued by a corporation limited by shares are always freely transferable. Such transfer is made through the delivery to the acquirer of the share certificates incorporating the shares.

Registered shares issued by a corporation limited by shares are also freely transferable unless its articles of association subject such transfer to the consent of the board of directors. The transfer of shares cannot however be per se prohibited.

If the transfer of registered shares issued by a privately held company is restricted, the articles of association can set out circumstances in which the board of directors is legitimately allowed to refuse its consent and therefore prevent the transfer of the shares. Such circumstances typically relate to the composition of the company's shareholding (ie to limit a concentration of shares in one shareholder) or to the independence of the company (ie to prevent the company from being acquired by a competitor). The board of directors may also refuse its consent if the would-be acquirer does not confirm that it is acquiring the shares for itself and for its own account. The board of directors may also refuse its consent without giving any reason for such refusal, but in such a case the board of directors has to offer to buy back the shares for a price which corresponds to the value of the company as a going concern. If the registered shares are acquired through inheritance, liquidation of matrimonial regime or through debt enforcement proceedings, the board of directors may only refuse its consent if it offers to buy back the shares for a price which corresponds to the value of the company as a going concern. If there is a dispute between the company and the shareholder on such price, the price will be determined by the courts in the context of an appraisal proceeding or by an expert if the parties agree to such appointment.

If the transfer of registered shares issued by a publicly held company is restricted, the company can only refuse its consent if the articles of association provide for a maximum shareholding's threshold and such threshold is exceeded or if the would-be acquirer has not confirmed that it is acquiring the shares for itself and for its own account. The consent of the board of directors cannot be withheld if the shares have been acquired through inheritance, liquidation of matrimonial regime or through debt enforcement proceedings. If the shares with restriction of transfer issued by a publicly listed company are acquired on an exchange, the transfer of title from the seller to the acquirer occurs immediately but the acquirer cannot exercise its voting rights and other related rights until the transfer is approved by the board of directors. If the consent of the board of directors is validly denied, the acquirer will be registered as a non-voting shareholder in the shareholders' register.

With respect to equity quotas issued by a limited liability company, Swiss corporate law provides that the transfer of such quotas require the approval of the GM. The articles of association can provide that the transfer can be made without the consent of the GM. The articles of association can also set out circumstances in which the GM may legitimately refuse its consent. The rules governing such limitations are similar to those applicable to privately held corporations limited by shares. Furthermore, the articles of the limited liability company can also provide that the transfer of quotas is *per se* prohibited, it being specified that a quota holder may exercise an exit right for good cause.

29. Are shareholders entitled to pledge their stock?

Shareholders of a corporation limited by shares are entitled to pledge their stock. In practice it is important for the pledgee to review the articles of association of the company for any provisions which may limit or hinder enforcement of the pledge. Limitations in the articles on the transferability of the shares or the percentage of stated capital or voting rights which can be held by a single shareholder may impact the value of a share pledge. It is common for shareholders of a Corporation to restrict their ability to pledge their shares through a shareholders' agreement.

Quota holders of a limited liability company are entitled to pledge their quotas, except when the articles prohibit the transfer of quotas. In such a case, the pledge of the quotas is also prohibited. The articles of association may also submit the pledge to the approval of a majority of quota holders.

30. Are there financial assistance issues to be considered and other prohibitions to be evaluated in the context of a leveraged buyout transaction?

The provisions of Swiss corporate law aimed at protecting the stated capital of a Corporation limit the ability of a Corporation to guarantee the obligations of an acquirer who would have borrowed heavily to purchase the entire share capital of such Corporation.

A Swiss Corporation can only guarantee the obligations of its controlling shareholder up to an amount which is equal to the accrued earnings and reserves of such Corporation which could be freely distributed by way of a dividend at the time the guarantee is called.

The possibilities of a 'debt push-down' (through a merger of the Corporation with the acquisition vehicle) are severely limited due to Swiss tax considerations. The tax authorities will typically refuse to consider as deductible any interest paid by the Corporation on the acquisition debt.

The answer is identical with respect to an LLC.

31. May a company buy back its own stock and if so under which cases and subject to which limitations?

A Corporation or an LLC may acquire its own shares or equity quotas only if it has freely disposable reserves to pay the purchase price and if the aggregate nominal value of such shares does not exceed 10 per cent of the nominal value of the share capital. The voting rights and associated rights attached to shares or quotas will lie dormant as long as they are owned by the company. If shares are acquired due to the restrictions of transfer applicable to the shares or equity quota, such limit of 10 per cent is increased to 20 per cent of the stated capital for Corporations and to 35 per cent for LLCs. Shares repurchased by a Swiss Corporation or LLC do not carry any rights to vote at shareholders' meetings. Additionally, when a company buys back its own shares, a transfer of distributable profits or freely disposable assets must be made to an undistributable capital redemption reserve in the amount of the purchase price of the acquired shares or quotas on its balance sheet. Furthermore, in the event that the 10 per cent threshold is exceeded, the company shall either dispose of the shares (or equity quotas) in excess or cancel them within two years from their acquisition.

The abovementioned conditions do not apply if a GM resolves that a company shall buy back shares in order to cancel them so as to reduce the share capital. Moreover, there are no specific restrictions under Swiss law in relation to financial assistance by a corporation to persons intending to purchase shares of that corporation (although the board of directors has to ensure that such transactions are in compliance with general principles of corporate law and certain tax directives).

Listed companies intending to implement a share buyback programme may be subject to additional requirements stemming from the Swiss takeover rules. Indeed, all public offers by a listed company of its own shares are deemed to be tender offers, but after reviewing the offer, the Swiss Takeover Board may exempt certain conditions from the obligations to comply with the takeover rules.

From a Swiss tax perspective, share buybacks followed by a subsequent capital reduction are deemed partial liquidations of the company, resulting in income and withholding tax duties for private sellers on the difference between the redemption price and the nominal value of the shares. Share repurchase programmes with subsequent capital reduction are therefore attractive only for Swiss holding companies and tax exempt entities, although the negative consequences for the non-exempt sellers may be avoided by using various schemes. Share repurchases with a subsequent capital reduction are not however considered as a partial liquidation of the company if the corporate law requirements are satisfied and the redeemed shares are not held for a period of more than six years.

32. Is there a legal right to withdraw from the company and, if so, under what circumstances? How is the shareholders' stock valued and paid in such a case?

There is no legal right to withdraw from a corporation limited by shares. A shareholder may never request the company in which it has invested to repurchase its shares. Correspondingly a shareholder may in principle not be deprived of its shares by the company in which it has invested. There are however four exceptions to this principle:

(i) a shareholder has not fully paid up the subscription price of its shares and fails to pay up the balance after being requested to do so by the company – in this situation the shareholder will forfeit its shares;

(ii) in a situation where the company is over-indebted and needs financial restructuring, the stated capital of the company is reduced to zero and is then immediately increased back to its initial level and the shareholder fails to participate in such share capital increase – in such a situation the shares held by the shareholder will be cancelled without compensation;

(iii) in the context of a public tender offer if the offeror holds more than 98 per cent of the voting rights of the target company;

(iv) shareholders representing less than 10 per cent of the stated capital of a company may be squeezed out upon merger of such company into another entity. In such instance, the minority shareholders will receive cash instead of shares as merger consideration. This cash consideration will be determined by the companies party to the merger agreement and can be challenged by the minority shareholders in court should this consideration be inadequate.

33. In which circumstances can dividends be distributed among shareholders? Is it possible to exclude or limit the right of certain shareholders to dividends? Does a certain portion of the profits need to be set aside in a reserve fund where it cannot be distributed to the shareholders? Are advances on dividends allowed and, if so, under which circumstances? Can advances on dividends be reclaimed by the company?

Dividends may only be distributed by a Corporation or an LLC if such company has accrued earning or distributable reserves. The distribution of a dividend by a Corporation or LLC requires a resolution of the shareholders. Five per cent of the yearly profits have to be allocated to the legal reserves of the company until such reserve amounts to 20 per cent of its stated capital, it being specified that the articles of association may increase the five per cent and 20 per cent thresholds. In addition, 10 per cent of the portion of the dividend exceeding five per cent of the stated capital has to be allocated to the legal reserves of the company unless such company qualifies as a holding company. As long as they do not reach 50 per cent of the stated capital of the company, the legal reserves cannot be distributed to the shareholders and can only be used to cover losses, unless the company qualifies as a holding company. The portion of the legal reserves exceeding 50 per cent of the stated capital can be distributed to the shareholders by way of a dividend. Swiss corporate law provides that dividends can only be distributed based on the last audited annual accounts, so in theory the payment of an interim dividend (ie dividend of the profit of the current financial year) is not possible. In practice, an interim dividend is admissible provided that it is based on interim audited accounts showing distributable profits.

34. What are the rights of shareholders in the case of an issue of new stock (increase of the company's corporate capital) (pre-emption rights)?

Each shareholder has a right of first subscription with respect to any issuance of new shares by the company. Such right can only be limited or suppressed by a resolution of a qualified majority of the shareholders and only if the company has good cause to do so. Financing new acquisitions or supporting employee stock option plans are examples of good cause justifying the suppression of the right of first subscription.

35. May minority shareholders ban or limit the company's capital structure in any manner?

No.

36. Which financial assistance prohibitions are in force?

There is no formal prohibition on a Swiss Corporation or LLC extending a loan to an existing or future shareholder who will then use such loan to subscribe new shares issued by such Corporation or LLC. In practice, the executive organs of a Corporation or LLC should be extremely careful before extending such a loan as they could be held liable towards the company, the other shareholders or even the company's creditors in the event that the borrower defaults on the loan.

37. Apart from publicly listed companies, in which cases (if any) are shareholders obligated to obtain an authorisation from, or provide information to, a public authority about events that have an impact on their stock interest in the company?

With respect to privately held Corporations, Swiss corporate law does not provide for any authorisation or information requirement. However, Corporations which are active in a regulated industry, such as banks, securities dealer, etc, may be required to obtain an authorisation or provide information with respect to material changes in the composition of their shareholding.

The quota holders of an LLC are registered in the commercial register so any transfer of quotas in an LLC has to be announced and registered with the commercial register.

SHAREHOLDERS' RIGHTS IN CASE OF EXTRAORDINARY TRANSACTIONS AND/OR WINDING-UP

38. What rights are available to shareholders in the case of a sale of all or a substantial portion of the company's assets? In case of a merger or de-merger?

As a general rule, the decision to sell the company assets lies with the board of directors, not the GM. However, if the Corporation is selling all or substantially all of its assets, it may be considered either as a fundamental change of the corporate purpose of the Corporation or a liquidation of the Corporation, which in both cases would require a resolution of the GM approved by a qualified majority. Minority shareholders could therefore challenge a resolution of the board of directors approving the sale of all or substantially all of the assets of the Corporation on the ground that the board of directors is not the competent organ to pass such a resolution. If the sale of all or substantially all of the assets is approved by the required qualified majority of the GM, the minority shareholders may no longer challenge the transaction itself but may obtain a judicial review of the terms of the transaction, determining in particular whether the assets were sold or transferred for adequate consideration.

Merger and de-merger require a resolution of the GM approved by a qualified majority. In principle, the rights of minority shareholders have to be maintained in the merger or de-merger and the minority shareholders have to retain an adequate stake in the merged entity or the company (or companies) created as a result of the de-merger. Swiss merger law however provides that consideration other than shares in the surviving company may be granted to minority shareholders. The merging companies may even provide in the merger agreement that the minority shareholders have to accept the settlement if at least 90 per cent of the votes of the absorbed company consent (squeeze-out merger).

Shareholders, who consider that their rights have not been adequately maintained or compensated in a merger or de-merger, may request a court to set an adequate monetary compensation for their shares. This request has to be filed within two months of the merger or de-merger resolution. Besides this request for monetary compensation, the minority shareholders do not have a cause of action to challenge the merger or de-merger itself, unless such merger or de-merger has been made in breach of the law.

39. Which rights are available to shareholders in the case of conversion of the company into a European Company (SE) or into another type of company?

Swiss law does not know the concept of European Company (SE). In a situation where a Swiss corporation or limited liability company is converted into another type of company, the same remedies are available to the minority shareholders as in a situation of merger or de-merger.

40. Which rights are available to shareholders of a company in liquidation?

Upon resolving on the dissolution of the company, the GM may decide to completely discharge the board of directors and to appoint third parties to act as liquidators of the company.

Each shareholder shall be entitled to a share of the liquidation proceeds to the extent that the articles of association do not provide for another use of the net assets of the company in liquidation.

Unless otherwise provided for by the articles of association, the net assets of the company in liquidation, shall be distributed to the shareholders in proportion to the amount paid in and with due regard to the preferential rights associated to each class of shares.

Liquidation proceeds may be distributed at the earliest upon the expiry of one year from the date upon which the call for the filling of claims was issued for the third time. However, a distribution may already be made after a three-month period if a specifically qualified auditor confirms that the liabilities have been satisfied and that, under the circumstances, it may be assumed that no third party interests are jeopardised.

41. Can shareholders cause the liquidation of the company? How?

The company may be dissolved by a resolution of the GM made in the form of a notarised deed. This resolution may be passed at any time. At least two-thirds of the votes represented and the absolute majority of the par value of shares represented at the GM are required for such resolution to be passed.

COMPANY GROUPS

42. Is the concept of 'group' recognised as such under specific legislation? What are the implications?

The concept of 'group' is not recognised as such under Swiss law and there are no specific rules applicable to groups in Switzerland. Swiss corporate law provides however the obligation to maintain consolidated group accounts for the company that comprises by a majority of votes or in another way one or more companies under common management (ie a group of companies).

The absence of specific group legislation is particularly problematic in situations of group meltdown. Since each of the various companies composing the group is considered as a separate legal entity, there is no consolidation of all the assets of the various group companies for the satisfaction of all group creditors. The Swiss Supreme Court has developed an exception to the principle that each group company is only liable for its own obligations. Under the so-called 'trust liability', the Swiss Supreme Court has ruled that a parent company could be held liable to third parties for the obligations of its subsidiary if it had created the expectation with such third party that the parent company would provide its subsidiary with the sufficient financial means to satisfy its obligations.

Furthermore, under Swiss case law, a parent may be liable under certain circumstances for the acts of its subsidiary in application of the doctrine of piercing the corporate veil.

43. Does a controlling company have any particular duties *vis-à-vis* its controlled company shareholders?

Swiss law does not provide for any specific duty of the controlling company towards its controlled company shareholders besides the preparation of group accounts. The controlling company has to comply with the provisions of Swiss corporate law regarding the organisation and functioning of its controlled subsidiaries. If the controlling company does not comply with these provisions, it runs the risk of being considered a *de facto* organ of the controlled subsidiaries and be held liable towards third parties (including minority shareholders) in this capacity.

44. What are the rights of company shareholders when the controlling company puts in place actions and/or transactions that can be prejudicial to the shareholders?

If the controlling company is passing shareholders' resolutions or board resolutions which are not in compliance with law or the articles of association of the company, the minority shareholders can challenge such resolutions in court. If the controlling company is usurping powers of the shareholders' meeting or the board of directors, it could be held liable to the minority shareholders as a *de facto* organ of the company. If the representatives of the controlling company on the board of directors are in breach their fiduciary duties towards the company, they could be held liable to the shareholders and creditors for any damage that arises.

45. What are the limitations, if any, to the possibility of owning reciprocal stock interests in companies?

There is no limitation on the possibility of owning reciprocal stock interests in companies as long as none of these reciprocal interests is a majority holding. Once a company holds a majority holding in a company, which holds a stock interest in such controlling company, this stock interest will be considered to be treasury shares. Under Swiss corporate law, a company cannot hold either directly or through subsidiaries, more than 10 per cent of its own stock.

United Arab Emirates

Afridi & Angell Amjad Ali Khan

BASIC INFORMATION ON THE TYPES OF LIMITED LIABILITY COMPANIES AND ON THE RIGHTS OF SHAREHOLDERS

1.   What types of companies enjoy limited liability? If more than one, which ones have shareholders, ie holders of share certificates? Which one is the most common? Which one is mostly used by foreign investors?

The following companies offer limited liability:
*   limited liability companies;
*   public joint stock companies; and
*   private joint stock companies.

Each of the abovementioned companies has shareholders. Limited liability companies are the most common corporate structure in the UAE and are also the most common corporate structure used by foreign investors. However, its shareholders do not hold share certificates. Instead they own a percentage of the capital of the limited liability company which does not issue transferable share certificates.

2.   Are there minimum capital requirements and/or thin capitalisation rules in force?

The following companies have the following minimum capital requirements:
*   limited liability companies: AED 150,000 (AED 300,000 in the Emirate of Dubai) or other amount adequate for the business of the company;
*   public joint stock companies: AED 10 million; and
*   private joint stock companies: AED 2 million.

3.   Describe the types of shares that can be issued by a company and the different rights that they attribute to their owners, as well as any other financial instruments (bonds or other) and other instruments of a participatory nature in the company's capital that can also be issued by the company.

Limited liability companies

Shareholders of limited liability companies can have different rights in relation to profit participation and management of the company. A minority shareholder can be entitled to a majority of the profits and to complete control of the management of the company pursuant to the provisions agreed in the memorandum of association of the company.

Public joint stock companies

The share capital of a public joint stock company is comprised of shares of equal nominal value. All shares have equal rights and obligations.

The shares of a public joint stock company are freely transferable. Fifty-one per cent of the shares of all companies must be held by UAE nationals or companies wholly owned by UAE nationals. Also, founders must hold their shares for a two-year period after listing.

The company may not issue bearer shares.

A public joint stock company may issue public debentures. The value of the debentures must not exceed the capital. All the rights of debenture holders in respect of a single issue must be equal. Debentures may be convertible into shares of the company if so stipulated in the conditions of issue.

A limited liability company may not issue public debentures.

Private joint stock companies

Except for provisions regarding the public subscription of shares and debentures, the provisions governing public joint stock companies are applicable to a private joint stock company.

4.   Can a company have only one shareholder and still enjoy limited liability?

All companies must have at least two shareholders. A minimum of two shareholders is required in a limited liability company and three in a private joint stock company. There must be at least 10 founders of a public joint stock company.

5.   Are the rights of shareholders the same in any type of company?

Shareholders have limited liability in the three types of limited companies. Shareholders in limited liability companies have a statutory right of pre-emption and can agree to different profit and management rights attaching to different shares.

6.   What are the basic rights of any shareholder? Describe briefly the rights of minority shareholders and indicate which thresholds, if any, are required to allow the minority shareholders to exercise any such rights.

Shareholders have the following basic rights:
*   the right to vote in the annual general assembly in the election of directors;
*   subject to a minimum holding period for founders of public joint stock companies and pre-emption rights of other shareholders of limited liability companies, shareholders have the right to transfer their shares; and
*   subject to certain statutory conditions and any restrictions in

the memorandum and articles of association regarding reserves, shareholders have the right to share in the profits of the company.

There are no explicit statutory protections for minority shareholders. Minority rights may be protected through shareholder agreements' and/ or through the incorporation of such protections in the memorandum and articles of association of a company.

While shareholders' agreements are generally enforced in the UAE courts, these agreements are essentially private contracts among the shareholders. To be effective against all parties, the relevant provisions should be incorporated into the memorandum and articles of association.

Minority shareholders holding in excess of 25 per cent of the capital of the company have veto power in relation to various shareholder decisions which require the approval of shareholders representing three-quarters of the capital of the company.

7. Do all shareholders enjoy the same rights or can some shareholders be attributed specific rights, whether by reason of the particular class of stock owned or other? Are such rights generally provided for at the level of the company's by-laws and/or in shareholders' agreements?

The Companies Law (CL) does not permit the issuance of different classes or series of shares in private and public joint stock companies. All shareholders in such companies must have the same rights and obligations. Shares in limited liability companies can have different rights pursuant to the memorandum of association of the company with regard to participation in management and share of profits.

8. May the rights of shareholders, generally speaking, be limited, modified, suppressed or waived in any way? If so, how? Are such modifications or limitations provided for in the company's by-laws and/or in shareholders' agreements?

It is possible to modify certain rights of shareholders of limited liability companies through amendments to the memorandum of association of such companies. Such amendments require a minimum approval of shareholders representing three-quarters of the capital of the company. However, practically (on account of the procedure for amendment of the memorandum of association) it requires the consent of all shareholders.

Shareholders may enter into a shareholders' agreement to modify their rights and obligations. However, as noted above, this is a private contract and therefore, to be effective against all parties, the relevant provisions of the shareholders' agreement should be incorporated into the memorandum of association of a limited liability company.

GENERAL MEETING OF SHAREHOLDERS (GM) AND VOTING RIGHTS

9. Which decisions are reserved to the competence of the GM?

A GM shall be competent to consider all questions relating to the company except for those questions reserved by statute or the memorandum and articles of association of the company as being within the competence of an extraordinary GM (Article 129, CL).

The following matters are reserved by statute to the competence of an extraordinary GM (Article 137, CL):

- to amend the memorandum and articles of association and the by-laws;
- to increase or reduce the capital;
- to dissolve the company or merge it into another;
- to sell or otherwise dispose of substantially all of the assets; and
- to extend the duration of the company.

10. How does a shareholder participate in a GM? Are there any limitations to having a minimum number of shares? May a shareholder delegate attendance to another shareholder or to the board? May a shareholder obtain assistance from the courts or any other governmental body to intervene in a GM or to cause one to be held in some particular cases?

Every shareholder has the right to attend the GM (Article 125, CL). Shareholders must register their names in a special register prior to the scheduled GM. The register should include the names of the shareholders and the number of shares held, together with the submission of any proxies (Article 142, CL).

A shareholder of a public or private joint stock company may delegate its right to attend by special proxy to any person it chooses, other than a member of the board of directors. The person appointed must not in this capacity hold more than five per cent of the capital of the company (Article 126, CL). A shareholder of a limited liability company may only appoint another shareholder as its proxy. A shareholder who is a director of the limited liability company may not be a proxy.

Shareholders may obtain the assistance of the Ministry of Economy and the concerned local authority of the relevant Emirate (eg the Dubai Department of Economic Development) to call a GM. If the shareholders requisition a GM and the board of directors fails to issue invitations to the shareholders in respect of such a meeting, then the Ministry of Economy, after consultation with the concerned local authorities, will issue an invitation to shareholders (Article 121, EL) to attend a GM. The Ministry of Economy and the concerned local authorities send representatives to attend the GM as observers.

11. May a GM be called and held at the request of any shareholder? Is there a threshold regarding the percentage of the stock interest owned in the company that may entitle a shareholder to such a right?

If at least 10 shareholders of a public or private joint stock company holding not less than 30 per cent of the capital request that a GM be held, then the board of directors must issue an invitation to shareholders within 15 days from the date of the requisition. The invitation to all shareholders is communicated by publication in two local daily Arabic newspapers and by registered letter at least 21 days before the date of the scheduled meeting (Article 121, CL).

12. May a shareholder bring up an issue to be resolved upon and put it to a vote if it is not included on the agenda? May a shareholder require more information from the GM and/or the board, concerning the agenda of the GM, to be put in a better position to exercise their vote?

A shareholder may not raise matters which are not included in the agenda. However, a shareholder has the right to discuss important issues that come up in the course of the GM (Article 129, CL).

If a shareholder or a number of shareholders representing not less than one-tenth of the capital request(s) the inclusion of a new issue in the agenda, then the board of directors must grant such a request. If the board of directors does not grant the request, the GM shall have the right to decide whether to include the issue on the agenda (Article 129, CL).

13. May a GM be held by telecommunication means and/or by correspondence (ie by written consent)?

There are no statutory provisions prohibiting a GM of a limited liability company from being held via teleconference or correspondence. Its memorandum of association will typically specify the methods acceptable for conducting the GM. General meetings of public and private joint stock companies must be physically held.

14. Are voting rights always proportionate to the stock held by each shareholder or can they vary by share class?

Voting rights in public and private joint stock companies are equivalent to the number of shares held by a shareholder. Public and private joint stock companies may not issue different classes or series of shares.

15. Are there non-voting shares? Is there a maximum percentage of capital represented by non-voting shares?

All shares of public and private joint stock companies have voting rights. In relation to limited liability companies, shares can be made practically non-voting in relation to management issues by giving certain shareholders all management rights.

16. Can shareholders group their shares in order to exercise their voting rights (eg, by trust, shareholders' agreement or otherwise)?

There are no statutory provisions restricting shareholders from entering into voting agreements in respect of their shares.

17. Under what circumstances can a shareholder challenge the resolutions adopted by the GM? Are there thresholds concerning the stock interest owned to be able to bring such a claim?

Resolutions duly adopted by the GM are binding on all shareholders. However, any resolution adopted to further or to harm the interests of one group of shareholders over another or to confer a special benefit upon any member of the board of directors without consideration for the interests of the company may be void (Articles 135/136, CL).

18. What are the terms and procedures to challenge a resolution of the GM?

The law is silent on the procedure for challenging resolutions passed at the GM. In practice a complaint can be made with the Ministry of Economy, the regulator, and if the Ministry fails to resolve the issue, an action can be filed in the civil courts.

SHAREHOLDERS' RIGHTS VERSUS DIRECTORS AND DUTIES OF OTHER CORPORATE BODIES IN THE COMPANY

19. What is the procedure for the appointment/replacement/revocation of directors and of statutory auditors, if any?

The procedure for the appointment of directors of a public or private joint stock company is election by secret ballot at the GM of the shareholders. However, the founders may appoint from among themselves the members of the first board of directors, provided that the duration of such a first term does not exceed three years (Article 96, CL).

Unless the by-laws provide otherwise, the board of directors may appoint a director to a vacant position, provided that the appointment is presented for approval to the shareholders at the next GM. The new member shall complete the term of the predecessor. If the vacant positions reach one-quarter of the number of the members of the board of directors, then a GM must be called to meet within no more than three months from the date the last position became vacant to elect directors to fill the vacant positions (Article 102, CL).

The GM may dismiss any and all members of the board of directors, even if the by-laws provide otherwise. The GM of the shareholders must then elect new members to the board of directors to replace those dismissed. The Ministry of Economy and the concerned local authority of the relevant Emirate must be notified of such actions (Article 116, CL).

The auditor is appointed by the GM for a one-year renewable term. The compensation of the auditor is also approved by the GM.

20. May shareholders challenge the resolutions of the board of directors? Is there a minimum percentage of capital required to challenge a board resolution?

Resolutions which are validly adopted by the GM are binding on all shareholders (Article 135, CL). However, any resolutions adopted to further or to harm the interests of certain groups of shareholders or to confer a special benefit upon members of the board of directors or others without consideration of the interests of the company may be void (Article 136, CL). Any shareholder may challenge such resolution but see question 21 below.

21. Are shareholders entitled to bring a legal action against the directors of the company? In which circumstances? Please describe briefly the principles of directors' liability.

Shareholders may commence legal action against the directors of the company. Directors are liable to the company and the shareholders in respect of any fraud or abuse of power, for all violations of applicable laws and the memorandum and articles of association, and for all errors in the management of the company (Article 111, CL).

The company has a right of action against the board of directors due to errors causing loss or damage to the shareholders. A resolution must be passed by the GM appointing a person to initiate proceedings in the company's name (Article 113, CL). A shareholder shall also have the right individually to make a claim in the event the company fails to do so if the mistake caused damage directly to the shareholder, provided the shareholder notifies the company (Article 114, CL).

22. What are the rights in connection with transactions where the directors have a conflict of interest situation?

A member of the board of directors may not participate, whether directly or indirectly, in any activity which competes with the company or its business without prior permission from the GM. This permission must be renewed annually (Article 108, CL).

If a member of the board of directors participates in a competing activity without obtaining prior permission from the GM, the company may request compensation or require that the transaction which the director entered into on their own behalf be considered as having been entered into on behalf of the company.

A member of the board of directors who has an interest which conflicts with the interests of the company in respect of a transaction duly brought before the board of directors, is obligated to notify the board of such a conflict and to not participate in the voting on the decision made in respect of the said transaction (Article 109, CL).

INFORMATION RIGHTS ON THE COMPANY'S BUSINESS

23. What information may be requested by the shareholders from the board concerning the general state of the company's business or any specific transaction? Are information rights different depending on the number of shares owned? Are shareholders entitled to receive written information before, during or after the GM about the meeting agenda and to what extent? Is it possible for a shareholder to obtain a copy of the minutes of the GM?

Each shareholder has the right to discuss subjects on the agenda of the GM and to pose questions to the members of the board of directors. The board members must answer the questions to the extent that the responses do not expose the company to harm (Article 130, CL). The shareholders are not generally entitled to information about the company's business outside the GM.

A shareholder may review the minutes of the GM. The review of the records and documents of the company by a shareholder is by permission of the board of directors or the GM in accordance with the by-laws of the company (Article 170, CL).

24. Do shareholders have the right/duty to resolve in the GM upon matters which were not on the agenda?

The law is silent on whether shareholders must or have the right to vote on matters which were not on the agenda of the GM. However, to the extent that these matters arise from issues on the agenda or are put on the agbenda by the shareholders during the GM and are important, the Ministry of Economy will probably approve such a vote.

25. Are shareholders entitled to inspect the corporate books and/or any other corporate or accounting documents? To what extent? Can they do it through external counsel or advisors?

Records and documents of the company can be made available following permission from the board of directors or the GM in accordance with the by-laws of the company (Article 170, CL). A shareholder is not otherwise allowed to inspect the books and records of the company.

SHAREHOLDERS' AGREEMENTS

26. Are shareholders' agreements validly enforceable? What are their typical contents and term of duration? Are they enforceable by or against third parties and, if so, to what extent?

Shareholders' agreements are enforceable in the UAE courts as private contracts. It is difficult to insist on the rights contained therein in dealings with government authorities or third parties.

Shareholders' rights may be enforceable against third parties if such rights are contained in the memorandum and articles of association of the company.

27. Do shareholders' agreements have to be disclosed to the public or registered in any public registry?

Shareholders' agreements do not have to be disclosed to the public or registered.

ECONOMIC RIGHTS AND RIGHTS OVER THE STOCK

28. Is the stock always freely transferable? Are there any legal limitations? Are there any restrictions on contractual limitations?

Whether shares are freely transferable depends on the type of company: eg, shares of public joint stock companies (Article 64, CL) are freely transferable; shares of limited liability companies have restrictions on transfer (Article 221, CL).

The transfer of shares is also subject to minimum national ownership requirements (Article 22, CL).

29. Are shareholders entitled to pledge their stock?

Shareholders in public and private joint stock companies may pledge shares by delivering them to the pledgor (Article 164, CL). As indicated above, limited liability companies do not issue transferable share certificates.

30. Are there financial assistance issues to be considered and other prohibitions to be evaluated in the context of a leveraged buyout transaction?

No. A parent or subsidiary company may provide assistance to the other.

31. May a company buy back its own stock and, if so, under what circumstances and subject to which limitations?

Generally a company may not purchase its own shares except when this is done for the reduction of the capital (Article 168, CL).

It is permissible for a company to purchase a portion of its shares not exceeding 10 per cent for the purpose of reselling, provided:

(a) the company obtains the prior consent of the Securities and Commodities Authority;

(b) the board of directors carries out the purchase transaction within one year from the date of obtaining approval from the Securities and Commodities Authority; and

(c) the company has surplus funds to meet the purchase requirements (the capital or the legal reserve must not be used to purchase the shares).

32. Is there a legal right to withdraw from the company and, if so, under what circumstances? How is the shareholders' stock valued and paid in such a case?

There is no right to withdraw from a company under the Companies Law.

33. In which circumstances can dividends be distributed among shareholders? Is it possible to exclude or limit the right of certain shareholders to dividends? Does a certain portion of the profits need to be set aside in a reserve fund where it cannot be distributed to the shareholders? Are advances on dividends allowed and, if so, under which circumstances? Can advances on dividends be reclaimed by the company?

Shareholders are entitled to their share of net profits upon a resolution of the GM to distribute such net profits (Article 194, CL).

All shareholders of a public or private joint stock company are entitled to share the profits of the company in proportion to their holding of shares of the company.

A company must allocate at least 10 per cent of the company's net profit to a legal reserve. The GM may suspend such contributions once the legal reserve equals half of the capital. The legal reserve may not be distributed to the shareholders. However, the portion that exceeds half of the paid up capital may be used in the distribution of the profits to the shareholders during years in which the company does not attain net profit sufficient to distribute the percentage specified in the by-laws.

Shareholders of limited liability companies can agree in the memorandum of association of the company to distribute profits in a ratio other than that of the ownership of the company provided no shareholder is excluded from participation in profits.

34. What are the rights of shareholders in the case of an issue of new stock (increase of the company's corporate capital) (pre-emption rights)?

Shareholders have priority in the subscription of new shares (Article 204, CL). Any provision to the contrary in the memorandum and articles of association, or in the resolution adopted to increase the capital of the company, is void.

New shares are allocated to shareholders in proportion to their current shareholding, provided that the allocation does not exceed the amount each shareholder has subscribed for. Any unallocated shares are allocated to shareholders who applied for more than their proportionate number of shares, and any remaining shares are offered for public subscription (Article 206, CL).

35. May minority shareholders ban or limit the company's capital structure in any manner?

Increases in capital may be vetoed by minority shareholders holding 25 per cent or more of the shares of the company. As a practical matter on account of the requirement to amend the memorandum of association of a company to give effect to a change in capital, all shareholders have a veto on any change in the capital structure.

36. Which are the financial assistance prohibitions in force?

There are none.

37. Apart from publicly listed companies, in which cases (if any) are shareholders obligated to obtain an authorisation from, or provide information to, a public authority about events that have an impact on their stock interest in the company?

The capital of a company may not be reduced without obtaining the prior approval of the Ministry of Economy (Article 209, CL). The Ministry of Economy and the concerned local authority of the relevant Emirate have broad rights to supervise public and private joint stock companies to verify that these companies are in compliance with the law (Article 318, CL).

SHAREHOLDERS' RIGHTS IN THE CASE OF EXTRAORDINARY TRANSACTIONS AND/OR WINDING-UP

38. What rights are available to shareholders in the case of a sale of all or a substantial portion of the company's assets? In the case of a merger or de-merger?

There are no special rights available to shareholders in the case of the sale of all or a substantial portion of the assets of the company. The merger of a company with another will require the consent of shareholders representing three-quarters of the capital of the company.

39. Which rights are available to shareholders in the case of conversion of the company into a European Company (SE) or into another type of company?
A company may be converted from one form to another by a resolution of at least three-quarters of the shares represented at an extraordinary GM of the company (Articles 143; 273, CL).

40. Which rights are available to shareholders of a company in liquidation?
Shareholders have the right to receive their proportionate share of the company's assets following liquidation (Article 169, CL). Proceeds from the liquidation are distributed to the shareholders following payment of the company's debts (Article 308, CL). In the case of limited liability companies, following payment of debt and return of the capital contributed by shareholders, the balance assets are distributed to shareholders in the proportion to which they are entitled to participate in the profits of the company.

41. Can shareholders cause the liquidation of the company? How?
A company may be liquidated by a resolution of shareholders representing at least three-quarters of the capital at an extraordinary GM of the company (Articles 137; 141, CL).

COMPANY GROUPS
42. Is the concept of 'group' recognised as such under specific legislation? What are the implications?
Such a concept is not recognised.

43. Does a controlling company have any particular duties *vis-à-vis* its controlled company shareholders?
Not applicable.

44. What are the rights of company shareholders when the controlling company puts in place actions and/or transactions that can be prejudicial to the shareholders?
Not applicable.

45. What are the limitations, if any, to the possibility of owning reciprocal stock interests in companies?
Not applicable.

United Kingdom

Travers Smith LLP Spencer Summerfield, Oliver Barnes & Laura Brocklehurst

BASIC INFORMATION ON THE TYPES OF LIMITED LIABILITY COMPANIES AND ON THE RIGHTS OF SHAREHOLDERS

1. What types of companies enjoy limited liability? If more than one, which ones have shareholders, ie, holders of share certificates? Which one is the most common? Which one is mostly used by foreign investors?

In the UK a company is a limited company if the liability of its members is limited by its constitution. Limited companies may be private or public and the liability of their members may be limited by shares or by guarantee. Private companies with liability limited by shares are most common and would mostly be used by foreign investors unless a public company was particularly required.

2. Are there minimum capital requirements and/or thin capitalisation rules in force?

Public companies must have a minimum allotted share capital of at least £50,000 (or the prescribed euro equivalent), one quarter of which must be paid-up. There are no minimum capital requirements for private companies.

3. Describe the types of shares that can be issued by a company and the different rights that they attribute to their owners, as well as any other financial instruments (bonds or other) and other instruments of a participatory nature in the company's capital that can also be issued by the company.

The most common shares are ordinary shares. Share rights will be set out in the company's constitution and will usually relate to entitlement to dividends and to payment on the winding up of the company as well as entitling the holders to participate in meetings of the company. Companies may also issue preference shares which customarily give the holder preferential rights, particularly in relation to entitlement to dividends and on a winding-up, but limited voting rights. Shares may be redeemable or non-redeemable. They can also be convertible (into other classes of shares) or deferred. Companies may also issue instruments giving rights to subscribe or convert into shares, such as options, warrants and unsecured loan stock but, until converted, these do not form part of the company's capital.

4. Can a company have only one shareholder and still enjoy limited liability?

Yes. And that shareholder may itself be a company with limited liability.

5. Are the rights of shareholders the same in any type of company?

Shareholders will usually have the same basic rights regardless of whether the company is private or public. The rights of shareholders depend on the rights which the company's constitution gives to their shares. These may include special rights, eg, relating to the appointment of directors, rights to be consulted or informed before the company takes a particular action or weighted voting rights. There is no limit on the number of different classes of shares a company may have.

6. What are the basic rights of any shareholder? Describe briefly the rights of minority shareholders and indicate which thresholds, if any, are required to allow the minority shareholders to exercise any such rights.

See questions 3 and 5.

Minority shareholders' rights include the following:

Percentage of shares/voting rights in the company	Rights of shareholders
At least five per cent	• apply to court to prevent conversion of a public company to a private company; • requisition general meeting; • require written resolution of private company to be circulated to members; and • requisition resolution at annual general meeting of a public company
At least 10 per cent	Call for a poll on a resolution
More than 25 per cent	Prevent passing of special resolution.

7. Do all shareholders enjoy the same rights or can some shareholders be attributed specific rights, whether by reason of the particular class of stock owned or other? Are such rights generally provided for at the level of the company's by-laws and/or in shareholders' agreements?

See question 5. Different shareholders can enjoy different rights but this is usually effected by a company having different classes. So, for example all the A shareholders will have the same rights and all the B shareholders will have the same rights – but the rights of the A shareholders and B shareholders do not need to be the same. These rights are usually provided for in the company's articles of association.

8. May the rights of shareholders, generally speaking, be limited, modified, suppressed or waived in any way? If so, how? Are such modifications or limitations provided for in the company's by-laws and/or in shareholders' agreements?

See questions 3 and 5. The rights of shareholders may be limited, modified or waived, except that shareholders cannot, in their capacity as shareholders, be financially liable for more than the amount unpaid on their shares. Shareholders may agree with the company and/or between themselves that their rights may be restricted so, for example, a share may be non-voting (ie, the holder is not able to vote at a meeting of the company) or may not entitle the holder to payment of a dividend. The constitutional document of a company (known as its articles of association) may entrench certain rights so that, for example, a set percentage of the shareholders must vote in favour of changing a right. Under legislation expected to become effective shortly, such provisions must be made either on the formation of the company or by an amendment of the articles of association agreed to by all the shareholders. If a company has more than one class of shares then the articles of association will often contain a provision to the effect that the rights of that class cannot be varied by changing the rights of another class, without the consent of the holders of the first class of shares. Modifications to rights would usually be contained in the company's articles of association although they could be contained in a shareholders' agreement if the modification applied solely between two or more shareholders.

GENERAL MEETING OF SHAREHOLDERS (GM) AND VOTING RIGHTS
9. Which decisions are reserved to the competence of the GM?
There are a number of actions which, in accordance with the Companies Act 2006 (the '2006 Act'), must be approved by shareholders, including:
- amending the company's articles of association;
- approving a reduction of capital or share buy-back;
- converting the company from one form to another, eg, from a private company to a public company;
- approving the payment of a political donation;
- approving a loan to or a substantial property transaction involving a director;
- approving a payment for loss of office to a director;
- removing an auditor from office; and
- approving a liability limitation agreement between an auditor and the company.

Listed companies are required to obtain further shareholder approvals at GMs in respect of certain transactions.

10. How does a shareholder participate in a GM? Are there any limitations to having a minimum number of shares? May a shareholder delegate attendance to another shareholder or to the board? May a shareholder obtain assistance from the courts or any other governmental body to intervene in a GM or to cause one to be held in some particular cases?

All shareholders have the right to attend, speak and vote at a GM. There is no minimum number of shares which a shareholder must hold before being able to participate in a GM. Shareholders may appoint proxies (or, in the case of a corporate shareholder, a corporate representative) to attend, speak and vote on their behalf. A proxy need not be a shareholder and is commonly the chairman of the meeting. Proxies must be appointed before the meeting starts in accordance with the company's articles of association.

Shareholders could obtain an injunction from the courts to prevent a meeting being held. Conversely, the 2006 Act allows a court to order that a GM should be held. This applies if for any reason it is impracticable to call a meeting of a company in any manner in which meetings of that company may be called or to conduct the meeting in the manner prescribed by the company's articles of association or the 2006 Act. The court can order a meeting either of its own volition or if a director or shareholder applies to the court and the court may give such directions as it thinks expedient.

11. May a GM be called and held at the request of any shareholder? Is there a threshold regarding the percentage of the stock interest owned in the company that may entitle a shareholder to such a right?

The directors of a company are required to call a GM once a request is received from members representing at least five per cent of shares with voting rights.

12. May a shareholder bring up an issue to be resolved upon and put it to a vote if it is not included on the agenda? May a shareholder require more information from the GM and/or the board concerning the agenda of the GM, to be put in a better position to exercise their vote?

Shareholders in a public company can require the company to give notice of a resolution which may be properly proposed, and is intended to be proposed, at an annual general meeting (AGM). In order to compel the company to act on this, the request must be made by:

- members representing at least five per cent of the total voting rights of all the members who have a right to vote on resolutions at the AGM to which the request relates; or
- at least 100 members who have a right to vote on the resolution at that meeting and hold shares in the company on which there has been paid up an average sum, per shareholder, of at least £100.

Shareholders in companies which are listed on a regulated market (ie, on the Official List of the UK Listing Authority (the 'official list')) may request the company to include in the business to be dealt with at an AGM any matter (other than a proposed resolution) which may properly be included in the business of the meeting. The threshold to enable shareholders to exercise that power is as set out above.

Shareholders of either a private or public company may also require the company to circulate to other shareholders a statement of not more than 1,000 words about a matter referred to in a proposed resolution to be dealt with at a meeting or other business to be dealt with at the meeting. Again, the threshold for making such a request is as set out above.

If shareholders require further information, they should engage directly with the company. In large listed public companies, corporate governance guidelines encourage companies to engage with their shareholders, particularly in relation to any potentially contentious resolutions, but price-sensitive information should not be released on a selective basis.

13. May a GM be held by telecommunication means and/or by correspondence (ie, by written consent)?

There is no reason why a GM may not be held by telecommunication means, unless the company's articles of association specifically prohibit this. It is important that everyone attending the meeting can hear everyone else taking part.

Private companies may pass resolutions in writing so, rather than a meeting being physically held, the resolution is sent to shareholders who indicate their agreement to it by signing and returning it to the company. This usually only works in the case of small private companies with relatively few shareholders.

14. Are voting rights always proportionate to the stock held by each shareholder or can they vary by share class?

Unless the articles of association provide otherwise, each shareholder has one vote on a show of hands and, on a poll, one vote for each share they hold. However, different classes of shares may have different voting rights and a company's articles of association may provide for weighted voting rights – for example, a share may have more than one vote on a poll on a particular category of resolution.

15. Are there non-voting shares? Is there a maximum percentage of capital represented by non-voting shares?

Yes, shares may be non-voting. There is no maximum percentage but at least one share in the company must hold voting rights.

16. Can shareholders group their shares in order to exercise their voting rights (eg, by trust, shareholders' agreement or otherwise)?

Shareholders can work together to exercise their voting rights either formally through shareholders' agreements or informally on a one-off basis. However, in the case of public companies, they must be particularly careful that they are not deemed, for the purposes of the City Code on Takeovers and Mergers (UK Takeover Code) or the rules of the Financial Services Authority (FSA), to be acting in concert. If parties are treated as acting in concert (eg, by working together to ensure a resolution to remove a director is approved) this could trigger a mandatory bid for a company or require earlier than expected public disclosure of information about their shareholdings by the relevant shareholders to the listed company and to the market.

17. Under what circumstances can a shareholder challenge the resolutions adopted by the GM? Are there thresholds concerning the stock interest owned to be able to bring such a claim?

Any shareholder may challenge the decisions of a GM on procedural grounds, eg, failure to give proper notice of the meeting, or the fact that insufficient shareholders were present and the meeting was therefore inquorate. However, decisions taken at such a meeting may stand depending on the circumstances. For example, deliberate failure to give notice would invalidate the proceedings but it is likely that accidental failure to give notice would not invalidate decisions made at the meeting.

Shareholders of a quoted company may require an independent assessor to report on any poll taken or to be taken at a GM. The request must be made by:

- shareholders representing not less than five per cent of the total voting rights of all the members who have a right to vote on the matter to which the poll relates; or
- by not less than 100 members who have a right to vote on such a matter and hold shares in the company on which there has been paid up an average sum, per member, of not less than £100.

The independent assessor's report should cover whether the procedures adopted in relation to the poll were adequate, whether the votes cast were fairly and accurately reported and counted, whether the validity of any proxy appointments was fairly assessed and whether the notice of the meeting complied with the relevant provisions of the 2006 Act.

18. What are the terms and procedures to challenge a resolution of the GM?

See question 17. Where the meeting has suffered from some form of organisational irregularity then a shareholder would usually raise this with the board of the company. If the board refused to cooperate then the shareholder might seek an order from the court to prevent the company relying on the result of the meeting. Alternatively, if the meeting has not yet taken place then the shareholder might ask the company to postpone the meeting or seek a remedy such as an injunction to prevent the meeting from taking place.

SHAREHOLDERS' RIGHTS VERSUS DIRECTORS AND DUTIES OF OTHER CORPORATE BODIES IN THE COMPANY

19. What is the procedure for the appointment/replacement/ revocation of directors and of statutory auditors, if any?

A company's articles of association will usually set out the provisions relating to the appointment of a director and the termination of that appointment. The standard model articles which apply to private and public companies by default in accordance with the 2006 Act provide that a director may be appointed by ordinary resolution (ie, with the approval of 50 per cent of the shareholders) or by a decision of the board of directors.

The appointment of a director may be terminated in various ways – eg, if they are prohibited by law from being a director, a bankruptcy order is made against them or if the director resigns in accordance with the provisions of the articles of association. A director of a public company will normally be required, in accordance with corporate governance requirements and the articles of association, to retire by rotation every three years. If they wish they will be eligible to be re-appointed by an ordinary resolution of shareholders. A director can also be removed from office in accordance with the 2006 Act if the shareholders pass the necessary ordinary resolution.

20. May shareholders challenge the resolutions of the board of directors? Is there a minimum percentage of capital required to challenge a board resolution?

There is no formal procedure for shareholders to challenge a resolution passed by the board. However, a 75 per cent majority may direct the board to take certain action. If shareholders are unhappy with a decision of the board or are aware that the required procedures or legal requirements, such as the declaration of any interests in the matters under discussion, were not followed then this should be raised with the chairman or other appropriate board member such as, in the case of a listed company, the senior independent director. See question 21.

21. Are shareholders entitled to bring a legal action against the directors of a company? In which circumstances? Please describe briefly the principles of directors' liability.

This is a very complex area of English company law but, in brief, shareholders may in certain circumstances bring an action against the directors as follows:

- shareholders may, subject to obtaining court approval, bring a derivative claim on behalf of the company against the directors for negligence, default, breach of duty or breach of trust;
- minority shareholders may bring what is called an unfair prejudice claim seeking relief against the acts of the controlling directors of the company. Alternatively the shareholders might, in respect of any oppressive acts against them, seek the winding up of the company on a just and equitable basis;
- where the shareholder has a personal cause of action against the director – perhaps as a result of a direct contract between the director and shareholder; or
- where, in exceptional circumstances, the director has breached the company's constitution and the action is for some reason incapable of ratification by the shareholders. The shareholder could seek to enforce the constitutional term.

Directors may also have liability to creditors in insolvency situations where they have carried on trading in circumstances where it was probable that the company would go into insolvent liquidation.

They may also have liability to fines or imprisonment for breaches of statutory provisions.

22. What are the rights in connection with transactions where the directors have a conflict of interest situation?

Under the 2006 Act, directors must avoid situations which do or could conflict with the interests of the company. The directors may authorise the situation (provided, in the case of public companies, that their constitution permits such authorisation). In relation to conflicts arising out of a proposed transaction or arrangement with the company, directors must declare the nature and extent of their interest in advance either at a specific board meeting or in writing. The declaration must be updated if the interest changes. There are exceptions to this regime – for example, if the interest cannot reasonably be regarded as giving rise to a conflict or if it relates to a director's service contract. A company's constitution may often contain provisions which allow, subject to declaration of the conflict, the relevant director to take part in and vote on the matter which gives rise to the conflict.

INFORMATION RIGHTS ON THE COMPANY'S BUSINESS

23. What information may be requested by the shareholders from the board concerning the general state of the company's business or any specific transaction? Are information rights different depending on the number of shares owned? Are shareholders entitled to receive written information before, during or after the GM about the meeting agenda and to what extent? Is it possible for a shareholder to obtain a copy of the minutes of the GM?

Unless shareholders have a separate agreement with the company, they will have no special entitlement to information (other than information already in the public domain) about the company's business or any specific transactions regardless of how many shares they hold. Listed companies may require shareholder approval for larger or significant transactions and will therefore have to send a circular to shareholders about the transaction and call a meeting to obtain their consent.

All shareholders are entitled to receive notice of a GM. The notice must state the general nature of the business to be dealt with at the meeting. In practice, notices will usually set out the actual resolutions to be approved at the meeting and may include an explanation of the resolution. Listed companies will always include the resolutions for the GMs and detailed explanations about them. There are additional notice requirements for listed companies.

Every company must keep records comprising minutes of all proceedings of general meetings as well as copies of all shareholder resolutions passed otherwise than at meetings, ie, in writing. Such records must be kept available for inspection by any shareholder free of charge.

24. Do shareholders have the right/duty to resolve in the GM upon matters which were not on the agenda?

A resolution which is not set out in the agenda may be capable of being proposed, but only if it is within the scope of the business of the meeting. A resolution which is not clearly related to the business set out in the agenda will not be permitted. To avoid doubt, shareholders wishing to propose resolutions should use the powers of requisition referred to under question 12.

25. Are shareholders entitled to inspect the corporate books and/or any other corporate or accounting documents? To what extent? Can they do it through external counsel or advisors?

All shareholders have the right to inspect in person and free of charge the company's registers of members, directors, secretaries and charges and also copies of the directors' service contracts. Shareholders may also inspect, for a limited time, certain other documents in connection with a transaction a company is carrying out, eg, the directors' statement and auditor's report in connection with the payment out of capital for redemption or purchase of own shares. However, they may not inspect management accounts or board briefing papers.

Shareholders have the right to be sent a copy of the company's annual accounts and reports. In addition shareholders can demand, without paying any fee, copies of a company's last annual accounts, last directors' report and auditors' report and, for quoted companies, the last directors' remuneration report.

SHAREHOLDERS' AGREEMENTS
26. Are shareholders' agreements validly enforceable? What are their typical contents and term of duration? Are they enforceable by or against third parties and, if so, to what extent?

In general, shareholders' agreements are as enforceable as any other contract. (Note, however, that the company itself cannot contract to limit its statutory powers – for example to alter its articles or issue share capital – and so should not be a party to such a restriction.) A shareholders' agreement may be for a fixed or indeterminate period of time or may be expressed to last until one or more named shareholders no longer hold shares. In order to be of continuing enforceability, it will be necessary to provide that no transfer of shares can be made unless the transferee enters into a deed by which they adhere to and become bound by the shareholders' agreement.

Shareholders' agreements may contain almost any arrangements and will normally cover matters which the shareholders would prefer not to be made public (as would be the case if the subject matter were instead contained in the articles of association). Frequently they contain voting undertakings or voting restrictions which would, if not contained in a separate shareholders' agreement, require the creation of different classes of shares carrying special voting rights. In the case of private companies, they may also entitle the shareholder to receive information about the company which is not available to other shareholders.

If a third party contracts in good faith with a company, without notice of any restrictions imposed by a shareholders' agreement, the third party will not be affected by the restrictions.

27. Do shareholders' agreements have to be disclosed to the public or registered in any public registry?

An agreement which has been agreed to by all the shareholders (or all of a class of shareholders) which, if not so agreed to, would not have been effective for its purpose unless passed by a special resolution (or a particular majority of the relevant class) must be registered with the Registrar of Companies and will then be available for public inspection. To the extent, therefore, that a shareholders' agreement overrides or contradicts provisions in the company's articles of association, it will need to be registered. However, if it merely expands on the articles or deals with completely different subject matter, it should not need to be registered or disclosed to the public.

ECONOMIC RIGHTS AND RIGHTS OVER THE STOCK
28. Is the stock always freely transferable? Are there any legal limitations? Are there any restrictions on contractual limitations?

Unless the company's articles of association provide otherwise, shares are freely transferable. For listed companies it is a requirement that their shares be freely transferable, unless, in exceptional circumstances, the FSA otherwise agrees. A restriction on the transfer of such shares is generally permissible where the holder or any other person who appears to be interested in the shares has failed to respond to a notice requiring it to disclose the nature and extent of the interests. This restriction would normally appear in the company's articles of association. Companies quoted on the London Stock Exchange's alternative investment market (AIM) may also restrict transfers where they are seeking to limit the number of shareholders in a particular country to ensure that they do not become subject to foreign statutes or regulations. For private companies there are no restrictions on contractual limitations. These companies often have restrictions on transfer, by providing that shares must be offered to existing shareholders before being transferred to third parties. It is also possible for private companies to provide in their articles of association that the directors may refuse to register the transfer of any shares to persons of whom they do not approve.

29. Are shareholders entitled to pledge their stock?

Shareholders are entitled to pledge their shares, although in publicly traded companies, such pledges, if made by directors or senior managers, will need to be disclosed to the market.

30. Are there financial assistance issues to be considered and other prohibitions to be evaluated in the context of a leveraged buyout transaction?

Leveraged buyouts often involve the target company giving some security to secure the debt financing. This gives rise to considerations of financial assistance if the target is a public company, although since the financial assistance provisions no longer generally apply to private companies, the lending bank will often wish to ensure that the target company converts to a private company before entering into any security. As with any transaction, the directors will need to be satisfied that the giving of security is in the interests of the company.

31. May a company buy back its own stock and, if so, under what circumstances and subject to which limitations?

The 2006 Act prohibits a company acquiring its own shares (section 658), but the 2006 Act sets out a number of exceptions to this general rule. In particular, sections 690 and following set out procedures and conditions which must be followed for a share buyback to be permitted, including shareholder approval. A public company may only use distributable profits or the proceeds of a fresh issue of shares to pay for the buyback. A private company may finance the purchase out of capital, subject to a number of conditions, including shareholder approval and the making of statements by the directors and auditors as to the company's financial position and prospects.

32. Is there a legal right to withdraw from the company and, if so, under what circumstances? How is the shareholders' stock valued and paid in such a case?

Shareholders may normally only withdraw by selling their shares to a third party. Some private companies may have provisions in their articles of association giving a shareholder a right to require other shareholders to buy their shares in certain circumstances or requiring them to transfer their shares if, for example, they leave the employment of the company. The articles may pre-determine the price or provide that if the parties cannot agree, the value will be determined by an independent third-party valuer. It is possible for the shares to be bought back by the company, subject to shareholder approval, as referred to in question 31, although this is not very common.

33. In which circumstances can dividends be distributed among shareholders? Is it possible to exclude or limit the right of certain shareholders to dividends? Does a certain portion of the profits need to be set aside in a reserve fund where it cannot be distributed to the shareholders? Are advances on dividends allowed and, if so, under which circumstances? Can advances on dividends be reclaimed by the company?

A company may only pay dividends out of 'profits available for distribution'. These are defined by the 2006 Act (section 830(2)) as its accumulated realised profits (so far as not previously distributed or capitalised) less its accumulated, realised losses (so far as not previously written off in a reduction or reorganisation of capital). Realised profits and losses are determined in accordance with technical guidance produced by the Institute of Chartered Accountants in England and Wales.

It is possible to create shares which by their terms of issue, have no, or very limited, rights to dividends. Holders of shares which carry normal rights to dividends, may, by virtue of the company's articles of association, be deprived of their rights to dividends while there is a default in providing information as to the nature and extent of any interest in their shares (see question 27).

There is no requirement to set any part of the profits aside in a reserve. However, the directors of the company should ensure that the company has sufficient cash and reserves for its future development and needs and may be in breach of their duties if they recommend a distribution of all the profits, with the result that the company's financial position is compromised.

As well as paying a final dividend, approved by shareholders, the directors may pay an interim dividend, without shareholder approval, if they are satisfied that the profits of the company and the future financial requirements of the company justify this. However, interim dividends are not strictly an advance of the final dividend and, once paid, may not be reclaimed.

34. What are the rights of shareholders in the case of an issue of new stock (increase of the company's corporate capital) (pre-emption rights)?

Any issue of shares (or grant of rights to subscribe or convert into shares), other than under an employees' share scheme, must first be approved by the company's articles of association or by a majority vote of shareholders (section 549 2006 Act). This does not apply to private companies with only one class of shares which may allot freely, subject to their articles.

Any equity shares must be offered pre-emptively to existing shareholders. However, this provision only applies to issues for cash and may be disapplied by shareholders passing a special resolution (requiring a 75 per cent majority of those voting) or, in the case of a private company, if the articles of association exclude or disapply it. Listed companies are subject to additional guidelines imposed by institutional investors, which state that non pre-emptive issues for cash should normally be limited to five per cent of the company's issued ordinary share capital in any year and to 7.5 per cent over a rolling three-year period.

35. May minority shareholders ban or limit the company's capital structure in any manner?

Except where a special resolution is required to issue shares non pre-emptively (see question 34), minority shareholders have no rights to limit the company's capital structure. This is subject to the general right of a minority shareholder to apply to the courts if the company's affairs are being conducted in a manner that is unfairly prejudicial to all or some of the shareholders (section 994 2006 Act – see question 21). Issues of shares may be limited by a shareholders' agreement or by special share rights giving minority shareholders a veto over changes to the share capital.

36. Which are the financial assistance prohibitions in force?

Public companies are prohibited from giving financial assistance directly or indirectly for the purpose of the acquisition of their shares. This prohibition is wide and covers the giving of loans, guarantees and security and other financial assistance which materially reduces the company's net assets, or where the company has no net assets. It also prohibits the giving by a public company of financial assistance for the purpose of the acquisition of shares in its private holding company. Private companies are no longer subject to these restrictions (other than private companies giving assistance for the purchase of shares in their public holding companies). However, they are still bound by the general rule that companies should not unlawfully reduce their capital.

37. Apart from publicly listed companies, in which cases, if any, are shareholders obligated to obtain an authorisation from, or provide information to, a public authority about events that have an impact on their stock interest in the company?

Shareholders in publicly traded (listed and AIM) companies are obliged to notify significant interests in shares. For private companies there are no such notification requirements.

SHAREHOLDERS' RIGHTS IN THE CASE OF EXTRAORDINARY TRANSACTIONS AND/OR WINDING-UP

38. What rights are available to shareholders in the case of a sale of all or a substantial portion of the company's assets? In the case of a merger or de-merger?

Such transactions, if carried out by a public listed or AIM traded company, would require the prior approval of shareholders. No such approval is required by private companies.

The shareholders have no direct right to the proceeds of a sale of the company's assets. To the extent that they represent distributable profits, they may be distributed by way of dividend. Otherwise they may be returned to shareholders by means of a reduction of capital or by a winding-up.

In the case of a merger involving the disposal of shares, all shareholders would have to be treated equally and so any consideration received would be divided between them in proportion to their shareholdings.

39. Which rights are available to shareholders in the case of conversion of the company into a European Company (SE) or into another type of company?

A public company may be transformed into an SE with the approval of at least 75 per cent of the shareholder votes cast.

An SE is not a common type of company in the UK. At the end of March 2009 (in the latest Statistical Tables on Companies Registration Activities 2008-2009 compiled by Companies House), only 14 SEs had been registered in Great Britain.

40. Which rights are available to shareholders of a company in liquidation?

On a liquidation the liquidator collects in and realises the assets of the company. The liquidator must pay the assets in the following statutory order of priority:

- fixed charges;
- expenses of the winding-up;
- preferential debts;
- floating charges; and
- ordinary unsecured creditors (*pro rata*).

If the company is solvent after paying the above categories in full, any surplus will be distributed to the shareholders of the company in accordance with their shareholdings. Preference shareholders may have a preferential right to the surplus ahead of ordinary shareholders.

41. Can shareholders cause the liquidation of the company? How?

Yes. There is a statutory provision in the Insolvency Act 1986 permitting shareholders to adopt a special resolution (requiring a 75 per cent majority of those voting to approve it) for a voluntary winding-up. The shareholders appoint a liquidator for the purpose of winding up the company and distributing its assets. If the collection and distribution of assets takes more than one year, the liquidator must call a GM at the end of the first year and each successive year to keep the shareholders informed. A final meeting of the shareholders is held prior to dissolution.

The usual practical difficulty is the inability to get the majority needed for a special resolution for a voluntary winding-up. The alternative provided by the legislation is for a shareholder to ask the court to order that the company be wound up. The court cannot make a winding-up order unless one of the circumstances set out in section 122(1) of the Insolvency Act 1986 exists. The circumstance that shareholders invariably rely on is section 122(1)(g): 'the court is of the opinion that it is just and equitable that the company should be wound up'. See question 21.

COMPANY GROUPS

42. Is the concept of 'group' recognised as such under specific legislation? What are the implications?

There is no general definition of 'group' in UK company legislation. However, it is common to call a holding company and its subsidiaries a 'group'. The terms 'holding company', 'subsidiary' and 'wholly owned subsidiary' are defined in section 1159 of the 2006 Act.

The 2006 Act does recognise the concept of a 'group' in particular circumstances, eg, for the purposes of consolidated group accounts. In this context, 'group' means the parent undertakings and its subsidiary undertakings (such terms are defined in section 1162 of the 2006 Act).

Groups are also recognised under tax legislation.

43. Does a controlling company have any particular duties *vis-à-vis* its controlled company shareholders?

A controlling company has no particular duties under law towards other shareholders in its subsidiaries.

44. What are the rights of company shareholders when the controlling company puts in place actions and/or transactions that can be prejudicial to the business of the shareholders?

See question 21.

45. What are the limitations, if any, to the possibility of owning reciprocal stock interests in companies?

A subsidiary is prohibited from holding shares in its holding company and any allotment or transfer of shares in a company to its subsidiary is void (section 136(1) 2006 Act).

United States

Kirkland & Ellis LLP Susan J. Zachman
Richards Layton & Finger, P.A. Megan W. Shaner

BASIC INFORMATION ON THE TYPES OF LIMITED LIABILITY COMPANIES AND ON THE RIGHTS OF SHAREHOLDERS

1. What types of companies enjoy limited liability? If more than one, which ones have shareholders, ie holders of share certificates? Which one is the most common? Which one is mostly used by foreign investors?

In the United States the three types of general use, for-profit companies that enjoy limited liability are corporations, limited liability companies (LLCs) and limited partnerships (LPs). Corporations are the most common form of company structure, but for sophisticated transactions there has been a move towards using the LLC structure, which allows more freedom to contractually arrange ownership rights and the operation of the entity. Foreign investors commonly use a corporation to establish a US business and an LLC or an LP to establish an investment vehicle for a portfolio of investments, although such choices are highly fact specific to a particular investor's tax circumstances, a discussion of which is beyond the scope of this chapter.

Unless otherwise noted, the responses in this chapter refer to the statutory and case law of the State of Delaware, which is the jurisdiction of choice for the formation of many US entities, and has the most developed business law jurisprudence. While many contracts provide that the laws of the State of New York will be used to interpret the contract, and the federal or state courts in the State of New York used to decide any related disputes, the contracting entities need not be incorporated or formed in the State of New York in order to make such contract choices.

None of the Delaware statutory regimes governing corporations (the General Corporation Law of the State of Delaware (the DGCL)), LLCs (the Delaware Limited Liability Company Act) or LPs (the Delaware Revised Uniform Limited Partnership Act) require that stakeholders be issued share certificates to reflect their ownership position, however, it is common for share certificates to be issued to shareholders of corporations and for ownership interests in LLCs and LPs to remain uncertificated.

In general, private corporations in the United States are not listed on any stock exchange. Public corporations that are listed on stock exchanges are governed by the rules of the US Securities and Exchange Commission and the rules of the particular stock exchange on which they are listed, in addition to the laws of the state of their incorporation.

2. Are there minimum capital requirements and/or thin capitalisation rules in force?

Generally no; provided, however, that if the stock of a corporation is issued with par value, then the consideration received for such stock, as determined by the corporation's board of directors, must be at least equal to the par value of such stock as required by DGCL §153(a). Because most corporate stock is issued with a *de minimis* par value, such as $0.01 per share or less, there is not a true minimum capital requirement.

3. Describe the types of shares that can be issued by a company and the different rights that they attribute to their owners, as well as any other financial instruments (bonds or other) and other instruments of a participatory nature in the company's capital that can also be issued by the company.

Corporations may issue one or more classes of common or preferred stock or one or more series of common or preferred stock within any class thereof (DGCL §151(a)). If provided in the certificate of incorporation or resolution of the board of directors providing for the issuance of a class or series of stock, stock of any class or of any series may also be convertible into, or exchangeable for, either at the option of the holder or the corporation, or upon the happening of a specified event, shares of any other class or classes or any other series of the same or different class or classes of stock of the corporation. Corporations may also issue options, warrants, stock appreciation rights and other similar contractual instruments that may be exercisable or convertible into common or preferred stock, as well as debt securities of the corporation (which also may be convertible into common or preferred stock). The default statutory rights of the common shareholders are described in the DGCL, but may be altered in the certificate of incorporation, the by-laws, shareholders' agreements and the grant, subscription or purchase agreements under which the securities are granted or issued. As distinguished from common stock, preferred stock is stock that enjoys certain defined rights, powers and preferences generally relating to dividend and liquidation priorities, which are set forth in the corporation's certificate of incorporation or the resolutions of the board of directors providing for the issuance of such stock.

Similar types of ownership can be effectuated in an LLC or an LP through contractual provisions in the Limited Liability Company Agreement or Limited Partnership Agreement that governs the economics of ownership interests in the LLC or the LP, respectively.

4. Can a company have only one shareholder and still enjoy limited liability?

Yes. There is no requirement under the DGCL that a corporation have more than one shareholder.

5. Are the rights of shareholders the same in any type of company?

Default shareholder rights are delineated in more detail for corporations under the DGCL and relevant case law, but as discussed above, such default rights can in many instances be modified in the corporation's certificate of incorporation or by agreement among the relevant shareholders and the corporation. The statutory and case law regimes for LLCs and LPs map out less detailed default provisions for shareholder rights in LLCs and LPs (technically ownership holdings are denoted in 'units' and ownership percentages, respectively, as opposed to shares of stock).

6. What are the basic rights of any shareholder? Describe briefly the rights of minority shareholders and indicate which thresholds, if any, are required to allow the minority shareholders to exercise any such rights.

As a general matter, ownership of stock of a corporation gives the shareholder the right to share in the earnings of the corporation, as they may be declared from time to time in the form of dividends, and to receive a *pro rata* share of the assets of the corporation on dissolution, after all of its debts have been paid.

Corporations in the United States are managed by the board of directors of the corporation, which then may delegate the day-to-day functions to the management of the corporation (DGCL §141(a)). Shareholders do not have the right to participate in the general management of the corporation, however, certain matters do require shareholder approval. Shareholders generally are charged with the selection and removal of the board of directors (although interim period replacements or designation of board members for vacancies and newly created seats may generally be carried out by the board itself), approval of amendments to the corporation's certificate of incorporation and by-laws (although generally the board can amend the by-laws as well), sales, leases or exchanges of all or substantially all of the assets of the corporation, mergers, dissolutions and liquidations.

Such approval rights are generally granted to all shareholders (without a holding size threshold). Additionally, shareholders, including minority shareholders, can use the information rights or the appraisal rights described in questions 23 and 38 below.

7. Do all shareholders enjoy the same rights or can some shareholders be attributed specific rights, whether by reason of the particular class of stock owned or other? Are such rights generally provided for at the level of the company's by-laws and/or in shareholders' agreements?

Shareholders of corporations may be attributed specific rights, by reason of the particular class of stock owned, by reason of the identity of the particular shareholder or otherwise. Rights granted to particular classes of stock are generally laid out in the certificate of incorporation or the resolutions of the board of directors establishing the class or series of stock, but may also appear in the by-laws, shareholders' agreements or the grant or subscription agreements under which the shares were issued. Rights attributed to a shareholder other than by reason of the particular class of stock owned are most often found in a shareholders' agreement or the grant or subscription agreements governing the issuance of such securities. In the case of some fundamental rights negotiated by a certain class of shareholders, such rights may be included in the certificate of incorporation in order to ensure that if such rights are violated they may be declared void, as opposed to simply creating a cause of action for damages in a contract dispute.

8. May the rights of shareholders, generally speaking, be limited, modified, suppressed or waived in any way? If so, how? Are such modifications or limitations provided for in the company's by-laws and/or in shareholders' agreements?

The DGCL generally allows the shareholders to limit, modify, suppress or waive default shareholder rights provided in the statute. Such modification of rights must in some cases be outlined in the certificate of incorporation or the by-laws of the corporation, but in other cases modification in shareholders' agreements is permitted.

Economic holders in LLC and LP entities may generally limit, modify, suppress or waive any of their default rights under the relevant statute in the LLC or LP Agreement of the organisation.

GENERAL MEETING OF SHAREHOLDERS (GM) AND VOTING RIGHTS

9. Which decisions are reserved to the competence of the GM?

Any topic of business that is a proper matter for shareholder action under applicable law, such as the matters discussed above in question 6, may be raised at either a special or annual general meeting of the shareholders in accordance with the procedural rules set forth in the DGCL and any other rules set forth in the certificate of incorporation and the by-laws of the corporation. Generally, with respect to a special meeting of the shareholders, only those matters that are stated in the notice for the special meeting may be considered at such meeting.

Unless the members of the board of directors are chosen by written consent in lieu of an annual meeting in accordance with DGCL §211(b), an annual meeting of the shareholders for the purpose of electing directors must be held within 13 months after the latest to occur of:
(i)   the organisation of the corporation;
(ii) the corporation's last annual meeting; or
(iii) the last action by written consent to elect directors in lieu of an annual meeting (DGCL §211(c)).

10. How does a shareholder participate in a GM? Are there any limitations to having a minimum number of shares? May a shareholder delegate attendance to another shareholder or to the board? May a shareholder obtain assistance from the courts or any other governmental body to intervene in a GM or to cause one to be held in some particular cases?

Any shareholder may participate in an annual general meeting, without regard to the number of shares such holder owns. If authorised by DGCL §211(a)(1) or the corporation's organisational documents, the board of directors may determine that shareholders not present at the meeting may participate through means of remote communication. Shareholders may also delegate attendance, voting and acting by written consent to a proxyholder in accordance with DGCL §212, however, the formalities of granting valid proxies may also be governed by state laws other than the law of the state of incorporation of the entity.

If a corporation has not held an annual general meeting or effectuated the election of the board of directors through a written consent within 13 months of its last such action, then any shareholder may seek the intervention of the Delaware Court of Chancery to order such a meeting (DGCL §211(c)).

11. May a GM be called and held at the request of any shareholder? Is there a threshold regarding the percentage of the stock interest owned in the company that may entitle a shareholder to such a right?
Special meetings of the shareholders may be called by the board of directors, or by those persons who have been given such rights under the certificate of incorporation or by-laws of the corporation (DGCL §211(d)). A corporation's organisational documents may provide limitations on who has the ability to call a special meeting of the shareholders, including requiring shareholders to hold a specific percentage of the corporation's capital stock.

12. May a shareholder bring up an issue to be resolved upon and put it to a vote if it is not included on the agenda? May a shareholder require more information from the GM and/or the board concerning the agenda of the GM to be put in a better position to exercise its vote?
Other than the above-mentioned right to call a meeting to elect the board of directors (see question 10), the DGCL does not give the shareholders of a corporation specific rights to place items on the agenda or to call for a vote. Such rights, however, are often granted contractually to certain shareholders in the certificate of incorporation, by-laws, shareholders' agreement or the grant or subscription agreement documents governing the issuance of securities of the corporation.

A corporation's organisational documents may provide for procedures that a shareholder must follow in order to properly submit nominees for the election of directors or other business matters for consideration by the shareholders at an annual general meeting or special meeting. The ability of shareholders to bring up issues for a vote at the annual general meeting or special meeting, as well as the inclusion by shareholders of information about such issues in the proxy materials mailed out to the shareholders by the corporation in connection with the meeting, is currently the topic of much discussion in the United States in the case of publicly-traded listed companies.

Notice of meetings, generally required to be delivered between 10 and 60 days before the meeting, must include the date, time and place (if any) of the meeting, the means of remote communication for participation, if permitted, and the record date for determination of the shareholders entitled to vote (DGCL §222(a)). Certain matters such as the approval of a merger or the sale, lease or exchange of all or substantially all of a corporation's property and assets, require more than the minimum 10 days notice (see DGCL §§251, 271). In the case of a special meeting (as opposed to regularly-scheduled annual general meeting) the purpose or purposes of the meeting must also be contained in the notice pursuant to DGCL §222(a). Delaware law imposes on the board of directors the general fiduciary duty to disclose the material facts within its control that would have significant effect on a shareholder vote, however there is no requirement that the corporation or the board of directors must disclose all information (*Stroud v. Grace*, 606 A.2d 75 (Del. 1992)). The standard of disclosure under Delaware law closely resembles the standard under the federal securities laws, accordingly an omitted fact is material if it would 'significantly alter the total mix of information made available' (*Gantler v. Stephens*, 965 A.2d 695, 710 (Del. 2009)). While no specific process is outlined in the statute for shareholders to obtain further information regarding agenda items, shareholders are also permitted to examine the books and records of the corporation for any proper purpose, as described in question 23 below.

13. May a GM be held by telecommunication means and/or by correspondence (ie by written consent)?
Generally, yes, in accordance with DGCL §§211(a)(2) and 228.

14. Are voting rights always proportionate to the stock held by each shareholder or can they vary by share class?
No. The default voting right is one vote per share, but voting rights may be modified in the corporation's certificate of incorporation (DGCL §212(a)).

15. Are there non-voting shares? Is there a maximum percentage of capital represented by non-voting shares?
A corporation may issue stock which may have full, limited, or no voting powers, with differing classes of stock having differing voting rights (DGCL §151(a)). A corporation will generally need at least one voting share in order to operate effectively under the DGCL, and the corporation must have at least one share of voting stock outstanding after redemption of its shares by the corporation (DGCL §151(b)), but otherwise there is no statutory minimum.

16. Can shareholders group their shares in order to exercise their voting rights (eg, by trust, shareholders' agreement or otherwise)?
Yes. The most common method of effectuating agreements between shareholders is a contractual shareholders' agreement, which is permitted under DGCL §218(c). For sophisticated parties, such agreements are often drafted without the use of a grant of a specific proxy to any particular entity or person. DGCL §218(a) and (b) also permit the use of voting trusts.

17. Under what circumstances can a shareholder challenge the resolutions adopted by the GM? Are there thresholds concerning the stock interest owned to be able to bring such a claim?

A formal challenge to a resolution of the shareholders adopted at an annual or special meeting of the shareholders may be brought against the corporation, its board of directors or its officers in the form of direct or derivative litigation on such grounds as insufficient notice, lack of required disclosure, invalid voting mechanics or a challenge to the transaction or action that was approved by the shareholders at the meeting. In the case of a shareholder vote that was not in accordance with the terms of a shareholders' agreement, a claim for breach of contract may also be brought against the breaching shareholders.

A derivative claim may only be brought if the plaintiff in such suit was a shareholder of the corporation at the time of the transaction that the shareholder is protesting (DGCL §327). In a derivative suit, a shareholder must also either: (i) make a demand on the corporation that it bring the claims itself and that demand is refused; or (ii) show that such a demand would be futile.

18. What are the terms and procedures to challenge a resolution of the GM?

The claims described in question 17 may be brought against the corporation, its board of directors or its officers in the Delaware courts, including the Delaware Chancery Court, as well as the courts of other states, provided that standing and personal and subject matter jurisdictional requirements are met. Claims against another shareholder for breach of the terms of a shareholders' agreement would usually be brought in a court in the jurisdiction dictated by the provisions of such shareholders' agreement.

SHAREHOLDERS' RIGHTS VERSUS DIRECTORS AND DUTIES OF OTHER CORPORATE BODIES IN THE COMPANY

19. What is the procedure for the appointment/replacement/ revocation of directors and of statutory auditors, if any?

The directors of a corporation are generally elected at the annual shareholders meeting, or by written shareholder consent in accordance with DGCL §228, and serve until their successors are duly elected and qualified or their earlier disqualification, resignation, removal or death. The number of directors, and any detailed procedures for their election or removal, may be fixed in the certificate of incorporation or in the by-laws. Directors need not be shareholders of the corporation, unless required by the corporation's organisational documents. The holders of a majority of the shares entitled to vote at the election of the directors may remove, with or without cause, any director or the entire board of directors unless:

(i)   the certificate of incorporation provides for a classified board, in which case shareholders may only effect removal for cause;

(ii) the corporation has cumulative voting, in which case if less than the entire board is being removed, no director may be removed without cause if the votes cast against such removal would be sufficient to elect such director if cumulatively voted at an election of the board; or

(iii) the certificate of incorporation gives the right to elect certain directors to a particular class or series of stock, in which case the majority of such class shall have such right to remove such directors (DGCL §141(k)).

Under Delaware law, directors may not remove other directors. Unless otherwise provided in a corporation's organisational documents, vacancies and newly created directorships may be filled by a majority of the directors then in office, even if less than a quorum, or by a sole remaining director. (DGCL §223(a)(1)). Stockholders may also fill vacancies or newly created directorships unless they are otherwise prohibited or restricted in a corporation's organisational documents. When the holders of a class or classes of stock or series thereof are entitled to elect one or more directors pursuant to the corporation's certificate of incorporation, vacancies and newly created directorships of such class or classes or series may be filled by a majority of the directors elected by such class or classes or series thereof then in office. Under DGCL §223, in certain instances the officers or stockholders may apply to the Court of Chancery for a decree ordering an election of directors (DGCL §223(a), (c)).

The board of directors of the corporation, or often the audit committee of the board of directors, is entrusted with the appointment and replacement of the independent auditors of the corporation.

20. May shareholders challenge the resolutions of the board of directors? Is there a minimum percentage of capital required to challenge a board resolution?

Except for the types of decisions outlined in question 6, the board of directors has the right to govern the corporation. A formal challenge to a decision by the board of directors that is within the powers of the board may be brought in the form of direct or derivative litigation, as discussed in question 17.

21. Are shareholders entitled to bring a legal action against the directors of the company? In which circumstances? Please describe briefly the principles of directors' liability.

Yes, as discussed in questions 17 and 20.

The principles of director liability under Delaware law have largely been developed in the case law. The concepts of the fiduciary duties of care and loyalty, which also include duties of good faith, oversight and disclosure, are not explicitly laid out in the DGCL, rather, they are outlined in various lines of court cases, which continue to be refined. The importation of these various director duties may largely be avoided by the use of the LLC or the LP entity form and a very carefully drafted LLC or LP agreement.

The personal liability of directors may be limited or eliminated pursuant to DGCL §102(b)(7), which enables a Delaware corporation to include in its original certificate of incorporation, or an amendment to it, a provision eliminating or limiting (ie, providing a limit on monetary liability either per director or for the board collectively) the personal liability of its directors (but not officers) to the corporation or its shareholders for monetary damages for breach of fiduciary duty. However, a §102(b)(7) exculpatory provision in a corporation's certificate of incorporation may not eliminate or limit the liability of a director:

(i)   for any breach of the director's duty of loyalty to the corporation or its shareholders;
(ii) for acts or omissions not in good faith or which concern intentional misconduct or a knowing violation of law;
(iii) for unlawful payments of dividends or unlawful stock purchases or redemptions under DGCL §174; or
(iv) for any transaction from which the director derived an improper personal benefit.

In addition to the limitation or elimination of liability allowed under DGCL §102(b)(7), Delaware's general statutory framework also contains provisions dealing with indemnification and advancement of expenses for directors, officers, employees and agents of a corporation. DGCL §145 generally authorises a corporation to indemnify and advance litigation expenses to any person who is or was a party to a proceeding or threatened proceeding by reason of the fact that such person is or was a director, officer, employee or agent of the corporation or is or was serving another entity in such capacity at the request of the corporation. Except in certain circumstances, to obtain indemnification under DGCL §145, the individual must:

(i)   have acted in good faith;
(ii) in a manner that they reasonably believed to be in or not opposed to the best interests of the corporation in respect of the claim made against such person; and
(iii) with respect to criminal cases, have reasonable cause to believe their action was not unlawful.

In addition, in connection with the advancement of expenses, an officer or director may be required to execute an undertaking promising to repay those amounts advanced to them in the event that it is ultimately determined that the officer or director is not entitled to be indemnified.

Additionally, DGCL §145(g) allows a Delaware corporation to purchase liability insurance on behalf of its directors or officers, and in practice, corporations generally do purchase directors' and officers' liability insurance that is designed to defray the cost of any indemnification provided to such individuals.

DGCL §145(f) further provides that the statutory rights and procedures regarding indemnification and advancement of expenses are not exclusive and permits a Delaware corporation to include in its organisational documents provisions granting rights to indemnification and advancement of expenses and setting forth the procedures to be followed in connection with the provision of such rights beyond those provided by statute. Further, many corporations enter into separate indemnification agreements with their directors, officers, and in some cases employees and agents.

22. What are the rights in connection with transactions where the directors have a conflict of interest situation?

The actions of a corporation, as effectuated by the board of directors, are not considered void or voidable solely because of a conflict of interest with a director if the details of the conflict are:

(i)   fully disclosed to the board of directors and approved by a majority of the disinterested directors;

(ii) fully disclosed to the shareholders and approved by the shareholders (in the case of transactions in which the shareholders are entitled to vote); or

(iii) the transaction is fair as to the corporation at the time it was approved by the board of directors (or the shareholders, if applicable) (DGCL §144).

Provisions regarding interested party transactions are also often negotiated into shareholders' agreements.

INFORMATION RIGHTS ON THE COMPANY'S BUSINESS

23. What information may be requested by the shareholders from the board concerning the general state of the company's business or any specific transaction? Are information rights different depending on the number of shares owned? Are shareholders entitled to receive written information before, during or after the GM about the meeting agenda and to what extent? Is it possible for a shareholder to obtain a copy of the minutes of the meetings of the GM?

Any shareholder, without regard to the size of such person's shareholdings or the length of time such person has been holding such shares, is entitled under DGCL §220 to inspect for any proper purpose (defined as a purpose reasonably related to such person's interest as a shareholder) the corporation's stock ledger, a list of its shareholders and its other books and records. In the case of requests for access to the books and records of a corporation, the burden of showing a proper purpose falls on the requesting shareholder.

As discussed in question 12, shareholders are entitled to notice of an annual or special meeting, which in the case of a special meeting shall include the purpose of the meeting. A shareholder may request a copy of the minutes of the meeting in accordance with DGCL §220.

24. Do shareholders have the right/duty to resolve in the GM upon matters which were not on the agenda?

Generally a corporation's organisational documents will provide for the procedures governing the nominations or other business matters that may be properly submitted for consideration at a meeting of the shareholders and only those nominations and other matters may then be considered by the shareholders. Where a corporation's organisational documents are silent as to how nominations and other business matters are to be submitted for consideration at a meeting of the shareholders, it is possible that nominations and other business matters may be brought before the shareholders for consideration even when such matters were not on the agenda.

25. Are shareholders entitled to inspect the corporate books and/or any other corporate or accounting documents? To what extent? Can they do it through external counsel or advisors?

As discussed in question 23 above, shareholders have a statutory right to inspect a corporation's stock ledger, list of shareholders and its books and records for a proper purpose. Where a shareholder is seeking access to such information through external counsel or an agent, the demand for access must be accompanied by a power of attorney or other written authorisation that such person is acting on behalf of the shareholder (DGCL §220(b)).

Additional information rights are also commonly provided for by contract in shareholders' agreements.

SHAREHOLDERS' AGREEMENTS

26. Are shareholders' agreements validly enforceable? What are their typical contents and term of duration? Are they enforceable by or against third parties and, if so, to what extent?

Shareholders' agreements are permissible under DGCL §218(c) and are considered validly enforceable under the law using the same criteria as any other contract.

Typical contents of a shareholders' agreement include: provisions such as the right to nominate certain directors; the specific procedures under which such directors may be elected or removed; transfer restrictions; information rights; veto rights on certain types of decisions; and the governing law, jurisdiction and venue for any disputes under the shareholders' agreement. Provisions of shareholders' agreements often terminate if the shareholder benefiting from the provision transfers a significant portion of its shareholdings, or if the corporation becomes a publicly-traded company.

Third parties do not generally have standing to enforce a shareholders' agreement, so in practice all relevant parties, including the corporation, should be made party to the agreement.

27. Do shareholders' agreements have to be disclosed to the public or registered in any public registry?

The existence of a shareholders' agreement that affects the rights and privileges of certain shares is usually evidenced by a legend printed on the reverse side of the affected share certificate, if the shares are in certificated form, and is required to be so legended if the agreement contains transfer restrictions, as discussed below in question 28.

ECONOMIC RIGHTS AND RIGHTS OVER THE STOCK

28. Is the stock always freely transferable? Are there any legal limitations? Are there any restrictions on contractual limitations?

Shares of stock of a corporation are generally freely transferable under the DGCL but may be restricted under the organisational documents of the corporation or by contract. Such contractual restrictions are governed by DGCL §202(c), which broadly allows most types of transfer restrictions. Under DGCL §202(a), a restriction on the transfer or registration of transfer of stock or on the amount of stock that may be owned by any person or group of persons must be noted conspicuously on the certificate or certificates representing the stock, or in the case of uncertificated shares, contained in a notice or notices sent to the shareholder. Further, no restriction shall be binding with respect to stock issued prior to the adoption of the restriction unless the holders of the stock are parties to the agreement providing for the restriction or voted in favour of the restriction (DGCL §202(b)).

29. Are shareholders entitled to pledge their stock?
Yes, in general, shareholders may pledge shares of their stock.

30. Are there financial assistance issues to be considered and other prohibitions to be evaluated in the context of a leveraged buyout transaction?
While there are no special statutory rules relating to financial assistance in the US, leveraged buyouts should be structured so as to avoid potential future civil claims of fraudulent conveyance brought by creditors or bankruptcy trustees on behalf of the bankruptcy debtor estate.

31. May a company buy back its own stock and if so under what circumstances and subject to which limitations?
Subject to any shareholder rights set forth in the corporation's organisational documents or other contractual rights of any specific shareholders, a corporation may buy back shares of its stock upon resolution of the board of directors. The corporation need not make the same repurchase offer to all of its shareholders, or to all shareholders of the same class, and need not offer a fair market price. The corporation must have enough surplus capital or net profits as dictated by DGCL §160 in order to make the purchase, and wilful or negligent disregard of such provisions may result in personal liability of the directors involved. Further, the Delaware courts have held that a corporation may not purchase shares of its stock where it is doing so for an improper purpose.

As opposed to the right of the corporation to purchase its own stock when such right has not been built in to the specific terms of the class or series of stock as discussed above, DGCL §151(b) also provides that shares of any class or series may be made subject to pre-negotiated redemption by the corporation at its option or at the option of the holders of such stock or upon the happening of a specified event, provided that immediately following any such redemption the corporation shall have outstanding one or more shares of one or more classes or series of stock with full voting powers.

32. Is there a legal right to withdraw from the company and, if so, under what circumstances? How is the shareholders' stock valued and paid in such a case?
There is no statutory right to voluntarily withdraw from a corporation.

33. In which circumstances can dividends be distributed among shareholders? Is it possible to exclude or limit the right of certain shareholders to dividends? Does a certain portion of the profits need to be set aside in a reserve fund where it cannot be distributed to the shareholders? Are advances on dividends allowed and, if so, under which circumstances? Can advances on dividends be reclaimed by the company?
Subject to any restrictions in the certificate of incorporation, the board of directors of a corporation has the right to declare and pay dividends to the shareholders so long as there is available surplus (as defined in DGCL §§154 and 244) or net profits (DGCL §170). One class or series of shareholders may be granted a right to receive dividends in preference over another if such rights are set forth in the certificate of incorporation or the resolution of the board of directors providing for the issuance of such class or series of stock.

Since each dividend distributed to the shareholders must be approved by the board of directors, and a determination must be made in connection with such approval that there is surplus or net profits available to make such payment, dividends are not generally advanced.

34. What are the rights of shareholders in the case of an issue of new stock (increase of the company's corporate capital) (pre-emption rights)?
Unless expressly provided for in a corporation's certificate of incorporation, there are no statutory pre-emptive rights under the DGCL (DGCL §102(b)(3)). If the issuance of new stock requires an amendment to the certificate of incorporation, the shareholders of the corporation have the right to vote (and in some instances a specific right to vote separately as a class) on the approval of such amendment in accordance with DGCL §242 after the board of directors first approves the amendment in a resolution declaring its advisability.

35. May minority shareholders ban or limit the company's capital structure in any manner?
There are no statutory minority rights with respect to a corporation's capital structure, but such rights are often negotiated by certain classes of shareholders in the organisational documents of the corporation or in contracts between the corporation and its shareholders.

36. Which are the financial assistance prohibitions in force?
The considerations discussed in question 30 above also apply to transactions other than leveraged buyouts.

37. Apart from publicly listed companies, in which cases (if any) are shareholders obligated to obtain an authorisation from, or provide information to, a public authority about events that have an impact on their stock interest in the company?

Private companies operating in certain regulated business spheres may be subject to reporting requirements to government agencies. For example, corporations that own educational institutions may be subject to share ownership reporting requirements to the US Department of Education.

In the context of mergers and acquisitions of companies over a certain threshold value, information about the proposed transaction and share ownership must be given to the US Federal Trade Commission and the Department of Justice under the Hart-Scott-Rodino Antitrust Improvements Act.

SHAREHOLDERS' RIGHTS IN CASE OF EXTRAORDINARY TRANSACTIONS AND/OR WINDING-UP

38. What rights are available to shareholders in the case of a sale of all or a substantial portion of the company's assets? In case of a merger or de-merger?

A majority vote of the outstanding shares of stock of a corporation entitled to vote on the matter is required in order to sell, lease or exchange all or substantially all of the assets of a corporation (DGCL §271) or to effectuate a merger (DGCL §§251, 252), other than in certain statutorily specified circumstances such as the case where at least 90 per cent of the shares of each class of stock is owned by a parent corporation (DGCL §253).

In certain circumstances, shareholders may have the right to an appraisal of the 'fair value' of their shares, as determined by the Delaware Court of Chancery, in accordance with DGCL §262. The procedures provided for in DGCL §262 must be strictly followed in order to perfect a shareholder's right to appraisal of such shareholder's shares of stock.

39. Which rights are available to shareholders in the case of conversion of the company into a European Company (SE) or into another type of company?

A US corporation is not convertible into a European Company (SE).

DGCL §266 allows the conversion of a Delaware corporation into another form of entity by the recommendation of the board of directors and the approval of all of the shareholders of the corporation.

40. Which rights are available to shareholders of a company in liquidation?

In general, a shareholder in a corporation has that right to receive a pro rata share of the assets of the corporation on dissolution or liquidation after all of its debts have been paid, if any assets remain available. Trustees or receivers can be appointed by the Court of Chancery under DGCL §279 on the application of any creditor, shareholder or director. The Court of Chancery, on the application of any creditor or shareholder, may also appoint a receiver to take charge of the assets and affairs of the corporation in the case where the corporation has become insolvent, but in practice in such cases many companies use proceedings under the US Federal Bankruptcy Code, 11 U.S.C. § 101 *et seq* to reorganise and shed excess debt.

41. Can shareholders cause the liquidation of the company? How?
See question 40 above.

COMPANY GROUPS
42. Is the concept of 'group' recognised as such under specific legislation? What are the implications?
There is no specific recognition of the concept of a company 'group' under the DGCL, although there are specific provisions that relate to actions of parent and subsidiary corporations.

US tax law, and certain other US statutes including the Employee Retirement Income Security Act of 1974, as amended and the Comprehensive Environmental Response, Compensation and Liability Act of 1980, as amended do sometimes implicate interrelated groups of corporations, but such discussion is beyond the scope of this chapter.

43. Does a controlling company have any particular duties *vis-à-vis* its controlled company shareholders?
Not in addition to any duty a majority shareholder in any corporation would have with respect to minority shareholders.

44. What are the rights of company shareholders when the controlling company puts in place actions and or transactions that can be prejudicial to the shareholders?
No additional minority rights are granted to minority shareholders in the case of a majority shareholder being a related corporate entity.

45. What are the limitations, if any, to the possibility of owning reciprocal stock interests in companies?
There is no prohibition of a corporation owning its own stock or that of a related entity.

Contact details

GENERAL EDITORS
Alessandro Varrenti
CBA Studio Legale e Tributario
Galleria San Carlo
Milano
Italy
6 – 20122
T: +39 02 778061
F: +39 02 76002790
E: alessandro.varrenti@cbalex.it
www.cbalex.it

Fernando de las Cuevas
Gómez-Acebo Pombo
Castellana, 216
Madrid
Spain
28046
T: +34 91 582 91 00
F: +34 91 582 91 14
E: fcuevas@gomezacebo-pombo.com
www.gomezacebo-pombo.com

Matthew Hurlock
Kirkland & Ellis International LLP
30 St Mary Axe
London, EC3A 8AF
United Kingdom
T: +44 20 7469 2000
F: +44 20 7469 2001
E: matthew.hurlock@kirkland.com
www.kirkland.com

ARGENTINA
Roberto H. Crouzel,
Miguel C. Remmer, Constanza P.
Connolly, Germán G. Pennimpede &
Nicolás C. D'Odorico.
Estudio Beccar Varela
Tucumán 1, piso 3
Buenos Aires
Argentina
C1049AAA

T: +54 11 4379 6800,
  +54 11 4379 4700
F: +54 11 4379 6860/6869/4777
E: estudio@ebv.com.ar
www.ebv.com.ar

BRAZIL
Alexandre Bertoldi, Roberta S.R. Bilotti
Demange, Sofia Toledo Piza, Vânia
Marques Ribeiro Moyano
Pinheiro Neto Advogados
Rua Hungria, 1100
São Paulo
Brazil
01455-000
T: +55 11 3247 8567
F: +55 11 3247 8600
E: abertoldi@pn.com.br;
  rdemange@pn.com.br;
  spiza@pn.com.br;
  vmoyano@pn.com.br
www.pinheironeto.com.br

CHILE
Francisco Javier Illanes, Pedro Lluch,
Carolina Flisfisch
Cariola Diez Perez-Cotapos &
Compania Limitada
Av. Andres Bello 2711, piso 19
Las Condes
Santiago, Region Metropolitana
Chile
7550611
T: +56 (2) 360 4046
F: +56 (2) 360 4030
E: fjillanes@cariola.cl;
  plluch@cariola.cl;
  cflisfisch@cariola.cl
www.cariola.cl

PEOPLE'S REPUBLIC OF CHINA

Chuanjie Zhou
Fangda Partners
21/F, China World Tower,
No. 1, Jian Guo Men Wai Avenue
Beijing
People's Republic of China
100004
T: +86 10 5769 5600
F: +86 1350 108 7197
E: cjzhou@fangdalaw.com
www.fangdalaw.com

XY Li, Chuan Li, Mark Horvick &
Jing Li
Kirkland & Ellis International LLP
11th Floor, HSBC Building, Shanghai
IFC
8 Century Avenue, Pudong New
District
Shanghai
People's Republic of China
200120
T: +8621 3857 6300
F: +8621 3857 6301
E: xy.li@kirkland.com;
   chuan.li@kirkland.com;
   mark.horvick@kirkland.com;
   jing.li@kirkland.com;
www.kirkland.com

David Patrick Eich & Daniel Wang
Kirkland & Ellis International LLP
26th Floor, Gloucester Tower
The Landmark, 15 Queen's Road
Central
Hong Kong
T: +852 3761 3300
F: +852 3761 3301
E: david.eich@kirkland.com;
   daniel.wang@kirkland.com
www.kirkland.com

COLOMBIA

Dario Cárdenas
Cárdenas & Cárdenas Abogados

Cra 7 No. 71 – 52 Torre B, Piso 9
Colombia
T: +571 313 7800
F: +571 312 2410
E: dcardenas@cardenasycardenas.com
www.cardenasycardenas.com

CZECH REPUBLIC

Judr. Michael Mullen & Mgr. Jan
Koval
Havel & Holásek, s.r.o.
Týn 1049/3
Prague 1
Czech Republic
110 00
T: +420 224 895 950
F: +420 224 895 980
E: michael.mullen@havelholasek.cz;
   jan.koval@havelholasek.cz
www.havelholasek.cz

DENMARK

Niels Heering & Niels Bang
Gorrissen Federspiel
H.C. Andersens Boulevard 12
Copenhagen V
Denmark
1553
T: +45 33 41 41 41
F: +45 33 41 41 33
E: nh@gorrissenfederspiel.com;
   nba@gorrissenfederspiel.com
www.gorrissenfederspiel.com

FRANCE

Yvon Dréano
Jeantet Associés
87, avenue Kléber
Paris
Cedex 16
75784
France
T: +33 (0)1 45 05 80 08
F: +33 (0)1 44 05 95 69
E: ydreano@jeantet.fr
www.jeantet.fr

GERMANY
Dr. Ingo Theusinger
Noerr LLP
Speditionstraße 1
Düsseldorf
Germany
40221
T: +49 211 4998 6248
F: +49 211 4998 6100
E: ingo.theusinger@noerr.com
www.noerr.com

GREECE
Christina Faitakis
Karatzas & Partners
8 Omirou Street
Athens
Greece
105 64
T: +30 210 3713600
F: +30 210 3234363
E: ch.faitakis@karatza-partners.gr
www.karatza-partners.gr

HONG KONG
John Richardson & Alexander Que
Deacons
5th Floor Alexandra House,
18 Chater Road
Hong Kong
Hong Kong
T: +852 2825 9211
F: +852 2810 0431

Pierre-Luc Arsenault &
David Patrick Eich
Kirkland & Ellis International LLP
26th Floor, Gloucester Tower
The Landmark, 15 Queen's Road
Central
Hong Kong
T: +852 3761 3300
F: +852 3761 3301
E: pierre.arsenault@kirkland.com;
david.eich@kirkland.com
www.kirkland.com

HUNGARY
Dr Pál Rahóty & Richard Lock
Lakatos, Köves and Partners Ügyvédi
Iroda
Madách Trade Center
Madách Imre út 14.
Budapest
Hungary
1075
T: +36 1 429 1300
F: +36 1 429 1390
E: richard.lock@lakatoskoves.hu;
pal.rahoty@lakatoskoves.hu
www.lakatoskoves.hu

INDIA
Neeraj Kumar, Sanjeev Kaul, Abhinav
Rastogi & Jay Badola
Dua Associates
Tolstoy House
15, Tolstoy Marg
New Delhi
India
110001
T: +91 (11) 23714408
F: +91 (11) 23317746,
+91 (11) 23357097
E: duadel@duaassociates.com
www.duaassociates.com

ISRAEL
Ido Gonen & Michal Matthews
Goldfarb Levy Eran Meiri Tzafrir & Co
2 Weizmann Street
Tel Aviv
Israel
64239
T: +972 3 608 9999
F: +972 3 608 9909
E: ido.gonen@goldfarb.com
www.goldfarb.com

ITALY
Alessandro Varrenti
CBA Studio Legale e Tributario
Galleria San Carlo
Milano

Italy
6 – 20122
T: +39 02 778061
F: +39 02 76002790
E: alessandro.varrenti@cbalex.it
www.cbalex.it

JAPAN
Tsuyoshi Shimizu
Nagashima Ohno & Tsunematsu
Kioicho Building, 3-12, Kioicho
Chiyoda-ku
Tokyo
Japan
102-0094
T: +81 3 3511 6182
F: +81 3 5213 2282
E: tsuyoshi_shimizu@noandt.com
www.noandt.com

LUXEMBOURG
Stef Oostvogels
Oostvogels Pfister Feyten
291 Route d'Arlon
Luxembourg City
Luxembourg
B.P.603/L-2016
T: +352 46 83 83
F: +352 46 84 84
E: soostvogels@oostvogels.com
www.oostvogels.com

MEXICO
Daniel Antonio del Rio Loaiza &
Amilcar Garcia Cortes
Basham Ringe Y Correa S.C.
Paseo de los Tamarindos No. 400-A
Piso 9, Col. Bosques de las Lomas
Mexico
Federal District
Mexico
D.F. 05120
T: +52 (55) 5261 0432
F: +52 (55) 5261 0496
E: delrio@basham.com.mx;
   daniel.delrio@basham.com.mx;
www.basham.com.mx

THE NETHERLANDS
Michiel Pannekoek, Marleen van
Uchelen, Yvon Tang, Ariane Smits,
Angela van Lamsweerde, Maurits de
Haan
Houthoff Buruma
Weena 355
3013 AL,
Rotterdam
Holland
T: +31 (0)10 217 20 00
F: +31 (0)10 217 27 00
E: m.pannekoek@houthoff.com;
   m.van.uchelen@houthoff.com;
   y.tang@houthoff.com;
   a.smits@houthoff.com;
   a.van.lamsweerde@houthoff.com;
   m.g.de.haan@houthoff.com
www.houthoff.com

POLAND
Arkadiusz Ruminski LLM, Marta
Szczepanik & Krzysztof Banaszek
Noerr Sp. z o.o. Spiering Sp. k.
Al. Armii Ludowej 26
Warsaw
Poland
00-609
T: +48 22 579 3060
F: +48 22 579 3070
E: arkadiusz.ruminski@noerr.com
   marta.szczepanik@noerr.com
   krzysztof.banaszek@noerr.com
www.noerr.com

PORTUGAL
Teresa Baptista
Gómez-Acebo & Pombo
Avenida da Liberdade
Lisbon
Portugal
131 – 1250
T: +351 21 340 86 00
F: +351 21 340 86 08
E: tbaptista@gomezacebo-pombo.com
www.gomezacebo-pombo.com

REPUBLIC OF IRELAND
Bryan Bourke & Joanne Conlon
William Fry
Fitzwilton House
Wilton Place
Dublin 2
Ireland
T: +353 1 639 5000
F: +353 1 639 5333
E: bryan.bourke@williamfry.ie;
   joanne.conlon@williamfry.ie
www.williamfry.ie

RUSSIA
Yulia Solovykh & Dr Thomas Mundry
Noerr
1-ya Brestskaya ul. 29
Moscow
Russia
125047
T: +7 495 7995696
F: +7 495 7995697
E: yulia.solovykh@noerr.com;
   thomas.mundry@noerr.com
www.noerr.com

SLOVAK REPUBLIC
Judr. Michael Mullen &
Mgr. Jan Koval
Havel & Holásek, s.r.o.
Týn 1049/3
Prague 1
Czech Republic
110 00
T: +420 224 895 950
F: +420 224 895 980
E: michael.mullen@havelholasek.cz;
   jan.koval@havelholasek.cz
www.havelholasek.cz

SPAIN
Fernando de las Cuevas
Gómez-Acebo & Pombo
Castellana, 216
Madrid
Spain
28046

T: +34 91 582 91 00
F: +34 91 582 91 14
E: fcuevas@gomezacebo-pombo.com
www.gomezacebo-pombo.com

SWITZERLAND
David Ledermann & Andreas Rötheli
Lenz & Staehelin
Route de Chene 30
Geneva 17
Switzerland
1211
T: +41 58 450 70 00
F: +41 58 450 70 01
E: david.ledermann@lenzstaehelin.com;
   andreas.roetheli@lenzstaehelin.com
www.lenzstaehelin.com

UNITED ARAB EMIRATES
Amjad Ali Khan
Afridi & Angell
Emirates Towers – Level 35
Sheikh Zayed Road
Dubai
United Arab Emirates
T: +971 4 330 3900
F: +971 4 330 3800
E: akhan@afridi-angell.com
www.afridi-angell.com

UK
Spencer Summerfield, Oliver Barnes
& Laura Brocklehurst
Travers Smith LLP
10 Snow Hill
London
England
EC1A 2AL
T: +44 20 7295 3000
F: +44 20 7295 3500
E: spencer.summerfield@
traverssmith.com;
   oliver.barnes@traverssmith.com;
   laura.brocklehurst@traverssmith.com
www.traverssmith.com

USA

Susan J. Zachman
Kirkland & Ellis LLP
601 Lexington Avenue
New York
NY 10022
T: +1 212 446 4947
F: +1 212 446 6460
E: susan.zachman@kirkland.com
www.kirkland.com

Megan W. Shaner
Richards Layton & Finger, P.A.
One Rodney Square
920 North King Street
Wilmington
Delaware
19801
T: +1 302 651 7647
F: +1 302 498 7647
E: mshaner@rlf.com
www.rlf.com